PENGUIN BOOKS

MASTERING THE ART OF FRENCH COOKING

Julia Child was born in Pasadena, California in 1912. She graduated from Smith College and worked for the OSS during World War II in Sri Lanka and China, where she met Paul Child. After they married they lived in Paris, where she studied at *Le Cordon Bleu* and worked under various distinguished French chefs. In 1951 she started her own cooking school in Paris, L'Ecole des Trois Gourmandes, with Simone Beck and Louisette Bertholle and the three women started compiling this cookbook. *Mastering the Art of French Cooking* (1961) grew out of the work they had done to translate classic French cooking techniques and recipes for their English-speaking pupils. Published in 1961, the book was an instant success. In 1963, Julia Child began appearing on the hugely popular US television series *The French Chef*, which earned her the Peabody Award in 1965 and an Emmy in 1966. Several public television shows and numerous acclaimed cookbooks followed. Julia Child received the French Legion of Honour in 2000. She died in 2004, two days before her 92nd birthday.

Mastering the Art of

FRENCH COOKING

By

SIMONE BECK

LOUISETTE BERTHOLLE

JULIA CHILD

Illustrations by Sidonie Coryn

PENGUIN BOOKS

PENGUIN BOOKS

Published by the Penguin Group
Penguin Books Ltd, 80 Strand, London WC2R ORL, England
Penguin Group (USA) Inc., 375 Hudson Street, New York, New York 10014, USA
Penguin Group (Canada), 90 Eglinton Avenue East, Suite 700, Toronto, Ontario, Canada M4P 2Y3
(a division of Pearson Penguin Canada Inc.)
Penguin Ireland, 25 St Stephen's Green, Dublin 2, Ireland (a division of Penguin Books Ltd)
Penguin Group (Australia), 250 Camberwell Road, Camberwell, Victoria 3124, Australia
(a division of Pearson Australia Group Pty Ltd)
Penguin Books India Pvt Ltd, 11 Community Centre, Panchsheel Park, New Delhi – 110 017, India
Penguin Group (NZ), 67 Apollo Drive, Rosedale, North Shore 0632, New Zealand
(a division of Pearson New Zealand Ltd)
Penguin Books (South Africa) (Pty) Ltd, 24 Sturdee Avenue, Rosebank, Johannesburg 2196, South Africa

Penguin Books Ltd, Registered Offices: 80 Strand, London WC2R ORL, England

www.penguin.com

First published in the USA 1961
First published in the UK by Cassell & Co. Ltd 1963
First published in Penguin Books 1966
This paperback edition published by Penguin Books 2009

5

Printed in England by Clays Ltd, St Ives plc

ISBN: 978–0–141–04841–3

www.greenpenguin.co.uk

TO

La Belle France

WHOSE PEASANTS, FISHERMEN, HOUSEWIVES,
AND PRINCES—NOT TO MENTION HER CHEFS—
THROUGH GENERATIONS OF INVENTIVE AND
LOVING CONCENTRATION HAVE CREATED ONE
OF THE WORLD'S GREAT ARTS

FOREWORD

THIS IS A BOOK for the servantless cook who can be unconcerned on occasion with budgets, waistlines, timetables, children's meals, or anything else which might interfere with the enjoyment of producing something wonderful to eat. Written for those who love to cook, the recipes are as detailed as we have felt they should be so that the reader knows exactly what is involved and how to go about it. This makes them a bit longer than usual, and some of the recipes are quite long indeed. No out-of-the-ordinary ingredients are called for. In fact the book could well be titled 'French Cooking from the Supermarket', for the excellence of French cooking, and of good cooking in general, is due more to cooking techniques than to anything else. And these techniques can be applied wherever good basic materials are available. We have purposely omitted cob-webbed bottles, the *patron* in his white cap bustling among his sauces, anecdotes about charming little restaurants with gleaming napery, and so forth. Such romantic interludes, it seems to us, put French cooking into a 'never-never' land instead of the Here, where happily it is available to everybody. Anyone can cook in the French manner anywhere, with the right instruction. Our hope is that this book will be helpful in giving that instruction.

Cooking techniques include such fundamentals as how to sauté a piece of meat so that it browns without losing its juices, how to fold beaten egg whites into a cake mixture to retain their maximum volume, how to add egg yolks to a hot sauce so that they will not curdle, where to put the tart in the oven so that it will puff and brown, and how to chop an onion quickly. Although you will perform with different ingredients for different dishes, the same general processes are repeated over and over again. As you enlarge your repertoire, you will find that the seemingly endless babble of recipes begins to fall rather neatly into groups of theme and variations; that *homard à l'américaine* has many technical aspects in common with *coq au vin*, that *coq au vin* in turn is almost identical in technique to *boeuf bourguignon*; all of them are types of fricassees, so follow the fricassee pattern. In the sauce realm, the cream and egg-yolk sauce for a *blanquette* of veal is the same type as that for a sole in white-wine sauce, or for a *gratin* of scallops. Eventually you will rarely need recipes at all, except as reminders of ingredients you may have forgotten.

All of the techniques employed in French cooking are aimed at one goal: how does it taste? The French are seldom interested in unusual combinations or surprise presentations. With an enormous background of traditional dishes to choose from (*1000 Ways to Prepare and Serve Eggs* is the title of one French book on the subject) the Frenchman takes his greatest pleasure from a well known dish impeccably cooked and served. A perfect *navarin* of lamb, for instance, requires a number of operations including brownings, simmerings, strainings, skimmings, and flavourings. Each of the several steps in the process, though simple to accomplish, plays a critical role, and if any is eliminated or combined with another, the texture and taste of the *navarin* suffer. One of the main reasons that pseudo-French cooking, with which we are all too familiar, falls far below good French cooking is just this matter of elimination of steps, combination of processes, or skimping on ingredients such as butter, cream—and time. 'Too much trouble', 'Too expensive', or 'Who will know the difference' are death knells for good food.

Cooking is not a particularly difficult art, and the more you cook and learn about cooking, the more sense it makes. But like any art it requires practice and experience. The most important ingredient you can bring to it is love of cooking for its own sake.

SCOPE

A complete treatise on French cooking following the detailed method we have adopted would be about the size of an unabridged dictionary; even printed on India paper, it would have to be placed on a stand. To produce a book of convenient size, we have made an arbitrary selection of recipes that we particularly like, and which we hope will interest our readers. Many splendid creations are not included, and there are tremendous omissions. One may well ask: 'Why is there no *pâte feuilletée*? Where are the *croissants*?' These are the kinds of recipes, in our opinion, which should be demonstrated in the kitchen, as each requires a sense of touch which can only be learned through personal practice and observation. Why only five cakes and no *petits fours*? No boiled, souffléed, or mashed potatoes? No courgettes? No tripe? No *poulet à la Marengo*? No green salads? No pressed duck or *sauce rouennaise*? No room!

A NOTE ON THE RECIPES

All of the master recipes and most of the sub-recipes in this book are in step-by-step form. The ingredients for each step, often including some special piece of equipment needed, are in bold type. Below them follows the paragraph of instruction. Thus what to cook and how to cook it, at each stage in the proceedings, are always brought together in one sweep of the eye. Master recipes are headed in large, bold type; a special sign, *, precedes those which are followed by variations. Most of the recipes contain this sign, (*), in the body of the text, indicating up to what point a dish may be prepared in advance. Wine and vegetable suggestions are included with all master recipes for main-course dishes.

Our primary purpose in this book is to teach you how to cook, so that you will understand the fundamental techniques and gradually be able to divorce yourself from a dependence on recipes. We have therefore divided each category of food into related groups or sections, and each recipe in one section belongs to one family of techniques. Fish fillets poached in white wine, starting on page 189, are a good example, or the chicken fricassees starting on page 233, or the group of *quiches* on pages 132 to 138. It is our hope that you will read the introductory pages preceding each chapter and section before you start on a recipe, as you will then understand what we are about. For the casual reader, we have tried to make every recipe stand on its own. Cross references are always a problem. If there are not enough, you may miss an important point, and if there are too many you will become enraged. Yet if every technique is explained every time it comes up, a short recipe is long, and a long one forbidding.

QUANTITIES

Most of the recipes in this book are calculated to serve six people with reasonably good appetites. The amounts called for are generally twice what would be considered sufficient for a typical French menu comprising hors d'œuvre, soup, main course, salad, cheese, and dessert. We hope that we have arrived at quantities which will be correct for most of our readers. If a recipe states that the ingredients listed will serve 4 to 6 people, this means the dish should be sufficient for 4 people if the rest of your menu is small, and for 6 if it is large.

SOME WORDS OF ADVICE

Our years of teaching cookery have impressed upon us the fact that all too often a learner cook will start enthusiastically on a new dish without ever reading the recipe first. Suddenly an ingredient, or a process, or a time sequence will turn up, and there is astonishment, frustration, and even disaster. We therefore urge you, however much you have cooked, always to read the recipe first, even if the dish is familiar to you. Visualize each step so that you will know exactly what techniques, ingredients, time, and equipment are required and you will encounter no surprises. Recipe language is always a sort of shorthand in which a lot of information is packed, and you will have to read carefully if you are not to miss small but important points. Then, to build up your over-all knowledge of cooking, compare the recipe mentally to others you are familiar with, and note where one recipe or technique fits into the larger picture of theme and variations.

We have not given estimates for the time of preparation, as some people take half an hour to slice three pounds of mushrooms while others take five minutes.

Pay close attention to what you are doing while you work, for precision in small details can make the difference between passable cooking and fine food. If a recipe says, 'cover casserole and regulate heat so that liquid simmers very slowly', 'heat the butter until its foam begins to subside', or 'beat the hot sauce into the egg yolks drop by drop', follow it. You may be slow and clumsy at first, but with practice you will pick up speed and style.

Allow yourself plenty of time. Most dishes can be assembled, or started, or partially cooked in advance. If you are not an old campaigner, do not plan more than one long or complicated recipe for a meal or you will wear yourself out and derive no pleasure from your efforts.

If food is to be baked or grilled, be sure your oven or grill is hot before the dish goes in. Otherwise soufflés will not rise, pie crusts will collapse, and *gratinéed* dishes will overcook before they brown.

A pot saver is a self-hampering cook. Use all the pans, bowls, and equipment you need, but soak them in water as soon as you are through with them. Clean up after yourself frequently to avoid confusion.

Train yourself to use your hands and fingers; they are wonderful instruments. Train yourself also to handle hot foods; this will save time. Keep your knives sharp.

Above all, have a good time.

S. B., L. B., J. C.

ACKNOWLEDGMENTS

Our FRIENDS, students, families, and husbands who have gracefully and often courageously acted as guinea-pigs for years are owed a special thank-you from the authors. But there are others toward whom we feel particular gratitude because of help of a different kind. The Agricultural Research Service of the U.S. Department of Agriculture has been one of our greatest sources of assistance and has unfailingly and generously answered all sorts of technical questions ranging from food to plastic bowls. The Meat Institute of Chicago, the National Livestock and Meat Board, and the Poultry and Egg National Board have answered floods of inquiries with prompt and precise information. Wonderfully helpful also have been the Fish and Wildlife Service of the Department of the Interior, and the California Department of Fish and Game. Sessions with *L'École Professionelle de la Boucherie de Paris* and with the *Office Scientifique et Technique de la Pêche Maritime* have been invaluable in our research on French meat cuts and French fish. During our years of practical kitchen-training in Paris, *Chef de Cuisine* Max Bugnard and *Chef Pâtissier* Claude Thillmont have been our beloved teachers. More recently we have also had the good fortune to work with Mme Aimée Cassiot, whose long years as a professional *cordon bleu* in Paris have given her a vast store of working knowledge which she has willingly shared with us. We are also greatly indebted to *Le Cercle des Gourmettes* whose bi-monthly cooking sessions in Paris have often been our proving grounds, and whose culinary ideas we have freely used. We give heartfelt thanks to our editors whose enthusiasm and hard work transformed our manuscript-in-search-of-a-publisher into this book. Finally there is Avis DeVoto, our foster mother, wet nurse, guide, and mentor. She provided encouragement for our first steps, more than ten years ago, as we came tottering out of the kitchen with the gleam of authorship lighting our innocent faces.

CONTENTS

ILLUSTRATIONS

* THIS SYMBOL preceding a recipe title indicates that variations follow.

(*) WHEREVER you see this symbol in the body of recipe texts you may prepare the dish ahead of time up to that point, then complete the recipe later.

KITCHEN EQUIPMENT

Batterie de Cuisine

THEORETICALLY A GOOD COOK should be able to perform under any circumstances, but cooking is much easier, pleasanter, and more efficient if you have the right tools. Good equipment which will last for years does not seem outrageously expensive. A large frying pan can be bought for the price of a leg of lamb, and a fine paring knife may cost less than two steaks. One of the best places to shop for reasonably priced kitchenware is in a hotel and restaurant equipment shop where objects are sturdy, professional, and made for hard use.

STOVES

Always check your oven with a portable thermometer; thermostats have a way of becoming unreliable, which can be disastrous if you are cooking a soufflé or a cake, and will put your timing out when roasting.

You should be able to perform fast changes of heat from the bare simmer to the rolling boil on your burners. Gas is certainly the most supple heat source, but if gas pressure is low, it is wise to have one strong electric hot plate for sautés and for boiling large pans of water.

POTS, PANS, AND CASSEROLES

Pots, pans, and casseroles should be heavy-bottomed so that they will not tip over, and good heat conductors so that foods will not stick and scorch. With the exception of heavy copper, the best all-purpose material, in our opinion, is heavy, enamelled cast iron. It conducts heat very well, its enamelled surface does not discolour foods, and it is easy to clean. Stainless steel with a wash of copper on the bottom for looks is a poor heat conductor—the copper bottom should be $\frac{1}{8}$ inch thick to be of any value. Stainless steel with a cast aluminium bottom, on the other hand, is good, as the thick aluminium spreads the heat. Glazed

A

earthenware is all right as long as it has not developed cracks where old cooking grease collects and exudes whenever foods are cooked in it. Ovenglass and heat-proof porcelain are fine but fragile. Thick aluminium and iron, though good heat conductors, will discolour foods containing white wine or egg yolks. Because of the discolouration problem, we shall specify an enamelled saucepan in some recipes to indicate that any non-staining material is to be used, from enamel to stainless steel, lined copper, ovenglass, glazed pottery, or porcelain.

A Note on Copper Pots

Copper pots are the most satisfactory of all to cook in, as they hold and spread the heat well, and their tin lining does not discolour foods. A great many decorative types are currently sold; these are thin and glittering, and have shiny brass handles. To get the full benefit out of cooking in copper, the metal must be $\frac{1}{8}$ inch thick, and the handle should be of heavy iron. The interior of the pot is lined with a wash of tin, which must be renewed every few years when it wears off and the copper begins to show through. A copper pot can still be used when this happens if it is scrubbed just before you cook with it, and if the food is removed as soon as it is done. If cooked food remains in a poorly lined pot, some kind of a toxic chemical reaction can take place. It is thus best to have the pot re-tinned promptly.

In addition to re-tinning, there is the cleaning problem, as copper tarnishes quickly. There are quick modern copper cleaners available. A good home-made mixture is a quarter of a pint of white vinegar, and one ounce each of table salt and scouring powder. Rub the mixture over the copper, using steel wool if the pot is badly tarnished, then rinse in hot water. The tin lining is cleaned with steel wool and scouring powder, but do not expect it ever to glitter brightly again once you have used the pot for cooking.

Never let a copper pot sit empty over heat, or the tin lining will melt. For the same reason, watch your heat when browning meats in copper. If the tin begins to glisten brightly in places, lower your heat.

Any of the following items are made in enamelled cast iron:

Oval Casseroles

Oval casseroles are more practical than round ones as they can hold a chicken or a joint of meat as well as a stew or a soup. A good pair would be the

3-pint size about 6 by 8 inches across and 3½ inches high; and a 6- to 7-quart size about 9 by 12 inches across and 6 inches high.

Baking Dishes

Round and oval baking dishes can be used for roasting chicken, duck, or meats, or can double as *gratin* dishes.

Saucepans

Saucepans in a range of sizes are essential. One with a metal handle can also be placed in the oven.

Frying pan and
Sauté Pan

A frying pan, *poêle,* has sloping sides and is used for browning and tossing small pieces of food like mushrooms or chicken livers; the long handle makes it easy to toss rather than turn the food. A sauté pan, *sautoir,* has straight sides and is used for sautéing small steaks, liver, or veal scallops, or foods like chicken that are browned then covered to finish their cooking in the sauté pan.

Besides the usual array of pots, roasting tins, vegetable peelers, spoons, and spatulas, here are some useful objects which make cooking easier:

Knives and
Sharpening Steel

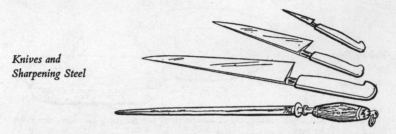

A knife should be as sharp as a razor or it mashes and bruises food rather than chopping or cutting it. It can be considered sharp if just the weight of it, drawn across a tomato, slits the skin. No knife will hold a razor-edge for long. The essential point is that it takes an edge, and easily. If the steel is too hard, the knife is very difficult to sharpen, and for this reason stainless steel knives are often unsatisfactory. You will be far better off with plain, rustable, carbon steel knives that can be sharpened quickly on a butcher's steel. The French chef's knife is the most useful general-purpose shape, as it can be used equally well for chopping or paring. If you cannot find good knives, consult your butcher or a professionally trained chef.

Knives should be washed separately and by hand as soon as you have finished using them. Tarnished blades are cleaned easily with steel wool and scouring powder.

Wooden and
Rubber Spatulas

A wooden spatula is more practical for stirring than a wooden spoon; its flat surfaces are easily scraped off on the side of a pan or bowl. You will usually find wooden spatulas only at stores specializing in French imports. The rubber spatula, which can be bought almost anywhere, is indispensable for scraping sauces out of bowls and pans, for stirring, folding, creaming, and smearing.

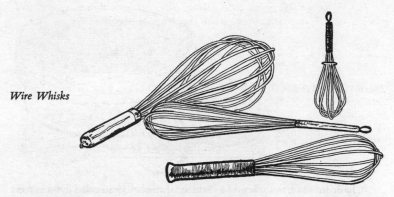

Wire Whisks

Wire whisks are wonderful for beating eggs, sauces, tinned soups, and for general mixing. They are easier to use than the rotary egg beater because you use one hand only. Whisks range from minute to gigantic, and the best selections are in restaurant equipment shops. You should have several sizes including the balloon whisk for beating egg whites, shown at the far left; its use is illustrated on page 144.

Bulb Baster and
Poultry Shears

The bulb baster is particularly good for basting meats or vegetables in a casserole, and for degreasing roasts as well as basting them. Some plastic models collapse in very hot fat; a metal tube-end is usually more satisfactory. Poultry shears are a great help in disjointing broilers and fryers; regular steel is more practical than stainless, as the shears can be sharpened more satisfactorily.

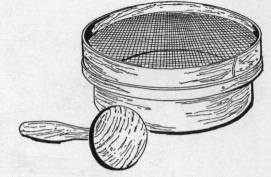

Drum Sieve and Pestle

The drum sieve, *tamis*, is used in France when one is instructed to force food through a sieve. The ingredients, such as pounded lobster shells and butter, are placed on the screen and rubbed through it with the pestle. An ordinary sieve placed over a bowl or a moulinette can take the place of a *tamis*.

Moulinette and
Garlic Press

Two wonderful inventions, the moulinette and the garlic press. The moulinette purées soups, sauces, vegetables, fruits, raw fish, or mousse mixtures. The best type has 3 removable discs about $5\frac{1}{2}$ inches in diameter, one for fine, one for medium, and one for coarse puréeing. The garlic press will purée a whole, unpeeled clove of garlic, or pieces of onion.

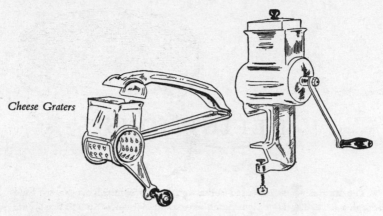

Cheese Graters

It is always best to grate cheese yourself just before you use it.

Mortar and Pestle

Small mortars of wood or porcelain are useful for grinding herbs, pounding nuts, and such like. The large mortars are of marble, and are used for pounding or puréeing shellfish, forcemeats, and so on. The electric liquidizer, mincer, and moulinette take the place of a mortar and pestle in many instances.

DEFINITIONS

We have tried, in this book, to use ordinary cooking terms familiar to anyone who has been around a kitchen, but we list a few definitions here to avoid possible misunderstanding.

BASTE, *arroser*   To spoon melted butter, fat, or liquid over foods.

BEAT, *fouetter*   To mix foods or liquids thoroughly and vigorously with a spoon, fork, or whisk, or an electric beater. When you beat, train yourself to use your lower-arm and wrist muscles; if you beat from your shoulder you will tire quickly.

BLANCH, *blanchir*   To plunge food into boiling water and to boil it until it has softened, or wilted, or is partially or fully cooked. Food is also blanched to remove too strong a taste, such as for cabbage or onions, or for the removal of the salty, smoky taste of bacon.

BLEND, *mélanger*   To mix foods together in a less vigorous way than by beating, usually with a fork, spoon, or spatula.

BOIL, *bouillir*   Liquid is technically at the boil when it is seething, rolling, and sending up bubbles. But in practice there are slow, medium, and fast boils. A very slow boil, when the liquid is hardly moving except for a bubble at one point, is called to simmer, *mijoter*. An even slower boil with no bubble, only the barest movement on the surface of the liquid, is called 'to shiver', *frémir*, and is used for poaching fish or other delicate foods.

BRAISE, *braiser*   To brown foods in fat, then cook them in a covered casserole with a small amount of liquid. We have also used the term for vegetables cooked in butter in a covered casserole, as there is no English equivalent for *étuver*.

COAT A SPOON, *napper la cuillère* This term is used to indicate the thickness of a sauce, and it seems the only way to describe it. A spoon dipped into a cream soup and withdrawn would be coated with a thin film of soup. Dipped into a sauce destined to cover food, the spoon would emerge with a fairly thick coating.

DEGLAZE, *déglacer* After meat has been roasted or sautéed, and the pan degreased, liquid is poured into the pan and all the flavourous coagulated cooking juices are scraped into it as it simmers. This is an important step in the preparation of all meat sauces from the simplest to the most elaborate, for the deglaze becomes part of the sauce, incorporating into it some of the flavour of the meat. Thus sauce and meat are a logical complement to each other.

DEGREASE, *dégraisser* To remove accumulated fat from the surface of hot liquids.

Sauces, Soups, and Stocks

To remove accumulated fat from the surface of a sauce, soup, or stock which is simmering, use a long-handled spoon and draw it over the surface, dipping up a thin layer of fat. It is not necessary to remove all the fat, as this will be done later.

When the cooking is done, remove all the fat. If the liquid is still hot, let it settle for 5 minutes so that the fat will rise to the surface. Then spoon it off, tipping the pot or pan so that a heavier fat deposit will collect at one side and can more easily be removed. When you have taken up as much as you can—it is never a quick process—draw strips of absorbent paper over the surface until the last floating fat globules have been blotted up.

It is easier, of course, to chill the liquid, for then the fat congeals on the surface and can be scraped off.

Roasts

To remove fat from a tin while the meat is still roasting, tilt the tin and scoop out the fat which collects in the corner. Use a big spoon. It is never necessary to remove all the fat at this time, just the excess. This degreasing should be done quickly, so that your oven will not cool. If you take a long time over it, add a few extra minutes to your total roasting figure.

After the roast has been taken from the tin, tilt the tin, then with a spoon remove the fat that collects in one corner, but do not take up the browned juices, as these will go into your gravy. Usually a tablespoon or two of fat is left in the tin, as it will give a little body and flavour to the gravy.

Another method—and this can be useful if you have lots of juice—is to place a trayful of ice cubes in a sieve lined with 2 or 3 thickness of damp cheesecloth and place over a saucepan. Pour the fat and juices over the ice

A*

cubes; most of the fat will collect and congeal on the ice. As some of the ice will melt and combine with the juices in the saucepan, rapidly boil down the juices to concentrate their flavour.

Casseroles

For stews, *daubes*, and other foods which cook in a casserole, tip the casserole and the fat will collect at one side. Spoon it off. Or strain off all the gravy into a pan, by placing the casserole cover askew and holding the casserole in both hands with your thumbs clamped to the cover while you pour out the liquid. Then degrease the gravy in the pan, and return the gravy to the casserole.

DICE, *couper en dés*   To cut food into cubes the shape of dice, usually about ⅛ inch in size as illustrated on page 23.

FOLD, *incorporer*   To blend a fragile mixture, such as beaten egg whites, delicately into a heavier mixture, such as a soufflé base. This is described and illustrated in the Soufflé section on page 146. To fold also means to mix delicately without breaking or mashing, such as folding cooked artichoke hearts or brains into a sauce.

GRATINÉ   To brown the top of a sauced dish, usually under a hot grill. A sprinkling of bread crumbs or grated cheese, and dots of butter, help to form a light brown covering (*gratin*) over the sauce.

MACERATE, *macérer*; MARINATE, *mariner*   To place foods in a liquid so that they will absorb flavour, give off flavour, or become more tender. Macerate is the term usually reserved for fruits, such as: cherries macerated in sugar and alcohol. Marinate is used for meats: beef marinated in red wine. A marinade is a pickle, brine, or souse, or a mixture of wine or vinegar, oil, and condiments.

NAP, *napper*   To cover food with a sauce which is thick enough to adhere, but supple enough so that the outlines of the food are preserved.

POACH, *pocher*   Food submerged and cooked in a liquid that is barely simmering or shivering. The term can also be used poetically for such things as 'chicken breasts poached in butter'.

PURÉE, *réduire en purée*   To render solid foods into a mash, such as apple sauce or mashed potatoes. This may be done in a mortar, a mincer, a moulinette, an electric liquidizer, or through a sieve.

REDUCE, *réduire*   To boil down a liquid, reducing it in quantity, and concentrating its taste. This is a most important step in sauce making.

REFRESH, *rafraîchir*   To plunge hot food into cold water in order to cool it quickly and stop the cooking process, or to wash it off.

SAUTÉ, *sauter*   To cook and brown food in a very small quantity of very hot fat, usually in a frying pan. You may sauté food merely to brown it, as you brown the beef for a stew. Or you may sauté until the food is cooked through, as for slices of liver. Sautéing is one of the most important of the primary cooking techniques, and it is often badly done because one of the following points has not been observed:

(1) The sautéing fat must be very hot, almost smoking, before the food goes into the pan, otherwise there will be no sealing-in of juices, and no browning. The sautéing medium may be fat, oil, or butter and oil. Plain butter cannot be heated to the required temperature without burning, so it must either be fortified with oil or be clarified—rid of its milky residue as described on page 12.

(2) The food must be absolutely dry. If it is damp, a layer of steam develops between the food and the fat, preventing the browning and searing process.

(3) The pan must not be crowded. Enough air space must be left between each piece of food or it will steam rather than brown, and its juices will escape and burn in the pan.

TOSS, *faire sauter*   Instead of turning food with a spoon or a spatula, you can make it flip over by tossing the pan. The classic example is tossing a pancake so that it flips over in mid-air. But tossing is also a useful technique for cooking vegetables, as a toss is often less bruising than a turn. If you are cooking in a covered casserole, grasp it in both hands with your thumbs clamped to the cover. Toss the pan with an up-and-down, slightly jerky, circular motion. The contents will flip over and change cooking levels. For an open saucepan use the same movement, holding the handle with both hands, thumbs up. A back-and-forth slide is used for a frying pan. Give it a very slight upward jerk just as you draw it back toward you.

INGREDIENTS

Eхcept for wines and spirits, and possibly *foie gras* and truffles, all the ingredients called for in this book are available in the average grocers. The following list is an explanation of the use of some items:

BACON, *lard de poitrine fumé* The kind of bacon used in French recipes is fresh, unsalted, and unsmoked, *lard de poitrine frais*. As this is fairly difficult to find, we have specified smoked bacon; its taste is usually fresher than that of salt pork. It is always blanched in simmering water to remove its smoky taste. If this were not done, the whole dish would taste of bacon.

Blanched Bacon

Place the bacon strips in a pan of cold water, about $1\frac{1}{2}$ pints for each 4 ounces. Bring to the simmer and simmer 10 minutes. Drain the bacon and rinse it well in fresh cold water, then dry it thoroughly.

BUTTER, *beurre* French butter is made from matured cream rather than from sweet cream, is unsalted, and has a special almost nutty flavour. Lightly salted or unsalted butters are interchangeable with French butter for the cooking of any French recipe with the exception of certain desserts and cake icings; for these we have specified unsalted butter.

Clarified Butter, beurre clarifié

When ordinary butter is heated until it liquefies, a milky residue sinks to the bottom of the saucepan. The clear, yellow liquid above it is clarified butter. It burns less easily than ordinary butter, as it is the milky particles in ordinary butter which blacken first when butter is heated. Clarified butter is used for sautéing the rounds of white bread used for canapés, or such delicate items as boned and skinned chicken breasts. It is also the base for brown butter sauce, and is used rather than fat in the brown *roux* for particularly fine brown sauces. To clarify butter, cut it into pieces and place it in a saucepan over moderate heat. When the butter has melted, skim off the foam, and strain the clear yellow liquid into a bowl, leaving the milky residue in the bottom of the pan. The residue may be stirred into soups and sauces to serve as an enrichment.

Butter Temperatures, Butter Foam

Whenever you are heating butter for an omelette, or butter and oil for a sauté, your recipe will direct you to wait until the butter foam looks a certain way. This is because the condition of the foam is a sure indication of how hot the butter is. As it begins to melt, the butter will foam hardly at all, and is not hot enough to brown anything. But as the heat increases, the liquids in the butter evaporate and cause the butter to foam up. During this full-foaming period the butter is still not very hot, only around 212 degrees Fahrenheit. When the liquids have almost evaporated, you can see the foam subsiding. When you see practically no foam, you will observe the butter begin to turn light brown, then dark brown, and finally a burnt black. Butter fortified with oil will heat to a higher temperature before browning and burning than will plain butter, but the observable signs are the same. Thus the point at which you add your eggs to the omelette pan or your meat to the frying pan is when the butter is very hot but not browning, and that is easy to see when you look at the butter. If it is still foaming up, wait a few seconds; when you see the foam begin to subside, the butter is hot enough for you to begin.

CHEESE, *fromage* The two cheeses most commonly used in French cooking are Swiss and Parmesan. Imported Swiss cheese is of two types, either of which may be used: the true *Gruyère* with small holes, and the *Emmenthal* which is fatter, less salty, and has large holes. *Petit suisse,* which is sometimes called for in French recipes, is a cream cheese.

CREAM, *crème fraîche, crème double* (slightly fermented); *fleurette* (sweet) French cream is matured cream, that is, lactic acids and natural ferments have been allowed to work in it until the cream has thickened and taken on a nutty flavour. It is not sour. Commercially made sour cream with a butterfat content of 18 to 20 per cent. is no substitute; furthermore, it cannot be boiled without curdling. British double cream and French *crème double* both have a butterfat content of at least 30 per cent., therefore British cream may be substituted for *crème fraîche* in any original French recipe. If British double cream is allowed to stand and thicken with a little sour cream, the result will taste quite a bit like French cream, can be boiled without curdling, and will keep for 10 days or more under refrigeration; use it on fruits or desserts, or in cooking.

1 tbl sour cream   **½ pt. double cream**

Stir the sour cream into the double cream and heat to lukewarm—not over 85 degrees Fahrenheit. Pour the mixture into a loosely covered jar and let it stand at a temperature of not over 85 degrees Fahrenheit nor under 60 degrees Fahrenheit until it has thickened. This will take 5 to 8 hours on a hot day, 24 to 36 hours at a low temperature. Stir, cover, and refrigerate.

FLOUR, *farine* Whether flour is made of soft wheat, hard wheat, or a blend is of great importance when you are making bread, pastry, and cakes. Soft wheats have little gluten or strength, and do not bulk up satisfactorily when used for breads. Hard wheats, with their strong gluten content, are difficult to manage when used for pie doughs as they become rubbery when rolled out or manipulated. Fortunately, British and French plain white flour are about equivalent: soft wheat blended with some harder wheats to give added strength. Thus a French pastry recipe should turn out perfectly in Great Britain. Cake flour is a bleached, very finely granulated milling of soft wheat; it produces a lighter, finer, and puffier cake than plain flour. Except for cakes, all references to flour in the following recipes apply to British plain white flour.

NOTE: In a French recipe 1 *cuillère de farine* usually means 1 heaped French tablespoon, or 15 to 20 grams.

GLACÉ FRUITS, CRYSTALLIZED FRUITS, *fruits confits* These are fruits such as cherries, orange peel, citron, apricots, and angelica, which have undergone a preserving process in sugar. They are sometimes coated with sugar so that they are not sticky; at other times they *are* sticky, depending on the specific process they have been through. Glacé fruits are called for in a number of the dessert recipes; most grocers stock selections or mixtures in jars or packets.

HERBS, *herbes* Classical French cooking uses far fewer herbs than most people would suspect. Parsley, thyme, bay, and tarragon are the standbys, plus fresh chives and chervil in season. A mixture of fresh parsley, chives, tarragon, and chervil is called *fines herbes*. Mediterranean France adds to the general list basil, fennel, oregano, sage, and saffron. The French feeling about herbs is that they should be an accent and a complement, but never a domination over the essential flavours of the main ingredients. Fresh herbs are, of course, ideal; but excellent also are most of the dried herbs now available. Be sure any dried herbs you use retain most of their original taste and fragrance.

HERB BOUQUET, *bouquet garni* This term means a combination of parsley, thyme, and bay leaf for flavouring soups, stews, sauces, and braised meat and vegetables. If the herbs are fresh and in sprigs or leaf, the parsley is folded around them and they are tied together with string. If the herbs are dried, they are wrapped in a piece of washed cheesecloth and tied. A bundle is made so that the herbs will not disperse themselves into the liquid or be skimmed off it, and so that they can be removed easily. Celery, garlic, fennel, or other items may be included in the bouquet, but are always specifically mentioned, such as 'a medium herb bouquet with celery stalk'. A small herb bouquet should contain 2 parsley sprigs, 1 bay leaf, and 1 sprig or ⅛ teaspoon of thyme.

MARROW, *moelle* The fatty filling of beef leg-bones, marrow is poached and used in sauces, garnitures, and on canapés. It is prepared as follows:

A beef marrowbone about 5 inches long

Stand the bone on one end and split it with a cleaver. Remove the marrow in one piece if possible. Slice or dice it with a knife dipped in hot water.

Boiling bouillon or boiling salted water

Shortly before using, drop the marrow into the hot liquid. Set aside for 3 to 5 minutes until the marrow has softened. Drain, and it is ready to use.

OIL, *huile* Classical French cooking uses almost exclusively odourless, tasteless vegetable oils for cooking and salads. These are made from peanuts, corn, cottonseed, sesame seed, poppy seed, or other analogous ingredients. Olive oil, which dominates Mediterranean cooking, has too much character for the subtle flavours of a delicate dish. In recipes where it makes no difference which you use, we have just specified 'oil'.

SHALLOTS, *échalotes* Shallots with their delicate flavour and slightest hint of garlic are small members of the onion family. They are used in sauces, stuffings, and general cooking to give a mild onion taste. In place of shallots you may use the finely chopped white part of spring onions, *ciboules*; these are ordinary onions pulled from the beds before the onion has developed. If you cannot obtain these, substitute very finely chopped onion dropped for one minute in boiling water, rinsed, and drained. Or omit them altogether.

TRUFFLES, *truffes* Truffles are round, pungent, wrinkled, black fungi usually an inch or two in diameter which are dug up in certain regions of France and Italy from about the first of December to the end of January. They are always expensive. If you have ever been in France during this season, you will never forget the exciting smell of fresh truffles. Tinned truffles, good as they are, give only a suggestion of their original glory. But their flavour can be much enhanced if a spoonful or two of Madeira is poured into the tin half an hour before the truffles are to be used. Truffles are used in decorations, with scrambled eggs and omelettes, in meat stuffings and *pâtés,* and in sauces. The juice from the tin is added to sauces and stuffings for additional truffle flavour. A partially used tin of truffles may be deep frozen.

MEASURES

A PINT OF WATER weighs a pound and a quarter except in America, where 'a pint's a pound the world around', and all measurements in this book are level. Here are some tables for those who wish to translate foreign terms and weights into their nearest British equivalents or vice versa. You will note that the American fluid ounce is slightly larger than the Imperial fluid ounce, however British and American dry or avoirdupois ounces and pounds are similar, as are linear measures for inches and feet. All spoon measurements in this book should be regarded as level spoonfuls.

WEIGHTS

GRAMMES (gr.)	OUNCES (oz.)	GRAMMES	OUNCES
1,000 (1 kilogramme)	$35\frac{1}{5}$ (2·2 lbs.)	85	3
500 (1 livre)	$17\frac{3}{5}$	80	$2\frac{7}{8}$
454	16 (1 lb.)	75	$2\frac{5}{8}$
250	$8\frac{7}{8}$	50	$1\frac{3}{4}$
150	$5\frac{1}{4}$	30 (28·3)	1
125	$4\frac{1}{2}$	25	$\frac{7}{8}$
100	$3\frac{1}{2}$	10	$\frac{1}{3}$

A PINCH, *une pincée* The amount of any ingredient you can take up between your thumb and forefinger. There are large and small pinches.

A SPOONFUL OF FLOUR, *une cuillère de farine* In French this usually means a heaped spoonful: 15 to 20 grams, or $\frac{1}{2}$ to $\frac{2}{3}$ ounce.

LINEAR MEASURE

5 centimetres = 2 inches

30 centimetres = 1 foot

100 centimetres = 1 metre or 40 inches

LIQUID MEASURES

BRITISH TERMS	IMPERIAL FLUID OUNCE	FRENCH TERMS	CENTILITRES	AMERICAN TERMS	AMERICAN FLUID OUNCE
1 quart (qt.)	40		114		38½
	35	1 *litre* (l.)	100		33½
	33⅓		95	1 quart	32
1 pint (pt.)	20		57		19
	16½		47	1 pint	16
1 cup=½ pint (British Standard)	10		28½		9½
	9	¼ *litre*	25		8½
	8⅓		23½	1 cup=½ pint	8
1 gill=¼ pint	5		14		5
	3½	1 *décilitre* (dl.) or 1 *demi-verre*	10		3⅓
	1·04		2·96	1 fluid ounce	1
1 fluid ounce (fl. oz.)	1		2·84		0·96
1 tablespoon (tbl)=1/16 cup	⅝		1⅔		⅝
	½	1 *cuillère à soupe*, 1 *cuillère à bouche* or 1 *verre à liqueur*	1½	1 tablespoon =1/16 cup	½
1 dessertspoon (dsp)	⅓		1		⅓
1 teaspoon (tsp)	⅙	*cuillère à café*	½	1 teaspoon	⅙

CONVERSION FORMULAE

TO CONVERT	MULTIPLY	BY
Ounces to grammes	the ounces	28·35
Grammes to ounces	the grammes	0·035
Litres to British quarts	the litres	0·88
Litres to American quarts	the litres	0·95
British quarts to litres	the quarts	1·14
American quarts to litres	the quarts	1·057
Inches to centimetres	the inches	2·54
Centimetres to inches	the centimetres	0·39

TEMPERATURES

Fahrenheit and Centigrade

TO CONVERT FAHRENHEIT (° F.) INTO CENTIGRADE (° C.),
subtract 32, multiply by 5, divide by 9.

Example: 212 (Fahrenheit) minus 32 equals 180
180 multiplied by 5 equals 900
900 divided by 9 equals 100, or the temperature of boiling water in
centigrade

TO CONVERT CENTIGRADE (° C.) INTO FAHRENHEIT (° F.),
multiply by 9, divide by 5, add 32.

Example: 100 (centigrade) multiplied by 9 equals 900
900 divided by 5 equals 180
180 plus 32 equals 212, or the temperature of boiling water in
Fahrenheit

TEMPERATURE CONVERSION TABLE
British—French

FAHRENHEIT DEGREES	CENTIGRADE DEGREES	BRITISH OVEN TEMPERATURE TERMS	BRITISH REGULO OVEN THERMOSTAT SETTINGS	FRENCH OVEN TEMPERATURE TERMS AND FAIRLY STANDARD THERMOSTAT SETTINGS
160	71			1
170	77			
200	93			Très Doux; Étuve
212	100			
221	105			2
225	107			
230	110			3
240	116	Very slow	$\frac{1}{4}$	Doux
250	121			
265	130		$\frac{1}{2}$	
275	135			
290	143	Slow	1	Moyen; Modéré
300	149			
302	150			4
310	154		2	
325	163			
335	168		3	
350	177			
355	179	Moderate	4	Assez Chaud; Bon Four
375	190			5
380	193		5	
390	200			
400	205	Moderately hot	6	
410	210			
425	218		7	6
428	220	Hot		Chaud
437	225			
445	229		8	
450	232			
470	243	Very hot	9	Très Chaud; Vif
475	246			
490	253		10	
500	260			7
510	265		11	
525	274		12	8
550	288			9

CUTTING

Chopping, Slicing, and Dicing

FRENCH COOKING requires a good deal of chopping, slicing, dicing, and fancy cutting, and if you have not learned to wield a knife rapidly a recipe calling for eight ounces of finely diced vegetables and 2 pounds of sliced mushroom caps is often too discouraging to attempt. It takes several weeks of off-and-on practice to master the various knife techniques, but once learned they are never forgotten. You can save a tremendous amount of time, and also derive a modest pride, in learning how to use a knife professionally.

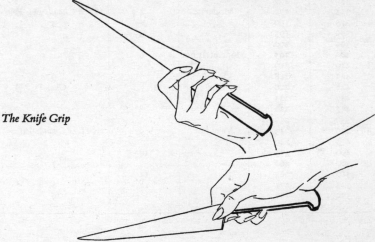

The Knife Grip

For cutting and slicing, hold the knife with your thumb and index finger gripping the top of the blade, and wrap your other fingers around the handle.

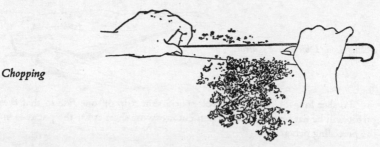

Chopping

For chopping, hold the knife blade by both ends and chop with rapid up-and-down movements, brushing the ingredients repeatedly into a heap again with the knife.

Slicing Round Objects (a)

To slice potatoes or other round or oval objects, cut the potato in half and lay it cut-side down on the chopping board. Use the thumb of your left hand as a pusher, and grip the sides of the potato with your fingers, pointing your fingernails back toward your thumb so that you will not cut them.

Slicing Round Objects (b)

Cut straight down, at a right angle to board, with a quick stroke of the knife blade, pushing the potato slice away from the potato as you hit the board. The knuckles of your left hand act as a guide for the next slice. This goes slowly at first, but after a bit of practice, 2 pounds of potatoes can be sliced in less than 5 minutes.

Slicing Long Objects like Carrots

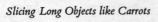

   To slice long objects like carrots, cut a thin strip off one side so that the carrot will lie flat on the board. Then cut crosswise slices as for the potatoes in the preceding paragraph.

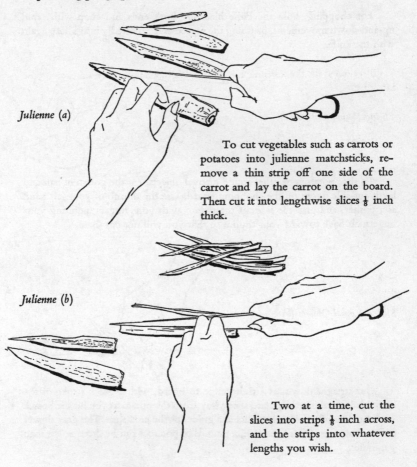

Julienne (a)

   To cut vegetables such as carrots or potatoes into julienne matchsticks, remove a thin strip off one side of the carrot and lay the carrot on the board. Then cut it into lengthwise slices ⅛ inch thick.

Julienne (b)

   Two at a time, cut the slices into strips ⅛ inch across, and the strips into whatever lengths you wish.

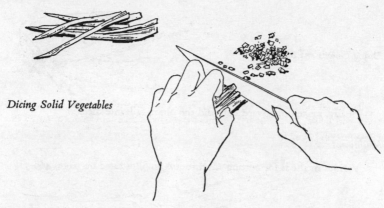

Dicing Solid Vegetables

Proceed as for the julienne, but cut the strips, a handful at a time, crosswise into dice.

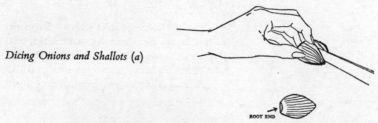

Dicing Onions and Shallots (a)

ROOT END

Once mastered, this method of dicing onions or shallots goes like lightning. Cut the onion in half through the root. Lay one half cut-side down, its root-end to your left. Cut vertical slices from one side to the other, coming just to the root but leaving the slices attached to it, thus the onion will not fall apart.

Dicing Onions and Shallots (b)

Then make horizontal slices from bottom to top, still leaving them attached to the root of the onion.

Dicing Onions and Shallots (c)

Finally, make downward cuts and the onion falls into dice.

Mushrooms

Various methods for cutting mushrooms are illustrated on pages 469-71.

WINES

I. *Cooking with Wine*

Food, like the people who eat it, can be stimulated by wine or spirits. And, as with people, it can also be spoiled. The quality in a white or red wine, vermouth, Madeira, or brandy which heightens the character of cooking is not the alcohol content, which is usually evaporated, but the flavour. Therefore any wine or spirit used in cooking must be a good one. If it is excessively fruity, sour, or unsavoury in any way, these tastes will only be emphasized by the cooking, which ordinarily reduces volume and concentrates flavour. If you have not a good wine to use, it is far better to omit it, for a poor one can spoil a simple dish and utterly debase a noble one.

WHITE WINE

White wine for cooking should be strong and dry, but never sour or fruity. A most satisfactory choice is white Mâcon, made from the Pinot Blanc or the Chardonnay grape. It has all the right qualities and is not unduly expensive.

RED WINE

A good, young, full-bodied red wine is the type you should use for cooking. In France you would pick a Mâcon, one of the lesser Burgundies, one of the more full-bodied clarets such as St.-Émilion, or a good local wine having these qualities.

FORTIFIED WINES, SPIRITS, AND LIQUEURS

Fortified wines, spirits, and liqueurs are used principally for final flavourings. As they must be of excellent quality they are always expensive; but usually only a small quantity is called for, so that your supply should last quite a while. Here, particularly, if you do not want to spend the money for a good bottle, omit the ingredient or pick another recipe.

RUM and LIQUEURS are called for in desserts. Dark Jamaican rum is the best type to use here, to get a full rum flavour. Among liqueurs, orange is most frequently specified; good imported brands as touchstones for flavour are Cointreau, Grand Marnier, and curaçao.

MADEIRA and PORT are often the final flavour-fillip for sauces, as in a brown Madeira sauce for ham, or chicken in port wine. These wines should be the genuine imported article of a medium-dry type, but can be the more moderately priced examples from a good firm.

SHERRY and MARSALA are rarely used in French cooking. If used in place of port or Madeira they tend to give an un-French flavour to most French recipes.

BRANDY is the most ubiquitous spirit in French cooking, from desserts to sauces, consommés, aspics, and *flambées*. Because there are dreadful concoctions bottled under the label of brandy, we have specified cognac whenever brandy is required in a recipe, as a reminder that you use a good brand. You do not have to buy the most expensive, but whatever you use should compare favourably in taste with a good cognac.

II. *Wine and Food*

The wonderful thing about French wines is that they go so well with food. And there is always that enjoyable problem of just which of the many possible choices you should use for a particular occasion. If you are a novice wine drinker, the point to keep in mind in learning about which wine to serve with which dish is that the wine should complement the food and the food should accentuate and blend with the qualities of the wine. A robust wine overpowers the taste of a delicate dish, while a highly spiced dish will kill the flavour of a light wine. A dry wine tastes sour if drunk with a sweet dessert, and a red wine often takes on a fishy taste if served with fish. Great combinations of wine and food are unforgettable: kidneys and one of the great red Burgundies, where each rings reminiscent changes on the characteristics of the other; sole in one of the rich white wine sauces and a fine white Burgundy; *soufflé à la liqueur* and a Château d'Yquem. And then there are the more simple pleasures of a stout red wine and a strong cheese, white wine and oysters, red wine and a beef stew, chilled *rosé* and a dish of cold meats. Knowledge of wines is a lifetime hobby, and the only way to learn is to start drinking and enjoying them, and comparing types, vintages, and good marriages of certain wines with certain foods.

Wine suggestions go with all the master recipes for main courses. Here is a list of generally accepted concordances to reverse the process. As this is a book on French cooking, we have concentrated on French wines.

SWEET WHITE WINES (*not champagnes*)

The best known of these are probably the Sauternes, the greatest of which is Château d'Yquem. They may range from noble and full bodied to relatively light, depending on the vineyard and vintage.

Sweet white wines are too often neglected. Those of good quality can be magnificent with dessert mousses, creams, soufflés, and cakes. And a fine Sauternes is delicious with foie gras *or a pâté of chicken livers. In the old days sweet wines were drunk with oysters.*

LIGHT, DRY, WHITE WINES

Typical examples are Alsatian Riesling, Muscadet, Sancerre, and usually Pouilly-Fumé, Pouilly-Fuissé, and Chablis. Local wines, *vins du pays*, often fall into this category.

Serve with oysters, cold shellfish, boiled shellfish, grilled fish, cold meats, egg dishes, and entrées.

FULL-BODIED DRY, WHITE WINES

White Burgundy, Côtes du Rhône, and the dry Graves are examples.

Serve with fish, poultry, and veal in cream sauces. White Burgundy can also be drunk with foie gras, *and it is not unheard of to serve a Meursault with Roquefort cheese.*

ROSÉS

Rosés *can be served with anything, but are usually reserved for cold dishes,* pâtés, *eggs, and pork.*

LIGHT-BODIED RED WINES

These are typically clarets from the Médoc or Graves districts. Many of the regional wines and local *vins du pays* can also be included here.

Serve clarets with roast chicken, turkey, veal, or lamb; also with fillet of beef, ham, liver, quail, pheasant, foie gras, and soft fermented cheese like Camembert. Regional wines and vins du pays *go especially well with informal dishes such as beef or lamb stew, daubes, bouillabaisse, hamburgers, steaks, and pâtés.*

FULL-BODIED RED WINES

All of the great Burgundies and Rhônes fall into this category; the full-bodied clarets from St.-Émilion may be included also.

Serve with duck, goose, kidneys, well-hung game, meats marinated in red wine, and authoritative cheeses such as Roquefort. They are called for wherever strong-flavoured foods must meet strong-flavoured wines.

CHAMPAGNE
Brut
Serve as an apéritif, *or at the end of an evening. Or it may accompany the whole meal.*

Dry, Sec
Serve as an apéritif, *or with crustaceans, or* foie gras, *or with nuts and dried fruits.*

Sweet, Doux, Demi-sec
Sweet champagne is another neglected wine, yet is the only kind to serve with desserts and pastries.

III. *The Storage and Serving of Wine*

Except for champagne, which has sugar added to it to produce the bubbles, great French wines are the unadulterated, fermented juice from the pressings of one type of grape originating in one vineyard during one harvest season. Lesser wines, which can be very good, may also be unadulterated. On the other hand, they may be fortified with sugar during a lean year to build up their alcoholic strength, or they may be blended with wines from other vineyards or localities to give them more body or uniformity of taste. The quality of a wine is due to the variety of grape it is made from, the locality in which it is grown, and the climate during the wine-growing year. In exceptional years such as 1929 and 1947, even lesser wines can be great, and the great ones become priceless. Vintage charts, which you can procure from your wine merchant, evaluate the various wines by region for each year.

Wine is a living liquid containing no preservatives. Its life cycle comprises youth, maturity, old age, and death. When not treated with reasonable respect it will sicken and die. If it is left standing upright for a length of time, the cork will dry out, air will enter the bottle, and the wine will spoil. Shaking of any kind is damaging to it, as are extreme fluctuations of heat and cold. If it is to be laid down to grow into maturity it should rest on its side in a dark, well-ventilated place at a temperature of around 50 degrees Fahrenheit. If it is to be kept only for a year or two, it can be laid in any dark and quiet corner as long as the temperature remains fairly constant and is neither below 50 degrees Fahrenheit nor over 65.

Even the most modest wine will improve if allowed to rest for several days before it is drunk. This allows the wine to reconstitute itself after its journey from shop to home. Great wines, particularly the red ones, benefit from a rest of at least two to three weeks.

TEMPERATURE AT WHICH WINE SHOULD BE SERVED

Red wines, unless they are very young and light, are generally served at a normal room temperature of around 65 degrees Fahrenheit. At lower temperatures they do not show off their full qualities. At least four hours in the dining room are required to bring them slowly up from the temperature of a 50-degree-Fahrenheit cellar. Never warm a wine artificially; an old wine can be ruined if the bottle is heated. It is better to pour it out too cold, and let it warm in the glass.

White wines, champagnes, and *rosés* are served chilled. As a rule, the sweeter the wine, the colder it should be. A Sauternes or sweet champagne will take four to five hours in the refrigerator. For other white wines, two to three hours are sufficient; if they are too cold, they lose much of their taste.

UNCORKING

Most red wines should be uncorked for a certain amount of time before serving, to allow the release of pent-up gases. There is no set rule, and one vintage may differ from another. In general, a light young red wine needs half an hour, a Burgundy about an hour, and a claret three to four hours. If you cannot uncork the wine ahead of time, decant it, which will aerate it. White wines, champagnes, and *rosés* are uncorked just before serving.

WINE BASKETS, DECANTERS, AND GLASSES

Old red wines that throw a deposit in the bottom of the bottle must be handled so as not to disturb the deposit and circulate it through the wine. Either pour the wine into a decanter leaving the deposit behind, or serve it from a wine basket where it will remain in a prone position. When serving from a basket, pour very smoothly so that the wine does not slop back into the bottle and agitate the sediment.

Young red wines, white wines, *rosés,* and champagnes throw no deposit, so the use of a wine basket is silly. The bottle is stood upright after the wine is poured.

The bigger the wine, the bigger the glass. A small glass gives no room for the bouquet to develop, nor for the drinker to swirl it. A good all-purpose glass is tulip-shaped and holds about ¼ pint. It should be filled to just below the halfway mark.

CHAPTER ONE

SOUP

Potages et Soupes

An EXCELLENT LUNCH or light supper need be no more than a good soup, a salad, cheese and fruit. And combined according to your own taste, a good home-made soup in these days of the tin opener is almost a unique and always a satisfying experience. Most soups are simple to make, and the major portion of them can be prepared several hours before serving. Here is a varied handful of good recipes.

A NOTE ON ELECTRIC LIQUIDIZERS AND PRESSURE COOKERS

Although we are enthusiastic about the electric liquidizer for many things, we almost always prefer a moulinette to a liquidizer when a soup must be puréed. There is something un-French and monotonous about the way a liquidizer reduces soup to universal baby pap.

A pressure cooker can save time, but the vegetables for a long-simmered soup should have only 5 minutes under 15 pounds pressure; more gives them a pressure-cooker taste. Then the pressure should be released and the soup simmered for 15 to 20 minutes so that it will develop its full flavour.

---

* POTAGE PARMENTIER

[Leek or Onion and Potato Soup]

Leek and potato soup smells good, tastes good, and is simplicity itself to make. It is also versatile as a soup base; add watercress and you have a watercress soup, or stir in cream and chill it for a *vichyssoise*. To change the formula a bit, add carrots, string beans, cauliflower, broccoli, or anything else you think would go with it, and vary the proportions as you wish.

For about 3 pints serving 6 to 8 people

A 5- to 6-pt. saucepan or pressure cooker
1 lb. peeled potatoes, sliced or diced

1 lb. thinly sliced leeks including the tender green; or onions
3 pts. of water
1 dsp salt

Either simmer the vegetables, water, and salt together, partially covered, for 40 to 50 minutes until the vegetables are tender; or cook under 15 pounds pressure for 5 minutes, release pressure, and simmer uncovered for 15 minutes.

Mash the vegetables in the soup with a fork, or pass the soup through a moulinette. Correct seasoning. (*) Set aside uncovered until just before serving, then reheat to simmering point.

4 to 6 tbl cream or 1 to 1½ oz. softened butter

2 to 3 tbl chopped parsley or chives

Away from heat, and just before serving, stir in the cream or butter by spoonfuls. Pour into a tureen or soup cups and decorate with the herbs.

VARIATIONS

Potage au Cresson

[Watercress Soup]

This simple version of watercress soup is very good. See also the more elaborate recipe on page 35.

For 6 to 8 people

Ingredients for the leek and potato soup, omitting cream or butter enrichment until later

¼ lb. of watercress leaves and tender stems

Follow the preceding master recipe, but before puréeing the soup, stir in the watercress and simmer for 5 minutes. Then purée in a moulinette and correct seasoning.

4 to 6 tbl cream or 1 to 1½ oz. softened butter
Optional: a small handful of

watercress leaves boiled ½ minute in water, rinsed in cold water, and drained

Away from heat, and just before serving, stir in the cream or butter by spoonfuls. Decorate with the optional watercress leaves.

Cold Watercress Soup

Use the following *vichyssoise* recipe, adding watercress to simmer for 5 minutes before puréeing the soup.

Vichyssoise

[Cold Leek and Potato Soup]

This is an invention based on the leek and potato soup in the preceding master recipe.

For 6 to 8 people

¾ lb. peeled, sliced potatoes   Salt to taste
1 lb. sliced white of leek
2½ pts. of white stock, chicken
   stock, or chicken broth

Simmer the vegetables in stock or broth instead of water as described in the master recipe. Purée the soup either in the electric liquidizer, or through a moulinette and then through a fine sieve.

¼ to ½ pt. cream   Salt and white pepper

Stir in the cream. Season to taste, oversalting very slightly as salt loses savour in a cold dish. Chill.

Chilled soup cups   2 to 3 tbl chopped chives

Serve in chilled soup cups and decorate with chopped chives.

OTHER VARIATIONS on Leek and Potato Soup

Using the master recipe for leek and potato soup on page 31, ¼ to ½ pound of one or a combination of the following vegetables may be added as indicated. Proportions are not important here, and you can use your imagination to the full. Many of the delicious soups you eat in French homes and little restaurants are made just this way, with a leek and potato base to which leftover vegetables or sauces and a few fresh items are added. You can also experiment with your own combinations for cold soups, by stirring ½ pint or more of cream into the cooked soup, chilling it, then sprinkling on fresh herbs just before serving. You may find you have invented a marvellous concoction, which you can keep as a secret of the house.

To be simmered or cooked in the pressure cooker with the potatoes and leeks or onions at the start

Sliced or diced carrots or turnips   Half-cooked dried beans, peas, or
Peeled, seeded, and chopped   lentils, including their cooking
   tomatoes, page 465; or   liquid
   strained tinned tomatoes

B

To be simmered for 10 to 15 minutes with the soup after it has been puréed

Fresh or frozen diced cauliflower, cucumbers, broccoli, butter beans, peas, string beans, or courgettes	**Shredded lettuce, spinach, sorrel, or cabbage**

To be heated in the soup just before serving

Diced, cooked leftovers of any of the preceding vegetables	**Tomatoes, peeled, seeded, juiced, and diced, page 465**

POTAGE VELOUTÉ AUX CHAMPIGNONS

[Cream of Mushroom Soup]

Here is a fine, rich, mushroom soup either for grand occasions or as the main course for a Sunday supper.

For 6 to 8 people

A 4-pt. heavy-bottomed enamelled saucepan	**4 tbl chopped onions**
	1½ oz. butter

Cook the onions slowly in the butter for 8 to 10 minutes, until they are tender but not browned.

1½ oz. flour

Add the flour and stir over moderate heat for 3 minutes without browning.

2½ pts. boiling white stock or chicken stock; or chicken broth and 2 parsley sprigs, 1 bay leaf, and ⅛ tsp thyme	**Salt and pepper to taste**
	The chopped stems from ¾ to 1 lb. fresh mushrooms

Away from heat, beat in the boiling stock or broth and blend it thoroughly with the flour. Season to taste. Stir in the mushroom stems, and simmer partially covered for 20 minutes or more, skimming occasionally. Strain, pressing juices out of mushroom stems. Return the soup to the pan.

1 oz. butter	**¼ tsp salt**
An enamelled saucepan	**1 tsp lemon juice**
The thinly sliced caps from ¾ to 1 lb. fresh mushrooms	

Melt the butter in a separate saucepan. When it is foaming, toss in the mushrooms, salt, and lemon juice. Cover and cook slowly for 5 minutes.

Pour the mushrooms and their cooking juices into the strained soup base. Simmer for 10 minutes.

(*) If not to be served immediately, set aside uncovered, and film surface with a spoonful of cream or milk. Reheat to simmering point just before proceeding to the step below, which will take 2 or 3 minutes.

2 egg yolks	A wire whisk
¼ pt. cream	A wooden spoon
A 5-pt. mixing bowl	

Beat the egg yolks and cream in the mixing bowl. Then beat in hot soup by spoonfuls until ½ pint has been added. Gradually stir in the rest. Correct seasoning. Return the soup to the pan and stir over moderate heat for a minute or two to poach the egg yolks, but do not let the soup come near simmering point.

½ to 1½ oz. softened butter	and lemon juice; and/or
Optional: 6 to 8 fluted mushroom	2 or 3 tbl chopped fresh
caps, page 470, cooked in butter	chervil or parsley

Away from heat, stir in the butter by tablespoons. Pour the soup into a tureen or soup cups, and decorate with optional mushrooms and herbs.

---

* POTAGE CRÈME DE CRESSON

[Cream of Watercress Soup]

This is a lovely soup, and a perfect one for an important dinner.

For 6 servings

6 tbl chopped onion, or spring	1½ oz. butter
onions	A heavy-bottomed, 4-pt. saucepan

Cook the onions slowly in the butter in a covered saucepan for 5 to 10 minutes, until tender and translucent but not browned.

½ to ¾ lb. of fresh watercress leaves	½ tsp salt
and tender stems, washed, and	
dried in a cloth	

Stir in the watercress and salt, cover, and cook slowly for about 5 minutes or until the leaves are tender and wilted.

1½ oz. flour

Sprinkle in the flour and stir over moderate heat for 3 minutes.

2½ pts. boiling white stock or
  chicken broth

Away from heat, beat in the boiling stock. Simmer for 5 minutes, then purée
through a moulinette. Return to saucepan and correct seasoning.

(*) If not to be served immediately, set aside uncovered. Reheat to simmering
point before proceeding.

2 egg yolks	A wire whisk
¼ pt. cream	½ to 1 oz. softened butter
A 5-pt. mixing bowl	

Blend the yolks and cream in the mixing bowl. Beat ½ pint of hot soup into
them drop by drop. Gradually beat in the rest of the soup in a thin stream.
Return soup to saucepan and stir over moderate heat for a minute or two to
poach the egg yolks, but do not bring the soup to simmering point. Remove
from heat, stir in the enrichment butter a little at a time.

A handful of watercress leaves	water, refreshed in cold
dropped for ½ minute in boiling	water, and drained

Pour the soup into a tureen or soup cups and decorate with optional watercress
leaves.

TO SERVE COLD: Omit final butter enrichment and chill. If too thick,
stir in more cream before serving.

VARIATIONS

Potage Crème d'Oseille or Potage Germiny

[Cream of Sorrel Soup]

Potage Crème d'Épinards

[Cream of Spinach Soup]

Follow the recipe for the preceding *crème de cresson,* using sorrel or spinach
leaves instead of watercress, but cut the leaves into chiffonade (thin slices or
shreds). Do not purée the soup.

---

* SOUPE À L'OIGNON

[Onion Soup]

The onions for an onion soup need a long, slow cooking in butter and oil,
then a long, slow simmering in stock for them to develop the deep, rich flavour

which characterizes a perfect brew. You should therefore count on 2½ hours at least from start to finish. Though the preliminary cooking in butter requires some watching, the actual simmering can proceed almost unattended.

For 6 to 8 servings

1½ lbs. thinly sliced onions	A heavy-bottomed, 6-pt.
1½ oz. butter	covered saucepan
1 tbl oil	

Cook the onions slowly with the butter and oil in the covered saucepan for 15 minutes.

1 tsp salt
¼ tsp sugar (helps the onions to
   brown)

Uncover, raise heat to moderate, and stir in the salt and sugar. Cook for 30 to 40 minutes stirring frequently, until the onions have turned an even, deep, golden brown.

1½ oz. flour

Sprinkle in the flour and stir for 3 minutes.

3¼ pts. boiling brown stock, beef bouillon, or 1½ pts. of boiling water and 1½ pts. of stock or bouillon	¼ pt. dry white wine or dry white vermouth Salt and pepper to taste

Away from heat, blend in the boiling liquid. Add the wine, and season to taste. Simmer partially covered for 30 to 40 minutes or more, skimming occasionally. Correct seasoning.

(*) Leave aside uncovered until ready to serve. Then reheat to simmering point.

3 tbl cognac	¼ to ½ lb. grated Swiss or Parmesan
Rounds of hard-toasted French bread (see recipe following)	cheese

Just before serving, stir in the cognac. Pour into a soup tureen or soup cups over the rounds of bread, and pass the cheese separately.

GARNISHINGS FOR ONION SOUP

Croûtes—hard-toasted French bread

12 to 16 slices of French bread
   cut ¾ to 1 in. thick

Place the bread in one layer in a roasting tin and bake in a preheated oven 325° F.,

Mark 2, for about half an hour, until it is thoroughly dried out and lightly browned.

Olive oil or beef dripping   **A cut clove of garlic**

Halfway through the baking, each side may be basted with a teaspoon of olive oil or beef drippings; and after baking, each piece may be rubbed with cut garlic.

Croûtes au Fromage—cheese *croûtes*

Grated Swiss or Parmesan cheese   **Olive oil or beef dripping**

Spread one side of each *croûte* with grated cheese and sprinkle with drops of olive oil or beef dripping. Brown under a hot grill before serving.

VARIATIONS

Soupe à l'Oignon Gratinée

[Onion Soup *Gratinéed* with Cheese]

The preceding onion soup
A fireproof tureen or casserole or
**   individual onion soup pots**
2 oz. Swiss cheese cut into very thin
**   slivers**
1 tbl grated raw onion

12 to 16 rounds of hard-toasted
**   French bread**
4 to 6 oz. grated Swiss, or Swiss and
**   Parmesan cheese**
1 tbl olive oil or melted butter

Preheat oven to 325° F., Mark 2.
Bring the soup to the boil and pour into the tureen or soup pots. Stir in the slivered cheese and grated onion. Float the rounds of toast on top of the soup, and spread the grated cheese over it. Sprinkle with the oil or butter. Bake for 20 minutes in the oven, then set for a minute or two under a preheated grill to brown the top lightly. Serve immediately.

Soupe Gratinée des Trois Gourmandes

[Onion Soup *Gratinéed de Luxe*]

A final fillip to the preceding onion soup may be accomplished in the kitchen just before serving or by the server at the table.

A 3-pt. bowl   **1 tsp Worcester sauce**
1 tsp cornflour   **3 tbl cognac**
1 egg yolk

Beat the cornflour into the egg yolk, then the Worcester sauce and the cognac.

The preceding onion soup   **A serving fork**
A soup ladle

Just before serving the soup, lift up an edge of the crust with a fork and remove a ladleful of soup. In a thin stream of drops, beat the soup into the egg yolk mixture with a fork. Gradually beat in two more ladlefuls, which may be added more rapidly.

Again lifting up the crust, pour the mixture back into the soup. Then reach in under the crust with the ladle and stir gently to blend the mixture into the rest of the soup. Serve.

SOUPE AU PISTOU

[Provençal Vegetable Soup with Garlic, Basil and Herbs]

Early summer is the Mediterranean season for *soupe au piston,* when fresh basil, fresh white beans, and broad *mange-tout* beans are all suddenly available, and the market women shout in the streets, *'Mesdames, faites le bon piste, faites le pistou!'* The *pistou* itself, like the Italian *pesta,* is a sauce made of garlic, basil, tomato and cheese, and is just as good on spaghetti as it is in this rich vegetable soup. Fortunately, this soup is not confined to summer and fresh vegetables, for you can use tinned haricot beans or runner beans, fresh or frozen French beans, and a fragrant dried basil. Other vegetables in season may be added with the French beans as you wish, such as peas, diced courgettes, and green or red peppers.

For 6 to 8 servings

5 pts. water
½ lb. each: diced carrots, diced
   boiling potatoes, diced white of
   leek or onions

1 tbl salt
(If available, ½ lb. fresh white
   beans, and omit the haricot beans
   farther on)

Either boil the water, vegetables, and salt slowly in a 5-quart pan for 40 minutes; or pressure-cook for 5 minutes, release pressure, and simmer uncovered for 15 to 20 minutes. Correct seasoning.

½ lb. diced French beans or 1
   packet frozen 'cut' beans
½ lb. cooked haricot or runner
   beans

1 oz. broken spaghetti or vermicelli
1 slice stale white bread, crumbled
⅛ tsp pepper
Pinch of saffron

Twenty minutes before serving, so that the green vegetables will retain their freshness, add the beans, spaghetti or vermicelli, bread and seasonings to the boiling soup. Boil slowly for about 15 minutes, or until the French beans are just cooked through. Correct seasoning again.

4 cloves mashed garlic　　　　　　2 oz. grated Parmesan cheese
6 tbl fresh tomato purée, page 69,　⅛ to ¼ pt. fruity olive oil
　or 4 tbl tomato paste
4 tbl chopped fresh basil or 1 tbl
　fragrant dried basil

Prepare the following *pistou* while the soup is cooking: place the garlic, tomato purée or paste, basil, and cheese in the soup tureen and blend to a paste with a wooden spoon; then, drop by drop, beat in the olive oil. When the soup is ready for serving, beat ½ pint gradually into the *pistou*. Pour in the rest of the soup. Serve with hot French bread, or hard-toasted bread rounds basted with olive oil, page 37.

---

* *AÏGO BOUÏDO*

[Garlic Soup]

Enjoying your first bowl of garlic soup, you might never suspect what it is made of. Because the garlic is boiled, its after-effects are at a minimum, and its flavour becomes exquisite, aromatic, and almost undefinable. Along the Mediterranean, an *aïgo bouïdo* is considered to be very good indeed for the liver, blood circulation, general physical tone, and spiritual health. A head of garlic is not at all too much for 3 pints of soup. For some addicts, it is not even enough.

For 6 to 8 people

1 separated head or about 16 cloves
　whole, unpeeled garlic

Drop garlic cloves in boiling water and boil 30 seconds. Drain, run cold water over them, and peel.

3 pts. water　　　　　　　　¼ tsp thyme
2 tsp salt　　　　　　　　　½ bay leaf
Pinch of pepper　　　　　　4 parsley sprigs
2 cloves　　　　　　　　　　3 tbl olive oil
¼ tsp sage　　　　　　　　　A 5-pt. saucepan

Place the garlic and the rest of the ingredients in the saucepan and boil slowly for 30 minutes. Correct seasoning.

A wire whisk　　　　　　　A soup tureen
3 egg yolks　　　　　　　　2 to 3 tbl olive oil

Beat the egg yolks in the soup tureen for a minute until they are thick and sticky. Drop by drop, beat in the olive oil as for making a mayonnaise.

A strainer   4 oz. grated Swiss or Parmesan
Rounds of hard-toasted French   cheese
  bread, page 37

Just before serving, beat a ladleful of hot soup into the egg mixture drop by
drop. Gradually strain in the rest, beating, and pressing the juice out of the
garlic. Serve immediately, accompanied by the bread and cheese.

VARIATIONS

Soupe à l'Oeuf, Provençale

[Garlic Soup with Poached Eggs]

The preceding garlic soup,   6 very fresh eggs
  omitting the egg yolk and olive
  oil liaison

After the soup has been simmered for half an hour, strain it into a wide, shallow
saucepan. Correct seasoning and bring to simmering point. Following directions
on page 104, poach the eggs in the soup.

6 to 8 rounds of hard-toasted French   2 to 3 tbl chopped parsley
  bread, page 37   4 oz. grated Parmesan cheese

Place a round of bread in each soup plate and top with a poached egg. Pour in
the soup and decorate with parsley. Pass the cheese separately.

Soupe à l'Ail aux Pommes de Terre

[Saffron-flavoured Garlic Soup with Potatoes]

Ingredients for garlic soup,   ¾ lb. diced boiling potatoes
  omitting the egg yolk and olive   Pinch of saffron
  oil liaison

After the garlic soup has simmered for 30 minutes, strain it and return it to the
saucepan. Simmer the potatoes in the soup with the saffron for about 20 minutes
or until tender. Correct seasoning. Serve with French bread and grated Swiss or
Parmesan cheese.

SOUPE AUX CHOUX—GARBURE

[Main-course Cabbage Soup]

This fine and uncomplicated peasant soup is a comforting dish for a cold
winter day. In the Basque country, a good cabbage soup must always include a
B*

chunk of *lard rance,* their slightly rancid and much appreciated salt pork; otherwise, the dish is considered to lack distinction. In neighbouring Béarn, *confit d'oie*—preserved goose—is added to the pot to warm up in the soup at the end of its cooking.

For about 8 people

5 pts. water
¾ lb. peeled, quartered boiling potatoes

A 1½-lb. chunk of lean salt pork, lean bacon, or smoked, unprocessed ham

Place the water, potatoes, and meat in the pan and bring it to the boil.

2 lbs. of roughly sliced cabbage
8 crushed peppercorns or a big pinch of ground chilli peppers
Salt as necessary, added near the end
6 parsley sprigs tied with 1 bay leaf
½ tsp marjoram
½ tsp thyme
4 cloves mashed garlic

2 medium onions studded with 2 cloves
2 peeled, quartered carrots
Optional additions:
2 to 4 peeled, quartered turnips
2 to 3 sliced celery stalks
¼ to ½ lb. fresh white beans, or half-cooked haricot beans

Add the cabbage and all the other ingredients. Simmer partially covered for 1½ to 2 hours or until the meat is tender. Discard parsley bundle. Remove the meat, slice it into serving pieces, and return it to the pan. Correct seasoning. Skim off accumulated fat.

(*) If not to be served immediately, set aside uncovered. Reheat to simmering point before serving.

Rounds of hard-toasted French bread, page 37

Serve in a tureen or soup plates, accompanied by the bread.

TWO MEDITERRANEAN FISH SOUPS

How to make a real Mediterranean fish soup is always a subject of lively and utterly dogmatic discussion among French experts; and if you do not happen to live on the Mediterranean, you cannot obtain the particular rockfish, gurnards, mullets, weavers, sea eels, wrasses, and breams which they consider absolutely essential. But you can make an extremely good fish soup even if you have only frozen fish to work with because the other essential flavourings of tomatoes, onions or leeks, garlic, herbs, and olive oil are always available.

Fish soups are usually made from lean fish. The flavour of the soup is more interesting if as many varieties of fish are included as possible, and the soup has more body if a proportion of gelatinous fish such as halibut, eel, and some of the firmer-fleshed type are used. Here are some suggestions:

Cod or Ling	Red or Grey Mullet
Conger or Sea Eel	Rock or Sea Bass
Gurnard or Gurnet	Sea Bream
Haddock	Sea Devil, Frogfish, or Angler
Hake or Whiting	Fresh-water Trout; Sea Trout
Halibut	Turbot
John Dory	Weever
Lemon Sole	Wrasse
Perch	Shellfish—Scallops, Mussels, Crab,
Plaice	Lobster
Pollack, Coalfish or Saithe	

To prepare the fish for cooking, have them cleaned and scaled. Discard the gills. Save heads and trimmings for fish stock. Cut large fish into crosswise slices 2 inches wide. Scrub and soak the mussels, page 204. Wash scallops. If using live crab or lobster, split them just before cooking. Remove the sand sac and intestinal tube from lobsters.

SOUPE DE POISSON

[Strained Fish Soup]

Soupe de poisson has the same taste as bouillabaisse, but the soup is strained and *pasta* is cooked in it to give a light liaison. If you are making the soup on the Mediterranean, you will come home with dozens of tiny, freshly caught fish all colours of the rainbow. Elsewhere, use whole fish, fish heads, bones, and trimmings, shellfish carcasses.

For 6 to 8 people

A large saucepan	¼ pt. olive oil
¼ lb. chopped onions	
3 oz. chopped leek, or 2 oz. more onions	

Cook the onions and leeks slowly in olive oil for 5 minutes or until almost tender but not browned.

4 cloves mashed garlic	or a small tin drained tomatoes,
1 lb. of ripe tomatoes roughly chopped,	or 3 tbl tomato paste

Stir in the garlic and tomatoes. Raise heat to moderate and cook 5 minutes more.

3½ pts. water	⅛ tsp pepper
6 parsley sprigs	1 tbl salt
1 bay leaf	3 to 4 lbs. lean fish, fish heads,
½ tsp thyme or basil	bones, and trimmings, shellfish
⅛ tsp fennel	remains, or frozen fish from the
2 big pinches of saffron	list, page 43
A 2-in. piece orange peel	

Add the water, herbs, seasonings, and fish to the pan and cook uncovered at a moderate boil for 30 to 40 minutes.

2 oz. spaghetti or vermicelli	A 5-pt. saucepan
broken into 2 in. pieces	

Strain the soup into the saucepan, pressing juices out of ingredients. Correct seasoning, adding a bit more saffron if you feel it necessary. Stir in the *pasta* and boil for 10 to 12 minutes or until tender. Correct seasoning again.

Rounds of hard-toasted French	Parmesan cheese and *rouille*
bread, page 37	(following recipe)
¼ to ½ lb. grated Swiss or	

Pour the soup into a tureen or soup plates over the bread rounds, and pass the cheese and *rouille* separately.

VARIATION

Substitute ¾ pound or 1 pound of diced potatoes for the *pasta,* or poach eggs in the soup as for the garlic soup on page 40.

Rouille

[Garlic, Pimento, and Chilli Pepper Sauce]

The following strong sauce is passed separately with fish soup or bouilla-baisse; each guest helps himself and stirs it into the soup.

For about ½ pint

1 oz. chopped red pepper simmered	1 medium potato cooked in the
for several minutes in salted	soup
water and drained, or tinned	4 cloves mashed garlic
pimento	1 tsp basil, thyme, or savory
A small chilli pepper boiled until	
tender, or drops of Tabasco	
sauce	

Pound all ingredients in a bowl or mortar for several minutes to form a very smooth, sticky paste.

4 to 6 tbl fruity olive oil   **Salt and pepper**

Drop by drop, pound or beat in the olive oil as for making a mayonnaise.
Season to taste.

2 to 3 tbl hot soup

Just before serving, beat in the hot soup drop by drop. Pour into a sauceboat.

BOUILLABAISSE
[Bouillabaisse]

You can make as dramatic a production as you want out of a bouillabaisse,
but remember it originated as a simple, Mediterranean fisherman's soup, made
from the day's catch or its unsaleable leftovers, and flavoured with the typical
condiments of the region—olive oil, garlic, leeks or onions, tomatoes, and herbs.
The fish are rapidly boiled in an aromatic broth and are removed to a dish; the
broth is served in a tureen. Each guest helps himself to both and eats them
together in a big soup plate. If you wish to serve wine, choose a *rosé*, or a light,
strong, young red such as a Côtes de Provence or Beaujolais, or a strong, dry,
white wine from the Côtes de Provence, or a Riesling.

Ideally you should pick six or more varieties of fresh fish, which is why a
bouillabaisse is at its best when made for at least six people. Some of the fish
should be firm-fleshed and gelatinous like halibut, eel, and angler, and some
tender and flaky like hake, baby cod, and lemon sole. Shellfish are neither
necessary nor particularly typical, but they always add glamour and colour if
you wish to include them.

The fish, except for live lobsters and crabs, may be cleaned, sliced, and
refrigerated several hours before the final cooking. The soup base may be boiled
and strained. The actual cooking of the fish in the soup will take only about 20
minutes, and then the dish should be served immediately.

For 6 to 8 people

Ingredients for the preceding   **Use fish heads, bones, and**
  soupe de poisson, minus the *pasta*.   **trimmings**

Boil the soup ingredients for 30 to 40 minutes as described in the fish soup recipe,
page 43. Strain, pressing juices out of ingredients. Taste carefully for seasoning
and strength. It should be delicious at this point, so it will need no further fussing
with later. You should have about 2 quarts in a high, rather narrow pan.

6 to 8 lbs. assorted lean fish, and shellfish
  if you wish, selected and prepared
  from the suggestions on page 43

Bring the soup to a rapid boil 20 minutes before serving. Add lobsters, crabs, and firm-fleshed fish. Bring quickly back to the boil and boil rapidly for 5 minutes. Add the tender-fleshed fish, the mussels, and scallops. Bring rapidly to the boil again and boil 5 minutes more or until the fish are just tender when pierced with a fork. Do not overcook.

A hot dish
A soup tureen
Rounds of hard-toasted French
  bread, page 37

3 tbl roughly chopped fresh parsley
Optional: A bowl of *rouille* (page
  44)

Immediately lift out the fish and arrange on the dish. Correct seasoning, and pour the soup into the tureen over rounds of French bread. Spoon a ladleful of soup over the fish, and sprinkle parsley over both fish and soup. Serve immediately accompanied by the optional *rouille*.

CHAPTER TWO

SAUCES

Sauces

SAUCES ARE the splendour and glory of French cooking, yet there is nothing secret or mysterious about making them. For while a roster of French sauces is stupendous, the individual sauces divide themselves into half a dozen definite groups and each one in a particular group is made in the same general way. For instance, each of the white sauces—béchamel and *velouté*—calls for an identical technique, but any change in ingredients or trimmings gives the sauce a different name. Béchamel with grated Swiss cheese is *sauce mornay*. Béchamel with cream is *sauce suprême*. A fish *velouté* enriched with cream, egg yolks, and butter becomes a *sauce normande*. The group which stems from hollandaise follows the same pattern. Hollandaise made with vinegar, shallots, pepper, and tarragon is called *sauce béarnaise*. Hollandaise made with white-wine fish stock is *sauce vin blanc*. If cream is added to a hollandaise, the sauce becomes a *mousseline*. Thus as soon as you have put into practice the basic formulas for the few mother sauces, you are equipped to command the whole towering edifice.

Rich sauces should be used sparingly, never more than one to a meal. And a sauce should never be considered as a disguise or a mask. Its role is to prolong, and complement the taste of the food it accompanies, to contrast with it, or to give variety to its mode of presentation. One of its most useful functions, also, is to make an interesting dish out of something simple and economical like hard-boiled eggs, plain poached fish, tinned food, or leftovers.

The French Family of Sauces

WHITE SAUCES

These stem from the two cousins, béchamel and *velouté*. Both use a flour and butter *roux* as thickening agent. Béchamel is moistened with milk; *velouté*, with white stock made from poultry, veal, or fish.

BROWN SAUCES

For the brown sauces, the butter and flour *roux* is cooked slowly until it turns a nut brown. Then a brown stock is added.

TOMATO SAUCE

EGG YOLK AND BUTTER SAUCES

Hollandaise is the mother of this family.

EGG YOLK AND OIL SAUCES

These are all variations of mayonnaise.

OIL AND VINEGAR SAUCES

Vinaigrette—French dressing—heads this family.

FLAVOURED BUTTERS

These include the hot butter sauces, and butters creamed with various herbs, seasonings, or purées.

WHITE SAUCES

Sauces Blanches

White sauces are rapidly made with a white *roux* (butter and flour cooked together) plus milk, or white stock. They go with eggs, fish, chicken, veal, and vegetables. They are also the base for cream soups, soufflés, and many of the hot hors d'œuvres.

Sauce béchamel in the time of Louis XIV was a more elaborate sauce than it is today. Then it was a simmering of milk, veal, and seasonings with an enrichment of cream. In modern French cooking, a béchamel is a quickly made milk-based foundation requiring only the addition of butter, cream, herbs, or other flavourings to turn it into a proper sauce.

Sauce velouté is made in exactly the same way, but its *roux* is moistened with chicken, veal, or fish stock, often with a wine flavouring. Milk or cream are included if you wish.

The roux

In French cooking, the flour and butter, which act as a thickening agent for the sauce, are always cooked slowly together for several minutes before any liquid is added. This is called a *roux*. The cooking eliminates that raw, pasty taste uncooked flour will give to a sauce, and also prepares the flour particles to absorb the liquid. The thickness of a sauce is in direct relation to the proportion of flour you use per pint of liquid. The following table is based on plain flour.

THIN SAUCE OR SOUP	$\frac{1}{2}$ ounce flour per $\frac{1}{2}$ pint of liquid
MEDIUM, GENERAL-PURPOSE SAUCE	$\frac{3}{4}$ ounce flour per $\frac{1}{2}$ pint of liquid
THICK SAUCE	1 ounce flour per $\frac{1}{2}$ pint of liquid
SOUFFLÉ BASE	$1\frac{1}{2}$ ounce flour per $\frac{1}{2}$ pint of liquid

Cooking time

Many of the old cookery books recommend that a white sauce, especially a *velouté*, be simmered for several hours, the object being to rid the sauce of its floury taste, and to concentrate flavour. However, if the flour and butter *roux* is properly cooked to begin with, and a concentrated, well-flavoured stock is used, both of these problems have been solved at the start. After a long simmering, a perfectly executed *velouté* will acquire a certain added finesse; and if you have the time to simmer, by all means do so. But for the practical purposes of this book, we shall seldom consider it necessary.

Saucepan note

White sauces should always be made in a heavy-bottomed enamelled, stainless steel, or tin-lined copper saucepan. If a thin-bottomed pan is used, it is a poor heat conductor and the sauce may scorch in the bottom of the pan. Aluminium tends to discolour a white sauce, particularly one containing wine or egg yolks.

A NOTE ON STOCKS FOR VELOUTÉ SAUCES

The recipe for home-made white stock is on page 98; for white chicken stock on page 213; for fish stock on page 103. Tinned chicken broth may be substituted for home-made white stock if you give it the following preliminary treatment:

Tinned chicken broth

$\frac{3}{4}$ pt. tinned chicken broth or strained clear chicken and vegetable soup

3 tbl each: sliced onions, carrots, and celery

$\frac{1}{4}$ pt. dry white wine or $\frac{1}{8}$ pt. dry white vermouth

2 parsley sprigs, $\frac{1}{8}$ bay leaf and a pinch of thyme

Simmer the chicken broth or soup with the vegetables, wine, and herbs for 30 minutes. Season to taste, strain, and it is ready to use.

* *SAUCE BÉCHAMEL*
SAUCE VELOUTÉ

[White Sauce]

This basic sauce takes about 5 minutes to make, and is then ready for the addition of flavours or enrichments. Suggestions for these are at the end of the master recipe.

For ¾ pint (*medium thickness*)

A 3-pt. heavy-bottomed enamelled, stainless steel or lined copper saucepan	1 oz. butter 1 oz. flour A wooden spatula or spoon

In the saucepan melt the butter over low heat. Blend in the flour, and cook slowly, stirring, until the butter and flour froth together for 2 minutes without colouring. This is now a white *roux*.

¾ pt. of milk and ¼ tsp salt heated to the boil in a small saucepan Or: ¾ pt. boiling white stock (see notes in preceding paragraph)	A wire whisk

Remove *roux* from heat. As soon as *roux* has stopped bubbling, pour in all the hot liquid at once. Immediately beat vigorously with a wire whisk to blend liquid and *roux,* gathering in all bits of *roux* from the inside edges of the pan. Set saucepan over moderately high heat and stir with the wire whisk until the sauce comes to the boil. Boil for 1 minute, stirring.

Salt and white pepper

Remove from heat, and beat in salt and pepper to taste. Sauce is now ready for final flavourings or additions.

(*) If not used immediately, clean sauce off inside edges of pan with a rubber spatula. To prevent a skin from forming on its surface, float a thin film of milk, stock, or melted butter on top. Set aside uncovered, keep it hot over simmering water, or refrigerate.

Remarks

If you follow the preceding directions, you will always obtain a smooth sauce of the correct consistency. But here are some remedial measures in case you need them:

If sauce is lumpy

If your *roux* is hot, and your liquid near the boil, you should never have a lumpy sauce. But if there are lumps, force the sauce through a very fine sieve. Then simmer it for 5 minutes.

If sauce is too thick

Bring the sauce to the simmering point. Thin it out with milk, cream, or stock, beaten in a tablespoon at a time.

If sauce is too thin

Either boil it down over moderately high heat, stirring continually with a wooden spoon, until it has reduced to the correct consistency;
Or blend ¼ ounce of butter into a paste with ¼ ounce of flour (*beurre manié*). Away from heat, beat the paste into the sauce with a wire whisk. Boil for 1 minute, stirring.

ENRICHMENTS FOR WHITE SAUCES

The three following enrichments complete the whole master system of white-sauce making. While a plain, well-seasoned béchamel or *velouté* may be served just as it is, the addition of butter, cream, or egg yolks transforms it into something infinitely more delicious.

Butter Enrichment

Fresh butter stirred into a sauce just before serving is the simplest of the enrichments. It smooths out the sauce, gives it a slight liaison, and imparts that certain French taste which seems to be present in no other type of cooking. For ½ pint of simple sauce, ¼ to ½ ounce of butter is sufficient; as much as 4 ounces may be beaten into a fine fish sauce. But if more than ½ ounce of butter is beaten into ½ pint of sauce, the sauce should then be served immediately. If it is reheated, or is kept hot, or if it is used for a *gratinéed* dish, the butter either liquefies and the sauce thins out just as though it had been diluted with milk, or the butter releases itself from suspension and floats on top of the sauce. However, if you make a mistake and heat a heavily buttered sauce, it will quickly reconstitute itself if you treat it like turned hollandaise, page 72.

To enrich ¾ pint of béchamel or velouté, page 50

1 to 4 oz. butter is the usual amount   A wire whisk

Just before serving the sauce, and after all the final flavourings have been added, remove it from heat. Stir in the butter, a little at a time, beating until each piece of butter has been absorbed into the sauce before adding the next. Spoon the sauce over the hot food, or pour the sauce into a warmed bowl, and serve immediately.

Cream Enrichment—Cream Sauce

[*Sauce Crème—Sauce Suprême*]

With the addition of cream, a béchamel becomes a *sauce crème*; and a *velouté*, a *sauce suprême*. As the cream thins out the sauce, the basic béchamel or *velouté* must be thick enough initially so that the finished sauce will be of the correct consistency.

Cream sauces are used for vegetables, eggs, fish, poultry, hot hors d'œuvres, and for dishes which are to be *gratinéed*.

For 1 pint

¾ pt. of thick béchamel or
  velouté, page 50 (1½ oz. flour,
  1½ oz. butter, and ¾ pt. liquid)

¼ pt. cream
Salt and white pepper
Lemon juice

Bring the sauce to simmering point. Beat in the cream by spoonfuls, simmering, until the sauce is the consistency you wish it to be. Season to taste with salt, pepper, and drops of lemon juice.

Optional: ½ to 1 oz. softened butter
(no butter if sauce is to be used
for a *gratinéed* dish)

Away from heat, and just before serving, beat in the optional butter a little at a time.

Egg Yolk and Cream Enrichment

[*Sauce Parisienne*—formerly *Sauce Allemande*]

Sauces enriched with egg yolks and cream are among the richest and most velvety in all the French repertoire. *Sauce parisienne,* or *sauce allemande,* is the generic term, but it invariably goes by another name according to its special flavourings or to the dish it accompanies. The simplest, *sauce poulette,* has a base of *velouté* flavoured with meat or fish, onions and mushrooms. The famous *sauce normande* is a *velouté* based on white-wine fish stock and the cooking liquors of mussels, oysters, shrimps, *écrevisses,* and mushrooms. The shellfish sauces such as *cardinal, Nantua,* and *Joinville* are shellfish *veloutés* with special trimmings and a shellfish butter enrichment beaten in at the end. As all of these sauces are a basic *velouté* with a final enrichment of egg yolks, cream, and usually butter, if you can make one, you can make all.

Success in making the egg yolk liaison is but a realization that egg yolks will curdle and turn granular unless they are beaten with a little cold liquid first, before a hot liquid is gradually incorporated into them so that they are slowly heated. Once this preliminary step has been completed, the sauce may be brought to the boil; and because the egg yolks are supported by a flour-based sauce they may boil without danger of curdling.

The *sauce parisienne* described in the following recipe is used with eggs, fish, poultry, hot hors d'œuvres, and dishes which are to be *gratinéed*. A heavily buttered *sauce parisienne* is used principally for fish poached in white wine, as described beginning on page 192 in the Fish chapter.

For 1 pint

¾ pt. thick béchamel or *velouté*, page 50 (1½ oz. flour, 1½ oz. butter, and ¾ pt. liquid)	A heavy-bottomed saucepan

Bring the sauce to the simmer in its saucepan.

2 egg yolks	A 3-pt. mixing bowl
¼ pt. cream	A wire whisk

Blend the egg yolks and cream in the mixing bowl with a wire whisk. A few drops at a time, beat in ¼ pint of hot sauce. Slowly beat in the rest of the sauce in a thin stream. Pour the mixture back into the saucepan.

A wooden spatula or spoon

Place on a moderately high heat and stir constantly with a wooden spoon, reaching all over the bottom of the pan until the sauce comes to the boil. Boil and stir for 1 minute.

Salt and white pepper	**More cream if necessary**
Lemon juice	

Strain the sauce through a fine sieve to remove coagulated bits of egg white which always cling to the yolk. Rinse out the saucepan and return the sauce to it. Simmer over low heat to check seasoning, adding salt, pepper, and drops of lemon juice to taste. If sauce is too thick, beat in more cream by spoonfuls.

(*) If not used immediately, clean off sides of pan, and float a film of cream or stock over the surface. Sauce will thicken and look custardy as it cools, which is normal. It will smooth out when it is reheated.

Optional: ½ to 1 oz. softened butter (occasionally more is called for;	**use no butter if sauce is for a *gratinéed* dish)**

Away from heat, and just before serving, stir in the optional butter a little at a time.

SAUCES DERIVED FROM BÉCHAMEL
AND VELOUTÉ

Here are some of the principal sauces derived from *sauce béchamel* and *sauce velouté*, the recipes for which are on page 50.

Sauce Mornay

[Cheese Sauce]

For: eggs, fish, poultry, veal, vegetables, *pastas*, and hot hors d'œuvres

Note: If the sauce covers foods which are to be baked or *gratinéed,* use the minimum amount of cheese suggested, and omit the butter enrichment at the end of the recipe. Too much cheese can make the sauce stringy, and a butter enrichment will exude from the top of the sauce.

¾ pt. of medium béchamel or *velouté*, page 50
1 to 2 oz. of coarsely grated Swiss

cheese, or a combination of coarsely grated Swiss and finely grated Parmesan

Bring the sauce to the boil. Away from heat, and beat in the cheese until it has melted and blended with the sauce.

Salt and pepper
Pinch of nutmeg

Optional: pinch of cayenne pepper and ½ to 1 oz. softened butter

Season to taste with salt, pepper, nutmeg, and optional cayenne. Away from heat and just before serving, stir in the optional butter a bit at a time.

Sauce Aurore

[Béchamel or *Velouté* with Tomato Flavouring]

For: eggs, fish, chicken, vegetables

¾ pt. béchamel or *velouté*, page 50, or the cream sauce, page 52

3 to 4 tbl cooked, fresh tomato purée, page 69, or tomato paste

Bring the sauce to the simmering point. Stir in the tomato, a spoonful at a time, until you have achieved the colour and flavour you wish. Correct seasoning.

½ to 1 oz. softened butter
Optional: 1 to 2 tbl chopped fresh

parsley, chervil, basil, or tarragon

Away from heat, and just before serving, stir in the butter and the optional herbs.

Sauce Chivry
Sauce à L'Estragon

[Herbal White Wine Sauce and Tarragon Sauce]

For: eggs, fish, vegetables, or poached chicken

A small enamelled saucepan
½ pt. dry white wine or ⅓ pt. dry
white vermouth
4 tbl chopped fresh chervil,
tarragon, and parsley, or tarragon
only; Or: 2 tbl dried herbs
2 tbl chopped minced shallots or
onions

Place all ingredients in the saucepan and boil slowly for 10 minutes, allowing the wine to reduce to about 2 tablespoons. This is now a herb essence.

¾ pt. béchamel or *velouté*, page 50,
or the cream sauce, page 52

Strain the essence into the sauce, pressing the juice out of the herbs. Simmer for 2 to 3 minutes.

3 to 4 tbl chopped fresh green herbs
or parsley, or tarragon
½ to 1 oz. softened butter

Away from heat, and just before serving, stir in the fresh herbs and the enrichment butter.

Sauce au Cari

[Light Curry Sauce]

For: fish, veal, lamb, chicken, turkey, eggs, and vegetables

Here the béchamel or *velouté* sauce is made simultaneously with the curry flavourings.

For 1 pint

2 oz. finely chopped white onions
2 oz. butter
A 3-pt. enamelled saucepan

Cook the onions and butter over low heat for 10 minutes without allowing the onions to colour.

2 to 3 tbl curry powder

Stir in the curry powder and cook slowly for 2 minutes.

1½ oz. flour

Add the flour and stir over low heat for 3 minutes more.

**¾ pt. boiling milk, white stock,
   or fish stock**

Away from heat, blend in the boiling liquid. Return sauce to heat and simmer
slowly for 10 to 15 minutes, stirring occasionally.

4 to 5 tbl cream   **Lemon juice**
Salt and pepper

Then stir in the cream by tablespoons, until sauce has thinned to consistency you
wish. Check seasoning, and add lemon juice to taste.

½ to 1 oz. softened butter
**Optional: 2 to 3 tbl chopped
   parsley**

Away from heat, and just before serving, stir in the butter a little at a time, then
the optional parsley.

Sauce Soubise

[Onion Sauce]

For: eggs, veal, chicken, turkey, lamb, vegetables, and foods which are to
be *gratinéed*

Another version of this excellent sauce is in the Veal section, page 326.

For about 1 pint

1 lb. of sliced onions   **A 4-pt. heavy-bottomed, enamelled**
¼ tsp salt   **saucepan**
3 oz. butter

Cook the onions slowly with salt and butter in a covered saucepan for 20 to 30
minutes, or until the onions are very tender but not browned.

1½ oz. flour

Add the flour and stir over low heat for 3 minutes.

**¾ pt. boiling milk, white stock,
   or fish stock**

Away from heat, blend in the boiling liquid. Then simmer the sauce slowly for
15 minutes, stirring occasionally. Force the sauce through a sieve or moulinette,
or purée it in the electric liquidizer.

¼ pt. cream   **Pinch of nutmeg**
Salt and pepper

Bring again to simmering point, and thin out to desired consistency with
spoonfuls of cream. Add salt, pepper, and nutmeg to taste.

½ to 1 oz. softened butter (no butter
   if sauce is to be used for *gratinéed*
   dish)

Away from heat, and just before serving, stir in the enrichment butter.

---

* *SAUCE BÂTARDE*
SAUCE AU BEURRE

[Mock Hollandaise]

For: boiled fish, boiled chicken, boiled lamb, boiled potatoes, asparagus, cauliflower, celery, broccoli

This quickly made and useful sauce does not belong to the béchamel and *velouté* family because it is made with an uncooked *roux,* or *beurre manié.* A golden colour is given it by the addition of an egg yolk, and when flavoured with enough butter it suggests a hollandaise.

For ¾ pint (*medium thickness*)

1 oz. melted or softened butter   A 4-pt. heavy-bottomed, enamelled
1 oz. flour   saucepan

Place the butter and flour in the saucepan and blend them into a smooth paste.

¾ pt. boiling white stock, or   A wire whisk
   vegetable cooking water, or
   water and ¼ tsp salt

Pour on all the boiling liquid at once and blend vigorously with a wire whisk.

1 egg yolk   Salt and white pepper
2 tbl cream   1 to 2 tbl lemon juice
A 3-pt. mixing bowl

Blend the egg yolk and cream with a wire whisk, then, a few drops at a time, beat in ¼ pint of sauce. Beat in the rest in a thin stream. Pour the mixture back into the saucepan. Bring to the boil over moderately high heat, beating, and boil 5 seconds. Remove from heat and season to taste with salt, pepper, and lemon juice.

(*) If not used immediately, film surface with a half-tablespoon of melted butter.

2 to 4 oz. softened butter

Away from heat, and just before serving, beat in the butter, a tablespoon at a time.

VARIATIONS

Sauce aux Câpres

[Caper Sauce]

For: boiled fish or boiled leg of lamb

¾ pt. *sauce bâtarde*	2 to 3 tbl capers

Just before stirring in the enrichment butter, beat in the capers. Then, away from heat, beat in the enrichment butter.

Sauce à la Moutarde

[Mustard Sauce]

For: grilled mackerel or herring

¾ pt. *sauce bâtarde* omitting final butter enrichment	2 to 4 oz. softened butter
2 tbl strong French prepared mustard	

Blend the mustard and butter together. Away from heat, and just before serving, beat the mustard/butter by tablespoons into the hot sauce.

Sauce aux Anchois

[Anchovy Sauce]

For: boiled fish or boiled potatoes

2 tbl tinned anchovies mashed into a purée or 1 tbl anchovy paste	¾ pt. *sauce bâtarde*

Just before buttering the sauce, beat in the anchovy mixture to taste. Then away from heat, and before serving, beat in the enrichment butter.

BROWN SAUCES

Sauces Brunes

The classic French brown sauce starts out with a long-simmered brown meat stock that goes into the making of an equally long-simmered, lightly thickened sauce base called an *espagnole*. The *espagnole* is simmered and skimmed for several hours more with additional stock and flavourings until it finally develops into the traditional mother of the brown sauces, *demi-glace*. This may take several days to accomplish, and the result is splendid. But as we are concerned with less formal cooking, we shall discuss it no further.

A good brown sauce may have as its thickening agent a brown *roux* of flour and butter, or cornflour, potato flour, rice flour, or arrowroot. A flour-thickened brown sauce must be simmered and skimmed for two hours at least if it is to develop its full flavour. Starch and arrowroot thickenings take but a few minutes; and when properly made they are very good indeed. Because they are far more useful in home cooking than the long simmered and more conventional sauce, we have used them in most of the main-course recipes throughout this book.

Following are three interchangeable methods for making a basic brown sauce. Any of them may rapidly be converted into one of the composed sauces starting on page 63.

A NOTE ON MEAT STOCKS FOR BROWN SAUCES

Recipes for making brown stocks are on pages 96-9. However, as one does not always have the time to prepare stock, one must have substitutes. The best prepared alternative is tinned beef bouillon, usually available in speciality shops. Tinned beef consommé tends to be sweetish, and we therefore do not recommend it. Bouillon cubes, with their often too characteristic flavour, are not as satisfactory as tinned bouillon, but you should not hesitate to use them in an emergency. Tinned bouillon or bouillon cubes and water may be substituted for stock in the first two of the following recipes for brown sauce. If they are used in recipe Number 3, for starch-thickened sauce, the flavour must be disguised and enriched as follows:

Beef Bouillon—from tinned beef bouillon or bouillon cubes

¾ pt. tinned beef bouillon, or ¾ pt. water and 3 to 4 bouillon cubes

3 tbl each: finely chopped onions and carrots

1 tbl finely chopped celery

¼ pt. red wine, dry white wine, or dry white vermouth

2 parsley sprigs

⅓ bay leaf

⅛ tsp thyme

Optional: 1 tbl tomato paste

Simmer the liquid with the rest of the ingredients listed for 20 to 30 minutes. Strain through a fine sieve, and the bouillon is ready to be turned into a sauce.

BROWN SAUCE (1)

SAUCE BRUNE

[Flour-based Brown Sauce]

This is the best of the group and the one most nearly approaching the traditional *demi-glace*. Its preliminaries are somewhat exacting, and it requires at least two hours of simmering; the longer it cooks the better it will be. It may be refrigerated for several days and deep freezes perfectly for several weeks.

A NOTE ON BROWN ROUX

Brown *roux,* which is the thickening for this type of sauce, is flour and fat cooked together until the flour has turned an even, nut-brown colour. For an ordinary sauce, the flour is cooked in rendered fresh pork fat, or in cooking oil. But if the sauce is to accompany a delicate dish, such as *foie gras,* eggs, or *vol-au-vent,* the flour should be cooked in clarified butter—meaning the butter is melted and decanted, leaving its milky particles behind, as these burn and taste bitter.

It is important that the *roux* be cooked slowly and evenly. If the flour is burned, it will not thicken the sauce as it should, and it will also impart an unpleasant taste.

For about 2 pints of brown sauce

A 3-pt. heavy-bottomed saucepan
2 oz. each: finely diced carrots,
    onions, and celery
3 tbl diced boiled ham (or diced
    lean bacon simmered for 10

minutes in water, rinsed, and
    drained)
6 tbl clarified butter, page 12,
    rendered fresh pork fat, or
    cooking oil

Cook the vegetables and ham or bacon slowly in the butter, fat, or oil for 10 minutes.

2 oz. flour   A wooden spatula or spoon

Blend the flour into the vegetables and stir continually over moderately low heat for 8 to 10 minutes, until the flour slowly turns a golden, nut brown.

A wire whisk
3 pts. boiling brown stock or
    beef bouillon
2 tbl tomato paste

A medium herb bouquet:
    3 parsley sprigs, $\frac{1}{2}$ bay leaf, and
    $\frac{1}{4}$ tsp thyme tied in cheesecloth

Remove from heat. With a wire whisk, immediately blend in all the boiling liquid at once. Beat in the tomato paste. Add the herb bouquet.

Simmer slowly, partially covered, for 2 hours or more, skimming off fat and scum as necessary. Add more liquid if sauce thickens too much. You should finish up with about 2 pints of sauce, thick enough to coat a spoon lightly.

Salt and pepper

Correct seasoning. Strain, pressing juice out of vegetables. Degrease thoroughly, and the sauce is ready to use.

(*) If not used immediately, clean off sides of pan, and float a film of stock over the top of the sauce to prevent a skin from forming. When cold, cover and refrigerate or deep-freeze.

BROWN SAUCE (2)

* *SAUCE RAGOÛT*

[Flour-based Brown Sauce with Giblets]

Sauce ragoût is essentially like the preceding brown sauce, but has more character, as it includes bones, trimmings, or giblets gathered from the game, beef, lamb, veal, goose, duck, or turkey the sauce is to be served with.

For about 2 pints

A 6- to 8-pt. heavy-bottomed
  saucepan
¼ to 1 lb. of giblets, bones, and meat
  trimmings, raw or cooked
2 oz. chopped carrots

2 oz. chopped onions
6 tbl clarified butter (page 12),
  rendered fresh pork fat, or
  cooking oil; more if needed

Brown the giblets, bones, meat trimmings and vegetables in hot clarified butter, fat, or oil. Remove them to a side dish.

2 oz. flour

Slowly brown the flour in the fat remaining in the saucepan, adding more fat if necessary.

3 pts. boiling brown stock or
  beef bouillon
Optional: ½ pt. dry white wine,
  red wine, or ⅓ pt. dry white
  vermouth

Optional: 3 tbl tomato paste
A medium herb bouquet: 3 parsley
  sprigs, ½ bay leaf, ¼ tsp thyme
  tied in cheesecloth

Away from heat, beat in the boiling liquid, optional wine, and optional tomato paste. Add the herb bouquet and return the browned ingredients. Simmer, skimming as necessary, for 2 to 4 hours. Strain, degrease, correct seasoning, and the sauce is ready to use.

VARIATIONS

Sauce Poivrade

[Brown Game Sauce]

This is the same as *sauce ragoût*. If the game has been marinated, ¼ to ½ pint of the marinade is used instead of the optional wine. The final sauce is highly seasoned with pepper.

Sauce Venaison

[Brown Sauce for Venison]

This is *sauce poivrade* with ¼ pint red currant jelly and ¼ pint cream beaten into it just before serving.

BROWN SAUCE (3)

* JUS LIÉ

[Starch-thickened Brown Sauce]

Jus lié is a most useful alternative to the preceding long-simmered brown sauces, and takes about 5 minutes to prepare. But it has no culinary interest whatsoever if it is not made with an excellent base, as it is only stock thickened with cornflour or arrowroot. The sauce is usually made with the liquids obtained from the simmering or stewing of meats, and therefore acquires a good, strong flavour. If it is made from dissolved bouillon cube, the bouillon should first be simmered with wine and seasonings as described under meat stocks on page 59. Cornflour is the thickening for ordinary brown sauces of this type. Arrowroot is used when the sauce is to be very clear and limpid, such as that for the ham braised in Madeira on page 361, or the duck with orange, page 251. (Potato flour and rice flour are French equivalents of cornflour.)

For ¾ pint

1 oz. cornflour or arrowroot   A 2-pt. saucepan
¾ pt. of excellent brown stock, or   A wire whisk
    beef bouillon simmered with wine
    and seasonings, page 59

Blend the cornflour or arrowroot with 2 tablespoons of cold stock, then beat in the rest of the stock. Simmer for 5 minutes, or until sauce has cleared and is lightly thickened. Correct seasoning.

Optional: ⅛ pt. Madeira, port, or
   cognac

Add optional wine or cognac, and simmer for 2 to 3 minutes, tasting, until the
alcohol has evaporated.

(*) Sauce may be set aside, and reheated when needed.

SAUCES DERIVED FROM BROWN SAUCE

   Following are some of the principal composed sauces which are made with
any of the three preceding brown sauces. They are almost always combined
with the cooking juices of the dishes they accompany, and thereby obtain
additional flavour.

Sauce Diable

[Peppery Brown Sauce]

   For: grilled chicken, roast or braised pork, pork chops, hot meat leftovers

A 2-pt. saucepan
1 to 2 tbl chopped shallots or spring
   onions

½ oz. butter or cooking fat
½ pt. dry white wine or ⅓ pt. dry
   white vermouth

Cook the shallots or spring onions slowly with the butter or cooking fat for
2 minutes without browning. Then add the wine and boil it down rapidly until
it has reduced to 2 or 3 tablespoons.

¾ pt. brown sauce, pages 59 to 63
Black pepper

Cayenne pepper

Pour in the sauce and simmer for 2 minutes. Season with enough pepper to give
it a spicy taste.

½ to 1½ oz. softened butter
2 to 3 tbl fresh chopped parsley or
   mixed green herbs

Away from heat, and just before serving, swirl butter into the sauce a bit at a
time. Stir in the parsley or herbs.

Sauce Piquante

[Brown Sauce with Pickles and Capers]

   For: roast or braised pork, pork chops, boiled or braised tongue, boiled
beef, and hot meat leftovers

The preceding sauce diable *plus:*

2 tbl finely chopped pickles   **2 tbl capers**

Just before removing the sauce from heat, stir in the pickles and capers. Simmer a moment, then, away from heat, beat in the butter and herbs.

Sauce Robert

[Brown Mustard Sauce]

For: roast or braised pork, pork chops, boiled beef, grilled chicken, or turkey, hot meat leftovers, hamburgers

A 3-pt. heavy-bottomed saucepan   **½ oz. butter**
1 oz. finely chopped onions   **1 tsp oil or cooking fat**

Cook the onions slowly with the butter and oil or fat, for 10 to 15 minutes until they are tender and lightly browned.

½ pt. dry white wine or ⅓ pt. dry
   vermouth

Add the wine and boil it down rapidly until it has reduced to 2 or 3 tablespoons.

¾ pt. brown sauce, pages 59 to 63

Add the brown sauce and simmer 10 minutes. Correct seasoning.

3 to 4 tbl French prepared mustard   **2 to 3 tbl fresh chopped parsley**
   creamed with 1 or 1½ oz.
   softened butter and ⅛ tsp sugar

Away from heat, and just before serving, beat the mustard mixture into the sauce, tasting. Beat in the parsley, and serve.

Sauce Brune aux Fines Herbes
Sauce Brune à l'Estragon

[Brown Herb or Tarragon Sauce]

For: sautéed chicken, veal, rabbit, braised vegetables, hot meat leftovers, and poached or baked eggs

A 2-pt. enamelled saucepan   **4 tbl fresh herbs or 2 tbl dried herbs**
½ pt. dry white wine or ⅓ pt. dry   **as follows: parsley, basil, chervil,**
   white vermouth   **rosemary, oregano, and tarragon**
2 tbl chopped shallots or spring   **only**
   onions

Place all the ingredients in the saucepan and boil slowly for 10 minutes, reducing the wine to 1 or 2 tablespoons. This is now a herb essence.

¾ pt. of brown sauce, pages 59 to 63   A 3 pt. saucepan

Strain the herb essence into the brown sauce, pressing the juices out of the herbs. Simmer for 1 minute.

1 to 1½ oz. softened butter
2 to 3 tbl fresh chopped parsley, mixed
   green herbs, or tarragon

Away from heat, and just before serving, beat the butter into the sauce a little at a time, then beat in the herbs.

Sauce Brune au Cari

[Brown Curry Sauce]

For: lamb, chicken, beef, rice, and egg dishes

A 3-pt. heavy-bottomed saucepan   1 oz. butter
6 oz. finely chopped onions   1 tsp oil

Cook the onions slowly in the butter and oil for about 15 minutes, until they are tender and lightly browned.

3 to 4 tbl curry powder

Blend in the curry powder and cook slowly for 1 minute.

Optional: 2 cloves mashed garlic

Stir in the optional garlic and cook slowly for half a minute.

¾ pt. brown sauce, pages 59 to 63

Add the brown sauce and simmer for 10 minutes.

2 to 3 tsp lemon juice

Correct seasoning and add lemon juice to taste.

½ to 1½ oz. softened butter   2 to 3 tbl fresh chopped parsley

Away from heat, and just before serving, beat in the butter a little at a time. Stir in the parsley.

Sauce Duxelles

[Brown Mushroom Sauce]

For: grilled or sautéed chicken, veal, rabbit, or for egg dishes, hot meat leftovers, or *pastas*

c

A 3-pt. heavy-bottomed saucepan   2 tbl shallots or spring onions
¼ lb. finely chopped fresh   ½ oz. butter
    mushrooms or mushroom stems   ½ tbl oil
    only

Sauté the mushrooms with the shallots or spring onions in hot butter and oil for
4 to 5 minutes.

¼ pt. dry white wine or ⅛ pt. dry
    white vermouth

Add the wine and boil it down rapidly until it has reduced almost completely.

¾ pt. brown sauce, pages 59 to 63   1½ tbl tomato paste

Stir in the brown sauce and tomato paste and simmer for 5 minutes. Correct
seasoning.

1 to 1½ oz. softened butter
3 to 4 tbl mixed green herbs or
    parsley

Away from heat and just before serving, stir in the butter a little at a time, then
the herbs or parsley.

Sauce Chasseur

[Brown Mushroom Sauce with Fresh Tomatoes, Garlic, and Herbs]

For: same as preceding *sauce duxelles*

Sauce chasseur is almost the same as *sauce duxelles,* but a bit more hearty in
flavour. The recipe for it is described in the Veal section under *escalopes de veau
chasseur* on page 338.

Sauce Madère

[Brown Madeira Sauce]

Sauce au Porto

[Brown Port-wine Sauce]

For: fillet of beef, or for ham, veal, chicken livers, and egg dishes, or to
sauce a garniture for *vol-au-vents*

¼ pt. Madeira or port   A 2-pt. saucepan

Boil the wine in the saucepan until it has reduced to about 2 tablespoons.

¾ pt. excellent brown sauce, pages
59 to 63
Optional: 1 to 2 tsp meat glaze,
page 99

3 to 4 tbl Madeira or port, if
necessary

Add the brown sauce and simmer for a minute or two. Taste carefully for
seasoning and strength, adding meat glaze if you have it and consider it
necessary. If more wine is needed, add it by tablespoons, simmering briefly to
evaporate the alcohol.

1 to 1½ oz. softened butter

Away from heat and just before serving, beat in the butter a little at a time.

Sauce Périgueux

[Brown Madeira Sauce with Truffles]

For: fillet of beef, fresh *foie gras*, ham, veal, egg dishes, and timbales

The preceding *sauce Madère*
2 to 4 diced tinned truffles and
their juice

Prepare the Madeira sauce as in the preceding recipe, but add the truffle juice
to reduce with the Madeira at the beginning. After flavouring the sauce, stir in
the truffles and simmer for a minute. Away from heat, beat the butter into the
sauce just before serving.

OTHER BROWN SAUCES

The following brown sauces are incorporated into recipes in other parts of
the book:

Brown deglazing sauce. This sauce is made by dissolving the coagulated cooking
juices in a roasting or sautéing pan with wine or stock after the meat has
been removed. The liquid is boiled down until it is syrupy. Away from the
heat a lump of butter is swirled in to give the sauce a slight liaison. It is one
of the most delicious, useful, and simple of all the brown sauces, and is
described in countless recipes. A good illustration is the deglazing sauce for
roast chicken, page 216.

Sauce à l'Italienne, a brown sauce with ham, mushrooms, and herbs, as described
under braised sweetbreads, page 376. The sauce may also be used for brains,
sautéed liver, egg dishes, and *pastas.*

Sauce Bordelaise, a red wine sauce with beef marrow, described in the Kidney
section under *rognons de veau à la bordelaise,* page 386. The sauce is also good
with steaks, hamburgers, and egg dishes.

Sauce à l'Orange, a brown sauce with orange flavouring and orange peel, as
described in the Duck section for *canard à l'orange,* page 251. The same sauce
could also be used with baked ham or roast pork.

Sauce Bourguignonne, a red wine sauce always accompanied by a garniture of
bacon, mushrooms, and braised onions, as described under poached eggs
à la bourguignonne on page 108. It also goes with sweetbreads or brains,
sautéed beef, and chicken. *Boeuf bourguignon* and *coq au vin* are examples,
pages 288 and 239.

TOMATO SAUCES

Sauces Tomate

SAUCE TOMATE

[Tomato Sauce]

This good basic tomato sauce is served just as it is, or may be flavoured
with herbs or combined with other sauces whenever you wish a tomato
flavouring. It is at its best with fresh tomatoes, but tinned tomatoes or tinned
tomato purée will also produce a good sauce. You will notice, during its
simmering, that it really should cook for about an hour and a half to develop its
full flavour.

For about 1 pint

A 4-pt. heavy-bottomed saucepan	for 10 minutes in water, rinsed,
1 oz. each: finely diced carrots,	and drained
onions, and celery	1½ oz. butter
2 tbl chopped boiled ham; Or: 2	2 tbl oil
tbl chopped lean bacon, simmered	

Cook the vegetables and the ham or bacon slowly in the butter and oil for 10
minutes without letting them brown.

¾ oz. flour

Blend the flour into the ham and vegetables, and cook slowly for 3 minutes,
stirring.

¾ pt. boiling stock or beef bouillon

Away from heat, beat in the stock or bouillon.

2 lbs. chopped, ripe, red tomatoes
which need not be peeled; Or:
1½ lb. tinned tomatoes; Or:
¾ pt. tinned tomato purée and ¾ pt.
water
¼ tsp salt

⅛ tsp sugar
2 unpeeled cloves garlic
4 parsley sprigs
½ bay leaf
¼ tsp thyme

Stir in the tomatoes, salt, and sugar. Add the garlic and herbs. Simmer for 1½ to 2 hours, skimming occasionally, and adding water if sauce reduces and thickens too much. You should finish up with about 1 pint of rich, fairly thick sauce.

1 to 2 tbl tomato paste, if necessary

Strain, pressing juice out of ingredients. Correct seasoning. Stir in 1 to 2 table-spoons of tomato paste if you feel the sauce lacks colour, and simmer again for 5 minutes.

(*) If not used immediately, film surface with stock or a few drops of oil. May be refrigerated or deep-frozen.

COULIS DE TOMATES À LA PROVENÇALE

[Fresh Tomato Purée with Garlic and Herbs]

For: grilled or boiled chicken, boiled beef, meat patties, hot meat leftovers, eggs, *pastas,* and pizzas

Here is a thick, concentrated tomato sauce with real Mediterranean flavour.

For about ¾ pint

A 5-pt. heavy-bottomed saucepan
3 oz. finely chopped onions

2 tbl olive oil

Cook the onions and olive oil slowly together for about 10 minutes, until the onions are tender but not browned.

2 tsp flour

Stir in the flour and cook slowly for 3 minutes without browning.

3 lbs. ripe red tomatoes, peeled,
seeded, juiced, and chopped,
page 465
⅛ tsp sugar
2 cloves mashed garlic
A medium herb bouquet: 4 parsley
sprigs, 1 bay leaf, and ¼ tsp
thyme tied in cheesecloth

⅛ tsp fennel
⅛ tsp basil
Small pinch of saffron
Small pinch of coriander
A 1-in. piece orange peel
½ tsp salt

Stir in the tomatoes, sugar, garlic, herbs, and seasonings. Cover pan and cook slowly for 10 minutes, so that the tomatoes will render more of their juice. Then uncover and simmer for about half an hour, adding spoonfuls of tomato juice or water if the sauce becomes so thick it risks scorching. The purée is done when it tastes thoroughly cooked and is thick enough to form a mass in the spoon. Remove herb bouquet.

1 to 2 tbl tomato paste, if necessary   **Salt and pepper**

If necessary, stir in 1 or 2 tablespoons of tomato paste for colour, and simmer 2 minutes. Correct seasoning. Strain the sauce if you wish.

(*) May be refrigerated or deep-frozen.

THE HOLLANDAISE FAMILY

SAUCE HOLLANDAISE

[Hollandaise Sauce: Egg Yolk and Butter Sauce flavoured with Lemon Juice]

Hollandaise sauce is made of warmed egg yolks flavoured with lemon juice, into which butter is gradually incorporated to make a thick, yellow, creamy sauce. It is probably the most famous of all sauces, and is often the most dreaded, as the egg yolks can curdle and the sauce can turn. It is extremely easy and almost foolproof to make in an electric liquidizer, and we give the recipe on page 72. But we feel it is of great importance that you learn how to make hollandaise by hand, for part of every good cook's general knowledge is a thorough familiarity with the vagaries of egg yolks under all conditions. The following recipe takes about 5 minutes, and is almost as fast as liquidizer hollandaise. It is only one of numerous methods for hollandaise, all of which accomplish the same result, that of forcing egg yolks to absorb butter and hold it in creamy suspension.

TWO POINTS TO REMEMBER when making hollandaise by hand

The heating and thickening of the egg yolks

So that the egg yolks will thicken into a smooth cream, they must be heated slowly and gradually. Too sudden heat will make them granular. Over-cooking scrambles them. You may beat them over hot water or over low heat; it makes no difference as long as the process is slow and gentle.

The butter

Egg yolks will readily absorb a certain quantity of butter when it is fed to them gradually, giving them time to incorporate each addition before another is presented. When too much is added at a time, particularly at first, the sauce will not thicken. And if the total amount of butter is more than the yolks can absorb, the sauce will curdle. About 3 ounces of butter is the usual maximum amount per yolk. But if you have never made hollandaise before, it is safer not to go over 2 ounces.

For ½ to ¾ pint hollandaise—serving 4 to 6 people

6 to 8 oz. butter   **A small saucepan**

Cut the butter into pieces and melt it in the saucepan over moderate heat. Then set it aside.

A 2-pt. medium-weight,   **A wire whisk**
    enamelled or stainless steel   **3 egg yolks**
    saucepan

Beat the egg yolks for about 1 minute in the saucepan, or until they become thick and sticky.

1 tbl cold water   **Big pinch of salt**
1 tbl lemon juice

Add the water, lemon juice, and salt, and beat for half a minute more.

½ oz. cold butter
A pan of cold water (to cool off the
    bottom of the saucepan if necessary)

Add the ½ ounce of cold butter, but do not beat it in. Then place the saucepan over very low heat or barely simmering water and stir the egg yolks with a wire whisk until they slowly thicken into a smooth cream. This will take 1 to 2 minutes. If they seem to be thickening too quickly, or even suggest a lumpy quality, immediately plunge the bottom of the pan in cold water, beating the yolks to cool them. Then continue beating over heat. The egg yolks have thickened enough when you can begin to see the bottom of the pan between strokes, and the mixture forms a light cream on the wires of the whisk.

½ oz. cold butter

Immediately remove from heat and beat in the cold butter, which will cool the egg yolks and stop their cooking.

The melted butter

Then beating the egg yolks with a wire whisk, pour on the melted butter drop by drop until the sauce begins to thicken into a very heavy cream. Then pour the butter a little more rapidly. Omit the milky residue at the bottom of the butter pan.

Salt and white pepper   **Drops of lemon juice**

Season the sauce to taste with salt, pepper, and lemon juice.

Keeping the sauce warm

Hollandaise is served warm, not hot. If it is kept too warm, it will thin out or curdle. It can be held perfectly for an hour or more near the very faint heat of a gas pilot light on the stove, or in a pan of lukewarm water. As hollandaise made with the maximum amount of butter is difficult to hold, use the minimum suggested in the recipe, then beat softened or tepid butter into the sauce just before serving.

A restaurant technique

A tablespoon or two of béchamel or *velouté* sauce, page 50, beaten into the hollandaise, or a teaspoon of cornflour beaten into the egg yolks at the beginning, will help to hold a sauce that is to be kept warm for a long period of time.

If the sauce is too thick

Beat in 1 to 2 tablespoons of hot water, vegetable cooking liquid, stock, milk, or cream.

If the sauce refuses to thicken

If you have beaten in the butter too quickly, and the sauce refuses to thicken, it is easily remedied. Rinse out a mixing bowl with hot water. Put in a teaspoon of lemon juice and a tablespoon of the sauce. Beat with a wire whisk for a moment until the sauce creams and thickens. Then beat in the rest of the sauce a dessertspoon at a time, beating until each addition has thickened in the sauce before adding the next. This always works.

If the sauce curdles or separates—'turned sauce'

If a finished sauce starts to separate, a tablespoon of cold water beaten into it will often bring it back. If not, use the preceding technique.

Leftover hollandaise

Leftover hollandaise may be refrigerated for a day or two, or may be deep-frozen. It is fine as an enrichment for *veloutés* and béchamels; beat it into the hot white sauce away from heat and a tablespoon at a time just before serving.

If the leftover sauce is to be used again as a hollandaise, beat 2 tablespoons of it in a saucepan over very low heat or hot water. Gradually beat in the rest of the sauce by spoonfuls.

Hollandaise Sauce made in the Electric Liquidizer

This very quick method for making hollandaise cannot fail when you add your butter drop by drop. If the sauce refuses to thicken, pour it out, then pour it back into the liquidizer drop by drop. As the butter cools, it begins to cream and forms itself into a thick sauce. If you are used to hand-made hollandaise, you may find the liquidizer variety lacks something in quality; this is perhaps due to complete homogenization. But as the technique is well within the capabilities of an 8-year-old child, it has much to recommend it.

For about ¼ pint

3 egg yolks   ¼ tsp salt
1 tbl each lemon juice and water   Pinch of pepper

Place the egg yolks, lemon juice, water, and seasonings in the liquidizer jar.

4 oz. butter

Cut the butter into pieces and heat it to foaming hot in a small saucepan.

A cloth, if you do not have a
   splatterproof liquidizer jar

Cover the jar and blend the egg yolk mixture at top speed for 2 seconds. Uncover, and still blending at top speed, immediately start pouring in the hot butter drop by drop. (You may need to protect yourself with a cloth during this operation.) By the time two-thirds of the butter has gone in, the sauce will be a thick cream. Omit the milky residue at the bottom of the butter pan. Taste the sauce, and blend in more seasonings if necessary.

(*) If not used immediately, place the jar in tepid, but not warm, water.

For more sauce

The amount of butter you can use in a liquidizer is only half the amount the egg yolks could absorb if you were making the sauce by hand, when 3 egg yolks can take 8 to 9 ounces of butter rather than the 4 ounces in the preceding recipe. However, if you added more butter to the liquidizer than the 4 ounces specified, the sauce would become so thick that it would clog the machine. To double your amount of sauce, then, pour it out of the liquidizer jar into a saucepan or bowl and beat into it an additional 4 oz. of melted butter, added very slowly.

OTHER MEMBERS OF THE HOLLANDAISE FAMILY

Except for the *mousseline sabayon* mentioned at the end of this section, all the other members of the family are made in exactly the same way as hollandaise sauce. The basic flavourings may be vinegar and herbs instead of lemon juice, or concentrated white-wine fish stock, but the technique does not vary.

c*

Stirred-in trimmings

A plain hollandaise may have a number of trimmings such as the following stirred into it:

HERBS

For poached eggs or boiled fish, stir in a mixture of chopped parsley, chives, and tarragon.

PURÉES

From 2 to 3 tablespoons of puréed artichoke hearts, asparagus tips, or cooked shellfish stirred into a hollandaise make it a good sauce for egg dishes. Or use finely chopped sautéed mushrooms—see the recipe for mushroom *duxelles* on page 475.

Hollandaise avec Blancs d'Oeufs

[Hollandaise with Beaten Egg Whites]

For: fish, soufflés, asparagus, egg dishes

Stiffly beaten egg whites folded into hollandaise swell and lighten the sauce so that it may serve more people.

2 or 3 stiffly beaten egg whites, $\frac{3}{4}$ pt. *sauce hollandaise*,
    page 144   page 70

Just before serving, fold the egg whites into the hollandaise.

Sauce Mousseline
Sauce Chantilly

[Hollandaise with Whipped Cream]

For: fish, soufflés, asparagus

$\frac{1}{4}$ pt. chilled cream

Beat the chilled cream in a chilled bowl with a chilled beater as described on page 534.

$\frac{3}{4}$ pt. *sauce hollandaise,* page 70

Fold it into the hollandaise just before serving.

Sauce Maltaise

[Orange-flavoured Hollandaise]

For: asparagus or broccoli

This sauce is made like an ordinary hollandaise except for the orange flavouring. Proceed as follows:

3 egg yolks	**Pinch of salt**
1 tbl lemon juice	**1 oz. cold butter**
1 tbl orange juice	**2½ to 5 oz. melted butter**

Beat the egg yolks until thickened, then beat in the liquids and salt. Add ½ ounce of cold butter, and thicken the mixture over low heat. Beat in the other ½ ounce of cold butter, then the melted butter.

2 to 4 tbl orange juice   **The grated peel of an orange**

Finish the sauce by beating in the orange juice by spoonfuls, then the orange peel.

HOLLANDAISE SAUCES FOR FISH

When a hollandaise type of sauce is to accompany fillets of fish poached in white wine, or a fish soufflé, the fish-poaching liquid is boiled down to a concentrated essence, or *fumet*, and is used in place of lemon juice as a flavouring for the sauce.

Sauce Vin Blanc

[Hollandaise with White-wine Fish *Fumet*]

½ pt. white-wine fish stock, page 103

Boil down the fish stock until it has reduced to 2 tablespoons. This is now a *fumet de poisson*. Allow it to cool.

**Ingredients for the *sauce hollandaise*,
page 70, omitting lemon juice
and water**

Proceed with the hollandaise as usual, substituting the fish *fumet* for the lemon juice and water.

Sauce Mousseline Sabayon

[Hollandaise with Cream and White-wine Fish *Fumet*]

The recipe for this extremely good sauce, in which the egg yolks are thickened with cream and fish *fumet*, is on page 154 under *soufflé de poisson*.

*   *Sauce Béarnaise*

[*Béarnaise* Sauce]

For: steaks, boiled or fried fish, grilled chicken, egg dishes, timbales

Béarnaise sauce differs from hollandaise only in taste and strength; instead of lemon juice, its basic flavouring is a reduction of wine, vinegar, shallots, pepper, and tarragon. The techniques for making the two sauces are similar.

For ½ pint

⅛ pt. wine vinegar	1 tbl chopped fresh tarragon or
⅛ pt. dry white wine or dry white	½ tbl dried tarragon
vermouth	⅛ tsp pepper
1 tbl chopped shallots or spring	Pinch of salt
onions	A small saucepan

Boil the vinegar, wine, shallots or spring onions, herbs, and seasonings over moderate heat until the liquid has reduced to 2 tablespoons. Let it cool.

3 egg yolks	2 tbl fresh chopped tarragon or
1 oz. cold butter	parsley
4 to 5 oz. melted butter	

Then proceed as though making a hollandaise, page 70. Beat the egg yolks until thick. Strain in the vinegar mixture and beat. Add ½ ounce of cold butter and thicken the egg yolks over low heat. Beat in the other ½ ounce of cold butter, then the melted butter drop by drop. Correct seasoning, and beat in the tarragon or parsley.

VARIATIONS

The two following sauces are also for steaks, fish, chicken, and eggs.

Sauce Choron

[Tomato-flavoured *Béarnaise*]

2 to 4 tbl tomato paste or purée	½ pt. *sauce béarnaise*

Beat the tomato by tablespoons into the *sauce béarnaise* and correct seasoning.

Sauce Colbert

[*Béarnaise* with Meat Glaze]

1 to 1½ tbl meat glaze, page 99,	½ pt. *sauce béarnaise*
melted in 1 tbl white wine	

Stir the melted meat glaze into the *sauce béarnaise*.

THE MAYONNAISE FAMILY

MAYONNAISE

[Mayonnaise: Egg Yolk and Oil Sauce]

Mayonnaise like hollandaise is a process of forcing egg yolks to absorb a fatty substance, oil in this case, and to hold it in thick and creamy suspension. But as the egg yolks do not have to be warmed, the sauce is that much simpler to make than hollandaise. Mayonnaise may be produced by hand, with an electric beater, or in an electric liquidizer. Liquidizer mayonnaise, see page 79, uses a whole egg rather than egg yolks; it is almost automatic, and no culinary skill whatsoever enters into its preparation. Mayonnaise made by hand or with an electric beater requires familiarity with egg yolks. And again, as with hollandaise, you should be able to make it by hand as part of your general mastery of the egg yolk. It is certainly far from difficult once you understand the process, and after you have done it a few times, you should easily and confidently be able to whip together a quart of sauce in less than 10 minutes.

POINTS TO REMEMBER when making mayonnaise by hand

Temperature

Mayonnaise is easiest to make when all ingredients are at normal room temperature. Warm the mixing bowl in hot water to take the chill off the egg yolks. Heat the oil to tepid if it is cold.

Egg yolks

Always beat the egg yolks for a minute or two before adding anything to them. As soon as they are thick and sticky, they are ready to absorb the oil.

Adding the oil

The oil must be added very slowly at first, drop by drop, until the emulsion process begins and the sauce thickens into a heavy cream. After this, the oil may be incorporated more rapidly.

Proportions

The maximum amount of oil one large egg yolk will absorb is about 6 fluid ounces. When this maximum is exceeded, the binding properties of the egg yolks break down, and the sauce thins out or curdles. If you have never made mayonnaise before, it is safest not to exceed 4 to 5 ounces, or a bare $\frac{1}{4}$ pint of oil per egg yolk.

Using an Electric Beater

The directions in the following recipe, for hand-beaten mayonnaise, apply equally well to mayonnaise made in an electric beater on a stand. Use the large bowl, and the moderately fast speed, the one usually indicated for whipping cream. Stop pouring in oil at frequent intervals and push the sauce into the beater blades, to be sure that all is being well mixed.

For ¾ to 1¼ pints of Hand-beaten Mayonnaise

A 3- to 4-pt. round-bottomed glazed pottery, glass, or stainless-steel mixing bowl. Place it in a heavy casserole or saucepan to keep it from slipping

3 egg yolks
A large wire whisk

Warm the bowl in hot water. Dry it. Add the egg yolks and beat for 1 to 2 minutes until they are thick and sticky.

1 tbl wine vinegar or lemon juice
½ tsp salt

¼ tsp dry or prepared mustard

Add the vinegar or lemon juice, salt, and mustard. Beat for a further 30 seconds.

½ to ¾ pt. of olive oil, salad oil, or a mixture of each. If the oil is cold, heat it to tepid; and if you

are a novice, use the minimum amount

The egg yolks are now ready to receive the oil, and while it goes in, drop by drop, you must not stop beating until the sauce has thickened. A speed of 2 strokes per second is fast enough. You can change hands or direction, it makes no difference as long as you beat constantly. Add the drops of oil with a teaspoon, or rest the lip of the bottle on the edge of the bowl. Keep your eye on the oil rather than on the sauce. Stop pouring and continue beating every 10 seconds or so, to be sure the egg yolks are absorbing the oil. After ⅛ to ¼ pint of oil has been incorporated, the sauce will thicken into a very heavy cream and the crisis is over. The beating arm may rest a moment.

Then beat in the remaining oil 1 to 2 tablespoons at a time, blending it thoroughly after each addition.

Drops of wine vinegar or lemon juice as needed

When the sauce becomes too thick and stiff, beat in drops of vinegar or lemon juice to thin it out. Then continue with the oil.

2 tbl boiling water
Vinegar, lemon juice, salt, pepper,
 and mustard

Beat the boiling water into the sauce. This is an anti-curdling insurance. Season to taste.

If the sauce is not used immediately, scrape it into a small bowl and cover it closely so that a skin will not form on its surface.

REMEDY FOR TURNED MAYONNAISE

You will never have trouble with freshly made mayonnaise if you have beaten the egg yolks thoroughly in a warmed bowl before adding the oil, if the oil has been added drop by drop until the sauce has commenced to thicken, and if you have not exceeded the maximum proportions of 6 fluid ounces of oil per egg yolk. A mayonnaise has turned when it refuses to thicken, or, in a finished mayonnaise, when the oil releases itself from suspension and the sauce curdles. In either case, the remedy is simple.

Warm a mixing bowl in hot water. Dry it. Add 1 teaspoon of prepared mustard and 1 tablespoon of sauce. Beat with a wire whisk for several seconds until they cream and thicken together. Beat in the rest of the sauce by teaspoons, thickening each addition before adding the next. This always works. Just be sure you add the turned sauce a little bit at a time, particularly at first.

REFRIGERATION

After several days under refrigeration, mayonnaise has a tendency to thin out, especially if it is stirred before it comes to room temperature. If it does turn, bring it back using the preceding system.

Mayonnaise made in the Electric Liquidizer

Mayonnaise in the electric liquidizer must be made with a whole egg, and is a lighter sauce than hand-made egg-yolk mayonnaise. It will keep several days longer in the refrigerator before it turns or thins out, but can be brought back just as easily as the hand-made sauce by blending 1 tablespoon of turned sauce with 1 teaspoon of prepared mustard for a few seconds until thickened. The rest of the sauce is blended in by teaspoons. Liquidizer mayonnaise, when thick enough, can be used to cover cold foods such as fish and eggs.

For almost ¾ pint

1 whole egg   **½ tsp salt**
¼ tsp dry mustard

Break the egg into the liquidizer jar. Add the mustard and salt. Cover and blend at top speed for 30 seconds, or until mixture is thick and foamy.

1 tbl lemon juice or wine vinegar

Pour in the lemon juice or vinegar, and blend for 10 seconds.

**A bare ½ pt. olive oil, salad oil, or a
   mixture of both**

Uncover jar, and blending at high speed, pour the oil into the centre of the egg mixture in a very thin stream of drops. It is important that the oil be added slowly. The sauce will begin to thicken after ¼ pint has gone in; continue adding oil very slowly until the sauce is too thick to whirl in the machine. Scrape into a bowl or jar, and stir in more seasonings to taste.

MAYONNAISE VARIATIONS

Mayonnaise aux Fines Herbes

[Mayonnaise with Green Herbs]

For: hors d'œuvres, eggs, fish, meats

3 to 4 tbl of fresh, chopped green herbs, such as tarragon, basil, chervil, chives, parsley, oregano	**¾ pt. mayonnaise, page 77 or 79**

If the sauce is to be kept for several days, blanch the herbs for 1 minute in boiling water. Drain, run cold water over them, and pat dry with a cloth. The herbs will look greener, and will not turn sour in the sauce. Stir them into the mayonnaise.

Mayonnaise Verte

[Green Herbal Mayonnaise]

For: hors d'œuvres, eggs, fish, meats

Ingredients for about 4 tbl of herb purée: **8 to 10 spinach leaves** **2 tbl chopped shallots or spring onions**	**1 oz. watercress leaves** **4 tbl parsley leaves** **1 tbl fresh tarragon or ½ tbl dried tarragon** **Optional: 2 tbl fresh chervil**

Bring ½ pint of water to the boil in a small saucepan. Add the spinach and shallots or spring onions and boil 2 minutes. Then add the rest of the ingredients and boil 1 minute more. Strain, run cold water over the herbs, and pat dry with a cloth.

Ingredients for ¾ pt. of mayonnaise,
  page 77 or 79

If you are making the mayonnaise in an electric liquidizer, add the herbs to the liquidizer with the egg, then proceed as usual. For a hand-made mayonnaise, either purée the herbs in a liquidizer, or chop them into a purée and force them through a sieve, then stir the herbs into the finished sauce.

Sauce Riviera

Beurre Montpellier

[Green Mayonnaise with Butter or Cream Cheese, Pickles, Capers, and Anchovies]

For: hors d'œuvres, sandwich spreads, eggs, fish, and as a spread for cold sliced veal, beef, or pork

For about 1 pint

2 tbl each: sour pickles, capers, and tinned anchovies or anchovy paste	**4 oz. softened butter or cream cheese** **The preceding *mayonnaise verte***

Chop the pickles, capers, and anchovies very finely, twist in the corner of a towel to extract their juice, then cream them with the butter or cheese. Beat the mixture, a tablespoon at a time, into the green mayonnaise.

Sauce Tartare

[Hard Yolk Mayonnaise]

The yolks of hard-boiled eggs will also absorb oil and turn into a mayonnaise, but with its own characteristic taste and consistency. When sieved egg whites are beaten into it, the sauce acquires a nice lightness and body which makes it useful for spooning over cold foods. This sauce cannot be made in an electric liquidizer; it turns so stiff the machine becomes clogged.

For about ¾ pint

4 hard-boiled egg yolks **1½ tbl prepared mustard**	**¼ tsp salt**

Pound and mash the egg yolks in a mixing bowl with the mustard and salt until you have a very smooth paste. Unless the yolks are smooth and free from lumps, they will not absorb the oil.

½ pt. oil
Wine vinegar or lemon juice as
  needed

Proceed as for normal mayonnaise, page 77, beating in the oil drop by drop at
first until the sauce has thickened, and thinning out with vinegar or lemon juice
as necessary.

3 to 4 tbl chopped sour pickles   **Optional: 2 or 3 sieved hard-boiled**
3 to 4 tbl chopped capers   **egg whites**
2 to 4 tbl chopped fresh green herbs
  such as parsley, chives, tarragon

Twist the chopped pickles and capers into a ball in the corner of a cloth to
extract their juice. Beat them gradually into the sauce. Then beat in the herbs,
and finally the optional egg whites. Correct seasoning.

Sauce Rémoulade

[Mayonnaise with Anchovies, Pickles, Capers, and Herbs]

With the addition of half a teaspoon or so of anchovy paste, *sauce rémoulade*
has the same flavourings as *sauce tartare*, but it is a normal mayonnaise rather than
one made with hard yolks.

Mayonnaise Collée

[Gelatine Mayonnaise—for Decorating Cold Dishes]

When gelatine is dissolved and congealed in mayonnaise, the sauce will
hold its shape and can be used for coating cold eggs, fish, and vegetables, or
may be squeezed out of a pastry bag to make fancy decorations.

For about ¾ pint

(This is the correct consistency for coating cold foods with a spoon. If the
mayonnaise is to be forced through a pastry bag, it must be stiffer; you would
use 1 ounce of gelatine dissolved in ¼ pint of liquid then beaten into ¾ pint of
mayonnaise.)

⅛ pt. of liquid as follows: **1 tbl wine vinegar**
2 tbl white wine or white   **2½ tbl chicken-, beef-, or fish-stock**
  vermouth   **½ oz. gelatine**

Pour the liquid into a small saucepan. Sprinkle the gelatine on it and let it
dissolve for several minutes. Then stir the mixture over low heat until the
gelatine is completely free of granules. Let it cool to tepid.

½ pt. mayonnaise, page 77 or 79

Beat the gelatine mixture gradually into the mayonnaise. Correct seasoning. The sauce will thin out, then gradually thicken as the gelatine sets.

Use it just before it sets. If it becomes too stiff, stir it briefly over gentle heat.

Sauce Aïoli

[Provençal Garlic Mayonnaise]

For: boiled fish, especially cod, *bourride* (Provençal fish soup), snails, boiled potatoes, French beans, and hard-boiled eggs

This rich, thick mayonnaise with its fine garlic flavour must be made in a fairly traditional way if it is to have its correct taste and consistency. The garlic should be pounded in a mortar until it is mashed into a very smooth paste. You cannot make it successfully in an electric liquidizer because for some unfortunate reason the garlic acquires a raw and bitter taste, and the egg white required for liquidizer-made sauce does not produce the fine, heavy texture that is characteristic of a proper Mediterranean *aïoli*.

For about ¾ pint

1 slice—⅜ in. thick—of stale, white home-made type bread   3 tbl milk or wine vinegar

Remove crusts and break the bread into a small bowl. Stir in the milk or vinegar and let the bread soak for 5 to 10 minutes into a soft pulp. Twist the bread into a ball in the corner of a towel to extract the liquid.

A heavy bowl or mortar   4 to 8 cloves mashed garlic
A wooden pestle

Place the bread and garlic in the bowl and pound with the pestle for at least 5 minutes to mash the garlic and bread into a very, very smooth paste.

1 egg yolk   ¼ tsp salt

Pound in the egg yolk and salt until the mixture is thick and sticky.

½ pt. good olive oil   3 to 4 tbl boiling water or fish stock
A wire whisk   2 to 3 tbl lemon juice

Then, drop by drop, pound and blend in the olive oil. When the sauce has thickened into a heavy cream, you may change from a pestle to a wire whisk and add the oil a little bit faster. Thin out the sauce as necessary with drops of water or stock, and lemon juice. Sauce should remain quite heavy, so that it holds its shape in a spoon. Correct seasoning.

NOTE: If the sauce turns or curdles, you can reconstitute it by following the directions for turned mayonnaise on page 79.

Fish Soup Note

If the *aïoli* is to be stirred into a fish soup, more egg yolks are used, usually one per person.

Sauce Alsacienne
Sauce de Sorges

[Herbal Mayonnaise made with Soft-boiled Eggs]

For: hot boiled beef, chicken, or fish

For about ¾ pint

2 eggs

Boil the eggs for 3 minutes (3½ if they are chilled). Place the yolks in a mixing bowl and put the whites—which should be just set—aside.

1 tbl prepared mustard	**1 tbl wine vinegar or lemon juice**
½ tsp salt	**½ pt. oil**

Proceed as for making mayonnaise, page 77, beating the yolks until they are thick and sticky, then beating in the mustard, salt, and vinegar or lemon juice. Finally beat in the oil, drop by drop at first.

⅛ pt. cream, sour cream, or beef, chicken, or fish stock	**3 to 4 tbl chopped parsley, tarragon, basil, etc.; or dill only**
1 tbl finely chopped shallots or spring onions	**The soft-boiled egg whites chopped or sieved**
1½ tbl capers	

Gradually beat the additional liquid into the sauce. Beat in the rest of the ingredients. Season to taste.

OIL AND VINEGAR SAUCES
Vinaigrettes

* *SAUCE VINAIGRETTE*

[French Dressing]

For: salads and simple marinades

The basic French dressing of France is a mixture of good wine vinegar, good oil, salt, pepper, fresh green herbs in season, and mustard if you like it. Garlic is employed usually only in southern France. Worcester sauce, curry, cheese, and tomato flavourings are not French additions, and sugar is heresy.

The usual proportion of vinegar to oil is one to three, but you should establish your own relationship. Lemon juice or a mixture of lemon and vinegar may be used, and the oil may be a tasteless salad oil, or olive oil. For salads, make the dressing in the empty bowl or a jar, so that all ingredients are well blended and flavoured before the salad is mixed with the dressing. And be sure the salad greens are perfectly dry so that the dressing will adhere to the leaves. Salad dressings are always best when freshly made; if they stand around for several days they tend to acquire a rancid taste.

For about ¼ pint

½ to 2 tbl good wine vinegar or a
   mixture of vinegar and lemon
   juice
⅛ tsp salt

Optional: ¼ tsp dry mustard
6 tbl salad oil or olive oil
Big pinch of pepper

Either beat the vinegar or lemon juice in a bowl with the salt and optional mustard until the salt is dissolved, then beat in the oil drop by drop and season with pepper, *or* place all ingredients in a screw-top jar and shake vigorously for 30 seconds to blend thoroughly.

Optional: 1 to 2 tbl chopped green
   herbs, such as parsley, chives, tarragon, basil; or pinch of dried herbs

Stir in the optional herbs and correct seasoning just before dressing the salad.

VARIATIONS

Sauce Ravigote

[Vinaigrette with Herbs, Capers, and Onion]

For: cold or hot boiled beef, boiled chicken, boiled fish, pig's feet, calfs' head, and vegetables

½ pt. vinaigrette, page 85   2 tbl chopped fresh green herbs,
1 tsp chopped capers   parsley, chives, tarragon, chervil,
1 tsp very finely chopped shallots or parsley only
 or spring onions

Stir all the ingredients into the vinaigrette and taste for seasoning.

Vinaigrette à la Crème

[Sour Cream Dressing—Dill Sauce]

For: cold eggs, vegetables, and cold or hot fish

1 egg yolk   2 tbl chopped fresh green herbs,
4 tbl cream or sour cream   parsley, chives, tarragon, chervil,
¼ pt. vinaigrette, page 85   burnet, or just dill
Lemon juice to taste

Beat the egg yolk and cream in a bowl until thoroughly blended. Then beat in
the vinaigrette in a stream of drops as though making a mayonnaise. Season to
taste with lemon juice, and stir in the herbs.

Sauce Moutarde

[Cold Mustard Sauce with Herbs]

For: cold beef, pork, and vegetables

2 tbl prepared French mustard   3 tbl boiling water

Rinse a small mixing bowl in hot water. Add the mustard and beat with a wire
whisk, adding the water by drops.

⅛ to ¼ pt. olive oil or salad oil

Again drop by drop, beat in the olive oil to make a thick, creamy sauce.

Salt and pepper   1 to 2 tbl parsley or chopped fresh
Lemon juice   green herbs

Beat in salt, pepper, and lemon juice to taste. Then beat in the herbs.

HOT BUTTER SAUCES
Sauces au Beurre

* ### BEURRE BLANC
BEURRE NANTAIS

[White Butter Sauce]

For: boiled, baked, or grilled fish, shellfish, asparagus, broccoli, cauliflower,
poached eggs

This famous sauce originated in Nantes, on the Loire river, and is traditionally served with pike, *brochet au beurre blanc*. Warm, thick, creamy, and butter-
coloured, *beurre blanc* is actually nothing but warm butter flavoured with shallots,
wine, vinegar, salt, and pepper. The trick in making it is to keep the butter from
turning oily; that is, it must retain its creamy appearance. A chemical process
takes place once the wine and vinegar base is boiled down and the acids are well
concentrated, so that when the butter is gradually beaten in, the milk solids in
the butter remain in suspension rather than sinking to the bottom of the pan as
they usually do when butter is melted. For this reaction to take place, the initial
amount of vinegar must be a strong one. Once the creaming process has started,
you can go on beating in butter to double the amount of that given in the recipe.
You can also beat in less, but if you do so the sauce may have too acid a taste.

For ½ pint

A 2½-pt. medium-weight enamelled   1 tbl very finely chopped shallots
  saucepan   or spring onions
⅛ pt. white wine vinegar   ¼ tsp salt
⅛ pt. dry white wine or lemon juice   ⅛ tsp white pepper

Boil the liquids, shallots or spring onions, and seasonings until they have
reduced to about 1 tablespoon.

A wire whisk   Salt and pepper
12 oz. best-quality, chilled butter   Lemon juice
  cut into 24 pieces

Remove saucepan from heat and immediately beat in 2 pieces of chilled butter.
As the butter softens and creams in the liquid, beat in another piece Then place
the saucepan over very low heat and, beating constantly, continue adding
successive pieces of butter when each previous piece has almost creamed into the
sauce. The sauce will be thick and ivory-coloured, the consistency of a light
hollandaise. Immediately remove from heat as soon as all the butter has been
used. Beat in additional seasoning to taste.

Transfer the sauce to a barely warmed bowl, and serve.

Holding the sauce

Beurre blanc will thin out and turn oily almost at once if it is reheated or if
it is kept over hot water. It must be held over water of a barely tepid temperature, just warm enough to keep the butter from congealing. Or place the sauce
near the very faint heat of a gas pilot light.

Turned sauce

Sauce that has thinned or turned oily may be made creamy again by beating
a spoonful in a cold mixing bowl, then gradually beating in the rest of the sauce

by small spoonfuls. It cannot be reheated, but you can beat 2 or 3 tablespoons of hot liquid into it a little at a time.

Leftover sauce

Beurre blanc congeals as it cools and looks like butter. It may be spread over grilled fish, used for making a hollandaise, or substituted for the butter enrichment in a béchamel or *velouté*.

VARIATION

Beurre au Citron

[Lemon Butter Sauce]

For: grilled or boiled fish, asparagus, broccoli, cauliflower

This is a minor variation of *beurre blanc,* and very nice with fish or vegetables.

For about ¼ pint

A 1-pt. medium-weight enamelled saucepan	⅛ tsp salt
⅛ pt. lemon juice	Pinch of white pepper

Boil down the lemon juice with the salt and pepper until it has reduced to 1 tablespoon.

A wire whisk
4 oz. chilled butter cut into 8
  pieces

Remove from heat and immediately beat in 2 pieces of chilled butter. Place over very low heat and beat in the rest of the butter, a piece at a time, to make a thick, creamy sauce. Immediately remove from heat.

2 to 3 tbl hot fish or vegetable
  stock or hot water

Just before serving, beat in the hot liquid drop by drop to warm the sauce. Correct seasoning and serve in a barely warmed sauceboat.

BEURRE NOIR
BEURRE NOISETTE

[Brown Butter Sauce]

For: shirred eggs, calf's brains, boiled or sautéed fish, chicken breasts, vegetables

A good brown butter sauce is rarely seen because not many cooks will take the trouble to make it so that it is a clear, unspeckled brown. It should never be black despite the poesy of the French title. To be really good, it must be made with clarified butter because the milk solids in regular butter turn black and bitter, speckling the sauce.

For about ¼ pint

6 oz. butter   **A small saucepan of medium weight**

Cut the butter into pieces and place in the saucepan over moderately low heat. When the butter has melted, skim off the foam, and decant the clear yellow liquid into a bowl. Omit all the milky residue at the bottom of the pan. Rinse out the pan, and strain the butter back into it.

3 tbl chopped parsley

Place over moderate heat. The butter will foam and crackle a bit, and as it ceases to sputter it will begin to brown. As soon as it has turned a golden nut brown, remove from heat and stir in the parsley. Pour it into another saucepan.

4 tbl wine vinegar or lemon juice   **Salt and pepper to taste**

Pour the vinegar or lemon juice into the empty butter-cooking pan and boil it down rapidly until it has reduced to about 1 tablespoon. Stir it into the browned butter. Season to taste with salt and pepper.

(*) Keep over hot water until ready to serve.

VARIATION WITH CAPERS

1 tbl capers

Stir the capers into the butter with the parsley.

COLD FLAVOURED BUTTERS
Beurres Composés

Butter can be put to a variety of appetizing uses when it has been creamed with herbs, wine, mustard, egg yolks, shellfish meat, or other flavourings.

On Hot Dishes

Place a piece of cold flavoured butter on top of grilled fish or meat just as it is sent to the table.

For Basting

Baste meat, fish, or mushrooms with flavoured butter while baking or grilling.

Sauce and Soup Enrichment

Stir flavoured butter into a sauce or soup just before serving.

Egg Filling or Sandwich Spread

Cream butter, egg yolks, and herbs together and use as a filling for hard-boiled eggs, or as a sandwich spread.

Decorations

Fill a pastry bag with chilled but still malleable flavoured butter and squeeze it out in fancy designs to decorate appetizers or cold dishes.

Cutout Designs

Spread flavoured butter on a plate and chill it. Then dip a knife or cutter in hot water and form fancy shapes for canapés or cold dishes.

HOW TO CREAM BUTTER

[*Beurre en Pommade*]

The butter must always be creamed or beaten before the flavouring is added to it. You can blend the butter to a cream in an electric beater, pound it in a bowl with a pestle, or mash it, a bit at a time, with the back of a wooden spoon, then beat it vigorously until it is light and creamy. Then the flavourings and the butter are creamed together, and the mixture is put in a cool place to firm up. If it is refrigerated, it will become as hard as an ordinary piece of chilled butter.

Beurre de Moutarde

[Mustard Butter]

For: kidneys, liver, steaks, grilled fish, and sauce enrichments

4 oz. butter
1 to 2 tbl prepared French mustard

Salt and pepper to taste
Optional: 2 tbl fresh chopped parsley or mixed green herbs

Cream the butter well. One teaspoon at a time, beat in the mustard. Beat in seasonings and optional parsley or mixed herbs to taste.

Beurre d'Anchois

[Anchovy Butter]

For: grilled fish, egg fillings, sandwiches, sauce enrichments

4 oz. butter	**Lemon juice to taste**
2 tbl mashed tinned anchovies or	**Optional: 1 to 2 tbl chopped parsley**
1 tbl anchovy paste	**or mixed green herbs**
Pepper	

Cream the butter well. One teaspoon at a time, beat in the anchovies or anchovy paste. Season to taste with pepper, drops of lemon juice, and optional herbs.

Beurre d'Ail

[Garlic Butter]

For: grilled or boiled fish, steaks, hamburgers, lamb chops, boiled potatoes, canapés, sauce and soup enrichments

The smoothest and best-tasting result will be obtained if the garlic is pounded to a paste with a pestle and the butter is gradually pounded into it. A garlic press may be used if you have not the time or patience to pound, but the result will not be as good either in flavour or in texture.

2 to 8 cloves garlic	**1½ pts. boiling water**

Place the unpeeled cloves of garlic in the boiling water, bring to the boil for 5 seconds. Drain, peel, and rinse under cold water. Bring to the boil again for 30 seconds, drain, and rinse. Pound to a smooth paste in a mortar (or put through a garlic press).

4 oz. butter	**Optional: 1 to 2 tbl chopped**
Salt and pepper	**parsley or mixed green herbs**

Pound or cream the butter and garlic together. Season to taste with the salt, pepper, and optional herbs.

Beurre à l'Oeuf

[Egg Yolk Butter]

For: sandwiches, canapés, hard-boiled eggs, and general decoration

4 oz. butter

Cream the butter well.

4 sieved hard-boiled egg yolks   Optional: 1 to 2 tbl chopped chives
Salt and pepper   or mixed green herbs

Beat the sieved egg yolks into the butter and season to taste with salt, pepper, and
optional herbs.

Beurre Maître d'Hôtel

[Parsley Butter]

Beurre de Fines Herbes

[Mixed Herb Butter]

Beurre d'Estragon

[Tarragon Butter]

For: grilled meats and fish, and for sauce and soup enrichments

4 oz. butter   (or dried tarragon and fresh
1 tbl lemon juice   parsley)
2 to 3 tbl fresh chopped parsley, or   Salt and pepper
   mixed green herbs, or tarragon

Cream the butter. Drop by drop, beat in the lemon juice. Then beat in the herbs,
and season to taste with salt and pepper.

Beurre Colbert

[Tarragon Butter with Meat Flavouring]

For: grilled meats and fish

Ingredients for the preceding butter   1 tbl melted meat glaze (meat stock
   using tarragon   reduced to a syrup), page 99

Drop by drop, beat the meat glaze into the tarragon butter.

Beurre pour Escargots

[Snail Butter]

For: snails, grilled meats and fish; for basting baked or grilled fish or
mushrooms; for grilled mussels, or oysters

4 oz. butter   depending on your taste for
2 tbl chopped shallots or spring   garlic
   onions   2 tbl chopped parsley
1 to 3 cloves mashed garlic,   Salt and pepper

Cream the butter well. Twist the shallots or spring onions into a ball in the
corner of a cloth to extract their juice. Beat them into the butter with the garlic
and parsley. Season to taste with salt and pepper.

Beurre Marchand de Vins

[Shallot Butter with Red Wine]

For: steaks, hamburgers, liver, and enrichment of brown sauces

⅛ pt. red wine	1 tbl meat glaze or ¼ pt. brown
1 tbl chopped shallots or spring	stock or beef bouillon
onions	Big pinch of pepper

Boil the wine with the shallots or spring onions, meat flavouring, and pepper until the liquid has reduced to about 1 tablespoon. Let it cool.

4 oz. butter	Salt and pepper
1 to 2 tbl chopped parsley	

Cream the butter well, then beat it, a tablespoon at a time, into the wine flavouring. Beat in the parsley, and season to taste.

Beurre Bercy

[Shallot Butter with White Wine]

For: steaks, hamburgers, liver, and enrichment of brown sauces

Ingredients for the preceding	white wine or vermouth for the
shallot butter, but substitute dry	red wine

Follow the preceding recipe, then proceed to the optional next step.

Optional: 3 to 4 tbl diced beef	minutes in hot salted water,
marrow softened for 3 or 4	page 15

Stir in the optional beef marrow along with the final seasonings.

Beurre de Crustacés

[Shellfish Butter]

For: sandwich spreads, canapés, hard-boiled eggs, decoration of cold dishes; for enrichment of shellfish sauces and bisques, and tinned and frozen shellfish soups

Shellfish butters are made with the cooked debris, such as legs, chests, eggs, and green matter of lobster, crab, crayfish, or shrimps. The red shells colour the butter a creamy rose, and both shell and bits of flesh give a lovely flavour to the mixture. You can also make shellfish butter with the meat alone, and colour the butter with a bit of tomato paste.

Traditionally, the shells and meat are placed in a large marble mortar, and are pounded into a purée with a heavy wooden pestle. Then they are pounded with the butter so that every bit is thoroughly mixed together. Finally the whole mass is forced through a fine-meshed drum sieve to remove all minute pieces of shell. This long and arduous process needs no further explanation. You just pound; the result is exquisite. An excellent butter may be made in an electric liquidizer in a fraction of the time:

For about ¼ pint

8 oz. cooked shellfish debris   **Or: 4 oz. cooked shellfish meat**
Or: 4 oz. cooked, whole, unpeeled   **and 1½ tbl tomato paste**
shrimps

Chop the debris or meat into ¼-inch pieces, or put it through a mincer.

4 oz. hot melted butter

Fill the electric liquidizer jar with hot water to heat it thoroughly. Empty and dry quickly. Then add the shellfish. Immediately pour in the hot melted butter, cover, and blend at top speed. The butter will cream into a stiff paste in a few seconds. Pour the mixture into a saucepan, heat until the butter has warmed and melted. Blend again. Repeat, if you feel it necessary.

A fine-meshed sieve set over a   **A pestle or wooden spoon**
bowl   **Salt and white pepper**

Rub through a very fine sieve, extracting as much butter and shellfish meat as possible. As the butter cools and partially congeals, beat it with a wooden spoon. Season to taste with salt and pepper.

(*) May be deep-frozen.

Second pressing

To extract the remaining butter and flavour from the debris left in the sieve, steep the debris in an equal amount of almost simmering water for 5 minutes in a saucepan over very low heat. Strain, and chill. The congealed butter on top of the liquid may be used for sauce enrichments. The liquid itself may serve as the basis for a fish stock.

OTHER SAUCES

Following is a list of regional or special sauces described in recipes elsewhere in this book.

Sauce Spéciale à l'Ail pour Gigot, a special garlic sauce for roast lamb, page 306.

Sauce Moutarde à la Normande, a cream and mustard sauce for pork, page 350.

Sauce Nénette, cream, mustard, and tomato sauce for pork or boiled beef, page 355.

Sauce Fondue de Fromage, a creamy, wine-flavoured cheese sauce with a whiff of garlic, in the Poached Egg section, page 106. This is also good for vegetables, fish, chicken, or *pastas* which are to be *gratinéed* under a grill, or as a spread for hot hors d'œuvres that are to be browned quickly in the oven or under the grill.

Sauce Chaud-froid, Blanche-neige, a reduction of heavy cream, meat, poultry, or fish stock, and tarragon, plus gelatine. For coating cold chicken, fish, or cold moulded mousses. This is an excellent cold sauce, and in our opinion far more delicate than the traditional *sauce chaud-froid* made from a flour-thickened *velouté*. See the recipes for cold breast of chicken on page 508, for crab on page 511, and for fish mousse on page 519.

STOCKS AND ASPICS
Fonds de Cuisine—Gelée

The wonderful flavour of good French food is the result, more often than not, of the stock used for its cooking, its flavouring, or its sauce. The French term *fonds de cuisine* means literally the foundation and working capital of the kitchen. A stock is the liquid obtained from the simmering together of meat, bones—or fish trimmings—with vegetables, seasonings, and water. This liquid, strained, and boiled down to concentrate its flavour if necessary, is the basis for soups, the moistening element for stews, braised meats, or vegetables, and the liquid used in making all the sauces that have a meat or fish flavouring. Stocks are extremely easy to make, and can simmer quietly by themselves with little or no attention from the cook. They may be deep-frozen and stored for weeks, or they may be boiled down until all their water content has evaporated, and they become a *glace de viande,* or flavour concentrate.

SUBSTITUTES FOR HOME-MADE STOCK

If you do not have home-made stock in the larder, a recipe for improving tinned beef bouillon or bouillon cubes is on page 59; for tinned chicken broth, on page 49. Tinned consommé tends to be sweet and we do not recommend it as a substitute except in the case of aspics.

INGREDIENTS FOR MAKING STOCKS

The most luxurious stocks are made from fresh soup bones, fresh meat, and vegetables. But unless you intend to make a stock for an absolutely remarkable consommé, use what you have on hand and add any fresh ingredients you wish to buy. It is a good idea to make a collection in the refrigerator of beef, veal, and poultry bones, and meat scraps. Then when a sufficient amount has accumulated, you can boil up a stock. Both meat and bones give flavour, and the bones, in addition, contain a certain amount of gelatine which gives body to the stock. Raw veal bones, especially the knuckle, and calf's feet, if you can find them, contain the most gelatine. If you want a stock that will jelly naturally include these in the proportions listed on page 101.

Lamb, Ham, and Pork

A few pork bones may be added to the stock pan, but too much pork tends to give the stock a sweet flavour. Lamb or ham bones should not be used; their flavour is too strong for a general-purpose stock. But lamb or ham stocks are made in the same way as simple stock.

Vegetables

Carrots, onions, celery, and leeks are the usual soup vegetables. A parsnip or two may be included if you wish. Starchy vegetables will cloud the stock. Turnips, cauliflower, and the cabbage family in general have too strong a flavour for a general-purpose stock.

THE PRESSURE COOKER

One would expect a pressure cooker to be the ideal stock-making instrument; but our experiments have shown otherwise. After about 45 minutes of cooking under 15 pounds of pressure, a meat stock acquires its maximum pressure-cooked flavour. To reach its optimum flavour, it must then be simmered quietly in an open pot an hour or two more. Poultry stock, in our experience, acquires an unpleasant flavour if cooked for more than 20 minutes under 15 pounds of pressure. After this lapse of time the pressure should be released and the stock allowed to simmer, uncovered, for an hour or so longer.

---

* FONDS DE CUISINE SIMPLE

[Simple Meat Stock]

This is the general formula for a simple stock made from a miscellaneous collection of bones and meat scraps. It may be employed for meat sauces, the braising of meats and vegetables, the flavouring of soups, and for deglazing a roasting tin. The stock may be made from bones alone, but will have more character if some meat is included; ideal proportions are about half and half. The more elaborate stocks follow exactly the same cooking procedure.

For 3 to 4 pints

5 pts. of meat and bones chopped into 2- to 3-in. pieces (raw or cooked veal or beef bones and meat, and/or poultry carcasses, scraps, and giblets)	A 4- to 5-qt. saucepan Cold water

Place the meat and bones in the saucepan and add cold water to cover them by 2 inches. Place over moderate heat. As the liquid comes slowly to the simmering point, scum will start to rise. Remove it with a spoon or ladle for 5 minutes or so, until it almost ceases to accumulate.

2 medium-sized scraped carrots	1 bay leaf
2 medium-sized peeled onions	6 parsley sprigs
2 medium-sized celery stalks	2 unpeeled garlic cloves
The following tied in washed cheesecloth:	2 whole cloves
¼ tsp thyme	2 tsp salt
	Optional: 2 washed leeks

Add all the ingredients above, and more water if the liquid does not cover the ingredients by a full inch. When liquid is simmering again, skim as necessary. Partially cover the pan, leaving a space of about 1 inch for steam to escape. Maintain liquid at a very quiet simmer—just a bubble or two of motion at the surface—for 4 to 5 hours or more. Accumulated fat and scum may be skimmed off occasionally. Boiling water should be added if the liquid evaporates below the level of the ingredients.

Never allow the liquid to boil; fat and scum incorporate themselves into the stock and will make it cloudy.

Cooking may be stopped at any time, and continued later.

Never make the saucepan airtight unless its contents have cooled completely, or the stock will sour.

When your taste convinces you that you have simmered the most out of the ingredients, strain the stock out of the saucepan into a bowl.

TO DEGREASE

Either let the stock settle for 5 minutes, remove the fat from its surface with a spoon or ladle, then draw scraps of absorbent paper over the top of the stock to blot up the last globules of fat;

Or place the stock, uncovered, in the refrigerator until the fat has hardened on the surface and can be scraped off.

FINAL FLAVOURING

Taste the degreased stock for strength. If its flavour is weak, boil it down to evaporate some of its water content and to concentrate its strength. Correct seasoning, and it is ready to use.

D

When the stock is cold, cover and refrigerate it, or bottle and deep-freeze it. Stock kept in the refrigerator must be brought to the boil every 3 or 4 days to keep it from spoiling.

VARIATIONS

The following are traditional recipes for classical stocks made with fresh ingredients. You can, of course, vary the proportions according to your store of leftover bones and meat scraps. These are all simmered in exactly the same way as the simple stock in the preceding master recipe.

Fonds Blanc

[White Stock—Veal Stock]

White stock is used when you want to make a particularly fine white *velouté* sauce or soup. Raw veal releases a tremendous amount of grey and granular scum that can cloud your stock if it is not completely removed. The easiest way to deal with this problem is to blanch the veal as described here.

For 3 to 4 pints

3 lbs. lean, raw veal shank meat   **4 lbs. cracked, raw veal bones**

Place the meat and bones in a saucepan. Cover with cold water, bring to the boil and boil slowly for 5 minutes. Drain, and rinse the bones and meat under cold water to remove all scum. Rinse the saucepan clean.

Same vegetables, herbs, and
  seasonings as for the master
  recipe, page 96

Place the bones and meat again in the saucepan, cover with cold water, bring to simmering point, and skim as necessary. Then add the vegetables, herbs, and seasonings. Simmer the stock for 4 to 5 hours or more as described in the master recipe.

Fonds Blanc de Volaille

[White Poultry Stock]

This stock is used for soups and sauces. Employ the same method and ingredients as for the preceding white veal stock, but add a whole or parts of a boiling fowl to the saucepan along with the vegetables. The chicken may be removed when tender, and the stock simmered several hours longer.

Fonds Brun

[Brown Stock]

Brown stock is used for brown sauces, consommés, and for the braising of vegetables and red meats. To give the stock a good colour, the meat, bones, and vegetables are browned before they go into the saucepan, otherwise the cooking procedure is the same as for a simple stock, which may also be turned into a brown stock if you brown the ingredients.

For 2 to 3 quarts

3 lbs. beef shank meat	2 scrubbed, quartered carrots
3 to 4 lbs. cracked beef and veal	2 halved, peeled onions
bones	A shallow roasting tin

Heat oven to 425° F., Mark 7. Arrange the meat, bones, and vegetables in the roasting pan and place in the middle portion of the oven. Turn the ingredients occasionally so that they will brown evenly, in 30 to 40 minutes.

A 6- to 8-quart saucepan

Remove from oven and drain fat out of roasting tin. Transfer the browned ingredients to a saucepan. Pour ½ pint of water into the pan, place over heat, and scrape up all coagulated browning juices. Pour them into the saucepan.

2 tsp salt	the master recipe, page 96,
2 celery stalks	tied in cheesecloth
Herbs and flavourings listed in	

Then, following the procedure in the master recipe on page 96, cover the ingredients in the saucepan with cold water, bring to the simmering point, skim. Add all the ingredients above and proceed with the recipe. Simmer the stock 4 to 5 hours or more.

Fonds Brun de Volaille

[Brown Poultry Stock]

The recipe for a simple brown poultry stock is on page 213 in the Poultry chapter. You will note that poultry bones and scraps should be browned in a frying pan, as they tend to burn and to acquire an unpleasant flavour if browned in the oven.

Glace de Viande

[Meat Glaze]

Meat glaze is any one of the preceding stocks boiled down until it has reduced to a syrup that becomes a hard jelly when it is cold. Five pints of stock will reduce to ¾ pint or less of glaze, so it is easily stored. A teaspoon stirred into a sauce or a soup will often give it just that particular boost of flavour which it lacks. Meat glaze dissolved in hot water may always be used in place of stock. It is thus a most useful commodity to have on hand and almost invariably has a better flavour than commercial meat extracts and bouillon cubes.

**1 to 2 qts. of any home-made
    stock**

Strain the stock and degrease it thoroughly Bring it to the boil in an uncovered saucepan and boil it slowly until it has reduced to about 1½ pints. Strain it through a very fine sieve into a smaller saucepan and continue to boil it down until it has reduced to a syrup which coats the spoon lightly. Watch it during the last stages to be sure it does not burn. Strain it into a jar. When it is cold and has turned to a jelly, cover and refrigerate, or deep-freeze it.

Meat glaze will keep for weeks under refrigeration. If it develops a few spots of mould, no harm is done. Take it out of the jar, wash it under warm water. Then simmer it in a saucepan over low heat with a spoonful of water until it has again reduced to a thick syrup.

CLARIFICATION OF STOCKS

Clarification du Bouillon

If you wish to serve a rich home-made consommé, jellied soup, or aspic, you should clarify your stock so that it is beautifully clear and sparkling. This is accomplished by beating egg whites into cold stock, then heating it to just below the simmering point for 15 minutes. The egg-white globules dispersed into the stock act as a magnet for all its minute cloudy particles. These gradually rise to the surface, leaving a crystal-clear liquid below them.

Clarification is a simple process if you remember that the stock must be perfectly degreased, that all equipment must be absolutely free of grease, and that you must handle the stock gently so that the egg whites are not unduly disturbed.

For about 1½ pints

2 pts. cold stock   **A very clean 4-pt. saucepan**
Salt and pepper

Degrease the stock thoroughly; any fat particles will hinder the clarification process. Taste carefully for seasoning and oversalt slightly if stock is to be served cold; salt loses savour in a cold dish.

A very clean 3-pt. mixing bowl
A wire whisk
2 egg whites
Optional: 2 oz. of absolutely lean,
  scraped, or minced beef; 1 oz.

chopped green leek tops or spring
onion tops; 2 tbl chopped parsley;
and ½ tbl tarragon or chervil

Beat ½ pint of stock in the mixing bowl with the egg whites and add optional ingredients for richer flavour. Bring the rest of the stock to the boil in the saucepan. Then, beating the egg-white mixture, gradually pour on the hot stock in a very thin stream. Pour the mixture back into the saucepan and place over moderate heat. Until the stock starts to simmer, agitate it slowly and continually with a wire whisk so that the egg whites, which will begin to turn white, are being constantly circulated throughout the liquid. Immediately the simmering point is reached, stop stirring. The egg whites now will have mounted to the surface. Gently move the saucepan to the side of the heat so that one edge of the liquid is barely bubbling. In 5 minutes, rotate the saucepan a quarter turn. Turn it again in 5 minutes, and once more for a final 5 minutes.

5 layers of well-washed, damp
  cheesecloth
A very clean colander

A very clean 5-pt. bowl
A very clean ladle
⅛ pt. Madeira, port, or cognac

Line the colander with the cheesecloth and place it over the bowl. The colander should be of a size so that its base will remain above the surface of the liquid which is to be poured into the bowl. Very gently ladle the stock and egg whites into the cheesecloth, disturbing the egg whites as little as possible. The clarified stock will drain through the cheesecloth, leaving the egg-white particles behind. Allow the egg whites to drain undisturbed for 5 minutes, then remove the colander, and stir the wine or cognac into the clarified stock.

JELLIED STOCKS—ASPICS

Gelée

Home-made Jellied Stock

Calf's feet and veal knuckles contain enough natural gelatine to make a stock jelly by itself; pork rind helps the process. They are added to simmer with any of the stocks on pages 96 to 99 and will provide about 5 pints of jelly. Prepare them as follows:

Either: 2 calf's feet

These can usually be ordered from your butcher, and come skinned and cleaned. Scrub them under cold water. Soak them for 8 hours in several changes of cold water. Then cover them with cold water, boil for 5 minutes, and wash under cold water. They are now ready to use, and are added to the stock along with the vegetables.

Or: 1 lb. cracked veal knuckles

Cover the knuckles with cold water, boil for 5 minutes, then wash under cold water. Add the knuckles to the stock along with the vegetables.

And: ¼ lb. fresh or salt pork rind

Scrub the pork rind in cold water. Cover with cold water and simmer for 10 minutes. Rinse under cold water. Add the rind to the stock along with the vegetables and the calf's feet or knuckles.

USING COMMERCIAL GELATINE

Plain stock, clarified stock, bouillon, and tinned consommé are turned into aspic (or meat jelly) by adding unflavoured gelatine in the following proportions:

For jellied soup: ¼ ounce of gelatine for each pint of liquid

For aspics or for the decoration of cold dishes: ¼ ounce of gelatine for each ¾ pint of liquid

For lining a mould: ¼ ounce of gelatine for each ½ pint of liquid

Gelatine can be obtained in either powder or sheet form, both sold by weight. If you are living in France you will usually buy gelatine in sheets: 1 sheet of French gelatine equals 2 grams; 4 sheets are the equivalent of ¼ ounce of powdered gelatine.

How to Use Powdered Gelatine

Sprinkle ¼ ounce of gelatine into ⅛ to ¼ pint of cold stock and let it soften for 3 to 4 minutes. Then blend it into the rest of the stock and stir over moderate heat for several minutes until the gelatine has completely dissolved and the liquid is absolutely free of granules.

How to Use Sheet Gelatine

Soak the sheets in cold water for about 10 minutes, until they are soft. Drain them, then stir them in the stock over gentle heat until the gelatine has completely dissolved.

Wine Flavouring

The wine used for flavouring a jelly is almost always port, Madeira, or cognac. From 1 to 2 tablespoons per ½ pint is usually sufficient. Stir the wine or cognac into the hot stock after the gelatine has been dissolved. As most of the alcohol will evaporate, this small additional amount of liquid will not disturb the proportions of gelatine.

TESTING JELLIES

Always test out a jelly before using it; the few minutes you spend can save you from disaster. Pour ½ inch of jelly into a chilled saucer and refrigerate it for about 10 minutes until it has set. Then break it up with a fork and leave it at room temperature for 10 minutes. For jellied soups it should hold its shape softly. For aspics its broken lumps should stand alone, but not be rubbery. A jelly that is to line a mould should be stiffer, so that it can support the ingredients it is to enclose. If the jelly is too hard, add unjellied stock and test again. If the jelly is too soft, add more gelatine and test again.

FISH STOCK

Fumet de Poisson

Fumet de Poisson au Vin Blanc

[White-wine Fish Stock]

The following proportions are for the production of a fine, well-flavoured fish stock to be used as the basis of a fish *velouté* sauce. A smaller quantity of fish would produce a lighter stock suitable for fish-poaching, or fish soups.

For about ¾ pint

A 5- to 6-qt. enamelled or stainless steel saucepan

2 lbs. lean, fresh fish, fish heads, and/or bones and trimmings (halibut, whiting, or plaice are recommended, or use frozen fish of good quality. Fresh or cooked shellfish leftovers may be included)

1 thinly sliced onion

6 to 8 parsley stems—not the leaves, which will darken the stock

1 tsp lemon juice

¼ tsp salt

½ pt. dry white wine or ⅓ pt. dry white vermouth

Cold water to cover ingredients

Optional: 2 oz. fresh mushroom stems

Place all the ingredients in the saucepan. Bring to simmering point, skim, then simmer uncovered for 30 minutes. Strain through a fine sieve, and correct seasoning. Fish stock may be refrigerated or deep-frozen. If refrigerated, boil it up every 2 days to keep it from spoiling.

CHAPTER THREE

EGGS

Oeufs

ONCE AN EGG is taken out of the breakfast category and put to use as a hot entrée, a luncheon, or a supper dish, it offers a great variety of presentations and you can draw on practically your whole cooking experience for its saucing and garnishing. In the following selection of recipes, we have concentrated on poaching, shirring, baking, scrambling, and omelette making, with a fundamental recipe for each, and a group of variations.

Wine and eggs have no great sympathy for each other, but as one usually likes to serve wine with an entrée, the best choice would be a fairly dry white wine with some body—such as Graves, Chablis, or Pouilly-Fuissé—or a *rosé*.

---

* POACHED EGGS

[Oeufs Pochés]

A poached egg is one that has been dropped without its shell into a pan of barely simmering liquid and cooked for about 4 minutes until the white is set but the yolk remains liquid. A perfect specimen is neat and oval in shape, and the white completely masks the yolk. The most important requirement for poaching is that the eggs be very fresh; the yolk stands high, the white clings to it in a cohesive mass and only a small amount of watery liquid falls away from the main body of the white. A stale egg with a relaxed and watery white is unpoach-able because the white trails off in wisps in the water leaving the yolk exposed. If the eggs are not quite as fresh as you could wish, simmer them in their shells for 8 to 10 seconds before poaching. This will often firm up the white just enough to make it hold its shape around the yolk when the egg is broken into the water. Another solution is to use the 5-minute boiled eggs on page 106; these do not require exceptional freshness, and, when peeled, can substitute for poached eggs in any recipe. *We are not discussing the egg poacher with its circular rings to hold each egg; it produces a neat, mechanically circular result out of even the stalest egg. By all means use an egg poacher if you do not wish to attempt the free-floating traditional method described here.*

How to poach eggs

To transfer the egg from the shell to the water you may either break it directly into the water as described below, or break it into a saucer, tilt the saucer directly over the water, and slip the egg in.

A saucepan or a frying pan 8 to   **Vinegar (which helps the eggs to**
   10 ins. in diameter and 2½ to 3 ins.   **hold their shape)**
   deep

Pour 2 inches of water into the pan or frying pan and add 1 tablespoon of vinegar per pint of water. Bring to simmering point.

4 very fresh eggs   **A slotted spoon**
A wooden spoon or spatula

Break one of the eggs, and, holding it as closely over the water as possible, let it fall in. Immediately and gently push the white over the yolk with a wooden spoon for 2 to 3 seconds. Maintain the water at barely simmering point and proceed with the other eggs in the same manner.

A bowl of cold water

After 4 minutes, remove the first egg with the slotted spoon and test with your finger. The white should be set, the yolk still soft to the touch. Place the egg in the cold water; this washes off the vinegar and stops the cooking. Remove the rest of the eggs as they are done, and poach others in the same water if you are doing more.

(*) The eggs may remain for several hours in cold water, or may be drained and refrigerated.

A bowl of hot water containing   **A clean cloth**
   1½ tsp salt per pt.

To reheat the eggs, trim off any trailing bits of white with a knife. Place them in hot salted water for about half a minute to heat them through. Remove one at a time with a slotted spoon. Holding a folded cloth under the spoon, roll the egg back and forth for a second to drain it, and it is ready to serve.

D*

A SUBSTITUTE FOR POACHED EGGS

Oeufs Mollets

[Five-minute Boiled Eggs]

This is a boiled egg with a set white and a soft yolk which can be peeled and substituted for poached eggs.

2 qts. boiling water   **6 eggs with uncracked shells**

Lower the eggs into the boiling water and boil slowly according to the following table, adding 1 minute if the eggs are chilled.

Small Eggs	5 mins
Standard Eggs	5½ mins
Large Eggs	6 mins

As soon as the time is up, drain off the boiling water and run cold water into the pan for a minute to set the white, and to cool the eggs enough to remove the shells. Tap gently on a hard surface to break the shells, peel carefully under a stream of water.

If to be served cold, refrigerate. If to be served hot, warm for a minute in a bowl of hot water.

OEUFS SUR CANAPÉS
OEUFS EN CROUSTADES

[Poached Eggs on Canapés, Artichoke Bottoms, Mushroom Caps, or in Pastry Shells]

A practically limitless series of elegant little hot first courses or luncheon dishes may be concocted with poached eggs, sauces, minces, and imagination. Here are some ideas:

Oeufs à la Fondue de Fromage

[Poached Eggs on Canapés with Cheese Fondue Sauce]

This is a particularly good sauce for eggs; it is creamy, wine-flavoured, cheesy, and has just a whiff of garlic. *Sauce mornay* (béchamel with cheese), page 54, may always be substituted.

For 6 servings (¾ pint)

A 2-pt. saucepan   ½ oz. butter
1 tbl chopped shallots or spring   A small clove mashed garlic
  onions

Cook the shallots or spring onions for 1 to 2 minutes in the butter without
browning. Add garlic and cook 30 seconds more.

¼ pt. dry white wine or ⅛ pt. dry   ⅛ pt. stock or beef bouillon
  white vermouth

Then add the wine and stock and boil rapidly until liquid has reduced to 3 or 4
tablespoons.

¾ oz. cornflour   A small mixing bowl
½ pt. cream

Blend the cornflour with 2 tablespoons of the cream, then stir in half of the
remaining cream. Pour it into the wine and shallots and simmer, stirring, for 2
minutes. Add more cream by spoonfuls to thin the sauce—it should coat a spoon
fairly heavily.

2 to 3 oz. grated Swiss cheese   Pinch of nutmeg
Salt and pepper

Stir in the cheese and simmer, stirring, until the cheese has melted and the sauce
is smooth and creamy. Add more spoonfuls of cream if necessary. Correct
seasoning, set aside, and reheat when needed.

6 poached eggs or 5-minute boiled   bread sautéed in clarified butter),
  eggs   page 181
6 canapés (oval slices of white

Prepare the eggs and canapés.

3 tbl grated Swiss cheese   A grill pan or fireproof serving
½ oz. melted butter   dish

Shortly before serving, preheat grill to very hot. Place a cold drained egg on
each canapé, spoon the sauce over, sprinkle with cheese and butter. Place for
about a minute under the hot grill to reheat the eggs but not to overcook them,
and to brown the top of the sauce lightly. Serve on a dish or on serving plates.

Other Ideas

Mix a spoonful or two of cooked, chopped spinach, or chopped sautéed
ham with a little of the sauce and spread over each canapé to act as a bed for the

108 CHAPTER THREE: EGGS

egg. Use pastry shells, grilled mushroom caps, or cooked artichoke bottoms instead of canapés.

Oeufs en Croustades à la Béarnaise

[Poached Eggs and Mushrooms, Béarnaise Sauce]

For 8 servings

1 lb. finely chopped fresh mushrooms	3 tbl chopped shallots or spring onions
1½ oz. butter	An enamelled frying pan

A handful at a time, twist the mushrooms into a ball in the corner of a cloth to extract their juice. Sauté the mushrooms in hot butter with the shallots or spring onions for 7 to 8 minutes, until the pieces begin to separate from each other.

¾ oz. flour

Sprinkle on the flour and stir over moderate heat for 3 minutes.

⅛ pt. Madeira or port	½ tsp salt
¼ pt. cream	Pinch of pepper

Stir in the wine and boil for a minute. Then stir in two-thirds of the cream. Add the seasonings. Simmer for 2 to 3 minutes, adding more cream by spoonfuls if the mushroom mixture becomes too thick. Correct seasoning and set aside.

8 cooked pastry shells 2 to 2½ ins. in diameter and 1½ ins. high, page 182	¾ to 1 pt. *sauce béarnaise*, or *sauce choron* (béarnaise with tomato), *page 76*
8 poached eggs or 5-minute boiled eggs	

Just before serving, reheat the mushrooms, pastry shells, and eggs. Put 2 or 3 tablespoons of the mushroom mixture into each shell, lay an egg over it, and coat with the sauce. Serve immediately on a dish or individual serving plates.

Other Ideas

Instead of mushrooms, use creamed shellfish; follow the recipe for *fondue de crustacés* on page 184, and top with hollandaise. Grilled mushroom caps, grilled tomatoes, or cooked artichoke bottoms may replace pastry shells.

Oeufs à la Bourguignonne

[Eggs Poached in Red Wine]

This is a good dish for a light supper or a winter luncheon, and can be made more important if it is garnished with sautéed chicken livers or braised onions, and sautéed or grilled mushrooms. Accompany it with a light red Burgundy or Beaujolais. Traditionally the eggs are poached in the wine, but they may be done in water in the usual way, if you wish.

For 8 servings

¾ pt. of brown stock or beef
  bouillon
¾ pt. good, young red wine

An 8-in. saucepan
8 very fresh eggs

Bring the stock and wine to the simmer and poach the eggs in it. Remove the eggs to a fireproof dish, add a very little of poaching liquid, and set aside. About 5 minutes before serving, set the dish uncovered over simmering water to reheat the eggs.

½ bay leaf tied with 2 or 3 parsley
  sprigs
¼ tsp thyme
1 clove mashed garlic

1 tbl chopped shallots or spring
  onions
Pinch of cayenne pepper
Pinch of pepper

After poaching the eggs, add the herbs, garlic, shallots or spring onions, and seasonings to the wine and boil it down rapidly until it has reduced to ¾ pint. Remove parsley and bay leaf.

¾ oz. softened butter
¾ oz. flour

Optional: 1 tbl red currant jelly

Blend the butter and flour to a smooth paste—*beurre manié*. Away from heat, beat it into the wine mixture with a wire whisk. Boil for 30 seconds. Beat in the optional currant jelly for colour and flavour, and correct seasoning.

(*) If not to be used immediately leave aside uncovered, top dotted with part of the enrichment butter.

½ to 1 oz. softened butter

Just before serving, reheat the sauce to the simmering point. Away from heat, beat in the butter.

8 canapés (ovals of white bread
  sautéed in clarified butter,
  page 181. They may be rubbed

with a cut clove of garlic if you
  wish)
2 to 3 tbl fresh chopped parsley

Place a hot egg on each canapé and arrange on a dish or serving plates. Surround with whatever garniture you may have chosen, and spoon the hot sauce over. Decorate with parsley, and serve.

Oeufs en Gelée

[Poached Eggs in Aspic]

This recipe is in the chapter on cold buffets, page 504.

---

* SHIRRED EGGS

[Oeufs sur le Plat—Oeufs Miroir]

A shirred egg is one that is broken into a small, flat, buttered dish and cooked quickly under the grill. The white is softly set and tender, and the yolk is liquid, but covered by a shimmering, translucent film. Shirred eggs should never be attempted in the oven, as it toughens them.

For each serving

Preheat grill to very hot.

A shallow, fireproof dish about   ¼ oz. butter
4 ins. in diameter   1 or 2 eggs

Place the dish over moderate heat and add the butter. As soon as it has melted, break the egg or eggs into the dish and cook for about 30 seconds until a thin layer of white has set in the bottom of the dish. Remove from heat, tilt dish, and baste the egg with the butter. Set aside.

Salt and pepper

A minute or so before serving, place the dish an inch below the hot grill. Slide it in and out every few seconds and baste the egg with the butter. In about a minute the white will be set, and the yolk filmed and glistening. Remove, season, and serve immediately.

VARIATIONS

Using the technique of the preceding recipe, shirred eggs may be dressed up in the following ways:

Au Beurre Noir

[With Black Butter Sauce]

Substitute *beurre noir,* page 88, for plain butter.

Aux Fines Herbes

[With Herb Butter]

Substitute herb or tarragon butter, page 92, for plain butter.

À la Crème

[With Cream]

Use half the amount of butter. After bottom of egg has been lightly cooked on top of the stove, pour 2 tablespoons of cream over the egg, then set it under the grill. Basting is not necessary.

Gratinés

[Browned with Cheese]

This is the same as *à la crème,* but sprinkle a teaspoon of grated cheese over the cream, and dot with butter.

Pipérade

[With Tomatoes, Onions, and Peppers]

Prepare the *pipérade* mixture of cooked onions, green peppers, and tomatoes described on page 124. Then proceed as for the main recipe, spooning the *pipérade* around the egg before it goes under the grill.

Other Suggestions

Just before serving, surround the egg with sautéed mushrooms, kidneys, chicken livers, sausages, asparagus tips, grilled tomatoes, tomato sauce, or whatever else strikes your fancy.

---

* EGGS BAKED IN RAMEKINS

[Oeufs en Cocotte]

These are individual servings of 1 or 2 eggs baked in porcelain, ovenglass, or earthenware ramekins. The ramekins must be set in a pan of boiling water, otherwise the intense heat of the oven toughens the outside layer of egg before the inside has cooked.

For each serving

Preheat oven to 375° F., Mark 5.

1 tsp butter
1 ramekin 2½ to 3 ins. in diameter
   and about 1½ ins. high
2 tbl cream

A pan containing ¾ in. of simmering
   water
1 or 2 eggs

Butter the ramekin, saving a dot for later. Add 1 tablespoon of cream and set the ramekin in the simmering water over moderate heat. When the cream is hot, break into it one or two eggs. Pour the remaining spoonful of cream over the egg and top with a dot of butter.

Place in middle level of the moderate oven and bake for 7 to 10 minutes. The eggs are done when they are just set but still tremble slightly in the ramekins. They will set a little more when the ramekins are removed, so they should not be overcooked.

Salt and pepper

Season with salt and pepper, and serve.

(*) The ramekins may remain in the pan of hot water, out of the oven, for 10 to 15 minutes before serving. To prevent overcooking, remove eggs from oven when slightly underdone.

VARIATIONS

Aux Fines Herbes

[With Herbs]

Add a teaspoon of mixed fresh parsley, chives, and chervil, or tarragon to the cream in the preceding recipe.

Sauces

Instead of cream, use one of the brown sauces on pages 63 to 67, especially those with herbs, mushrooms, or tomatoes. Or substitute one of the white sauces, pages 54 to 56, of which *sauce soubise* with onions, or *sauce au cari* (curry sauce) are especially good. The tomato sauces on pages 68 to 69 are other alternatives.

Other Suggestions

A spoonful or two of any of the following cooked ingredients may be put in the bottom of the ramekins along with either cream or sauce:

Chopped mushrooms, asparagus, spinach, artichoke hearts
Diced lobster, shrimp, crab
Diced truffles, and/or a slice of *foie gras*

* *SCRAMBLED EGGS*

[Oeufs Brouillés]

Scrambled eggs in French are creamy soft curds that just hold their shape from fork to mouth. Their preparation is entirely a matter of stirring the eggs over gentle heat until they slowly thicken as a mass into a custard. No liquid or liquid-producing ingredients such as tomatoes should be beaten into them before cooking, as this is liable to turn them watery.

For 4 or 5 servings

A fork or a wire whisk	¼ tsp salt
8 eggs, or 7 eggs and 2 yolks	Pinch of pepper
A mixing bowl	

Beat the eggs in the bowl with the seasonings for 20 to 30 seconds to blend yolks and whites.

1 oz. softened butter	7 to 8 ins. in diameter. Depth of
A heavy-bottomed, enamelled,	eggs in pan should be ⅔ to 1 in.
ovenglass, earthenware, or stain-	A rubber spatula, wooden spoon,
less steel saucepan or frying pan	or wire whisk

Smear the bottom and sides of the pan with the butter. Pour in the eggs and set over moderately low heat. Stir slowly and continually, reaching all over the bottom of the pan. Nothing will seem to happen for 2 to 3 minutes as the eggs gradually heat. Suddenly they will begin to thicken into a custard. Stir rapidly, moving pan on and off heat, until the eggs have almost thickened to the consistency you wish. Then remove from heat, as they will continue to thicken slightly.

¾ to 1 oz. softened butter or cream	Parsley sprigs
A warm buttered dish	

Just as soon as they are of the right consistency, stir in the enrichment butter or cream, which will stop the cooking. Season to taste, turn out on to the dish, decorate with parsley, and serve.

(*) The eggs may be kept for a while in their saucepan over tepid water, but the sooner they are served the better.

VARIATIONS

Aux Fines Herbes

[With Herbs]

Beat a tablespoon of chopped fresh herbs such as parsley, chervil, chives, and tarragon into the eggs at the start. Sprinkle more herbs over the eggs just before serving.

Au Fromage

[With Cheese]

Stir 4 to 6 spoonfuls of grated Swiss cheese into the eggs along with the enrichment butter at the end.

Aux Truffes

[With Truffles]

Stir 1 or 2 diced truffles into the eggs before scrambling them. Sprinkle a bit of chopped truffle over the eggs before serving.

Garnishings

Apart from ham, bacon, or sausages, the dish may be garnished with such things as: grilled or sautéed mushrooms, kidneys, or chicken livers; sautéed aubergines or courgettes; grilled tomatoes, tomato sauce, or the *pipérade* mixture on page 124; diced sautéed potatoes; buttered peas, asparagus tips, or artichoke hearts.

OMELETTES

A good French omelette is a smooth, gently swelling, golden oval that is tender and creamy inside. And as it takes less than half a minute to make, it is ideal for a quick meal. There is a trick to omelettes, and certainly the easiest way to learn is to ask an expert to give you a lesson. Nevertheless we hope one of the two techniques we describe will enable you, if you have never made an omelette before, to produce a good one. The difficulty with all written recipes for omelettes is that before you even start to make one you must read, remember, and visualize the directions from beginning to end, and practise the movements. For everything must go so quickly once the eggs are in the pan that there is no time at all to stop in the middle and pore over your book in order to see what comes next. Learning to make a good omelette is entirely a matter of practice. Do one after another for groups of people every chance you get for several days, and even be willing to throw some away. You should soon develop the art, as well as your own personal omelette style.

The two methods set forth here are rapid, professional techniques. The first is the simpler. The second takes more manual skill.

OMELETTE PANS

An omelette cannot be made in a sticky pan. The eggs must be able to slide around freely. This is why it is a good idea to have one pan that is reserved for omelettes only. Various omelette makers like different kinds of pans: stainless steel, plain or treated aluminium, or plain or enamelled iron. We prefer the French type of plain iron pan ⅛ inch thick, like the one illustrated in the next few pages. Eggs never stick to it when the pan is properly cared for; and its 2-inch sloping sides and long handle make it a perfect shape for omelettes done in the professional manner. Such pans are inexpensive and can be ordered from one of the shops importing French kitchenware, or can be bought in many restaurant equipment shops. Ask for a chef's iron pan with a bottom diameter of 7 inches. This is the perfect size for the 2- to 3-egg omelette. The pan must be treated before you use it. First scrub it with steel wool and scouring powder. Rinse and dry it. Then heat it for a minute or two, just until its bottom is too hot for your hand. Rub it with cooking oil and let it stand overnight. Just before making your first omelette, sprinkle a teaspoon of table salt in the pan, heat it, and rub vigorously for a minute with paper. Then rub the pan clean and it is ready for an omelette. If the pan is used only for omelettes, it needs no washing afterwards; merely rub it clean with paper. If the pan *is* washed, you should dry, warm, and oil it before putting it away. If the pan sticks a bit after a period of non-use, heat it gently, and rub it with salt. Never allow any type of pan to be left empty over heat; this does something to its internal structure so that foods stick to it ever after.

EGGS AND HOW TO BEAT THEM

An omelette can contain up to 8 eggs, but the individual 2- to 3-egg omelette is usually the tenderest, and by far the best size to practise making. At under 30 seconds an omelette, a number of people can be served in a very short time. In fact, unless you are extremely expert and have a restaurant-size heat source, we do not recommend larger omelettes at all. But if you do want to attempt them, be sure to have the correct size of pan. The depth of the egg mass in the pan should not be over ¼ inch, as the eggs must cook quickly. A pan with a 7-inch bottom is right for the 2- to 3-egg omelette; a 10- to 11-inch pan is required for 8 eggs.

Just before heating the butter in the pan, break the eggs into a mixing bowl and add salt and pepper. With a large fork, beat the eggs only enough to blend the whites and yolks thoroughly. From 30 to 40 vigorous strokes should be sufficient.

If you are making several 2- to 3-egg omelettes, beat the necessary number of eggs and seasonings together in a large mixing bowl, and provide yourself with a ladle or measure. Two large eggs measure about 6 tablespoons; 3 eggs, about 9 tablespoons. Measure out the required quantity for each omelette as you are ready to make it, giving the eggs 4 or 5 vigorous beats before dipping them out with your measure.

TRANSFERRING THE OMELETTE FROM PAN TO PLATE

In each of the methods described, the finished omelette ends up in the far lip of the pan. This is the way to transfer it from the pan to the plate.

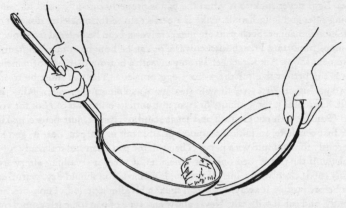

Hold the plate in your left hand. Turn the omelette pan so that its handle is to your right. Grasp the handle with your right hand, thumb on top. Rest the lip of the pan slightly off the centre of the plate so that the omelette will land in the middle of the plate. Then tilt plate and pan against each other at a 45-degree angle.

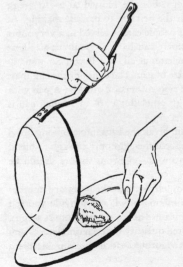

Quickly turn the pan upside down over the plate and the omelette will drop into position.

If it has not formed neatly, push it into shape with the back of a fork. Rub the top of the omelette with softened butter and serve as soon as possible, for omelettes toughen if they are kept warm.

I. L'OMELETTE BROUILLÉE

[Scrambled Omelette]

This is best done in a French omelette pan, but a frying pan can be used.

For 1 omelette, 1 to 2 servings. Time: Less than 30 seconds of cooking

2 or 3 eggs
Big pinch of salt
Pinch of pepper
A mixing bowl
A fork

Beat the eggs and seasonings in the mixing bowl for 20 to 30 seconds until the whites and yolks are just blended.

½ oz. butter
An omelette pan 7 ins. in
  diameter at the bottom
A fork

Place the butter in the pan and set over very high heat. If you have an electric heat element, it should be red hot. As the butter melts, tilt the pan in all directions to film the sides. When you see that the foam has almost subsided in the pan and the butter is on the point of colouring, it is an indication that it is hot enough to pour in the eggs.

Hold the pan handle with your left hand, thumb on top, and immediately start sliding the pan back and forth rapidly over the heat. At the same time, fork in right hand, its flat side against the bottom of the pan, stir the eggs quickly to spread them continuously all over the bottom of the pan as they thicken. In 3 or 4 seconds they will become a light, broken custard. (*A filling would go in at this point.*)

Then lift the handle of the pan to tilt it at a 45-degree angle over the heat, and rapidly gather the eggs at the far lip of the pan with the back of your fork.

Still holding the pan tilted over the heat, run your fork around the lip of the pan under the far edge of the omelette to be sure it has not adhered to the pan.

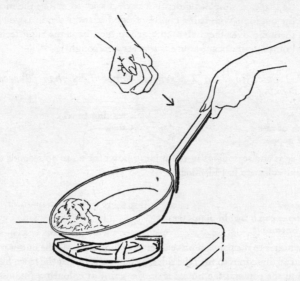

Give 4 or 5 short, sharp blows on the handle of the pan with your right fist to loosen the omelette and make the far edge curl over on to itself.

Hold the pan tilted over heat for 1 or 2 seconds to brown the bottom of the omelette very lightly, but not too long or the eggs will overcook. The centre of the omelette should remain soft and creamy.

A warm plate   **Softened butter**

Turn the omelette on to the plate as illustrated on page 116, rub the top with a bit of butter, and serve as soon as possible.

II. L'OMELETTE ROULÉE

[Rolled Omelette]

This omelette should be made in a French omelette pan and a high gas flame is usually more successful than an electric heat element. The rolled omelette is the most fun of any method, but requires more practice. Here the pan is jerked over high heat at an angle so that the egg mass is continually hurled against the far lip of the pan until the eggs thicken. Finally, as the pan is tilted further while it is being jerked, the eggs roll over at the far lip of the pan, forming an omelette shape. A simple-minded but perfect way to master the movement is to practise outdoors with half a cupful of dried beans. As soon as you are able to make them flip over themselves in a group, you have the right feeling; but the actual omelette-making gesture is sharper and rougher.

For 1 omelette, 1 to 2 servings. Time: Less than 30 seconds of cooking

2 or 3 eggs   **A mixing bowl**
Big pinch of salt   **A fork**
Pinch of pepper

Beat the eggs and seasonings in the mixing bowl for 20 to 30 seconds until the whites and yolks are just blended.

½ oz. butter   **A fork**
An omelette pan 7 ins. in diameter
  at the bottom

Place the butter in the pan and place over very high heat. As the butter melts, tilt the pan in all directions to film the sides. When you see that the foam has almost subsided in the pan and the butter is on the point of colouring (indicating it is hot enough), pour in the eggs. It is of utmost importance in this method that the butter be of the correct temperature.

Let the eggs settle in the pan for 2 or 3 seconds to form a film of coagulated egg in the bottom of the pan.

Grasp the handle of the pan with both hands, thumbs on top, and immediately begin jerking the pan vigorously and roughly toward you at an even, 20-degree angle over the heat, one jerk per second.

It is the sharp pull of the pan toward you which throws the eggs against the far lip of the pan, then back over its bottom surface. You must have the courage to be rough or the eggs will not loosen themselves from the bottom of the pan. After several jerks, the eggs will begin to thicken. (*A filling would go in at this point.*)

Then increase the angle of the pan slightly, which will force the egg mass to roll over on itself with each jerk at the far lip of the pan.

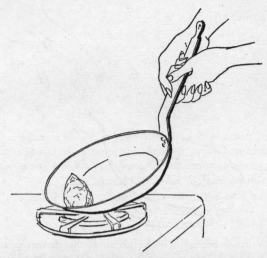

As soon as the omelette has shaped up, hold it in the angle of the pan to brown the bottom a pale golden colour, but only a second or two, for the eggs must not overcook. The centre of the omelette should remain soft and creamy. If the omelette has not formed neatly, push it with the back of your fork.

Turn the omelette on to the plate as illustrated on page 116, rub the top with a bit of butter, and serve as soon as possible.

GARNISHINGS AND FILLINGS FOR OMELETTES

Aux Fines Herbes

[With Herbs]

Beat into the eggs at the beginning 1 tablespoon of chopped fresh herbs such as chervil, parsley, chives, and tarragon. Sprinkle more of the same over the finished omelette.

Au Fromage

[With Cheese]

After the eggs have set for 2 or 3 seconds in the pan at the point indicated in either of the two omelette recipes, sprinkle in 1 or 2 tablespoons of grated Swiss or Parmesan cheese and finish the omelette. If you wish, sprinkle more cheese over the completed omelette, dot with butter, and place quickly under a very hot grill to melt and brown the cheese.

Aux Épinards

[With Spinach]

Beat 2 or 3 tablespoons of cooked purée of spinach, page 431, into the eggs at the beginning, then proceed with the omelette as usual.

Other Suggestions

Sprinkle 2 ounces of any of the following cooked ingredients over the eggs after they have set for 2 or 3 seconds in the pan at the point indicated in either of the two omelette recipes, then proceed with the omelette as usual:

Diced sautéed potatoes and chopped herbs
Diced truffles
Diced sautéed ham, chicken livers, or mushrooms
Diced cooked asparagus tips or artichoke hearts
Diced cooked shrimps, crab, or lobster
Cubes of stale white bread sautéed in butter

Omelettes Gratinées à la Tomate

[Tomato-filled Omelettes *Gratinéed* with Cream and Cheese]

Here is a delicious supper or luncheon dish that can be prepared ahead and *gratinéed* just before serving.

For 4 to 6 people

4 two-egg omelettes or 2 three-egg omelettes **A buttered plate**	**A shallow, buttered, fireproof serving dish**

Cook the omelettes according to one of the master recipes, but leave them slightly underdone. Slip each as it is made on to a buttered plate, then slide it on to the buttered dish, arranging the omelettes side by side.

½ pt. fresh tomato purée, page 69

Cut a slit along the length of each omelette to within ½ inch of the 2 ends. Fill the slits with the tomato purée.

(*) If not to be used immediately, rub tops of omelettes with softened butter and cover with greaseproof paper.

Preheat grill to very hot.

⅛ to ¼ pt. cream or *crème fraîche*,
   page 13

1½ oz. grated Swiss cheese
¼ oz. melted butter

Just before serving, pour the cream over the omelettes, and sprinkle with cheese
and melted butter. Set dish 3 inches below hot grill for 1 or 2 minutes to reheat
the omelettes and to brown the cheese lightly, but do not let the omelettes
overcook. Serve immediately.

Pipérade

[Open-faced Omelette Garnished with Onions, Peppers, Tomatoes, and
Ham]

This is a Basque speciality, and quick to make if the *pipérade* mixture has
been prepared in advance. As the omelette is not folded, and is served in its
cooking vessel, it is not a disaster if it sticks a little on the bottom. You may
therefore cook the eggs in a low, glazed pottery dish, or a fancy frying pan.

For 4 to 6 servings

8 to 12 strips of ham ¼ in. thick and
   about 2 by 3 ins. across

2 tbl olive oil or butter
An 8- to 9-in. enamelled frying pan

Brown the ham slices lightly on both sides in hot oil or butter. Set them aside,
and reheat just before using them at the end of the recipe.

3 oz. thinly sliced onions
3 oz. thinly sliced green or red
   peppers

Salt and pepper to taste

In the same oil or butter in which you browned the ham, cook the onions and
peppers slowly, covering the frying pan, until they are tender but not browned.
Season to taste with salt and pepper.

½ clove mashed garlic
Speck of cayenne pepper
2 or 3 firm, ripe, red tomatoes

peeled, seeded, juiced, and sliced,
   page 465
Salt and pepper

Stir in the garlic and pepper. Lay the tomatoes over the onions and sprinkle with
salt. Cover and cook slowly for 5 minutes. Uncover, raise heat, and boil for a
few minutes, shaking the pan occasionally until the juice from the tomatoes has
almost entirely evaporated. Season to taste, and reheat just before using.

(*) Recipe may be prepared ahead to this point.

1½ tbl olive oil or butter
An 11- to 12-in. shallow, fireproof
   serving dish
8 to 10 eggs beaten lightly with a
   pinch of pepper and ¼ tsp salt

A large fork
2 to 3 tbl chopped parsley or mixed
   fresh green herbs

Heat the oil or butter in the dish. When very hot, pour in the eggs. Stir rapidly with a fork until the eggs have just set into a creamy mass. Remove from heat and spread over them the hot *pipérade*, mixing a bit of it delicately into the eggs. Lay the warm ham strips over the *pipérade*. Sprinkle with the herbs and serve immediately.

CHAPTER FOUR

ENTRÉES AND LUNCHEON DISHES

PASTRY CRUSTS
Pâte Brisée

PÂTE BRISÉE
[Short Crust Pastry]

A good French pastry crust is tender, crunchy, and buttery. The best one, *pâte brisée fine,* is made in the proportions of 5 parts flour to 4 parts butter. As British plain white flour and French flour are roughly equivalent, both being soft wheat blended with some hard wheat, the French method and proportions are used here. If, however, you happen to be living in a foreign country, such as America, where plain flour is predominantly hard wheat, you will achieve a more tender crust if you use a proportion of white vegetable fat or leaf lard with your butter; vegetable fat or lard helps counteract the brittle quality of hard wheat. In this case, when your recipe calls for 4 ounces of butter, take instead 3 ounces of butter and 1 ounce of fat or lard. You will note in the following recipe for blending pastry that the French system calls for a *fraisage* at the end of the operation; this is a quick smearing out of the dough by bits, with the heel of the hand, to ensure an even blending of fat and flour.

Directions for making short crust pastry

The following proportions are sufficient for an 8- to 9-inch shell, giving enough extra for easy rolling. For a 10- to 11-inch shell, use 1½ times this amount.

The mixing of pastry should be accomplished rapidly, particularly if your kitchen is warm, so that the butter will soften as little as possible. Use very quick, light finger movements, and do not linger on the dough at all with the warm palms of the hands. A necessary part of learning how to cook is to get the feel of the dough in your fingers. *Il faut mettre la main à la pâte!*

5 oz. plain white flour
Scant ½ tsp salt
Big pinch sugar

4 oz. chilled butter cut into ½ in.
   pieces
4 to 4½ tbl cold water

Place flour, salt, sugar, and butter in a big mixing bowl. Rub the flour and fat together rapidly between the tips of your fingers until the fat is broken into pieces the size of oatmeal flakes. Do not overdo this step as the fat will be blended more thoroughly later.

Add the water and blend quickly with one hand, fingers held together and slightly cupped, as you rapidly gather the dough into a mass. Sprinkle up to 1 tablespoon more water by drops over any unmassed remains and add them to the main body of the dough. Then press the dough firmly into a roughly shaped ball. It should just hold together and be pliable, but not be damp and sticky.

Place the dough on a lightly floured pastry board. With the heel of one hand, not the palm which is too warm, rapidly press the pastry by two-spoonful bits down on the board and away from you in a firm, quick smear of about 6 inches. This constitutes the final blending of fat and flour, or *fraisage*.

With spatula, gather the dough again into a mass; knead it briefly into a fairly smooth round ball. Sprinkle it lightly with flour and wrap it in greaseproof paper. Either place it in the freezing compartment of the refrigerator for about 1 hour until the dough is firm but not congealed, or leave it for 2 hours or overnight in the refrigerator.

Uncooked pastry dough will keep for 3 to 4 days under refrigeration, or may be deep-frozen for several weeks. In either case, wrap it airtight in greaseproof paper and a polythene bag.

Rolling out the dough

Because of its high butter content, roll out the dough as quickly as possible, so that it will not soften and become difficult to handle.

Place the dough on a lightly floured board or marble. If the dough is hard, beat it with the rolling pin to soften it. Then knead it briefly into a fairly flat circle. It should be just malleable enough so that it can be rolled out without cracking.

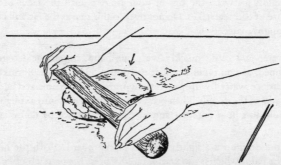

Lightly flour the top of the dough. Place rolling pin across centre and roll the pin back and forth with firm but gentle pressure to start the dough moving. Then, with a firm, even stroke, and always rolling away from you, start just below the centre of the dough and roll to within an inch of the far edge.

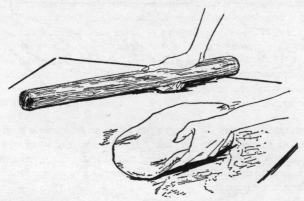

Lift dough and turn it at slight angle.

Give it another roll. Continue lifting, turning, and rolling, and, as necessary, sprinkle board and top of dough lightly with flour to prevent sticking. Roll it into a circle ⅛ inch thick and about 2 inches larger all around than your baking tin or flan ring. If your circle is uneven, cut off a too-large portion, moisten the edge of the too-small portion with water, press the two pieces of pastry together, and smooth them with your rolling pin.

The dough should be used as soon as it has been rolled out, so that it will not soften.

Making a pastry shell

Flan ring, false-bottomed cake tin

A French tart, *quiche*, or pie is straight sided and open faced, and stands supported only by its pastry shell. In France the shell is moulded in a bottomless metal flan ring that has been set on a baking sheet. When the tart is done, the ring is removed and the tart is slid from the baking sheet to a rack or the serving dish. You can achieve the same effect by moulding your pastry in a false-bottomed, straight-sided, cake tin 1 to 1½ inches deep. When the shell is ready for unmoulding, the tin is set over a jar and the false bottom frees the shell from the sides of the tin. It is then, with the aid of a long-bladed spatula, slid off its false bottom and on to a rack or the serving dish. You can also make pastry shells using two matching pie tins; once in a while the weight of the filling forces the outward-slanting sides of the shell to collapse, so we do not recommend it.

Quiches

E

Partially baked pastry shells are used for *quiches* and for tarts whose filling cooks in the shell. Fully baked shells are for tarts filled with cooked ingredients that need only a brief reheating, or for fresh fruit tarts that are served cold.

Butter the inside of the tin. If you are using a flan ring, butter the baking sheet also.

Either reverse the dough on to the rolling pin, and unroll it over the tin; *or* fold the dough in half, in half again, then lay it in the tin and unfold it.

Press the dough lightly into the bottom of the cake tin, or on to the baking sheet if you are using a flan ring. Then lift the edges of the dough and work it gently down the inside edges of tin with your fingers, taking in about ⅜ inch of dough all around the circumference. This will make the sides of the pastry shell a little thicker and sturdier. Trim off excess dough by rolling the pin over the top of the tin.

Then with your thumbs, push the dough ⅛ inch above the edge of the tin, to make an even, rounded rim of dough all around the inside circumference of the tin.

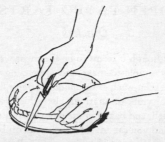

Press a decorative edge around the rim of the pastry with the dull edge of a knife.

Prick bottom of pastry with a fork at ½-inch intervals.

To keep the sides of the pastry shell from collapsing and the bottom from puffing up, *either* butter the bottom of another tin, weight it with a handful of dry beans, and place it inside the pastry; *or* line the pastry with buttered, light-weight foil, or buttered brown paper. Press it well against the sides of the pastry, and fill it with dried beans. The weight of the beans will hold the pastry against the tin during the baking.

Refrigerate if not baked immediately.

For a partially cooked shell
Bake on the middle shelf of a preheated 400° F., Mark 6 oven for 8 to 9 minutes until pastry is set. Remove tin or foil and beans. Prick bottom of pastry with a fork to keep it from rising. Return to oven for 2 to 3 minutes more. When the shell is starting to colour and just beginning to shrink from sides of tin, remove it from the oven. If it seems to you that the sides of the shell are fragile, or are liable to crack or leak with the weight of the filling to come, do not unmould until your tart or *quiche* is filled and finally baked.

For a fully cooked shell
Bake 7 to 10 minutes more, or until the shell is very lightly browned. When the shell is done, unmould it and slip it on to a rack. Circulation of air around it while it cools will prevent it from getting soggy.

OPEN-FACED TARTS
Quiches

Quiche Lorraine, although it seems to be the most well known, is only one of a series of generally simple-to-make and appetizing entrées. A *quiche* is a mixture of cream and bacon, such as the *quiche Lorraine*, or cheese and milk, or tomatoes and onions, or crab, or anything else which is combined with eggs, poured into a pastry shell, and baked in the oven until it puffs and browns. It is practically foolproof, and you can invent your own combinations. Serve it with a salad, hot French bread, and a cold white wine; follow it with fruit, and you have a perfect lunch or supper menu. Or let it be the first course of your dinner. You can also make tiny *quiches* for hot hors d'œuvres.

The following recipes are all designed for pastry shells 8 inches in diameter. The *quiche* ingredients should fill the shell by no more than three-fourths, to allow room for puffing. An 8-inch shell will hold about ¾ pound of filling and serves 4 to 6 people. A 10-inch shell, serving 6 to 8, will hold one and a half times this amount of filling or slightly more.

The partially cooked shell may be baked hours ahead of time, and the filling prepared and refrigerated in its mixing bowl. Half an hour before serving, the filling is poured into the shell and the *quiche* is set in a 375° F., Mark 5 oven. In 25 to 30 minutes it will have puffed and the top browned. A knife plunged into the centre should come out clean, and the *quiche* is ready to serve. It will stay puffed for about 10 minutes in the turned-off hot oven with the door ajar. As it cools, it sinks down. It may be reheated, but will not puff again. A cold *quiche* makes a good snack and is easy to take along on a picnic.

---

* *QUICHE LORRAINE*

[Cream and Bacon *Quiche*]

The classic *quiche Lorraine* contains cream, eggs, and bacon, no cheese. The bacon is usually blanched in simmering water to remove its smoky, salty taste, but this step is optional. Diced, cooked ham, sautéed briefly in butter, may replace the bacon.

For 4 to 6 servings

Preheat oven to 375° F., Mark 5.

3 to 4 oz. lean bacon (6 to 8 slices,   An 8-in. partially cooked pastry
  medium thickness)   shell placed on a baking sheet,
1½ pts. water   page 131

Cut bacon into pieces about an inch long and ¼ inch wide. Simmer for 5
minutes in the water. Rinse in cold water. Dry. Brown lightly in a frying pan.
Press bacon pieces into bottom of pastry shell.

3 eggs or 2 eggs and 2 yolks   Pinch of pepper
½ to ¾ pt. cream or half cream and   Pinch of nutmeg
  half milk   ½ to 1 oz. butter cut into pea-sized
½ tsp salt   dots

Beat the eggs, cream or cream and milk, and seasonings in a mixing bowl
until blended. Check seasonings. Pour into pastry shell and distribute the butter
pieces on top.

Place in top part of preheated oven and bake for 25 to 30 minutes, or until *quiche*
has puffed and browned. Slide *quiche* on to a hot dish and serve.

Quiche au Fromage de Gruyère

[Swiss Cheese *Quiche*]

Follow the preceding recipe, but stir 2 to 4 ounces grated Swiss cheese into
the egg and cream mixture. The bacon is usually omitted, and you may use all
milk instead of cream.

---

* QUICHE AU ROQUEFORT

[Roquefort Cheese *Quiche*]

For 4 to 6 servings

Preheat oven to 375° F., Mark 5.

3 oz. Roquefort or blue cheese   Cayenne pepper to taste
6 oz. (2 small packets) cream   ¼ tbl chopped fresh chives or ½ tsp
  cheese or cottage cheese   chopped spring onion tops
1 oz. softened butter   An 8-in. partially cooked pastry
3 tbl cream   shell placed on a baking sheet,
2 eggs   page 131
Salt and white pepper

Blend the cheese, butter, and cream with a fork, then beat in the eggs. Force the
mixture through a sieve, to get rid of the lumps. Season to taste and stir in the
chives or spring onion tops. Pour into the pastry shell and place in top part of
preheated oven. Bake for 25 to 30 minutes, or until *quiche* has puffed and top has
browned.

Quiche au Camembert

[Camembert Cheese *Quiche*]

Instead of Roquefort cheese, use the same amount of Camembert, or Brie, but remove the outside crust of the cheese. Or use a mixture of all or some of these, including Roquefort cheese, if you have leftovers.

QUICHE À LA TOMATE, NIÇOISE

[Fresh Tomato *Quiche* with Anchovies and Olives]

For 4 to 6 servings

Preheat oven to 375° F., Mark 5.

An 8- to 9-in. enamelled or stainless steel frying pan	**1 oz. chopped onions**
	2 tbl olive oil

Cook the onions slowly in the olive oil for 5 minutes or so, until tender but not browned.

1¾ to 2 lbs. firm, ripe, red tomatoes	**½ tsp oregano, basil, or thyme**
1 large clove mashed garlic	**½ tsp salt**
	⅛ tsp pepper

Peel, seed, and juice the tomatoes, page 465, and chop the pulp roughly. Stir the tomatoes into the frying pan and add the garlic, herbs, and seasonings. Cover frying pan and cook for 5 minutes over low heat. Uncover, raise heat and cook for 5 minutes or so more, shaking pan occasionally, to evaporate the juice almost entirely. Allow to cool slightly.

1 egg and 3 egg yolks	**3 tbl tomato paste**
8 chopped anchovy fillets	**3 tbl chopped parsley**
3 tbl olive oil (including oil from anchovy tin)	**1 tsp paprika**
	Pinch of cayenne pepper

Beat the egg, egg yolks, anchovies, oil, tomato paste, parsley and seasonings in a mixing bowl until blended. Gradually fold in the cooked tomatoes. Check seasoning.

An 8-in. partially cooked pastry shell on a baking sheet, page 131	**1 oz. grated Parmesan or Swiss cheese**
12 stoned black olives (the dry Mediterranean type)	**1 tbl olive oil**

Spread tomato mixture in pastry shell. Place olives over the top in a decorative design. Spread on the cheese and pour the oil over it. Bake in top part of pre-heated oven for 25 to 30 minutes, or until *quiche* has puffed and browned on top.

QUICHE AUX FRUITS DE MER

[Shrimp, Crab, or Lobster *Quiche*]

For 4 to 6 servings

Preheat oven to 375° F., Mark 5.

2 tbl chopped shallots or spring onions	¼ tsp salt
1½ oz. butter	Pinch of pepper
¼ lb. cooked fresh or tinned crab, or diced cooked fresh or potted shrimps or lobster	2 tbl Madeira or dry white vermouth

Cook the shallots or spring onions in the butter for 1 to 2 minutes over moderate heat until tender, but not browned. Add shellfish meat and stir gently for 2 minutes. Sprinkle on salt and pepper. Add wine, raise heat, and boil for a moment. Allow to cool slightly.

3 eggs	¼ tsp salt
¼ pt. cream	Pinch of pepper
1 tbl tomato paste	

Beat the eggs in a mixing bowl with the cream, tomato paste, and seasonings. Gradually blend in the shellfish and taste for seasoning.

An 8-in. partially cooked pastry shell on a baking sheet, page 131	1 oz. grated Swiss cheese

Pour mixture into pastry shell and sprinkle the cheese over it. Bake in top part of preheated oven for 25 to 30 minutes, until *quiche* has puffed and browned.

QUICHE AUX OIGNONS

[Onion *Quiche*]

For 4 to 6 servings

2 lbs. chopped onions	1 tbl oil
1½ oz. butter	

Cook the onions in a heavy frying pan with the oil and butter over very low heat, stirring occasionally until they are extremely tender and a golden yellow. This will take about an hour.

¾ oz. flour

Sprinkle with the flour, mix well, and cook slowly for 2 or 3 minutes. Allow to cool slightly.

Preheat oven to 375° F., Mark 5.

2 eggs or 3 yolks
¼ pt. cream
1 tsp salt
⅛ tsp pepper
Pinch of nutmeg

2 oz. grated Swiss cheese
An 8-in. partially cooked pastry
    shell on a baking sheet, page 131
½ oz. butter cut into pea-sized dots

Beat the eggs or egg yolks in a mixing bowl with the cream and seasonings until blended. Gradually mix in the onions and half of the cheese. Check seasoning. Pour into tart shell. Spread on the rest of the cheese and distribute the butter over it. Bake in upper part of preheated oven for 25 to 30 minutes, until *quiche* has puffed and browned.

PISSALADIÈRE NIÇOISE

[Onion Tart with Anchovies and Black Olives]

This is not a *quiche*, properly speaking, because it contains no eggs. In Nice it is made either in a pastry shell or on a flat round of bread dough like the Italian pizza.

For 4 to 6 servings

2 lbs chopped onions
4 tbl olive oil
1 medium herb bouquet: 4 parsley
    sprigs, ¼ tsp thyme, and ½ bay
    leaf tied in washed cheesecloth

2 cloves unpeeled garlic
½ tsp salt
1 pinch of powdered cloves
⅛ tsp pepper

Cook the onions very slowly in the olive oil with the herb bouquet, garlic, and salt for about 1 hour, or until very tender. Discard herb bouquet and garlic. Stir in cloves and pepper, and taste carefully for seasoning.

Preheat oven to 400° F., Mark 6.

An 8-in. partially cooked pastry
    shell on a baking sheet, page 131
8 tinned anchovy fillets

16 stoned black olives (the dry
    Mediterranean type)
1 tbl olive oil

Spread the onions in the pastry shell. Arrange anchovy fillets over it in a fan-shaped design. Place the olives at decorative intervals. Sprinkle on the oil. Bake in top part of the preheated oven for 10 to 15 minutes, or until bubbling hot.

* FLAMICHE—QUICHE AUX POIREAUX

[Leek *Quiche*]

For 4 to 6 servings

Preheat oven to 375° F., Mark 5.

1 lb. sliced white of leek	1 tsp salt
¼ pt. water	1½ oz. butter

Boil the leeks over moderately high heat in a heavy-bottomed, covered saucepan with the water, salt, and butter until liquid has almost evaporated. Lower heat and stew gently for 20 to 30 minutes until leeks are very tender.

3 eggs	An 8-in. partially cooked pastry
½ pt. cream	shell on a baking sheet, page 131
Pinch of nutmeg	1 oz. grated Swiss cheese
⅛ tsp pepper	½ oz. butter cut into pea-sized dots

Beat the eggs, cream, and seasonings in a mixing bowl to blend. Gradually stir in the leeks. Check seasoning. Pour into pastry shell. Spread on the cheese and distribute the butter over it. Bake in top part of preheated oven for 25 to 30 minutes, or until puffed and browned.

Quiche aux Endives

[Chicory or Belgian Endive *Quiche*]

Follow the preceding recipe, using sliced chicory rather than leeks; add a teaspoon of lemon juice to their cooking water.

Quiche aux Champignons

[Mushroom *Quiche*]

Use the same proportions of cream, eggs, grated cheese, and dots of butter as for the preceding leek *quiche* and an 8-inch partially cooked pastry shell. Prepare the mushrooms as follows:

2 tbl chopped shallots or spring onions	1 tsp salt
	1 tsp lemon juice
1½ oz. butter	Optional: 2 tbl Madeira or port
1 lb. sliced fresh mushrooms	

Cook the shallots or spring onions in a heavy-bottomed saucepan with the butter for a moment. Stir in the mushrooms, salt, lemon juice and optional wine. Cover pan and cook over moderately low heat for 8 minutes. Uncover. Raise heat and boil for several minutes until liquid is completely evaporated and mushrooms are beginning to sauté in their butter.

E*

Gradually stir the mushrooms into the eggs and cream. Pour into pastry shell, sprinkle with cheese, dot with butter, and bake for 25 to 30 minutes in a preheated 375° F., Mark 5 oven.

Quiche aux Épinards

[Spinach Quiche]

Use the same proportions of cream, eggs, cheese, and butter as for the leek quiche, page 137, and an 8-inch partially cooked pastry shell. Prepare the spinach as follows:

An enamelled saucepan	page 430, or frozen spinach,
2 tbl finely chopped shallots or	page 437
spring onions	½ tsp salt
1 oz. butter	⅛ tsp pepper
½ lb. chopped blanched spinach,	Pinch of nutmeg

Cook the shallots or spring onions for a moment in the butter. Add the spinach and stir over moderate heat for several minutes to evaporate all its water. Stir in salt, pepper, and nutmeg and taste carefully for seasoning. Gradually stir the spinach into the eggs and cream. Pour into pastry shell, sprinkle with cheese, dot with butter, and bake for 25 to 30 minutes in a preheated 375° F., Mark 5 oven.

GRATINÉED DISHES

Gratins

Any of the quiche mixtures in the preceding section may be baked in a shallow fireproof dish or ovenglass pie plate rather than a pastry shell. They then officially become gratins. Most of the following, although they look more grand in a shell, are so substantial that they are perhaps better in a dish.

RÂPÉE MORVANDELLE

[Gratin of Shredded Potatoes with Ham and Eggs and Onions]

For 4 people

Preheat oven to 375° F., Mark 5.

2 oz. finely chopped onions	1 oz. butter
2 tbl olive oil	

Cook the onions slowly in the oil and butter for 5 minutes or so, until tender but not browned.

3 oz. finely diced cooked ham

Raise heat slightly, stir in ham, and cook a moment more.

4 eggs	3 oz. grated Swiss cheese
½ clove crushed garlic	4 tbl cream or milk
2 tbl chopped parsley and/or chives	Pinch of pepper
and chervil	¼ tsp salt

Beat the eggs in a mixing bowl with the garlic, herbs, cheese, cream or milk, and seasonings. Then blend in the ham and onions.

3 medium-sized potatoes (about 10 oz.)

Peel the potatoes and grate them, using large holes of grater. A handful at a time, squeeze out the water. Stir potatoes into egg mixture. Check seasoning.

(*) May be prepared ahead to this point.

1 oz. butter	individual baking dishes about 6
An 11- to 12-in. baking dish or	ins. in diameter
frying pan about 2 ins. deep or	¼ oz. butter cut into pea-sized dots

Heat the butter in the dish. When foaming, pour in the potato and egg mixture. Dot with butter. Set in top part of preheated oven and bake for 30 to 40 minutes, or until top is nicely browned. Serve directly from the dish or frying pan.

---

* GRATIN DE POMMES DE TERRE AUX ANCHOIS

[*Gratin* of Potatoes, Onions, and Anchovies]

For 4 people

Preheat oven to 375° F., Mark 5.

3 oz. chopped onions	1 oz. butter

Cook the onions slowly in butter for 5 minutes or so, until tender but not browned.

½ lb. diced raw potatoes

Drop potatoes in boiling salted water and cook for 6 to 8 minutes, or until barely done. Drain thoroughly.

A 1 to 1½-pt. baking dish, 1½ to 2 ins.   8 to 10 anchovy fillets packed in
   deep, such as an 8-in. ovenglass   olive oil
   pie plate

Butter the baking dish. Spread half the potatoes in the bottom, then half the cooked onions. Over them lay the anchovy fillets, then the rest of the onions, and finally the remaining potatoes.

3 eggs beaten with ½ pt. cream,   Or: ¾ pt. well-seasoned béchamel
   ½ tsp salt and ⅛ tsp pepper;   sauce, page 50

Pour the eggs and cream, or the béchamel sauce, over the potatoes and shake dish to send liquid to bottom.

1 oz. grated Swiss cheese
1 tbl oil from anchovy tin or
   butter

Spread on the cheese. Sprinkle on the oil, or dot with the butter.

(*) May be prepared ahead to this point.

Bake for 30 to 40 minutes in top part of oven until top is nicely browned.

VARIATIONS

Gratin de Pommes de Terre et Saucisson

[*Gratin* of Potatoes, Onions, and Sausages]

Follow the preceding master recipe, but cut the potatoes in slices rather than dice, and substitute sliced uncooked Polish sausage for the anchovies, interspersing the sausage between the potato slices.

Gratin de Poireaux

[*Gratin* of Leeks with Ham]

Use the same amount of eggs and cream or of béchamel sauce, as in the preceding potato and anchovy *gratin*, or substitute a *sauce mornay* (béchamel with cheese), page 54, and prepare the leeks as follows:

12 leeks, ¾ in. thick

Use the white of the leeks only. Cut each into crosswise sections about 2 inches long.

A heavy-bottomed saucepan   1 oz. butter
½ tsp salt   ½ pt. water

Boil the leeks in a covered saucepan over moderately high heat with salt, butter, and water until liquid has almost completely evaporated. Lower heat and stew gently for 20 to 30 minutes until the leeks are very tender.

6 to 8 thin slices of cooked ham

Wrap each piece of leek in a piece of ham, arrange in buttered dish, cover with eggs and cream, or sauce, and bake as in the preceding master recipe.

Gratin d'Endives

[*Gratin* of Chicory or Belgian Endive with Ham]

Use whole chicory braised in butter, page 453, wrap in ham, cover with eggs and cream, or béchamel sauce, and bake as in the preceding master recipe.

---

*   GRATIN AUX FRUITS DE MER

[*Gratin* of Creamed Salmon or Other Fish]

A quick and delicious main-course dish can be made by combining a good cream sauce with tinned salmon, or leftover cooked fish or shellfish. If you are using a baking dish, all may be prepared ahead, then set in the oven shortly before serving, but a pastry shell should not be filled until just before it goes into the oven. The following recipe is for salmon, but other fish may be substituted:

For 4 to 6 people

Preheat oven to 425° F., Mark 7.

1 oz. finely chopped onions   A 3-pt. heavy-bottomed saucepan
1½ oz. butter

Cook the onions in butter in the saucepan over low heat for 5 minutes or so until onions are tender but not browned.

1½ oz. flour

Stir in the flour, and cook slowly for 2 minutes without colouring.

½ pt. boiling milk   ¼ tsp salt
⅛ pt. dry white wine or dry white   Pinch of pepper
  vermouth   ¼ tsp oregano
Juice from salmon tin, if any   4 to 6 tbl cream

Away from heat, beat in the boiling milk, then the wine, salmon juice, and the
seasonings. Now bring this sauce to boil over moderately high heat, stirring.
Boil several minutes to evaporate the alcohol in the wine, and allow the sauce
to thicken considerably. Then thin it out to a medium consistency with tablespoons of cream. Taste carefully for seasoning.

6 oz. cooked or tinned salmon   to 2 ins. deep, or a cooked pastry
Optional: sautéed mushrooms;   shell, page 131
  sliced hard-boiled eggs   1 oz. grated Swiss cheese
An 8-in., shallow, baking dish 1½   ½ oz. butter

Fold the salmon and optional ingredients into the sauce, and check seasoning
again. Spread in baking dish or pastry shell. Sprinkle on the cheese, and distribute the butter in small dots. Bake in top part of preheated oven for about 15
minutes, or until top is nicely browned.

VARIATIONS

> *Gratin de Volaille*
> *Gratin de Cervelles*
> *Gratin de Ris de Veau*
>
> [*Gratin* of Chicken, Turkey, Brains, or Sweetbreads with Mushrooms]
>
> Exactly the same system as that for the preceding master recipe for fish
> *gratin* may be followed, using diced cooked chicken, turkey, brains, or sweet-
> breads. Combine with sautéed mushrooms, and warm the mixture briefly in
> butter with shallots or onions. If you are short of meat, or wish to make the dish
> more filling, include cooked rice or noodles. Concentrated chicken stock or
> mushroom juice, or leftover chicken sauce may be substituted for part of
> the milk in the béchamel sauce. If your sauce is carefully flavoured, this is an
> attractive way to use leftovers.

SOUFFLÉS

A soufflé, quickly described, is a sauce containing a flavouring or purée into
which stiffly beaten egg whites are incorporated. It is turned into a mould and
baked in the oven until it puffs up and the top browns.

EGG WHITES

The glory and lightness of a French soufflé are largely a matter of how voluminously stiff the egg whites have been beaten and how lightly they have been folded into the body of the soufflé. It is the air, beaten into the whites in the form of little bubbles, which expands as the soufflé is cooked and pushes it up into its magnificent puff. Correctly beaten egg whites mount to 7 or 8 times their original volume, are perfectly smooth and free from granules, and are firm enough to stand in upright peaks when lifted in the wires of the beater as illustrated further on. Another test of their perfect stiffness is that they will support the weight of a whole egg if one is placed on top of them.

Warning

Egg whites will not mount stiffly if they contain any particles of egg yolk, or if either the bowl they are beaten in or the beater itself is moist or even slightly greasy. Have your egg whites at room temperature if possible; they will mount more rapidly and voluminously than chilled egg whites.

Beating bowls and cream of tartar

If beaten egg whites are to remain stable, that is, if they are not to lose their velvety, voluminous, just-beaten texture, they must contain a little acid; without it, they gradually turn granular and tend to leak. French chefs beat egg whites in unlined copper because the slight acidity of the copper acts as a stabilizer. Cream of tartar, which is an acid, also acts as a stabilizer. Therefore, if you do not have an unlined copper bowl, use stainless steel, glass, or glazed pottery—aluminium may give the egg whites a greyish cast. After you have beaten the egg whites for about 30 seconds and they are foamy, beat in a small pinch of cream of tartar per egg white: 4 egg whites take a bare ¼ level teaspoon. (Copper bowls may be ordered from a restaurant equipment shop; best size is 10 inches at top diameter.)

The beater

Although it requires muscular exertion, hand-beating is much the best method for anyone who is serious about cooking. Beaten with a large balloon whisk, egg whites mount faster and more effectively than with a household electric beater—2 to 3 minutes by hand in contrast to about 8 with a machine. This is just because the balloon whisk is bigger—5 to 6 inches across—and can keep almost the whole mass of egg whites in continual, air-circulating motion. Balloon whisks may be bought in hotel and restaurant equipment shops. Directions for both hand- and machine-beating follow.

How to beat egg whites by hand—for 2 to 8 egg whites

Provide yourself with a clean, dry, balloon whisk or a large wedge-shaped wire whisk, and a clean, dry, round-bottomed bowl 9 to 10 inches in diameter and 5 to 6 inches deep. To keep the bowl from jumping about, place it in a heavy pot or casserole.

Place the egg whites in the bowl and add a pinch of salt. The salt gives a slight flavour to the egg whites, and is added even for sweet soufflés.

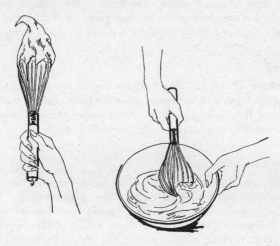

Start beating at a speed of 2 strokes per second with a vertical, circular motion for 20 to 30 seconds until the egg whites have begun to foam. (If you are not using a copper bowl, add cream of tartar at this point; see proportions on preceding page.) Use your lower-arm and wrist muscles for beating; shoulder muscles tire quickly. Then increase the beating speed to 4 strokes per second, beating as much air as possible into the mixture, and circulating the bowl so all the egg whites are entering into the action. Start testing as soon as the whites seem to be stiff by gathering a quantity in the wires of the whisk and holding it upright. If peaks are formed like those in the illustration, you have achieved 'stiffly beaten egg whites'. If not, beat a few seconds more and test again. When the right consistency has been arrived at, the egg whites should be folded almost immediately into the soufflé mixture.

How to beat egg whites by machine—for 2 to 8 egg whites

A hand-held beater which you can circulate around the bowl to incorporate air into the egg whites is most satisfactory for machine-beating. If you must use a stationary beater, continually push the whites into the blades with a rubber spatula; the whites will not, unfortunately, mount as high as with the hand-held beater.

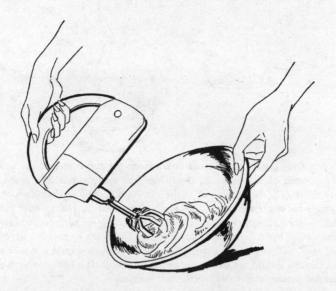

Starting out as described for hand-beating, use a slow beating speed for about a minute until the egg whites are foaming. Gradually increase the speed to moderate while tilting the bowl and circulating the beater around its sides and up from the middle, to beat as much air as possible into the mixture. Start testing as soon as the egg whites seem stiff, as described for hand-beating in the preceding directions.

Folding in the egg whites

After the main ingredients of the soufflé have been blended together and seasoned, the beaten egg whites are incorporated gently and delicately so that they will retain as much of their volume as possible. This process is known as folding, and is accomplished as follows:

First stir a big spoonful of egg whites into the soufflé mixture to lighten it. Then with a rubber spatula, scoop the rest of the egg whites on top. Finally,

still using your rubber spatula, cut down from the top centre of the mixture to the bottom of the saucepan, then draw the spatula quickly toward you against the edge of the pan, and up to the left and out, as illustrated. You are thus bringing a bit of the soufflé mixture at the bottom of the pan up over the egg whites. Continue the movement while slowly rotating the saucepan, and rapidly cutting down, toward you, and out to the left, until the egg whites have been folded into the body of the soufflé. The whole process should not take more than a minute, and do not attempt to be too thorough. It is better to leave a few unblended patches than to deflate the egg whites.

AHEAD-OF-TIME NOTES

After your soufflé mould has been filled and is ready for the oven, you may set it aside in a warm place free from draughts. Cover it with a big empty pot. As long as it is protected, it will not begin to collapse for an hour.

SOUFFLÉ DISHES

Although a soufflé can be cooked in a fairly shallow porcelain or ovenglass dish—the usual type sold in Britain for this purpose—a more practical one is the cylindrical, metal mould known in France as a *charlotte*. *Charlotte* moulds come in the following sizes and are inexpensive.

CHARLOTTE MOULDS

HEIGHT	BOTTOM DIAMETER	APPROXIMATE CAPACITY
3⅜ inches	4⅝ inches	1¼ pints
3½ inches	5½ inches	2¼ pints
4 inches	6 inches	3 to 3½ pints

If you do not have one of these, use a porcelain or ovenglass dish holding whatever capacity your recipe specifies. Give it added height by tying a double strip of buttered foil or brown paper around the dish and removing it when the soufflé is done. We have found this a nuisance, but if you like this method, calculate the capacity of the mould-plus-paper-collar according to the height and diameter measurements in the preceding table.

Soufflé
Moulds

Preparing the mould for the soufflé

So that the soufflé may slide easily up during its rise, butter the sides and bottom of the mould heavily. Then roll grated cheese or breadcrumbs around in it, paying particular attention to the inner circumference, which must be lightly but evenly coated. Turn the mould upside down and knock it on the table to dislodge excess cheese or breadcrumbs.

PLACEMENT IN THE OVEN

A soufflé will always perform as it should if it is placed on a rack in the middle of a preheated 400° F., Mark 6 oven and the temperature is immediately reduced to 375° F., Mark 5.

GENERAL PROPORTIONS

Whether your soufflé is made with cheese, fish, spinach, or anything else, the proportions with few exceptions remain the same.

INGREDIENTS	AMOUNTS FOR A 2½-PINT MOULD	AMOUNTS FOR A 3-PINT MOULD
Thick béchamel or *velouté* sauce	2 oz. butter 1½ oz. flour ½ pt. liquid	2¼ oz. butter 2 oz. flour ¾ pt. liquid
Egg yolks, beaten into sauce	4	6
Flavouring added: cheese, fish, meat, vegetables	3 to 6 oz.	5 to 10 oz.
Stiffly beaten egg whites folded in	5	7 or 8

WHEN IS IT DONE?

After 25 to 30 minutes of baking in a 375° F., Mark 5 oven, the soufflé will have risen 2 or 3 inches over the rim of the mould and will have browned on top. If you like the centre creamy, it may be served at this point, but it is fragile and will sink rapidly. It will collapse less readily if you allow it to cook 4 to 5 minutes more, until a trussing needle or thin knife plunged into the centre through the side of the puff comes out clean. A well-cooked soufflé will stay puffed for about 5 minutes in the turned-off hot oven, door ajar. As it cools, the masterpiece begins to sink. Therefore, there should be no lingering when a soufflé is to be eaten.

HOW TO SERVE A SOUFFLÉ

Puncture the top of the soufflé lightly with a serving spoon and fork—held vertically—and spread it apart for each serving.

---

* SOUFFLÉ AU FROMAGE

[Cheese Soufflé]

This recipe is intended as a detailed guide to those that follow. All main-course soufflés follow this general pattern:

For 4 people

The soufflé sauce base

A 2½-pt. soufflé mould, page 147

Preheat oven to 400° F., Mark 6.

1 tsp butter
1 tbl grated Swiss or Parmesan cheese

Measure out all your ingredients. Butter inside of soufflé mould and sprinkle with cheese.

2 oz. butter	**A wire whisk**
A 4-pt. saucepan	**½ tsp salt**
1½ oz. flour	**⅛ tsp pepper**
A wooden spatula or spoon	**A pinch of cayenne pepper**
½ pt. boiling milk	**Pinch of nutmeg**

Melt the butter in the saucepan. Stir in the flour with a wooden spoon and cook over moderate heat until butter and flour foam together for 2 minutes without browning. Remove from heat; when mixture has stopped bubbling, pour in all the boiling milk at once. Beat vigorously with a wire whisk until blended. Beat in the seasonings. Return over moderately high heat and boil, stirring with the wire whisk, for 1 minute. Sauce will be very thick.

4 egg yolks

Remove from heat. Immediately start to separate the eggs. Drop the white into the egg-white bowl, and the yolk into the centre of the hot sauce. Beat the yolk into the sauce with the wire whisk. Continue in the same manner with the rest of the eggs. Correct seasoning.

(*) May be prepared ahead to this point. Dot top of sauce with butter. Heat to tepid before continuing.

> *The egg whites and cheese*

5 egg whites	**3 oz. coarsely grated Swiss, or Swiss**
A pinch of salt	**and Parmesan, cheese**

Add an extra egg white to the ones in the bowl and beat with the salt until stiff, as described and illustrated, page 144. Stir a large spoonful (about one-quarter of the egg whites) into the sauce. Stir in all but a tablespoon of the cheese. Delicately fold in the rest of the egg whites.

> *Baking*

Turn the soufflé mixture into the prepared mould, which should be almost three-quarters full. Tap bottom of mould lightly on the table, and smooth the surface of the soufflé with the flat of a knife. Sprinkle the remaining cheese on top.

Place on a rack in middle of preheated 400° F., Mark 6 oven and immediately turn heat down to 375° F., Mark 5. (Do not open oven door for 20 minutes.) In 25 to 30 minutes the soufflé will have puffed about 2 inches over the rim of the mould, and the top will be nicely browned. Bake 4 to 5 minutes more to firm it up, then serve at once.

VARIATION

Soufflé Vendôme

[Soufflé with Poached Eggs]

For 4 people

Prepare the soufflé mixture as in the preceding master recipe. Turn half of it into the prepared mould. Arrange 4 to 6 cold poached eggs (page 104) over the soufflé, and cover with the rest of the soufflé mixture. Sprinkle with cheese and bake for 25 to 30 minutes in a 375° F., Mark 5 oven. Dig carefully into the soufflé so as to lift out an unbroken egg with each serving. Poached eggs also may be baked in the following spinach soufflé:

* SOUFFLÉ AUX ÉPINARDS

[Spinach Soufflé]

For 4 people

A 2½-pt. soufflé mould, page 147

Butter the mould and sprinkle with cheese. Preheat oven to 400° F., Mark 6. Measure out your ingredients.

An enamelled saucepan	**(or chopped frozen spinach—**
1 tbl chopped shallots or spring	**which will take several minutes**
onions	**more cooking)**
½ oz. butter	**¼ tsp salt**
6 oz. blanched chopped spinach	

Cook the shallots or spring onions for a moment in the butter. Add spinach and salt, and stir over moderately high heat for several minutes to evaporate as much moisture as possible from the spinach. Remove from heat.

The soufflé sauce base, page 148

Prepare the soufflé sauce base. After the egg yolks have been beaten in, stir in the spinach. Correct seasoning.

5 egg whites   **1½ to 2 oz. grated Swiss cheese**
A pinch of salt

Beat the egg whites and salt until stiff, page 144. Stir one-quarter of them into the sauce. Stir in all but a tablespoon of the cheese. Fold in the rest of the egg whites and turn mixture into prepared mould. Sprinkle with remaining cheese and place on a rack in the middle of preheated oven. Turn heat down to 375° F., Mark 5 and bake for 25 to 30 minutes.

VARIATIONS to be added to the preceding spinach soufflé:

Ham

2 oz. finely chopped boiled ham

Cook the ham with the butter and shallots for a moment before adding the spinach.

Mushrooms

¼ lb. finely chopped mushrooms   **Salt and pepper**
½ oz. butter

A handful at a time, twist the mushrooms in the corner of a cloth to extract their juice. Sauté in the butter for 5 minutes or so until the mushroom pieces begin to separate from one another. Season to taste. Stir them into the soufflé mixture with the spinach.

Other vegetable soufflés

These are all done in exactly the same manner as the spinach soufflé. Use 6 ounces of cooked vegetables, finely diced or puréed, such as mushrooms, broccoli, artichoke hearts, or asparagus tips.

---

*   SOUFFLÉ DE SAUMON

[Salmon Soufflé]

For 4 people

A 2½-pt. soufflé mould, page 147	1 tbl grated Swiss or Parmesan
½ oz. butter	cheese

Butter the mould and sprinkle with cheese. Preheat oven to 400° F., Mark 6. Measure out all your ingredients.

2 tbl chopped shallots or spring onions	½ tsp salt
2 oz. butter	⅛ tsp pepper
A 4-pt. saucepan	1 tbl tomato paste (for colour)
1½ oz. flour	½ tsp oregano or marjoram
½ pt. boiling liquid (juice from tinned salmon, if any, and milk)	

Cook the shallots or spring onions in the butter for a moment in the saucepan. Add the flour and cook 2 minutes. Away from heat, beat in the boiling liquid, then the seasonings, tomato paste, and herbs. Bring to boil, stirring, for 1 minute.

4 egg yolks	2 oz. grated Swiss cheese
6 oz. shredded cooked or tinned salmon	

Away from heat, beat in the egg yolks one by one. Then beat in the salmon and all but a tablespoon of cheese.

5 egg whites	A pinch of salt

Beat the egg whites and salt until stiff, see page 144. Stir a quarter of them into the soufflé mixture. Fold in the rest. Turn into prepared mould and sprinkle with the remaining cheese. Place in middle of preheated oven. Turn heat down to 375° F., Mark 5 and bake for about 30 minutes.

VARIATIONS

With the same method and proportions, you can make a soufflé using 6 ounces of any of the following:

Flaked tinned tuna or any cooked fish

Finely diced or minced cooked lobster, shrimp, or crab

Minced cooked chicken or turkey

Puréed cooked sweetbreads or brains.

If you wish to use raw fish or chicken, mince it, add it to the sauce base with the boiling milk, and boil for 2 minutes. Then beat in the egg yolks and proceed with the recipe.

FISH SOUFFLÉS FROM THE HAUTE CUISINE

These are only more complicated than the preceding soufflés in that each requires fish fillets poached in white wine, and each is accompanied by a delicious type of hollandaise called *sauce mousseline sabayon*. The fish may be poached ahead of time and the soufflé sauce base as well as the hollandaise may also be prepared in advance. Remember that if the hollandaise is to wait, it must be kept barely warm or it will thin out. If it is set aside to cool, reheat it very gently and not too much.

---

* SOUFFLÉ DE POISSON

[Fish Soufflé]

For 4 to 6 people

A 2½-pt. soufflé mould, page 147
1 tsp butter

1 tbl grated Swiss or Parmesan cheese

Butter the mould and sprinkle with cheese. Measure out ingredients. Preheat oven to 400° F., Mark 6.

Preparing the fish

¾ lb. skinless sole, brill, whiting or plaice fillets
¼ tsp salt
Pinch of pepper

1 tbl chopped shallots or spring onions
¼ pt. dry white wine or dry white vermouth

Mince half the fish; you will have 5 to 6 ounces of purée. Set it aside. Following directions for fish fillets in white wine on page 189, season the rest of the fillets, arrange them in a buttered baking dish with the shallots or spring onions, wine, and enough water barely to cover them. Bring to the simmering point, cover with buttered paper, and bake in bottom part of oven for 8 to 10 minutes or until a fork just pierces them easily. Strain out all the cooking liquor, boil it down in an enamelled saucepan until it has reduced to ⅛ pint, and set it aside until later for your *sauce mousseline sabayon*.

The soufflé mixture

2 oz. flour	**½ tsp salt**
1½ oz. butter	**⅛ tsp pepper**
A 3-pt. saucepan	**The minced fish**
½ pt. boiling milk	

Cook the flour and butter together slowly in the saucepan for 2 minutes without colouring. Away from heat, beat in the boiling milk, salt, pepper, and minced fish. Boil, stirring, for 2 minutes.

4 egg yolks

Remove from heat and immediately beat in the egg yolks one by one. Taste for seasoning.

5 egg whites	**1½ oz. grated Swiss cheese**
A pinch of salt	

Beat the egg whites and salt until stiff, page 144. Stir a quarter of them into the soufflé mixture. Stir in the cheese. Delicately fold in the rest of the egg whites.

Filling the mould

Turn a third of the soufflé mixture into the prepared mould. Cut the poached fish fillets into 2-inch strips about ½ inch wide, and arrange half of them over the soufflé. Cover them with half the remaining soufflé mixture, and arrange the rest of the fillets over it. Cover them with the last of the soufflé mixture.

Baking the soufflé

1 tbl grated Swiss cheese

Sprinkle the cheese on top, and place the mould in the middle of the preheated, 400° F., Mark 6 oven. Immediately reduce heat to 375° F., Mark 5, and bake for about 30 minutes, or until the soufflé has puffed and browned and a needle or knife plunged into the side of the puff comes out clean. While the soufflé is cooking, prepare the following sauce as an accompaniment. Serve the soufflé as soon as it is done.

Sauce Mousseline Sabayon (¾ pint)

3 egg yolks	**A 2-pt. enamelled saucepan**
¼ pt. cream	**A wire whisk**
The ⅓ pint concentrated fish liquor	

Beat the egg yolks, cream, and fish liquor over low heat until they gradually thicken into a light cream that coats the wires of the whisk (165° F.). Do not overheat or the egg yolks will scramble.

6 oz. softened butter divided into
    10 pieces

Away from heat, beat in the butter a piece at a time, beating until each is almost absorbed before adding another. The sauce will thicken like a hollandaise.

Salt and pepper   **Lemon juice, if necessary**

Taste carefully for seasoning, and add drops of lemon juice if you feel they are needed. Keep sauce over tepid—not hot—water, and when the soufflé is done, pour the sauce into a warm sauceboat to accompany the soufflé.

VARIATIONS

Soufflé de Homard
Soufflé de Crabe
Soufflé aux Crevettes

[Lobster, Crab or Shrimp Soufflé]

Use the same soufflé mixture as in the preceding recipe, with about 6 ounces of minced fish fillets. Instead of poached fish fillets in the centre of the soufflé, use:

4 oz. cooked diced lobster, crab,	**Pinch of pepper**
or shrimps	**3 tbl Madeira, sherry, or dry white**
1 oz. butter	**vermouth**
¼ tsp salt	

Cook the diced shellfish gently in the butter and seasonings for 3 minutes. Then add the wine, cover the pan, and simmer for 1 minute. Raise heat and let liquid boil off quickly.

Filets de Poisson en Soufflé

[Fish Soufflé Baked on a Dish]

A soufflé will also rise impressively when baked on a dish. This recipe is lighter than the preceding fish soufflé as it has no minced fish in its sauce base and only one egg yolk.

For 6 people

Preheat oven to 350° F., Mark 4.

½ lb. skinless turbot, sole, or brill fillets	½ tsp salt
¼ pt. dry white wine or dry white vermouth	Pinch of pepper
	1 tbl chopped shallots or spring onions

Measure out ingredients. Poach the fish fillets for 8 to 10 minutes in wine, seasonings, and shallots or spring onions as described in fillets poached in white wine, page 189. Drain out all the cooking liquor and boil it down in an enamelled saucepan until it has reduced to ⅛ pint. Set it aside for your *sauce mousseline sabayon*. Turn oven up to 425° F., Mark 7.

2 oz. butter	½ tsp salt
1½ oz. flour	Pinch of pepper
A 4-pt. saucepan	Pinch of nutmeg
½ pt. boiling milk	1 egg yolk

Cook the butter and flour slowly in the saucepan for 2 minutes without colouring. Away from heat, beat in the boiling milk and seasonings. Boil, stirring, for 1 minute. Away from heat, beat in the egg yolk. Check seasoning.

4 or 5 egg whites	2 oz. coarsely grated Swiss cheese
Pinch of salt	

Beat the egg whites and salt until stiff, page 144. Stir a quarter of them into the soufflé base. Stir in all but two tablespoons of the cheese. Delicately fold in the rest of the egg whites.

A buttered oval fireproof dish
  about 16 ins. long

Spread a ¼-inch layer of soufflé in the bottom of the dish. Flake the poached fish fillets and divide into 6 portions on the dish. Heap the rest of the soufflé mixture over the fish, making 6 mounds. Sprinkle with the remaining cheese and place on a rack in top part of preheated 425° F., Mark 7 oven. Bake for 15 to 18 minutes, or until soufflé has puffed and browned on top.

Ingredients for ¾ pt. *sauce mousseline*
  ***sabayon*, page 154**

Meanwhile, prepare the sauce as directed in the master fish soufflé recipe. Pass it separately in a warm sauceboat.

SOUFFLÉ DÉMOULÉ, MOUSSELINE

[Unmoulded Soufflé]

Most unmoulded soufflés are heavy, pudding-like affairs, but this one is light and delicious. You bake it slowly in a tin of water for over an hour, and then unmould it. Although it does not rise as high as its moulded relatives, it sinks only a little, and may be kept warm for a good 30 minutes before it is served. You may adapt any of the soufflé combinations in the preceding recipes for unmoulding if you use the same number of egg yolks and egg whites, and the same cooking method specified in the following recipe. Unmoulded cheese soufflé makes a handsome first course, and a fine main course surrounded by or accompanied with chicken livers, sausages, mushrooms, green peas, or asparagus tips.

For 6 people as a first course; 4, as a main course

Preheat oven to 350° F., Mark 4.

**½ pt. tomato sauce or fresh tomato
    purée, page 68 or 69**

Prepare the tomato sauce and let it simmer while the soufflé bakes.

¼ oz. butter	**2 tbl finely grated Swiss or**
A 3-pt. soufflé mould, preferably	**Parmesan cheese**
one 4 ins. deep	

Butter your mould heavily, especially on the bottom so that the soufflé will unmould easily. Roll cheese around in it to cover the bottom and sides.

1½ oz. butter	**A wire whisk**
1 oz. flour	**½ tsp salt**
A 4-pt. saucepan	**Big pinch of pepper**
A wooden spoon	**Pinch of nutmeg**
¼ pt. boiling milk	

Stir the butter and flour over moderate heat in the saucepan until they foam and froth together for 2 minutes without colouring. Away from heat, vigorously beat in the boiling milk, then the seasonings. Boil over moderate heat, stirring, for 1 minute. Remove from heat.

3 egg yolks	**A wire whisk**

One by one, beat the egg yolks into the hot sauce. Correct seasoning.

6 egg whites	**or a combination of Swiss and**
A pinch of salt	**Parmesan**
4 oz. coarsely grated Swiss cheese,	

In a separate bowl, beat the egg whites and salt until stiff peaks are formed, page 144. Stir a quarter of the egg whites into the sauce base; then stir in the cheese. Delicately fold in the rest of the egg whites.

Turn the mixture into the prepared mould, which the soufflé will fill by about two-thirds. Place in a tin and pour boiling water around the mould to come up to the level of the soufflé mixture. Place in middle of preheated oven and bake for about 1¼ hours. Regulate heat so that the water in the tin never quite simmers—this is important; soufflé must cook slowly. The soufflé is done when it has risen about half an inch over the top of the mould, is brown and crusty, and has just begun to show a faint line of shrinkage from the sides of the mould.

Turn a warm serving plate over the soufflé; reverse them. Then, clamping mould and plate together, give a sharp downward jerk or two, and the soufflé will dislodge itself. If the mould was properly buttered, and the soufflé sufficiently cooked, it will unmould perfectly, and present a golden brown exterior. Surround the soufflé with the tomato sauce, and serve. In the case of blemishes, pour the sauce over the soufflé and decorate with parsley.

(*) If there is a wait of 30 minutes or so, leave the soufflé unmoulded in its tin of hot water, and return to hot, turned-off oven and leave door ajar.

SOUFFLÉ AUX BLANCS D'OEUFS

[Cheese Soufflé with Egg Whites Only]

The following light soufflé with its strong cheese flavour is one way of using leftover egg whites. Remember that egg whites take well to freezing, so you can make a collection and do the soufflé when you have the right amount. One egg white equals 2 tablespoons.

If you wish to make this type of soufflé with other flavourings, substitute 6 ounces of minced fish, chicken, sweetbreads, ham, or vegetables for two-thirds of the diced cheese.

For 4 people

Preheat oven to 400° F., Mark 6.

A 2½-pt. soufflé mould

Butter the soufflé mould and sprinkle with grated cheese, page 147. Measure out the ingredients.

1½ oz. butter	½ tsp salt
1 oz. flour	⅛ tsp pepper
A 3-pt. saucepan	Big pinch of nutmeg
¼ pt. simmering cream	

Cook the butter and flour slowly together in the saucepan for 2 minutes without colouring. Away from heat, beat in the simmering cream and seasonings. Boil, stirring, for 1 minute. Remove from heat.

6 or 7 egg whites	3 oz. coarsely grated Swiss cheese
Big pinch of salt	3 oz. Swiss cheese cut into ¼ in. dice

Beat the egg whites and salt until stiff, page 144. Stir one-fourth of them into the soufflé mixture. Stir in all but a tablespoon of the grated cheese, then the diced cheese. Fold in the rest of the egg whites.

Turn mixture into the prepared mould, sprinkle with the remaining cheese, and place in middle of preheated, 400° F., Mark 6 oven. Immediately reduce heat to 375° F., Mark 5 and bake for 25 to 30 minutes, until soufflé has puffed and browned. Serve immediately.

---

* TIMBALES DE FOIES DE VOLAILLE

[Unmoulded Chicken Liver Custards]

These delicate little entrées (also called *mousses, pains,* and *soufflés*) are usually baked in individual ramekins and served hot with a *béarnaise* sauce. Or you can bake the ingredients in one large ring mould and fill the centre with the sauce. It can be prepared very quickly in an electric liquidizer, but if you do not have one, put the livers through a mincer, push them through a sieve, then beat in the rest of the ingredients.

For 1½ pints serving 8 people

Preheat oven to 350° F., Mark 4.

1¼ oz. butter	¼ tsp salt
1 oz. flour	Pinch of pepper
½ pt. boiling milk	

Make a thick béchamel sauce in a small saucepan by cooking the butter and flour together until they foam for 2 minutes without colouring. Away from heat, beat in the boiling milk and seasonings. Boil, stirring, for 1 minute. Allow to cool while preparing other ingredients, beating occasionally.

1 lb. of chicken livers	¼ tsp salt
2 eggs	⅛ tsp pepper
2 egg yolks	

Place the livers, eggs, egg yolks, and seasonings in the liquidizer, cover, and blend at top speed for 1 minute.

6 tbl cream   **2 tbl port, Madeira, or cognac**

Add the cool béchamel sauce, cream, and wine to the liver and blend for 15 seconds. Strain through a sieve into a bowl.

Optional: 1 chopped, tinned truffle

Stir in the optional truffle and correct seasoning.

(*) If not used immediately, cover and refrigerate.

½ oz. butter
8 ramekins of ¼ pt. capacity, or a
    1½-pt. ring mould

Butter the interior of the ramekins or mould heavily. Pour in the liver mixture, filling each ramekin or the mould to within about ⅛ inch of the top.

A pan containing 1 to 1½ ins. of
    boiling water

Place in tin of boiling water, then place on a rack in middle of preheated oven for 25 to 30 minutes, until a needle or knife plunged into the centre comes out clean, and the timbales have just begun to show a line of shrinkage from the ramekins.

(*) If not served immediately, leave in hot turned-off oven, with door ajar, for 15 to 20 minutes.

¾ pt. *sauce béarnaise*, page 76

Run a knife around the edge of each timbale and reverse on to a serving dish or plates. Top each with a spoonful of sauce, and pass the rest of the sauce separately.

VARIATIONS

Using the same proportions and method, substitute for the chicken livers any of the following cooked ingredients: ham, chicken, turkey, sweetbreads, salmon, lobster, crab, scallops, mushrooms, asparagus tips, or spinach.

Other Sauces

Sauce Aurore, béchamel or *velouté* with cream and a flavouring of tomato paste, page 54

    Sauce Madère, brown sauce with Madeira wine, page 66

    Sauce Périgueux, brown sauce with truffles, page 67

    Sauce Estragon, brown sauce with tarragon, page 64

PUFFS, GNOCCHI, AND QUENELLES

* *PÂTE À CHOUX*

[Cream Puff Pastry]

Pâte à choux is one of those quick, easy, and useful preparations like béchamel sauce which every cook should know how to make. Most people do not realize cream puff pastry is only a very, very thick white sauce or *panade* of flour, water, seasonings, and butter, into which eggs are beaten. The eggs make the pastry swell as it cooks.

Baked just as it is in the following recipe or mixed with cheese, *pâte à choux* becomes puffs for hors d'œuvres. Sweetened with sugar, it is ready to be cream puffs. When mashed potato or cooked semolina is beaten in, it turns into *gnocchi*. And with minced fish, veal, or chicken, it is quenelle paste, or can become a mousse.

For about 1¼ lbs.

A 3-pt. heavy-bottomed saucepan	1 tsp salt
½ pt. water	⅛ tsp pepper
3 oz. butter cut into pieces	Pinch of nutmeg

Bring water to boil with the butter and seasonings and boil slowly until the butter has melted. Meanwhile measure out the flour.

4 oz. sifted flour	A wooden spoon

Remove from heat and immediately pour in all the flour at once. Beat vigorously with a wooden spoon for several seconds to blend thoroughly. Then beat over moderately high heat for 1 to 2 minutes until mixture leaves the sides of the pan and the spoon, forms a mass, and begins to film the bottom of the pan.

4 standard, 2oz. eggs

Remove saucepan from heat and make a well in the centre of the pastry with your spoon. Immediately break an egg into the centre of the well. Beat it into the pastry for several seconds until it is absorbed. Continue with the rest of the eggs, beating them in one by one. The third and fourth eggs will be absorbed more slowly. Beat for a moment more to be sure all is well blended and smooth.

Pâte à choux for Dessert Puffs

For dessert puffs, only a suggestion of sugar—1 teaspoon—is added to boil with the water and butter in the preceding recipe, and the salt is reduced from 1 teaspoon to a pinch. Otherwise there is no difference in ingredients or method.

Leftover pâte à choux

Pâte à choux is usually employed as soon as it is made, and while it is still warm. If it is not used immediately, rub the surface with butter and cover with greaseproof paper to prevent a skin from forming over it. If your recipe then specifies warm *pâte à choux*, beat it vigorously in a heavy-bottomed saucepan over low heat for a moment until it is smooth and free from lumps and is barely warm to your finger. Be very careful not to warm it to more than tepid or the pastry will lose its ability to puff. *Pâte à choux* may be kept under refrigeration for several days, or it may be deep-frozen. Reheated gently as just described, it will produce a good small puff; large puffs may not always rise as high as those made with fresh pastry.

If you wish to make hot hors d'œuvres in a hurry, leftover *pâte à choux* can help you. Beat 3 or 4 tablespoons of cream into ¼ pint of warmed *pâte à choux*, then several tablespoons of grated cheese or chopped ham. Spread the mixture on biscuits, toast, or triangles of bread, pop them into a hot oven, and in 15 minutes you will have lovely puffed canapés.

PUFF SHELLS
Choux

You cannot fail with puff shells—as mounds of *pâte à choux* puff and brown automatically in a hot oven—if you take the proper final measures to ensure the shells remain crisp. A perfect puff is firm to the touch, tender and dry to the taste. Hot puffs will seem perfectly cooked when taken from the oven, but, if left as they are, they will become soggy as they cool because there is always an uncooked centre portion that gradually spreads its dampness through to the outside crust. To prevent this sad effect, small puffs are punctured to release steam; large puffs are slit, and often their uncooked centres are removed. This is actually the only secret to puff making.

F

When you have done puff shells once or twice you will find that it takes less than 30 minutes from start to finish to make them ready for the oven, and that they are a wonderfully useful invention. Hot, bite-sized, filled puffs make delicious appetizers. Large ones may contain creamed fish, meat, or mushrooms and be a hot first course. And sweet puffs with ice-cream or custard filling and chocolate or caramel topping are always an attractive dessert.

Forming Puffs

A forcing bag makes the neatest puffs. If you do not have one, drop the pastry on the baking sheet with a spoon.

Small Puffs

For 36 to 40 puffs 1¼ to 1½ inches in diameter

Preheat oven to 425° F., Mark 7.

| Ingredients for 1¼ lbs. warm *pâte à choux* from the preceding recipe | A forcing bag with ½-in. nozzle |

Make the *pâte à choux*.
Fold the top 3 inches of the forcing bag over your left hand as illustrated. Using a spoon, fill the bag with the warm *choux* pastry.

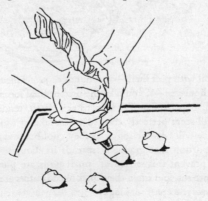

2 buttered baking sheets

Squeeze the pastry on to the baking sheets, making circular mounds about 1 inch in diameter and ½ inch high. Space the mounds 2 inches apart.

1 egg beaten with ½ tsp water in a   **A pastry brush**
small bowl

Then dip your pastry brush into the beaten egg and flatten each puff very slightly with the side of the brush. Avoid dripping egg down the puff and on to the baking sheet, as this will prevent the puff from rising.

Place the sheets in the top and lower parts of your preheated, 425° F., Mark 7 oven, and bake for about 20 minutes. The puffs are done when they have doubled in size, are a golden brown, and firm and crusty to the touch. Remove them from the oven and pierce the side of each puff with a sharp knife. Then place in the turned-off oven and leave the door ajar for 10 minutes. Cool the puffs on a rack.

Large Puffs

For 10 to 12 puffs about 3 inches in diameter

Use the same ingredients as in the preceding recipe, but provide a ¾-inch nozzle for the pastry bag. Squeeze the *choux* pastry on to the baking sheets in mounds 2 to 2¼ inches in diameter and 1 inch at the highest point. Space the mounds 2 inches apart. Flatten each mound slightly with the flat of your pastry brush dipped into the beaten egg. Place the baking sheets in the top and lower parts of a preheated, 425° F., Mark 7 oven and bake for 20 minutes, or until the puffs have doubled in size and are lightly browned. Then reduce heat to 375° F., Mark 5 and bake for 10 to 15 minutes more, or until the puffs are golden brown, and firm and crusty to the touch. Remove from oven, and make a 1-inch slit in the side of each puff. Return the puffs to the hot, turned-off oven, and leave its door ajar for 10 minutes. Then open one puff as a test. If its centre is damp, *either* reach into the other puffs through their slits with the handle of a teaspoon and remove their damp centres, *or* cut all the puffs in two horizontally, and scrape out the uncooked portions with a fork. Allow the halves to cool and crisp, then re-form the puffs.

Deep-Freezing Puff Shells

Puff shells deep-freeze perfectly Just before using frozen puffs, place them in a 425° F., Mark 7 oven for 3 to 4 minutes to thaw and crisp them.

Filling Puff Shells

For appetizer or entrée puffs, use any of the cream fillings on pages 183 to 185. *Either* place the filling in a forcing bag, slit the sides of the puffs, and squeeze in the filling, *or* remove the tops of the puffs and insert the filling with a spoon.

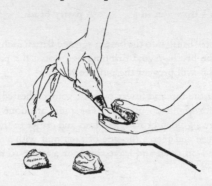

Reheat for 2 to 3 minutes in a 425° F., Mark 7 oven. For dessert puffs, use ice-cream, or the custard filling, *crème pâtissière* on page 543, plain or with beaten egg whites.

Petits Choux au Fromage

[Cheese Puffs]

As cocktail appetizers, these may be served hot or cold, and need no filling. Because of the large amount of cheese, they do not rise as high as plain puffs.

For about 40 puffs, 1½ inches in diameter when baked

Preheat oven to 425° F., Mark 7.

4 oz. grated Swiss, or Swiss and Parmesan cheese	1¼ lbs. warm *pâte à choux*, page 160

Beat the cheese into the warm *pâte à choux*. Correct seasoning. Squeeze into circular mounds on a baking sheet, paint with beaten egg, and bake as in the preceding recipe for small puffs. After painting with egg, you may, if you wish, sprinkle each puff with a pinch of grated cheese.

GNOCCHI

Gnocchi and quenelles are types of dumplings made of *pâte à choux* into which a purée is beaten. They are shaped into ovals or cylinders and are poached for 15 to 20 minutes in salted water or bouillon until they swell almost double in size. After they have drained, they may be covered with a hot sauce, or they may be *gratinéed* with cheese and butter, or with a sauce.

Both *gnocchi* and quenelles are relatively simple to make, and as they may be poached ahead of time and either refrigerated or deep-frozen, they are a useful addition to one's cooking repertoire.

---

* GNOCCHI DE POMMES DE TERRE

[Potato *Gnocchi*]

These make a good luncheon dish, or may be used as a starchy vegetable to accompany a roast.

For about 12 gnocchi, 3 by 1½ inches when cooked

**3 to 4 medium-sized baking
potatoes (1 lb.)**

Peel and quarter the potatoes. Boil in salted water until tender. Drain and put through a mincer. You should have about 12 oz.

Dry out the potatoes by stirring them in a heavy-bottomed saucepan over moderate heat for a minute or two until they film the bottom of the pan. Remove from heat.

**6 oz. warm *pâte à choux,* page 160
1½ oz. grated Swiss, or Swiss and
Parmesan cheese**

Beat the *pâte à choux* and the cheese into the potatoes. Correct seasoning.

Take the mixture by dessertspoonfuls and roll it with the palms of your hands on a lightly floured board to form cylinders about 2½ inches long and 1 inch in diameter.

**A 12-in. frying pan of simmering
salted water**

Slip the *gnocchi* into the simmering water and poach, uncovered, for 15 to 20 minutes. Water should remain almost but not quite at the simmering point throughout the cooking. If it boils, the *gnocchi* may disintegrate. When they have swelled almost double, and roll over easily in the water, they are done. Drain on a rack or a cloth. Serve as in the following suggestions:

TO SERVE

Gnocchi Gratinés au Fromage

[*Gnocchi* Baked with Cheese]

The preceding *gnocchi*   **1 oz. butter cut into pea-sized dots**
2 oz. grated Swiss or Parmesan
   cheese

Arrange the drained *gnocchi* in a shallow, buttered, baking dish. Spread the cheese over them and dot with the butter. Set aside uncovered.

Ten minutes before serving time, reheat and brown them slowly under a moderately hot grill.

Gnocchi Mornay

[*Gnocchi* Baked with Cheese Sauce]

For about 1¼ pints of sauce

2 oz. butter   **¾ tsp salt**
2 oz. flour   **⅛ tsp pepper**
A 3-pt. saucepan   **Big pinch of nutmeg**
1¼ pts. boiling milk

Cook the butter and flour together slowly in the saucepan for 2 minutes without colouring. Off heat, beat in the boiling milk and seasonings. Boil, stirring, for 1 minute.

3 oz. coarsely grated Swiss cheese

Remove from heat and beat for a moment to cool slightly. Then beat in the cheese and correct seasoning.

The potato *gnocchi*, page 165   **½ oz. butter cut into pea-sized dots**
3 tbl finely grated Swiss cheese

Arrange the *gnocchi* in a buttered baking dish about 2 inches deep. Spoon the cheese sauce over them, sprinkle with cheese, and dot with the butter. Leave aside uncovered.

About 10 minutes before serving time, reheat and brown slowly under a moderately hot grill.

ADDITIONS TO THE POTATO GNOCCHI PASTE on page 165.

Any of the following may be mixed into the *gnocchi* paste along with the cheese, and are especially good if your *gnocchi* are to be served as a main course.

3 to 4 tbl chopped fresh green herbs, such as chives and parsley
2 to 3 ounces chopped cooked ham or bacon
2 to 3 ounces sautéed diced mushrooms or chicken livers

GNOCCHI DE SEMOULE AVEC PÂTE À CHOUX—PATALINA

[Semolina *Gnocchi*]

Italian *gnocchi* are made of semolina with butter and seasonings. This French version with *pâte à choux* gives the semolina a puff and a lighter texture. Semolina is the residue of middle-sized particles left over from the sifting of durum wheat, the type of wheat used for making macaroni. It cooks in 10 to 20 minutes, depending on the fineness of the grind.

For about 12 pieces, 3 by 1½ inches when cooked

½ pt. water   ⅛ tsp pepper
½ oz. butter   Pinch of nutmeg
½ tsp salt

Bring the water to the boil in a saucepan with the butter and seasonings.

2 oz. semolina

Stirring the boiling water with a wooden spoon, gradually sprinkle in the semolina. Boil, stirring, until the cereal is tender, and thick enough to form a mass on the back of the spoon.

2 oz. grated Swiss or Parmesan   1¼ lbs. warm *pâte à choux*, page 160
cheese

Beat the semolina, then the cheese, into the *pâte à choux*. Correct seasoning.

Roll the *gnocchi* paste into cylinders on a floured board, poach in salted water, drain, and brown under the grill with grated cheese or cheese sauce as for the potato *gnocchi* in the preceding recipes.

QUENELLES

A quenelle, for those who are not familiar with this delicate triumph of French cooking, is *pâte à choux* with a purée of raw fish, veal, or chicken which is formed into ovals or cylinders and poached in seasoned liquid. Served hot in a good sauce, quenelles make a distinguished first course or luncheon dish. A good quenelle mixture is almost as light as a soufflé, and has just enough body to hold its shape when it goes into the poaching liquid. If the paste is too solid, the quenelle will taste dry and heavy, and if it is not solid enough it will disintegrate as it cooks. Of all the quenelle-making techniques we have tried, from the classical mortar and drum-sieve method of the ancients to the electric liquidizer the process described here seems to us to be the simplest and best. The initial paste can take as little as 15 minutes to prepare.

A chilled white Burgundy or Graves is perfect with quenelles in a cream sauce. A good claret such as Médoc goes with veal or chicken quenelles in a brown sauce.

---

* QUENELLES DE POISSON

[Fish Quenelles]

Fish quenelles in France are usually labelled *quenelles de brochet,* and are presumably made from pike, a fish of excellent flavour but so webbed with little bones that a quenelle is the most convenient way of eating it. If pike fillets are used, the fish must be pounded in a mortar and then pushed through a fine-meshed sieve to eliminate the bones. Boneless fish fillets may be puréed in a mincer and need not be sieved. The electric liquidizer is not suitable for this type of purée.

Beating equipment

Quenelle paste requires a fairly thorough beating at the end of the process when cream is added to it. As the pastry is thick and sticky, the pastry blender attachment for an electric mixer is excellent. Otherwise you must beat by hand with a wooden spoon because the regular egg-beating attachment for a mixer becomes hopelessly clogged.

Choice of fish

The type of fish to use for quenelles is one with lean, fairly close-grained flesh of a slightly gelatinous quality, which will combine solidly enough with the *pâte à choux* so that a good amount of cream can be beaten in. Flimsy, light-textured fish will absorb little cream and thus produce a rather dull and dry quenelle. Substitutes for pike are: coalfish, coley, pollack or saithe (*colin*), conger eel (*congre*), brill (*barbue*), whiting (*merlan*), and chicken halibut.

For about 16 quenelles

Pâte à choux (for 1 lb.)

½ pt. water	4 oz. sifted flour
A 3-pt. heavy-bottomed saucepan	2 eggs
1 tsp salt	2 egg whites
2 oz. butter	A 5-pt. mixing bowl

Following the general directions for *pâte à choux* on page 160, bring the water to the boil in the saucepan with the salt and butter. As soon as the butter has melted, remove the saucepan from heat and beat in all the flour at once with a wooden spoon. Then beat over moderately high heat for several minutes until the mixture forms a mass. Remove from heat and one by one, beat in the eggs, then the egg whites. Turn the *pâte à choux* into the mixing bowl.

The fish

1¼ lbs. skinless and boneless lean fish fillets from the preceding suggestions	½ tsp salt
	¼ tsp white pepper
2 tbl finely chopped truffle; Or: a big pinch of nutmeg	

Put the fish twice through the mincer. You should have 1 pound of purée; beat vigorously into the *pâte à choux* along with the truffles or nutmeg, and seasonings. (Use the pastry-blender attachment for your mixer, or a wooden spoon.) Set the paste in the coldest part of the refrigerator until it is thoroughly chilled. This will stiffen it so it will have sufficient body to absorb cream.

Adding the cream

2 to 6 tbl chilled cream

Just before you are ready to poach the quenelles, vigorously beat chilled cream into the chilled paste by dessertspoons. How much to add will depend on the consistency of the paste. It must be firm enough to hold its shape when it is formed into quenelles, but if too much cream is incorporated the paste will become too soft. If you have any doubts, test the paste by dropping a spoonful into barely simmering water as described in the following directions.

Shaping quenelles and poaching them

The spoon method described here makes the most delicate quenelles. A neater-looking but less light-textured alternative is to roll them into cylinders on a floured board as for the *gnocchi* on page 165.

2 dessertspoons in a cup of cold water	3 to 4 ins. of barely simmering fish stock or salted water
A 12-in. frying pan containing F*	

With a wet spoon, dip out a rounded mass of the cold quenelle paste. Transfer the spoon to your left hand. Smooth the top of the paste with the inverted bowl of the second wet spoon. Then slip the bowl of the second spoon under the

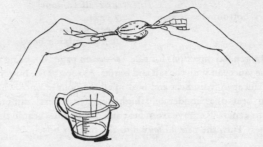

quenelle to loosen it and drop it into the barely simmering liquid. Rapidly form quenelles with the rest of the paste in the same manner. Poach them uncovered for 15 to 20 minutes, never allowing the water to come beyond the barest suggestion of a simmer. The quenelles are done when they have about doubled in size and roll over easily. Remove with a slotted spoon, and drain on a rack or a cloth.

(*) If the quenelles are not to be served immediately, arrange them in a lightly buttered dish, brush them with melted butter, cover with greaseproof paper, and refrigerate. They will keep perfectly for one to two days.

Fish Mousse

In Case of Disaster

If by any chance your quenelle paste turns out to be too soft to poach as quenelles, it will taste every bit as good if you declare it to be a mousse. Pack it into a buttered soufflé mould, a ring mould, or individual serving moulds. Set in a tin of boiling water and bake in a preheated 350° F., Mark 4 oven until the mousse has risen and shows a faint line of shrinkage from the sides of the mould. Unmould and serve with any of the fish sauces suggested on pages 194 to 196, or with the delicious *sauce mousseline sabayon* in the fish soufflé recipe on page 154.

Sauces for Quenelles

Quenelles may be served as in the following recipe, in which they may be sauced ahead of time and *gratinéed* just before serving; or hot quenelles may be coated with a hot sauce. If you choose the latter system and the quenelles have been prepared in advance, cover them and heat them through in a buttered dish for 10 to 15 minutes in a 350° F., Mark 4 oven. Then sauce them. Fish quenelles may be substituted for poached fish fillets in any of the recipes for fish on pages

194 to 196, which include the fine, rich, buttery sauces such as *Nantua* and *normande*.

Gratin de Quenelles de Poisson

[Quenelles *Gratinéed* in White Wine Sauce]

Sauce suprême de poisson (1½ pints) enough for 16 poached quenelles, page 168

2¼ oz. butter	½ pt. boiling, concentrated, white-
2 oz. flour	wine fish stock, page 103
A 3-pt. enamelled saucepan	½ tsp salt
½ pt. boiling milk	⅛ tsp white pepper

Cook the butter and flour slowly together in the saucepan for 2 minutes without colouring. Away from heat, beat in the boiling milk, fish stock, and seasonings. Boil, stirring, for 1 minute. Sauce will be very thick.

¼ to ½ pt. cream	Lemon juice
Salt and pepper	

Slowly simmering the sauce, thin it out with the cream, stirred in by tablespoons. Sauce should be thick enough to coat the spoon fairly heavily. Taste carefully for seasoning, adding salt, pepper and drops of lemon juice as you feel it necessary.

A lightly buttered baking dish	3 tbl grated Swiss cheese
2 ins. deep	½ oz. butter cut into pea-sized dots

Pour ¼ inch of sauce in the baking dish. Arrange the drained quenelles on top and spoon the rest of the sauce over them. Sprinkle with cheese and dot with the butter. Leave aside uncovered.

About 10 to 15 minutes before serving time, reheat and brown slowly under a moderate grill.

Quenelles aux Huîtres

[Fish Quenelles with Oysters]

½ tbl chopped shallots or spring	¼ pt. dry white wine or ⅛ pt. dry
onions	white vermouth
½ oz. butter	¼ tsp salt
12 large oysters, shelled	Pinch of pepper

Sauté the shallots or spring onions in butter for a moment in a small saucepan. Add the oysters, wine, and seasonings. Poach at just below the simmering point for 3 to 4 minutes, until the oysters swell. Drain the oysters. Boil the poaching liquid over high heat until it is reduced by half, and reserve it for your sauce.

Ingredients for the fish quenelle paste, page 160

Roll one oyster into each cylinder of the fish quenelle paste. Poach and sauce the quenelles in the same manner as the fish quenelles in the preceding recipes.

Quenelles de Saumon

[Salmon Quenelles]

Use exactly the same proportions and method as given in the master recipe for the fish quenelles, page 168, substituting 1 pound of raw salmon, or well-drained tinned salmon, for the white-fleshed fish. You may wish to include a tablespoon of tomato paste for added colour. Serve with the fish *velouté* sauce, or with any of the other sauces suggested for fish quenelles.

Quenelles de Crustacés

[Shrimp, Lobster, or Crab Quenelles]

Using exactly the same proportions and method as given in the master recipe for the fish quenelles on page 168, substitute 1 pound of raw, cooked, or tinned shrimps, lobster, or crab for the fish. The same sauces also apply.

Quenelles de Veau
Quenelles de Volaille

[Veal, Chicken, or Turkey Quenelles]

Veal, chicken, and turkey quenelles use the same proportions and methods as the master recipe for quenelles, with the following slight alterations:

Ingredients for quenelles, page 168, but substitute the following for the 1 lb. of fish: 1 lb. raw veal, chicken, or turkey, minus all skin, bones, and gristle	A 12-in. buttered frying pan Boiling well-seasoned chicken or veal stock, or salted water

Put the meat twice through the mincer, and beat it into the *pâte à choux*. Chill. Then beat in the cream and seasonings. Form into quenelles and arrange in the frying pan. Cover by 2 inches with boiling stock or water. Poach for 15 to 20 minutes. Drain. Serve in one of the following ways:

TO SERVE

Quenelles au Gratin. Use the same proportions and method as for the *velouté* with cream in the *gratin* recipe, page 171, substituting the veal or chicken stock in which you poached the quenelles for the fish stock and all or part of the milk.

Or use the cheese sauce in the *gnocchi* recipe on page 166.

Quenelles, Sauce Madère. Pour over the hot quenelles a brown sauce flavoured with Madeira: *sauce madère*, page 66, or *sauce périgueux* (with truffles), page 67.

FRENCH PANCAKES
Crêpes

Every French household makes use of *crêpes*, not only as a festive dessert for Mardi Gras and Candlemas Day, but as an attractive way to turn leftovers or simple ingredients into a nourishing main-course dish. *Crêpes* may be rolled around a filling of fish, meat, or vegetables, spread with sauce, and browned under the grill. More spectacular is a *gâteau de crêpes* in which the pancakes are piled upon each other in a stack of 24, each spread with a filling. This is then heated in the oven and *gratinéed* with a good sauce. Or the *crêpes* may be piled in a soufflé mould with alternating layers of filling, heated in the oven, unmoulded, and coated with sauce. Whatever system you decide upon, including rolled *crêpes*, your dish may be prepared in advance and heated up when you are ready to serve.

Dessert *crêpes*, called *crêpes sucrées*, and entrée *crêpes*, *crêpes salées*, have slightly different proportions, but their batters are blended and cooked in the same way. The following recipe is made with an electric liquidizer, because it is so quick. If you do not have one, gradually blend the eggs into the flour, beat in the liquid by spoonfuls, then the butter, and strain the batter to get rid of any possible lumps. *Crêpe* batter should be made at least 2 hours before it is to be used; this allows the flour particles to expand in the liquid and ensures a tender, light, thin *crêpe*.

PÂTE À CRÊPES

[*Crêpe* Batter]

For about 12 crêpes, 6 to 6½ inches in diameter

¾ pt. cold liquid (½ water, ½ milk)	½ lb. sifted flour
	4 tbl melted butter
4 eggs	A rubber spatula
½ tsp salt	

Put the liquids, eggs, and salt into the liquidizer jar. Add the flour, then the butter. Cover and blend at top speed for 1 minute. If pieces of flour adhere to sides of jar, dislodge with a rubber spatula and blend for 2 to 3 seconds more. Cover and refrigerate for at least 2 hours.

The batter should be a very light cream, just thick enough to coat a wooden spoon. If, after making your first *crêpe,* it seems too heavy, beat in a bit of water, a spoonful at a time. Your cooked *crêpe* should be about $\frac{1}{8}$ inch thick.

Method for making Crêpes

The first *crêpe* is a trial one to test the consistency of your batter, the exact amount you need for the pan, and the heat.

An iron frying pan or a *crêpe* pan with a 6½- to 7-in. bottom diameter	**A piece of fat bacon or pork-rind; Or: 2 to 3 tbl cooking oil and a pastry brush**

Rub the frying pan with the rind or brush it lightly with oil. Place over moderately high heat until the pan is just beginning to smoke.

Iron Crêpe Pans

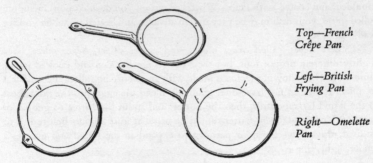

Top—French
Crêpe Pan

Left—British
Frying Pan

Right—Omelette
Pan

A ladle or measure to hold 3 to 4 tbl or ⅛ pt.

Immediately remove from heat and, holding handle of pan in your right hand, pour with your left hand a scant ⅛ pint of batter into the middle of the pan. Quickly tilt the pan in all directions to run the batter all over the bottom of the pan in a thin film. (Pour any batter that does not adhere to the pan back into your bowl; judge the amount for your next *crêpe* accordingly.) This whole operation takes but 2 or 3 seconds.

Return the pan to heat for 60 to 80 seconds. Then jerk and toss pan sharply back and forth and up and down to loosen the *crêpe*. Lift its edges with a spatula and if the under side is a nice light brown, the *crêpe* is ready for turning.

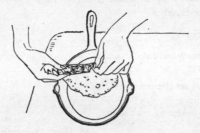

Turn the *crêpe* by using 2 spatulas; *or* grasp the edges nearest you in your fingers and sweep it up toward you and over again into the pan in a reverse circle; *or* toss it over by a flip of the pan.

Brown lightly for about ½ minute on the other side. This second side is rarely more than a spotty brown, and is always kept as the underneath or nonpublic aspect of the *crêpe*.

Slide *crêpe* on to a plate. Grease the frying pan again, heat to just smoking, and proceed with the rest of the *crêpes*. *Crêpes* may be kept warm by covering them with a dish and setting them over simmering water or in a slow oven. Or they may be made several hours in advance and reheated when needed.

As soon as you are used to the procedure, you can keep 2 pans going at once, and make 24 *crêpes* in less than half an hour.

* *Gâteau de Crêpes à la Florentine*

[Mound of French Pancakes Filled with Cream Cheese, Spinach, and Mushrooms]

An amusing entrée or main-course dish can be made by piling *crêpes*, a filling between each, in a shallow baking dish. (It looks like a many-layered cake or cylindrical mound.) Then the whole mound is covered with a good sauce and heated in the oven. Instead of the spinach, cheese, and mushrooms suggested, use any type of filling you wish, even three or four different kinds rather than one or two. Like the cream fillings on pages 183-5, they are all a combination of well-flavoured sauce and a purée of cooked fish, shellfish, veal, ham, chicken or chicken livers, to which are added cooked vegetables such as asparagus tips, aubergine, tomatoes, spinach, or mushrooms if you wish. Other sauce suggestions, depending on your filling, are tomato sauce, page 68, brown Madeira sauce, page 66, *sauce soubise* (béchamel with puréed onions), page 56. You may use one or more types of sauce for the fillings, and still another to top the mound of *crêpes*.

This type of dish may be made ready for the oven in the morning, and heated up at dinner-time.

For 4 to 6 people

Batter for 24 *crêpes* 6½ ins. in diameter, page 173

Make the *crêpes* and set them aside.

Sauce Mornay (*béchamel with cheese*)

2 oz. flour	**A 2½-pt. saucepan**
2 oz. butter	

Cook the flour and butter slowly together in the saucepan for 2 minutes without colouring

1 pt. boiling milk	**⅛ tsp pepper**
½ tsp salt	**Big pinch of nutmeg**

Away from heat, beat in the boiling milk and seasonings. Boil, stirring, for 1 minute.

⅛ pt. cream	**4 oz. coarsely grated Swiss cheese**

Reduce to the simmering point and stir in the cream by tablespoons. Sauce should be thick enough to coat the spoon fairly heavily. Remove from heat and correct seasoning. Stir in all but two tablespoons of the cheese. Film top of sauce with milk to prevent a skin from forming.

The spinach filling

1 tbl chopped shallots or spring onions	**12 oz. blanched chopped spinach, page 430**
1 oz. butter	**¼ tsp salt**

Cook the shallots or onions in butter for a moment in an enamelled saucepan. Add spinach and salt, and stir over moderately high heat for 2 to 3 minutes to evaporate moisture. Stir in about ¼ pint of the cheese sauce. Cover and simmer slowly for 8 to 10 minutes, stirring occasionally. Correct seasoning and set aside.

The cheese and mushroom filling

8 oz. cottage cheese or cream cheese	**Salt and pepper**
	1 egg

Mash the cheese in a mixing bowl with the seasonings. Beat in ¼ pint of the cheese sauce, and the egg.

| ¼ lb. chopped mushrooms | ½ oz. butter |
| 1 tbl chopped shallots or spring onions | ½ tbl oil |

Sauté the mushrooms and shallots or spring onions in butter and oil for 5 to 6 minutes in a frying pan. Stir them into the cheese mixture, and correct seasoning.

Forming the mound

| A round baking dish about 9 ins. in diameter and 1½ ins. deep | 3 tbl grated cheese |
| | ¼ oz. butter |

Butter the baking dish, and centre a *crêpe* in the bottom. Spread it with a layer of cheese and mushroom filling. Press a *crêpe* on top and spread it with a layer of spinach filling. Continue with alternating layers of *crêpes* and filling, ending with a *crêpe*. Pour the remaining cheese sauce over the top and sides of the mound. Sprinkle with the 3 tablespoons of cheese and dot with 3 or 4 small pieces of butter. Leave aside.

Baking

About 25 to 30 minutes before serving time, place in upper part of a preheated 350° F., Mark 5 oven to heat through thoroughly and brown the top lightly. To serve, cut in pie-shaped wedges.

VARIATIONS

Timbale de Crêpes

[Moulded French Pancakes with Various Fillings]

For 6 people

| A 2½-pt. cylindrical mould, preferably a charlotte, about 3½ ins. high and 6¼ ins. in diameter | diameter and 12 *crêpes* 6 ins. in diameter |
| 10 cooked *crêpes* 6½ to 7 ins. in | 1½ pts. of cream fillings, pages 183 to 185, one or several varieties |

Butter the mould. Cut the 10 large *crêpes* in half. Line the mould with them—their best sides against the mould, their pointed ends meeting at the bottom centre of the mould, and the other ends folded down the outside of the mould. Fill the mould with alternating layers of stuffing and *crêpes*. Fold the dangling ends of the halved *crêpes* over the last layer of stuffing and top with a final *crêpe*

1 pt. of sauce, such as tomato, cheese, or whatever will go with fillings

Set mould in a tin of boiling water and bake in lower part of a preheated 350° F., Mark 5 oven for 30 to 40 minutes, or until thoroughly heated. Unmould on a buttered serving dish and cover with whatever sauce you have chosen.

Crêpes Farcies et Roulées

[Stuffed and Rolled French Pancakes]

Place a big spoonful of filling on the lower third of each *crêpe* and roll the *crêpes* into cylinders.

Either sauté in butter, remove to a hot serving dish and sprinkle with parsley;

Or arrange in a shallow baking dish, cover with sauce, sprinkle with cheese and brown slowly under a moderate grill.

The shellfish or chicken fillings on pages 184-5 are especially good for this if you wish to be fairly elaborate. Both call for a good *sauce velouté*; in making it, use half the sauce to mix with an equal amount of shellfish or chicken for your filling. Thin out the rest with a small amount of cream, and use that for coating the *crêpes*.

COCKTAIL APPETIZERS

Hors d'Œuvres

For those who enjoy making pastries, here are a few good hot hors d'œuvres and one cold one. The series of canapés and tartlets starting on page 181, and the *chaussons* on page 186, can be made larger, and served as a first course or luncheon dish.

AMUSE-GUEULES AU ROQUEFORT

[Roquefort Cheese Balls—Cold]

For about 24

½ lb. Roquefort or blue cheese
2 to 3 oz. softened butter
1 tbl chives or chopped spring onion tops
1 tbl finely chopped celery

Pinch of cayenne pepper
Salt if needed
⅛ tsp pepper
1 tsp cognac or a few drops of Worcester sauce

Crush the cheese in a bowl with 3 tablespoons of the butter and work it into a smooth paste. Beat in the chives or spring onion tops, celery, seasonings, and cognac or Worcester sauce. If mixture is very stiff, beat in more butter by fractions. Check seasoning carefully. Roll into balls about ½ inch in diameter.

1½ oz. fine, stale, white breadcrumbs   2 tbl very finely chopped parsley

Toss breadcrumbs and parsley in a plate. Roll the cheese balls in the mixture so that they are well covered. Chill.

Serve as they are or pierced with a cocktail stick.

CHEESE BISCUITS

Bouchées, Galettes, Baguettes

Any of the following are more attractive when hot, but are quite good served cold. They may be baked, then deep-frozen, and reheated for 5 minutes or so in a hot oven.

* GALETTES AU FROMAGE

[Cheese Wafers]

These featherweight wafers are often made of Swiss cheese, but you can use other cheese or a mixture of cheeses if you wish, and thus employ leftovers. The dough contains just enough flour to hold the *galettes* together while they bake, and 3 ounces of flour is usually right for Swiss cheese. You will probably need more if you are using soft cheeses, and should always bake one as a test.

For about 30 wafers

Preheat oven to 425° F., Mark 7.

½ lb. grated Swiss cheese or a mixture of cheeses	¼ tsp pepper Pinch of cayenne pepper
½ lb. softened butter	Salt to taste
3 oz. sifted flour, more if needed	

Knead all ingredients together in a bowl or on a board. The mixture will be sticky. Roll 1 tablespoonful of mixture into a ball in the palms of your hands, then flatten it into a cake ¼ inch thick. Bake 10 to 15 minutes in hot oven to observe how it holds together; it should spread slightly, puff lightly, and brown. If it spreads out more than you wish, or is too fragile, knead in 1 ounce more flour and make another test.

Lightly buttered baking sheets	A pastry brush
1 egg beaten with ½ tsp water in a small bowl	2 oz. Swiss cheese A cooling rack

When you are satisfied, form the rest of the dough into cakes and place on baking sheets. Paint the tops with beaten egg and top each with a pinch of grated cheese. Bake for 10 to 15 minutes until the *galettes* have puffed, and browned lightly. Cool them on a rack.

Galettes au Roquefort

[Roquefort Cheese Biscuits]

The dough for these *galettes* may also serve as a pastry dough for tarts and turnovers.

For about 30 biscuits

¼ lb. Roquefort or blue cheese	2 tbl cream
A 3-pt. mixing bowl	1 egg yolk
¼ lb. softened butter	6 oz. flour

Mash the cheese in the bowl with a mixing fork. Beat in the butter, cream, and egg yolk. Then knead in the flour. Form into a ball, wrap in greaseproof paper, and chill until firm. Roll out ¼ inch thick, cut into 1½ inch rounds, brush with egg, and bake as in the preceding recipe.

Galettes au Camembert

[Camembert Biscuits]

This dough may be substituted for the usual pastry dough for tarts and turnovers.

For about 50 biscuits

6 to 8 oz. ripe Camembert or Brie cheese	½ tsp salt
	⅛ tsp pepper
A 3-pt. mixing bowl	Pinch of cayenne pepper
3 oz. softened butter	8 oz. sifted flour
2 eggs	

Scrape off the crusts and mash the cheese in the bowl with a mixing fork. Blend in the butter, then beat in the eggs and seasoning. Work in the flour and knead everything together for a moment to make a smooth and fairly supple dough. Knead in a tablespoon or so more flour if dough seems too soft. Wrap in grease-proof paper and chill until firm. Roll out ¼ inch thick, cut into 1½-inch rounds, and brush with egg as in the preceding master recipe for cheese biscuits. Bake in upper part of a preheated 350° F., Mark 4 oven for about 15 minutes, or until lightly browned.

BOUCHÉES PARMENTIER AU FROMAGE

[Potato Cheese Sticks]

Mashed potato gives these little cheese mouthfuls a nice, tender quality.

For about 60 pieces

½ lb. baking potatoes (2 medium
  potatoes)

Peel and quarter the potatoes. Boil in salted water until tender. Drain, and mash well. You should have 6 ounces.

Stir the potatoes over moderate heat in a heavy-bottomed saucepan for 2 to 3 minutes until they form a light film on the bottom of the pan, indicating that most of their moisture has been evaporated.

4 oz. sifted flour	$\frac{1}{8}$ tsp white pepper
4 oz. softened butter	Pinch of nutmeg
1 egg	Pinch of cayenne pepper
4 oz. grated Swiss cheese	Salt as needed

Beat the flour into the potatoes, then the butter by fractions, then the egg, cheese, and seasonings. Taste for seasoning.

Preheat oven to 425° F., Mark 7.

2 lightly buttered baking sheets

With a fluted pastry nozzle $\frac{1}{4}$ inch diameter in a forcing bag, squeeze the mixture into 2$\frac{1}{2}$-inch lengths spaced $\frac{1}{2}$ inch apart on to the baking sheets.

Bake both sheets at a time in preheated oven for about 15 minutes, or until sticks are lightly browned.

CANAPÉS, BREAD CASES, AND TARTLET SHELLS

Although Melba toast and biscuits make good foundations for hot appetizers, the following are more elegant. They may be used interchangeably. all of them may be prepared ahead, and they may also be filled and browned, then reheated. When bread is specified, use only a home-made type of white bread with body, not the soft squashy type. French recipes call for *pain de mie*.

Canapés—Croûtons

[Plain or Sautéed Bread Rounds]

Plain, sliced, white bread works perfectly well for canapés when cut into triangles or rounds, spread with a filling, then placed in a preheated 425° F., Mark 7 oven until the bread is toasted on the bottom and the filling has puffed and browned on top. But if you wish to be more elaborate, proceed as follows:

Slice the bread $\frac{1}{4}$ inch thick, and cut it into rounds 1$\frac{1}{2}$ to 2 inches in diameter with a fluted cutter. Heat 2 tablespoons of clarified butter (page 12) in a frying pan and sauté the rounds on each side until very lightly browned, adding more butter as necessary. (These are called *croûtons* when they are triangular and garnish an entrée.)

Heap the filling (recipes are on following pages) upon each canapé in a ½-inch dome. Top with a pinch of grated cheese, and a drop of melted butter. Arrange on a baking sheet and place for a moment under a hot grill to brown the tops lightly. If prepared in advance, reheat in a 350° F., Mark 4 oven for several minutes.

Croûtes

[Toasted Bread Cases]

Slice off the crust. Cut the bread into 1-inch slices, and the slices either into 1-inch cubes or, with a cutter, into rounds. Cut out a well in the centre of each. Press down the bread on the sides and bottom of the well with your finger to make an open-topped case about ¼ inch thick. Paint the tops and sides with melted butter. Place on a baking sheet and brown lightly for 5 minutes in the upper part of a preheated 450° F., Mark 8 oven.

Place filling (following pages) in the hollow centres. Top with a pinch of grated cheese and a drop of melted butter. Brown top of filling delicately under a hot grill for a moment. Reheat, if they have been prepared in advance, in a 350° F., Mark 4 oven for several minutes.

Tartelettes

[Little Pastry Shells]

Following the general procedure for pastry and for pastry shells, pages 126 to 131, roll the pastry a bit less than ⅛ inch thick. Line buttered pastry moulds ½ inch deep and 2 to 2½ inches in diameter, with the pastry. Flute the rims with the back of a knife. Prick the bottom of the pastry with a fork. Fill each mould or cup with a round of buttered brown paper and a small handful of dried beans; or set another mould on the pastry. Either will keep the bottom from puffing up and the sides from collapsing. Bake in a preheated 400° F., Mark 6 oven for 7 to 8 minutes, or until pastry will hold its shape. Remove paper and beans or empty moulds. Prick bottom of shells again and return to oven for 2 to 3 minutes more, or until shells are just beginning to colour and to shrink from sides of moulds. Remove shells and cool on a rack.

Place a filling (following) in the centre. Top with a pinch of cheese and a drop of melted butter. Arrange on a baking sheet and place in a 450° F., Mark 8 oven for 5 minutes or so, until filling has browned on top. If cooked beforehand, reheat in a 350° F., Mark 4 oven for several minutes.

SPREADS AND FILLINGS
Farces

Use these multipurpose cream fillings for the sautéed bread rounds, bread cases or *tartelettes*. They may also garnish the cream puffs on page 161, the pastry turnovers on page 186, the croquettes on page 185, and the *crêpes* on pages 173 to 178.

---

* *FONDUE AU GRUYÈRE*

[Cream Filling with Swiss Cheese]

For about ¾ pint

1¼ oz. butter
1¼ oz. flour
A 3-pt. saucepan
A wire whisk
½ pt. boiling milk or boiling cream

½ tsp salt
⅛ tsp pepper
Pinch of nutmeg
Pinch of cayenne pepper

Cook the butter and flour slowly together in the saucepan for 2 minutes without colouring. Away from heat, beat in the boiling milk or cream, then the seasonings. Boil, stirring, for 1 minute. The sauce should be very thick. Taste for seasoning.

1 egg yolk
4 oz. coarsely grated Swiss, or
 Swiss and Parmesan, cheese

1 oz. butter

Remove sauce from heat. Place egg yolk in centre of sauce and immediately beat it in vigorously with the wire whisk. Beat for a moment to cool slightly, then beat in the cheese, and finally the butter. Taste carefully for seasoning. If not used immediately, dot top of sauce with butter to prevent a skin from forming.

VARIATIONS

Garlic and Wine Flavouring

¼ oz. butter
1 tbl chopped shallots or spring
 onions

1 small clove mashed garlic
¼ pt. dry white vermouth

Using a small enamelled saucepan, cook the shallots or spring onions and garlic slowly in butter for a moment. Add wine, raise heat, and boil down rapidly until wine is reduced to ⅛ pint. Substitute this for ⅛ pint of milk in the master recipe.

Ham

3 oz. chopped ham   ¼ oz. butter

Sauté the ham for a moment in butter. Substitute it for half of the cheese in the master recipe.

Mushrooms or Chicken Livers

¼ lb. diced mushrooms or chicken   ½ oz. butter
    livers   Salt and pepper

Sauté the mushrooms or chicken livers in the butter. Season to taste, and substitute for half of the cheese in the master recipe.

---

* FONDUE DE CRUSTACÉS

[Cream Filling with Shellfish]

For about ¾ pint

1 tbl chopped shallots or spring   vermouth; or 3 to 4 tbl Madeira
    onions   or sherry
1 oz. butter   Salt and pepper to taste
10 oz. diced or flaked, cooked or   Optional: 1 tbl chopped fresh herbs
    tinned shellfish   such as tarragon or chervil; or
⅛ pt. dry white wine or dry white   1 tsp dried tarragon or oregano

Using a 3-pint saucepan or a small enamelled frying pan, cook the shallots or spring onions in the butter for a moment over low heat. Stir in the shellfish and cook slowly for 2 minutes over low heat. Add the wine. Cover and simmer for 1 minute. Uncover, raise heat, and boil rapidly until liquid has almost evaporated. Season to taste and stir in optional herbs.

1 oz. butter   ⅛ tsp pepper
1 oz. flour   Salt to taste
½ pt. boiling liquid (milk, plus—if
    you have it—concentrated fish
    stock or mushroom juice)

In a separate 3-pint saucepan, cook the butter and flour slowly together for 2 minutes without colouring. Away from heat, beat in the boiling liquid, pepper, and salt to taste. Boil, stirring, for 1 minute.

egg yolk   ¼ pt. cream

Beat egg yolk and cream in a bowl. Remove sauce from heat and beat it into the bowl a tablespoonful at a time. Return to saucepan and boil, stirring, for 1 minute. Sauce should be very thick. Correct seasoning.

1 oz. grated Swiss cheese

Fold the previously prepared shellfish, then the cheese into the sauce, and check seasoning again. If not used immediately, dot top of sauce with butter to prevent a skin from forming.

VARIATION

Fondue de Volaille

[Cream Filling with Chicken or Turkey]

Using exactly the same method and proportions as for the preceding *fondue de crustacés*, substitute 8 ounces of diced, cooked chicken, turkey, duck, or game for the shellfish.

CROQUETTES
Crèmes Frites, Fondues, Cromesquis

Any of the preceding fondues, starting on page 183, may be chilled, cut into squares or balls, rolled in egg and breadcrumbs, then browned in deep fat. The secret of doing them is that they need a double layer of egg and crumbs which is firmly patted on to enclose the cream completely. It will then not burst when fried. It is also advisable, but not imperative, to allow the crumbed croquettes to stand an hour or more before frying; this sets the crumbs more firmly. Fry only a few at a time so as not to lower the temperature of the fat. Made larger, they also provide a delicious first course or luncheon dish.

For about 30 pieces

¾ pt. cream filling, such as cheese,   **Buttered dish**
   shellfish, or chicken (preceding   **Melted butter**
   pages)

Spread the filling in a smooth 1-inch layer on the buttered dish. Film surface with melted butter. Chill until firm.

4 oz. flour

Spread the flour on a plate.

2 eggs   **A pinch of salt and pepper**
1 tbl oil

Beat the eggs with the oil and seasoning until well blended in a soup plate.

6 oz. stale white breadcrumbs

Spread the crumbs on a plate.

Cut the chilled cream filling into 1-inch cubes. One at a time, roll each cube in the flour, dip in beaten egg being sure egg covers the cube completely, shake off excess egg, then roll in the breadcrumbs. Pat crumbs into place with the flat of a knife. When all cubes have been done, roll each again in beaten egg, then in crumbs; be sure each cube is well covered all over with crumbs. If possible, let them stand for an hour before frying.

Heat the frying fat or oil to 385° F. and fry the croquettes, a few at a time, for several minutes until lightly browned. Drain on absorbent paper and keep hot in a 350° F., Mark 4 oven. If they must be reheated, use a 400° F., Mark 6 oven.

TURNOVERS

Chaussons

PETITS CHAUSSONS AU ROQUEFORT

[Pastry Turnovers with Roquefort Cheese]

These nice little mouthfuls are made of pastry rolled out and cut into squares, ovals, or circles. In the centre a small lump of filling is placed. The edges of the pastry are moistened with beaten egg, then either another piece of pastry is placed on top, or the original pastry is folded over upon itself to enclose the filling. They are then baked in a hot oven until they puff and brown. In making them, avoid putting in so much filling that the pastry cannot be sealed, and be sure to seal carefully so that the turnovers do not burst while baking.

Turnovers may enclose a variety of stuffings other than Roquefort, such as the cream fillings on pages 183 to 185, or any of the liver, sausage, or veal mixtures in the *pâté* section, pages 520 to 525, or the minced meat mixtures in the Beef, Lamb, or Veal sections. You can also use little pork sausages or shop-bought sausage meat. *Chaussons* may be made in any size or shape, from about 2½ inches for appetizers to 12 inches for an entrée.

For about 40 pieces

½ lb. Roquefort or blue cheese
A 5-pt. mixing bowl
¼ lb. softened butter
2 egg yolks

1 to 2 tbl kirsch or cognac
1¼ tsp pepper
2 tbl chopped chives or chopped
    spring onion tops

Mash the cheese in the bowl with a mixing fork. Beat in the butter, then the egg yolks, kirsch or cognac, pepper, and chives or onion tops.

2 to 6 tbl cream

Beat in the cream by tablespoons but do not let the mixture thin out too much. It should remain a fairly thick paste. Correct seasoning.

**Chilled pastry made from 1 lb. of
  flour, page 126**

Roll out the dough into a rectangle $\frac{1}{8}$ inch thick. With a knife, cut the dough into 2$\frac{1}{2}$-inch squares.

Preheat oven to 425° F., Mark 7.

**1 egg beaten in a bowl with $\frac{1}{2}$ tsp   A pastry brush
  water   Lightly buttered baking sheets**

Place 1 teaspoon of filling in the centre of each square. One by one, paint a $\frac{1}{4}$-inch border of beaten egg around the edges of the pastry. Fold the pastry over on itself into a triangle. Press the edges together firmly with your fingers. Press them again, making a design with the prongs of a fork. Place on a buttered baking sheet and continue with the rest of the turnovers. Paint the tops with beaten egg. Make shallow crosshatch lines with the point of a knife, and poke a $\frac{1}{8}$-inch hole through the centre of each pastry top so that cooking steam can escape.

Bake in top part of preheated oven for about 15 minutes, or until puffed and lightly browned.

Turnovers may be baked, then reheated. Baked turnovers may also be deep-frozen, then placed in a 425° F., Mark 7 oven for 5 minutes or so to thaw and heat through.

CHAPTER FIVE

FISH

Poisson

THE FRENCH are magnificent with fish. Not only is fresh fish abundant all the year round, but the art of its cooking and saucing is accomplished with great taste and skill.

This chapter includes two fine recipes for scallops, three for lobster, and a group for mussels. But the main emphasis is on the important and typically French method of poaching fillets of fish in white wine and serving them in a wine sauce, starting with the simplest type of sauce and ending with several of the most famous of *la grande cuisine*. These last, as you will observe, are fish *veloutés* (flour and butter *roux* simmered with the fish cooking liquid), which are then enriched with cream and egg yolks. They are all the same basic sauce described in detail on page 52 in the Sauce chapter. Under numerous disguises and with various flavourings, this sauce appears throughout almost every phase of French cookery.

A NOTE ON BUYING FISH

Fish must be fresh smelling and fresh tasting. If it is whole, its eyes are bright and full, not filmed, opaque, and flat. Its gills are bright red, its flesh firm to the touch, its skin fresh and glistening.

Frozen fish should be bought from a dealer who has the proper facilities to store it at a constant temperature of zero degrees. It should be solidly frozen. A block of frozen juices at the bottom of the packet is proof that it has been thawed and refrozen. Before cooking, defrost it in the refrigerator, or under cold running water.

SERVING SUGGESTIONS

A beautifully sauced fish can well be considered as a separate course and needs nothing but French bread and a good wine to go with it. If it is a main course, include *risotto* or steamed rice for shellfish, boiled potatoes for other fish. A salad or vegetable should come afterwards, so as not to disturb the harmony of the fish, the sauce, and the wine.

FISH FILLETS IN WHITE WINE SAUCE
THE FISH FILLETS

Most of the famous French dishes involving fillets of fish centre around sole poached in white wine, then covered with a lovely, creamy sauce made from the poaching liquid. Sole is ideal for poaching in fillets as its delicious, close-grained flesh does not flake apart during cooking. Other excellent choices are brill, chicken turbot, and John Dory. Fillets of plaice, lemon sole, whiting, and fresh-water trout may also be used, but as they tend to flake after poaching, it is best to cook, sauce, and serve them in the original poaching dish. Any of the fish mentioned in this paragraph may replace sole in the following recipes.

---

* *FILETS DE POISSON POCHÉS AU VIN BLANC*

[Fish Fillets Poached in White Wine]

For 6 people

Preheat oven to 350° F., Mark 4.

A buttered, 10- to 12-in., fireproof baking and serving dish, 1½ to 2 ins. deep	Salt and pepper
	¾ oz. butter cut into pieces
2 tbl finely chopped shallots or spring onions	½ to ¾ pt. cold, white-wine fish stock made from heads, bones, and trimmings, page 103; Or: a mixture of ¾ pt. dry white wine or vermouth and water
2½ lbs. skinless and boneless sole fillets	

Sprinkle half the shallots or spring onions in the bottom of the dish. Season the fillets lightly with salt and pepper and arrange them in one slightly overlapping layer in the dish. If fillets are thin, they may be folded in half so that they make triangles. Sprinkle the fillets with the remaining shallots or onions, and dot with butter. Pour in the cold liquid and enough water so that the fish is barely covered.

Buttered brown paper or grease-proof paper (do not use	aluminium foil—it will discolour the wine)

Bring almost to simmering point on top of the stove. Lay the buttered paper over the fish. Then place dish in bottom half of preheated oven. Maintain liquid

almost at simmering point for about 8 minutes, thicker fillets from the alternative
fish choices on page 189 will take a few minutes longer. The fish is done when
a fork pierces the flesh easily. Do not overcook; the fish should not be dry and
flaky.

An enamelled saucepan

Place a cover over the dish and drain out all the cooking liquid into an enamelled
saucepan.

(*) The fish is now poached and ready for saucing. It may be covered and kept
warm for a few minutes over hot, but not simmering, water. Or place it aside,
covered with its piece of paper, and reheat later for a few minutes over simmering water. Be very sure that the fish does not overcook as it reheats. Before
saucing the fish, drain off any liquid which may have accumulated in the dish.

*   *Filets de Poisson Bercy aux Champignons*

[Fish Fillets Poached in White Wine with Mushrooms]

Bercy is the simplest of the white-wine fish sauces. The poaching liquid is
thickened with *beurre manié*—a flour and butter paste—then enriched with
cream. This combination of fish, mushrooms, and cream sauce is an informal
version of *sole bonne femme*. Serve with it a white Burgundy, Graves, or
Traminer.

For 6 people

¾ lb. sliced fresh mushrooms	⅛ tsp salt
1 oz. butter	Pinch of pepper
An enamelled frying pan	

Toss the mushrooms in hot butter over moderately high heat for a minute or
two without browning. Season with salt and pepper, and leave aside.

2½ lbs. fillets of sole and the ingredients for poaching them in white wine (see preceding recipe)	A 3-pt. enamelled or stainless steel saucepan

Arrange the seasoned fillets in a buttered baking dish as described in the master
recipe. Spread the mushrooms over them. Pour in the liquids, and poach the
fish. Then drain the poaching liquid into the saucepan. Preheat grill.

Rapidly boil down the poaching liquid until it has reduced to ½ pint.

1 oz. flour blended to a paste with 1½ oz. softened butter	Salt and pepper
¼ to ½ pt. cream	Lemon juice

Away from heat, beat the flour and butter paste into the hot liquid, then ¼ pint of the cream. Bring to the boil. Thin out the sauce with additional tablespoons of cream until it coats the spoon nicely. Season to taste with salt, pepper, and drops of lemon juice.

| 1 oz. grated Swiss cheese | ½ oz. butter cut into pieces |

Spoon the sauce over the fish. Sprinkle with the cheese, and dot with butter. Place dish 6 to 7 inches below a hot grill for 2 to 3 minutes to reheat fish and brown top of sauce lightly. Serve as soon as possible.

(*) Dish may be prepared ahead and reheated as follows: After sprinkling with the cheese and butter, place aside. Before serving, reheat just to simmering point on top of the stove, then place for a minute or two under a hot grill to brown the top of the sauce.

VARIATION

Filets de Poisson à la Bretonne

[Fish Fillets Poached in White Wine and a Julienne of Vegetables]

This is the same recipe, but with a julienne of carrots, onions, celery, and mushrooms cooked in butter, then spread over the fish. It makes a pretty dish with a delicious flavour.

| Ingredients for the preceding recipe, but use only ¼ lb. of mushrooms, and the following vegetables: | 2 leeks, white part only; or 2 onions |
| 1 carrot | 2 tender celery stalks |

Cut the vegetables into julienne matchsticks 1½ inches long and ⅛ inch across. Keep the mushrooms separate. Cook the other vegetables slowly in butter for about 20 minutes in a covered saucepan, until they are tender but not browned. Then add the mushrooms and cook for 2 minutes. Season with salt and pepper.

Spread the vegetables over the seasoned fish fillets, cover with the liquids, and poach the fish. Make the sauce as in the preceding recipe.

* Filets de Poisson Gratinés, à la Parisienne

[Fish Fillets Poached in White Wine; Cream and Egg Yolk Sauce]

In the following recipe, the fish poaching liquid is cooked with a flour and butter *roux* to make a fish *velouté*. The *velouté* is then combined with cream and egg yolks to produce a delicious, velvety sauce called a *parisienne*. Although it uses almost the same elements as the *sauce Bercy*, because of its cooked *roux* and its egg yolks, *sauce parisienne* is far more subtle in taste and texture. It is the basis for all the great fish sauces described later. When the sauce is to be used for a *gratin*, as in this recipe, the whole dish may be prepared ahead of time, and reheated later. Before the fish is sauced, it may be surrounded with various cooked shellfish as suggested at the end of the recipe. Serve with this a chilled white Burgundy, or an excellent Graves.

For 6 people

½ lbs. sole fillets poached in white
   wine, page 189

poach the fish in white wine as described in the master recipe. Drain the poaching liquid into an enamelled saucepan and rapidly boil it down until it has reduced to ½ pint.

Sauce Parisienne

A 3-pt. heavy-bottomed enamelled or stainless steel saucepan	A wooden spoon
	The boiling fish-poaching liquid
1½ oz. butter	¼ pt. milk
1½ oz. flour	A wire whisk

Melt the butter, blend in the flour, and cook slowly, stirring, until they foam and froth together for 2 minutes without colouring. Away from heat, beat in the boiling liquid, then the milk. Boil, stirring, for 1 minute. Sauce will be very thick.

Preheat grill.

2 egg yolks	A wooden spoon
¼ pt. cream	More cream as needed
A 3-pt. mixing bowl	Salt and white pepper
A wire whisk	Lemon juice

Blend the yolks and cream in the mixing bowl. Beat in drops of hot sauce until ¼ pint has been added. Beat in the rest of the hot sauce in a thin stream. Return the sauce to the pan. Place over moderately high heat and stir with wooden spoon, reaching all over the bottom of the pan, until the sauce comes to the boil. Boil and stir for 1 minute. Thin out with additional spoonfuls of cream until the sauce coats the spoon nicely. Season carefully to taste with salt, pepper, and drops of lemon juice. Strain.

2 tbl grated Swiss cheese, to help brown top of sauce	½ oz. butter cut into pieces

Spoon the sauce over the fish. Sprinkle with cheese, and dot with butter.

(*) If not to be served immediately, leave aside.

Just before serving, reheat slowly almost to simmering point on top of the stove. Place under hot grill to brown the top of the sauce.

SHELLFISH GARNITURES

Before saucing the fish in the preceding or following recipes, you may surround it with one or various types of cooked shellfish meat. Their cooking juices are added to reduce with the liquid in which the fish fillets were poached, giving it even more character.

The following brief directions include the cooking of the raw shellfish, and then the warming of the meat in butter and seasonings to give it additional flavour. If you are using previously cooked or tinned meat, it will need only the final warming in butter.

Lobster

Steam the lobster in wine and aromatic flavourings as described at the beginning of the lobster Thermidor recipe on page 199. When the lobster is cool, remove the meat and dice or slice it. Sauté the meat for 2 to 3 minutes in 1 to 2 ounces of hot butter, 1 tablespoon of chopped shallots or spring onions, and salt and pepper. Stir in 3 tablespoons of dry white wine or dry white vermouth and boil for 1 minute until the liquid has almost completely evaporated. The lobster is now ready to be used.

Shrimps

Follow the preceding directions for lobster, but simmer the whole, unpeeled shrimps for 5 minutes only. Allow them to cool in the cooking liquid. Then peel them, and warm them in butter, seasonings, and wine.

Écrevisses

These fresh-water shellfish are also called crayfish. They look exactly like baby lobsters but are only 4 to 5 inches long. Prepare them like the shrimps in the preceding directions. Only the tail meat is used as a garnish. The chests and the rest of the shells may be ground up to make a shellfish butter, page 93.

Shelled Fresh Oysters

Poach the oysters at just below simmering point for 3 or 4 minutes in their natural juices until they swell. Drain them, and they are ready to use.

Mussels

Scrub and soak 1½ pints of fresh mussels as directed on page 204. Then place them in a covered enamel or stainless steel saucepan with ½ pint of dry white wine or ¼ pint of dry white vermouth, 3 tablespoons of chopped shallot or spring onions, 3 parsley sprigs, and a pinch of pepper. Boil rapidly for about 5 minutes, tossing several times, until the shells swing open. Remove the mussels from their shells, and they are ready to use.

G

SOME CLASSIC COMBINATIONS

The same cream and egg-yolk fish sauce described in the recipe for *filets de poisson gratinés à la parisienne* on page 191 becomes even richer and more velvety if a fairly large quantity of butter is beaten into it just before serving. The more you beat in, the more delicious the sauce becomes. But as in all heavily buttered sauces, it cannot be kept warm once buttered or the butter will liquefy and either thin out the sauce, or rise up and float on top. Here in outline are some traditional combinations of poached fish fillets and various shellfish garnitures to give you an idea of what you can do. You can, of course, make up your own selection. In each case, in the following recipes, the sauce takes on the name of the dish. Serve your finest white Burgundy with any of these, and they should be considered a separate course, accompanied only by hot French bread.

---

* SOLE À LA DIEPPOISE

[Fish Fillets with Mussels and Shrimps]

This recipe is the model for the variations to follow.

For 6 people

Poaching the fish

2½ lbs. sole fillets poached in white
    wine, page 189
1½ pts. fresh mussels steamed in
    white wine, page 193

½ lb. shelled shrimps warmed in
    butter and seasonings, page 193

Arrange the poached fish fillets on a lightly buttered serving dish and surround them with the mussels and shrimps. Just before serving, cover the dish and reheat the fish for a few minutes over simmering water. Drain off any accumulated liquid before covering the fish with the following sauce:

For 1 pint of sauce

A 3-pt. enamelled saucepan
1½ oz. butter
1½ oz flour
The fish-poaching and mussel-
    steaming liquids combined and
    boiled down to ½ pt.

¼ pt. milk
2 egg yolks and ¼ pt. cream blended
    in a 3-pt. mixing bowl
Salt and pepper
Drops of lemon juice

Following the technique for *sauce parisienne* on page 192, cook the flour and butter slowly together until they foam and froth for 2 minutes. Away from heat, beat in the hot fish cooking liquid, then the milk. Boil 1 minute. Beat the hot sauce drop by drop into the yolks and cream. Return mixture to saucepan and boil, stirring, for 1 minute. Thin out with more cream if necessary, and correct seasoning. Strain. Film top of sauce with a tablespoonful of melted butter if not to be served immediately.

2 to 8 oz. softened butter (3 to 4 oz. is usual)

Just before serving the fish, bring the sauce to simmering point. Then remove it from heat and beat in the butter a little at a time.

Final assembly

6 whole cooked shrimps in their shells   **6 to 12 thin slices of tinned truffles**

Immediately spoon the sauce over the hot fish and shellfish. Decorate with the shrimps and truffles and serve.

VARIATIONS

The following are all constructed in exactly the same manner as the preceding *sole à la dieppoise*. Directions for poaching the fish are on page 189; for the shellfish garnitures, on page 193.

Sole à la Normande

[Fish Fillets with Shellfish and Mushrooms]

Follow the preceding recipe, but to the garniture add oysters, mushrooms, and *écrevisses*, if available. Decorate the sauced fish with whole shrimps or *écrevisses*, truffle slices, and *croûtons* (triangles of white bread sautéed in butter), page 181.

Sole Walewska

[Fish Fillets with Shellfish and Truffles]

Same as the *sole à la dieppoise*, but the fillets are garnished with *écrevisses* or shrimps, and lobster meat, and instead of beating plain butter into the sauce, use the shellfish butter on page 93. Decorate the sauced fish with truffle slices, and cooked lobster claws or whole shrimps.

Sole à la Nantua

[Fish Fillets with *Écrevisses*]

Same as the *sole à la dieppoise*, but the fish is garnished with *écrevisses*, and shellfish butter, page 93, rather than plain butter is beaten into the sauce.

Sole Bonne Femme

(Fish Fillets with Mushrooms]

Poach the fish fillets in white wine and sliced mushrooms as for the *sole Bercy* on page 190. Make the sauce following the recipe for the *sole à la dieppoise*. Garnish the sauced fish with 6 fluted mushroom caps, page 470, which have been stewed in butter and lemon juice, page 471.

Filets de Sole Farcis

[Stuffed Fish Fillets]

Into ½ pound of the fish quenelle mixture on page 168 mix 4 tablespoons of finely diced mushroom *duxelles*, page 475, and 2 to 3 tablespoons additional cream. Place a spoonful in the centre of each seasoned, raw fillet, and fold or roll the fillet to enclose the filling. Tie with white string. Poach, garnish, and sauce the fillets following any of the preceding suggestions.

COQUILLES ST. JACQUES À LA PARISIENNE

[Scallops and Mushrooms in White Wine Sauce]

Exactly the same *sauce parisienne* as that for the poached fish fillets in the preceding recipes is delicious with scallops *gratinéed* in their shells. This dish may be prepared ahead, and *gratinéed* just before serving. A fine, chilled white Burgundy or a very good Graves would go well with it. Scallops are usually served as a first course, or as a light luncheon dish.

For 6 scallop shells

Cooking the scallops

½ pt. dry white wine or ⅓ pt. dry white vermouth	2 tbl chopped shallots or spring onions
½ tsp salt	A 3-pt. enamelled or stainless steel saucepan
Pinch of pepper	
½ bay leaf	

Simmer the wine and flavourings together for 5 minutes.

16 to 20 medium-sized washed scallops   **½ lb. sliced fresh mushrooms**

Add the scallops and mushrooms to the wine, and pour in enough water barely to cover ingredients. Bring to simmering point. Cover, and simmer slowly for 5 minutes. Remove scallops and mushrooms with a slotted spoon, and leave aside in a bowl.

The sauce

Rapidly boil down the cooking liquid until it has reduced to ½ pint.

A 3-pt. enamelled or stainless	2 egg yolks
steel saucepan	¼ pt. cream, more if needed
1½ oz. butter	Salt and pepper
1½ oz. flour	Drops of lemon juice
¼ pt. milk	

Following the directions in *sauce parisienne*, page 192, cook the butter and flour slowly together for 2 minutes. Away from heat, blend in the boiling cooking liquid, then the milk. Boil 1 minute. Blend the egg yolks and cream in a bowl, then beat the hot sauce into them by drops. Return the sauce to the pan and boil, stirring, for 1 minute. Thin out with more cream if necessary. Season to taste with salt, pepper, and lemon juice. Strain.

Final assembly

6 scallop shells or ovenglass or
    porcelain shells of ⅛ pt. capacity

Cut the scallops into crosswise pieces about ⅛ inch thick.

¼ oz. butter	¾ oz. butter cut into 6 pieces
6 tbl grated Swiss cheese	

Blend two-thirds of the sauce with the scallops and mushrooms. Butter the shells. Spoon the scallops and mushrooms into them, and cover with the rest of the sauce. Sprinkle with cheese and dot with butter. Arrange the shells on a grill pan.

(*) Leave aside or refrigerate until ready to *gratiné*.

Fifteen minutes before serving, place the scallops 8 to 9 inches below a moderately hot grill to heat through gradually, and to brown the top of the sauce. Serve as soon as possible.

A RECIPE FROM PROVENCE

COQUILLES ST. JACQUES À LA PROVENÇALE

[Scallops *Gratinéed* with Wine, Garlic, and Herbs]

This good recipe may be prepared in advance and *gratinéed* just before serving. The following proportions are sufficient for a first course. Double them for a main course. Serve a chilled *rosé*, or a dry white wine such as Côtes de Provence.

For 6 scallop shells

1 medium chopped onion	1 clove chopped garlic
1 oz. butter	
1½ tbl chopped shallots or spring onions	

Cook the onions slowly in butter in a small saucepan for 5 minutes or so, until tender and translucent but not browned. Stir in the shallots or spring onions, and garlic, and cook slowly for 1 minute more. Leave aside.

24 to 30 medium-sized washed scallops	Salt and pepper
	4 oz. flour in a dish

Dry the scallops and cut into slices ¼ inch thick. Just before cooking, sprinkle with salt and pepper, roll in flour, and shake off excess flour.

1 oz. butter	A 10-in. enamelled frying pan
1 tbl olive oil	

Sauté the scallops quickly in very hot butter and oil for 2 minutes to brown them lightly.

¼ pt. dry white wine, or ⅛ pt. dry white vermouth and 4 tbl water	½ bay leaf
	⅛ tsp thyme

Pour the wine, or the vermouth and water, into the frying pan with the scallops. Add the herbs and the cooked onion mixture. Cover the frying pan and simmer for 5 minutes. Then uncover, and if necessary boil down the sauce rapidly for a minute until it is lightly thickened. Correct seasoning, and discard bay leaf.

6 buttered scallop shells, or porcelain or ovenglass shells, of ⅛ pt. capacity	1 oz. grated Swiss cheese
	1 oz. butter cut into 6 pieces

Spoon the scallops and sauce into the shells. Sprinkle with cheese and dot with butter.

(*) Leave aside or refrigerate until ready to *gratiné*.

Just before serving, place under a moderately hot grill for 3 to 4 minutes to heat through, and to brown the cheese lightly.

TWO FAMOUS LOBSTER DISHES

A NOTE ON DEALING WITH LIVE LOBSTERS

If you object to steaming or splitting a live lobster, it may be killed almost instantly just before cooking if you plunge the point of a knife into the head between the eyes, or sever the spinal cord by making a small incision in the back of the shell at the juncture of the chest and the tail.

HOMARD THERMIDOR

[Lobster Thermidor—*Gratinéed* in its Shell]

So many steps are involved in the preparation of a really splendid lobster Thermidor, no wonder it costs a fortune in any restaurant! But it is not a particularly difficult dish to execute, and everything may be prepared in advance and heated up just before serving. This is an especially attractive recipe for lobster Thermidor because the meat is stirred in hot butter before it is sauced, and turns a rosy red. Buy lobsters weighing a good 2 pounds each, so that the shells will be large enough to hold the filling.

For 6 people

Steaming the lobsters

A large covered, enamelled or
  stainless steel saucepan with tight-
  fitting cover
1¼ pt. dry white wine (or ¾ pt. dry
  white vermouth) and ¾ pt. water
A large onion, a medium carrot,
  and a celery stalk, all thinly
  sliced

6 parsley sprigs
1 bay leaf
¼ tsp thyme
6 peppercorns
1 tbl fresh or dried tarragon
3 live lobsters, 2 lbs. each

Simmer wine, water, vegetables, herbs, and seasonings in the pan for 15 minutes. Then bring to a rolling boil and add the live lobsters. Cover and boil for about 20 minutes. The lobsters are done when they are bright red and the long head-feelers can be pulled from the sockets fairly easily.

½ lb. sliced fresh mushrooms
½ oz. butter
1 tsp lemon juice

¼ tsp salt
A covered enamelled or stainless
  steel saucepan

While the lobsters are steaming, stew the mushrooms slowly in the covered saucepan with the butter, lemon juice, and salt for 10 minutes.

The sauce

When the lobsters are done, remove them from the pan. Pour the mushroom cooking juices into the lobster steaming juices in the pan and boil down rapidly until liquid has reduced to about 1 pint.

A 1½-pt. enamelled or stainless
  steel saucepan

Strain into the saucepan and bring to simmering point.

2½ oz. butter	A wooden spoon
2 oz. flour	A wire whisk
A 2½-pt. heavy-bottomed,	1 tbl cream
enamelled or stainless steel	
saucepan	

Cook the butter and flour slowly together in the second saucepan for 2 minutes without browning. Away from heat, beat in the simmering lobster-cooking liquid. Boil, stirring, for 1 minute. Leave aside. Film top of sauce with the cream.

A 5-pt. mixing bowl	¼ pt. cream
1 tbl dry mustard	Pinch of cayenne pepper
2 egg yolks	

Split the lobsters in half lengthwise, keeping the shell halves intact. Discard sand sacs in the heads, and the intestinal tubes. Rub lobster coral and green matter through a fine sieve into the mixing bowl, and blend into it the mustard, egg yolks, cream, and pepper. Beat the sauce into this mixture drop by drop.

4 to 6 tbl more cream

Return the sauce to the pan and, stirring with a wooden spoon, bring it to the boil and boil slowly for 2 minutes. Thin out with tablespoons of cream. Sauce should be thick enough to coat a spoon fairly heavily. Taste carefully for seasoning. Leave aside, the top filmed with a spoonful of cream.

Sautéing the lobster meat

Remove the meat from the lobster tails and claws, and cut it into ⅜-inch cubes.

A 12-in. enamelled or stainless	2 oz. butter
steel frying pan	⅛ pt. cognac

Place the frying pan with the butter over moderate heat. When the butter foam begins to subside, stir in the lobster meat and sauté, stirring slowly, for about 5 minutes until the meat has turned a rosy colour. Pour in the cognac and boil for a minute or two, shaking the frying pan, until the liquid has reduced by half.

Final assembly

Preheat oven to 425° F., Mark 7.

Fold the cooked mushrooms and two-thirds of the sauce into the frying pan with the lobster meat.

A shallow roasting tin or fireproof   1 oz. butter cut into pieces
  serving dish
2 oz. grated Parmesan or Swiss
  cheese

Arrange the split lobster shells in the roasting tin. Heap the lobster mixture into
the shells; cover with the remaining sauce. Sprinkle with cheese and dot with
butter

(*) May be prepared ahead up to this point and refrigerated.

Place in top part of 425° F., Mark 7 oven for 10 to 15 minutes, until lobster is
bubbling and the top of the sauce is nicely browned. Serve immediately on a
dish or serving plates.

VARIATION

Homard aux Aromates

[Lobster Steamed in Wine with Herb Sauce]

This is not a variation of lobster Thermidor at all, but it fits well into this
niche.

**Ingredients for steaming 3 lobsters
in wine, herbs, and aromatic
vegetables as in the preceding
Thermidor recipe**

Steam the lobsters for about 20 minutes as described in the preceding recipe.
Remove them. Rapidly boil down their cooking liquid until it has reduced to
¾ pint. The sliced carrots and onions need not be removed.

¾ oz. flour blended to a paste with   About ½ pt. of cream
  ¾ oz. softened butter

Away from heat, beat in the flour and butter paste. Then bring to the boil for
15 seconds. Reduce to simmering point and stir in the cream by tablespoons
until the sauce is the consistency of a light cream soup. Correct seasoning and
stir in the herbs.

**3 to 4 tbl fresh chopped green
  herbs: parsley, chervil, and
  tarragon, or parsley only**

Split the lobsters in two, lengthwise. Remove sand sacs in the heads and
intestinal tubes. Arrange the lobsters in a serving dish, pour the sauce over them,
and serve.

G*

HOMARD À L'AMÉRICAINE

[Lobster Simmered with Wine, Tomatoes, Garlic, and Herbs]

Homard à l'américaine is live lobster chopped into serving pieces, sautéed in oil until the shells turn red, then flamed in cognac, and simmered with wine, aromatic vegetables, herbs, and tomatoes. In France, unless you are at a formal dinner, the meat is left in the shells and guests dig in, flanked by finger bowl and napkin. We have noticed that many non-French people prefer the meat to be removed from the shells before the dish is served, which is too bad, as it makes more work for the cook.

The origin of *homard à l'américaine* is a subject for discussion. Some authorities call it *à l'armoricaine*, after the ancient province of Armorique in Brittany where lobsters grow. Others say *armoricaine* is nonsense because the tomato flavouring is quite untypical of Brittany and that the recipe is far more likely the product of a Paris chef with Provençal inclinations who titled his dish after an American client, or after the exotic origins of the tomato. In any case it is a splendid creation for lobster.

Risotto simmered in fish stock, or steamed rice, and a dry white wine with body such as Burgundy, Côtes du Rhône, or Graves would make fine accompaniments.

For 6 people

Three 1½-lb. live lobsters

Split the lobsters in two lengthwise. Remove sand sacs in the heads and intestinal tubes. Reserve coral and green matter. Remove claws and joints and crack them. Separate tails from chests.

2 tbl olive oil
A heavy 12-in. enamelled frying pan
or casserole

Heat the oil in the frying pan until it is very hot but not smoking. Add the lobster pieces, meat-side down, and sauté for several minutes, turning them, until the shells are bright red. Remove lobster to a side dish.

1 medium carrot, finely diced   **1 medium onion, finely diced**

Stir in the diced carrot and onion, and cook slowly for 5 minutes or until almost tender.

Preheat oven to 350° F., Mark 4.

Salt and pepper
3 tbl chopped shallots or spring
  onions
1 clove mashed garlic
⅛ pt. cognac
1 lb. fresh, ripe tomatoes, peeled,
  seeded, juiced, and chopped,
  page 465

2 tbl tomato paste
½ pt. fish stock, page 103
¾ pt. dry white wine or ½ pt. dry
  white vermouth
Optional: ½ tbl meat glaze, page 99
2 tbl chopped parsley
1 tbl fresh tarragon or 1 tsp dried
  tarragon

Season the lobster, return it to the frying pan, and add the shallots or spring onions, and the garlic. With the frying pan over moderate heat, pour in the cognac. Avert your face and ignite the cognac with a lighted match and shake the frying pan slowly until the flames have subsided. Stir in all the ingredients and bring to simmering point on top of the stove. Cover and place in the middle part of preheated oven. Regulate heat so that lobster simmers quietly for 20 minutes.

3 oz. softened butter
The lobster coral and green matter

A 5-pt. mixing bowl

While the lobster is simmering, force the lobster coral and green matter with the butter through a fine sieve into the mixing bowl and set aside.

When the lobster is done, remove it to a side dish. Take the meat out of the shells if you wish. Place frying pan with its cooking liquids over high heat and boil down rapidly until sauce has reduced and thickened slightly. It will acquire more body later when the butter and coral mixture is added. Taste very carefully for seasoning.

(*) Recipe may be completed to this point, and finished later.

Return the lobster to the sauce and bring to simmering point to reheat the lobster. Beat ½ pint of hot sauce by drops into the coral and butter mixture, then pour the mixture into the frying pan with the lobster. Shake and swirl the frying pan over low heat for 2 to 3 minutes to poach the coral and green matter, but do not bring the sauce near simmering point again.

A ring of *risotto*, page 491, or of
  steamed rice, page 488

2 to 3 tbl chopped parsley, or
  parsley and fresh tarragon

Arrange the lobster and sauce in the rice ring, decorate with herbs, and serve immediately.

MUSSELS

Moules

Mussels, with their long, oval, blue-black shells and delicious pink-orange flesh are often called the poor man's oyster. Clinging to rocks and piers along the sea coasts everywhere, they can be had for the picking at low tide. If you are gathering mussels yourself, take them only from places washed by clear, clean, sea water.

SCRUBBING AND SOAKING MUSSELS

Before they can be cooked, mussels must have a rather long and careful cleaning process to remove all possible sand from their interiors, and to rid the shells of any slime and dirt which might spoil the excellent juices they render as they steam open. Discard any mussels that are not firmly closed, or which feel lighter in weight than the rest. Discard also any too-heavy mussels, as they may be nothing but sand enclosed between two mussel shells. Scrub each mussel very clean with a rough brush under running water. Then with a small knife, scrape off the tuft of hairs, or beard, which protrudes from between one side of the closed shell halves. Place the mussels in a basin or bucket of fresh water for an hour or two so that they disgorge their sand and also lose a bit of their saltiness. Lift the mussels out of the water into a colander, wash and drain them again, then they are ready to cook.

Note: Some cooks add flour to the soaking water on the theory that while the mussels eat the flour and become fatter and more succulent, they are at the same time disgorging their sand more thoroughly. Use 2 ounces of flour for each 3 pints of water, beating the flour and a little water with a whisk first, to mix it thoroughly. Then, after soaking the mussels, lift them into a colander, and rinse them in cold water.

TINNED MUSSELS

Beware of sand if you are using tinned mussels. If there is any sand at all in the juices at the bottom of the tin, soak the mussels in several changes of cold water. Eat one, and if it is sandy, continue washing the mussels. Good quality tinned mussels may be substituted for fresh mussels in all but the first two of the following recipes; the tinned juices may be used as stock for the sauce. Simmer the juices with a little white wine or vermouth, and fill out the quantity of stock called for in your recipe with boiling milk.

MOULES À LA MARINIÈRE—I

[Fresh Mussels Steamed Open in Wine and Flavourings]

Here is the simplest version of this most typical of French methods for cooking mussels. They are steamed open in a big pot with wine and flavourings, which takes only about 5 minutes. Then the mussels, shells and all, are ladled out into soup plates, and the cooking liquor is poured over them. Each guest removes the mussels one by one from their shells with fingers or a fork and discards the shells into a side dish. In addition to shell dish and fork, provide your guests with a soup spoon for drinking up the mussel juices, a big napkin, and a finger bowl. Together with the mussels serve French bread, butter, and a chilled, light, dry white wine such as Muscadet, dry Graves, or one of the Pouillys.

For 6 to 8 people

¾ pt. of light, dry white wine or ½ pt. dry white vermouth	8 parsley sprigs ½ bay leaf
A 5- to 6-qt. enamelled pan with cover	¼ tsp thyme ⅛ tsp pepper
8 tbl chopped shallots, or spring onions, or very finely chopped onions	3 oz. butter

Bring the wine to the boil in the pan with the rest of the ingredients listed. Boil for 2 to 3 minutes to evaporate its alcohol and to reduce its volume slightly.

5 qts. scrubbed, soaked mussels, page 204

Add the mussels to the pan. Cover tightly and boil quickly over high heat. Frequently grasp the pan with both hands, your thumbs clamped to the cover, and toss the mussels in the pan with an up and down slightly jerky motion so that the mussels will change levels and cook evenly. In about 5 minutes the shells will swing open and the mussels are done.

8 tbl roughly chopped parsley

With a big spoon, dip the mussels into wide soup plates. Allow the cooking liquid to settle for a moment so that any sand will sink to the bottom. Then ladle the liquid over the mussels, sprinkle with parsley and serve immediately.

MOULES À LA MARINIÈRE—II

[Mussels Steamed with Wine, Flavourings, and Breadcrumbs]

In this quite different method, breadcrumbs cook with the mussels and give a liaison to the sauce. Here you must be sure that the mussels are most carefully washed and soaked so that there will be no sand to mix itself with the crumbs.

For 6 to 8 people

¾ lb. finely chopped onions   A 8- to 10-qt. enamelled pan with
¼ lb. butter   cover

Cook the onions slowly in the butter for about 10 minutes, until they are tender
and translucent but not browned.

¾ pt. light, dry white wine or   8 tbl chopped parsley
    ½ pt. dry white vermouth   ⅛ tsp pepper
4 oz. fine, dry, white breadcrumbs   1 bay leaf
    from home-made type of bread   ¼ tsp thyme

Stir in all the ingredients, cover the pan, and simmer very slowly for 10 minutes,
stirring occasionally, and making sure the mixture does not scorch. Remove
bay leaf.

5 qts. scrubbed, soaked mussels,   6 tbl chopped parsley
    page 204

Add the mussels. Cover and toss them in the pan. Place over high heat, tossing
frequently until the mussel shells swing open. Ladle the mussels and sauce into
soup plates, sprinkle with parsley, and serve.

MOULES AU BEURRE D'ESCARGOT
MOULES À LA PROVENÇALE

[Mussels on the Half Shell, *Gratinéed*]

These are delicious as a first course. Serve them with French bread and a
rather strong, dry, white wine such as Mâcon, Côtes de Provence, white Chianti,
or equivalent.

For 4 to 6 people

48 extra large, scrubbed and
    soaked mussels, page 204

For this recipe you may steam the mussels open as for *moules à la marinière I*,
preceding, or you may open the raw mussels with a knife. We prefer the latter
method. When the mussels are open, discard the empty shell halves. Arrange the
remaining half shells holding the mussels in a shallow baking and serving dish,
or individual fireproof dishes.

6 oz. softened butter	1 to 3 cloves mashed garlic,
A 3-pt. mixing bowl	depending on your love of garlic
A wooden spoon	4 tbl chopped parsley
3 tbl finely chopped shallots or	1½ oz. fine, white, dry breadcrumbs
spring onions	Salt and pepper to taste

Beat the butter in the mixing bowl until it is light and creamy. Beat in the rest of the ingredients and taste for seasoning. Spread a little of the mixture over each mussel.

(*) May be prepared ahead of time to this point. Cover the mussels with grease-proof paper and refrigerate.

About 2 or 3 minutes before serving, place the mussels under a very hot grill until the butter is bubbling in the shells and the crumbs have browned lightly. Serve immediately.

SALADE DE MOULES

[Mussels Marinated in Oil and Herbs]

¾ pt. of cooked, fresh mussels (or
   tinned or bottled mussels)

Steam fresh mussels open as directed in *moules à la marinière I*, page 204. Discard shells.

4 tbl light olive oil or salad oil	3 tbl chopped parsley or a mixture
1 tbl dry white vermouth and 1 dsp	of fresh green herbs
lemon juice	Pinch of pepper
2 tbl finely chopped shallots or	
spring onions	

Toss the mussels in a bowl with the ingredients and allow them to marinate half an hour before serving. They may be served just as they are, or you may drain them and fold into them ¼ pint of mayonnaise, page 77. Place them in a bowl or individual shells.

---

* MOULES EN SAUCE
MOUCLADES
MOULES À LA POULETTE
MOULES À LA BÉARNAISE

[Sauced Mussels Served in Scallop Shells]

This is a more formal recipe for mussels. They are steamed open with wine and flavourings, then a rich, creamy, buttery sauce is made with their cooking liquid This is the same heavily buttered *sauce parisienne* found on page 192, but with a quite different flavour. If the mussels are served on the half shell, as they often are in Brittany, they are called *mouclades*. We have suggested in the following recipe that they be shelled, sauced, and served in scallop shells; done this way they may be prepared ahead of time. There are naturally many versions and flavourings for mussels served in a sauce. For instance, if you omitted the curry, garlic, and fennel in the recipe, and substituted 2 ounces of mushroom stems, your mussel dish would be *à la poulette*. Also, if you omitted the special flavourings, and the cream, egg yolks, and butter enrichment, then stirred ½ pint of *béarnaise* sauce into your *velouté* just before serving, you would have *moules à la béarnaise*.

For 6 people

4 to 5 qts. scrubbed, soaked mussels, page 204. (A 2-hour soaking is advisable here to rid the mussels of as much salt as possible)	**The wine and flavouring for *moules à la marinière I*, page 204, plus:** ¼ tsp curry powder A pinch of fennel 1 clove mashed garlic

Steam the mussels open in wine and flavourings, following the method for *moules à la marinière I*, page 204. Shell the mussels and place them in a bowl. Strain the mussel cooking liquor into an enamelled saucepan and rapidly boil it down over high heat to concentrate its flavour. Taste it frequently as it boils; you may find that if you reduce it too much, the salt content will be overpowering. Measure out ¾ pint of the concentrated liquor to be used in the following sauce:

1½ oz. butter **1½ oz. flour** **A 3-pt. heavy-bottomed enamelled saucepan**	**A wooden spoon**

Stir the butter and flour over low heat in the saucepan until they foam and froth together for 2 minutes without colouring. Remove *roux* from heat.

A wire whisk

Strain the hot mussel cooking liquor into the flour and butter *roux*, being sure not to add any sand that may have collected at the bottom of the mussel pan. Beat *roux* and liquid with a wire whisk to blend thoroughly. Bring to the boil, stirring, for 1 minute. The sauce will be very thick.

2 egg yolks **¼ pt. cream** **A mixing bowl** **A wire whisk**	**A wooden spoon** **Salt and pepper** **Drops of lemon juice**

Blend the egg yolks and cream in the mixing bowl. Gradually beat in the hot sauce, in a thin stream of drops. Pour the sauce back into the pan. Place over moderately high heat and stir with a wooden spoon, reaching all over the bottom of the pan, until the sauce comes to the boil. Boil 1 minute, stirring. Remove from heat and taste carefully for seasoning, stirring in salt, pepper, and drops of lemon juice if necessary. Fold the mussels into the sauce.

(*) If not to be served immediately, clean sauce off sides of pan and film top of sauce with milk. Leave aside uncovered, and reheat to simmering point when ready to use.

2 to 4 oz. softened butter	Parsley sprigs
6 buttered scallop shells or	
porcelain or ovenglass shells of	
¼ pt. capacity	

Just before serving, and away from heat, fold the butter into the hot sauce and mussels a little at a time. Fold until each bit is absorbed before adding the next. Heap the mixture into the shells, decorate with parsley, and serve immediately.

VARIATIONS

Pilaf de Moules

[Sauced Mussels in a Rice Ring]

Prepare and sauce the mussels exactly as in the preceding recipe, but serve them in a ring of *risotto*, page 491.

Soupe aux Moules

[Mussel Soup]

The very same recipe may also be turned into a mussel soup. After enriching the sauce with cream and egg yolks, thin it out to a cream soup consistency with one or two pints of boiling milk. Then add the mussels, and bring just to simmering point. Away from heat, and just before serving, fold in 1 ounce of butter. Decorate with chopped parsley or chervil.

OTHER RECIPES—OTHER SAUCES

Fish Recipes Appearing in Other Chapters

FISH SOUFFLÉS

Fish Timbales, pages 158-9
Fish Quenelles, page 168
Creamed Shellfish, page 184
Shellfish *Quiche*, open-faced tart, page 135
Gratin of Tinned Salmon, or of Fish Leftovers, page 141
Bouillabaisse, page 45
Crab or Lobster in Aspic, pages 506, 511
Salmon Mousse, page 518
Fish and Shellfish Mousse, pages 519, 520

Sauces for Boiled or Baked Fish

Hollandaise and Variations, pages 70 to 76
Mock Hollandaise and Variations, page 57
White Butter Sauce and Lemon Butter Sauce, pages 86 and 88
Brown Butter Sauce, page 88
Sauce Chivry, white-wine herb sauce, page 55
Aïoli, garlic mayonnaise, page 83
Sauce Alsacienne, herbal mayonnaise with soft-boiled eggs, page 84
Sauce Ravigote, vinaigrette with herbs, capers and onions, page 85
Sour Cream Dressing, page 86

Sauces for Sautéed or Grilled Fish

Mustard Sauce, page 58
Brown Butter Sauce, page 88
Many of the Flavoured Butters, pages 89 to 94

Sauces for Cold Fish

Mayonnaise and Variations, pages 77 to 84
Sauce Ravigote, vinaigrette with herbs, capers, and onions, page 85
Sour Cream Dressing, page 86

CHAPTER SIX

POULTRY

Volaille

CHICKEN

Poulet—Poularde

SOME OF THE most glorious dishes of the French *cuisine* have been created for chicken, and almost all the fundamentals of French cookery and sauce-making are to be found somewhere in the chicken realm. The most important aspect of chicken cooking is that you procure a good and flavoursome bird. Modern poultry raising has done wonders in making it possible to grow a fine-looking chicken in record time and to sell it at a most reasonable price, but rarely does anyone in the country discuss flavour. If you are interested in price alone, you will often end up with something that tastes like the stuffing inside a teddy bear and needs strong dousings of herbs, wines, and spices to make it at all palatable. A chicken should taste like chicken and be so good in itself that it is an absolute delight to eat as a perfectly plain, buttery roast, sauté, or grill. So when you buy chicken, make every attempt to find a shop which takes special pride in the quality and flavour of its poultry.

CHICKEN TYPES

Chickens fall into several categories, all of which relate to age. Age dictates the cooking method. A poussin, for instance, may be grilled, or roasted, but its very tender flesh becomes dry and stringy if it is fricasseed. The full-flavoured boiling fowl, on the other hand, must be fricasseed or stewed, as its flesh is too firm to be cooked in any other way.

DEFROSTING FROZEN CHICKEN

The best method for defrosting frozen chicken, according to those in the business, is the slowest: leave it in its transparent wrapper and let it thaw in the

refrigerator. It will lose much less of its juice and flavour. The best alternative
is to unwrap it and thaw it in a basin of cold, running water, removing the
package of giblets from the cavity as soon as it can be pried loose, and pulling
the legs and wings away from the body as soon as they will move.

Sometimes frozen chickens can be quite tough and stringy. Apparently this
is usually the result of their having been frozen while they were too fresh. If the
frozen chicken is flavourless, it may have thawed and been refrozen several
times, so that the juices escaped; or it may be too young a bird to have a
developed flavour.

BRITISH CHICKEN	NEAREST FRENCH EQUIVALENT	WEIGHTS READY TO COOK (AND UNDRAWN)	COOKING METHOD
POUSSIN Baby or squab chicken, available most of the year. About 2 months old	Poussin Coquelet	¾ to 1¼ lbs. (Undrawn: 1 to 1½ lbs.)	Grill, Roast
SMALL SPRING CHICKEN or BROILER Usually obtainable all year, the product of broiler farms. 2 to 3 months old	Petit Poulet	1½ to 2½ lbs. (Undrawn: 1¾ to 3½ lbs.)	Grill, Roast
FRYER or SMALL ROASTER (large spring chicken, cockerel, or pullet). Obtainable all year round. 3 to 5 months old	Poulet de Grain (small) Poulet Reine (larger)	2 to 3 lbs. (Undrawn: 3 to 4 lbs.)	Fry, Sauté, Roast, Casserole Roast, Fricassee, Poach
LARGE ROASTER or FAT FOWL 5½ to 9 months old	Poulet Gras Poularde	4 lbs. and over (Undrawn: 5 lbs. and over)	Roast, Casserole Roast, Poach, Fricassee
CAPON Usually 7 to 10 months old	Chapon	Usually over 4 lbs. (Undrawn: over 5 lbs.)	Roast, Casserole Roast, Poach, Fricassee
BOILING FOWL Over 10 months old	Poule	Over 3½ lbs. (Undrawn: over 4½ lbs.)	If still tender: Stew, Fricassee If tough: Soup stock, Forcemeat, Pâté; Pressure cook

WASHING AND DRYING

If you wash the chicken, though the French do not wash theirs, as they feel
it destroys flavour and hastens spoilage—do so rapidly under cold, running
water. Dry it thoroughly inside and out. It will not brown if it is damp.

Usually chickens have been plucked absolutely clean. If not, pluck and squeeze out feather follicles, then turn the chicken rapidly over a gas or alcohol flame to burn off any hairs or feather bits.

---

* CHICKEN STOCK

A little concentrated chicken stock is easy to make with the giblets and neck of a chicken and will always give more character to your sauce, however simple it may be.

Brown Chicken Stock

For about ½ pint

A 3-pt. heavy-bottomed saucepan
The chicken neck, gizzard, heart,
  and miscellaneous scraps
1 sliced onion

1 sliced carrot
1 tbl rendered fresh pork fat or
  cooking oil

Chop the chicken into pieces of 1½ inches or less. Brown them with the vegetables in hot fat or oil.

¾ pt. white or brown stock, or
  beef bouillon or chicken broth
2 parsley sprigs

⅓ bay leaf
⅛ tsp thyme

Pour out the browning fat. Add the liquid, the herbs, and enough water to cover the chicken by ½ inch. Simmer, partially covered, for 1½ hours or more, skimming as necessary. Strain, degrease, and the stock is ready to use.

White Chicken Stock

Same brown chicken stock, but do not brown the ingredients, and use white stock or tinned chicken broth.

Stuffings may be prepared in advance, but a chicken should never be stuffed until just before it is cooked, as the mixture may sour inside the chicken and spoil the meat.

A whole chicken should be trussed so that the legs, wings, and neck skin are held in place during its cooking, and the bird will make a neat and attractive appearance on the table. The following French method calls for a trussing or mattress needle and white string. There are two ties, one at the tail end to secure the drumsticks, and one at the breast end to fasten the wings and neck skin.

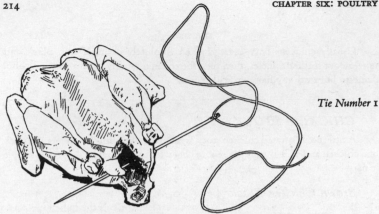

Tie Number 1

Thrust the needle through the lower part of the carcass.

Come back over one drumstick, through the tip of the breastbone, and over the second drumstick. Tie.

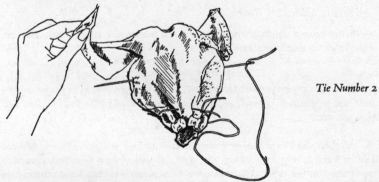

Tie Number 2

Push the needle through the carcass where the second joint and drumstick join, coming out at the corresponding point on the other side.

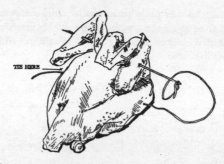

TIE HERE

Turn the chicken on its breast. Fold the wings akimbo. Thread the needle through one wing, catch the neck skin against either side of the backbone, and pull the needle out through the other wing. Draw the string tight and tie.

The chicken is now ready for oven roasting, or spit roasting.

HOW TO TELL WHEN A CHICKEN IS DONE

A boiling chicken is done when its meat is tender if pierced with a fork. Roasting chickens and fryers are tender to begin with and are done when the flesh is cooked through so that the juices, when the meat is pricked deeply with a fork, run clear yellow with no trace of rosy colour. For a whole chicken, the last drops of juice drained from the vent will run clear yellow with no rosy traces. While an underdone chicken is not fit to eat, it is a shame to overcook chicken, allowing the meat to dry out and lose its juice and flavour. However, we have noticed that the French criterion of doneness seems like underdoneness to some British palates. We consider a chicken to be cooked at a meat-thermometer reading of 175 to 180° F., and have based our recipes on these figures.

TIMETABLE FOR WHOLE CHICKENS: Oven Roasting, Casserole Roasting, and Spit Roasting.

This table is based on unchilled, unstuffed chicken. Oven temperature for open-pan roasting is 350° F., Mark 4, for covered roasting, 325° F., Mark 2. Meat-thermometer reading is 175 to 180° F. You will note that larger chickens require less cooking time per pound than smaller chickens. A 4-pound chicken takes an hour and 10 to 20 minutes, while a 7-pound bird requires only 20 to 30 minutes more. Stuffed chicken will take 10 to 30 minutes additional roasting than the total time indicated.

ROASTING TIMETABLE—OVEN TEMPERATURE: 350° F., Mark 4

READY-TO-COOK WEIGHT	UNDRAWN WEIGHT	NUMBER OF PEOPLE SERVED	APPROXIMATE TOTAL COOKING TIME
¾ lb.	1 lb.	1 or 2	30 to 40 minutes
1¼ lbs.	2 lbs.	2	40 to 50 minutes
2 lbs.	3 lbs.	2 or 3	50 to 60 minutes
3 lbs.	4 lbs.	4	1 hour and 10 to 20 minutes
4 lbs.	5 lbs.	4 or 5	1 hour and 15 to 30 minutes
4½ lbs.	6 lbs.	5 or 6	1 hour and 25 to 40 minutes
5¼ lbs.	7 lbs.	6 or 8	1 hour and 30 to 45 minutes

ROAST CHICKEN

* *POULET RÔTI*

[Roast Chicken]

You can always judge the quality of a cook or a restaurant by roast chicken. While it does not require years of training to produce a juicy, brown, buttery, crisp-skinned, heavenly bird, it does entail such a greed for perfection that one is under compulsion to hover over the bird, listen to it, above all see that it is continually basted, and that it is done just to the proper turn. Spit roasting, where the chicken is wrapped in fat and continually rotated, is far less exacting than oven roasting where you must constantly turn and baste.

Small French chickens are frequently roasted without a stuffing. The cavity is seasoned with salt and butter, and the skin rubbed with butter. For oven roasting, it is browned lightly for 10 to 15 minutes at a temperature of 425° F., Mark 7, then the temperature is reduced to 350° F., Mark 4, and the chicken is turned and basted until it is done. A simple, short deglazing sauce is made with stock and the juices in the pan, giving just a bare spoonful for each serving.

VEGETABLE SUGGESTIONS

Grilled tomatoes, buttered French beans or peas, and sautéed, roasted, souffléed, or fried potatoes, or potato *crêpes*, page 481.

One of the potato casseroles on page 482, and green peas or French beans.

Stuffed mushrooms, glazed carrots, and glazed onions.

Ratatouille (aubergine casserole), page 463, and sautéed potatoes.

WINE SUGGESTIONS

A light claret such as Médoc, or a *rosé*.

For 4 people

Estimated roasting time for a 3-pound chicken: 1 hour and 10 to 20 minutes.

Preheat oven to 425° F., Mark 7.

A 3-lb. ready-to-cook roasting or frying chicken	**¼ tsp salt** **1 oz. softened butter**

Sprinkle the inside of the chicken with the salt, and smear in half the butter. Truss the chicken, page 213. Dry it thoroughly, and rub the skin with the rest of the butter.

A shallow roasting tin just large enough to hold the chicken easily **To flavour the sauce: a small sliced carrot and onion**	**For basting: a small saucepan containing 1 oz. melted butter, 1 dsp good cooking oil; a basting brush**

Place the chicken breast up in the roasting tin. Strew the vegetables around it, and place it on a rack in the middle of the preheated oven. Allow the chicken to brown lightly for 15 minutes, turning it on the left side after 5 minutes, on the right side for the last 5 minutes, and basting it with the butter and oil after each turn. Baste rapidly, so that the oven does not cool off.

Reduce oven to 350° F., Mark 4. Leave the chicken on its side, and baste every 8 to 10 minutes, using the fat in the roasting tin when the butter and oil are exhausted. Regulate oven heat so that the chicken is making cooking noises, but fat is not burning.

¼ tsp salt

Halfway through estimated roasting time, salt the chicken and turn it on its other side. Continue basting.

¼ tsp salt

Fifteen minutes before end of estimated roasting time, salt again and turn the chicken breast up. Continue basting.

Indications that the chicken is almost done are: a sudden rain of splutters in the oven, a swelling of the breast and slight puff of the skin, the drumstick is tender when pressed and can be moved in its socket. To check further, prick the thickest part of the drumstick with a fork. Its juices should run clear yellow. As a final check, lift the chicken and drain the juices from its vent. If the last drops are clear yellow, the chicken is definitely done. If not, roast another 5 minutes, and test again.

When done, discard trussing strings and place the chicken on a hot dish. It should stand at room temperature for 5 to 10 minutes before being carved, so that its juices will retreat back into the tissues.

½ tbl chopped shallots or spring onions	Salt and pepper
½ pt. brown chicken stock, chicken broth, or beef bouillon	½ to 1 oz. softened butter

Remove all but one tablespoon of fat from the tin. Stir in the chopped shallots or spring onions and cook slowly for 1 minute. Add the stock and boil rapidly over high heat, scraping up coagulated roasting juices with a wooden spoon and allowing the liquid to reduce to about ¼ pint. Season with salt and pepper. Away from heat and just before serving, swirl in the enrichment butter in pieces until it has been absorbed. Pour a spoonful of the sauce over the chicken, and send the rest to the table in a sauceboat.

(*) AHEAD–OF–TIME NOTE

Roast chicken can wait for 20 to 30 minutes in the turned-off hot oven, the door ajar. It cannot be reheated or it loses its fresh and juicy quality.

Poulet à la Broche

[Spit-roasted Chicken]

Estimated roasting time: same as for oven-roasted chicken, see chart on page 216.

3 to 4 strips of blanched bacon, page 12 (never use plain smoked bacon; it will flavour the whole chicken)

Season and truss the chicken as described in the preceding master recipe. Push the spit through it starting at the breast end. Dry it thoroughly, rub with butter and sprinkle with salt. Secure the strips of blanched bacon over the breast and thighs with white string. Because of the bacon, no basting is necessary until the very end.

If you have a rotisserie, use the moderate heat and roast with the door closed. Remove bacon 15 minutes before the end, and baste with the tin drippings until the chicken is browned and done.

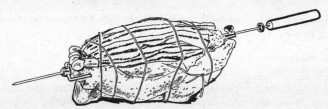

If you have a spit attachment in the oven, use a moderate grill temperature, and place a tin under the chicken to catch the fat and juices. Fifteen minutes before the end, turn up the heat element over the chicken, remove the bacon, continue roasting, basting frequently, until the chicken is browned and done.

Use the same tests as for oven roasting in determining when the chicken is done, and the same method for making the sauce.

Poulet Rôti à la Normande

[Roast Chicken Basted with Cream, Herb and Giblet Stuffing]

In this lush combination, the chicken is roasted as usual, but is basted for the last minutes with cream, which rolls off the buttery, brown chicken skin and combines with the tin and stuffing juices.

VEGETABLE SUGGESTIONS

Serve sautéed mushrooms and sautéed potatoes, or green peas and braised onions.

WINE SUGGESTIONS

A chilled white Burgundy or Graves, or a claret such as Médoc would be appropriate.

For 4 or 5 people

Herb and giblet stuffing

The chicken gizzard, peeled and chopped	**The chicken heart, chopped**
½ oz. butter	1 to 4 chopped chicken livers
⅛ tsp oil	1 tbl chopped shallots or spring onions
A small frying pan	

Sauté the gizzard in hot butter and oil for 2 minutes. Then stir in the heart, liver, and shallots or spring onions. Sauté for 2 minutes more, or until the liver has stiffened but is still rosy inside. Scrape into a mixing bowl.

1 oz. coarse dry crumbs from home-made type of white bread	2 tbl chopped parsley
2 tbl cream cheese	⅛ tsp tarragon or thyme
½ oz. softened butter	⅛ tsp salt
	Pinch of pepper

Blend in the rest of the ingredients and taste carefully for seasoning. Allow the stuffing to cool.

A 3-lb. ready-to-cook roasting or frying chicken	¼ tsp salt
	½ oz. butter

Sprinkle salt inside the chicken, and loosely fill with the stuffing. Sew or skewer the vent. Truss and dry the chicken, and rub its skin with butter.

Roasting the chicken

½ pt. cream

Roast it either in the oven, page 216, or on a spit, page 218. About 10 minutes before the end of the estimated roasting time, remove all but 1 spoonful of fat from the roasting-tin. Start basting with 2 or 3 tablespoons of cream every 3 to 4 minutes until the chicken is done. The cream will probably look curdled in the tin, but this will be corrected later.

¼ tsp salt

Remove the chicken to a hot dish and sprinkle with salt.

The sauce

2 tbl strong brown chicken stock or canned beef bouillon

Add the stock or bouillon to the cream in the roasting tin and boil rapidly for 2 to 3 minutes, scraping up coagulated chicken roasting juices.

2 to 3 tbl cream	Drops of lemon juice
Salt and pepper	

Just before serving, remove from heat and stir in additional cream by spoonfuls to smooth out the sauce. Correct seasoning, and add drops of lemon juice to taste.

Spoon a bit of sauce over the chicken and send the rest to the table in a warmed sauceboat.

Poulet au Porto

[Roast Chicken Steeped with Port Wine, Cream, and Mushrooms]

Chicken, cream, and mushrooms occur again and again, as it is one of the great combinations. This perfectly delicious recipe is not difficult, but it cannot be prepared ahead of time or the chicken will lose its fresh and juicy quality. The chicken is roasted, then carved, flamed in cognac, and allowed to steep for several minutes with cream, mushrooms, and port wine. It is the kind of dish to do when you are entertaining a few good, food-loving friends whom you can receive in your kitchen.

VEGETABLE SUGGESTIONS

Nothing should interfere with these special flavours. It would be best to serve only potatoes sautéed in butter, page 486, or a perfectly seasoned *risotto*, page 491. Peas, or asparagus tips, or braised onions, page 442, could be added if you feel the necessity for more vegetables.

WINE SUGGESTIONS

Serve very good, chilled, white Burgundy such as a Meursault or Montrachet, or an excellent château-bottled white Graves.

For 4 people

A 3-lb. ready-to-cook, roasting or
**   frying chicken**

Roast the chicken as described in the master recipe on page 216. Be sure not to overcook it.

1 lb. fresh mushrooms

Meanwhile, trim and wash the mushrooms. Quarter them if large, leave them whole if small.

A 3-pt. enamelled or stainless steel $\frac{1}{4}$ **oz. butter**
**   saucepan** $\frac{1}{2}$ **tsp lemon juice**
$\frac{1}{8}$ **pt. water** $\frac{1}{4}$ **tsp salt**

Bring the water to the boil in the saucepan with the butter, lemon, and salt. Toss in the mushrooms, cover, and boil slowly for 8 minutes. Pour out the cooking liquid and reserve.

$\frac{1}{2}$ **pt. cream**   **Salt and pepper**
$\frac{1}{4}$ **oz. cornflour blended with 1 tbl**
**   of the cream**

Pour the cream and the cornflour mixture into the mushrooms. Simmer for 2 minutes. Correct seasoning, and leave aside.

When the chicken is done, remove it to a carving board and let it rest at room temperature while completing the sauce.

½ tbl chopped shallots or spring onions	The mushrooms in cream
⅛ pt. medium-dry port	Salt and pepper
The mushroom cooking liquid	Drops of lemon juice

Remove all but 1 tablespoon of fat from the roasting tin. Stir in the shallots or spring onions and cook slowly for 1 minute. Add the port and the mushroom juice, and boil down rapidly, scraping up coagulated roasting juices, until liquid has reduced to about ⅛ pint. Add the mushrooms and cream and simmer for 2 to 3 minutes, allowing the liquid to thicken slightly. Correct seasoning and add lemon juice to taste.

A fireproof casserole or a chafing dish	½ oz. butter
	⅛ tsp salt

Smear the inside of the casserole or chafing dish with butter. Rapidly carve the chicken into serving pieces. Sprinkle lightly with salt, and arrange in the casserole or chafing dish.

⅛ pt. cognac

Place over moderate heat or an alcohol flame until you hear the chicken begin to sizzle. Then pour the cognac over it. Avert your face, and ignite the cognac with a lighted match. Shake the casserole slowly until the flames have subsided. Then pour in the mushroom mixture, tilting the casserole and basting the chicken. Cover and steep for 5 minutes without allowing the sauce to boil. Serve.

(*) Chicken may remain in its casserole over barely simmering water or in the turned-off hot oven with door ajar, for 10 to 15 minutes, but the sooner it is served, the better it will be.

Coquelets sur Canapés

[Small Roast Chickens with Chicken Liver Canapés and Mushrooms]

Also for: pigeons, partridge, quail, dove

This is one of the classic French recipes for serving small roast birds. The livers are chopped, seasoned, and spread over sautéed bread rectangles; just before serving, these are placed under the grill. Then the roast birds are placed on them, and the dish is garnished with a wine-flavoured deglazing sauce and sautéed mushrooms.

VEGETABLE SUGGESTIONS

Only sautéed, matchstick, or souffléed potatoes, or home-made potato chips are suggested.

WINE SUGGESTIONS

Serve a claret such as Médoc for chicken, or pigeon; claret, such as St. Émilion, or red Burgundy for game.

For 6 people, 1 bird apiece

A Note on the Order of Battle: Although the mushrooms and canapés may be prepared while the birds are roasting, it seems best to do them ahead and relieve pressure, for the roast birds should be served almost as soon as they are done.

The mushrooms

1½ lbs. fresh mushrooms	1 tbl oil
1 oz. butter	A 10- to 12-in. enamelled frying pan

Trim and wash the mushrooms. Leave whole if small, quarter if large. Dry on a cloth. Sauté for 5 to 6 minutes in hot butter and oil until they are very lightly browned.

1 tbl chopped shallots or spring onions	½ clove mashed garlic

Stir in the shallots or spring onions, and garlic, and cook over moderate heat for 2 minutes. Leave aside.

The canapés

Home-made type of white bread

Cut 6 slices of bread ¼ inch thick. Remove crusts, and cut slices into rectangles 2 by 3½ inches.

4 oz. clarified butter, page 12	A frying pan

Sauté the bread lightly on each side in hot clarified butter.

6 poultry or game livers from the birds	¼ tsp salt
2 tbl fresh, raw pork fat; Or: fat bacon simmered in water for 10 minutes, rinsed, and dried	Big pinch of pepper
	1 tbl Madeira, port, or cognac
	Optional: 2 to 3 tbl *foie gras*

Trim the livers, cutting off any black or green spots. Chop very fine, almost into a purée, with the pork fat or bacon. Then blend the liver in a bowl with the seasonings, wine, and optional *foie gras*. Spread the mixture on one side of each rectangle of sautéed bread. Arrange on a grill pan and place aside. (Preheat grill in time to cook the canapés just before serving.)

Roasting the birds

Preheat oven to 400° F., Mark 6.

Six 10- to 12-oz. ready-to-cook
 small roast chickens, pigeons,
 or game birds
1 dsp salt
2 tbl finely chopped shallots or
 spring onions

½ tsp dried tarragon
2 oz. butter
6 strips of bacon simmered in water
 for 10 minutes, rinsed, and dried

Season the cavities of the birds with a sprinkling of salt, shallots or spring onions, and tarragon, and 1 teaspoon of butter. Truss the birds, dry them, and rub with butter. Cut the blanched bacon in half, crosswise, and tie 2 strips over the breast and thighs of each bird.

A shallow roasting tin just large
 enough to hold the birds easily on
 their sides

1½ oz. butter melted with ½ tbl good
 cooking oil
A basting brush

Place the birds in the roasting tin and place on a rack in the middle of the preheated oven. Baste and turn the birds every 5 to 7 minutes until they are done:

CHICKENS will take from 30 to 40 minutes; they are done when the last drops of juice from their vents run clear yellow with no trace of rose.

PARTRIDGE and QUAIL, if young and tender, may be judged like chicken; if older, like game hens.

PIGEON and DOVE may be served slightly underdone if you wish, when their juices run a very pale rose rather than a clear yellow.

1 tsp salt

When done, remove trussing strings, sprinkle the birds with salt, and place them on a warm dish. Place in turned-off oven, the door ajar.

The sauce

1 tbl chopped shallots or spring
 onions
½ pt. brown chicken stock, brown
 stock, or beef bouillon

⅛ pt. Madeira or port
½ to 1 oz. softened butter

Remove all but 1 tablespoon of fat from the roasting pan. Stir in the shallots or spring onions and cook slowly for 1 minute. Add the stock or bouillon and wine and boil rapidly, scraping up coagulated cooking juices until liquid has reduced to about ¼ pint. Correct seasoning. Remove from heat and just before serving, swirl the butter into the sauce.

Final assembly

Just before serving, place the liver canapés under a hot grill for a minute, until they are sizzling.

½ oz. butter   **Pinch of pepper**
¼ tsp salt

Toss the mushrooms over moderately high heat with the butter, salt, and pepper.

A handful of watercress leaves
or parsley sprigs

Place a canapé under each bird. Surround with the mushrooms, and decorate with watercress or parsley. Spoon the sauce over the birds, and serve.

CASSEROLE-ROASTED CHICKEN

* *POULET POÊLÉ À L'ESTRAGON*

[Casserole-roasted Chicken with Tarragon]

For: roasters and large fryers

When a chicken is cooked this way, it is trussed, browned in butter and oil, then left to roast in a covered casserole with herbs and seasonings. It is a very good method, as the buttery, aromatic steam in the casserole gives the chicken great tenderness and flavour. While oven cooking is more even, the top of the stove may be used if your casserole is heavy; then the chicken must be turned and basted frequently, and the cooking will be a little longer than for oven cooking.

VEGETABLE AND WINE SUGGESTIONS

They are the same as for a roast chicken, page 216.

For 4 people

Estimated roasting time: 1 hour and 10 to 20 minutes for a 3-lb. bird. See chart on page 216 for other sizes.

Preheat oven to 325° F., Mark 2.

A 3-lb. ready-to-cook roasting   **1 oz. butter**
  chicken   **3 or 4 sprigs of fresh tarragon or**
¼ tsp salt   **¼ tsp of dried tarragon**
Pinch of pepper

Season the cavity of the chicken with salt, pepper, and ½ ounce of the butter. Insert the tarragon leaves, or sprinkle in dried tarragon. Truss the chicken, page 213. Dry it thoroughly and rub the skin with the rest of the butter.

H

| A heavy fireproof casserole just large enough to hold the chicken on its back and on its side | 1 oz. butter ½ tbl oil, more if needed |

Place the casserole over moderately high heat with the butter and oil. When the butter foam has begun to subside, lay in the chicken, breast down. Brown for 2 to 3 minutes, regulating heat so that butter is always very hot but not burning. Turn the chicken on another side, using 2 wooden spoons or a cloth. Be sure not to break the chicken skin. Continue browning and turning the chicken until it is a nice golden colour almost all over, particularly on the breast and legs. This will take 10 to 15 minutes. Add more oil if necessary to keep the bottom of the casserole filmed.

1½ oz. butter, if necessary

Remove the chicken. Pour out the browning fat if it has burned, and add fresh butter.

| 1 medium sliced onion 1 small sliced carrot ¼ tsp salt | 3 or 4 sprigs of fresh tarragon or ½ tsp dried tarragon |

Cook the carrots and onions slowly in the casserole for 5 minutes without browning. Add the salt and tarragon.

| ¼ tsp salt A bulb baster Aluminium foil | A tight-fitting cover for the casserole |

Salt the chicken. Set it breast up over the vegetables and baste it with the butter in the casserole. Lay a piece of aluminium foil over the chicken, cover the casserole, and reheat it on top of the stove until you hear the chicken sizzling. Then place the casserole on a rack in the middle of the preheated oven.

Roast for 1 hour and 10 to 20 minutes, regulating heat so that chicken is always making quiet cooking noises. Baste once or twice with the butter and juices in the casserole. The chicken is done when its drumsticks move in their sockets, and when the last drops of juice drained from its vent run clear yellow.

Remove the chicken to a serving dish and discard trussing strings.

Brown tarragon sauce

| ¾ pt. brown stock or beef bouillon and tinned chicken broth combined to make ¾ pt. ½ oz. cornflour blended with 1 tbl Madeira or port | 2 tbl fresh chopped tarragon or parsley ½ oz. softened butter |

Add the stock or bouillon and broth to the casserole and simmer for 2 minutes, scraping up coagulated roasting juices. Then skim off all but a tablespoon of fat. Blend in the cornflour mixture, simmer a minute, then raise heat and boil rapidly until sauce is lightly thickened. Taste carefully for seasoning, adding more tarragon if you feel it necessary. Strain into a warmed sauceboat. Stir in the herbs and the enrichment butter.

To serve

Optional but attractive: 10 to 12 fresh tarragon leaves blanched for 30 seconds in boiling water then   **rinsed in cold water, and dried on absorbent paper**

Pour a spoonful of sauce over the chicken, and decorate the breast and legs with optional tarragon leaves. Dish may be garnished with sprigs of fresh parsley or— if you are serving them—sautéed potatoes and grilled tomatoes.

(*) AHEAD–OF–TIME NOTE

If the chicken is not to be served for about half an hour, make the sauce except for its butter enrichment, and strain it into a saucepan. Return the chicken to the casserole. Place aluminium foil over it and set the cover askew. Keep the casserole warm over almost simmering water, or in the turned-off hot oven, the door ajar. Reheat and butter the sauce just before serving.

OPTIONAL:

Farce Duxelles

[Mushroom Stuffing]

A chicken will need 10 to 15 minutes more cooking if you fill it with this stuffing.

For a 3-lb. chicken

¾ lb. finely chopped fresh mushrooms
½ oz. butter
1 dsp oil

1 tbl chopped shallots or spring onions
A 10-in. frying pan

A handful at a time, twist the mushrooms into a ball in the corner of a cloth to extract their juice. Sauté them in hot butter and oil with the shallots or spring onions for 5 to 8 minutes, until the pieces begin to separate from each other. Place them in a mixing bowl.

The chicken gizzard, peeled and   ½ oz. butter
   chopped   A small frying pan
The chopped chicken liver

Sauté the gizzard for 2 minutes in hot butter. Add the liver and sauté 2 minutes more. Add to the mixing bowl.

⅛ pt. Madeira or port

Pour the wine into the mushroom-cooking pan and boil down rapidly until reduced to a spoonful. Scrape into the mixing bowl.

1 oz. dry, white crumbs from   2 tbl chopped parsley
   home-made type of bread   ¼ tsp salt
2 tbl cream cheese   Big pinch of pepper
½ oz. softened butter
½ tsp chopped fresh or dried
   tarragon

Blend the rest of the ingredients into the mixing bowl and season carefully to taste. Let the stuffing cool. Pack it loosely into the chicken. Sew or skewer the vent and truss the chicken. Then brown and roast it as described in the preceding master recipe.

VARIATION

Poulet en Cocotte Bonne Femme

[Casserole-roasted Chicken with Bacon, Onions, and Potatoes]

    This is an all-in-one dish where bacon and vegetables are cooked with the chicken and each item takes on a little flavour from its neighbours. No other vegetables are needed to make up a main course, but you may wish to serve grilled tomatoes along with it for colour.

A ¼-lb. chunk of bacon   ½ oz. butter
A fireproof casserole for cooking
   the chicken

Remove the rind and cut the bacon into *lardons* (rectangular strips ½ inch wide and 1½ inches long). Simmer for 10 minutes in 3 pints of water. Rinse in cold water, and dry. In the casserole, sauté the bacon for 2 to 3 minutes in butter until very lightly browned. Remove to a side dish, leaving the fat in the casserole.

A 3-lb. ready-to-cook roasting
   chicken, trussed and buttered

Brown the chicken in the hot fat, as described in the master recipe on page 225. Remove it to a side dish and pour the fat out of the casserole.

Preheat oven to 325° F., Mark 2.

**15 to 25 peeled onions about 1 inch
in diameter**

Drop the onions in boiling, salted water and boil slowly for 5 minutes. Drain and leave aside.

**1 to 1½ lbs. boiling potatoes or small
new potatoes**

Peel the potatoes and trim them into uniform ovals about 2 inches long and 1 inch in diameter. Cover with cold water, and bring to the boil. Drain immediately.

1½ oz. butter
¼ tsp salt
**A medium herb bouquet: 4 parsley
sprigs, ½ bay leaf, and ¼ tsp thyme
tied in washed cheesecloth**

A bulb baster
Aluminium foil
**A tight-fitting cover for the
casserole**

Heat the butter in the casserole until it is foaming. Add the drained potatoes and roll them around over moderate heat for 2 minutes to evaporate their moisture; this will prevent their sticking to the casserole. Spread them aside, salt the chicken, and place it breast up in the casserole. Place the bacon and onions over the potatoes, and the herb bouquet. Baste all ingredients with the butter in the casserole, lay the aluminium foil over the chicken, and cover the casserole.

Heat the casserole on top of the stove until the contents are sizzling, then place in the middle of the preheated oven and roast for 1 hour and 10 to 20 minutes or until the chicken is done, page 215. Baste once or twice with the butter and juices in the casserole. No sauce is necessary.

SAUTÉED CHICKEN

* *POULET SAUTÉ*

[Sautéed Chicken]

For: frying chickens

In a true sauté the cut-up chicken is cooked entirely in butter, or butter and oil, with seasonings. No liquid comes in contact with it until the very end. It is a quick and delicious way to cook chicken, but should be served as soon as possible after it is done or it loses the fresh and juicy characteristics of a sauté. The fricassees, however, as they cook in a sauce, take well to reheating.

A NOTE ON DISJOINTING THE CHICKEN

French chicken is disjointed so that each wing includes a strip from the lower part of the breast. The breast minus ribs is cut in two, crosswise. The drumsticks are separated from the second joints. This makes 8 good serving pieces, plus the back cut in two, crosswise, if you wish to include it.

Chicken in Great Britain is usually disjointed into 2 drumsticks, 2 second joints, the 2 halves of the breast, and the 2 wings with no breast meat attached. So that the breasts will cook evenly, slip a knife under the ribs and remove them. Each breast half may be chopped in two, crosswise, if you wish.

WINE AND VEGETABLE SUGGESTIONS

These are the same as for roast chicken, page 216.

For 4 to 6 people

Total cooking time: 30 to 35 minutes.

Browning the chicken (8 to 10 minutes)

2½ to 3 lbs. of cut-up frying chicken

Dry each piece of chicken thoroughly. It will not brown if it is damp.

A heavy, 10-in. casserole, frying pan, or electric frying pan	**necessary to keep bottom of pan filmed with fat**
1 oz. butter and 1 dsp oil, more if	**Tongs for turning the chicken**

Place the casserole or frying pan over moderately high heat with the butter and oil (360° F. for an electric frying pan). When you see that the butter foam has almost subsided, add as many chicken pieces, skin-side down, as will fit easily in one layer. In 2 to 3 minutes, when the chicken has browned to a nice golden colour on one side, turn it to brown on another side. Regulate heat so that fat is always very hot but not burning. Remove browned pieces as they are done and add fresh ones until all pieces have browned.

Finishing the cooking (20 to 25 minutes)

Salt and pepper	**tarragon, or tarragon only; or**
Optional: 1 to 2 tsp fresh green herbs: thyme, basil, and	**1 tsp dried herbs**
	1 to 1½ oz. butter, if necessary

Season the dark meat with salt, pepper, and optional herbs. (The wings and breasts are done later, as they cook faster.) If the browning fat has burned, pour it out of the casserole and add the fresh butter. Place over moderate heat (300° F. for an electric frying pan). Add the dark meats, cover the casserole, and cook slowly for 8 to 9 minutes.

Salt and pepper   **A bulb baster**

Season the white meat, add it to the dark meat, and baste the chicken with the butter in the casserole. Cover and continue cooking for about 15 minutes, turning and basting the chicken 2 or 3 times.

The meat is done when the fattest part of the drumsticks is tender if pinched and the chicken juices run clear yellow when the meat is pricked deeply with a fork.

Remove the chicken to a hot serving dish. Cover and keep warm for 2 to 3 minutes while finishing the sauce.

Brown deglazing sauce

1 tbl chopped shallots or spring onions

Optional: $\frac{1}{4}$ pt. dry white wine or $\frac{1}{8}$ pt. dry white vermouth

$\frac{1}{4}$ to $\frac{1}{2}$ pt. brown chicken stock, beef bouillon, or tinned chicken broth

$\frac{1}{2}$ to 1 oz. softened butter

Optional: 1 to 2 tbl chopped parsley or fresh green herbs

Remove all but about 2 tablespoons of fat from the casserole. Add the shallots or spring onions and cook slowly for 1 minute. Pour in the optional wine, and the stock. Raise heat and boil rapidly, scraping up coagulated sauté juices and reducing liquid to about $\frac{1}{8}$ pint. Correct seasoning. Remove from heat and just before serving, swirl in the enrichment butter and optional herbs.

Arrange around the dish whatever vegetables you have chosen. Pour the sauce over the chicken and serve.

(*) FOR A WAIT UP TO HALF AN HOUR

Finish the sauce except for its final buttering. Arrange the cooked chicken in an enamelled, glazed, ovenglass, or stainless steel casserole and baste it with the sauce. Cover loosely and place over barely simmering water. Just before serving, and away from heat, tip casserole, add enrichment butter, and baste the chicken with the sauce.

(*) PARTIAL COOKING IN ADVANCE

The chicken may be browned, the dark meat cooked for 8 to 9 minutes, and the white meat added and cooked for 5 minutes more. Then leave the casserole aside, uncovered. About 10 to 15 minutes before serving time, cover and finish the cooking on top of the stove; or heat the casserole and set it in a preheated 350° F., Mark 4 oven for 15 to 20 minutes.

OTHER SAUCES

Poulet Sauté à la Crème

[Deglazing Sauce with Cream]

1 tbl chopped shallots or spring onions	½ pt. cream
¼ pt. dry white wine or ⅛ pt. dry white vermouth	

Sauté the chicken as described in the preceding recipe and place it on a hot dish. Remove all but 1 tablespoon of fat from the casserole. Stir in the shallots or spring onions and cook slowly for 1 minute. Then add the wine and boil it rapidly down to about 2 tablespoons, scraping up coagulated cooking juices. Add the cream and boil it down until it has thickened slightly.

½ to 1 oz. softened butter
Optional: 1 to 2 tbl chopped
    parsley or mixed green herbs

Correct seasoning. Remove from heat and just before serving, swirl in the butter and optional herbs.

Pour the sauce over the chicken.

Poulet Sauté Chasseur

[Tomato and Mushroom Sauce]

Use the same technique as for the veal scallops on page 338, *escalopes de veau chasseur*

VARIATION

Poulet Sauté aux Herbes de Provence

[Chicken Sautéed with Herbs and Garlic, Egg Yolk and Butter Sauce]

Basil, thyme or savoury, a pinch of fennel, and a bit of garlic give this sauté a fine Provençal flavour that is even more pronounced if your herbs are fresh. The sauce is a type of hollandaise, as the herbal, buttery pan juices are beaten into egg yolks to make a thick and creamy liaison. Serve this dish with potatoes sautéed in butter or potato *crêpes*, pages 486 or 481, grilled tomatoes and a chilled *rosé* wine.

For 4 to 6 people

A heavy, 10-in. fireproof casserole, frying pan, or electric frying pan set at 300° F.	1 tsp thyme or savoury
	1 tsp basil
¼ lb. butter	¼ tsp ground fennel
2½ to 3 lbs. of cut-up frying chicken dried in a cloth	Salt and pepper
	3 cloves unpeeled garlic

Heat the butter until it is foaming, then turn the chicken pieces in it for 7 to 8 minutes, not letting them colour more than a deep yellow. Remove the white meat. Season the dark meat with herbs, salt, and pepper, and add the garlic to the casserole. Cover and cook slowly for 8 to 9 minutes. Season the white meat and add it to the casserole, basting the chicken with the butter. Cook for about 15 minutes, turning and basting 2 or 3 times, until the chicken is tender and its juices run pale yellow when the meat is pricked with a fork.

When the chicken is done, remove it to a hot dish, cover, and keep warm.

¼ pt. dry white wine or ⅛ pt. dry white vermouth

Mash the garlic cloves in the casserole with a spoon, then remove the garlic peel. Add the wine and boil it down over high heat, scraping up coagulated sauté juices until the wine has been reduced by half.

2 egg yolks	A small enamelled saucepan
1 tbl lemon juice	A wire whisk
1 tbl dry white wine or white vermouth	

Beat the egg yolks in the saucepan until they are thick and sticky. Beat in the lemon juice and wine. Then beat in the casserole liquid, a half-teaspoon at a time, to make a thick creamy sauce like a hollandaise.

Optional: 1 to 1½ oz. softened butter	2 tbl fresh chopped basil, fresh fennel tops, or parsley

Beat the sauce over very low heat for 4 to 5 seconds to warm and thicken it. Remove from heat and beat in more butter a tablespoonful at a time if you wish. Beat in the herbs, and correct seasoning. Spoon the sauce over the chicken, and serve.

CHICKEN FRICASSEE

For: fryers, roasters, and young boiling chicken

One frequently runs into chicken recipes labelled sautés which are actually fricassees, and others labelled fricassees which are actually stews. The fricassee

H*

is halfway between the two. No liquid is included in the cooking of a sauté. For a stew, the chicken is simmered in liquid from the start of its cooking. When chicken is fricasseed, the meat is always cooked first in butter—or butter and oil—until its flesh has swelled and stiffened, then the liquid is added. There is a subtle but definite difference in taste between the three methods. Fricassees can be white, like the following recipe, or brown, like the *coq au vin* on page 239. It is an ideal technique for ahead-of-time dishes, as the chicken loses none of its essential qualities if it is allowed to cool in its sauce and is then reheated.

TYPE OF CHICKEN TO USE

The following recipes are all based on frying chicken. Younger chickens, such as poussins, should never be used; their flesh is so soft and tender that it dries out and becomes stringy. Older chickens need longer cooking than the 25 to 30 minutes of simmering required for a fryer.

Roasting chicken. 35 to 45 minutes of simmering.

Young boiling chicken. 1½ hours or more of simmering, or until the flesh is tender when pricked with a fork.

---

* FRICASSÉE DE POULET À L'ANCIENNE*

[Old-fashioned Chicken Fricassee with Wine-flavoured Cream Sauce, Onions, and Mushrooms]

For this traditional Sunday dinner dish, which is not difficult to execute, the chicken pieces are turned in hot butter, sprinkled with flour and seasonings, then simmered in wine and white stock. The sauce is a reduction of the cooking liquid, enriched with cream and egg yolks. Braised onions and mushrooms accompany the chicken. Include also steamed rice or *risotto*, pages 488 or 491, or buttered noodles. If you want other vegetables, buttered peas or asparagus tips may serve as a garnish.

WINE SUGGESTIONS

Serve a chilled, fairly full-bodied white Burgundy, Côtes du Rhône, or Graves.

For 4 to 6 people

Preliminary cooking in butter

2½ to 3 lbs. of cut-up frying chicken

Dry the chicken thoroughly in a cloth.

A heavy, 10-in. fireproof casserole   **2 oz. butter**
  or electric frying pan
1 thinly sliced onion, carrot, and
  celery stalk

Cook the vegetables slowly in the butter for about 5 minutes, or until they are almost tender but not browned (260° F. for an electric frying pan). Push them to one side. Raise heat slightly (290° F.), and add the chicken. Turn it every minute for 3 or 4 minutes until the meat has stiffened slightly, without colouring to more than a light golden yellow.

Lower heat (260° F. for an electric frying pan), cover, and cook very slowly for 10 minutes, turning the chicken once. It should swell slightly, stiffen more, but not deepen in colour.

Adding the flour

½ tsp salt   **2 oz. flour**
⅛ tsp white pepper

Sprinkle salt, pepper, and flour on all sides of the chicken, turning and rolling each piece to coat the flour with the cooking butter. Cover and continue cooking slowly for 4 minutes, turning it once.

Simmering in stock and wine

1¼ pts. boiling white chicken stock,   **A small herb bouquet: 2 parsley**
  white stock, or chicken bouillon   **sprigs, ⅓ bay leaf and ⅛ tsp thyme**
½ pt. dry white wine or ¼ pt. dry   **tied in washed cheesecloth**
  white vermouth

Remove from heat and pour in the boiling liquid, shaking casserole to blend the liquid and flour. Add the wine, the herb bouquet, and more stock, or water, so that the liquid just covers the chicken. Bring to simmering point. Taste for seasoning, and salt lightly if necessary.

Cover and maintain at a slow simmer for 25 to 30 minutes (180 to 190° F. for an electric frying pan). The chicken is done when the drumsticks are tender if pinched and the chicken juices run clear yellow when the meat is pricked with a fork. When done, remove the chicken to a side dish.

Onion and mushroom garniture

16 to 20 braised onions, page 442   **butter, lemon juice, and water,**
½ lb. fresh mushrooms stewed in   **page 471**

While the chicken is cooking, prepare the onions and mushrooms. Add their cooking juices to the chicken cooking sauce in the next step.

The sauce

Simmer the cooking liquid in the casserole for 2 to 3 minutes, skimming off fat. Then raise heat and boil rapidly, stirring frequently, until the sauce reduces and thickens enough to coat a spoon well. Correct seasoning. You should have ¾ pint.

| 2 egg yolks | A 3-pt. mixing bowl |
| ¼ pt. cream | A wire whisk |

Blend the egg yolks and cream in the mixing bowl with a wire whisk. Continue beating, and add the hot sauce by small tablespoonfuls until about ½ pint has been added. Beat in the rest of the sauce in a thin stream.

A wooden spoon

Pour the sauce back into the casserole, or into an enamelled or stainless steel saucepan (do not use aluminium). Set over moderately high heat and, stirring constantly, reach all over the bottom and sides of the casserole, until the sauce comes to the boil. Boil for 1 minute, stirring.

| **Salt and white pepper** | **Pinch of nutmeg** |
| **Drops of lemon juice** | |

Correct seasoning, adding drops of lemon juice to taste, and a pinch of nutmeg. Strain the sauce through a fine sieve.

Final assembly

A clean casserole

Arrange the chicken, and the onion and mushroom garniture, in the casserole. Pour the sauce over it.

(*) Except for reheating, and the final buttering of the sauce, the dish is now ready and can wait indefinitely. To prevent a skin from forming over the sauce, spoon over it a film of cream, stock, or milk. Leave aside uncovered.

Reheating and serving

Place casserole over moderate heat and bring to simmering point. Cover and simmer very slowly for 5 minutes, or until the chicken is hot through, basting it frequently with the sauce.

½ to 1 oz. softened butter

Remove from heat and just before serving, tilt casserole, add enrichment butter, and baste the chicken with the sauce until the butter has absorbed into it.

Sprigs of fresh parsley

Serve the chicken from the casserole; or arrange it with the onions and mush-rooms on a hot dish, surrounded with rice or noodles, and covered with the sauce. Decorate with sprigs of fresh parsley.

VARIATIONS: SAUCES

Using the preceding recipe, you may vary the sauce in a number of ways. The egg yolk liaison at the end may be omitted and a cream sauce substituted; just reduce the cooking liquid until it is quite thick, then simmer it slowly while thinning it out with spoonfuls of cream until it is the consistency you wish it to be. Here are some other ideas:

VARIATIONS

Fricassée de Poulet à l'Indienne

[Curry Sauce]

½ to 1 oz. fragrant curry powder

After the chicken has had its preliminary turning of 5 minutes in butter, blend in the curry powder. Cover, and proceed with the 10-minute cooking period. Then continue with the recipe.

Fricassée de Poulet au Paprika

[Paprika Sauce]

1 tbl fresh-smelling and fragrant paprika

After the chicken has had its preliminary turning of 5 minutes in butter, blend in the paprika. Cover, and proceed with the 10-minute cooking period. Then continue with the recipe.

1 tsp more paprika, if necessary

After completing the sauce, stir in more paprika if the sauce needs colour. It should be a creamy pink.

Fricassée de Poulet à l'Estragon

[Tarragon Sauce]

4 or 5 sprigs fresh tarragon or 2 tsp dried tarragon

Add the tarragon to the wine and stock for the simmering of the chicken.

2 tbl fresh chopped tarragon or
  parsley

Stir fresh tarragon or parsley into the finished sauce.

FONDUE DE POULET À LA CRÈME

[Chicken Simmered with Cream and Onions]

In this rich and delectable dish, the chicken is cooked in butter and onions, then simmered with wine and cream. Serve it with steamed rice or *risotto*, page 491, buttered green peas or baked cucumbers, page 459, and a fairly full-bodied white Burgundy or Graves.

For 4 to 6 people

2½ to 3 lbs. of cut-up frying chicken   A heavy, 10-in. fireproof casserole
1½ oz. butter

Dry the chicken thoroughly. Turn it in hot butter for 4 to 5 minutes, until the meat has stiffened slightly but has not browned. Remove it to a side dish.

½ lb. thinly sliced onions

Stir the onions into the butter in the pan. Cover and cook very slowly for 5 minutes, or until the onions are fairly tender but not browned.

Return the chicken to the casserole, cover and cook slowly for 10 minutes until it swells slightly and stiffens, but does not brown. Turn it once during this period.

½ tsp salt   ⅛ pt. cognac, Calvados, Madeira,
⅛ tsp white pepper   or port; or ¼ pt. dry white wine
¼ tsp curry powder   or ⅛ pt. dry white vermouth

Season the chicken with salt, pepper, and curry powder. Pour in the spirits or wine, raise heat, and boil rapidly until the liquid has almost entirely evaporated.

1¼ pts. cream brought to the boil
   in a small saucepan

Pour on the hot cream, bring to simmering point, baste the chicken, and cover the casserole. Maintain at the barest simmer for 30 to 35 minutes, or until the chicken is tender and its juices run a clear yellow when the meat is pricked with a fork. The cream may look slightly curdled, but will be smoothed out later.

Remove the chicken to a hot dish, cover, and keep warm for 5 minutes while finishing the sauce.

Salt and white pepper   **2 to 3 tbl cream**
Drops of lemon juice

Skim fat off the sauce, then boil it rapidly, stirring, until it reduces enough to coat the spoon lightly. Correct seasoning, adding lemon juice to taste. Away from heat, beat in additional cream by spoonfuls to smooth out the sauce.

Sprigs of fresh parsley

Pour the sauce over the chicken, decorate with parsley, and serve.

COQ AU VIN

[Chicken in Red Wine with Onions, Mushrooms, and Bacon]

This popular dish may be called *coq au Chambertin, coq au riesling,* or *coq au* whatever wine you use for its cooking. It is made with either white or red wine but the red is more characteristic. In France it is usually accompanied only by parsley potatoes; buttered green peas could be included if you wish a green vegetable. Serve with it a young, full-bodied red Burgundy, Beaujolais, or Côtes du Rhône.

For 4 to 6 people

A 3- to 4-oz. chunk of lean bacon

Remove the rind and cut the bacon into *lardons* (rectangles ¼ inch across and 1 inch long). Simmer for 10 minutes in 2 quarts of water. Rinse in cold water. Dry.

A heavy, 10-in. fireproof casserole   **1 oz. butter**
   or an electric frying pan

Sauté the bacon slowly in hot butter until it is very lightly browned (temperature of 260° F. for an electric frying pan). Remove to a side dish.

2½ to 3 lbs. cut-up frying chicken

Dry the chicken thoroughly. Brown it in the hot fat in the casserole (360° F. for the electric frying pan).

½ tsp salt   **⅛ tsp pepper**

Season the chicken. Return the bacon to the casserole with the chicken. Cover and cook slowly (300° F.) for 10 minutes, turning the chicken once.

⅛ pt. cognac

Uncover, and pour in the cognac. Averting your face, ignite the cognac with a lighted match. Shake the casserole back and forth for several seconds until the flames subside.

1¼ pts. young, full-bodied red wine   1 dsp tomato paste
   such as Burgundy, Beaujolais,   2 cloves mashed garlic
   Côtes du Rhône, or Chianti   ¼ tsp thyme
½ to ¾ pt. brown chicken stock,   1 bay leaf
   brown stock, or beef bouillon

Pour the wine into the casserole. Add just enough stock or bouillon to cover the chicken. Stir in the tomato paste, garlic, and herbs. Bring to simmering point. Cover and simmer slowly for 25 to 30 minutes, or until the chicken is tender and its juices run a clear yellow when the meat is pricked with a fork. Remove the chicken to a side dish.

12 to 24 brown-braised onions,   ½ lb. sautéed mushrooms, page 473
   page 444

While the chicken is cooking, prepare the onions and mushrooms.

Salt and pepper

Simmer the chicken cooking liquid in the casserole for a minute or two, skimming off fat. Then raise heat and boil rapidly, reducing the liquid to about 1 pint. Correct seasoning. Remove from heat, and discard bay leaf.

1 oz. flour   A rubber spatula
1 oz. softened butter   A wire whisk
A saucer

Blend the butter and flour together into a smooth paste (*beurre manié*). Beat the paste into the hot liquid with a wire whisk. Bring to simmering point, stirring, and simmer for a minute or two. The sauce should be thick enough to coat a spoon lightly.

Arrange the chicken in the casserole, place the mushrooms and onions around it, and baste with the sauce.

(*) If the dish is not to be served immediately, film the top of the sauce with stock or dot with small pieces of butter. Leave aside uncovered. It can now wait indefinitely.

Shortly before serving, bring to simmering point, basting the chicken with the sauce. Cover and simmer slowly for 4 to 5 minutes, until the chicken is hot through.

Sprigs of fresh parsley

Serve from the casserole, or arrange on a hot dish. Decorate with sprigs of parsley.

GRILLED CHICKEN

POULETS GRILLÉS À LA DIABLE

[Chicken Grilled with Mustard, Herbs, and Breadcrumbs]

Here is a fine method for grilled chicken which is good either hot or cold. The chicken is partially cooked under the grill, then smeared with mustard and herbs, rolled in fresh breadcrumbs, and returned to the grill to brown and finish cooking. A practical attribute is that it can be almost entirely cooked ahead of time, left aside or refrigerated, and then finished off in the oven. With the mustard dip, a sauce is not a necessity. But if you want one, serve melted butter mixed with lemon juice and chopped herbs, or *sauce diable* (herbal brown sauce with shallots and wine), page 63. Baked, whole tomatoes and French beans would go well with it, and a chilled *rosé* wine.

For 4 to 8 people

Preheat grill to moderately hot.

Two ready-to-cook, 2½-lb. small spring chickens or broilers, halved or quartered	A pastry brush
	A grilling pan minus rack
	Salt
A saucepan containing 3 oz. melted butter and 2 tbl oil	

Dry the chicken thoroughly, paint it with butter and oil, and arrange it skin-side down in the bottom of the grilling pan. Place it so that the surface of the chicken is 5 to 6 inches below the hot grill element and grill 10 minutes on each side, basting every 5 minutes. The chicken should be very lightly browned. Salt it lightly.

6 tbl prepared French mustard	½ tsp thyme, basil, or tarragon
3 tbl finely chopped shallots or spring onions	⅛ tsp pepper
	Pinch of cayenne pepper

Blend the mustard with the shallots or spring onions, herbs, and seasonings in a bowl. Drop by drop, beat in half the basting fat to make a mayonnaise-like cream. Reserve the rest of the basting fat for later. Paint the chicken pieces with the mustard mixture.

½ lb. fresh, white crumbs from home-made type of bread (make	the crumbs in an electric liquidizer, 3 or 4 slices of bread at a time)

Pour the crumbs into a big plate, then roll the chicken in the crumbs, patting them on so that they will adhere.

A grilling pan with rack   **The rest of the basting fat**

Arrange the chicken pieces skin-side down on the rack in the grill pan and pour half the remaining basting fat over them. Brown slowly for 10 minutes under a moderately hot grill. Turn, baste with the last of the fat, and brown 10 minutes more on the other side. The chicken is done when the thickest part of the drumstick is tender, and, when the meat is pricked with a fork, the juices run clear yellow.

Transfer to a hot dish and serve.

(*) AHEAD-OF-TIME NOTES

If you wish to do most of the cooking in advance, brown the crumbed chicken under the grill for 5 minutes only on each side. It may then be finished off several hours later, placed in a preheated 350° F., Mark 4 oven for 20 to 30 minutes. Do not allow it to overcook.

CHICKEN BREASTS
Suprêmes de Volaille

Breast of chicken when it is removed raw from one side of the bird in a skinless, boneless piece is called a *suprême*. Each chicken possesses two of these. If the upper part of the wing is left on, the *suprême* becomes a *côtelette*. The breast of a cooked chicken is not a *suprême*, but a *blanc de poulet*, or white meat of chicken. A *suprême* may be poached in butter in a covered casserole *à blanc*, or sautéed or grilled with butter *à brun*. It is never, in good French cooking, simmered in a liquid. The *suprême* is an easy morsel to cook, but attention must be exercised to be sure it is not overdone, as even a minute too much can toughen the meat and make it dry. The flesh of a perfectly cooked *suprême* is white with the faintest pinky blush, its juices run clear yellow, and it is definitely juicy. Its point of doneness is easily determined as it cooks. Press the top of it with your finger; if it is still soft and yields slightly to the touch, it is not yet done. As soon as the flesh springs back with gentle resilience, it is ready. If there is no springiness, it is overcooked. As a *suprême* cooks in only 6 to 8 minutes and may be served very simply, it can make an exquisite quick meal.

PREPARING THE SUPRÊMES FOR COOKING

Choose whole or half breasts from a 2½- to 3-lb. fryer. Slip your fingers between skin and flesh, and pull off the skin. Then cut against the ridge of the breastbone to loosen the flesh from the bone. Disjoint the wing where it joins the carcass and continue down along the rib cage, pulling flesh from bone as you cut until the meat from one side of the breast separates from the bone in one piece. Remove the wing. Cut and pull out the white tendon that runs about two-thirds of the way down the underside of the meat. Trim off any jagged edges and flatten the *suprêmes* lightly with the side of a heavy knife. They are now ready for cooking. If they are not to be used immediately, wrap in grease-proof paper and refrigerate.

---

* SUPRÊMES DE VOLAILLE À BLANC

[Breast of Chicken with Cream]

Serve these with buttered asparagus tips, green peas, artichoke hearts, or creamed spinach, a good *risotto* cooked in chicken stock, and a bottle of chilled white Burgundy or Alsatian Traminer.

For 4 people

Preheat oven to 400° F., Mark 6.

4 *suprêmes* (boned breasts from two frying chickens; see directions in paragraph preceding recipe)	A heavy, covered, fireproof casserole about 10 ins. in diameter
½ tsp lemon juice	A round of greaseproof paper 10 ins. in diameter and buttered on one side
¼ tsp salt	
Big pinch white pepper	2 oz. butter

Rub the *suprêmes* with drops of lemon juice and sprinkle lightly with salt and pepper. Heat the butter in the casserole until it is foaming. Quickly roll the *suprêmes* in the butter, lay the buttered paper over them, cover casserole and place in hot oven. After 6 minutes, press top of *suprêmes* with your finger. If still soft, return to oven for a moment or two. When the meat is springy to the touch it is done. Remove the *suprêmes* to a warm dish and cover while making the sauce (2 to 3 minutes).

For the sauce:

⅛ pt. white or brown stock or beef bouillon	½ pt. cream
⅛ pt. port, Madeira, or dry white vermouth	Salt and pepper
	Lemon juice as needed
	2 tbl fresh chopped parsley

Pour the stock or bouillon and wine into the casserole with the cooking butter and boil down quickly over high heat until liquid is syrupy. Stir in the cream and boil down again over high heat until cream has thickened slightly. Away from heat, taste carefully for seasoning, and add drops of lemon juice to taste. Pour the sauce over the *suprêmes*, sprinkle with parsley, and serve at once.

VARIATIONS

Suprêmes de Volaille Archiduc

[Chicken Breasts with Paprika, Onions, and Cream]

This is a delicious combination, the onions giving the chicken and the sauce a subtle flavour, while the paprika lends fragrance and rosiness to the finished dish.

3 oz. finely chopped onions	1 tbl fragrant red paprika
2½ oz. butter	⅛ tsp salt

Drop the chopped onions into boiling water for 1 minute. Drain, run cold water over them, and drain again. Cook the onions with the salt, paprika, and butter in the covered casserole for about 10 minutes over very low heat until the onions are tender and translucent, but not browned.

4 *suprêmes* and the sauce ingredients
   in the preceding master recipe

Following the master recipe, cook the *suprêmes* in the onions, paprika, and butter. Remove when done, leaving the onions in the casserole. Complete the sauce, also as described in the master recipe.

Suprêmes de Volaille à l'Écossaise

[Chicken Breasts with Diced Aromatic Vegetables and Cream]

The following vegetables cut into	1 to 2 tender celery stalks
neat $\frac{1}{8}$-in. cubes, making	1 medium onion
3 to 4 oz. in all:	
1 medium carrot	

Cook the diced vegetables slowly with the salt and butter for about 10 minutes in the covered casserole until tender, but not browned.

⅛ tsp salt	4 *suprêmes* and the sauce ingredients
2½ oz. butter	in the master recipe

Following the master recipe, cook the *suprêmes* in the vegetables and butter. Remove them when done, leaving the vegetables in the casserole. Complete the sauce, as described in the master recipe.

Suprêmes de Volaille aux Champignons

[Chicken Breasts with Mushrooms and Cream]

2½ oz. butter	¼ lb. diced or sliced fresh
1 tbl chopped shallots or spring	mushrooms
onions	⅛ tsp salt

Place the butter in the casserole over moderate heat until foaming. Stir in the chopped shallots or spring onions and sauté a moment without browning. Then stir in the mushrooms and sauté lightly for a minute or two without browning. Sprinkle with salt.

**4 suprêmes and the sauce ingredients
in the master recipe**

Following the master recipe, cook the *suprêmes* in the mushrooms and butter. Remove when done, leaving the mushrooms in the casserole. Complete the sauce, as described in the master recipe.

---

* *SUPRÊMES DE VOLAILLE À BRUN*

[Chicken Breasts Sautéed in Butter]

Here the chicken breasts are lightly dusted with flour and are sautéed in clarified butter. (Ordinary butter will burn and form black specks on the *suprêmes*. Clarified butter may be heated to a higher temperature before burning.) A good accompaniment for this dish would be grilled or stuffed tomatoes, buttered green peas or French beans, and potato balls sautéed in butter. Serve with it a Médoc claret.

For 4 people

**4 *suprêmes* (boned breasts from
2 frying chickens), page 242**
¼ tsp salt

Big pinch of pepper
4 oz. flour spread on an 8-in. plate

Just before sautéing, sprinkle the *suprêmes* with salt and pepper, roll them in the flour, and shake off excess flour.

An 8- to 9-in. frying pan
**3 to 4 oz. clarified butter, page 12
(note that you will need 2 oz.
more for your sauce)**

A hot dish

Pour clarified butter into frying pan to a depth of about $\frac{1}{16}$ inch. Place on a moderately high heat. When the butter begins to deepen in colour very slightly, put in the *suprêmes*. Regulate heat so that butter is always hot but does not turn more than a deep yellow. After 3 minutes, turn the *suprêmes* and sauté on the other side. In two minutes, press tops of *suprêmes* with your finger. As soon as they are springy to the touch, they are done. Remove to a hot dish, leaving the butter in the frying pan.

Brown Butter Sauce (Beurre Noisette)

3 tbl clarified butter   1 tbl lemon juice
3 tbl chopped parsley

Add additional clarified butter to frying pan and place over a moderately high heat until the butter has turned a very light golden brown (a minute or two). Immediately remove from heat, stir in parsley and lemon juice, and taste for seasoning. Pour over the *suprêmes* and serve.

VARIATIONS

Brown Deglazing Sauce with Wine

1 tbl chopped shallots or spring   ¼ pt. brown stock or beef
  onions   bouillon
⅛ pt. port or Madeira   2 tbl chopped parsley

After removing the sautéed *suprêmes*, stir chopped shallots or spring onions into frying pan and sauté a moment. Then pour in the wine and stock or bouillon and boil down rapidly over high heat until liquid is lightly syrupy. Pour over the *suprêmes*, sprinkle with parsley, and serve.

Deglazing Sauce with Truffles

1 chopped tinned truffle and the   Ingredients for the preceding brown
  juice from its tin   deglazing sauce minus the parsley

After sautéing the shallots or onions, as in the preceding master recipe, add the wine, stock or bouillon, and the truffle and its juice. Boil down liquid until syrupy, and pour over the *suprêmes*.

Suprêmes de Volaille à la Milanaise

[Chicken Breasts Rolled in Parmesan Cheese and Fresh Breadcrumbs]

4 *suprêmes* (boned breasts from two   beaten together in an 8-in. soup
  frying chickens), page 242   plate
¼ tsp salt   2 oz. freshly grated Parmesan
Big pinch of pepper   cheese and 1 oz. fine, white,
4 oz. flour spread on an 8-in. plate   fresh breadcrumbs mixed together
1 egg, ⅛ tsp salt, and ½ tsp olive oil   in an 8-in. dish

Season the *suprêmes* with salt and pepper. One at a time, roll them in the flour and shake off excess. Dip in beaten egg. Then roll in the cheese and breadcrumbs, patting them in place with the flat of a knife. Lay the *suprêmes* on greaseproof paper and allow cheese and breadcrumbs to set for 10 to 15 minutes or several hours.

Ingredients for brown butter sauce,
   master recipe

Sauté on both sides in clarified butter until resilient to the pressure of your finger. Serve with brown butter sauce as described in the master recipe.

DUCK

Canard—Caneton

Only the genuine duckling or *caneton*—a bird under 6 months old—is good for roasting. It generally weighs 4 to 5 pounds ready to cook and has been beautifully plucked and cleaned. If it has been deep-frozen, a state to which it takes much better than chicken, it needs only to be thawed out in the refrigerator or in a basin of cold, running water, and it is ready for cooking.

A NOTE ON FRENCH DUCKS

French ducks are of various breeds. These are: the *nantais*, which rarely weighs over 3 pounds and is the most common table duckling; the *rouennais*, famous as pressed duck; and the *canard de barbarie*, often older and always larger, which is used for braising.

PREPARING A DUCK FOR ROASTING

Pull out all loose fat from the cavity and from around the neck. To make the carving of the breast meat easier, cut out the wishbone. The lower part of the wing is mostly bone; chop it off at the elbow and add it to the stock pot. Be sure the fat glands on the back at the base of the tail have been removed, dig out any yellow residue that may remain, and rub the area with salt and lemon juice. To help the layer of subcutaneous duck fat to escape during cooking, prick the skin at $\frac{1}{2}$-inch intervals along the thighs, the back, and the lower part of the breast. After seasoning the cavity, or stuffing it, sew or skewer the legs, wings, and neck skin to the body so that the bird will make a neat appearance on the table; see the illustrated directions for trussing a chicken on page 213, which may be adapted for duck.

DUCK STOCK

The neck, heart, gizzard, and lower wings may be used for the making of a duck stock. Follow the same method as for chicken stock, page 213.

CARVING NOTE

Duck has far more carcass and far less meat than a chicken of the same weight; a $4\frac{1}{2}$-lb. duck will serve only 4 or 5 people. The French method of carving is to make as many thin slices of breast meat as possible, 4 to 6 per side, as follows: After the second joints and drumsticks have been removed, the duck is turned on its side, its tail facing the carver. Thin slices of meat are cut diagonally starting from the lower part of the breast nearest the tail and running toward the breastbone. The same system is used for the other side, cutting in the opposite direction.

ROASTING TIMETABLE

French taste is for ducks roasted to a medium rare—the juices run slightly rosy when the meat is pricked. If the duck is to be served well done, its juices should run clear yellow. Overcooked duck meat is brown, dry, and disappointing.

The following table is for unstuffed, unchilled duck. Add 20 to 30 minutes to the times listed if the duck is stuffed.

READY-TO-COOK (AND UNDRAWN) WEIGHTS	NUMBER OF PEOPLE SERVED	OVEN AT 350° F.	
		MEDIUM RARE	WELL DONE
3½ lbs. (Undrawn: 5 lbs.)	3 or 4	65 to 70 minutes	1 hour and 15 to 25 minutes
4½ lbs. (Undrawn: 5¾ lbs.)	4	1 hour and 15 to 20 minutes	1 hour and 25 to 35 minutes
5½ lbs. (Undrawn: 7 lbs.)	5 or 6	1 hour and 25 to 30 minutes	1 hour and 35 to 40 minutes

VEGETABLE SUGGESTIONS

Caneton aux petits pois, duckling with green peas, is one of the favourite French combinations, especially in the spring. Other vegetable suggestions are broccoli or Brussels sprouts, or braised lettuce, celery, celeriac, onions, or turnips. Among starchy vegetables, if you wish to serve one, are braised or puréed chestnuts, potatoes mashed with celery root or turnips, or a purée of lentils or haricot beans.

WINE SUGGESTIONS

Serve full red wine, such as Burgundy, Côtes du Rhône, Châteauneuf-du-Pape, or a claret such as St. Émilion. Or a chilled Alsatian Traminer.

---

*   CANETON RÔTI

[Roast Duckling]

For 4 people

Estimated roasting time: 1 hour and 15 to 20 minutes.

Preheat oven to 425° F., Mark 7.

A 4½-lb. ready-to-cook duckling   **A pinch of thyme or sage**
½ tsp salt   **A small sliced onion**
⅛ tsp pepper

Season the inside of the duck with salt, pepper, herbs, and the sliced onion.
Secure the legs, wings, and neck skin to the body. Prick the skin around the
thighs, back, and lower breast. Dry the duck thoroughly.

A shallow roasting tin just large   **1 medium sliced carrot**
enough to hold the duck easily   **1 medium sliced onion**

Place the duck breast up in the roasting tin, strew the vegetables around it, and
place it in the middle of the oven for 15 minutes to brown lightly.

A bulb baster

Reduce oven to 350° F., Mark 4, and turn the duck on its side. Regulate heat so
that the duck is always making cooking noises but the fat is not burning.
Remove accumulated fat occasionally (a bulb baster will suck it up easily).
Basting is not necessary.

About 30 minutes later, or about half-way through, turn the duck on its other
side.

½ tsp salt

Fifteen minutes before the end of the estimated roasting time, salt the duck and
turn it breast up.

The duck is done to a medium rare if the juices from the fattest part of the thigh
or drumstick run faintly rosy when the meat is pricked, and when the duck is
lifted and drained, the last drops of juice from the vent are a pale rose. The duck
is well done when the juices run pale yellow.

When done, discard trussing strings, and place the duck on a serving dish. Place
in turned-off oven and leave the door open while preparing the sauce, which
will take 3 to 4 minutes.

½ to ¾ pt. brown duck stock, beef   **Optional: 2 to 3 tbl port**
stock, or beef bouillon

Tilt the roasting tin and spoon out all but 1 tablespoon of fat. Add the stock or
bouillon and boil rapidly, scraping up coagulated roasting juices, and crushing
the vegetables, until liquid is reduced at least by half. Correct seasoning. Add
optional wine and simmer a minute to evaporate its alcohol.

½ to 1 oz. softened butter

Remove from heat and just before serving, swirl the butter into the sauce and strain it into a sauceboat. Pour a bit of sauce over the duck, and serve.

(*) AHEAD-OF-TIME NOTE

Roast duck may be left in the turned-off hot oven, the door ajar, for about 30 minutes before serving.

SPIT ROASTING

Duck does very well indeed on a rotary spit. Follow the directions for spit-roasted chicken on page 218, but omit the bacon wrapping. No basting is necessary. Roasting time is the same as for oven roasting on the chart, page 248.

VARIATIONS

Caneton Rôti à l'Alsacienne

[Roast Duck with Sausage and Apple Stuffing]

Apples and duck are a fine combination, and sausages make it an even better one. The dish may be garnished with more apples and sausages if you wish, braised onions, and sautéed potatoes or potato *crêpes*. A chilled Alsatian Traminer would go well with it, or rough cider.

For 4 people

Estimated roasting time for a 4½ duck: 1 hour and 35 to 50 minutes.

Sausage and apple stuffing

½ lb. pork sausages

Sauté the sausages in a frying pan until they are lightly browned. Drain them. Mash them roughly with a fork in a mixing bowl.

4 or 5 crisp eating apples

Peel, quarter, and core the apples. Cut the quarters into 2 or 3 lengthwise segments. Sauté them, a few at a time, in the hot sausage fat in the frying pan. They should be very lightly browned, and almost tender, but still retain their shape.

1 tbl sugar	¼ tsp sage
¼ tsp cinnamon	2 tbl cognac
¼ tsp salt	

Place them on a dish and sprinkle with the seasonings and cognac.

⅛ pt. port   ⅛ pt. stock or beef bouillon

Pour the fat out of the frying pan. Add the wine and stock or bouillon and boil
rapidly until liquid has reduced to about 2 or 3 tablespoons. Pour it over the
cooked sausages.

When both apples and sausages have cooled, mix them delicately together. Stuff
loosely into the duck. Sew or skewer the vent, truss the duck, and roast it
according to the preceding master recipe.

* *Caneton à l'Orange*

[Roast Duck with Orange Sauce]

One of the most well known of all the duck dishes, *caneton à l'orange*, is
roast duck decorated with fresh orange segments and accompanied by an
orange-flavoured brown sauce. Its most important element is its sauce—a rich,
strong, meaty, duck essence darkened with caramel, flavoured with wine and
orange peel, and given a light liaison of arrowroot. You can and should prepare
the sauce well ahead of time so that when the duck is roasted, the dish is within
2 to 3 minutes of being ready.

VEGETABLE AND WINE SUGGESTIONS

Nothing should interfere with the flavours of the duck, the sauce, and the
oranges. Sautéed or matchstick potatoes, or home-made potato chips are your
best choice. Serve a good claret such as Médoc, or a chilled white Burgundy—
Meursault, Montrachet, or Corton-Charlemagne.

For 4 people

Note: Under the ingredients needed for the sauce is ¾ pint of excellent duck
stock. This should be prepared ahead of time, as it must simmer about 2 hours.

Blanching the orange peel

4 brightly coloured navel oranges

Remove the orange part of the skin in strips with a vegetable peeler. Cut into
julienne (small strips 1/16 inch wide and 1½ inches long). Simmer for 15 minutes
in a quart of water. Drain. Pat dry.

Roasting the duck

A 4½-lb. ready-to-cook duckling   Pinch of pepper
½ tsp salt

Season the duck cavity with salt and pepper, add a third of the prepared orange
peel, and truss the duck. Roast it according to the master recipe, page 248.

The sauce base

A 1½-pt. saucepan
3 tbl granulated sugar
⅛ pt. red wine vinegar
¾ pt. strong, brown duck stock
  (follow directions for brown
  chicken stock, page 213, using

duck giblets instead of chicken
  giblets)
1 oz. arrowroot blended with 2 tbl
  port or Madeira
The rest of the blanched orange
  peel

While the duck is roasting, make a sweet-and-sour caramel colouring as follows:
Boil the sugar and vinegar over moderately high heat for several minutes until
the mixture has turned into a mahogany-brown syrup. Immediately remove
from heat and pour in ¼ pint of the duck stock. Simmer for a minute, stirring,
to dissolve the caramel. Then add the rest of the stock, beat in the arrowroot
mixture, and stir in the orange peel. Simmer for 3 to 4 minutes or until the sauce
is clear, limpid, and lightly thickened. Correct seasoning, and leave aside.

The orange segments

The 4 oranges, skinned

Cut the 4 oranges into neat, skinless segments and place in a covered dish.

Final assembly

When the duck is done, discard trussing strings, and place it on a dish. Place it in
the turned-off hot oven, leaving the door ajar.

¼ pt. port or Madeira

Remove as much fat as you can from the roasting tin. Add the wine and boil it
down rapidly, scraping up coagulated roasting juices and reducing the liquid to
2 or 3 tablespoons.

The prepared sauce base
2 or 3 tbl good orange liqueur

Drops of orange bitters or lemon
juice

Strain the wine reduction into the sauce base and bring to the simmer. Stir in the
orange liqueur by spoonfuls, tasting. The sauce should have a pleasant orange
flavour but not be too sweet. Add drops of orange bitters or lemon juice as a
corrective.

1 oz. softened butter

Just before serving, and away from heat, swirl in the butter enrichment, and
pour the sauce into a warmed sauceboat.

Place a line of orange segments over the length of the duck and heap the rest at
the two ends of the dish. Spoon a little of the sauce with peel over the duck, and
serve.

VARIATIONS

Caneton aux Cerises
Caneton Montmorency

[Roast Duck with Cherries]

Cherries or peaches are also good as a garnish for roast duck. Roast the bird as directed in the master recipe, page 248. Make the caramel-coloured and arrowroot-thickened sauce described for the preceding *caneton à l'orange*, omitting the orange peel and orange liqueur. The fruit is heated in the sauce as follows:

36 to 48 red or black stoned cherries	**1 tbl lemon juice**
A 1½-pt. enamelled saucepan	**3 tbl port or cognac**
	2 tbl granulated sugar

Toss the cherries in the saucepan with the lemon juice, port or cognac, and sugar. Let them soak for at least 20 to 30 minutes.

After the duck has roasted, and the tin juices have been deglazed with wine and added to the sauce, pour the sauce into the cherries. Heat to below simmering point for 3 to 4 minutes to poach the cherries (if liquid simmers the fruit may shrivel). Remove the cherries with a slotted spoon and distribute them over and around the duck.

1 oz. softened butter

Boil the sauce rapidly to reduce and thicken it slightly. Correct seasoning. Away from heat, swirl in the enrichment butter. Pour the sauce into a warmed bowl, spoon a little over the duck, and serve.

Caneton aux Pêches

[Roast Duck with Peaches]

3 large or 6 small, firm, ripe, peaches (or drained, tinned peaches, minus the sugar below)	**2 tbl lemon juice**
	2 to 3 tbl port or cognac
	2 to 3 tbl granulated sugar

If using fresh peaches, peel and halve them not more than 30 minutes before serving so that they will not discolour. Arrange the peaches in a fireproof dish and baste them with the liquids and sugar. Baste several times more before using.

After the duck has roasted and the tin juices have been deglazed with wine and added to the sauce, pour the sauce over the peaches. Proceed as for the preceding duck with cherries recipe.

CANETON POÊLÉ AUX NAVETS

[Casserole-roasted Duck with Turnips]

In casserole roasting, the duck is browned on all sides, then left to roast in a covered casserole. Cooked in its own steam, the duck's flesh becomes wonderfully tender, and the layer of subcutaneous fat is even more effectively dissolved than by roasting. The turnips, which finish their cooking with the duck absorbing cooking juices, are particularly succulent. No other vegetable is necessary, but you could serve green peas or broccoli. A claret, Beaujolais, or Côtes du Rhône would be the choice of wines.

For 4 people

Estimated roasting time: 1 hour and 15 to 35 minutes.

Preheat oven to 325° F., Mark 2.

A 4½-lb. ready-to-cook duckling
½ tsp salt
⅛ tsp pepper
A heavy, oval casserole just large
  enough to hold the duck easily

2 tbl rendered fresh pork fat or
  cooking oil

Season the inside of the duck with salt and pepper, truss it, prick the skin around the thighs, back, and lower part of the breast. Dry it thoroughly. Brown it slowly on all sides in hot fat in the casserole—as for browning a chicken, page 230.

½ tsp salt
A medium herb bouquet: 4 parsley
  sprigs, ½ bay leaf, and ¼ tsp thyme
  tied in washed cheesecloth

Pour out the browning fat. Salt the duck and place it breast up in the casserole. Add the herb bouquet, cover the hot casserole, and place it in the middle of the preheated oven. Roast for 40 to 50 minutes, regulating heat so that the duck is always making quiet cooking noises. Basting is not necessary.

2 lbs. firm, crisp, white or yellow
  turnips

While the duck is cooking, prepare the turnips: Peel them and cut into large olive shapes about 1¾ inches long, or into ¾-inch dice. Drop into boiling, salted water, and boil slowly for 5 minutes. Drain.

A bulb baster

After the duck has roasted for 40 to 50 minutes, or 30 to 40 minutes before the end of its estimated cooking time, degrease casserole with bulb baster. Arrange the turnips around the duck, cover the casserole, and return it to the oven. Baste turnips occasionally with the juices in the casserole.

The duck is done when its juices run a pale rose for medium rare, or a clear yellow for well done.

2 to 3 tbl chopped parsley

Drain the duck, discard trussing strings, and place it on a hot dish. Remove the turnips with a slotted spoon, arrange them around the duck, and decorate with parsley. Degrease the cooking juices, correct seasoning, pour into a warmed sauceboat, and serve.

(*) AHEAD-OF-TIME NOTE

The duck, turnips, and degreased cooking juices can be returned to the hot casserole. Place the cover askew, and keep it warm for 30 minutes in the turned-off hot oven, or over barely simmering water.

VARIATIONS

Canard Braisé avec Choucroute—à la Badoise
[Duck Braised in Sauerkraut]

Canard Braisé aux Choux Rouges
[Duck Braised in Red Cabbage]

These two classic combinations are both done in the same way: after the sauerkraut or cabbage is about two-thirds braised, the browned duck is added to cook in the casserole, and all ingredients benefit from their mutual exchange of flavours. Parsley potatoes or braised chestnuts and a chilled Alsatian Traminer go well with this.

For 4 people

Ingredients for 2 lbs. of braised sauerkraut, page 458, or braised red cabbage, page 457

A casserole large enough to include the duck as well

Follow the recipe for braised sauerkraut or braised red cabbage, and cook for 3½ hours.

A 4½-lb. ready-to-cook duckling

Season, truss, prick, and dry the duck. Brown it in hot fat as described in the preceding recipe. Salt it and bury it in the casserole with the sauerkraut or cabbage. Cover, and braise for about 1½ hours more, or until the duck is done.

Parsley sprigs

When done, remove the duck to a hot dish and discard trussing strings. Lift out the sauerkraut or cabbage, draining its juices back into the casserole, and arrange it about the duck. Decorate with parsley.

Degrease the cooking juices. Place casserole over high heat and boil rapidly until the liquid has reduced and its flavour is concentrated. Strain into a sauceboat, pour a spoonful over the duck, and serve.

CANETON BRAISÉ AUX MARRONS

[Braised Duck with Chestnut and Sausage Stuffing]

Follow the recipe for braised goose with chestnut and sausage stuffing, page 260. Use the timetable for roast duck on page 248, adding 30 minutes more because of the stuffing.

CANARD EN CROÛTE

[Boned, Stuffed Duck Baked in a Crust]

This recipe is on page 527.

GOOSE

Oie

Goose, like duck, can only be considered gastronomically interesting when it is under 6 months old. If frozen, it should be defrosted either in the refrigerator or in a pan with cold, running water. It is prepared for cooking like duck, page 247.

GOOSE FAT

Goose fat is extremely good as a sauté or basting medium, or as a flavouring for braised cabbage or sauerkraut. Once rendered, it will keep for weeks in the refrigerator. To render the fat, pull out all the loose fat from inside the goose. Chop it up into ½-inch pieces. Simmer it in a covered saucepan with ½ pint of water for 20 minutes to draw the fat out of the tissues. Then uncover the pan and boil the liquid slowly to evaporate the water. As the moisture evaporates, the fat will make spluttering noises. As soon as these have stopped, the fat is rendered, the liquid will be a pale yellow, and the fat particles will have browned very lightly. Strain the liquid into a jar.

Frittons
Grattons

[Goose Cracklings]

The browned fat particles may be turned into a spread for *croûtons*, toast, or biscuits. Pound them in a mortar or put them through the mincer. Warm them briefly in a frying pan and stir in salt, pepper, and allspice to taste. Pack them into a jar. When cold, pour a ⅛-inch layer of hot goose fat over them to seal them. They will keep for several weeks in the refrigerator.

GOOSE STOCK

A good goose stock is easy to make with the gizzard, neck, heart, and wing tips of the goose. The liver may be included, unless you wish to treat it like chicken liver, or add it to your stuffing. Follow the general procedure for chicken stock, page 213. It should simmer for 2 hours or so.

STUFFINGS FOR GOOSE

Goose may be cooked with or without a stuffing. Besides the prune and *foie gras*, and the chestnut stuffing, both of which are described in the pages following, another good one for goose is the apple and sausage mixture in the Duck section, page 250. In estimating the amount of stuffing required, use a graduated pint or quart measure marked in fluid ounces and count on 6 to 8 ounces of stuffing for each ready-to-cook pound of goose. An 8-lb. bird, for instance, will take 48 to 64 ounces on your measure. Although you may prepare a stuffing ahead of time, never stuff the goose until just before cooking, or both goose and stuffing may spoil.

TIMETABLE FOR ROAST OR BRAISED GOOSE

The following table is based on unstuffed, unchilled goose cooked to the well-done stage—when its juices run pale yellow. Be sure not to overcook your goose, or the breast meat especially will be dry and disappointing. You will see in the table that the larger the goose, the less time per pound it takes to cook. A 9-lb. goose requires about 2 hours, and a 12½-lb. bird, only about 30 minutes longer. The best sizes to buy are from 9 to 11 pounds; larger geese may be a bit older and tougher. Oven temperature for roasting is 350° F., Mark 4; for braising, 325° F., Mark 2. A meat thermometer should register 180° F.

READY-TO-COOK (AND UNDRAWN) WEIGHTS	NUMBER OF PEOPLE SERVED	APPROXIMATE TOTAL COOKING TIME (UNSTUFFED GOOSE)*
8 lbs. (Undrawn: 10 lbs.)	6	1 hour and 50 to 55 minutes
9 lbs. (Undrawn: 11 lbs.)	6 to 8	About 2 hours
9½ lbs. (Undrawn: 12 lbs.)	8 to 9	2 hours and 10 to 15 minutes
10½ lbs. (Undrawn: 13 lbs.)	9 to 10	2 hours and 15 to 20 minutes
11½ lbs. (Undrawn: 14 lbs.)	10 to 12	2 hours and 20 to 30 minutes
12½ lbs. (Undrawn: 15 lbs.)	12 to 14	2 hours and 30 to 40 minutes

* For a stuffed goose, add from 20 to 40 minutes to the times given.

OIE RÔTIE AUX PRUNEAUX

[Roast Goose with Prune and *Foie Gras* Stuffing]

Goose is roasted exactly like duck, the only exception being that the goose is basted every 15 to 20 minutes with boiling water to help in the dissolution of its subcutaneous fat, which is more copious for goose than for duck. Prunes and goose are an exceptionally fine combination. With the goose you can serve braised onions and chestnuts, and a full red wine such as a Burgundy or Châteauneuf-du-Pape.

For 6 to 8 people

Estimated roasting time: About 2½ hours.

Note: A good brown goose stock will give you an excellent sauce, but it must be prepared in advance; see preceding remarks.

Prune and foie gras stuffing

40 to 50 prunes

Soak the prunes in hot water until soft. Stone them as neatly as possible.

½ pt. white wine or ¼ pt. dry white vermouth   **¾ pt. brown goose stock, brown stock, or beef bouillon**

Simmer them slowly in a covered saucepan with the wine and stock or bouillon for about 10 minutes, or until they are just tender. Drain them and reserve the cooking liquid.

The goose liver, minced	$\frac{1}{2}$ oz. butter
2 tbl finely chopped shallots or	
spring onions	

Sauté the goose liver and shallots or spring onions in butter, using a small frying pan, for 2 minutes. Scrape into a mixing bowl.

$\frac{1}{4}$ pt. port

Boil the wine in the same frying pan until it is reduced to 2 tablespoons. Scrape it into the mixing bowl with the liver.

4 oz. of *foie gras* (goose liver), or	Pinch of thyme
very good liver paste	Salt and pepper to taste
Pinch of allspice	2 to 3 tbl breadcrumbs

Blend the *foie gras* or liver paste and flavourings into the mixing bowl with the sautéed liver. If mixture seems too soft for easy stuffing, beat in breadcrumbs. Taste carefully for seasoning. Fill each prune with a teaspoon of the stuffing.

Preheat oven to 425° F., Mark 7.

| A 9-lb. ready-to-cook young | 1 tsp salt |
| roasting goose | A shallow roasting tin |

Salt the cavity of the goose. Stuff it loosely with the prunes. Sew or skewer the vent. Secure the legs, wings, and neck skin to the body. Prick the skin over the thighs, back, and lower breast. Dry thoroughly, and place it breast up in the roasting tin.

| Boiling water | A bulb baster |

Following directions for roast duck, page 248, brown the goose for 15 minutes in the hot oven. Turn goose on its side, lower heat to 350° F., Mark 4, and continue roasting. Baste every 15 to 20 minutes with 2 or 3 tablespoons of boiling water, and remove excess accumulated fat. A bulb baster is useful for this; tilt the tin and draw the fat off. Turn goose on its other side at the half-way mark, and on its back 15 minutes before the end. The goose should be done in 2 hours and 20 to 30 minutes, when the drumsticks move slightly in their sockets, and, when the fleshiest part of one is pricked, the juices run a pale yellow. Do not allow the goose to overcook or the meat will dry out.

When done, discard trussing strings and place the goose on a dish.

| The prune cooking juices | Salt and pepper |
| Optional: $\frac{1}{8}$ to $\frac{1}{4}$ pt. port | 1 oz. softened butter |

Tilt the tin and spoon out the fat, but leave the brown roasting juices. Pour in the prune cooking juices and optional port. Boil down rapidly, scraping up coagulated roasting juices, until liquid has reduced and is full of flavour. Correct seasoning. Remove from heat and just before serving, swirl in the enrichment butter in pieces. Pour into a warmed sauceboat, spoon a little sauce over the goose, and serve.

(*) AHEAD-OF-TIME NOTE

Roast goose may wait for 30 to 40 minutes in the turned-off hot oven with the door ajar.

OIE BRAISÉE AUX MARRONS

[Braised Goose with Chestnut and Sausage Stuffing]

There are many who prefer braised goose to roast goose because the meat is more tender and more flavourful, and the closed, moist cooking of a braise renders out more fat than open-tin roasting. A good combination to go with this would be more chestnuts, either braised or puréed, and braised lettuce, onions or leeks. Brussels sprouts, or braised green or red cabbage are other choices. Serve a red Burgundy, Côtes du Rhône, Châteauneuf-du-Pape, or chilled Alsatian Traminer.

For a 9-lb. bird, serving 8 to 10 people—because of the meat stuffing the goose will go further.

Estimated roasting time: $2\frac{1}{2}$ hours.

Sausage and chestnut stuffing

$1\frac{1}{2}$ lbs. of fresh chestnuts, or 1 lb. of drained, tinned, and unsweetened chestnuts

If using fresh chestnuts, peel them, and simmer them in stock and seasonings as described on page 479. Drain, and allow them to cool.

2 lbs. of the fresh minced veal and pork stuffing described on page 522

The goose liver, chopped, and sautéed in butter

Prepare the stuffing and beat the sautéed liver into it. Sauté a spoonful to check seasoning.

Preheat oven to 450° F., Mark 8.

| A 9-lb. ready-to-cook young | ½ tsp salt |
| roasting goose | A shallow roasting tin |

Season the cavity of the goose with salt. Starting with the meat stuffing, loosely pack alternate layers of stuffing and of chestnuts into the goose, leaving a good inch of unfilled space at the vent. Sew or skewer the vent, truss the goose, and prick its skin. Dry it thoroughly, and set it breast up in the roasting tin.

Brown the goose lightly in the hot oven for 15 to 20 minutes, turning it several times so that it will colour evenly.

1 tsp salt
A covered roasting tin just large
  enough to hold the goose easily

Salt the goose and place it breast up in the roasting tin. Turn oven down to 325° F., Mark 2.

The goose neck, wing tips, gizzard,	3 tbl rendered goose fat, rendered
and heart	fresh pork fat, or cooking oil
6 oz. sliced onions	A frying pan
2 oz. sliced carrots	

Brown the goose bits and vegetables in hot fat in the frying pan.

2 oz. flour

Stir the flour into the frying pan and brown slowly for several minutes.

| 1½ pts. boiling brown stock or | 1¼ pts. dry white wine or ¾ pt. dry |
| beef bouillon | white vermouth |

Away from heat, blend in the boiling stock or bouillon, and then the wine. Simmer for a moment. Then pour the contents of the frying pan into the roasting tin around the goose. Add additional stock if necessary, so that liquid reaches about one-third the way up the goose.

Bring to simmering point on top of the stove. Cover, and place in the middle of the preheated 325° F., Mark 2 oven.

A bulb baster

Braise for about 2 hours and 20 to 30 minutes, regulating oven heat so that liquid simmers very quietly. Basting is not necessary. Accumulated fat should be removed occasionally with the bulb baster. The goose is done when its drumsticks move slightly in their sockets, and, when their fleshiest part is pricked, the juices run pale yellow.

Remove the goose to a serving dish and discard trussing strings.

Salt and pepper to taste $\frac{1}{8}$ to $\frac{1}{4}$ pt. port

Skim the fat out of the roasting tin (degreasing directions are on page 256), boil the cooking liquid down rapidly until it has thickened enough to coat a spoon lightly. Correct seasoning. Stir in the port and simmer a minute or two to evaporate its alcohol. Strain the sauce into a bowl or a saucepan, pressing juice out of the ingredients. You should have about $1\frac{1}{2}$ to 2 pints of sauce. Pour a spoonful over the goose, and serve.

(*) AHEAD–OF–TIME NOTE

For a 30- to 40-minute wait, return the goose to the roasting tin, and set the cover askew. Place in turned-off hot oven with the door ajar, or over barely simmering water.

CHAPTER SEVEN

MEAT

Viandes

Faced with the awesome problem of what to choose from among the wonderful store of French recipes for beef, lamb, pork, ham, sweetbreads, kidneys, liver, and brains, we have picked those which seemed to us especially French, or of particular interest to British cooks. We have not gone into roast beef or grilled chops as they are practically the same everywhere. Besides numerous traditional dishes, we have included a number of French regional recipes for *ragoûts*, stews, and *daubes*; their comparative economy and ease of execution, in addition to their robust flavours, make them most appealing.

For those who have collections of original French recipes, or who are living in France, we have in most instances given translations, approximations, or explanations of French meat cuts. Cross-cultural comparisons are a maze of complication as the systems of the two countries are entirely different: the French cut meat following muscle separations, while British butchers usually cut across the grain. Identification is made more confusing as the same cut may have a different name in another region of the same country. We have used London butcher's terminology for British cuts, and Paris terminology for French cuts.

BEEF

Boeuf

Any cook or housewife is well advised to learn as much as possible about cuts and quality of beef, as a vague beef-buyer is open to countless unnecessary disappointments and expenses. Cut and quality determine the cooking method; if you are going to braise or boil beef, it is wasteful to buy a roasting cut. And if you want a fine steak, you will be bitterly disappointed if you have bought a tough piece from the leg. The best way to learn is to look carefully at beef every time you go to the butcher's shop. Try to familiarize yourself with each cut, starting for instance with topsides and silversides, then moving to chucks, clods, and leg of mutton cuts. Ask questions; your butcher will be much more interested in serving you well if you show interest in his meat.

Here are some points to look for in choosing beef of best quality: lean meat is bright cherry red after it has been cut and is exposed to the air; flesh from old or poorly fed animals does not brighten after cutting. The fat is creamy white, firm, and brittle; yellow, oily fat comes from an old or poorly fed animal. The lean meat is resilient, smooth, has a slight sheen, and shows a minimum of gristle or graininess. The lean meat, particularly for those cuts intended for grilling or roasting, is marbled with fat; that is, little spots or a network of fat is distributed through the lean. Marbling increases flavour and tenderness. Reputable butchers hang, or age, their meat; this tenderizes roasting and grilling cuts, and improves flavour.

STEAKS
Biftecks

French and British methods of cutting up a beef carcass are so dissimilar that it is rarely possible to find in Great Britain the same steak cut you could find in France. But this is a point of small significance as the various steak recipes differ from one another only in their sauces, butters, or garnitures.

In France the undercut of the loin, or fillet, which runs from the thirteenth rib to the rump, is usually removed in one piece. The uppercut of the loin, under which the fillet was removed, is boned and used for steaks or roasts. Thus there is no loin left intact. The wing end of the ribs and the fore ribs are usually boned and cut into rib steaks called *entrecôtes*.

CUTS FOR STEAK
Since you often find French steak names on a menu, here is a list explaining them.

Entrecôte. Rib steak, cut from the fore- and wing-end parts of the rib-roast section, ribs 9 to 11.

Romsteck, or *Rumsteck.* Rump steak, cut from the part of the rump which faces the large end of the fillet. Rump steaks must be from a best quality, well-aged carcass to be tender.

Faux Filet, or *Contre Filet.* The boneless uppercut of the loin, as opposed to the undercut or fillet. It corresponds to the larger and less tender part of a porterhouse or T-bone steak.

Bifteck. This is cut from the larger and less tender end of the fillet which also makes up the best part of a rump or hip steak. In France the term *bifteck* can also include any lean, boneless steak from any reasonably tender part of the animal. We shall also include T-bone, porterhouse, hip and rump steaks as *biftecks.*

FILLET OF BEEF

If the fillet is taken from a large, fine carcass, the meat should be 3½ to 4 inches in diameter at the heart, and the slices delicately marbled with fat. Because many butchers reserve their best beef carcasses for loin roasts and porterhouse steaks, it is not always possible to find a fillet of this quality.

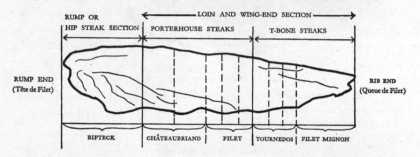

Whole Fillet of Beef

Bifteck, or the large end of the fillet situated in the loin end of the rump and fillet cut, is considered to be the less tender part of the fillet and is classified in the preceding list of steaks.

Châteaubriand (which can also be spelled with a final 't' rather than 'd') corresponds to the undercut or fillet portion of a porterhouse steak. It is 2 inches thick, should weigh a pound or more before trimming, and is always grilled. A thinner steak cut from this portion is called a *filet.*

Untrimmed Centre Cut of Fillet, the Châteaubriand Section

I*

Tournedos and *filet mignons* become progressively smaller as they near the tail of the fillet.

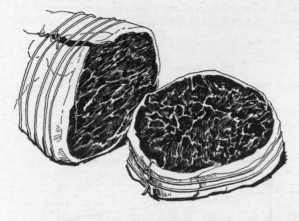

*Tournedos
Wrapped in a
Strip of Pork Fat*

WINE SUGGESTIONS

With all but the fillet steaks, which are discussed separately, serve a good, rather young red wine with a certain amount of body, such as a Côtes du Rhône, a St. Émilion claret, or Beaujolais.

VEGETABLE SUGGESTIONS

Bifteck et pommes frites are just as popular in France as they are in Britain. A good change from the old rhythm would be the garlic mashed potatoes on page 480, or one of the scalloped potato casseroles on pages 482 to 485, or potatoes sautéed in butter, page 486. Vegetables which would go well include the following:

Buttered green peas, page 425, or French beans, page 409, or Brussels sprouts, pages 413 to 418

Baked or stuffed tomatoes, pages 466 to 468

Grilled or stuffed mushrooms, pages 472 and 476

Ratatouille, aubergine casserole, page 463

Turnips, including the excellent casserole on page 449

Braised celery, leeks, or lettuce, pages 450 to 456.

Here are some of the classical French vegetable garnitures for a steak dish:

Beauharnais, stuffed mushrooms, page 476, artichoke hearts cooked in butter, page 397

Brabançonne, Brussels sprouts with cheese sauce, page 416, potato balls sautéed in butter, page 487

Catalane, stuffed tomatoes, page 467, artichoke hearts cooked in butter, page 397

Chartres, stuffed mushrooms, page 476, braised lettuce, page 450

Choron, artichoke hearts filled with buttered peas, page 397, potato balls sautéed in butter, page 487

Maillot, glazed turnips, page 448, carrots, page 440, and onions, page 442, with braised lettuce, page 450, and buttered green peas and French beans

Sévigné, braised lettuce, page 450, grilled mushrooms, page 472, potatoes sautéed in butter, page 486.

---

* *BIFTECK SAUTÉ AU BEURRE*

[Sautéed Steak]

Sautéed steak is very French and also a very nice method for cooking small steaks. None of the juice essences are lost, and it is easy to tell when the steak is done.

A 1-inch steak takes 8 to 10 minutes to cook, and the sauce, or pan gravy, 1 to 2 minutes to prepare after the steak is on its dish. The sauce, you will observe, is a deglazing of the pan with stock, wine, or water, and a swirl of butter at the end. It is purely an extension of the pan juices, and amounts to only 1 or 2 tablespoons of buttery, concentrated essence per serving.

KIND OF STEAK TO BUY

In France you would select an *entrecôte, romsteck, faux-filet,* or *bifteck*. In Great Britain buy any tender, well-aged ¾- to 1-inch steak or steaks which will fit easily into a frying pan such as:

Entrecôte or Rib Steak   Tender Steaks from:
Rump or Hip Steak   Thick Flank, Topside
Uppercut of Loin   Leg of Mutton Cut.

AMOUNT TO BUY

One pound of boneless steak will serve 2 people, 3 if the rest of the menu is copious. For large rump and porterhouse steaks, count on about ¾ pound per person.

PREPARATION FOR COOKING

Trim off excess fat. Cut small incisions around the circumference of the steak wherever there is a layer of gristle, usually between the fat and the meat. This will prevent the steak from curling as it cooks. Dry the steak thoroughly. It will not brown if it is moist.

For 4 to 6 people, depending on your menu

| One or two heavy frying pans just large enough to hold the meat easily in one layer | rendered fresh beef suet, more if needed |
| 1¼ oz. butter and 1 tbl oil, or | 2 to 2½ lbs. steak ¾ to 1 in. thick |

Put the butter and oil, or beef suet, in the frying pan and place over moderately high heat until you see the butter foam begin to subside, or the beef fat almost smoking; this indicates the fat is hot enough to sear the meat. Sauté the steak on one side for 3 to 4 minutes, and regulate the heat so that the fat is always very hot but is not burning. Turn the steak and sauté the other side for 3 to 4 minutes. The steak is done to a medium rare (*à point*) the moment you observe a little pearling of red juice beginning to ooze at the surface of the steak. Another test is to press the steak with your finger; it is medium rare when it just begins to take on a suggestion of resistance and spring in contrast to its soft raw state. If you have any doubts at all, cut a small incision in the steak.

A hot dish   **Salt and pepper**

Remove the steak to a hot dish and season it quickly with salt and pepper. Keep warm for a moment while completing the sauce.

| ¼ pt. stock, beef bouillon, red wine, dry white wine, dry white vermouth, or water | 1 to 1½ oz. softened butter |

Pour the fat out of the frying pan. Add the liquid, and place the frying pan over high heat. Scrape up coagulated juices with a wooden spoon while rapidly boiling down the liquid until it is reduced almost to a syrup. Away from heat, swirl the butter into the liquid until it is absorbed; the butter will thicken the liquid into a light sauce. Pour the sauce over the steak and serve.

VARIATIONS: FLAVOURED BUTTERS

Any of the following are delicious when beaten into your sauce in place of plain butter. They are simply butters creamed with flavourings. If you are serving a grilled steak, spread one of the butters over it just before taking it to the table.

Parsley Butter, page 92
Herb Butter, page 92
Mustard Butter, page 90
Shallot Butter, page 93
Garlic Butter, page 91
Snail Butter (with shallots, garlic, and herbs), page 92.

VARIATIONS

Bifteck Sauté Bercy

[Sautéed Steak, with Shallot and White Wine Sauce]

For grilled steak, use a *beurre Bercy*, page 93, and spread it over the steak just before serving.

For 4 to 6 people, depending on your menu

2 to 2½ lbs. steak	3 tbl chopped shallots or spring
½ oz. butter	onions

Sauté the steak as described in the master recipe and remove it to a hot dish. Pour the fat out of the frying pan. Add the butter. Stir in the shallots or spring onions and cook slowly for a minute.

¼ pt. dry white wine or dry white
  vermouth

Pour the wine into the frying pan and boil it down rapidly, scraping up the coagulated juices from the bottom of the pan until the liquid has reduced almost to a syrup.

2 to 3 oz. softened butter	Optional: 2 to 3 tbl diced, poached
Salt and pepper to taste	beef marrow, page 15
2 to 3 tbl chopped parsley	

Away from heat, beat in the butter a spoonful at a time until it is absorbed and has thickened the sauce. Beat in salt and pepper to taste, then the parsley. Fold in the optional beef marrow. Spread the sauce over the steak and serve.

Bifteck Sauté Marchand de Vins
Bifteck Sauté à la Bordelaise

[Sautéed Steak with Red Wine Sauce]

Use the same procedure described for the preceding *Bercy* sauce, but substitute red wine for white. If you add the optional beef marrow, the sauce becomes a *bordelaise*.

Bifteck Sauté Béarnaise

[Sautéed Steak with *Béarnaise* Sauce]

For 4 to 6 people, depending on your menu

2 to 2½ lbs. steak   ¼ pt. *sauce béarnaise*, page 76
⅛ pt. brown stock, beef bouillon,
   dry white wine, or dry white
   vermouth

Sauté the steak as described in the master recipe, preceding. Deglaze frying pan
with stock, bouillon, or wine, boiling it down rapidly to reduce it to 1½
spoonfuls. Beat the liquid by drops into the *sauce béarnaise*.

Sautéed or fried potatoes   A warmed sauceboat
Fresh watercress

Decorate the steak dish with sautéed or fried potatoes and fresh watercress. Serve
the sauce in a warmed sauceboat.

Steak au Poivre

[Pepper Steak with Brandy Sauce]

Steak au poivre can be very good when it is not so buried in pepper and
doused with flaming brandy that the flavour of the meat is utterly disguised. In
fact, we do not care at all for flaming brandy with this dish; it is too reminiscent
of restaurant show-off cooking. And the alcohol taste, as it is not boiled off
completely, remains in the brandy, spoiling the taste of the meat.

For 4 to 6 people, depending on your menu

2 tbl of a mixture of several kinds
   of peppercorns, or white peppercorns

Place the peppercorns in a big mixing bowl and crush them roughly with a
pestle or the bottom of a bottle.

2 to 2½ lbs. steak ¾ to 1 in. thick

Dry the steaks. Rub and press the crushed peppercorns into both sides of the
meat with your fingers and the palms of your hands. Cover with greaseproof
paper. Let them stand for at least half an hour; two or 3 hours are even better, so
that the flavour of the pepper will penetrate the meat.

A hot dish   Salt

Sauté the steak in hot oil and butter as described in the preceding master recipe.
Remove to a hot dish, season with salt, and keep warm for a moment while
completing the sauce.

½ oz. butter
2 tbl chopped shallots or spring
    onions
¼ pt. stock or beef bouillon

⅛ pt. cognac
1½ to 2 oz. softened butter
Sautéed or fried potatoes
Fresh watercress

Pour the fat out of the frying pan. Add the butter and shallots or spring onions and cook slowly for a minute. Pour in the stock or bouillon and boil down rapidly over high heat while scraping up the coagulated cooking juices. Then add the cognac and boil rapidly for a minute or two more to evaporate its alcohol. Away from heat, swirl in the butter a dessertspoon at a time. Decorate the dish with the potatoes and watercress. Pour the sauce over the steak, and serve.

FILLET STEAKS

Filets, Tournedos, Filet Mignons

Filets, tournedos, and *filet mignons* are steaks 1 inch thick cut from the fillet of beef as illustrated on page 265. The *filet,* the largest, should be 3 to 3½ inches in diameter, the *tournedos* about 2½ inches, and the *filet mignon* can be as small as 1½ inches. Since they are all cooked and served in the same way, we shall refer to all three as *tournedos* in French, and as fillet steaks in English. Fillet steaks are trimmed of all fat and surrounding filament. The circumference is usually wrapped in a strip of fresh pork fat or blanched bacon, and tied with string so that the steaks will keep their neat circular shape while they are being cooked. The string is removed before serving and also, if you wish, the strip of fat or bacon. Although fillet steaks may be grilled, they are usually sautéed quickly in hot butter to a nice brown on the outside and a juicy red inside.

Fillet steaks may be sauced and served exactly like the steaks in the preceding recipes, but because of their expense they are usually surrounded with fine wines and truffles or other elaborations. They cook in 8 to 10 minutes, and the sauce takes about 2 minutes, so that you can afford to spend a bit of time on the vegetables and garniture you wish to serve with them. Here are three classical combinations. See also the vegetable suggestions for steak on page 266.

* *TOURNEDOS SAUTÉS AUX CHAMPIGNONS*
TOURNEDOS SAUTÉS CHASSEUR

[Fillet Steaks with Mushroom and Madeira Sauce]

A handsome presentation for these steaks would be a dish decorated with whole baked tomatoes, artichoke hearts cooked in butter, and potato balls sautéed in butter. Serve with them a good claret from the Médoc district.

For 6 steaks

6 crustless rounds of white bread,   **1½ to 2 oz. clarified butter, page 12**
2½ ins. in diameter and $\frac{3}{16}$ in. thick

Sauté bread rounds in hot clarified butter to brown very lightly on each side.
Reheat them for a minute in a 350° F., Mark 4 oven just before serving.

½ lb. fresh mushrooms, whole if   **2 tbl chopped shallots or spring**
very small, quartered if large   **onions**
1 oz. butter   **¼ tsp salt**
1 tbl oil   **Pinch of pepper**

Sauté mushrooms in hot butter and oil for 5 minutes to brown them lightly.
Stir in the shallots or spring onions and cook slowly for a minute or two more.
Season, and leave aside.

6 fillet steaks 1 in. thick and 2½ ins.   **1 oz. butter, more if needed**
in diameter, each wrapped in a   **1 tbl oil**
strip of fat as illustrated on page   **1 or 2 heavy frying pans just large**
266   **enough to hold the steaks easily**

Dry the steaks. Place the butter and oil in the frying pan and place over moderately high heat. When you see the butter foam begin to subside, indicating it is
hot enough to sear and brown the steaks, sauté them for 3 to 4 minutes on each
side. They are medium rare if, when pressed with your finger, they offer a
suggestion of resistance in contrast to their soft, raw state.

Salt and pepper   **A warm serving dish**

Immediately remove from heat. Discard the strings and, if you wish, the strip
of fat. Season quickly with salt and pepper. Place each steak on a canapé, and
keep warm for several minutes while preparing the sauce.

¼ pt. stock or beef bouillon   **1 tbl tomato paste**

Pour the fat out of the frying pan; stir in the stock or bouillon and tomato paste.
Boil rapidly, scraping up the coagulated cooking juices, until liquid is reduced
to 2 or 3 tablespoons.

⅛ pt. Madeira mixed with ¼ oz. of   **2 tbl chopped parsley, tarragon and**
arrowroot or cornflour   **chervil, or parsley only**

Pour in the starch and wine mixture; boil rapidly for a minute to evaporate the
alcohol and to thicken the sauce lightly. Then add the sautéed mushrooms and

simmer a minute more to blend flavours. Correct seasoning. Spread the sauce and mushrooms over the steaks, sprinkle with herbs, and serve.

VARIATIONS

Tournedos Henri IV

[Fillet Steaks with Artichoke Hearts and *Béarnaise* Sauce]

For 6 steaks

6 fillet steaks sautéed in oil and butter

6 canapés (rounds of white bread sautéed in clarified butter, page 181)

$\frac{1}{8}$ pt. Madeira, dry white wine, or dry white vermouth

$\frac{1}{8}$ pt. beef stock or beef bouillon

6 fresh artichoke hearts cooked in butter, page 397

$\frac{1}{4}$ to $\frac{1}{2}$ pt. *sauce béarnaise*, page 76

Potato balls sautéed in butter, page 487, and rolled in 2 tbl chopped parsley

Asparagus tips cooked in butter, page 404

Sauté the steaks as described in the master recipe. Season and place on canapés on a hot dish. Keep warm for a few minutes. Pour sauté fat out of frying pan, add wine and stock or bouillon, and boil down rapidly reducing liquid to 3 tablespoons while scraping coagulated sauté juices into it. Spoon liquid over steaks. Top each steak with a hot artichoke heart filled with *béarnaise*. Decorate dish with the hot potatoes and asparagus. Serve immediately.

Tournedos Rossini

[Fillet Steaks with Artichoke Hearts, *Foie Gras,* Truffles, and Madeira Sauce]

A dish of *tournedos Rossini* takes the fillet steak about as far as it can go. Were you living in France during the midwinter, the *foie gras* and truffles would, of course, be fresh. You may use canapés rather than artichoke bottoms as a bed for the steaks, but it seems too bad to compromise at all in this dish.

Fitting accompaniments would be potato balls sautéed in butter, buttered peas, asparagus tips, or braised lettuce, and an excellent, château-bottled claret from the Médoc district.

For 6 steaks

3 large, fresh artichoke hearts cooked in a *blanc,* page 396

Salt and pepper

$1\frac{1}{2}$ oz. melted butter

Slice each cooked artichoke heart in two, horizontally. Season with salt, pepper, and melted butter. Place in a covered dish. Fifteen minutes before serving, heat them in a 350° F., Mark 4 oven.

6 slices tinned 'block' *foie gras*,	**2 tbl Madeira**
¼ in. thick and about 1½ ins. in	**3 tbl rich stock, mushroom essence,**
diameter	**page 472, or beef bouillon**

Place the *foie gras* slices in a covered dish and baste with the Madeira and stock, essence, or bouillon. Ten minutes before serving, place over barely simmering water to heat through gently.

18 to 24 slices of tinned truffle,	**Pinch of pepper**
1/16 in. thick	**½ oz. butter**
2 tbl Madeira	

Place the truffle slices and their juices in a small saucepan with the Madeira, pepper, and butter. Five minutes before serving, warm over gentle heat.

6 fillet steaks 1 in. thick and 2½ ins.	**Salt and pepper**
in diameter	

Sauté the steaks as directed in the master recipe on page 271. Season with salt and pepper.

A warm serving dish

Arrange the hot artichoke bottoms on the serving dish and place a steak on each. Over each steak lay a warm slice of *foie gras,* and top with slices of truffle. Decorate the dish with whatever vegetables you have chosen, and keep warm for 2 to 3 minutes while finishing the sauce.

¼ pt. stock or bouillon	**Salt and pepper**
Juice from the *foie gras,* and truffles	**1½ to 2 oz. softened butter**
1 tsp arrowroot or cornflour blended	
with 1 tbl Madeira	

Pour the fat out of the steak frying pan. Pour in the stock or bouillon, and the juices from the *foie gras* and truffles. Boil down rapidly, scraping up all coagulated juices, until liquid has reduced by half. Pour in the starch and wine mixture and simmer for a minute. Correct seasoning. Away from heat, swirl in the butter. Pour the sauce over the steaks and serve.

MINCED BEEF—HAMBURGERS

Bifteck Haché

Shock is the reaction of some people we have encountered who learn that real French people living in France eat hamburgers. They do eat them, and when sauced with any of the suggestions in the following recipes, the French hamburger is an excellent and relatively economical main course for an informal party. Serve with them the same types of red wines and vegetables as listed for steaks on pages 266 to 267.

The best hamburgers are made from the leanest beef. Actually some of the least expensive cuts, chuck and neck, are the most flavourful. Top sirloin, rump, and round are really second choice for hamburgers although they are more expensive. Be fussy in choosing your meat; have all the fat and sinews removed, and have it minced before your eyes or even better, mince it yourself. The fat content of hamburger should be only 8 to 10 per cent., or 1¼ to 1½ ounces per pound. This may be in the form of butter, minced beef suet, beef marrow, or minced fresh pork fat.

---

* BIFTECK HACHÉ À LA LYONNAISE

[Minced Beef with Onions and Herbs]

For 6 hamburgers

3 oz. finely chopped onions	1 oz. butter

Cook the onions slowly in the butter for about 10 minutes until very tender but not browned. Place them in a mixing bowl.

1½ lbs. lean, minced beef	1½ tsp salt
1 oz. softened butter, ground beef suet, beef marrow, or fresh pork fat	⅛ tsp pepper
	⅛ tsp thyme
	1 egg

Add the beef, butter or fat, seasonings, and egg to the onions in the mixing bowl and beat vigorously with a wooden spoon to blend thoroughly. Correct seasoning. Form into patties ¾ inch thick. Cover with greaseproof paper and refrigerate until ready to use.

2 oz. flour spread on a plate

Just before sautéing, roll the patties lightly in the flour. Shake off excess flour.

½ oz. butter and 1 dsp oil, or sufficient to film the bottom of the frying pan	1 or 2 heavy frying pans just large enough to hold the patties easily in one layer

Place the butter and oil in the frying pan and place over moderately high heat. When you see the butter foam begin to subside, indicating it is hot enough to sear the meat, sauté the patties for 2 to 3 minutes or more on each side, depending on whether you like your hamburgers rare, medium, or well done.

A warm serving dish

Arrange the hamburgers on the serving dish and keep warm for a moment while finishing the sauce.

$\frac{1}{4}$ **pt. beef stock, beef bouillon, dry**   1 to 1$\frac{1}{2}$ **oz. softened butter**
    white wine, dry white vermouth,
    red wine, or $\frac{1}{8}$ pt. water

Pour the fat out of the frying pan. Add the liquid and boil it down rapidly, scraping up the coagulated pan juices until it has reduced almost to a syrup. Away from heat, swirl the butter by dessertspoons into the sauce until it is absorbed. Pour the sauce over the hamburgers and serve.

VARIATION

Bitokes à la Russe

[Hamburgers with Cream Sauce]

Ingredients for 6 plain beef
    hamburgers or the preceding
    flavoured hamburgers

Sauté the hamburgers in oil and butter as described in the preceding master recipe. Remove them to a hot serving dish.

$\frac{1}{8}$ **pt. stock or beef bouillon**   **Pinch of nutmeg**
$\frac{1}{4}$ **pt. cream**   **Drops of lemon juice**
Salt and pepper

Pour the fat out of the frying pan. Add the stock or bouillon and boil it down rapidly, scraping up coagulated cooking juices, until reduced almost to a syrup. Pour in the cream and boil it down rapidly for a minute or two until it has reduced, and thickened slightly. Season to taste with salt, pepper, nutmeg, and drops of lemon juice.

1 to 1$\frac{1}{2}$ **oz. softened butter**
2 **tbl chopped green herbs such as**
    parsley, chives, tarragon, chervil,
    or parsley only

Away from heat, swirl in the butter by dessertspoons until it is absorbed. Stir in the herbs, spoon the sauce over the hamburgers, and serve.

VARIATION: FLAVOURED BUTTERS

Any of the butters listed here may be swirled into the frying pan after it has been deglazed with stock, wine, or water.

Parsley Butter, page 92   Shallot Butter, page 93
Herb Butter, page 92   Garlic Butter, page 91
Mustard Butter, page 90   Snail Butter (with shallots, garlic,
                                     and herbs), page 92.

VARIATION: OTHER SAUCES

Any of the following sauces are made separately. After the hamburgers
have been sautéed and removed from the frying pan, the sauce is poured in and
boiled for a moment while the coagulated sauté juices are scraped into it. The
sauce is then poured over the hamburgers.

Sauce Tomate, or Coulis de Tomates, tomato sauce, pages 68 to 70

Sauce Poivrade, brown sauce with strong pepper flavouring, page 62

Sauce Robert, brown sauce with mustard, page 64

Sauce Brune aux Fines Herbes, brown sauce with herbs or tarragon, page 64

Sauce Madère, brown sauce with Madeira wine, page 66

Sauce au Cari, brown sauce with curry and onions, page 65

See also the red wine and the white wine sauce for steaks on page 269, and
the mushroom sauce for fillet steak on page 271.

FILLET OF BEEF

Filet de Boeuf

* FILET DE BOEUF BRAISÉ PRINCE ALBERT

[Braised Fillet of Beef Stuffed with Foie Gras and Truffles]

Here is a magnificent recipe for an important dinner, and it is not a difficult
one in spite of the luxury of its details. We have chosen braised fillet because it is
more unusual than roast fillet. Everything except the actual cooking of the meat
may be done in advance as indicated by the asterisk in the recipe.

Braised lettuce and potato balls sautéed in butter would go beautifully with
this, and you should accompany it with a fine château-bottled claret from the
Médoc district. See also other vegetables suggested for steaks on pages 266-7.

For 8 people

4 to 6 tinned truffles about 1 in.   2 tbl Madeira
   in diameter

Cut the truffles in quarters. Place in a small bowl with juice from the tin and the
Madeira. Cover and marinate while preparing the rest of the ingredients.

The braising vegetables (matignon)

3 oz. each: finely diced carrots and
  onions
2 oz. finely diced celery
2 tbl diced boiled ham
¼ tsp salt
Pinch of pepper

A small herb bouquet: 2 parsley
  sprigs, ⅓ bay leaf, ⅛ tsp thyme
  tied in cheesecloth
1½ oz. butter
⅛ pt. Madeira

Cook the vegetables, ham, seasonings, herbs, and butter slowly together in a
small covered saucepan for 10 to 15 minutes, until the vegetables are tender but
not browned. Then pour in the wine and boil it down rapidly until it has
almost entirely evaporated. Leave aside.

The foie gras stuffing

2 tbl very finely chopped shallots
  or spring onions
½ oz. butter
4 oz. *mousse de foie d'oie* (or
  'block' *foie gras*, which is much
  more expensive but also much
  better)

1 dsp Madeira
1 dsp cognac
Pinch of allspice
Pinch of thyme
⅛ tsp pepper

Cook the shallots or spring onions slowly in butter for 3 minutes in a small
saucepan without browning them. Scrape into a mixing bowl. Beat in the *foie
gras* and other ingredients. Correct seasoning.

A 3-lb. trimmed fillet of beef, at
  least 3 ins. in diameter

Salt and pepper

Cut a deep slit down the length of the least presentable side of the fillet, to within
¼ inch of the two ends and to within ¼ inch of the other side, or top. Season the
interior of the slit lightly with salt and pepper, and spread it with the *foie gras*
mixture. Insert the truffles in a line down the centre of the filled slit—reserve
their marinade for later. Do not stuff the fillet so full that the slit cannot be
closed.

A 2½-in. strip of fresh pork fat as
  long as the fillet (or strips of
  blanched bacon, page 12)

White string

Lay the pork fat or bacon strips the length of the closed slit. Tie securely but not
too tightly with loops of white string at 1-inch intervals.

Braising the fillet

Preheat oven to 350° F., Mark 4.

A heavy, oval, fireproof casserole just large enough to hold the fillet	1 dsp oil
	Salt and pepper
1 oz. butter	A meat thermometer

Brown the fillet lightly on all sides in the casserole in hot butter and oil. Discard the browning fat. Season the meat lightly with salt and pepper. (Insert meat thermometer.) Spread the cooked vegetables over the fillet.

(*) May be prepared in advance to this point.

¾ to 1 pt. good brown stock or beef bouillon (or a very good brown sauce, page 58, in which case the starch liaison at the end of the recipe is omitted)	An oval of aluminium foil
	A bulb baster

Pour in enough stock, bouillon, or sauce to come half-way up the sides of the fillet. Bring to a simmer on top of the stove. Lay foil over the meat. Cover the casserole and place in lower part of pre-heated oven for 45 to 55 minutes. Regulate heat so that the liquid remains at a very slow boil. Baste the meat with the braising stock 3 or 4 times during its cooking. The fillet is done at a meat-thermometer reading of 136° F. for rare beef, or 140° for medium rare, and if, when you press the fillet with your finger, it offers a slight resistance in contrast to its soft, raw state.

A hot serving dish

Place the fillet slit-side down on a hot serving dish after removing the trussing strings and pork fat or bacon. The meat should cool for 10 minutes or more before carving, so that its juices will retreat back into the tissues.

Sauce and serving

Wine marinade from the truffles

Skim the fat off the braising juices. Pour the truffle marinade into them, and rapidly boil down this liquid until it has reduced to about ¾ pint and its flavour is rich and concentrated.

½ oz. arrowroot or cornflour mixed with 1 tbl Madeira	Optional: 2 or 3 tbl diced truffles

Beat in the cornflour mixture (unless you have used the brown sauce) and the optional truffles. Simmer for 2 to 3 minutes, then correct seasoning. The diced *matignon* vegetables remain in the sauce.

Decorate the dish with whatever vegetables you have chosen. Pour a spoonful or two of the sauce and diced vegetables over the meat, and pass the rest of the sauce in a bowl. The fillet is carved into crosswise slices about ⅜ inch thick.

VARIATION

If you do not wish to stuff the fillet, cook it exactly the same way but without slitting and filling it. When you have placed it on a serving dish, you may garnish the top with grilled mushroom caps alternating with sliced truffles.

VARIATION

Marinade, for Fillet of Beef

The following marinade is particularly good if you do not have top-quality fillet.

¼ pt. dry white wine or dry white vermouth	¼ tsp basil
⅛ pt. Madeira	3 parsley sprigs
1 tbl cognac	3 tbl chopped shallots or spring onions
1 tsp salt	2 or more tinned truffles and their juice
6 peppercorns	
¼ tsp thyme	

Place the raw, trimmed fillet in a dish or casserole. Pour on the wines and mix in the seasonings, herbs, shallots or spring onions, and truffles. Cover and marinate for 6 hours or overnight, turning the meat and basting it several times. Drain and dry the meat thoroughly before browning it. Include the marinade, but not the truffles, with your braising liquid. Reserve the truffles for your sauce.

BOILED BEEF

Pot-au-feu

* POTÉE NORMANDE
POT-AU-FEU

[Boiled Beef with Pork, Chicken, Sausage, and Vegetables]

Here is a sumptuous family-style boiled dinner which will serve 12 or more, and always makes a great hit with guests. It is brought to the table in its pan or a reasonable facsimile, looking for all the world like a plain *pot-au-feu*. The host starts the proceedings as usual by spearing out the beef and placing it on a dish. Then he finds a sausage, and after that a big piece of pork. Finally, to wild acclaim, he brings out a chicken. Two or three sauces may be served, such as a cream sauce with mustard and tomato, a herbal mayonnaise, and a big bowl of the cooking stock. The *potée,* like all boiled dinners, is easy on the cook because it can simmer quietly by itself for 4 to 5 hours and if it is ready before serving time, it can remain in its pan where it will keep warm for a good hour.

VEGETABLE AND WINE SUGGESTIONS

Carrots, turnips, onions, and leeks cook along with the meats. Boiled potatoes, *risotto,* or buttered noodles are prepared and served separately. A nice, simple red wine goes well: Beaujolais, claret, or Chianti, or a chilled *rosé.*

BEEF CUTS FOR BOILING—POT-AU-FEU

First Choice: Rump—*Pointe de Culotte* or *Aiguillette de Rumsteck.*
Other Choices: Thick Flank—*Tranche Grasse*
                Silverside—*Gîte à la Noix*
                Bladebone or Chuck—*Paleron* or *Macreuse à Pot-au-feu*
                Brisket—*Milieu de Poitrine.*

For 12 to 16 people

A pan large enough to hold all the ingredients listed
Beef (cooking time 3½ to 4 hours): a 4-lb. boneless piece of rump, thick flank, silverside, chuck, or brisket
Pork (cooking time about 3 hours): a 4-lb. piece from the top back, short back, prime collar, or gammon hock

Chicken (cooking time 2½ to 3 hours): a 4-lb. ready-to-cook boiling fowl of good quality
Sausage (cooking time 30 minutes): 2 lbs. lightly smoked country or Polish sausage

All the meats and the vegetables listed above are simmered together in the pan, but are added at various times, depending on how long they take to cook. Start the cooking 5 hours before you expect to serve, to be sure the meats will be done. Trim excess fat off the beef and pork. Tie each piece so that it will hold its shape during cooking. Truss the chicken. To each piece of meat and to the chicken, tie a string long enough to fasten to the handle of the pan, so that the meats may be removed easily for testing.

Vegetable Garnish (cooking time 1½ hours): carrots, onions, turnips, and, if available, leeks; 1 to 2 of each vegetable per person

Prepare the vegetable garnish: Peel the carrots and turnips and quarter them lengthwise; peel the onions; trim and wash the leeks. Tie the vegetables in one or several bundles of washed cheesecloth so that they may be removed easily from the pan.

Soup Vegetables and Herbs:
   3 scraped carrots
   3 peeled onions, each stuck with
     a whole clove
   2 scraped parsnips
   2 celery stalks
   2 leeks, if available
   A large herb bouquet as follows:
     6 parsley sprigs, 1 bay leaf,
     $\frac{1}{2}$ tsp thyme, 4 garlic cloves,
     8 peppercorns tied in cheesecloth

Cooking Stock: sufficient meat
   stock to cover ingredients by
   6 ins.; Or 2 pts. of bouillon, 3
   tins of chicken broth, and water
Optional: raw or cooked beef or
   veal bones, meat scraps, poultry
   carcasses, necks, gizzards

Place the beef in the pan with the soup vegetables, herb bouquet, and optional bones and scraps. Cover with cooking stock by 6 inches. More liquid may be added later if necessary. Place pan over moderate heat, bring to the simmering point, skim. Partially cover the pan and simmer slowly for 1 hour, skimming occasionally.

Add the pork and chicken. Bring pan quickly back to simmering point. Skim. Simmer 1$\frac{1}{2}$ hours more and skim from time to time.

Then add the vegetable garnish and bring pan quickly back to simmering point. Taste cooking stock for seasoning and salt lightly if necessary. Simmer 1$\frac{1}{2}$ to 2 hours more, adding the sausage $\frac{1}{2}$ hour before the end. The meats and chicken are done when they are tender if pierced with a sharp-pronged fork or skewer. If any piece is tender before the others are done, remove to a bowl and keep moist with several ladlefuls of cooking stock. Return to pan to reheat before serving.

(*) If the *potée* is ready before you are, it will stay warm for at least 45 minutes in the pan, or may be reheated.

While the pan is simmering, prepare one or two of the sauces suggested at the end of the recipe, using some of the liquid from the pan if you need stock.

Serving

Drain the meats and the vegetable garnish. Discard trussing strings. Arrange vegetables on a large, hot dish and moisten them with a ladleful of cooking stock. Decorate with parsley. Either place the meats in a large casserole for presentation and carving at the table, or carve in the kitchen and arrange on a dish. Strain, degrease, and season enough cooking stock to fill a large serving bowl, and pass it along with whatever sauce or sauces you have chosen from the following suggestions.

Sauce suggestions

Make 2½ to 3 pints if only one sauce is to be served; 1½ pints each if two sauces are served.

Sauce Alsacienne, hard-boiled egg mayonnaise with herbs, capers, and cooking stock, page 84.

Sauce Nénette, cream simmered until it has reduced and thickened, then flavoured with mustard and tomato, page 355.

Sauce Tomate or *Coulis de Tomates*, a good tomato sauce, pages 68-70.

Sauce Suprême, a velouté sauce made with the cooking stock, and enriched with cream, page 52.

BRAISED BEEF—POT ROAST
Pièce de Boeuf Braisée
* *BOEUF À LA MODE*
[Beef Braised in Red Wine]

Braised beef is a wonderful party dish; it is not only delicious to smell, look at, and eat, but you have no worries about overdone meat, and you can cook it ahead of time if you need to. The following recipe calls for a 6- to 24-hour marination of the beef in red wine and aromatic vegetables before cooking. If you prefer to omit this step, pour the marinade ingredients into the casserole after browning the meat.

VEGETABLE AND WINE SUGGESTIONS

Boeuf à la mode is traditionally garnished with braised carrots and onions, and is usually accompanied by buttered noodles, parsley potatoes, or steamed rice. Other vegetables could be braised lettuce, celery, or leeks, or buttered green peas. Serve with it a good, characterful red wine, such as a Burgundy, Hermitage, Côte Rôtie, or Châteauneuf-du-Pape.

BEEF CUTS FOR BRAISING

Although it is not essential, beef for braising is usually larded. That is, strips of fresh pork fat are inserted into it, going in the direction of the grain. They baste the interior of the meat as it cooks, and make an attractive design when the meat is sliced. Most butchers will lard the meat for you.

Choose a piece of beef of at least 3 pounds, and, however long it is, its width should be at least 4 inches. It shrinks quite a bit during cooking. Count on 1 pound of boneless beef for 2 or 3 people.

First Choice: Rump—*Pointe de Culotte* or *Aiguillette de Rumsteck*.

Other Choices: Thick Flank—*Tranche Grasse*
Bladebone or Chuck—*Paleron* or *Macreuse à Pot-au-feu*
Topside—*Tende de Tranche*
Silverside—*Gîte à la Noix*
Eye of Silverside—*Rond de Gîte à la Noix*.

For 10 to 12 people

Red wine marinade

An enamelled, ovenglass, or porcelain bowl just large enough to hold all the ingredients listed
¼ lb. each: thinly sliced carrots, onions, and celery stalks
2 halved cloves unpeeled garlic
1 dsp thyme
2 bay leaves
4 tbl chopped parsley
2 whole cloves or 4 allspice berries

A 5-lb. piece of braising beef, trimmed and tied for cooking
1 dsp salt
¼ tsp pepper
2 pts. young red wine with body—Burgundy, Côtes du Rhône, Mâcon, or Chianti
⅛ pt. brandy
¼ pt. olive oil

Place half the vegetables, herbs, and spices in the bottom of the bowl. Rub the meat with salt and pepper and place it over the vegetables. Spread the rest of the vegetables and herbs over the meat. Pour on the wine, brandy, and olive oil. Cover and marinate for at least 6 hours (12 to 24 hours if the meat is refrigerated). Turn and baste the meat every hour or so.

Half an hour before cooking, drain the meat on a rack. Just before browning, dry it thoroughly. It will not brown if it is damp.

Browning and braising the beef

Preheat oven to 350° F., Mark 4.

A fireproof casserole or heavy roasting pan just large enough to hold the meat and braising ingredients

3 to 4 tbl rendered pork fat or cooking oil

Add the fat to the casserole and place over moderately high heat. When fat is on the point of smoking, brown the meat on all sides. This takes about 15 minutes. Pour out the browning fat.

(*) Recipe may be prepared in advance up to this point.

One or all of these to give body to the sauce:	1½ to 2½ pts. beef stock, or beef bouillon
1 or 2 cracked veal knuckles 1 or 2 split calf's feet 4 to 8 oz. fresh pork rind, bacon rind, or ham rind simmered 10 minutes in a quart of water, rinsed, and drained	

Pour in the wine marinade and boil it down rapidly until it has reduced by half. Then add the veal knuckles, calf's feet, and rind, and pour in enough stock or bouillon to come two-thirds of the way up the beef. Bring to simmering point on top of the stove, skim, cover tightly, and place in lower part of preheated oven. Regulate heat so that liquid remains at a gentle simmer for 3½ to 4 hours, and turn the meat several times during its braising. The beef is done when a sharp-pronged fork will pierce it easily.

2 lbs. quartered carrots braised in butter, page 438	24 to 36 small onions, brown-braised in stock, page 444

While the beef is being braised, cook the carrots and onions. Leave them aside until needed.

A hot serving dish

When the meat is tender, remove it to the dish. Discard trussing strings. Trim off any loose fat, and keep the meat warm while finishing the sauce (5 to 10 minutes).

½ oz. arrowroot or cornflour mixed with 1 tbl Madeira or port, if needed

Skim the fat off the braising juices, and strain them through a sieve into a saucepan, pressing the liquid out of the vegetables. Simmer for a minute or two, skimming, then boil rapidly until liquid is reduced to about 1¼ pints and is full of flavour. Taste carefully for seasoning. Sauce should be lightly thickened. If too thin, beat in the cornflour and wine mixture and simmer for 3 minutes. Then add the braised carrots and onions and simmer for 2 minutes to blend flavours.

A slotted spoon Parsley sprigs	A warmed sauceboat

Remove vegetables with a slotted spoon and arrange them around the meat. Decorate with parsley. Pour a little sauce over the meat and take the rest to the table in a warmed sauceboat. (Or carve the meat and arrange on the dish with the vegetables and parsley, and spoon some of the sauce over the meat.)

(*) AHEAD-OF-TIME NOTES

For a wait of up to one hour, return meat, vegetables and sauce to casserole, cover loosely, and place over barely simmering water.

For a longer wait, slice the meat and arrange it on a fireproof dish. Place the vegetables around the meat. Baste with the sauce. Half an hour before serving, cover and reheat in a 350° F., Mark 4 oven. Leftover braised beef will be just as good the next day, heated up the same way.

VARIATIONS

Cold Braised Beef

This recipe for beef braised in red wine may easily be turned into an aspic by following the directions for *boeuf mode en gelée*, page 513. Cold braised beef may also be served as a salad, by following the directions for *salade de boeuf à la parisienne*, page 501.

Pièce de Boeuf à la Cuillère

[Chopped Braised Beef Served in a Beef Shell]

From *la vieille cuisine française* comes an unusual way to serve braised beef for a dinner party. First the beef is braised; then meat is cut out from its top and centre to leave a shell of beef which is crumbed and browned in the oven. The removed beef is chopped, combined with sautéed mushrooms, chopped ham, and sauce, and is returned to the shell for serving. A nice thing about this recipe is that all may be made in advance and reheated for 5-10 minutes just before serving.

For 10 to 12 people

Braising the beef

Braise the beef and make the sauce following the master recipe, but simmer the meat only until it is almost tender, about 3 hours for a 5-pound piece. It should still be firm enough to hold its shape when the shell is made. Choose a solid, lean piece of topside with no muscle separations. It should weigh at least 5 pounds and be cut into an even rectangular block about 5 inches wide and 5 inches deep.

Making the shell

When the meat is done, remove it from the sauce. Place it under a board and a 2-pound weight to preserve its shape for about an hour while it cools to tepid. Then trim it, if necessary, into a neat rectangle. Hollow out the centre, leaving an open-topped rectangular trough or shell of meat with sides and bottom half

an inch thick. Chop the removed meat, including any trimmed-off pieces, into
⅛-inch pieces. Place them in a large, heavy-bottomed, enamelled saucepan, frying
pan, or casserole.

Preparing the filling

½ lb. fresh mushrooms, quartered and sautéed in oil and butter with 1 tbl chopped shallots or spring onions, page 473	4 oz. lean, chopped, boiled ham ½ to ¾ pt. sauce from the braised beef

Stir the mushrooms and ham into the chopped beef, and blend in the sauce.
Simmer slowly, covered, for 15 to 20 minutes, stirring frequently. Add a little
more sauce if the mixture becomes too thick. It should hold its shape fairly
solidly in a spoon. Carefully correct seasoning. Film top of mixture with a
spoonful of stock or a little melted butter and leave aside, uncovered, or
refrigerate, until needed.

Finishing the shell

A pastry brush 2 eggs beaten in a small bowl with 1 tsp water and a pinch of salt 6 oz. fine, dry, white breadcrumbs tossed with 2 oz. Parmesan cheese	4 oz. melted butter A rack placed on a roasting tin

Using a pastry brush, paint the whole beef shell with beaten egg. Pat on a layer
of cheese and breadcrumbs. Sprinkle with butter and place the shell on the rack.
Refrigerate until needed.

(*) Recipe may be completed even a day ahead up to this point.

Final assembly

Preheat oven to 450° F., Mark 8.

A vegetable garnish such as braised onions and carrots, and sautéed potatoes; Or: baked tomatoes, and French beans or braised lettuce	The rest of the sauce from the braised beef poured into a gravy boat A hot serving dish 2 tbl chopped parsley

About 5 to 10 minutes before serving, place the beef shell in the oven to brown
the crumb and cheese covering lightly. Reheat the filling to simmering point.
Heat the vegetable garniture and the sauce. Then place the browned shell on the
dish, heap with meat mixture, and sprinkle parsley over it. Arrange the
vegetables about the dish. Pass the sauce separately. Each guest cuts down the
crusty, tender shell with a serving spoon to help himself to part of it and its
filling.

BEEF STEWS
Ragoûts de Boeuf

Of the several types of beef stew in which the meat is browned, then simmered in an aromatic liquid, *boeuf bourguignon* is the most famous. The *daubes*, *estouffades*, and *terrines* usually require no browning, and are much simpler to do. To be technically correct, any recipe describing meat which is browned before it is simmered should be labelled a fricassee; we shall not always make the distinction here because stew has become current usage.

CUTS FOR STEWING

The better the meat, the better the stew. While cheaper and coarser cuts may be used, the following are most recommended. Count on 1 pound of boneless meat, trimmed of fat, for 2 people; 3 if the rest of the menu is large.

First Choice: Rump—*Pointe de Culotte* or *Aiguillette de Rumsteck*.
Other Choices: Bladebone or Chuck—*Paleron* or *Macreuse à Pot-au-feu*
                 Thick Flank—*Tranche Grasse*
                 Topside—*Tende de Tranche*
                 Silverside—*Gîte à la Noix*.

COOKING TIME

Beef stews take 3 to 4 hours of simmering depending on the quality and tenderness of the meat. If it has been marinated before cooking, it may take less time. Stews may be cooked either in the oven or on top of the stove; the oven is preferable because its heat is more uniform.

BOEUF BOURGUIGNON
BOEUF À LA BOURGUIGNONNE

[Beef Stew in Red Wine, with Bacon, Onions, and Mushrooms]

As is the case with most famous dishes, there are more ways than one to arrive at a good *boeuf bourguignon*. Carefully done, and perfectly flavoured, it is certainly one of the most delicious beef dishes concocted by man, and can well be the main course for a buffet dinner. Fortunately you can prepare it completely ahead, even a day in advance, and it only gains in flavour when reheated.

VEGETABLE AND WINE SUGGESTIONS

Boiled potatoes are traditionally served with this dish. Buttered noodles or steamed rice may be substituted. if you also wish a green vegetable, buttered

peas would be your best choice. Serve with the beef a fairly full-bodied, young
red wine, such as Beaujolais, Côtes du Rhône, a St. Émilion claret, or Burgundy.

For 6 people

A 6-oz. chunk of streaky bacon

Remove rind, and cut bacon into *lardons* (sticks, ¼ inch thick and 1½ inches long).
Simmer rind and bacon for 10 minutes in 2½ pints of water. Drain and dry.

Preheat oven to 450° F., Mark 8.

A 9- to 10-in. fireproof casserole	**1 tbl olive oil or cooking oil**
3 ins. deep	**A slotted spoon**

Sauté the bacon in the oil over moderate heat for 2 to 3 minutes to brown lightly.
Remove to a side dish with a slotted spoon. Leave casserole aside. Reheat until
fat is almost smoking before you sauté the beef.

3 lbs. lean stewing steak cut into
2-in. cubes (see preceding list of
cuts)

Dry the beef; it will not brown if it is damp. Sauté it, a few pieces at a time, in
the hot oil and bacon fat until nicely browned on all sides. Add it to the bacon.

1 sliced carrot	**1 sliced onion**

In the same fat, brown the sliced vegetables. Pour out the sautéing fat.

1 tsp salt	**1 oz. flour**
¼ tsp pepper	

Return the beef and bacon to the casserole and toss with the salt and pepper.
Then sprinkle on the flour and toss again to coat the beef lightly with the flour.
Place casserole uncovered in middle position of preheated oven for 4 minutes.
Toss the meat and return to oven for 4 minutes more. (This browns the flour
and covers the meat with a light crust.) Remove casserole, and turn oven down
to 325° F., Mark 2.

1¼ pts. of a full-bodied, young red	**1 tbl tomato paste**
wine such as one of those	**2 cloves mashed garlic**
suggested for serving, or a Chianti	**½ tsp thyme**
¾ to 1 pt. brown beef stock or	**A crumbled bay leaf**
beef bouillon	**The blanched bacon rind**

Stir in the wine, and enough stock or bouillon so that the meat is barely covered.
Add the tomato paste, garlic, herbs, and bacon rind. Bring to simmering point

K

on top of the stove. Then cover the casserole and place in lower part of pre-heated oven. Regulate heat so that liquid simmers very slowly for 3 to 4 hours. The meat is done when a fork pierces it easily.

18 to 24 small onions, brown-braised in stock, page 444

1 lb. quartered fresh mushrooms sautéed in butter, page 473

While the beef is cooking, prepare the onions and mushrooms. Leave them aside until needed.

When the meat is tender, pour the contents of the casserole into a sieve placed over a saucepan. Wash out the casserole and return the beef and bacon to it. Distribute the cooked onions and mushrooms over the meat.

Skim fat off the sauce. Simmer sauce for a minute or two, skimming off additional fat as it rises. You should have about 1 pint of sauce thick enough to coat a spoon lightly. If too thin, boil it down rapidly. If too thick, mix in a few tablespoons of stock or bouillon. Taste carefully for seasoning. Pour the sauce over the meat and vegetables.

(*) Recipe may be completed in advance to this point.

Parsley sprigs

FOR IMMEDIATE SERVING: Cover the casserole and simmer for 2 to 3 minutes, basting the meat and vegetables with the sauce several times. Serve in its casserole, or arrange the stew on a dish surrounded with potatoes, noodles, or rice, and decorated with parsley.

FOR SERVING LATER: When cold, cover and refrigerate. About 15 to 20 minutes before serving, bring to simmering point, cover, and simmer very slowly for 10 minutes, occasionally basting the meat and vegetables with the sauce.

CARBONNADES À LA FLAMANDE

[Beef and Onions Braised in Beer]

Beer is typical for the Belgian braise, and gives a quite different character to beef from the red wine of the *bourguignon*. A little brown sugar masks the beer's slightly bitter quality, and a little vinegar at the end gives character. Serve this with parsley potatoes or buttered noodles, a green salad, and beer.

For 6 people

A 3-lb. piece of lean beef from the chuck or rump	**A heavy frying pan**
2 to 3 tbl rendered fresh pork fat or good cooking oil	

Preheat oven to 325° F., Mark 2. Cut the beef into slices about 2 by 4 inches across and ½ inch thick. Dry well. Put a $\frac{1}{16}$-inch layer of fat or oil in the frying pan and heat until almost smoking. Brown the beef slices quickly, a few at a time, and leave them aside.

1½ lbs. of sliced onions	**4 cloves mashed garlic**
Salt and pepper	

Reduce heat to moderate. Stir the onions into the fat in the frying pan, adding more fat if necessary, and brown the onions lightly for about 10 minutes, stirring frequently. Remove from heat, season with salt and pepper, and stir in the garlic.

A 9- to 10-in. fireproof casserole about 3½ ins. deep	**Salt and pepper**

Arrange half the browned beef in the casserole and season lightly with salt and pepper. Spread half the onions over the beef. Repeat with the rest of the beef and onions.

½ pt. strong beef stock or beef bouillon	**1 large herb bouquet: 6 parsley sprigs, 1 bay leaf, and ½ tsp thyme tied in cheesecloth**
¾ to 1 pt. lager	
1 tbl light brown sugar	

Heat the stock or bouillon in the same frying pan, and scrape up coagulated cooking juices. Pour it over the meat. Add enough beer so that the meat is barely covered. Stir in the brown sugar. Bury the herb bouquet among the meat slices. Bring casserole to simmering point on top of the stove. Then cover the casserole and place in lower part of preheated oven. Regulate heat so that liquid remains simmering very slowly for 2½ hours at the end of which time the meat should be fork-tender.

¾ oz. arrowroot or cornflour
blended with 2 tbl wine vinegar

Remove herb bouquet. Drain the cooking liquid out of the casserole into a saucepan, and skim off fat. Beat the starch and wine vinegar mixture into the cooking liquid and simmer for 3 to 4 minutes. Carefully correct seasoning. You should have about ¾ pint of sauce. Pour the sauce back over the meat.

(*) May be prepared in advance to this point.

Parsley potatoes or buttered noodles	Parsley sprigs

When ready to serve, cover the casserole and simmer slowly for 4 to 5 minutes until the meat is thoroughly heated through. Either take the casserole to the table, or arrange the meat on a hot serving dish, spoon the sauce over it, surround with potatoes or noodles, and decorate with parsley.

---

* PAUPIETTES DE BOEUF
ROULADES DE BOEUF
PETITES BALLOTINES DE BOEUF

[Braised Stuffed Beef Rolls]

Paupiettes are thin slices of beef wrapped around a filling, and braised in wine and stock with herbs and aromatic vegetables. Although they follow the same general pattern as other fricassees of beef, their pork and veal stuffing gives them a special character. *Paupiettes* can be cooked in advance, and any leftovers may be reheated or may be served cold. Accompany hot *paupiettes* with rice, *risotto*, or noodles, and a garniture of sautéed mushrooms, braised onions, and carrots, or with buttered green peas or French beans, grilled tomatoes, and French bread. Serve a good simple red wine such as Beaujolais, Côtes du Rhône, Chianti, or a *rosé*.

For about 18 paupiettes serving 6 people

2 oz. finely chopped onions	A 4-pt. mixing bowl
½ oz. butter	

Cook the onions slowly in butter for 7 to 8 minutes until they are tender but not browned. Scrape them into the mixing bowl.

6 oz. lean pork minced with 6 oz. lean veal and 3 oz. fresh pork fat	Pinch of allspice
	Big pinch of pepper
A wooden spoon	¼ tsp salt
1 clove mashed garlic	4 tbl chopped parsley
⅛ tsp thyme	1 egg

Add all ingredients listed above to the mixing bowl; beat vigorously with a wooden spoon until thoroughly blended.

2½ lbs. lean beef (topside or rump) cut into 18 cross-grain slices ¼ in. thick and about 3 ins. in diameter	Salt and pepper
	White string

Flatten each slice of beef to a thickness of ⅛ inch by pounding it between 2 sheets of greaseproof paper with a wooden mallet or rolling pin. Lay the meat flat on a board and sprinkle lightly with salt and pepper. Divide the stuffing into 18 portions and place one on the lower third of each slice. Roll the meat around the stuffing to form cylinders about 4 inches long and 1½ inches thick. Secure each with 2 ties of string. Dry well.

Preheat oven to 325° F., Mark 2.

2 to 3 tbl rendered pork fat or good cooking oil	2 oz. sliced onions
A heavy fireproof casserole about 10 ins. in diameter and 2¼ to 3 ins. deep	1 oz. flour
2 oz. sliced carrots	½ pt. dry white wine or dry white vermouth
	¾ pt. brown stock or beef bouillon

Heat the fat or oil in the casserole until almost smoking. Brown the *paupiettes* lightly, a few at a time, and remove to a side dish. Lower heat to moderate and brown the vegetables slowly for 4 to 5 minutes, stirring. Then add the flour and brown it slowly for 2 to 3 minutes. Remove casserole from heat and immediately beat in the wine, then the stock or bouillon.

A 4-in square of fresh pork rind, bacon rind or salt-pork rind, simmered 10 minutes in 1½ pts. of water, then drained	1 large herb bouquet plus 2 cloves of garlic: 6 parsley sprigs, 1 bay leaf, ½ tsp thyme, and the garlic tied together in cheesecloth

Lay rind in the bottom of the casserole. Place the *paupiettes* over it, and add more stock or bouillon, or water, if necessary, to the liquid in the casserole so that *paupiettes* are barely covered. Add the herb bouquet.

Bulb baster

Bring to simmering point on top of the stove. Cover the casserole and place in lower part of preheated oven. Regulate heat so that the *paupiettes* simmer very slowly for 1½ hours. Baste them two or three times with the liquid in the casserole.

Remove the *paupiettes* to a side dish and cut off trussing strings. Strain the cooking liquid into a saucepan and degrease thoroughly. Boil down the sauce if necessary, to concentrate its flavour. You should have ½ to ¾ pint thick enough to coat a spoon lightly. Correct seasoning.

1 tbl prepared French mustard blended with ⅛ pt. cream	A wire whisk

Away from heat, beat the mustard and cream into the sauce. Simmer for 1 minute. Rearrange the *paupiettes* in the casserole or a fireproof serving dish, and pour the sauce over them.

(*) Recipe may be prepared in advance to this point. Film top of sauce with a spoonful of stock or melted butter. When cold, cover and refrigerate.

Parsley sprigs

About 10 minutes before serving, reheat barely to simmering point on top of the stove. Cover and simmer slowly for 5 minutes or so, basting the *paupiettes* frequently with the sauce. Serve from the casserole, or arrange the *paupiettes* on a dish, spoon the sauce over them, and surround with rice or noodles. Decorate with parsley.

VARIATIONS

Prepare, brown, and braise the *paupiettes* as in the preceding recipe but use the sauce ingredients and techniques outlined either for the *boeuf bourguignon* on page 288, or for the *carbonnades à la flamande* on page 290.

BOEUF À LA CATALANE

[Beef Stew with Rice, Onions, and Tomatoes]

Here is a hearty dish from the Spanish-Mediterranean corner of France. Serve it with a green salad, French bread, and a strong, young red wine.

For 6 people

Preheat oven to 325° F., Mark 2.

A ¼-lb. chunk of streaky bacon	A slotted spoon
2 tbl olive oil	A 5-pt. fireproof casserole about
A heavy, 10-in. frying pan	3 ins. deep

Remove rind and cut bacon into *lardons* (1½-inch strips, ⅜ of an inch thick). Simmer in 1½ pints of water for 10 minutes. Drain, dry, and brown lightly in oil in the frying pan. Remove with a slotted spoon to the casserole.

**3 lbs. lean stewing steak cut into
squares 2½ ins. across and 1 in.
thick (see cuts listed on page 288)**

Dry the meat. Heat fat in frying pan until almost smoking then brown the meat a few pieces at a time. Place it when browned in the casserole.

6 oz. sliced onions

Lower heat to moderate, and brown the onions lightly. Remove them with a slotted spoon and add to the casserole.

**8 oz. clean, unwashed, raw white
rice**

Still in the same fat, stir the rice over moderate heat for 2 to 3 minutes until it turns a milky colour. Scrape into a bowl and leave aside until later.

**½ pt. dry white wine or dry white
vermouth**

Pour any remaining fat out of the frying pan, add the wine and stir for a moment over heat to dissolve coagulated cooking juices. Pour into the casserole.

**¾ pt. to 1 pt. beef stock or beef
bouillon
Salt to taste
¼ tsp pepper**

**2 cloves mashed garlic
½ tsp thyme
Pinch of saffron
1 crumbled bay leaf**

Add stock or bouillon almost to the top of the meat. Salt lightly. Stir in the pepper, garlic, and herbs. Bring to simmering point on top of the stove, cover tightly, and place in lower part of preheated oven to simmer slowly for 1 hour.

**1 lb. ripe, red tomatoes, peeled,
seeded, juiced, and chopped,
page 465**

Remove casserole from oven. Stir in the tomatoes, bring to simmering point on top of the stove, cover, and return to the oven for an additional 1½ to 2 hours of very slow simmering. When the meat is almost fork-tender, remove casserole from oven. Raise oven heat to 375° F., Mark 5.

Sautéed rice from above   **Stock or bouillon if necessary**

Tilt casserole and skim off fat. You should have ¾ to 1 pint of liquid; add more stock or bouillon, or water, if necessary. Stir in the rice. Bring to simmering point on top of stove, cover, and place again in lower part of oven. Regulate heat to keep liquid fully simmering for 20 minutes so that the rice will cook. Do not stir the rice. At the end of this time it should be tender and have absorbed almost all the liquid. Remove from oven and correct seasoning.

(*) May be prepared in advance to this point. Leave aside, cover askew. To reheat, cover casserole and place in a pan of boiling water for about half an hour.

**4 oz. grated Swiss or Parmesan
cheese**

Just before serving, delicately fold the cheese with a fork into the hot beef and rice. Serve from the casserole or on a hot dish.

* *DAUBE DE BOEUF*
  ESTOUFFADE DE BOEUF
  TERRINE DE BOEUF

[Casserole of Beef with Wine and Vegetables—Hot or Cold]

Daube comes from *daubière*, a covered casserole. *Estouffade* is a stifling or smothering, in a covered casserole. Almost every region of France has its own *daubes*, *estouffades*, and *terrines*. Some of them are for a whole piece of braised beef; others are like a *boeuf bourguignon*. In many the meat is larded, and in most it is marinated in wine with vegetables before the cooking begins. Here is a savoury, country-style *daube*, an informal main dish to serve with boiled potatoes, *risotto*, or noodles, a green salad, and a simple red wine or a chilled *rosé*.

Note: We have not directed that the meat be larded, but you may do so if you wish, by inserting two ¼-inch strips of larding pork or blanched bacon through each piece of meat. You may also omit the marination of the meat, and add all the marinade ingredients to the casserole with the beef.

For 6 people

3 lbs. lean stewing steak cut into 2½-in. squares, 1 in. thick (beef cuts are listed on page 288)
A large glazed earthenware bowl
½ pt. dry white wine, dry white vermouth, or red wine
Optional: ⅛ pt. brandy, *eau de vie*, or gin

2 tbl olive oil
2 tsp salt
¼ tsp pepper
½ tsp thyme or sage
1 crumbled bay leaf
2 cloves mashed garlic
½ lb. thinly sliced onions
½ lb. thinly sliced carrots

Place the beef in the bowl and mix with the wine, optional spirits, olive oil, seasonings, herbs, and vegetables. Cover and marinate at least 3 hours (6 if refrigerated), stirring up frequently.

½ lb. streaky bacon cut into 1-in. slices ¼ in. thick and 2 inches long approximately
6 oz. sliced fresh mushrooms

1½ lbs. ripe, red tomatoes, peeled, seeded, juiced, and chopped, page 465 (this will make about 1 pt. tomato pulp)

Simmer the bacon for 10 minutes in 3 pints of water. Drain and dry. Prepare the mushrooms and tomatoes.

Remove the beef from the marinade and drain through a sieve.

Preheat oven to 325° F., Mark 2.

A 4- to 5-qt. fireproof casserole   **4 oz. sifted flour on a plate**
  3½ ins. deep

Line the bottom of the casserole with 3 or 4 strips of bacon. Strew a handful of
the marinade vegetables, mushrooms, and tomatoes over them. Piece by piece,
roll the beef in the flour and shake off excess. Place closely together in a layer
over the vegetables. Cover with a few strips of bacon, and continue with layers
of vegetables, beef, and bacon. End with a layer of vegetables and 2 or 3 strips of
bacon.

½ to ¾ pt. beef stock or beef bouillon

Pour in the wine from the marinade and enough stock or bouillon almost to
cover the contents of the casserole. Bring to simmering point on top of the stove,
cover closely, and place in lower part of preheated oven. Regulate heat so that
the liquid simmers slowly for 3 to 4 hours. The meat is done when a fork
pierces it easily.

Tip casserole and skim out fat. Correct seasoning.

(*) May be prepared ahead and reheated, and is good either hot or cold.

VARIATION

Daube de Boeuf à la Provençale

[Casserole of Beef with Garlic and Anchovy Sauce]

This is the same *daube* given a Provençal flavouring at the end. Any cold
leftovers are delicious, served with a green salad and French bread. Follow the
master recipe with these additions:

10 flat anchovy fillets packed in   **3 tbl olive oil from the anchovy tin**
  olive oil   **and/or plain olive oil**
2 tbl capers   **2 cloves mashed garlic**
A table fork   **2 tbl chopped parsley**
3 tbl wine vinegar

Using a fork, mash the anchovies and capers to a paste in a bowl. Beat in the
other ingredients. After the *daube* has cooked for 2½ hours remove it from the
oven and skim off the fat. Pour on the anchovy mixture and baste the beef with
the cooking juices in the casserole. Cover and return to oven until the meat is
tender.

  K*

BEEF SAUTÉS

Sauté de Boeuf

* SAUTÉ DE BOEUF À LA PARISIENNE

[Beef Sauté with Cream and Mushroom Sauce]

This sauté of beef is good to know about if you have to entertain important guests in a hurry. It consists of small pieces of fillet sautéed quickly to a nice brown outside and a rosy centre, and served in a sauce. The following recipe can easily be prepared in 30 minutes, or in less than half the time if the meat has been sliced and the mushrooms sautéed ahead. In the variations at the end of the recipe, all the sauce ingredients may be prepared in advance. If the whole dish is cooked ahead of time, be very careful indeed in its reheating that the beef does not overcook. The cream and mushroom sauce here is a French version of beef Stroganoff, but less tricky as it uses fresh rather than sour cream, so you will not run into the problem of curdled sauce.

Serve the beef in a casserole, or on a dish surrounded with steamed rice, *risotto*, or potato balls sautéed in butter. Buttered green peas or French beans could accompany it, and a good claret.

For 6 people

½ lb. sliced fresh mushrooms
A heavy, 9- to 10-in. enamelled
　frying pan
1 oz. butter and 1 dsp good cooking
　oil

3 tbl chopped shallots or spring
　onions
¼ tsp salt and a pinch of pepper

Following directions on page 473, sauté the mushrooms in the frying pan in hot butter and oil for 4 to 5 minutes to brown them lightly. Stir in the shallots or spring onions, and cook for a minute longer. Season the mushrooms, and scrape them into a side dish.

2½ lbs. fillet of beef; the rump and
　rib ends of the fillet are usually
　used (see illustrations, page 265)

Remove all surrounding fat and filament, and cut the fillet into 2-ounce pieces, about 2 inches across and ½ inch thick. Dry thoroughly.

1 oz. butter and 1 dsp cooking oil,
　more if needed

Place the butter and oil in the frying pan and place over moderately high heat. When the butter foam begins to subside, sauté the beef, a few pieces at a time, for 2 to 3 minutes on each side to brown the exterior but keep the interior rosy red. Place the beef on a side dish, and discard sautéing fat.

⅛ pt. Madeira (best choice), or dry white vermouth	½ pt. cream
¼ pt. good brown stock or beef bouillon	2 tsp cornflour blended with 1 tbl of the cream

Pour the wine and stock or bouillon into the frying pan and boil it down rapidly, scraping up coagulated cooking juices, until liquid is reduced to about ⅛ pint. Beat in the cream, then the cornflour mixture. Simmer 1 minute. Add the sautéed mushrooms and simmer 1 minute more. The sauce should have a slight liaison (be lightly thickened). Taste carefully for seasoning.

Salt and pepper

Season the beef lightly with salt and pepper and return it to the frying pan along with any juices which may have escaped. Baste the beef with the sauce and mushrooms; or transfer everything to a serving casserole.

1 oz. softened butter	Parsley sprigs

When you are ready to serve, cover the frying pan or casserole and heat to below simmering point for 3 to 4 minutes, being very careful not to overdo it or the pieces of fillet will be well done rather than rare. Remove from heat and just before serving, tilt casserole, add butter to sauce a little at a time while basting the meat until the butter is absorbed. Decorate with parsley, and serve at once.

VARIATIONS

Sauté de Boeuf à la Bourguignonne

[Beef Sauté with Red Wine, Mushrooms, Bacon, and Onions]

For 6 people

2½ lbs. fillet of beef prepared and sautéed as in preceding master recipe	½ pt. red wine
	½ pt. brown stock or beef bouillon
A 3-oz. chunk blanched streaky bacon, page 12	1 clove mashed garlic
	1 tbl tomato paste
	¼ tsp thyme

Sauté the beef and leave it aside. Cut the blanched bacon into 1-inch strips ¼ of an inch thick. Brown lightly in the frying pan and pour out fat. Add rest of ingredients above and slowly boil down by half.

½ oz. flour mashed to a paste with ½ oz. butter—beurre manié	A wire whisk

Remove from heat and beat in the flour-butter paste. Simmer for 1 minute, beating with wire whisk.

18 small braised onions, page 442   Salt and pepper
½ lb. sliced mushrooms sautéed in   A fireproof serving casserole
  butter, page 473

Add onions and mushrooms and simmer 2 minutes. Correct seasoning. Season
the sautéed beef, and arrange it and the sauce, bacon, and vegetables in the
serving casserole.

(*) Recipe may be prepared ahead to this point. Leave casserole aside uncovered.

1 oz. softened butter   Parsley sprigs

When ready to serve, cover and reheat at below simmering point for 3 to 4
minutes. Away from heat, add the butter in pieces, basting the meat and
vegetables with the sauce until the butter is absorbed. Decorate with parsley
and serve immediately.

Sauté de Boeuf à la Provençale

[Beef Sauté with Fresh Tomato Sauce, Olives, and Herbs]

For 6 people

2½ lbs. fillet of beef

Cut and sauté the beef as described in the preceding master recipe. Remove to
a side dish.

⅛ pt. dry white wine or dry white   2 oz. stoned black olives, preferably
  vermouth   the dryish Mediterranean type
¾ pt. fresh tomato purée with garlic 2 tbl mixed fresh green herbs, or
  and herbs, page 69   parsley

Pour the fat out of the frying pan and pour in the wine. Boil it down rapidly
until reduced to 1 tablespoon, scraping up coagulated sauté juices. Add the
tomato purée; simmer 1 minute. Then add the sautéed beef and reheat without
simmering. Decorate with olives and herbs or parsley, and serve immediately.

LAMB AND MUTTON
Agneau et Mouton

Although modern raising methods have made it possible to schedule lamb
crops for any time of the year, the normal cycle starts in April with spring lamb;
a tender-fleshed leg weighs only 3 to 4 pounds. Lamb cuts become heavier as the
seasonal cycle progresses, and in late winter a leg may weigh over 7½ pounds,

meaning it is almost a leg of mutton. Mutton, with its developed flavour and firmer flesh, comes from an animal one year old and usually under two years old. All the recipes in this section are interchangeable: either for lamb over 5 months old, or for mutton under two years old.

FRENCH TERMS FOR LAMB AND MUTTON

Agneau de Lait, Agneau de Pauillac. This is lamb between 2 and 3 months old. It is raised like veal, on milk, and is considered a great early spring delicacy. It is roasted whole with one of the stuffings beginning on page 308, or it may be cut up and grilled with a mustard coating following the general outline of *poulet grillé à la diable*, page 241.

Agneau Pascal. This is spring lamb, 3 to 4 months old, with delicate, pale red flesh. It is roasted, grilled, or may be stewed like the veal in *blanquette de veau*, page 332.

Agneau, Agneau de Pré-salé. The best French *agneaux* are considered to be those fed on the salty grasses of the northern coastal regions, *les prés salés*. French lamb is 5 to about 9 months old, and may, like British lamb, be roasted, braised, boiled, or fricasseed.

Mouton. The most famous French mutton is from *les prés salés*. It comes from an animal between one and two years of age, and is cooked like lamb.

LEG OR SHOULDER OF LAMB
Gigot ou Épaule de Pré-salé

If a fine leg or shoulder of lamb is to be tender and full of flavour it must be sufficiently aged. A too-fresh piece will be rubbery and tough no matter how you cook it. Ageing is particularly necessary for mutton. Most French recipes are very specific: *un beau gigot bien rassis*. So if you have any doubts, wrap the meat loosely and store it in the refrigerator for three to five days before cooking it.

PREPARING A LEG OF LAMB FOR COOKING

Trim off all but a thin layer of fat, and remove any loose fat. Shave off the purple inspection stamps.

In the recipes which follow, a leg of lamb means a whole, unboned leg, but as you will note from the illustration, you may buy a short leg if you wish. The chump makes a nice small roast, or may be cut into steaks. Although some meat experts object to any tampering at all with a leg of lamb, carving is much easier if some of the bones are removed. The tail and the pelvic bone may be cut out, and the meat sewn or skewered together to cover the rump knucklebone. Or if you wish only the shank to remain after the pelvic bone has been removed,

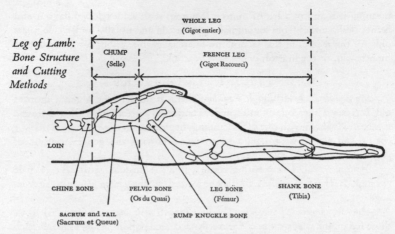

Leg of Lamb:
Bone Structure
and Cutting
Methods

the leg bone may be taken from inside the meat without making an outside incision; the meat is then sewn or skewered at the large end. If the leg is boned entirely, then rolled and tied, it makes a compact roast which may be cooked on a spit. Most butchers will perform any of these operations for you, but they are not too difficult to manage by yourself. The bones and trimmings may be turned into a good sauce for your roast, see *sauce ragoût,* page 61.

FLAVOURINGS AND STUFFINGS

For a mild garlic flavour, inset 3 or 4 slivers of garlic in the meat at the shank end. For a more pronounced flavour, make several incisions in the meat and insert more garlic slivers. See also the garlic and herb stuffing and other suggestions for boned lamb beginning on page 308, and the herbal–mustard coating on page 307.

SHOULDER OF LAMB OR MUTTON

Shoulder of lamb or mutton consists of the meat and bones of the scapula or bladebone, the arm-bone, and the shank. The shoulder may be roasted or braised as it is, but will be easier to carve and serve if it is boned, rolled, and tied. If you wish to serve it with a substantial stuffing, ask your butcher to cut the forequarter, of which the shoulder is a part, so that you will have the shoulder plus the middle neck, or shoulder chops (*épaule et côtes découvertes*). Otherwise you will have little room for stuffing. Boned shoulder may be substituted for leg of lamb or mutton in any of the recipes to follow.

TIMING FOR ROAST LAMB AND MUTTON

Lamb and mutton cooked in the French manner are seared for 15 minutes in a 450° F., Mark 8 oven, then the roasting is continued in a 350° F., Mark 4 oven until the meat is medium rare, pink, and juicy. If you prefer meat well done, do not go over a meat-thermometer reading of 170° F. or the meat will lose much of its juice and flavour; 160 to 165° F. is usually considered sufficient. A boned leg or shoulder will weigh approximately 30 per cent. less than a bone-in piece, but its cooking time per pound usually more than doubles, depending on the thickness of the meat. The estimates in the following list are based on unchilled meat, and the recipes refer to unboned meat unless otherwise specified.

A 6-pound leg or shoulder, bone in

Medium Rare—1 to 1¼ hours (10 to 12 minutes per pound)
Meat Thermometer Reading—145 to 150° F.
Well Done—1¼ to 1½ hours (13 to 15 minutes per pound)
Meat Thermometer Reading—160 to 165° F.

A 4-pound piece of boned and rolled leg or shoulder

Medium Rare—1¾ to 2 hours (25 to 30 minutes per pound)
Meat Thermometer Reading—147 to 150° F.
Well Done—2 to 2¼ hours (30 to 35 minutes per pound)
Meat Thermometer Reading—160 to 165° F.

VEGETABLE SUGGESTIONS FOR ROAST LAMB

Beans

Gigot, haricots—lamb and beans—are a favourite combination. The beans may be plain buttered French beans, page 409, or French beans and fresh haricot beans, or the dried beans on page 368. A mixture of the two is called *haricots panachés*. Another suggestion is French beans with tomatoes, page 411. Additional bean recipes are in the Bean section, pages 407 to 413.

Potatoes

With plain buttered green vegetables you could serve one of the potato casseroles, pages 482 to 485, or the garlic mashed potatoes on page 480. Potatoes sautéed in butter, page 486, go with either plain or sauced vegetables.

Other vegetables

Rice with mushrooms, page 490, could be accompanied by one of the recipes for peas, pages 424 to 429, and baked tomatoes, page 466.

Tomatoes stuffed with herbs or mushrooms, page 467, French beans, and sautéed potatoes are always good with roast lamb.

Aubergine and lamb are an excellent flavour combination. See the aubergine casserole, *ratatouille,* page 463, and the aubergine stuffed with mushrooms on page 461.

Brussels sprouts or broccoli, pages 413 to 419, or cauliflower, pages 419 to 424, are other ideas. If the vegetables are served plain, you could accompany them with one of the potato casseroles on pages 482 to 485.

TRADITIONAL GARNITURES

Here are some of the traditional French vegetable combinations for garnishing a roast of lamb:

Bruxelloise, braised chicory, page 453, Brussels sprouts braised in butter, page 414, potatoes sautéed in butter, page 486.

Châtelaine, quartered artichoke hearts braised in butter, page 397, whole baked tomatoes, page 466, braised celery, page 451, potatoes sautéed in butter, page 486.

Clamart, cooked artichoke hearts, page 397, filled with buttered peas, page 425, potatoes sautéed in butter, page 486.

Florian, braised lettuce. page 450, brown-braised onions, page 444, carrots braised in butter, page 438, potatoes sautéed in butter, page 486.

Judic, tomatoes stuffed with herbs or mushrooms, page 467, braised lettuce, page 450, potatoes sautéed in butter, page 486.

Provençale, whole baked tomatoes, page 466, baked stuffed mushrooms, page 476.

Viroflay, spinach braised with stock or cream, page 432, quartered artichoke hearts braised in butter, page 397, potatoes sautéed in butter, page 486.

WINE SUGGESTIONS

Lamb and mutton want red wine. A light claret, such as a Graves or Médoc, is best with the delicate flavour of young spring lamb. Serve a stronger red, a claret such as St. Émilion, with more mature lamb. Mutton, or lamb roasted with a strong, herbal stuffing or mustard coating, calls for a sturdier wine, Côtes du Rhône or Burgundy.

---

* GIGOT DE PRÉ-SALÉ RÔTI*

[Roast Leg of Lamb]

For 8 to 10 people

Preheat oven to 450° F., Mark 8,

A 6-lb. leg of lamb

Prepare the lamb for cooking as described in the preceding paragraphs, and wipe it dry.

3 tbl rendered fresh pork or beef
fat, or a mixture of melted
butter and cooking oil
A roasting tin 1½ ins. deep and just
large enough to hold the meat

A rack to fit the tin
A long-handled spoon

Brush the lamb with melted fat or butter and oil. Place it on the rack in the roasting tin and place in the upper part of the preheated oven. Turn and baste it every 4 to 5 minutes for 15 to 20 minutes, or until it has browned lightly on all sides. This sears the outside of the meat and prevents its juices from bursting out.

A meat thermometer
1 large carrot, roughly sliced
1 large onion, roughly sliced

Optional: 3 to 6 cloves unpeeled
garlic, added to tin ½ hour before
end of cooking

Reset oven for 350° F., Mark 4. Insert a meat thermometer into the fleshiest part of the lamb. Strew the vegetables in the bottom of the tin. Place lamb in middle of oven and roast until done. Basting is not necessary.

Total Cooking Time

Medium rare, 1 to 1¼ hours, 147 to 150° F. Meat is slightly resistant when pressed, and if the meat is pricked deeply with a fork, the juices run rosy, not red.

Well done, 1¼ to 1½ hours, 160 to 165° F. Meat is firmer when pressed, juices run clear yellow.

1 tsp salt
¼ tsp pepper

A hot dish

Discard any trussing strings or skewers. Season the lamb, and place it on a dish. It should rest at room temperature for 20 to 30 minutes before being carved, to let its juices retreat back into the tissues.

½ pt. brown lamb stock, beefstock,
or beef bouillon

A hot sauceboat

Remove the rack, and spoon the cooking fat out of the tin. Pour in the stock or bouillon and boil rapidly, scraping up coagulated roasting juices and mashing the vegetables into the stock. Taste for seasoning. Just before serving, strain into a hot sauceboat, pressing the juices out of the vegetables. Stir in any juices which may have escaped from the roast.

Watercress or parsley   **Hot plates**

Decorate the roast with watercress or parsley, and be sure to serve the lamb on
hot plates as lamb fat congeals when cold.

VARIATION: OTHER SAUCES

The preceding directions are for a deglazing sauce which furnishes about
a spoonful per serving. If you wish more sauce, prepare in advance ¾ to 1 pint
of *sauce ragoût* with the lamb bones and trimmings, page 61. Omit the stock in
the master recipe and stir the sauce into the degreased roasting juices; simmer a
moment, and pour into a sauceboat.

Sauce Spéciale à l'Ail pour Gigot

[Garlic Sauce for Roast Lamb]

This very good sauce uses a whole head of garlic which, after two blanch-
ings and a long simmering, becomes tamed and develops a delicious flavour.

For ½ to ¾ pint of sauce

1 large head of garlic
**A saucepan containing 3 pts. of cold
   water**

Separate the garlic cloves. Bring them to the boil in the saucepan and boil 30
seconds. Drain and peel. Place again in cold water, bring to the boil, and drain.

A 1½-pt. heavy-bottomed saucepan   **¼ tsp rosemary or thyme**
¼ pt. milk, more if needed   **1 tbl raw white rice**
⅛ tsp salt

In the saucepan bring the milk, salt, herbs, and rice to simmering point. Add the
garlic, and simmer very slowly for 45 minutes, putting in more milk by
spoonfuls if the rice is in danger of scorching.

½ pt. brown lamb stock, beef stock,   **Salt and pepper**
**   or beef bouillon**
**A sieve, a bowl, and a wooden
   spoon; or an electric liquidizer**

Pour in the stock or bouillon and simmer 1 minute. Then force through a sieve, or purée in the electric liquidizer. Correct seasoning. Place sauce aside and reheat when needed.

A hot gravy boat

After the lamb has been roasted as described in the master recipe and the roasting tin degreased, deglaze the tin with 2 to 3 tablespoons of stock or water, scraping up coagulated juices. Strain into the hot garlic sauce. Pass the sauce in a hot gravy boat.

VARIATION

Gigot à la Moutarde

[Herbal Mustard Coating for Roast Lamb]

When lamb is brushed with this mixture, garlic slivers and herbal stuffings are not necessary, and the lamb becomes a beautiful brown as it roasts.

For a 6-lb. leg of lamb

¼ pt. French prepared mustard	1 tsp ground rosemary or thyme
2 tbl soya sauce	¼ tsp powdered ginger
1 clove mashed garlic	1 tbl olive oil

Blend the mustard, soya sauce, garlic, herbs, and ginger together in a bowl. Beat in the olive oil drop by drop to make a mayonnaise-like cream.

A rubber spatula or brush

Paint the lamb with the mixture and place it on the rack of the roasting tin. The meat will pick up more flavour if it is coated several hours before roasting.

Roast in a 350° F., Mark 4 oven, 1 to 1¼ hours, for medium rare; or 1¼ to 1½ hours for well done. The searing step at the beginning of the master recipe is omitted.

---

* GIGOT OU ÉPAULE DE PRÉ-SALÉ, FARCI

[Stuffed Leg or Shoulder of Lamb]

Boned leg and shoulder of lamb lend themselves nicely to any of the following stuffings, and cold leftovers are particularly good. Lay the boned meat skin side down on a flat surface. Season lightly with salt and pepper. Spread the stuffing over the meat and into the pockets left by the bones. Then roll the meat into a cylindrical shape to enclose the stuffing completely. Sew or skewer if necessary, then tie loops of string around its circumference at 1-inch intervals so that the meat holds its shape. Roast either in the oven or on a spit, or braise it as described in the recipe on page 310. The following are for 3 to 4 pounds of boned meat.

Farce aux Herbes

[Garlic and Herb Stuffing]

8 tbl chopped parsley
½ tsp ground rosemary or thyme
2 tbl chopped shallots or spring
   onions

½ to 1 clove mashed garlic
¼ tsp powdered ginger
1 tsp salt
¼ tsp pepper

Mix all the ingredients together in a bowl. Spread the mixture on the lamb. Roll and tie as described in the preceding instructions.

Farce de Porc

[Pork and Herb Stuffing]

3 oz. finely chopped onions
1 oz. butter

A 4-pt. mixing bowl

Cook the onions and butter slowly together in a small saucepan until tender but not browned. Scrape into a mixing bowl.

2 oz. fresh white breadcrumbs
   (French or home-made type
   bread)

¼ pt. lukewarm stock or beef
   bouillon

Soak the breadcrumbs in stock or bouillon for 5 minutes. Drain through a sieve and press out as much liquid as you can. Save the liquid for your sauce, and place the breadcrumbs in the mixing bowl.

8 oz. lean, fresh pork minced with
   4 oz. fresh pork fat
1 clove mashed garlic
¼ tsp ground rosemary, sage, or
   thyme
4 tbl chopped parsley

Pinch of allspice
½ tsp salt
¼ tsp pepper
1 egg
A wooden spoon

Add the rest of the ingredients to the mixing bowl and beat vigorously with a wooden spoon until well mixed. Sauté a teaspoonful until cooked through, and taste for seasoning. Add more seasonings to the stuffing if you feel it necessary. Spread the stuffing on the lamb. Roll and tie as described at the beginning of this section.

Farce aux Rognons

[Rice and Kidney Stuffing]

4 tbl finely chopped onions	**¼ pt. white stock or tinned chicken**
½ oz. butter	**bouillon**
2½ oz. raw white rice	

In a small, heavy-bottomed saucepan, cook the onions in butter for 4 to 5 minutes until tender but not browned. Add the rice and stir over low heat for 2 to 3 minutes until it turns a milky colour. Pour in the stock or chicken bouillon, bring to the boil, cover, and simmer not too slowly for 15 minutes without stirring, at which point the liquid should be absorbed and the rice almost tender. It will finish cooking in the lamb.

½ tsp ground rosemary, sage, or	**¼ tsp pepper**
thyme	**½ clove mashed garlic**
Pinch of allspice	**Salt to taste**

Mix in the herbs, spice, pepper, and garlic with a fork. Add salt to taste.

4 lamb kidneys, or a mixture of	**½ oz. butter and 1 dsp oil**
lamb kidneys, heart, and liver	**Salt and pepper**
making about 8 oz. in all	

Dry the meat, and leave the pieces whole. Sauté quickly in hot butter and oil to brown very lightly, leaving the interior of the meat rosy. Cut into ⅛-inch slices. Season lightly with salt and pepper, and fold into the rice.

When the stuffing is cool, spread it on the lamb. Roll and tie the meat as described at the beginning of this section.

VARIATIONS: Other Stuffings Following the General Procedures Outlined

Farce Duxelles

[Ham and Mushroom Stuffing]

2 oz. chopped onions, cooked in	**4 oz. chopped, lean boiled ham**
butter	**2 oz. finely chopped fresh pork fat**
¼ lb. chopped fresh mushrooms,	**(or ham fat)**
cooked in butter	**Salt, pepper, herbs**

Farce aux Olives

[Olive and Minced Lamb Stuffing]

4 oz. minced lean lamb
2 oz. chopped onions, cooked in
   butter
3 oz. white breadcrumbs soaked in
   stock or bouillon and squeezed
   dry

12 stoned black Greek olives,
   simmered 10 minutes in 1½ pts of
   water, drained, and chopped
1 egg
Salt, pepper, herbs, allspice, and
   garlic

Farce Mentonnaise

[Salmon and Anchovy Stuffing]

An unlikely combination, but a good one

4 oz. drained, tinned salmon
6 drained, mashed anchovies
   (packed in olive oil)
4 oz. minced lean lamb

3 oz. chopped onions, sautéed in
   butter
Salt, pepper, herbs, garlic

GIGOT OU ÉPAULE DE PRÉ-SALÉ BRAISÉ (aux Haricots)

[Braised Leg or Shoulder of Lamb—with Beans]

Braising is a succulent way to do almost mature lamb or young mutton, particularly if it has been stuffed with any of the preceding suggestions. Beans may finish their cooking with the lamb, and will absorb a fine flavour from the braising liquid. If you do not wish to include them, serve with the lamb a purée of lentils or chestnuts, mashed potatoes, rice, or *risotto*. Other vegetables to serve with braised lamb are French beans, peas, Brussels sprouts, baked tomatoes, or a garniture of glazed carrots, turnips, onions, and sautéed mushrooms. A fairly full red wine goes well—Beaujolais, a St. Émilion claret, Côtes du Rhône, or Burgundy.

A NOTE ON TIMING

Almost mature lamb or young mutton is usually braised 40 to 50 minutes per pound, long enough for the meat, its stuffing, and the braising liquid to exchange flavours. This makes 3½ to 4 hours for a leg, and around 2½ hours for a shoulder. Boned and stuffed lamb will usually take an hour longer. The meat is done when a fork pierces it easily. You may, if you wish, cut the time by half, and cook the meat only until the thermometer indicates 150° F. for medium rare, or 160 to 165° F. for well done; in this case, there will be little exchange of flavour between the various elements.

Beans. If you are to use dry white beans, their soaking and precooking will take a good two hours. This is done while the lamb is braising.

For 8 to 10 people

Preheat oven to 350° F., Mark 4.

A 6- to 7-lb. leg or 4- to 5-lb.
shoulder of lamb, boned, and
stuffed, if you wish, with one of
the preceding fillings
The lamb bones, sawed or chopped
3 tbl rendered fresh pork fat or
cooking oil
A heavy fireproof casserole or
covered roasting tin just large
enough to hold all ingredients
2 large sliced carrots
2 large sliced onions
¾ pt. of dry white wine, or red
wine, or ½ pt. dry white
vermouth

½ tsp salt
¼ tsp pepper
1¼ to 1½ pts. beef stock or beef
bouillon
4 parsley sprigs
1 bay leaf
1 tsp rosemary, thyme, or sage
3 unpeeled cloves garlic
Optional: 2 tbl tomato paste
Aluminium foil

Brown the lamb on all sides, and then the bones in hot fat or oil in the casserole or roasting tin. This will take 15 to 20 minutes. Remove to a side dish. Then brown the vegetables for 2 to 3 minutes. Remove them with a slotted spoon to the dish. Pour out the browning fat. Add the wine or vermouth and boil it down rapidly, scraping up coagulated browning juices, until reduced by half. Season the lamb and place it, its fattiest side up, in the casserole or roasting tin. Surround it with the browned bones and vegetables. Pour in enough stock or bouillon to come two-thirds of the way up the meat. Stir in the herbs, garlic, and optional tomato paste. Bring to simmering point on top of the stove. Lay aluminium foil over the top of the casserole, then the casserole cover. Place in lower part of preheated oven and regulate so that the liquid is maintained at a slow simmer. Turn and baste the meat every half-hour.

Remove the lamb from the casserole when it is within half an hour of being done. (See A Note on Timing, at beginning of recipe.) Strain and degrease the cooking stock, and correct its seasoning. Return meat and stock to the casserole and surround with the beans which have been precooked as follows:

1 lb. white haricot beans
2½ pts. boiling water

A 3-qt. pan
1 tbl salt

Drop the beans into the boiling water. Bring quickly to the boil again and boil exactly 2 minutes. Leave aside for 1 hour. Immediately the soaking time is up, add the salt to the pan, bring to simmering point, and simmer 1 hour. Leave aside. The beans will finish their cooking later with the lamb. After the lamb stock has been degreased as described in the preceding paragraph, drain the beans and add them to the casserole with the lamb.

(*) May be prepared ahead to this point. See note at end of recipe.

Bring the casserole again to simmering point on top of the stove. Cover, and return to the oven until the meat is tender when pierced with a fork, about 30 minutes.

A hot dish   **A hot sauceboat**
Parsley sprigs

Drain the lamb, remove trussing strings, and place it on a hot dish. Strain the beans and place them around the meat. Decorate with parsley sprigs. Degrease the cooking stock, correct seasoning, and pour it into a hot sauceboat.

(*) AHEAD-OF-TIME NOTES

If you wish to cook the meat in advance, braise it until tender. Then strain and degrease the cooking stock and place meat and stock in the casserole. An hour before serving, reheat on top of the stove, then cover and place in a 350° F., Mark 4 oven. In 20 minutes, add the beans and continue cooking for about 30 minutes more. The meat should reach an internal temperature of about 130° F.

Or follow the recipe but carve the meat when it is done. Arrange it in a fireproof serving dish or casserole with the beans, and spoon part of the sauce over it. Cover and reheat slowly for 10 minutes before serving.

GIGOT EN CHEVREUIL

[Leg of Lamb or Mutton Marinated in Red Wine]

A large well-aged leg of lamb or a leg of young mutton marinated for several days in wine will taste very much like a marinated leg of venison. It is roasted and served, like venison, with a *sauce poivrade* or *chevreuil*. Braised red cabbage with chestnuts, and a purée of celery root and potatoes go well with it, plus a good red Burgundy wine. Any cold sliced leftovers will be delicious.

As the meat is marinated for a relatively long period of time, the marinade containing vegetables is cooked so that the vegetables will not turn sour. The second marinade with bay leaves needs no cooking.

Marinade Cuite

[Cooked Wine Marinade]

4 oz. thinly sliced onions
4 oz. thinly sliced carrots
2 oz. thinly sliced celery
2 halved cloves garlic

¼ pt. olive oil
A 2-qt. enamelled saucepan with cover

Cook the vegetables slowly in the olive oil in the covered saucepan for 5 minutes without allowing them to brown.

2½ pts. full-bodied, young red wine: Mâcon, Côtes du Rhône, Beaujolais, Burgundy, Chianti
⅛ pt. red wine vinegar
1 dsp salt
1 tsp peppercorns

2 cloves
5 parsley sprigs
2 bay leaves
1 tbl rosemary
½ tsp juniper berries, if available, or ⅛ pt. gin

Add the wine, the vinegar, and all the rest of the ingredients. Simmer, partially covered, for 20 minutes. Allow the marinade to cool completely before using it.

Marinade au Laurier

[Uncooked Wine Marinade with Bay Leaves]

2½ pts. red wine
½ pt. wine vinegar
¼ pt. olive oil

35 bay leaves
1 tbl salt
½ tsp peppercorns

This alternative marinade needs no cooking, and is just poured over the lamb.

Marinating and Roasting the Lamb

A 7- to 8-lb. leg of well-aged lamb or young mutton

Prepare the lamb for cooking as described on page 301. It may be boned if you wish.

Place it in an enamelled, ovenglass, porcelain, or stainless steel bowl, or roasting tin just large enough to hold it. Pour the marinade over it. Turn and baste the lamb 3 or 4 times a day for 4 to 5 days at room temperature, for 6 to 8 days if it is refrigerated.

Drain the lamb for half an hour or more on a rack. Just before roasting, dry it thoroughly. Following directions in the master recipe for roast lamb on page 304, baste it with fat and sear it for 15 to 20 minutes in a 450° F., Mark 8 oven then roast it at 350° F., Mark 4 to a medium rare, 147 to 150° F. on the meat thermometer.

If you are serving with it a *sauce poivrade*, page 62, or *sauce venaison*, page 62, include ¼ pint of the marinade liquid as part of the ingredients.

GIGOT À L'ANGLAISE
[Boiled Leg of Lamb with Onion, Caper, or Tomato Sauce]

This is a delicious and very easy way to cook a leg of lamb. Just simmer it in a pan of salted water until it is done, and you may leave it in its pan an hour or more before serving. The only essential is that the lamb be a particularly fine and well-aged piece, as its beauty resides entirely in its natural flavour and tenderness. It is not necessary to add soup vegetables and herbs to the cooking water since the lamb is simmered only until it is medium rare or barely well done, and, except for the salt, there is no exchange of flavours.

VEGETABLE AND WINE SUGGESTIONS
For a family-style vegetable garnish, carrots, turnips, onions, leeks, and potatoes may be cooked for an hour with the lamb; tie them in cheesecloth bundles for easy removal. For a more formal array, here are some other suggestions to be cooked separately and combined as you wish:

Purée of turnips and potatoes, page 448
Garlic mashed potatoes, page 480
Soubise (rice and onions), page 445
Brussels sprouts, pages 413 to 418
French beans, pages 407 to 413
Ratatouille (aubergine casserole), page 463.

If you choose onion sauce for the lamb, serve a claret from the Médoc district. With caper or tomato sauce, serve a chilled *rosé*.

For 8 to 10 people

A 6-lb. leg of lamb

Prepare the lamb for cooking as described on page 301. It may be boned, rolled, and stuffed if you wish.

A meat thermometer   **2 tsp salt per quart of water**
A pan of rapidly boiling water,
  large enough to hold the lamb
  completely submerged

Insert a meat thermometer into the fleshiest part of the lamb. Plunge the lamb into the boiling, salted water. When the water comes back to simmering point, begin timing: 12 to 15 minutes per pound, or 1¼ to 1½ hours (147 to 150° F. on the thermometer for medium rare, 160 to 165 for well done). The water must remain at a very slow simmer throughout the cooking.

(*) After the lamb has been removed from the pan, it should cool at room temperature for about 20 minutes before it is carved. But if it is to be served later than that, pour cold water into the pan to cool it to just below 150° F., so that the lamb will not continue to cook. (Add 1½ teaspoons salt per quart of water poured into the pan.) The lamb may rest thus for an hour or more, and the pan may be gently reheated if necessary.

1¼ pts. of one of the following sauces:
Sauce aux Câpres (mock hollandaise with egg yolks, cream, capers, and butter), page 58

Sauce Soubise (béchamel with onion purée), page 56
Coulis de Tomates (fresh tomato sauce with herbs), page 69

While the lamb is simmering, prepare the sauce: 5 minutes or less for caper sauce, about 30 for onion sauce, 1½ hours of simmering for tomato sauce.

1½ oz. melted butter
2 tbl chopped parsley

A hot dish
A warmed sauceboat

Drain the lamb when you are ready to serve, and place it on a hot dish. Baste it with the melted butter and sprinkle it with parsley. Pass the sauce in a warmed sauceboat.

LAMB STEW
Ragoûts, Navarins, et Haricots de Mouton

In France, mutton rather than lamb is preferred for stews because the flesh of the more mature animal has more character. Except for the tender fleshed stewing cuts of young spring lamb which are best in a *blanquette*, lamb or mutton may be used interchangeably. *Ragoût, navarin,* and *haricot* all mean stew. *Haricot* according to most linguists is a corruption of *halicoter*, to cut up. It does not therefore mean a lamb stew with beans. Stew meat is very inexpensive; one can only wonder why, but be grateful when a dish like a *navarin* is so delicious. Other lamb stews may be made like beef stew, and suggestions are listed at the end of the *navarin* recipe.

CUTS FOR STEWING

All of the lamb for a stew may be from the same cut, but a more interesting texture and sauce will be obtained if you use a mixture from the following suggestions. Chop and leg meat are not recommended as they become dry and stringy. Count on 1 pound of boneless meat for 2 people if your menu is small; for 3, if large.

Shoulder—*Épaule*. Lean and meaty, a bit dry.

Breast—*Poitrine*. Provides fat and texture.

Best End Short Ribs—*Haut de Côtelettes*. Provides fat and texture, and the bones give flavour.

Scrag end of Neck—*Collet*. Has a gelatinous quality which gives body to the sauce.

PREPARATION FOR COOKING

Have excess fat removed, and the meat cut into 2-inch cubes weighing 2 to 2½ ounces. Any bones left in the meat will give added flavour to the sauce. Most of them may be removed before serving.

TIMING

Allow about 2 hours for the cooking. Stews may be simmered on top of the stove but the more uniform and surrounding heat of the oven is preferable.

---

* NAVARIN PRINTANIER

[Lamb Stew with Spring Vegetables]

Navarin printanier, a most delectable lamb stew with its carrots, onions, turnips, potatoes, peas, and French beans, is presumably done in the spring when all the vegetables are young and tender. But as it can be made any time of the year, it is not a seasonal dish any more thanks to deep-freezing. Frozen beans and peas are discussed on pages 412 and 428. The written recipe is long as each detail is important if the *navarin* is to taste like a French masterpiece. But none of the steps is difficult and everything except the addition of the green vegetables at the very end may be made ready in the morning. The stew can then be finished in 10 to 15 minutes just before dinner time.

With the stew serve hot French bread, and a red Beaujolais or claret, a chilled *rosé*, or a fairly full-bodied, dry, chilled white wine such as a Mâcon, Hermitage, or one of the lesser Burgundies.

For 6 people

Preheat oven to 450° F., Mark 8.

3 lbs. lamb stew meat (see list preceding recipe)	A 10- to 12-in. frying pan A fireproof covered casserole
2 to 3 tbl rendered fresh pork fat or cooking oil	large enough to hold the meat, and all the vegetables to come

Cut the lamb into 2-inch cubes and dry. The meat will not brown if it is damp.

Brown a few pieces at a time in hot fat or oil in the frying pan. As they are browned, place them in the casserole.

1 tbl granulated sugar

Sprinkle the lamb in the casserole with sugar and toss over moderately high heat for 3 to 4 minutes until the sugar has caramelized. This will give a fine amber colour to the sauce.

1 tsp salt   **1 oz. flour**
¼ tsp pepper

Toss the meat with the salt and pepper, then with the flour. Place casserole uncovered in middle of preheated oven for 4 to 5 minutes. Toss the meat and return it to the oven for 4 to 5 minutes more. This browns the flour evenly and coats the lamb with a light crust. Remove casserole and turn oven down to 350° F., Mark 4.

¾ to 1 pt. brown lamb- or beef–   **2 cloves mashed garlic**
**   stock or beef bouillon**   **¼ tsp thyme or rosemary**
¾ lb. ripe, red tomatoes, peeled,   **1 bay leaf**
**   seeded, juiced, and chopped**
**   page 465; or 3 tbl tomato paste**

Pour out the fat; add ¾ pint of stock or bouillon to the frying pan. Bring to the boil and scrape up coagulated sauté juices. Then pour the liquid into the casserole. Bring to simmering point for a few seconds shaking and stirring to mix liquid and flour. Add the tomatoes or tomato paste and the other ingredients. Bring to simmering point for 1 minute, then add more stock if necessary; meat should be almost covered by liquid.

Put the lid on the casserole and place in lower part of preheated oven; regulate heat so that casserole simmers slowly and regularly for 1 hour. Then pour the contents of the casserole into a sieve placed over a bowl. Rinse out the casserole. Remove any loose bones and return the lamb to the casserole. Skim the fat off the sauce in the bowl, correct seasoning, and pour sauce back into casserole. Then add the vegetables which have been prepared as follows:

6 to 12 peeled boiling potatoes   **12 to 18 peeled onions about 1 in.**
6 scraped carrots   **   in diameter**
6 peeled turnips

While the lamb is simmering, trim the potatoes into ovals 1½ inches long, and cover with cold water until ready to use. Quarter the carrots and turnips, cut them into 1½ inch lengths, and, if you have the patience, trim the edges to round them slightly. Cut a cross in the root ends of the onions so that they will cook evenly.

Press the vegetables into the casserole around and between the pieces of lamb. Baste with the sauce. Bring to simmering point on top of the stove, cover and return to the oven. Regulate heat so that liquid simmers slowly and steadily for about an hour longer or until the meat and vegetables are tender when pierced with a fork. Remove from oven, tilt casserole, and skim off fat. Taste sauce again, and correct seasoning.

¼ lb. shelled green peas	5 pts. boiling water
¼ lb. French beans cut into ½-in. pieces	1 tbl salt

While the casserole is in the oven, drop the peas and beans into the boiling salted water and boil rapidly, uncovered, for 5 minutes or until the vegetables are almost tender. Immediately drain in a colander. Run cold water over them for 2 to 3 minutes to stop the cooking and to set the colour. Put aside until ready to use.

(*) May be prepared ahead to this point. Put casserole aside, cover askew. Bring to simmering point on top of the stove before proceeding with the recipe.

Shortly before serving, place the peas and beans in the casserole on top of the other ingredients and baste with the bubbling sauce. Cover and simmer for about 5 minutes or until the green vegetables are tender.

Serve the *navarin* from its casserole or arrange it on a very hot dish.

VARIATIONS

The preceding *navarin* is a model for other stews. You may, for instance, omit the French beans, peas, and potatoes, and add haricot beans or lentils simmered in salted water until almost tender, then finish them off for half an hour with the lamb. The following are prepared exactly like beef stews.

Civet de Mouton

[Lamb or Mutton Stew with Red Wine, Onions, Mushrooms, and Bacon]

Follow the recipe for *boeuf bourguignon*, page 288, braising the lamb 2 hours rather than the 3½ to 4 hours required for beef.

Pilaf de Mouton à la Catalane

[Lamb or Mutton Stew with Rice, Onions, and Tomatoes]

Follow the recipe for *boeuf à la catalane*, page 294, using boned shoulder or breast. Time the cooking for about 2 hours rather than the 3 or 4 required for beef.

Daube de Mouton

[Casserole of Lamb or Mutton with Wine, Mushrooms, Carrots, Onions, and Herbs]

Follow the recipe for *daube de boeuf*, page 296, using boned shoulder or breast. Cook the lamb for 2 hours rather than the 3 or 4 in the recipe.

Blanquette d'Agneau

[Spring Lamb Stew with Onions and Mushrooms]

This is a delicious stew for young spring lamb, and is cooked exactly like the *blanquette de veau* on page 332 in the Veal section.

LAMB PATTIES

Fricadelles d'Agneau

Delicious 'lamburgers' may be made using freshly minced neck or other lean meat and mixing it with any of the stuffing suggestions for boned lamb on pages 308–10.

Except for the garlic and herb stuffing, which is a flavouring only, use 1 part of stuffing for 3 to 4 parts of minced lamb. Sauté and sauce them according to directions in the hamburger recipes which begin on page 274.

MOUSSAKA

MOUSSAKA

[Lamb and Aubergine Mould]

Lamb can hardly be considered a leftover when it receives this elaborate treatment. A mould is lined with the skins of cooked aubergines, and filled with a carefully seasoned mixture of cooked lamb, aubergines, and mushrooms. It presents itself after baking and unmoulding as a shiny, dark purple cylinder surrounded with a deep red tomato sauce. It is delicious either hot or cold.

Serve the *moussaka* with steamed rice or *risotto*, and buttered French beans or a green salad. A fairly full-bodied, dry, chilled white wine such as a Mâcon or Hermitage goes well with it. *Moussaka* also makes a handsome cold dish served with tomato salad and French bread.

For 8 people

Preheat oven to 400° F., Mark 6, in time to bake the aubergine.

**Ingredients for 1 pt. of tomato
    sauce, page 68**

Prepare the tomato sauce and let it simmer while you work.

**5 lbs. of aubergines (five 1-lb.   1 tbl salt
    aubergines if possible, each 7 to 8   2 tbl olive oil
    ins. long)   A shallow roasting tin**

Remove green caps and slice aubergines in half lengthwise. Cut deep gashes in
the flesh of each half, but do not pierce the skin. Sprinkle flesh with salt and let
stand for 30 minutes. Wash under cold water, squeeze out juice, and dry. Rub
with olive oil and place aubergines skin side down in a roasting tin. Pour in ½
inch of water. Bake in upper part of preheated oven for about half an hour, or
until just tender.

**A 9- to 10-in. frying pan   1 dsp olive oil
3 oz. finely chopped onions   A 5-pt. mixing bowl**

While aubergines are baking, cook the onions slowly in olive oil for 10 to 15
minutes, until tender but not browned. Scrape into mixing bowl.

**½ lb. finely chopped mushrooms   1 tbl olive oil
2 tbl chopped shallots or spring
    onions**

A handful at a time, twist mushrooms into a ball in the corner of a cloth to
extract their juice. Add the juice to the tomato sauce. Sauté the mushrooms and
shallots or spring onions in olive oil for 5 minutes or so, until pieces separate
from each other. Add to mixing bowl.

2 tbl olive oil

When aubergines are tender, carefully scoop out the flesh with a spoon, leaving
the skin intact. Chop half the flesh and place in the mixing bowl. Dice or slice
the rest and toss it briefly in very hot olive oil to brown lightly. Put aside until
later.

**½ tsp olive oil
A 3-pt. cylindrical mould
    (preferably a *charlotte*) 4 ins. high
    and 7 ins. in diameter**

Oil the mould. Line it with the aubergine skins, their purple sides against the
mould; place each lengthwise, a pointed end at the centre of the bottom of the
mould, the other end falling down outside the mould.

1¼ lbs. minced cooked lamb	2 tbl tomato paste
1 tsp salt	3 eggs
½ tsp thyme	Aluminium foil
½ tsp pepper	
½ tsp rosemary	
1 medium clove crushed garlic	
¼ pt. thick brown sauce, pages 59 to 63 (preferably Numbers 1 or 2; but the quick sauce, Number 3, can be used)	

Reset oven to 375° F., Mark 5. Add all the ingredients above to the mixing bowl containing the onions, mushrooms, and chopped aubergines. Beat vigorously with a wooden spoon to blend thoroughly. Taste carefully for seasoning. Spread an inch of the mixture in the bottom of the mould. Arrange over that a layer of the previously sautéed aubergines. Continue thus, ending with a layer of lamb mixture. Fold the dangling ends of aubergine skin up over the surface. Cover the mould with foil and a lid or plate.

(*) May be prepared ahead to this point.

A pan of boiling water	The tomato sauce
A hot serving dish	A sauceboat

Place mould in a pan of boiling water. Bake in bottom part of oven for 1½ hours. Remove and let cool for 10 minutes. Reverse on a hot serving dish and surround with ¼ pint of the tomato sauce. Pass the rest of the sauce separately.

VEAL

Veau

Veal is an interesting and delicious meat when it is cooked well, and like chicken it lends itself to a variety of flavourings and sauces. The best quality of veal is milk-fed and is between 5 and 12 weeks old, and is the offspring of beef cattle rather than dairy cattle. The flesh is firm, smooth, fine-grained, and of a very pale pink colour. The fat, which is white and satiny, is concentrated almost entirely inside the carcass around the kidneys. The bones are soft and reddish and can easily be sawed without splintering. After about 12 weeks veal becomes calf and is of no further culinary interest until it develops into beef. At whatever age the veal animal leaves its milk diet and starts on grain or grass, its flesh becomes increasingly rosy until, when it is almost of calf age, it is frankly reddish. Train yourself when shopping for veal to look carefully at its colour. Once you are aware of what good quality should look like, you can avoid the reddish pieces.

L

CASSEROLE-ROASTED VEAL

Veau Poêlé

With no natural fat covering and no marblings of fat inside the meat, a roast of veal will always be juicier and have more flavour if it is cooked in a covered casserole with aromatic vegetables.

CUTS FOR ROASTING

Count on 1 pound of boneless meat for 2 or 3 people.

Leg or Fillet—*Cuisseau*. British duplication of French cuts for a leg of veal are difficult unless you can find a co-operative butcher with a large-sized milk-fed veal. A French leg is separated like beef, into the topside or *noix*, the silverside or *sous noix*, and the thick flank or *noix pâtissière*; these make compact, cylindrical roasts which carve into neat slices. Topside and thick flank are the choice morsels, and topside is also used for scallops. In Great Britain, the leg is usually formed into roasts by cutting directly across the grain, so that one piece contains topside, silverside, and thick flank.

Chump End of Loin—*Quasi* or *Culotte*. This should be boned and rolled.

Rib End of Loin—*Longe* or *Selle* or, if the kidneys are included, *Rognonnade*. This is the loin chop section; when used for roasts, it is usually boned and rolled. It is an expensive cut.

Shoulder or Oyster—*Épaule*. This should be boned and rolled.

PREPARATION FOR COOKING

Select a boneless roast from any of the veal cuts in the list. It should weigh at least 3 pounds. Have it tied to make, if possible, a compact cylindrical shape 4 to 5½ inches in diameter. As it is usually not the custom of British butchers to place thin strips of fresh pork fat along the top, bottom, and sides of a roast, we have suggested strips of blanched bacon in the recipes to follow; the bacon bastes the veal as it cooks.

TIMING AND TEMPERATURES

Veal is always cooked to well done; that is, until its juices run a clear yellow with no trace of rosy colour—about 175° F. on a meat thermometer. If the meat is at room temperature when it goes into the oven, estimate 30 to 40 minutes per pound depending on the thickness of the meat.

VEGETABLE SUGGESTIONS

Starchy vegetables

Risotto, page 491, or *soubise* (rice and onions), page 445.
Potatoes scalloped in cream, page 484, or sautéed in butter, page 486.
Buttered noodles.

Other vegetables

Braised lettuce, page 450, chicory, page 453, or celery, page 451, or baked cucumbers, page 459.

Spinach braised in cream or in stock, page 432.

Brussels sprouts with cream, page 417, or with cheese sauce, page 416.

Creamed, stuffed, or sautéed mushrooms, pages 473 to 475.

Buttered peas, page 425, and tomatoes stuffed with herbs, page 467.

A garniture of glazed carrots, page 440, onions, page 442, turnips, page 448, and sautéed mushrooms, page 473.

WINE SUGGESTION

A good claret from the Médoc district is usually the best choice.

---

* VEAU POÊLÉ

[Casserole-roasted Veal]

This is a very simple and savoury recipe for veal. The meat renders a certain amount of juice as it roasts, so that no special sauce is necessary if you are content with the French system of a spoonful per serving to moisten the meat.

For 6 people

Preheat oven to 325° F., Mark 2.

A 3-lb. roast of veal, boned and tied

Dry the veal.

A heavy fireproof casserole just large enough to hold the veal easily	**1 oz. butter** **1 tbl oil**

Place the casserole over moderately high heat with the butter and oil. When you see the butter foam begin to subside, brown the veal lightly on all sides; this takes 10 to 15 minutes. Remove the veal.

1½ oz. butter, if needed **2 sliced carrots** **2 sliced onions**	**A medium herb bouquet: 4 parsley sprigs, ½ bay leaf, and ¼ tsp thyme tied in cheesecloth**

If the browning fat has burned, pour it out and add butter. Stir in the vegetables and herb bouquet, cover, and cook over low heat for 5 minutes without browning.

½ tsp salt   **Aluminium foil**
¼ tsp pepper   **Bulb baster**
A meat thermometer
2 strips of fat bacon, simmered for
    10 minutes in 1½ pts. of water
    rinsed, drained, and dried

Sprinkle salt and pepper over the veal. Return it to the casserole and baste with the butter in the casserole. Insert meat thermometer. Lay the blanched bacon over the meat, then the foil. Cover the casserole and place in lower part of preheated oven. Regulate heat so that meat cooks slowly and steadily for about 1½ hours. Baste it 2 or 3 times with the juices in the casserole. The roast is done at a thermometer reading of 175° F., or as soon as its juices run clear yellow when the meat is pricked deeply with a fork.

A hot dish   A hot gravy boat
Salt and pepper

Place the veal on a hot dish and discard trussing strings. The veal and vegetables will have produced ½ pint or more of juice in the casserole. Remove all but 2 tablespoons of fat from them. Place casserole over moderate heat while scraping up any coagulated cooking juices from the bottom and sides with a wooden spoon, and mashing the vegetables into the liquid. Boil down rapidly if necessary; you should have ¼ to ½ pint. Correct seasoning, and strain into a hot gravy boat. Garnish the meat dish with whatever vegetables you have chosen, and serve.

(*) If you are not serving immediately, return the veal and sauce to the casserole, cover partially, and leave in turned-off hot oven where it will stay warm for half an hour at least.

VARIATION

Veau Poêlé à la Matignon

[Casserole-roasted Veal with Diced Vegetables]

⅛ pt. Madeira

Follow the master recipe for roast veal, but instead of slicing the carrots and onions, cut them into ⅛-inch dice. After browning the veal, remove it and cook the vegetables slowly in butter for 10 minutes. Then add the Madeira and boil it down rapidly until it has almost completely evaporated. Return the meat to the casserole and spread half the vegetables over it, leaving the rest in the bottom of the casserole. Proceed with the recipe.

½ pt. good brown stock or beef   Optional: 1 diced tinned truffle
   bouillon   and juice from the tin
½ oz. arrowroot or cornflour
   blended with 1 tbl Madeira

When the veal is done and has been removed from the casserole, add the stock
or bouillon and simmer for 5 minutes. Then remove the herb bouquet and
bacon, and degrease the sauce. Pour in the cornflour mixture and optional
truffles and truffle juice. Simmer for 5 minutes. Correct seasoning. Sauce should
be lightly thickened.

1 oz. softened butter   **A warmed sauceboat**

Remove from heat, and just before serving, add the butter in pieces, swirling
the sauce in the casserole until each addition has been absorbed. Ladle a spoonful
of sauce and vegetables over the meat. Pour the rest into the warmed sauceboat.

VEAU PRINCE ORLOFF

[Veal *Gratinéed* with Onions and Mushrooms]

This delicious creation is fine for a party as it may be prepared in the
morning and reheated in the evening. The veal is cooked and sliced, re-formed
with a spreading of onions and mushrooms between each slice, and covered
with a light cheese sauce. It is reheated and browned before serving. Braised
lettuce or chicory go particularly well with this roast, and either a claret from
the Médoc district or a chilled white Burgundy.

For 10 to 12 people

Roasting the veal

A 5-lb. boned and tied roast of veal

Brown the veal, and roast it for about 2½ hours (to 175° F. on a meat thermometer) in a covered casserole as described in the master recipe, page 323. Then
allow the meat to rest for 30 minutes at room temperature; it will be carved
when the preparations which follow are ready.

A 2-pt. saucepan

Strain the roasting juices into the saucepan and skim off the fat. Boil juices down
rapidly to reduce to ½ pint. These will go into the *velouté* sauce later.

While the veal is roasting, prepare the onions and mushrooms as follows:

Soubise (rice and onions)

2 oz. raw white rice	**1 dsp salt**
3 pts boiling water	

Drop the rice into boiling salted water. Boil 5 minutes. Drain.

1½ oz. butter	**1 lb. sliced onions**
A 3- to 4-pt. heavy, fireproof	**½ tsp salt**
casserole with cover	

Melt the butter in the casserole, stir in the onions and salt, and coat well with
butter; stir in the rice. (No liquid is added; the onions provide enough for the
rice.) Cover and cook over a very low heat or in the oven next to the veal for
45 minutes to 1 hour, until the rice and onions are very tender but not browned.

Mushroom duxelles

½ lb. finely chopped fresh	**1 dsp oil**
mushrooms	**An 8-in. enamelled frying pan or**
3 tbl chopped shallots or spring	**heavy-bottomed enamelled**
onions	**saucepan**
1 oz. butter	**Salt and pepper**

A handful at a time, squeeze the mushrooms in the corner of a cloth to extract
their juice. Then sauté them with the shallots or spring onions in hot butter and
oil for 5 to 6 minutes, or until the pieces begin to separate from each other.
Season to taste and leave aside.

When the roast is done, prepare the following sauce and the filling:

Thick velouté sauce

3 oz. butter	**A wire whisk**
A 3-pt. heavy-bottomed	**Pinch of nutmeg**
enamelled saucepan	**¼ tsp salt**
3 oz. flour	**⅛ tsp pepper**
A wooden spoon	
1¼ pts. boiling liquid: the veal-	
roasting juices plus milk	

Melt the butter in the saucepan. Stir in the flour and cook slowly together,
stirring, until they foam for 2 minutes without colouring. Remove from heat,
pour in all the boiling liquid at once and beat vigorously with wire whisk. Beat
in the seasonings. Bring to the boil, stirring, and boil for 1 minute. Correct
seasoning. Sauce will be very thick.

¼ pt. cream

Pour ½ pint of sauce into the cooked rice and onions. Beat the cream into the
rest of the sauce and place it in a pan of simmering water to continue cooking
slowly.

Rice, onion, and mushroom filling

The cooked rice and onions $\frac{1}{8}$ **pt. cream, more if needed**
The mushroom *duxelles*   **Salt and pepper**

Purée the rice and onions through a sieve or in an electric liquidizer. Add the purée to the mushrooms, pour in $\frac{1}{8}$ pint cream, and simmer for 5 minutes, stirring. The filling should be thick enough to hold its shape quite solidly in a spoon. Boil it down if it is not thick enough; thin out with spoonfuls of cream if too thick. Correct seasoning.

Final assembly

A lightly buttered, fireproof   **Salt and pepper**
 serving dish 1$\frac{1}{2}$ ins. deep and about **The filling**
 14 ins. long

Carve the veal into neat serving slices about $\frac{3}{16}$ of an inch thick, piling them to one side in the order in which you sliced them. The roast is now to be returned in slices to the serving dish: Place the last slice you carved in the dish, sprinkle lightly with salt and pepper, then spread it with a spoonful of the filling. Overlap the next slice of veal on the first, sprinkle with salt and pepper, spread with filling, and continue thus down the length of the dish. Spread any extra filling around and over the meat.

The remaining velouté sauce

1 to 2 tbl cream, if needed   **3 oz. grated Swiss cheese**

Bring the sauce to the simmer and correct seasoning. It should be thick enough to coat a spoon fairly heavily; thin out with more spoonfuls of cream, if necessary. Away from heat, beat in the cheese.

2 tbl grated Swiss cheese   **1$\frac{1}{2}$ oz. melted butter**

Spoon the sauce over the roast. Sprinkle the cheese over it, and pour on the melted butter.

(*) May be prepared ahead to this point. Leave aside uncovered until ready to reheat.

About 30 to 40 minutes before serving, place in the upper part of a preheated, 375° F., Mark 5 oven until the sauce is bubbling and the top has browned lightly. Do not overcook, or the meat will dry out and lose character.

Once ready, the dish will stay warm for 20 to 30 minutes in the turned-off hot oven, with the door ajar.

VEAU SYLVIE

[Veal Roasted with Ham and Cheese]

In this recipe, deep slits are cut in the roast of veal from one end to the other, and the meat is marinated in brandy, Madeira, and aromatic vegetables, then stuffed with slices of ham and cheese. It is roasted in a covered casserole and, when sliced, the ham and cheese appear to have melted into the veal. Serve with the roast any of the wine and vegetable suggestions on pages 322-3. *Veau Sylvie* also makes a good cold roast just as it is or glazed with aspic.

The French cut for this would be the *noix* or topside, as it is a long, cylindrical piece with no muscle separations. A cross-cut from the leg may be used but is a bit difficult to handle; a boned section of loin or best end would be better but more expensive alternatives.

For 10 to 12 people

A 5-lb. boneless roast of veal, as solid as possible and in a loaf shape

So that the roast may be stuffed, deep slits are cut from one end to the other to make it open like the leaves of a book: make a series of deep, parallel cuts 1 to 1½ inches apart starting at the top and going with the grain the length of the meat from one end of the roast to the other, and to within ½ inch of the bottom of the roast. You will thus have 3 or 4 thick pieces of meat which are free at the top and sides, but which are all attached together at the bottom of the roast. If your meat contains many muscle separations it will look very messy and uneven at this point, but the roast is tied into shape later.

¼ pt. cognac	1 bay leaf, ½ tsp thyme, and 6
¼ pt. Madeira	peppercorns tied in cheesecloth
2 tbl olive oil	*For the Stuffing*
3 oz. sliced carrots	6 or more large slices of boiled
3 oz. sliced onions	ham 1/16 in. thick
1 tbl salt	12 or more large slices of Swiss
A large herb bouquet with	cheese 1/16 in. thick
peppercorns: 6 parsley sprigs,	White string

Choose a glazed bowl large enough to hold the meat easily. Mix the marinade ingredients above in the bowl. Add the meat and baste it with the marinade. Turn and baste the meat every hour or so, and marinate for 6 hours or overnight. Then scrape off the marinade ingredients and dry the meat. Reserve the marinade. Lay the roast so that its base rests on a cutting board. Completely cover each leaf of meat with a layer of ham between two layers of cheese. The exterior of the two outside leaves is not covered. Then close the leaves of meat together to re-form the roast. Tie loops of white string around the circumference of the meat to hold it in shape. If the roast is not neat looking, no matter; it will firm up during its cooking. Dry the roast again so that it will brown nicely.

Preheat oven to 450° F., Mark 8.

2 oz. butter   **A bulb baster**
1 tbl oil
A covered fireproof casserole large
   enough to hold the meat

Strain the marinade, reserving the liquid. Cook the marinade vegetables slowly in the butter and oil in the casserole for 5 minutes. Push them to the sides of the casserole. Raise heat to moderately high, put the veal in, uncut side down, and let the base brown for 5 minutes. Then baste with the butter and oil in the casserole. Place the casserole uncovered in the upper part of the oven to brown the top and sides of the meat for about 15 minutes. Baste every 4 to 5 minutes with the butter in the casserole.

½ tsp salt   **A meat thermometer**
⅛ tsp pepper   **Aluminium foil**
2 strips of fat bacon simmered for
   10 minutes in 2 pts. of water,
   rinsed, drained, and dried

Turn oven down to 325° F., Mark 3. Remove the casserole, pour in the marinade liquid and boil it down rapidly on top of the stove until it is reduced to one-third of its volume. Season the meat with salt and pepper. Place the bacon over it. Insert a meat thermometer, lay the foil over the meat, cover the casserole and place it in the lower part of the oven. Regulate heat so that meat cooks slowly and steadily for about 2½ hours, or to a thermometer reading of 175° F. Baste 3 or 4 times with the juices in the casserole during this period.

Serve the veal and prepare the sauce as described in the master recipe, *veau poêlé*, on page 323.

The meat should rest at room temperature for about 20 minutes before being carved, and it is carved in crosswise slices so that each piece has lardings of cheese and ham.

VEAL STEW

Sauté de Veau—Blanquette de Veau

In France the favourite cut of veal for stews is *tendron*, the part of the breast which contains the cartilaginous false ribs. Its combination of meat and gelatine

L*

gives the sauce a fine body, and the cooked *tendron* has a special and slightly crunchy eating-quality all its own. However, this particular morsel does not charm all palates. Time and again we have noticed a guest push it off to the side of his plate, obviously indicating he has no intention of eating that inferior bit of cheap meat. Therefore, unless you know or can train your audience, it is probably wiser to choose other parts of the veal. A combination of cuts is the best alternative, some with bones, some with cartilage, and some lean meat. If you are using boneless meat, include ¼ pound or so of cracked veal bones with the stew so that your sauce will develop more flavour and body.

RECOMMENDED STEWING CUTS

Allow 1 pound of boneless meat for 2 or 3 people, depending on the rest of your menu; about ¾ pound per person for bone-in meat such as breast and ribs.

Breast—*Poitrine, Tendron.*

Short Ribs from Best End—*Haut de Côtes.*

Shoulder—*Épaule.*

Middle Neck—*Côtes Découvertes.*

Scrag—*Collet.*

Knuckle—*Gîte* or *Jarret.*

(Leg and Loin cuts tend to be dry and stringy when stewed, but you may use them if you wish.)

STEWING TIME

Allow 1½ to 1¾ hours.

SAUTÉ DE VEAU MARENGO

[Brown Veal Stew with Tomatoes and Mushrooms]

The flavours of Provence go into this uncomplicated and hearty dish. Steamed rice or noodles go well with it, and green peas or French beans. Serve a chilled *rosé* wine, or a strong, young, white wine. As with all stews, this one may be cooked in advance and reheated just before serving.

For 6 people

Preheat oven to 325° F., Mark 2.

3 lbs. veal stew meat from the preceding list, cut into 2-oz., 2-in. pieces	1 to 2 tbl olive oil, more if needed A 10- to 12-in. frying pan A 6-pt. fireproof casserole

Dry the veal. Heat the oil in the frying pan until almost smoking. Then brown the meat, a few pieces at a time, and arrange the browned pieces in the casserole.

¼ lb. chopped onions

Lower heat to moderate. Pour all but a tablespoon of oil out of the frying pan, and brown the onions lightly for 5 to 6 minutes.

1 tsp salt   1 oz. flour
¼ tsp pepper

While the onions are browning, toss the meat in the casserole with salt and pepper, then with the flour. Toss and stir over moderate heat for 3 to 4 minutes to brown the flour lightly. Remove from heat.

¾ pt. dry white wine or dry white
** vermouth**

Add the wine to the frying pan with the browned onions. Boil for 1 minute, scraping up coagulated sauté juices. Pour the wine and onions into the casserole and bring to simmering point, shaking and stirring to mix the liquid and flour.

1 lb. firm, ripe, red tomatoes,   ½ tsp basil or tarragon
** peeled, seeded, juiced, and   ½ tsp thyme**
** roughly chopped, page 465   A 3-in. strip of orange peel ½ in.**
Or: ½ pt. drained and strained   wide
** tinned tomatoes or tomato   2 cloves mashed garlic**
** purée   Salt and pepper to taste**

Stir the tomatoes into the casserole. Add the herbs, orange peel, and garlic. Bring again to simmering point and season lightly to taste. Cover and place in lower part of oven to simmer slowly for 1¼ to 1½ hours or until the meat is almost tender when pierced with a fork.

½ lb. fresh button mushrooms or
** quartered larger mushrooms**

Add the mushrooms to the casserole and baste them with the sauce. Bring again to simmering point on top of the stove. Then cover and return the casserole to the oven for 15 minutes more.

¼ oz. cornouflr mixed with 1 tbl water,
** if needed**

Remove casserole from oven. Pour contents into a sieve placed over a saucepan. Remove the strip of orange peel and return the meat and vegetables to the casserole. Skim the fat off the sauce in the saucepan and boil the sauce down rapidly until it has reduced to about 1 pint. It should be lightly thickened, and a rich reddish brown. If it is too thin, blend in the cornflour and water and simmer for 2 minutes. Correct seasoning, and pour the sauce back into the casserole over the veal.

(*) May be done ahead to this point. Leave aside, cover askew.

---

2 to 3 tbl chopped fresh tarragon,
basil, or parsley

Shortly before serving, cover and bring to simmering point for 5 to 10 minutes. Present the stew in its casserole, or on a dish surrounded by rice or noodles. Decorate with fresh herbs.

BLANQUETTE DE VEAU À L'ANCIENNE
[Veal Stew with Onions and Mushrooms]

Blanquette de veau, a much-loved stew in France, is veal simmered in a lightly seasoned white stock. It is served in a *sauce velouté* made from the veal cooking stock and enriched with cream and egg yolks. A *blanquette* is certainly not difficult to make, and except for the cream and egg yolk liaison at the end, which takes less than 10 minutes, all of it may be cooked in advance. However, as it is supposed to be a lovely and delicate dish, it should really not be attempted unless you can find veal of good quality and of the palest pink colour.

Serve it with noodles or rice, or boiled or mashed potatoes. No other vegetables are needed with the mushrooms and onions, but you could include green peas, artichoke hearts, or baked cucumbers. A Médoc claret or chilled *rosé* wine would go well.

TECHNICAL NOTE ON SCUM REMOVAL

As veal comes to simmering point it releases a tremendous amount of grey-brown scum which must be removed by one means or another. You can skim continually while the veal simmers for the first 30 to 40 minutes. You can let it simmer for 10 minutes, then remove the veal and wash it rapidly in cold water, wash out the casserole, strain the stock through several thicknesses of damp cheesecloth, and continue with the recipe. Or you can adopt the following blanching process, which is the simplest. As long as all the scum is removed, it makes no difference which method you use; pick the one which best suits your predilections and prejudices.

For 6 people

Cooking the veal

3 lbs. veal stew meat cut into 2-oz., 2-in. pieces (cuts are listed on page 330)

A 5- to 6-pt. fireproof, enamelled casserole

Place the veal in the casserole and cover with cold water by 2 inches. Bring to simmering point and simmer 2 minutes. Drain the veal and wash it rapidly under cold water to remove all traces of scum. Wash out the casserole. Return the meat to the casserole.

2 to 2½ pts. cold white stock or good   (not the leaves), ½ bay leaf,
   chicken broth   ½ tsp thyme, and 2 medium
1 large onion studded with 1 clove   celery stalks tied in cheesecloth
1 large carrot, scraped and quartered   Salt
A medium herb bouquet and 2
   celery stalks: 8 parsley stems

Pour on stock or broth to cover the veal by ½ inch. Bring slowly to simmering point, and skim as necessary for several minutes. Add the vegetables and herb bouquet. Taste for seasoning and salt lightly if necessary. Cover partially and simmer very slowly for 1¼ to 1½ hours, or until the veal is tender when pierced with a fork. It should not be overcooked.

The onions

18 to 24 peeled onions about 1 in.   ¼ tsp salt
   in diameter   ½ oz. butter
¼ pt. of stock dipped from the
   simmering veal casserole

While the *blanquette* is simmering, prepare the onions: Following directions for white-braised onions on page 442, cut a cross in the root ends and simmer for 30 to 40 minutes in a small, covered saucepan with the veal stock, salt, and butter. Put them aside.

When the veal is tender, pour the contents of the casserole into a colander placed over a bowl. Rinse out the casserole and return the meat to the casserole, removing any loose bones. Arrange the cooked onions over the meat.

Sauce velouté (1½ pints), and mushrooms

A 3-pt. heavy-bottomed, enamelled   A wire whisk
   saucepan   18 to 24 fresh mushroom caps
2 oz. butter   about 1 in. in diameter, tossed
2 oz. flour   with 1 tbl lemon juice
A wooden spoon   Salt and white pepper
1½ pts. of veal cooking stock   1 to 2 tbl lemon juice

In the saucepan, melt the butter, add the flour, and stir over low heat until they foam together for 2 minutes. Away from heat, pour in the veal stock, beating vigorously with a wire whisk. Bring the sauce to the boil, stirring. Simmer for 10 minutes, frequently skimming off the film which rises to the surface. Fold in the mushroom caps and simmer 10 minutes more, skimming. Taste the sauce very carefully for seasoning, adding salt, pepper, and lemon juice to taste.

2 tbl cream or stock

Pour the sauce and mushrooms over the veal. Film the top of the sauce with 2 spoonfuls of cream or stock to prevent a skin from forming. Leave aside, partially covered.

(*) May be done ahead to this point.

Cream and egg yolk enrichment

About 10 to 15 minutes before serving, reheat slowly to simmering point, basting the veal with the sauce. Cover and simmer for 5 minutes. Remove from the heat.

3 egg yolks	**A 2½-pt. mixing bowl**
¼ pt. cream	**A wire whisk**

Blend the egg yolks and cream in the bowl with wire whisk. Beat in by spoonfuls ½ pint of the hot sauce. Then pour the mixture into the casserole, tilting it and basting the veal and vegetables to blend the rest of the sauce with the egg yolk mixture.

Place over a moderate heat, gently shaking the casserole until sauce has thickened lightly, but do not let it come to simmering point. (If not served at once, film the top of the sauce with a spoonful or two of stock, partially cover the casserole, and keep warm over hot but not simmering water for 10 to 15 minutes.)

2 tbl chopped parsley

Serve from the casserole or on a dish surrounded with rice, noodles, or potatoes. Decorate with parsley.

VEAL SCALLOPS

Escalopes de Veau

French veal scallops are boneless slices of meat cut ⅜ inch thick which are flattened to a thickness of ¼ inch. So that each scallop will constitute a neat, flat serving piece, it is cut across the grain from a solid piece of veal which contains no muscle separations. Scallops take from 8 to 10 minutes to cook, may be elegantly or simply sauced, and are always an expensive delicacy. They may be breadcrumbed or floured but are best, in our opinion, when sautéed *au naturel*.

AMOUNT TO BUY

Allow 2 or 3 scallops per person, depending on the size of the pieces of meat.

QUALITY

Because it is cooked so quickly, the veal should be of good quality, tender, and of the palest pink you can find. Dark pink and reddish veal tends to be tough when cooked this way.

SCALLOPS CUT FROM THE LEG OR FILLET

In France, because of the French method of cutting the leg into lengthwise muscles, scallops are usually taken from what would correspond to the topside, or *noix*. This cut gives solid slices of meat with no muscle separations; they cook without curling. If you cannot persuade your butcher to cut the leg in this manner, get him to cut the leg into cross-grain slices ⅜ inch thick. You can then separate the slices yourself into their natural divisions. The largest piece is the topside, which you may divide in half. The silverside with its eye insert will furnish two more scallops. Usually one or more of reasonable size may be found among the muscle divisions which make up the thick flank, at the side nearest the bone. Save the smaller pieces for stewing or mincing.

SCALLOPS CUT FROM THE BEST END

Best end scallops are more expensive but easier to use and furnish scallops all of the same size. Ask your butcher to bone a section of best end and to cut the eye of the meat into ⅜-inch slices. Trimmings may be used for stewing or mincing; bones, for veal stock.

PREPARATION FOR COOKING

Remove any transparent filaments, skin or fat surrounding the scallops. If left on, the meat will curl up as it cooks. Place each scallop between sheets of greaseproof paper and pound briefly and not too roughly; use a mallet or a rolling pin to reduce the scallop to a thickness of ¼ inch. If they are not to be cooked immediately, wrap the scallops in greaseproof paper and refrigerate them.

---

* *ESCALOPES DE VEAU À LA CRÈME*

[Sautéed Veal Scallops with Mushrooms and Cream]

This recipe for veal scallops makes a perfect main course for a chic little luncheon. If you are reasonably quick you can complete it in 30 minutes or less, and you may prepare it in advance; it only needs a 5-minute heating before it is ready to eat. Serve with it buttered rice or *risotto*, French beans, peas, or braised chicory, and a chilled white Burgundy wine.

For 6 people

12 veal scallops prepared according to the preceding directions

Dry the scallops thoroughly. The meat will not brown if it is damp.

| 1 oz. butter and 1 dsp oil, more as necessary | A 10- to 12-in. enamelled frying pan |

Place the butter and oil in the frying pan over moderately high heat. When you see that the butter foam has almost subsided, arrange 3 or 4 pieces of veal in the frying pan. Do not crowd them together. Sauté on one side for 4 to 5 minutes, regulating the heat so that the fat is very hot but is not burning. Turn, and sauté the meat on its other side for 4 to 5 minutes. (Each scallop should be lightly browned and cooked to the point where the juices have turned from rose to yellow. It is done when it has just become resistant to the pressure of your finger.) Remove the scallops to a dish, and continue with the rest in the same manner, adding more butter and oil as needed.

| 3 tbl chopped shallots or spring onions | 1 oz. butter, if needed |

Pour all but 2 tablespoons of fat out of the frying pan. If fat has burned, discard it and add 1 ounce butter. Stir in the shallots or spring onions and cook slowly for 1 minute.

| ¼ pt. dry white wine or ⅛ pt. dry white vermouth or Madeira ¼ pt. brown stock or beef bouillon | A wooden spoon |

Pour the wine and stock or bouillon into the frying pan and scrape up all the coagulated cooking juices with wooden spoon. Boil rapidly until liquid has reduced to about ⅛ pint.

| ½ pt. cream ¼ oz. arrowroot or cornflour blended with 1 dsp water | Salt and pepper to taste |

Pour the cream and the cornflour mixture into the frying pan and boil for several minutes until cream has reduced and thickened slightly. Remove from heat and season with salt and pepper.

| ½ lb. sliced fresh mushrooms 1 oz. butter | 1 dsp oil Salt and pepper |

In a separate frying pan, sauté the mushrooms in very hot butter and oil for 4 to 5 minutes to brown them lightly. Season to taste with salt and pepper, and scrape them into the cream sauce. Simmer for 1 minute. Remove from heat and correct seasoning.

Salt and pepper

Sprinkle salt and pepper over the sautéed scallops and arrange in the frying pan, basting with the cream and mushrooms.

(*) May be done ahead to this point. Leave frying pan aside, partially covered.

Several minutes before serving, cover the frying pan and bring almost to simmering point for 4 to 5 minutes, to warm the veal thoroughly but not to overcook it.

A hot dish   **Parsley sprigs**

Arrange the scallops on a hot dish. Spoon the cream and mushrooms over them and surround, if you wish, with the rice or *risotto*. Decorate with parsley, and serve.

VARIATIONS

Escalopes de Veau à l'Estragon

[Sautéed Veal Scallops with Brown Tarragon Sauce]

Rice, noodles, or sautéed potatoes go well with this, and green peas or French beans. Accompany with a claret.

For 6 people

12 veal scallops

Prepare and sauté the veal as described in the preceding master recipe. Place on a plate while completing the following sauce.

3 tbl chopped shallots or spring onions
¼ pt. dry white wine or ⅛ pt. dry white vermouth
1 dsp fragrant tarragon, fresh or dried

½ pt. brown sauce, page 59, or ½ pt. brown stock or beef bouillon plus ½ oz. arrowroot or cornflour blended with 1 dsp water

Cook the shallots or spring onions for a minute in the frying pan, then deglaze the frying pan with the wine and tarragon, reducing the liquid to 2 or 3 spoonfuls. Add the brown sauce, or the stock and cornflour mixture, and boil for 2 to 3 minutes until the sauce has reduced and thickened lightly. Correct seasoning.

Salt and pepper
A hot dish
1 oz. softened butter

1 dsp fresh chopped tarragon or chopped parsley

Season the veal with salt and pepper. Return it to the frying pan, and baste with the sauce. Cover the frying pan and heat for 4 to 5 minutes without boiling.

Arrange the meat on a hot dish. Away from heat, swirl the butter into the sauce by small spoonfuls. Swirl in the herbs. Spoon the sauce over the veal and serve.

Escalopes de Veau Chasseur

[Sautéed Veal Scallops with Mushrooms and Tomatoes]

Serve rice, noodles, or sautéed potatoes with this, green peas or French beans, or sautéed aubergine, and a Beaujolais or chilled *rosé* wine.

For 6 people

12 veal scallops

Prepare and sauté the veal as described in the preceding master recipe. Place the meat on a plate while completing the following sauce:

4 tbl chopped shallots or spring onions	**½ tsp basil or tarragon**
¾ lb. firm, ripe, red tomatoes, peeled, seeded, juiced, and chopped, page 465	**¼ pt white wine or ⅛ pt. white vermouth**
½ clove mashed garlic	**¼ pt. brown sauce, page 58, or ⅛ pt. brown stock or beef bouillon plus ½ oz. arrowroot or cornflour blended with 1 dsp water**
¼ tsp salt	
Pinch of pepper	

Cook the shallots or spring onions for 1 minute in the frying pan. Stir in the tomatoes, garlic, seasonings, and herbs. Cover the frying pan and simmer for 5 minutes. Pour in the wine, and the brown sauce or the stock and starch. Boil rapidly for 4 to 5 minutes until the sauce has reduced and thickened. Correct seasoning and remove from heat.

½ lb. sliced fresh mushrooms	**1 dsp oil**
1 oz. butter	**Salt and pepper**

In a separate frying pan, sauté the mushrooms in very hot butter and oil to brown lightly. Season to taste and scrape them into the tomato sauce. Simmer for 1 minute and correct seasoning again.

A hot dish
2 tbl fresh chopped tarragon, basil, or parsley

Sprinkle the veal scallops with salt and pepper and return them to the frying pan Baste with the sauce. Cover and heat for 4 to 5 minutes without boiling. Serve on a hot dish and decorate with the herbs.

VEAL CHOPS OR CUTLETS
Côtes de Veau

The best treatment for veal chops, in our opinion, is the simple one of browning them, then cooking them slowly in a covered frying pan or casserole for 15 to 20 minutes until their juices have turned from rose to yellow. They are particularly good if aromatic herbs and vegetables are braised with them as veal usually needs other flavours to make it more interesting.

PREPARATION FOR COOKING

Buy loin chops 1 to 1¼ inches thick. Have the corner of the backbone at the top of the chop cut off so that the meat will lie as flat as possible on either side.

---

* *CÔTES DE VEAU AUX HERBES*
[Veal Chops Braised with Herbs]

This is an excellent basic recipe for all veal chops, whether they are served with a plain deglazing sauce made from the pan juices, or with any of the suggestions listed at the end of the recipe. Sautéed potatoes, grilled tomatoes, French beans, and a chilled *rosé* wine would go well with chops prepared in the following manner.

Cooking Note: For 2 or 3 chops, the final cooking may be done on top of the stove in a covered frying pan. For 6 chops, it is easier to finish cooking them in the oven.

For 6 people

Preheat oven to 325° F., Mark 2.

6 large veal chops cut 1 in. thick	Salt and pepper
A 10- to 12-in. frying pan	A heavy, 10- to 12-in. fireproof
1 oz. butter and 1 dsp oil, more if needed	casserole with cover

Dry the chops. Heat the butter and oil in the frying pan until you see that the butter foam has almost subsided, then brown the chops, two or three at a time, for 3 to 4 minutes on each side. As they are done, season with salt and pepper and arrange in the casserole, overlapping them slightly.

1½ oz. butter, if needed	¼ pt. dry white wine or dry white
3 tbl chopped shallots or spring onions	vermouth
Optional: 1 clove mashed garlic	1 tsp mixed basil and thyme, or tarragon

Pour all but 3 tablespoons of fat out of the frying pan. If fat has burned, pour it all out and add butter. Stir in the shallots or onions and optional garlic, and cook slowly for 1 minute. Then pour in the wine, add the herbs, and simmer for a few minutes, scraping up the coagulated sautéing juices. Scrape the mixture into the casserole over the chops.

Heat the casserole on top of the stove until the liquid is simmering. Cover and place in lower part of preheated oven for 15 to 20 minutes. Turn the chops and baste them with the liquid in the casserole 2 or 3 times during this period. The chops are done as soon as their juices run yellow when the meat is pierced with a fork.

A hot dish   **Salt and pepper**
⅛ pt. stock, bouillon, or cream   ½ to 1 oz. softened butter

Remove the chops to a hot dish. Add the stock, bouillon, or cream to the casserole and boil rapidly for a few minutes until the liquid has reduced and thickened slightly. Correct seasoning. Away from heat, swirl in the butter in pieces. Pour the sauce over the chops and serve.

(*) AHEAD-OF-TIME NOTE

Veal chops may be browned well in advance of their final cooking. Once cooked, they may be kept in the hot, turned-off oven, casserole cover askew, for about 20 minutes. But do not allow them to overcook or overheat for they will dry out.

VARIATIONS: SAUCES

In addition to the following sauces, you may use the mushrooms and cream, mushrooms and tomato, or brown tarragon sauces described in the recipes for veal scallops, pages 336 to 338.

Sauce Tomate or *Coulis de Tomates*,   *Sauce Duxelles*, brown sauce with
  tomato sauce, pages 68 to 70   diced mushrooms and herbs,
Sauce Madère, brown sauce with   page 65
  Madeira wine, page 66
Sauce Robert, brown sauce with
  mustard and onions, page 64

Before cooking the chops, prepare ½ to ¾ pint of one of the sauces listed above. When the chops are done, pour the sauce into the casserole, basting the chops. If not to be served immediately, leave aside. Shortly before serving, cover the casserole and reheat for 4 to 5 minutes without simmering. Arrange the chops on a dish. Away from heat, swirl ½ or 1 ounce of butter into the casserole, then pour the sauce over the chops.

OTHER VARIATIONS

The recipe for sautéed chicken *aux herbes de Provence*, page 232, has a herb and garlic type of hollandaise sauce which can be adapted for veal chops. Another idea is to place around the browned chops partially cooked small potatoes and small onions, and *lardons* of bacon (sticks of blanched bacon 1 inch long and ¼ inch thick, lightly browned); these will finish cooking with the chops, as in the *poulet en cocotte* on page 228. Or, following the same system, you can put into the casserole butter-braised carrots and artichoke hearts, and sautéed mushrooms.

VEAL STEAKS

Veal steaks 1 to 1¼ inches thick cut from the leg or the loin chump may be cooked in exactly the same way as veal chops.

MINCED VEAL PATTIES
Fricadelles de Veau

Here is a fine recipe for minced veal patties. Arranged on a bed of braised spinach, surrounded with baked or stuffed tomatoes, and served with a chilled *rosé* wine, they make a most attractive informal main course. Other vegetables are suggested in the list under roast veal on pages 322–3. Scrag, shoulder, or breast meat may be used for mincing; be sure that the meat has first been pared of gristle, tendons, and other miscellaneous matter. Always include a proportion of ham fat, pork fat, or sausage meat; otherwise the patties will be too dry.

---

* FRICADELLES DE VEAU À LA NIÇOISE

[Veal Patties with Tomatoes, Onions, and Herbs]

Onions, garlic, and tomatoes are particularly good mixed with minced veal. If you happened to have the remains of a *ratatouille* (aubergine and tomato casserole, page 463), ¼ pint of it could replace the tomatoes and onions in the following recipe.

For 6 people

2 oz. finely chopped onions　　　　　**1 oz. butter**

Cook the onions slowly with the butter in a small frying pan for 8 to 10 minutes, until they are tender but not browned.

2 medium tomatoes, peeled, seeded,	$\frac{1}{4}$ tsp salt
juiced, and chopped, page 465	$\frac{1}{2}$ tsp basil or thyme
1 clove mashed garlic	A 5-pt. mixing bowl

Add the tomatoes, and other ingredients. Cover and cook slowly for 5 minutes. Uncover, raise heat, and boil rapidly until the tomato juices have almost entirely evaporated. Scrape into the mixing bowl.

| $2\frac{1}{2}$ oz. stale white breadcrumbs and | Or: mince 2 oz. of cooked rice with |
| $\frac{1}{4}$ pt. milk | the veal |

While the tomatoes are cooking, soak the breadcrumbs in the milk for 5 minutes. Pour into a strainer and press out as much of the milk as you can. Add breadcrumbs to mixing bowl.

1 lb. lean raw veal, minced with	$\frac{1}{4}$ tsp pepper
2 oz. of boiled ham and 2 oz. of	3 tbl chopped parsley
ham fat or fresh pork fat	1 egg
1 tsp salt	A wooden spoon

Add the meat, seasonings, parsley, and egg to the mixing bowl and beat vigorously with wooden spoon to blend thoroughly. Taste carefully for seasoning, adding more if you feel it necessary. Form the mixture into 6 or 12 balls. Flatten them into patties $\frac{1}{2}$ inch thick with the palm of your hand. If they are not to be cooked immediately, cover with greaseproof paper and refrigerate.

2 oz. sifted flour spread on a dish

Just before sautéing, dredge the patties in the flour and shake off excess flour.

1 or 2 frying pans each containing
  1 oz. butter and 1 dsp oil

Place the frying pan or frying pans over a moderately high heat. When you see that the butter foam has almost subsided, brown the patties for 2 to 3 minutes on each side. Pour out the excess fat, cover and cook very slowly for 15 minutes, turning the patties once.

A hot dish

Arrange the meat on a hot dish with whatever vegetables you have chosen, and keep warm for a moment while finishing the sauce.

| $\frac{1}{4}$ pt. brown stock or beef bouillon | $\frac{1}{2}$ to 1 oz. softened butter |

Pour the fat out of the frying pan. Add the stock or bouillon and boil rapidly, scraping up coagulated cooking juices and reducing liquid to 3 or 4 spoonfuls.

Away from heat, swirl in the butter by small pieces. Pour the sauce over the patties, and serve.

(*) AHEAD-OF-TIME NOTE

After the patties have been browned, arrange them in a casserole. Deglaze the frying pan with stock and leave aside. About 20 to 30 minutes before serving, heat the casserole until the meat is sizzling, cover and finish cooking in a 325° F., Mark 2 oven. Reheat and butter the sauce just before pouring it over the patties.

VARIATION

Fricadelles de Veau à la Crème

[Veal Patties with Cream and Herb Sauce]

2 tsp tarragon or basil	1 oz. softened butter
¼ pt dry white wine, dry white vermouth, or stock	½ tbl fresh chopped tarragon, basil or parsley
⅛ to ¼ pt. cream	

Cook the patties and remove them to a hot dish as directed in the master recipe. Add the tarragon or basil and wine or stock to the degreased frying pan. Boil down liquid to 3 tablespoons, scraping up coagulated cooking juices. Then pour in the cream and boil it down rapidly to reduce and thicken it lightly. Away from heat, swirl in the butter in pieces, then swirl in the herbs. Pour over the patties.

VARIATIONS: SAUCES

Coulis de Tomates à la Provençale, fresh tomato sauce with herbs, page 69

Sauce Brune aux Fines Herbes or **à l'Estragon,** brown sauce with mixed green herbs or tarragon, page 64

Sauce Madère, brown sauce with Madeira wine, page 66

Sauce Robert, brown sauce with mustard and onions, page 64

Sauce Duxelles, brown sauce with diced mushrooms and herbs, page 65

After cooking the patties, deglaze the frying pan with ¼ pint of white wine or white vermouth, then add ½ to ¾ pint of any one of the sauces listed above. Simmer for a minute or two. Away from heat, swirl in 1 to 2 tablespoons of softened butter and pour the sauce over the meat.

OTHER VARIATIONS

Use the same mixture of minced veal, onions, and tomatoes as described in the master recipe on page 341.

Fricadelles de Veau Duxelles

[Veal Patties with Mushrooms]

**¼ lb. finely chopped fresh
mushrooms**

Squeeze the mushrooms, a handful at a time, in the corner of a cloth to extract
their juice. When the onions in the master recipe are tender, add the mushrooms.
Raise heat and sauté for 4 to 5 minutes. Then add the tomatoes and proceed
with the recipe.

Fricadelles de Veau Mentonnaise

[Veal Patties with Tuna and Anchovies]

This Italian and Mediterranean combination is especially good accompanied
by braised spinach and grilled or baked tomatoes, or fried or sautéed potatoes
and a salad of fresh tomatoes.

**4 oz. drained and mashed tinned
  tuna fish**

**6 tinned anchovy fillets drained and
  mashed, or 1 tbl anchovy paste**

Prepare the minced veal mixture as described in the master recipe and beat into
it the tuna and anchovies. Then proceed with the recipe.

Patties Using Cooked Minced Veal

Follow any of the preceding combinations, substituting cooked veal for
raw veal. To prevent the meat from being too dry, add to the mixture 4 ounces
of sausage meat or an additional 2 ounces of minced ham fat or pork fats.

Pain de Veau

[Veal Loaf]

Use any of the preceding minced veal combinations and pack the meat in a
loaf tin or a soufflé dish. Over the top of the meat lay 3 strips of blanched fat
bacon, page 12. Bake in a 350° F., Mark 4 oven for 1 to 1½ hours.

The loaf is done when the meat has shrunk slightly from the sides of the
dish and the surrounding juices are clear yellow with no trace of rosy colour, or
at a meat thermometer reading of 175 to 180° F. Unmould the loaf and serve it
with a tomato sauce, page 68. If the loaf is to be served cold, place a weight on
top of it after cooking to compress the meat as it cools.

PORK

Porc

MARINADES

Fresh pork, whether it is a large piece for roasting, or a thin piece for sautéing, will be more tender and have a more interesting flavour if it receives a marination before cooking. This is not an essential step, but you will find it most effective, and cold leftovers will be even better than usual. You may use a simple dry mixture of salt, herbs, and spices, or a liquid marinade of either lemon juice or wine and vinegar with herbs and aromatic vegetables.

Always marinate the meat in a non-corroding container: porcelain, oven-glass enamel, or stainless steel.

TIME REQUIRED

(If the meat is refrigerated, increase the minimum marination time by at least one-third.)

Chops and steaks—a minimum of 2 hours; 6 to 12 are even better.

Loin roasts—a minimum of 6 hours, but 24 are recommended.

leg, hand and spring—a minimum of 2 days, but 4 to 5 are more effective.

MARINADE SÈCHE

[Salt Marinade with Herbs and Spices]

Fine for all types of fresh pork. This is our favourite, as it tenderizes the pork and accentuates its natural flavour.

Per pound of pork

1 tsp salt	⅛ tsp ground bay leaf
⅛ tsp freshly ground pepper	Pinch of allspice
¼ tsp ground thyme or sage	Optional: ½ clove mashed garlic

Mix all the ingredients together and rub them into the surface of the pork. Place in a covered bowl. Turn the meat 2 or 3 times if the marinade is a short one; several times a day if it is of long duration.

Before cooking, scrape off the marinade, and dry the meat thoroughly.

MARINADE SIMPLE

[Lemon Juice and Herb Marinade]

For chops, steaks, and small, boned roasts. This is also an effective marinade, giving the pork a slightly different flavour to the dry one.

Per pound of pork

1 tsp salt
⅛ tsp pepper
3 tbl lemon juice
3 tbl olive oil

3 parsley sprigs
¼ tsp thyme or sage
1 bay leaf
1 clove mashed garlic

Rub salt and pepper into the meat. Mix the other ingredients in a bowl, add the pork and baste it. Place a lid over the bowl. Turn and baste the meat 3 or 4 times during its marination period.

Before cooking, scrape off the marinade, and dry the meat thoroughly.

MARINADE AU VIN

[Wine Marinade]

May be used for chops, steaks, and small roasts, but is usually reserved for legs. This is a special 2- to 4-day marinade which gives pork a taste akin to that of wild boar, *marcassin*.

[NOTE: If the pork is to be marinated for more than 3 days, cook the carrots, onions, and garlic very slowly in the olive oil before proceeding with the recipe.]

Per each 3 pounds of pork

1 dsp salt
½ pt. dry white wine or ⅓ pt. dry
  white vermouth
¼ pt. wine vinegar
4 tbl olive oil
3 halved cloves garlic
2 oz. thinly sliced carrots

2 oz. thinly sliced onions
½ tsp peppercorns
2 bay leaves
1 tsp thyme
Optional: ¼ tsp each of basil,
  tarragon, sage, and mint; 5
  coriander seeds; 5 juniper berries

Rub salt into the pork. Mix the other ingredients in a bowl, add the meat and baste it. Place a lid over the bowl. Turn and baste the meat 3 or 4 times a day. Before cooking, scrape off the marinade and drain the meat for half an hour or so. Then dry it thoroughly.

ROAST PORK

Rôti de Porc

Pork may be roasted slowly in an open tin in a 325° F., Mark 2 oven, and basted occasionally with a spoonful or two of wine, stock, or water to aid in the dissolution of its fat. But we think pork is more tender and juicy if it is browned in hot fat, then roasted like veal in a covered casserole. This slow, steamy cooking tenderizes the meat and renders out the fat very effectively.

PREPARATION OF ROASTS FOR COOKING

For pork roasted in the French manner, have the rind removed, all but a ⅛-inch layer of covering fat, and any loose interior fat or heavy layers of fat. You may save the rind and deep freeze it for several weeks, then add it to braised meat where it will combine with the braising juices and give body to your sauce. The flavours of a marinade will penetrate pork more thoroughly if the joint is boned; roll and tie the pork after marination.

CUTS FOR ROASTING OR BRAISING

One pound of boneless pork will serve 2 or 3 people. For bone-in roasts, particularly the loin, allow ¾ pound per person.

Loin of Pork—*Longe*. The loin is divided into the following cuts:

Chump End: Rump Section—*Pointe de Filet*. This should be boned, and makes a juicy roast with its combination of fat and lean.

Chump End: Fillet Section—*Milieu de Filet*. This is lean meat, and corresponds to the loin of beef, with both uppercut and fillet. If it is not boned and rolled, have the backbone part removed for easier carving.

Rib End—*Carré*. This is lean meat, corresponding to the rib of beef, with uppercut but no fillet. If it is not boned and rolled, have the backbone section removed.

Spare Rib—*Échine*. This combination of fat and lean is a favourite roasting cut in France; it should be boned.

Bladebone—*Palette*. This is also a combination of fat and lean; it should be boned.

Hand and Spring—No French equivalent for this. Part of the arm-bone is included in the *palette*; the shank and lower arm-bone are the *jambonneau*. This is lean meat and should be boned.

Leg—*Jambon Frais*. This is lean meat; it may be bought whole or in part, and may be boned if you wish.

TEMPERATURE AND TIMING FOR ROAST PORK

Pork, in our opinion, develops its best flavour and texture when it is cooked to an interior temperature of 180 to 185° F. on a meat thermometer. At this point all its juices have turned clear yellow with no trace of rosy colour, and the meat is somewhat grey with only a suggestion of pink overtone. It was authoritatively established as far back as the year 1919 that trichinae are killed at a meat temperature of 131° F. (137° F. for official purposes) or when the pork is still rare. In view of this fact there is no reason whatsoever for overcooking pork until it is dry and lifeless.

From 30 to 45 minutes per pound are required to roast a 3- to 8-pound piece of unchilled fresh pork to an internal temperature of 180 to 185° F. A long, thin, pork loin takes less time to roast than thick leg or hand and spring of the same weight. Boned roasts usually require 5 to 10 minutes per pound more than bone-in roasts. As it takes a good hour for a large roast to cool off when it is out of the oven, you can afford to allow yourself plenty of time. Here are some examples for covered roasting in a 325° F., Mark 2 oven:

A 3-*pound loin*
Bone In—1½ to 1¾ hours
Boned and Rolled—1¾ to 2 hours
A 5-*pound loin*
Bone In—2½ to 3 hours
Boned and Rolled—3 to 3½ hours
A 5-*pound leg or hand and spring*
Bone In—About 3½ hours
Boned and Rolled—About 4 hours

VEGETABLE SUGGESTIONS

Potatoes

Roast potatoes, which may cook with the pork.

Sautéed potatoes, which may be done in pork fat rather than butter, page 486.

Boiled potatoes, plain, mashed potatoes, or the garlic mashed potatoes on page 480.

Scalloped potatoes with stock and cheese, page 483, or with tomatoes and onions, page 485.

Other vegetables

Braised white cabbage, page 352, red cabbage, page 353, or sauerkraut, page 353, which may cook with the pork.

Brussels sprouts braised in butter, or with cheese, page 414 or 416.

Braised leeks, page 455, or braised celery root, page 453.

Stuffed tomatoes, page 467; *ratatouille* (aubergine and tomato casserole), page 463.

Glazed onions, page 442, or turnips, page 448, which may cook with the pork.

See also the fruit suggestions (apples, peaches, and cherries) in the Duck section, pages 250 to 253; and the prunes in the Goose section, page 258.

WINE SUGGESTIONS

Serve a dry white wine, Riesling, Traminer, white Côtes du Rhône, or a *rosé*.

* RÔTI DE PORC POÊLÉ

[Casserole-roasted Pork]

As most French recipes call for a boneless roast, we shall so specify in this recipe and its variations. The loin is the most expensive cut and also the most attractive looking. But any other cut among those listed on page 347 may be substituted, and may be boned or not.

For 6 people

A 3-lb. boneless roast of pork, previously marinated, if you wish, according to one of the suggestions on pages 345-6	3 tbl rendered pork fat, lard, or cooking oil A heavy fireproof casserole just large enough to hold the meat

Preheat oven to 325° F., Mark 2. Dry the meat thoroughly. Place the fat in the casserole and place over a moderately high heat. When fat is almost smoking, brown the pork on all sides. This will take about 10 minutes. Remove pork to a side dish.

1 oz. butter, if needed 1 sliced onion 1 sliced carrot Optional: 2 cloves unpeeled garlic	A medium herb bouquet: 4 parsley sprigs, ½ bay leaf, and ¼ tsp thyme tied in cheesecloth

Pour all but 2 spoonfuls of fat out of the casserole. If fat has burned, throw it all out and add more butter. Stir in the vegetables, optional garlic, and herb bouquet. Cover and cook slowly for 5 minutes.

A bulb baster

Place the meat in the casserole, its fattiest side up. (If pork was not marinated, season it with salt and pepper, and half a teaspoon of sage or thyme.) Cover the casserole and heat it until the meat is sizzling, then place in lower part of pre-heated oven for about 2 hours or to a meat thermometer reading of 180 to 185° F. Baste the roast 2 or 3 times during this period with the juices in the casserole, and regulate oven heat so that the pork is cooking slowly and evenly. The pork and vegetables will render about ½ pint of juices as they roast.

A hot dish

When it is done, place the pork on a hot serving dish and discard trussing strings.

¼ pt. dry white wine, stock, bouillon, or water	A hot gravy boat

Pour the liquid into the casserole and simmer slowly for 2 to 3 minutes. Then tilt the casserole and skim out all but a tablespoon or two of fat. Mash the vegetables into the juices; boil rapidly until you have about ½ pint. Strain into a hot gravy boat. Surround the pork roast with whatever vegetable garnish you have chosen, and serve.

(*) AHEAD-OF-TIME NOTE

If you are not serving immediately, return pork and sauce to casserole. Cover loosely and set in turned-off hot oven with the door ajar. The meat will stay warm for a good half-hour.

VARIATIONS: SAUCES

Any of the following sauces may be prepared while the pork is roasting, then simmered for a moment to blend with the degreased juices in the casserole.

Sauce Diable, peppery brown sauce, page 63.

Sauce Piquante, spicy brown sauce with pickles and capers, page 63.

Sauce Robert, brown mustard sauce, page 64.

Sauce Poivrade, peppery brown sauce with vinegar and wine for use especially if the pork has been marinated in wine, page 62.

Sauce Tomate, a good tomato sauce, page 68.

Sauce Moutarde à la Normande

[Mustard Sauce with Cream]

For about ¼ pint

After the pork has been cooked and placed on a dish, keep it warm for 10 to 15 minutes while preparing the sauce.

Strain the meat juices into a bowl and degrease them.

⅛ pt. cider vinegar	10 crushed peppercorns

Pour the vinegar and peppercorns into the casserole and boil until the vinegar has reduced to about a tablespoon. Pour in the meat juices and boil them down rapidly until they have reduced to about ¼ pint.

½ pt. cream	2 tsp dry mustard mixed with
Salt	2 tsp water

Add the cream and simmer for 5 minutes, stirring salt to taste. Beat in the mustard mixture and simmer 2 or 3 minutes more. Sauce should be thick enough to coat a spoon lightly. Correct seasoning.

½ to 1 oz. softened butter	A warm gravy boat

Remove from heat and just before serving, swirl in the butter in pieces, then pour the sauce into a warm gravy boat.

VARIATIONS

Rôti de Porc Grand' Mère

[Casserole-roasted Pork with Potatoes and Onions]

Onions and potatoes absorb a distinctive flavour when they are cooked with pork in this manner.

For 6 people

A 3-lb. boneless roast of pork
previously marinated in salt for
several hours, if you wish, page
345

Roast the pork in a covered casserole with seasonings as described in the master recipe, page 349, but omit the vegetables. After 1 hour, add potatoes and onions which have been prepared as follows:

12 to 18 peeled onions 1 to 1½ ins.
in diameter

Cut a cross in the root end of the onions, and boil them for 5 minutes in salted water. Drain.

12 to 18 small new potatoes or	**1 tbl rendered pork fat or cooking**
boiling potatoes, peeled and cut	**oil**
into 1½ in. ovals	**Salt and pepper**
A frying pan	

Drop the potatoes into a pan of boiling salted water. Bring to the boil and boil ½ minute. Drain. Just before adding the potatoes to the casserole, roll them for 1 to 2 minutes in hot fat in the frying pan to brown very lightly. Season with salt and pepper.

After the pork has cooked for an hour, arrange the potatoes and onions around it and baste them with the juices in the casserole. Cover the casserole and return it to the oven until the meat is done, basting the vegetables once or twice.

A hot dish   **1 to 2 tbl chopped parsley**

Remove the pork to a hot dish and arrange the vegetables around it. Decorate with chopped parsley. Degrease the meat juices and either pour them over the vegetables, or into a hot gravy boat.

Rôti de Porc aux Navets

[Casserole-roasted Pork with Turnips]

Turnips are wonderful when cooked in pork juices. Use the same general system described for the onions and potatoes in the preceding recipe. Peel and quarter the turnips; allow 4 to 6 pieces per person. Drop them in boiling water and boil 2 minutes. Drain. Add them to the casserole for the last hour of cooking.

Rôti de Porc aux Choux

[Casserole-roasted Pork with Cabbage]

This is a great dish for lovers of cabbage. Serve it with boiled potatoes and a dry Alsatian wine, or beer.

For 6 people

A 3-lb. boneless roast of pork
previously marinated for several
hours in salt, if you wish,
page 345

Roast the pork in a covered casserole with carrots, onions, and seasonings as described in the master recipe, page 349. After an hour, add the cabbage which has been prepared as follows:

1 lb. green or white cabbage cut
into ½-in. slices
A pan containing 5 to 6 qts. of
rapidly boiling water with 1½ tsp
salt per qt. of water

Drop the cabbage into the boiling water. Bring rapidly to the boil and boil uncovered for 2 minutes. Immediately drain in a colander, and run cold water over the cabbage for a minute or two. Drain thoroughly and leave aside.

½ tsp salt   **Optional: ½ tsp caraway seeds**
⅛ tsp pepper

After the pork has cooked for an hour, arrange the cabbage around it. Add salt, pepper, and the optional caraway seeds to the cabbage, and baste it with the juices in the casserole. Cover the casserole, bring to simmering point, and return it to the oven until the pork is done. Baste the cabbage several times with the meat juices during this period.

A hot dish   **Parsley sprigs**
Salt and pepper

Then remove the pork to a hot dish. Lift the cabbage out of the casserole with a fork and spoon so that it will drain, and arrange it around the meat. Season it with salt and pepper if necessary. Degrease the juices in the casserole and pour them over the cabbage. Decorate with sprigs of fresh parsley.

*   PORC BRAISÉ AUX CHOUX ROUGES

[Pork Braised with Red Cabbage]

A good dish of red cabbage is even better when a roast of pork is cooked with it. The casserole of cabbage cooks for 3 hours before the pork goes into it, and needs 2 hours more in the oven until the pork is done.

For 6 people

**Ingredients for the braised red
cabbage on page 457 (omit the
chestnuts if you wish, but they
are a good accompaniment)**

Braise the cabbage for 3 hours in a 325° F., Mark 2 oven, following the directions in the recipe.

**A 3-lb. boneless roast of pork,
previously marinated for several
hours in salt, if possible, page 345**

Brown the pork in hot fat in a frying pan. After the cabbage has cooked for 3 hours, place the pork in the casserole with the cabbage. Cover the casserole and return it to the oven to braise for two hours more or until the pork is done.

A hot dish   **Salt and pepper**

Then place the pork on a dish, drain the cabbage and arrange it around the pork. Correct seasoning. Degrease and season the cooking juices, and pour them over the cabbage.

VARIATION

Porc Braisé avec Choucroute

[Pork Braised with Sauerkraut]

Use exactly the same method as for red cabbage but substitute sauerkraut, page 458. After the sauerkraut has braised for 3 hours, brown the pork, add it to the casserole, and cook for another 2 hours or until the pork is done.

PORC SYLVIE

[Pork Stuffed with Cheese]

A loin of pork is cut lengthwise from the top almost to the bottom to make 3 or 4 long leaves or slices so that the roast may be opened up like a book.

M

It is marinated for several hours, then stuffed with slices of Swiss cheese and cooked in a covered casserole. Follow the recipe for *veau Sylvie*, page 328, but use one of the pork marinades on page 345, and omit the slices of ham.

PORK CHOPS AND STEAKS
Côtes de Porc

Pork chops and steaks are best, we think, when they are cut thick, browned on each side, then cooked in a covered casserole or frying pan like the preceding casserole roasts of pork.

Have the chops or steak cut between ¾ to 1¼ inches thick, and ask that the backbone corners of chops be levelled or removed so that the meat will lie perfectly flat on either side. All but a thin layer of fat should be trimmed off. The best chops are from the part of the chump end containing the fillet, or from the rib end. Second choices are the rump part of the chump end, the spare rib, the bladebone, and the hand and spring. Steaks are usually cut from the hand and spring or the leg.

Usually 1 thick chop per person is sufficient. For steaks, count on 1 pound for 2 or 3 people. As steaks or chops are interchangeable in these recipes, we will call everything chops.

VEGETABLE AND WINE SUGGESTIONS
These are the same as the suggestions for roast pork on page 348.

---

* CÔTES DE PORC POÊLÉES
[Casserole-sautéed Pork Chops]

Three or four chops may be cooked in a covered frying pan on top of the stove. For a larger quantity oven-cooking in a covered casserole is easier.

For 6 people

Preheat oven to 325° F., Mark 2.

6 pork chops cut 1 in. thick and previously marinated for several hours, if you wish, in salt, lemon juice, or wine, pages 345-6	2 tbl rendered pork fat, lard, or cooking oil A heavy, 10- to 12-in. fireproof casserole

Dry the pork chops. Heat the fat or oil in the casserole until it is almost smoking, then brown the chops, 2 or 3 at a time, on each side for 3 to 4 minutes. As they are browned, transfer them to a side dish.

If the chops have not been marinated, season them with salt, pepper, and ¼ teaspoon of thyme or sage.

1 oz. butter   **Optional: 2 halved cloves garlic**

Pour the fat out of the casserole and add the butter and optional garlic. Return the chops, overlapping them slightly. Baste them with the butter. Cover and heat the casserole until the meat is sizzling, then place in lower part of preheated oven for 25 to 30 minutes. Turn and baste the chops once or twice. They are done when the meat juices run a clear yellow with no trace of rose. Make a deep cut next to the bone if you have any doubts.

A hot dish
¼ pt. dry white wine, dry white
**   vermouth, brown stock, beef**
**   bouillon, or marinade liquid**

Arrange the chops on a hot dish with whatever vegetable garnish you have chosen. The chops will have rendered about ½ pint of juices during their cooking; remove all but 2 tablespoons of fat from them. Pour in the ¼ pint of liquid and boil rapidly, scraping up all coagulated cooking juices, until you have about ¼ pint of concentrated sauce. Taste for seasoning, and pour it over the chops.

(*) AHEAD-OF-TIME NOTE

If the chops are not to be served immediately, return them to the casserole, baste them with the sauce, cover loosely, and keep warm in turned-off oven for 20 minutes or so.

VARIATIONS: SAUCES

Any of the sauces suggested for roast pork on page 350 may also be used for pork chops. Here is another suggestion:

Côtes de Porc Sauce Nénette

[Pork Chops with Mustard, Cream, and Tomato Sauce]

While the pork chops are cooking according to directions in the master recipe, prepare the following:

½ pt. cream   **Pinch of pepper**
¼ tsp salt

Simmer the cream, salt, and pepper in a small saucepan for 8 to 10 minutes, or until it has reduced by one-third.

1 tbl dry English mustard   2 tbl tomato paste

Beat the mustard and tomato paste together in a small bowl, then beat in the hot cream. Leave aside.

2 tbl fresh chopped basil, chervil,
   or parsley

After removing the chops from the casserole and degreasing the meat juices, pour in the cream mixture and simmer for 3 or 4 minutes. Correct seasoning, stir in the herbs, and pour the sauce over the chops.

VARIATIONS

Côtes de Porc Robert
Côtes de Porc Charcutière

[Pork Chops Braised in Fresh Tomato Sauce]

Include sautéed potatoes and a chilled *rosé* wine on the menu with this good dish of pork chops. If you stir chopped pickles and capers into the sauce just before serving the chops, they become *côtes de porc charcutière*.

For 6 people

6 pork chops cut 1 in. thick and   A heavy, 10- to 12-in. fireproof
   previously marinated for several   casserole
   hours, if you wish, according to
   one of the formulas on page 345

Preheat oven to 325° F., Mark 2. Brown the chops in hot fat in the casserole as described in the master recipe, page 354, and leave them aside.

1 oz. butter   ½ tsp salt
¼ lb. chopped onions   ⅛ tsp pepper
½ oz. flour   ¼ tsp sage or thyme
1 lb. ripe tomatoes peeled, seeded,   1 large clove mashed garlic
   and chopped, page 465

Pour out the browning fat, add the butter and onions, cover and cook slowly for 10 minutes. Mix in the flour and stir over low heat for 2 minutes more. Stir in the tomatoes and other flavourings. Cover and cook slowly for 5 minutes.

½ pt. dry white wine or ⅓ pt. dry   ¼ pt. brown stock or beef bouillon
   vermouth (include marinade   1 to 2 tbl tomato paste
   liquid, if any)

Stir in the wine and stock or bouillon and simmer for 10 minutes. Correct seasoning and stir in enough tomato paste to deepen the flavour and colour of the sauce.

If the chops have not been marinated, season them with salt and pepper. Arrange them, slightly overlapping, in the casserole and baste them with the tomato sauce.

(*) May be done in advance to this point.

Cover the casserole and bring to simmering point on top of the stove, then place it in the lower part of the preheated oven. Regulate oven temperature so that the casserole simmers slowly and regularly for 25 to 30 minutes or until the chops are done.

A hot dish
1 to 2 tbl fresh chopped basil or
    parsley

Arrange the chops on a serving dish. Degrease the sauce and if necessary boil it down rapidly until it is lightly thickened. Correct seasoning and pour it over the chops. Sprinkle with herbs and serve.

VARIATIONS: VEGETABLE SUGGESTIONS

Browned pork chops may also finish their cooking for half an hour or so in a casserole of braised red cabbage, page 457, or braised sauerkraut, page 458. Or you can add blanched onions, carrots, new potatoes, or turnips to the casserole with the browned chops so that the meat and vegetables finish their cooking in the oven together.

PORK STEWS

Ragoûts de Porc

The following recipes for beef stew are very good with pork as well as beef. Use boneless pork cuts which contain a mixture of fat and lean, such as spare rib, rump part of chump end, or bladebone. Cooking time is 2 to $2\frac{1}{2}$ hours rather than the $3\frac{1}{2}$ hours required for beef.

Boeuf à la Catalane, stew with rice, onions, and tomatoes, page 294.

Daube de Boeuf, casserole with wine and vegetables, page 296.

Daube de Boeuf à la Provençale, casserole with wine, vegetables, anchovies, and garlic, page 297.

HAM

Jambon

Ham is a fine dish for large parties, but a parade of plain boiled or baked hams can become woefully monotonous especially around Christmas and Easter. Here is a handful of French recipes which will lift any ham into *la grande classe*.

VEGETABLE SUGGESTIONS

Classic accompaniment

Spinach braised with cream or with stock, page 432.

Other vegetables

Braised celery, page 451, celeriac, page 453, or lettuce, page 450.
Braised chestnuts, page 479, puréed chestnuts, page 478.
Braised onions, page 444, or leeks, page 455.
Mashed potatoes.

Fruits

The French do not go in much for fruits and ham, but if you like them, see the prunes in wine in the Goose section, page 258, and the fruits suggested for duck on pages 250 to 253.

WINE SUGGESTIONS

The best choice is a not-too-heavy red wine such as a claret from the Médoc, or a Beaujolais or Mâcon.

TYPE OF HAM

All of the recipes in this section call for boiled, mild-cured ham. In the recipes for whole braised ham, we have specified 8 to 10 pounds; a pound or two more will make little difference except to the braising time. You may buy gammon hock, which always looks more festive, or middle gammon. We have allowed about 1 pound of bone-in ham for 2 people. If the ham has been boned, 1 pound should serve 3 and possibly 4 people. Have the skin or rind removed, and cut off all but a ½-inch layer of covering fat.

* JAMBON BRAISÉ MORVANDELLE

[Ham Braised in Wine—Cream and Mushroom Sauce]

Ham heated in a covered roasting tin with aromatic vegetables, herbs, stock, and wine absorbs these different flavours, and the braising liquid is easily transformed into a good sauce.

For 16 to 20 people

¼ lb. sliced carrots	A heavy covered roasting tin or
¼ lb. sliced onions	fireproof casserole just large
1 oz. butter and 1 dsp oil, or 3 dsp	enough to hold the ham
rendered ham fat	

Preheat oven to 325° F., Mark 2. Sauté the vegetables in butter and oil or ham fat for about 10 minutes in the roasting tin or casserole until they are tender and very lightly browned.

An 8- to 10-lb. cooked ham,	3 whole cloves
skinned, and trimmed of excess	1½ pts. white Burgundy wine
fat	(Chablis or Pouilly-Fuissé) or
6 parsley sprigs	1 pt. dry white vermouth
1 bay leaf	1½ to 2½ pts. white or brown stock
6 peppercorns	or beef bouillon
½ tsp thyme	

Place the ham over the vegetables, its fattiest side up, and add the rest of the ingredients above, and bring to simmering point on top of the stove. Cover, and place the roasting tin or casserole in the middle of the preheated oven. Regulate heat so that the liquid barely simmers for about 2 hours. Baste every 20 minutes. The ham is done when a trussing needle or sharp-pronged fork will pierce the thickest part of it fairly easily.

Optional glazing

Icing sugar in a shaker
A shallow roasting tin containing
  a rack

When the ham is done, drain it. If you wish to glaze it, dust the top and sides with icing sugar, and place it on the rack in the roasting tin. Heat oven to 450° F., Mark 8. Place the ham in the upper part of the oven and let it brown lightly for 10 to 15 minutes. Basting is not necessary.

Remove the ham from the oven at least 20 minutes before carving. If it is to wait longer, put it in the turned-off hot oven with door ajar where it can be left for an hour. The braising liquid is turned into a sauce as follows:

Cream and Mushroom Sauce

Version I

2 lbs. sliced fresh mushrooms	A large enamelled frying pan
1½ oz. butter	Salt and pepper
1 dsp oil	
3 tbl chopped shallots or spring onions	

Dry the mushrooms in a cloth. Sauté them for 5 to 6 minutes in hot butter and oil until they are very lightly browned. Stir in the shallots or onions and sauté for a minute more. Season to taste and leave aside.

The ham braising liquid	2 oz. flour mixed to a paste with
⅛ pt. Marc de Bourgogne, Madeira, or port	2 oz. softened butter
A 4-pt. enamelled saucepan	¾ to 1 pt. cream

Degrease the braising liquid in the roasting tin. Set roasting tin over a high heat and boil rapidly until liquid has reduced to about 1 pint and is full of flavour. Add the *marc* or wine and simmer for a minute or two to evaporate the alcohol. Strain into a saucepan and beat in the flour and butter paste. Beat in ¾ pint of cream, then stir in the sautéed mushrooms. Simmer for 5 minutes. The sauce should be just thick enough to coat a spoon very lightly. Stir in more cream if sauce seems too thick. Taste carefully for seasoning.

(*) If not to be served immediately, leave aside uncovered, top of sauce filmed with a spoonful of cream to keep a skin from forming. Reheat when ready to serve.

Version II, with egg yolks

2 lbs. fresh sliced mushrooms	The ham braising liquid
1½ oz. butter	⅛ pt. Marc de Bourgogne, Madeira, or port
1 dsp oil	A 4-pt. enamelled saucepan
3 tbl chopped shallots or spring onions	

Following Version I of the sauce, sauté the mushrooms in butter and oil, adding the shallots or spring onions at the end. Degrease the ham braising liquid, reduce it to about 1¼ pints, add the *marc* or wine and simmer for a moment. Strain into the saucepan, add the sautéed mushrooms and simmer for 5 minutes.

5 egg yolks	A 3-pt. mixing bowl
1 tsp cornflour (anti-curdling insurance)	A wire whisk
	¾ pt. cream

Blend the egg yolks and cornflour in the mixing bowl with wire whisk. Beat in the cream. Then gradually beat in about ½ pint of the ham braising liquid from the saucepan. Pour the mixture back into the saucepan with the rest of the braising liquid and mushrooms.

(*) May be done in advance to this point.

A wooden spoon   **A warmed sauceboat**
$\frac{1}{4}$ to $\frac{1}{2}$ pt. cream

Shortly before serving, place the saucepan over a moderate heat and stir with a wooden spoon until the sauce thickens lightly, but do not let it come near to simmering point (maximum temperature, 165° F.) or the egg yolks will curdle. Stir in more cream by spoonfuls if the sauce seems too thick. It should coat a spoon lightly. Taste carefully for seasoning, pour into a warmed sauceboat, and serve.

VARIATION

Jambon Braisé au Madère

[Ham Braised in Madeira Wine]

The combined flavours of Madeira and ham have always been a favourite in France. Spinach braised in stock, grilled or stuffed mushrooms, and a Médoc-claret wine are good accompaniments for this dish.

For 16 to 20 people

$\frac{1}{4}$ lb. sliced onions $\frac{3}{4}$ pt. Madeira
$\frac{1}{4}$ lb. sliced carrots $1\frac{1}{4}$ pts. stock or beef bouillon
1 oz. butter   6 parsley sprigs
1 dsp oil   1 bay leaf
A covered roasting tin $\frac{1}{2}$ tsp thyme
An 8- to 10-lb. cooked ham,   Icing sugar in a shaker
   skinned and trimmed of excess
   fat

Following the general directions in the preceding master recipe, preheat oven to 325° F., Mark 2. Cook the vegetables in butter and oil in the roasting tin until lightly browned. Place the ham in the roasting tin, pour in the wine, the stock or bouillon, and add the herbs. Bring to simmering point on top of the stove, cover, and bake very slowly for 2 to 2$\frac{1}{2}$ hours, basting every 20 minutes. When the ham is tender, glaze it with icing sugar as described in the master recipe.

Degrease the braising liquid and boil it down rapidly to 1 pint. Strain it into a saucepan.
   M*

1½ oz. arrowroot (preferable to cornflour as it does not cloud the sauce)	2 or 3 chopped tinned truffles and their juice
1 tbl cold stock, wine, or truffle juice	Or: 2 oz. mushroom *duxelles* (finely diced, sautéed mushrooms), page 475

Blend the arrowroot with the cold liquid and beat it into the hot braising liquid. Stir in the truffles or mushrooms. Simmer for 5 minutes. Correct seasoning. Sauce will have a very light thickening; the butter enrichment will give it more body and character.

1½ oz. softened butter	A warmed sauceboat

Reheat when ready to serve. Away from heat, beat in the butter in pieces, and pour the sauce into a warmed sauceboat.

---

* JAMBON FARCI ET BRAISÉ

[Braised Ham with Mushroom Stuffing]

A fine dish for an important dinner is ham sliced into serving pieces, reconstructed with a stuffing between each slice, then braised in Madeira.

For 12 to 14 people

2 lbs. fresh mushrooms	2 oz. chopped shallots or spring onions
1½ oz. butter	
1 dsp oil	

Trim, wash, and chop the mushrooms. A handful at a time, twist them into a ball in the corner of a cloth to extract their juice. Sauté in the butter and oil with the shallots or onions for 8 to 10 minutes until the mushroom pieces begin to separate from each other.

⅛ pt. Madeira or port

Add the wine to the mushrooms and boil rapidly until the liquid has almost completely evaporated.

Salt and pepper	½ tsp sage or thyme
6 to 7 oz. *mousse de foie gras*, or *mousse de foie d'oie* (the latter is puréed liver from a plain goose and is much less expensive)	Pinch of allspice
	Optional: 1 or 2 diced, tinned truffles (reserve their juice for the sauce)

Scrape the mushrooms into a mixing bowl and season with salt and pepper. Blend in the rest of the ingredients. Taste carefully for seasoning, but do not salt too heavily because the ham is salted.

**A 10-lb. cooked ham, skinned, and   A large square of well washed
    trimmed of excess fat   cheesecloth, if needed**

Cut the upper two-thirds of the ham into neat, thin, horizontal serving slices,
piling them to one side in the order in which you slice them. Leave the lower
third of the ham intact to act as a cradle to hold the slices when you put them
back. Spread a spoonful of the mushroom stuffing in the centre of each slice and
pile the slices back on to the ham, reconstructing it into approximately its
original shape. If the slices have been arranged neatly and solidly on the ham, no
tying is necessary to keep them in place while the ham braises. But if you are
doubtful, wrap the ham in cheesecloth.

Then braise the ham for about 2½ hours with cooked vegetables, herbs, stock,
and Madeira as described in the braising recipe, page 361. Serve it with the same
Madeira sauce, and braised spinach, page 432.

VARIATION

Jambon Farci en Croûte

[Stuffed Ham Baked in a Pastry Crust]

A splendid way to serve the preceding sliced and stuffed ham is to bake
it in a pastry crust. To do so, after stuffing and braising it, allow it to cool for
about an hour. Then, following the directions for duck in a crust, page 527,
surround it with decorated pastry and bake it in a 375° F., Mark 5 oven for 30
to 40 minutes until the crust is cooked and nicely browned.

HAM SLICES

Tranches de Jambon

Sliced ham responds to a number of interesting preparations which are
relatively quick and simple to do.

TRANCHES DE JAMBON EN PIPÉRADE

[Ham Slices Baked with Tomatoes, Onions, and Peppers]

This savoury recipe for thick slices of smoked ham may be prepared for
baking several hours before it is placed in the oven. Sautéed potatoes, French
beans, and a light red wine or a *rosé* go well with it.

For 6 people

2½ to 3 lbs. of cooked ham, sliced ½ in. thick, and cut into serving pieces if you wish
2 tbl rendered ham fat or olive oil

A large frying pan
A shallow baking dish large enough to hold ham in one layer

Trim off excess fat, and dry the ham slice or slices. Heat the fat or olive oil in the frying pan until it is almost smoking, then brown the ham lightly for a minute or two on each side. Remove frying pan from heat and place the ham in the baking dish.

¼ lb. sliced onions   ¼ lb. sliced green peppers

Lower the heat, and stir the onions into the fat in the frying pan. Cover and cook slowly for 5 minutes. Stir in the peppers and cook 5 minutes more or until the vegetables are tender but not browned.

2 lbs. firm, ripe, red tomatoes, peeled, seeded, juiced, and sliced, page 465
2 cloves mashed garlic

⅛ tsp pepper
Pinch of cayenne pepper
¼ tsp sage or thyme

Spread the tomato pulp over the onions and peppers, add the garlic and seasonings. Cover and cook slowly for 5 minutes so that the tomatoes will render their remaining juice. Then uncover and boil for several minutes, shaking the frying pan, until the tomato juice has almost entirely evaporated.

Cover the browned ham with the vegetables.

(*) May be done in advance to this point.

2 to 3 tbl chopped parsley

Preheat oven to 350° F., Mark 4. About 20 to 30 minutes before serving time, cover the baking dish and place it in the middle of the oven and bake until the ham is heated through and tender when pierced with a fork. Baste with the juices in the dish and correct seasoning, adding salt if necessary. Decorate with parsley and serve.

TRANCHES DE JAMBON MORVANDELLE

[Sautéed Ham Slices—Cream and Madeira Sauce]

Placed on a bed of spinach braised in stock, surrounded with grilled mushrooms or sautéed potatoes, this is a delectable ham dish. Serve with it a light red wine, or a Chablis or Pouilly-Fuissé.

For 6 people

**2½ to 3 lbs. of cooked ham, sliced
  ¼ in. thick**

Trim off excess fat, and cut the ham into serving pieces. Dry.

1 oz. butter   **An enamelled frying pan**
1 dsp oil

A few pieces at a time, brown the ham lightly for a minute on each side in hot butter and oil. Put the ham aside.

1 oz. flour   **A wooden spoon**
**2 tbl chopped shallots or spring
  onions**

Pour all but 2½ tablespoons of fat out of the frying pan. Stir in the flour with a wooden spoon, then the shallots or spring onions, and cook slowly for 2 or 3 minutes without browning. Remove from the heat.

½ pt. very good ham stock, white   **A wire whisk**
  or brown stock, or beef bouillon   **1 tbl tomato paste**
¼ pt. Madeira or port   **Big pinch of pepper**

Bring the stock or bouillon and wine to simmering point in a small saucepan. Blend it into the flour in the frying pan with a wire whisk. Beat in the tomato paste and pepper.

½ pt. cream   **3 tbl cognac**

Bring the sauce to simmering point, stirring, then beat in the cream. Simmer for 4 or 5 minutes, allowing the sauce to reduce until it coats the spoon lightly. Taste carefully for seasoning but do not oversalt. Stir in the cognac. Then add the ham slices and spoon the sauce over them.

(*) May be done in advance to this point. Film surface with a spoonful of cream and leave aside.

**A hot dish on which, if you wish,
  is a mound of spinach braised in
  stock, page 432**

Shortly before serving, bring to simmering point, cover, and simmer slowly for a minute or two until the ham is tender when pierced with a fork. Taste again for seasoning. Transfer the ham to a dish, or place it over a bed of braised spinach. Spoon the sauce over the ham and serve.

VARIATION

Mix sliced, sautéed mushrooms into the sauce to simmer with the ham.

TRANCHES DE JAMBON À LA CRÈME

[Sautéed Ham Slices—Fresh Cream Sauce]

This famous recipe is the same idea as the preceding one, but is made with a richer and more delicate sauce.

For 6 people

2½ to 3 lbs. cooked ham, sliced   2 tbl shallots or spring onions
    ¼ in. thick   ¼ pt. Madeira or port and 2 tbl
1 oz. butter   cognac
1 dsp oil   A wooden spoon
A 9- to 10-in. frying pan

Trim off excess fat, cut the ham into serving pieces, and dry. Brown the slices lightly on each side in hot butter and oil and put them aside. Pour all but a tablespoon of sautéing fat out of the frying pan, stir in the shallots or spring onions, and cook slowly for 2 minutes. Pour in the wine and cognac and, scraping up the coagulated sauté juices with a wooden spoon, boil rapidly until the liquid has reduced to 3 or 4 tablespoons.

¾ pt. cream   Big pinch of pepper
2 tbl French prepared mustard
    mixed with 1 tbl tomato paste
    and 2 tbl cream

Add the cream to the frying pan, beat in the mustard mixture, and the pepper. Simmer slowly for 10 to 15 minutes, until the cream has reduced to about ½ pint and has thickened lightly. Correct seasoning, but do not oversalt.

Return the ham slices to the frying pan and baste them with the sauce.

(*) May be done ahead to this point.

A hot dish on which, if you wish,
    is a mound of spinach braised in
    stock, page 432

Shortly before serving, bring to simmering point, cover and simmer for several minutes until the ham is reheated and tender. Arrange the ham on a hot dish or on the bed of spinach. Spoon the sauce over the ham and serve.

FRENCH BAKED BEANS
Cassoulet

Cassoulet is a rich combination of beans baked with meats, typical of southwestern France. The composition of a *cassoulet* is, in typical French fashion, the subject of infinite dispute, so much so that if you have read or heard about *cassoulet* and never tasted it, you come to expect a kind of rare ambrosia rather than the nourishing country fare it actually is. As *cassoulet* is native to a relatively large region of France, each part of which has its own specialities, arguments about what should go into this famous dish seem based on local traditions. *Toulousains* insist that it must include among its meats preserved goose, *confit d'oie*, or it is not a real *cassoulet*. After all, something must be done with all the geese which housed the *foie gras*, and *cassoulet* is a natural solution in the Toulouse area. Then there are those who declare the *cassoulet* was born in Castelnaudary, and originally contained only beans, pork, and sausages. A heretical few suggest the *cassoulet* was not a French invention at all, but an adaptation from the Arab *fava* bean and mutton stew. And so on, with variations and dogmatisms rampant. Fortunately all the talk can be regarded as so much historical background, for an extremely good *cassoulet* can be made anywhere out of beans and whatever of its traditional meats are available: goose, game, pork, sausages, lamb, mutton. The important item is flavour, which comes largely from the liquid the beans and meats are cooked in. And truth to tell, despite all the to-do about preserved goose, once it is cooked with the beans you may find difficulty in distinguishing goose from pork.

The following recipe makes no attempt to cut corners, for the concoction of a good *cassoulet* is a fairly long process. You can prepare it in one day, but two or even three days of leisurely on-and-off cooking are much easier. It calls for a roast loin of pork, shoulder of lamb braised in wine, home-made sausage cakes, and beans cooked with pork rind, fresh bacon or salt pork, and aromatic vegetables. The meats are cut into serving pieces and arranged in a casserole with the beans and various cooking juices. Then the dish is baked in the oven for an hour to blend the flavours. Time could be saved if the lamb were roasted whole or if leftover roast were used, but flavour would be lost, and there would be no splendid braising liquid to give character to the *cassoulet*. Polish sausage could cook with the beans, replacing the home-made sausage cakes. But after you have made the dish once or twice, you will see that you can pretty well invent your own formula as long as you supply excellent flavour through one means or another. Suggestions for other meats are at the end of the recipe.

MENU SUGGESTIONS

Any *cassoulet* worthy of the name is not a light dish, and is probably best served as a midday dinner. The rest of the menu should consist of a simple first course, if any—a clear soup, jellied soup, or oysters—then a green salad and fruits. For wine, choose a strong, dry *rosé* or white, or a young, full-bodied red.

THE BEANS

Most French recipes specify simply 'dry white beans'. A few call for white beans from certain localities in France such as Cayence, Pamiers, Mazères, Lavelanet. Thus white haricot beans will be entirely satisfactory, but they should not be old and stale. If you wishto pressure-cook them instead of using the open-pot method, soak them as directed in the recipe, then add all the ingredients listed and, following the directions for your cooker, bring them quickly to 15 pounds pressure. Cook for exactly 3 minutes, then allow the pressure to go down slowly by itself, 15 to 20 minutes. Let the beans stand uncovered in the cooking liquid for at least 30 minutes so that they will absorb its flavour.

A NOTE ON THE ORDER OF BATTLE

All of the various steps leading up to the final assembly in the recipe below may be carried on at various times or almost simultaneously. Once the *cassoulet* is made ready for the oven, it may be refrigerated and baked a day or two later.

---

* *CASSOULET DE PORC ET DE MOUTON*

[Beans Baked with Loin of Pork, Shoulder of Mutton or Lamb, and Sausage]

For 10 to 12 people

The loin of pork

2¼ lbs. of boned loin of pork,
   excess fat removed. (It will taste
   even better if marinated overnight
   in salt and spices, page 345.)

Following directions on page 349, roast the pork to an internal temperature of 175 to 180° F. Put it aside to cool. Reserve cooking juices.

The beans

2 lbs. white haricot beans
A 7-qt. saucepan containing 4 qts.
   of rapidly boiling water

Drop the beans into the boiling water. Bring rapidly back to the boil and boil for 2 minutes. Remove from heat and let the beans soak in the water for 1 hour;

they will cook in the soaking water, and the cooking should proceed as soon as possible after the soaking process is completed.

½ lb. fresh pork rind or salt pork   A heavy saucepan
    rind   Large scissors

While the beans are soaking, place the rind in the saucepan and cover with 1½ pints of cold water. Bring to the boil and boil for 1 minute. Drain, rinse in cold water, and repeat the process. Then cut the rind into strips ¼ inch wide; cut the strips into small triangles. Cover the rind again with 1½ pints of cold water, bring to simmering point, and simmer very slowly for 30 minutes. Leave saucepan aside. This process freshens the rind, and softens it so that it will lose itself as it cooks with the beans.

A 1-lb. chunk fresh, unsalted,   A large herb bouquet, with garlic
    unsmoked streaky bacon (or very   and cloves: 6 to 8 parsley sprigs,
    good quality lean salt pork   4 unpeeled cloves garlic, 2 cloves,
    simmered for 10 minutes in   ½ tsp thyme, and 2 bay leaves tied
    3 pts. of water and drained)   in cheesecloth
4 oz. sliced onions   No salt until later if you have used
The pork rind and its cooking   salt pork; otherwise 1 dsp salt
    liquid

Place all the above ingredients in the pan with the soaked beans. Bring to simmering point. Skim off any scum which may rise. Simmer slowly, uncovered, for about 1½ hours or until the beans are just tender. Add boiling water if necessary during cooking, to keep beans covered with liquid. Season to taste near end of cooking. Leave beans in their cooking liquid until ready to use, then drain. Reserve cooking liquid. Remove the bacon or salt pork and leave aside. Discard the herb bag.

The lamb or mutton

2 to 2½ lbs. boned shoulder or breast   A heavy, 7-qt. fireproof casserole
    of mutton or almost mature   About 1 lb. cracked mutton or
    lamb, excess fat removed   lamb bones; some pork bones
3 to 4 tbl rendered fresh pork fat,   may be included
    pork-roast drippings, goose fat,   ½ lb. chopped onions
    or cooking oil; more if needed

Cut the lamb or mutton into chunks roughly 2 inches square. Dry each piece well. Pour a $\frac{1}{16}$-inch layer of fat into the casserole and heat until the fat is almost smoking. Brown the meat, a few pieces at a time, on all sides. Place the meat on a side dish. Brown the bones and add them to the meat. If fat has burned, discard it and add 3 tablespoons of fresh fat. Lower heat, and brown the onions lightly for about 5 minutes.

4 cloves mashed garlic
5 tbl fresh tomato purée, tomato
    paste, or 4 large tomatoes peeled,
    seeded, and juiced, page 465
½ tsp thyme
2 bay leaves

1 pt. dry white wine or ¾ pt. dry
    white vermouth
1½ pt. brown stock or 1 pts. beef
    bouillon and ½ pt. water
Salt and pepper

Return the bones and lamb or mutton to the casserole and stir in all ingredients above. Bring to simmering point on the top of the stove, season lightly with salt. Cover and simmer slowly on top of the stove or in a 325° F., Mark 2 oven for 1½ hours. Then remove the meat to a dish; discard the bones and bay leaves. Remove all but 2 tablespoons fat and carefully correct seasoning of cooking liquid.

Final flavouring of beans

Pour the cooked and drained beans into the lamb cooking juices. Stir in any juices you may have from the roast pork. Add bean cooking liquid, if necessary, so that the beans are covered. Bring to simmering point and simmer for 5 minutes, then let the beans stand in the liquid for 10 minutes to absorb flavour. Drain the beans when you are ready for the final assembly further on.

Home-made sausage cakes—a substitute for Saucisse de Toulouse

1 lb. lean fresh pork
6 oz. fresh pork fat
A mincer
A 5-pt. mixing bowl
A wooden spoon
2 tsp salt
⅛ tsp pepper

Big pinch allspice
⅛ tsp crumbled bay leaf
⅛ pt. armagnac or cognac
A small clove mashed garlic
Optional: 1 chopped truffle and
    the juice from the tin

Put the pork and fat through the mincer. Place in bowl and beat in the rest of the ingredients above. Then sauté a small spoonful and taste for seasoning, adding more to the mixture if you feel it necessary. Form into cakes 2 inches in diameter and ½ inch thick. Brown lightly over moderate heat in a frying pan. Drain.

Final assembly

A 7-qt. fireproof casserole 5 to 6 ins.
    high: brown earthenware glazed
    inside is typical, but other types
    of glazed pottery or enamelled
    iron will do nicely

6 oz. dry white breadcrumbs mixed
    with 8 tbl chopped parsley
2 to 3 tbl pork roasting fat or
    goose fat

Cut the roast pork into 1½ to 2 inch serving chunks. Slice the bacon or salt pork into serving pieces ¼ inch thick. Arrange a layer of beans in the bottom of the casserole, then continue with layers of lamb or mutton, roast pork, bacon slices, sausage cakes, and beans, ending with a layer of beans and sausage cakes. Pour on the meat cooking juices, and enough bean cooking juice so that the liquid comes just to the top layer of beans. Spread on the crumbs and parsley, and pour the fat on top.

(*) Leave aside or refrigerate until you are ready to take up the final cooking of about an hour. The *cassoulet* should be served soon after it has been baked, so that it will not dry out or overcook.

Baking

Preheat oven to 375° F., Mark 5. Bring the casserole to simmering point on top of the stove. Then place it in the upper part of the preheated oven. When the top has crusted lightly, in about 20 minutes, turn the oven down to 350° F., Mark 4. Break the crust into the beans with the back of a spoon, and baste with the liquid in the casserole. Repeat several times, as the crust forms again, but leave a final crust intact for serving. If the liquid in the casserole becomes too thick during the baking period, add a spoonful or two of bean cooking liquid. The *cassoulet* should bake for about an hour; serve it from its casserole.

VARIATIONS

Here are some additions or substitutions for the meats in the preceding recipe.

Preserved Goose, Confit d'Oie. This is goose, usually from the *foie gras* regions of France, which has been cut into wing, leg, and breast sections, poached in goose fat, and preserved in goose fat. It can usually be bought in tins from one of the food-importing shops. Use it instead of, or even in addition to, the roast pork in the recipe. Scrape the fat off the pieces of goose, and cut the goose into serving portions. Brown them lightly in some of the fat from the tin. Arrange the goose in the casserole with the beans and meats for the final baking.

Fresh Goose, Duck, Turkey, or Partridge. Roast or braise any of these, and carve into serving pieces. Use along with or instead of the roast pork in the recipe, arranging the pieces with the beans and meats in the casserole for the final baking.

Boiling Bacon or Veal Knuckle. Simmer either of these with the beans. Cut into serving pieces before arranging in the casserole for the final baking.

Polish Sausage. This sausage can usually be bought in any delicatessen, and is a good substitute for such French sausages as *de campagne, de ménage, à cuire, à l'ail,* or *de Morteau.* First simmer the whole sausage for ½ hour with the beans. Then cut it into ½-inch slices and arrange in the casserole with the beans and the other meats for the final baking. Polish sausage may be used instead of or in addition to the sausage cakes in the recipe.

SAUTÉED CALF'S LIVER

Foie de Veau Sauté

It is most important that calf's liver be sautéed in very hot butter and oil, so that a crust will form on the outside which will keep the juices in. Do not crowd the frying pan, use two frying pans if necessary, and do not use a frying pan too large for your source of heat. Sautéed liver should be pink inside, its juices will run a very pale rose when the meat is pricked with a fork. Have the liver cut into even slices ⅜ inch thick. Any surrounding filament should be peeled off each slice; if this is left on, the liver will curl as it cooks.

WINE AND VEGETABLE SUGGESTIONS

Grilled tomatoes, braised spinach, or *ratatouille* (aubergine and tomato casserole, page 463), and sautéed potatoes go well with liver. Wine choices would be chilled *rosé*, or a light red such as claret or Beaujolais.

---

* *FOIE DE VEAU SAUTÉ*

[Sautéed Calf's Liver]

For 6 people

6 to 12 slices of calf's liver ⅜ in. thick—surrounding filament removed	Salt and pepper 2 oz. of sifted flour on a large plate

Just before sautéing, season the slices with salt and pepper, roll in flour, and shake off excess flour.

1 or 2 heavy frying pans 1 oz. butter and 1 tbl oil for each frying pan	A hot dish A vegetable garniture, watercress, or parsley

Place the butter and oil in the frying pan or frying pans and place over a high heat until you see that the butter foam has almost subsided, indicating that it is hot enough. Then arrange the liver in the frying pan, leaving a ¼-inch space between each slice. Sauté for 2 to 3 minutes, regulating heat so that the butter is always very hot but not burning. Turn the liver and sauté for a minute or so on the other side. The liver is done when its juices run a very pale pink if a slice is pricked with a fork. Remove the liver to a hot dish and serve, surrounded by whatever garniture you have chosen, or decorated with watercress or sprigs of parsley.

SAUCES TO SERVE WITH SAUTÉED LIVER

Sauce Crème à la Moutarde

[Cream and Mustard Sauce]

For about ½ pint

¼ pt. brown stock or beef bouillon   **¼ pt. cream**

As soon as the liver has been removed to a dish, pour the stock or bouillon into the frying pan and boil down rapidly until it has been reduced by half. Then add the cream and boil for a moment to reduce and thicken it slightly.

1 tbl prepared mustard, mashed   **Parsley sprigs**
with 1 oz. softened butter

Away from heat, swirl the mustard-butter into the frying pan. Pour the sauce around the liver, decorate with parsley, and serve.

Other Sauces

The sauces in the following list can be prepared in advance; either serve them separately, or pour them around the sautéed liver. About ¾ pint should be sufficient.

Coulis de Tomates, fresh tomato purée with herbs, page 69.

Sauce Robert, brown sauce with mustard and onions, page 64.

Sauce Brune aux Fines Herbes, brown herb sauce, page 64.

Sauce à l'Italienne, tomato-flavoured brown sauce with diced mushrooms, diced ham, and herbs, page 67.

Beurres Composés, flavoured butters, pages 89 to 94. These include butter creamed with mustard, with herbs, with garlic, and with wine and herbs. Spread a spoonful over each slice of sautéed liver, or cut chilled, flavoured butter into pieces and pass separately.

FOIE DE VEAU À LA MOUTARDE

[Liver with Mustard, Herbs, and Breadcrumbs]

This is an appealing way to prepare liver. It is sautéed very briefly to brown lightly, then coated with mustard and herbs, rolled in fresh breadcrumbs, basted with melted butter, and placed under a hot grill to brown the crumbs. The preliminary sautéing and crumbing may be done several hours in advance of the final cooking, which takes about 5 minutes. For this recipe, the liver is sliced thicker, so that it will not cook too quickly.

For 6 servings

6 slices of calf's liver cut ½ in.   1 oz. butter
   thick—outside filament removed   1 dsp oil
Salt and pepper   A heavy frying pan
2 oz. sifted flour on a large plate

Season the liver with salt and pepper, dredge in the flour, and sauté for 1 minute on each side in very hot butter and oil. The slices should be very lightly browned and slightly stiffened, but not cooked through. Remove to a dish.

3 tbl prepared French mustard   Pinch of pepper
1 tbl finely chopped shallots or   6 oz. fine, white, fresh breadcrumbs
   spring onions   spread on a large plate
3 tbl chopped parsley   A greased grilling pan
½ clove mashed garlic

Beat the mustard in a small bowl with the shallots or spring onions and seasonings. Drop by drop, beat in the liver sautéing fat to make a mayonnaise-like cream. Coat the liver slices with the mixture. One by one, lay the slices in the breadcrumbs and heap breadcrumbs on top, gently shake off excess, and pat the adhering crumbs in place with the flat of a knife. Arrange the liver in the grilling pan.

(*) If not to be grilled immediately, cover with greaseproof paper and refrigerate.

Shortly before serving, heat grill to very hot.

3 oz. melted butter   A hot dish

Baste the liver with half the melted butter. Place so that its surface is about 2 inches below the grill to brown for a minute or two. Turn, baste with the remaining butter, and brown the other side quickly. Arrange on a hot dish and serve.

SWEETBREADS AND BRAINS

Ris de Veau et Cervelles

Sweetbreads and brains have much the same texture and flavour, but brains are more delicate. They both receive almost the same treatments. Both must be soaked for several hours in cold water before they are cooked, to soften the filament which covers them so that it may be removed, to dissolve their bloody patches, and to whiten them. Some authorities direct that they always be blanched before cooking—that is, poached in salted and acidulated water (see below) or a court bouillon; others do not agree. If the sweetbreads or brains are to be braised, blanching is a useless and flavour-losing step. If they are to be sliced and sautéed, blanching firms them up so that they are easier to cut, but removes some of their delicacy and tenderness. Both brains and sweetbreads are perishable, and if they are not to be cooked within 24 hours, they should be soaked and blanched, which will help to preserve them.

SOAKING SWEETBREADS AND BRAINS

Wash in cold water, then place in a bowl and soak in several changes of cold water or under a dripping tap for 1½ to 2 hours. Delicately pull off as much as you can easily of the filament which encloses them, without tearing the flesh. This is a rather slow process. Soak them again for 1½ to 2 hours, this time in several changes of cold water containing 1 tablespoon of vinegar per quart (acidulated water). Peel off as much more filament as you can, and they are then ready for trimming and cooking.

TRIMMING

A whole sweetbread, which is the thymus gland of a calf and usually weighs about 1 pound, consists of 2 lobes connected by a soft, white tube, the *cornet*. The smoother, rounder, and more solid of the two lobes is the kernel, heart, or *noix*, and choicest piece. The second lobe, called throat sweetbread or *gorge*, is more uneven in shape, broken by veins, and is often slit. Separate the two lobes from the tube with a knife. The tube may be added to the stock pot.

For brains, cut off white, opaque bits at the base.

BLANCHING SWEETBREADS

Sweetbreads, trimmed and soaked as in preceding directions	Cold water
An enamelled saucepan just large enough to hold them	Per qt. of water: 1 tsp salt and 1 tbl lemon juice

Place sweetbreads in saucepan and cover by 2 inches with cold water; add salt and lemon juice. Bring to simmering point and cook, uncovered, at breast simmer for 15 minutes. Drain and plunge into cold water for 5 minutes. Drain. The sweetbreads are now ready for sautéing.

BLANCHING BRAINS

Brains, trimmed and soaked as in   Boiling water
    preceding directions   Per qt. of water: 1 tsp salt and 1 tbl
An enamelled saucepan just large   lemon juice
    enough to hold them

Place the brains in saucepan and cover by 2 inches with boiling water; add salt
and lemon juice or vinegar. Heat to just below simmering point and maintain
water at a not-quite-simmering temperature, timing as follows:

Lamb brains, 15 minutes
Calf or pork brains, 20 minutes
Beef brains, 30 minutes.

Then leave saucepan aside and let the brains cool for 20 minutes in the cooking
liquid; if they are not to be used until later, place saucepan in refrigerator. Drain
the brains, and they are ready for sautéing, page 380.

PRESSING BLANCHED BRAINS OR SWEETBREADS UNDER A WEIGHT

Some cooks like to weight blanched sweetbreads or brains for 2 to 3 hours
under a heavy dinner-plate. This forces the water out of them, and flattens them
so that they are easy to cut into narrow slices. Follow this system or not, as you
wish.

SWEETBREADS

* RIS DE VEAU BRAISÉS

[Braised Sweetbreads]

Braising is a preliminary cooking for sweetbreads, and you will note that
no blanching is required. The soaked and peeled sweetbreads are first cooked
slowly in butter to firm them a little and to render some of their juices; they
are then baked with wine and other flavourings. After this cooking, or braising,
which may take place as long as the day before you are to use them, the sweetbreads are ready for saucing and serving. Sauced sweetbreads may be arranged
in a ring of rice or *risotto*, in a *vol-au-vent* or pastry shell, on a dish, or they may
be *gratinéed*. Drained, braised sweetbreads are also good cold, in a salad.

VEGETABLE AND WINE SUGGESTIONS

Rice or *risotto*, and buttered peas or creamed or braised spinach go well
with sweetbreads. Serve a light red wine such as a Médoc-claret, or a *rosé*
with sweetbreads in brown sauce; a white Burgundy or a white Graves with
sweetbreads in cream sauce.

For 6 people

1 oz. each: finely diced carrots, onions, celery, and diced ham	$\frac{1}{8}$ tsp salt
2 oz. butter	Pinch of pepper
A medium herb bouquet: 4 parsley sprigs, $\frac{1}{4}$ tsp thyme, and $\frac{1}{2}$ bay leaf tied in cheesecloth	A 10-in. enamelled frying pan

Cook the diced vegetables and ham slowly in the butter with the herb bouquet and seasonings for 10 to 15 minutes, until tender but not browned.

$\frac{1}{2}$ tsp salt
Big pinch of pepper
$1\frac{1}{2}$ to 2 lbs. sweetbreads previously soaked, peeled, and trimmed as directed on page 375

Season the sweetbreads. Arrange them in the frying pan and baste them with the butter and vegetables. Cover and cook slowly for 5 minutes. Turn, baste, and cook 5 minutes more. They will render quite a bit of juice.

A buttered fireproof casserole or baking dish about 7 ins. in diameter, or just large enough to hold the sweetbreads in one layer

Transfer the sweetbreads to the casserole.

Preheat oven to 325° F., Mark 2.

$\frac{1}{4}$ pt. dry white wine or $\frac{1}{8}$ pt. dry white vermouth
$\frac{1}{2}$ pt. brown stock or beef bouillon if you are serving a brown sauce; $\frac{1}{3}$ pt. white stock or chicken broth if you are serving a white sauce

Pour the wine into the frying pan with the sweetbread juices and vegetables, and boil down rapidly until the liquids have reduced to $\frac{1}{4}$ pint. Then pour the liquids, vegetables, and herb bouquet over the sweetbreads; add sufficient stock, bouillon, or broth barely to cover them.

Bring to simmering point on top of the stove. Cover the casserole and place in lower part of oven. Regulate heat so that the sweetbreads cook at the barest simmer for 45 minutes.

(*) Let the sweetbreads cool in their cooking stock until you are ready to use them.

VARIATIONS

Ris de Veau Braisés à l'Italienne

[Braised Sweetbreads with Brown Mushroom Sauce]

For 6 people

The braised sweetbreads in the
preceding recipe

Remove the sweetbreads from the braising casserole. Drain, cut into ½-inch slices, and leave aside.

½ oz. cornflour blended with 1 tbl   2 oz. diced, boiled ham
   dry white wine or vermouth   Salt and pepper
1 tbl tomato paste
½ lb. finely diced fresh mushrooms
   sautéed in butter, page 473

Rapidly boil down the cooking stock in the casserole to ½ pint. Remove from the heat and discard herb bouquet. (The braising vegetables and ham remain, and become a part of the sauce.) Beat in the cornflour mixture and the tomato paste. Stir in the mushrooms and additional ham; simmer for 3 minutes, stirring. Correct seasoning and fold in the sliced sweetbreads.

(*) If not to be served immediately, film sauce with a spoonful of stock.

2 tbl chopped green herbs such as
   parsley, chervil, and tarragon,
   or parsley only

Reheat for 2 to 3 minutes below simmering point just before serving. Arrange on a serving dish, or in a pastry shell or ring of rice. Sprinkle with herbs, and serve.

Ris de Veau à la Crème
Ris de Veau à la Maréchale

[Creamed Sweetbreads]

1½ to 2 lbs. braised sweetbreads,
   master recipe

Cut the braised sweetbreads into slices ½ inch thick and leave aside. Rapidly boil down their cooking stock until it has reduced to ½ pint.

A 2½-pt. enamelled saucepan   1¼ oz. flour
1¼ oz. butter

In a separate pan, cook the butter and flour slowly together until they foam for 2 minutes without browning. Away from heat, strain in the hot cooking stock and beat vigorously to blend. Bring to the simmer, stirring, for 1 minute. Sauce will be very thick.

¼ to ½ pt. cream   **Drops of lemon juice**
Salt and pepper

Beat in ¼ pint of cream, simmering, then beat in more by spoonfuls until the sauce thins out and coats the spoon nicely. Correct seasoning, adding drops of lemon juice if you feel it necessary.

Replace the sweetbreads in their original casserole, or in a fireproof serving dish, and pour the sauce over them.

(*) If not to be served immediately, film top with a spoonful of cream.

2 tbl chopped, mixed green herbs
or parsley

Reheat for 3 to 4 minutes below simmering point before serving, then decorate with the herbs.

Ris de Veau à la Crème et aux Champignons

[Creamed Sweetbreads with Mushrooms]

Ingredients for the preceding   **½ lb. sliced fresh mushrooms**
creamed sweetbreads

After making the sauce, stir in the mushrooms and simmer for 10 minutes, allowing the sauce to reduce slightly as the mushrooms will thin it out. Then proceed with the recipe.

Ris de Veau au Gratin

[Sweetbreads *au Gratin*]

Ingredients for the braised sweet-   **1 oz. grated Swiss cheese**
breads on page 376 and any of   **½ oz. butter, cut into pieces**
the preceding sauces

Arrange the sliced sweetbreads in a buttered baking dish or individual shells or dishes. Pour sauce over them. Sprinkle on the cheese, and dot with the butter. Leave aside until ready to serve.

About 10 minutes before serving, place 7 to 8 inches below a moderately hot grill to heat the sweetbreads through and to brown the top of the sauce lightly.

ESCALOPES DE RIS DE VEAU SAUTÉS

[Sweetbreads Sautéed in Butter]

These are done exactly like brains sautéed in butter, and are accompanied by any of the sauces suggested at the end of that recipe, page 381.

BRAINS

Although calf's brains are those most universally known, lamb's brains are equally good. Mutton, pork, and beef brains are less delicate in texture than calf brains and are best when braised, but you may sauté them if you wish. Soaking and peeling directions for brains are at the beginning of this section on page 375. We shall call everything in the following recipes calf's brains with the understanding that calf, lamb, mutton, pork, and beef brains are interchangeable though their cooking times differ slightly as indicated in the blanching directions on page 376.

---

* CERVELLES AU BEURRE NOIR

[Calf's Brains in Brown Butter Sauce]

Brown butter sauce and calf's brains are almost synonymous, they go so well together. To be at its best, the sauce should always be made separately, not in the pan in which you sautéed the brains. It is thus clear and unspeckled, and also much more digestible. In addition, as the brains can be sautéed only at the last minute, the dish will then be ready to serve almost at once.

Of the several methods for *cervelles au beurre noir*, we have chosen that of pre-cooking the brains, slicing them, marinating them in a vinaigrette, then sautéing and saucing them. As alternatives, you may simply pour a brown butter sauce over hot, blanched brains, or you may omit the pre-cooking and marination altogether. In this case, slice raw, soaked, and trimmed brains, season, dredge in flour, and sauté them; then pour the sauce over them.

VEGETABLE AND WINE SUGGESTIONS

This dish often constitutes a separate course, but if you wish to serve the brains as a main course, accompany them with mashed or parsley potatoes and either buttered green peas or the spinach braised in stock on page 432. Wine choices would be a claret, such as a Médoc, or a *rosé*; good but less usual would be a white Burgundy.

For 6 people as a main course

1½ lbs. calf's brains, previously
   soaked, trimmed, and blanched
   according to directions on pages
   375–6

Cut the blanched brains into slices ½ inch thick.

3 tbl lemon juice	Pinch of pepper
⅛ tsp salt	1 tbl olive oil
A 4-pt. mixing bowl	2 tbl chopped parsley

Beat the lemon juice and salt in the bowl until the salt has dissolved. Then beat in the pepper, oil, and parsley. Fold the sliced brains into the sauce. Marinate for 30 minutes, or until you are ready to sauté them.

½ pt. brown butter sauce, page 88,
   with or without capers

While the brains are marinating, prepare the sauce and keep hot over simmering water.

4 oz. flour sifted into a dish

Just before sautéing, drain the brains. Roll in the flour and shake off excess flour.

1 or 2 heavy frying pans
1 oz. butter and 1 tbl oil for each
   frying pan

Place the frying pan or frying pans over a moderately high heat with the butter and oil. As soon as you see that the butter foam has almost subsided, brown the brains lightly for 3 to 4 minutes on each side.

A hot dish

Arrange on a hot dish, pour the hot butter sauce over them, and serve.

VARIATIONS: SAUCES

Sauce à l'Italienne, tomato-flavoured brown sauce with diced mushrooms, diced ham, and herbs, page 67.

Coulis de Tomates, fresh tomato sauce with herbs, page 69.

CERVELLES BRAISÉES

[Braised Calf's Brains]

The brains are cooked in butter with aromatic vegetables, herbs, wine, and stock. Follow the recipe for braised sweetbreads, page 376, and use the same sauces, but the oven-simmering times are:

20 minutes for lamb brains
30 minutes for calf and pork brains
45 minutes for beef brains.

CERVELLES EN MATELOTE

[Calf's Brains in Red Wine with Mushrooms and Onions]

This dish makes a complete course in itself. Serve a light red Burgundy or Mâcon wine.

For 6 people

¾ pt. good, young, red wine (Mâcon or Burgundy)
½ pt. brown stock or beef bouillon
An enamelled saucepan just large enough to hold the brains in one layer
¼ tsp thyme

4 sprigs of parsley
½ bay leaf
1 clove mashed garlic
1½ lbs. calf's brains, previously soaked and peeled, page 375
A buttered, fireproof serving dish

Bring the wine and stock or bouillon to simmering point in the saucepan with the herbs and garlic. Add the brains, bring to simmering point, and cook uncovered at just below simmering point for 20 minutes. Allow the brains to cool in the cooking liquid for 20 minutes, so that they absorb flavour, and firm up. Then drain them, slice into ½-inch pieces, and arrange in the buttered serving dish.

1 dsp tomato paste
1 oz. flour mashed to a paste with 1 oz. softened butter

Salt and pepper

Beat the tomato paste into the cooking stock, and boil down rapidly until the liquid has reduced to ¾ pint. Away from heat, beat in the flour-butter paste. Boil, stirring, for 1 minute. Correct seasoning.

24 small, brown-braised onions, page 444

½ lb. fresh mushrooms sautéed in butter, page 473

Arrange the onions and mushrooms around the brains, and strain the sauce over the brains and vegetables.

(*) If not to be served immediately, film the sauce with a spoonful of stock or melted butter.

½ to 1 oz. softened butter

Just before serving, place over a low heat to warm through for 3 to 4 minutes without simmering. Away from heat, tip dish, add butter, a dessertspoon at a time, and baste brains and vegetables with the sauce until the butter is absorbed.

12 heart-shaped *croûtons* (white   **2 to 3 tbl chopped parsley**
bread sautéed in clarified butter),
page 181

Decorate with *croûtons* and parsley, and serve.

VEAL AND LAMB KIDNEYS
Rognons de Veau et de Mouton

Cooked kidneys should be tender and slightly pink near the centre. The bursting-out of juices is always a problem when they are sautéed in slices. Unless your source of heat is a very strong one, within a few seconds of placing the slices in the pan their juices pour out and the kidneys boil and toughen rather than sauté. An excellent solution—and, in fact, the best method for kidneys in our experience—is to cook the whole kidney in butter, then slice it, and warm the slices briefly in a sauce. However, if you prefer to sauté raw sliced kidneys, do so in very hot butter and oil for only 2 to 3 minutes. They do not brown; they just cook through, turning a uniform grey outside but remaining somewhat pink inside. Then remove the kidneys to a hot dish, make one of the sauces described in the following recipes, and return the kidneys to warm in the sauce without boiling.

Any of the following recipes may be made at the table in a chafing dish.

LAMB KIDNEYS

All of the following recipes are for veal kidneys, but are equally applicable to lamb kidneys. Allow 2 or 3 lamb kidneys per person. Cook them whole in butter as described in the master recipe, but only for 4 to 5 minutes rather than the 10 for veal kidneys. Then proceed with the recipe.

PREPARATION FOR COOKING

Both lamb and veal kidneys are encased in a layer of fat which has usually been peeled off, presumably without breaking the kidneys, before you buy them. Under this is a thin filament surrounding the kidney; this should also be peeled off. Cut out most of the button of fat on the underside of lamb kidneys, and most of the knob of fat under a veal kidney. A trimmed veal kidney will weigh 6 to 8 ounces; a lamb kidney, 1½ to 2 ounces. Kidneys should have a good, fresh odour and only the faintest suggestion, if any, of an ammonia smell. Veal and lamb kidneys should never be washed or soaked in water, as they absorb too much of it.

---

* *ROGNONS DE VEAU EN CASSEROLE*

[Kidneys Cooked in Butter—Mustard and Parsley Sauce]

If you want to serve this as a main course rather than as a hot hors d'œuvre, potatoes sautéed in butter and braised onions make good accompaniments. Red Burgundy goes especially well with kidneys.

For 4 to 6 people

2 oz. butter
A fireproof casserole or chafing dish which will just hold the kidneys easily side by side

3 veal kidneys, peeled and trimmed of fat
A hot plate and cover

Heat the butter in the casserole or chafing dish until you see the foam begin to subside. Roll the kidneys in the butter, then cook them uncovered for about 10 minutes; turn them every minute or two. Regulate heat so that the butter is always very hot but is not discolouring. A little juice from the kidneys will exude and coagulate in the bottom of the casserole. The kidneys should stiffen but not become hard, brown very lightly, and be pink at the centre when sliced. Remove them to a hot plate and cover to keep warm for a few minutes.

1 tbl chopped shallots or spring onions
¼ pt. dry white wine or dry vermouth

1 tbl lemon juice

Stir the shallots or spring onions into the butter in the casserole and cook for 1 minute. Then add the wine or vermouth and lemon juice. Boil, scraping up coagulated cooking juices, until the liquids have reduced to about 4 tablespoons.

1½ tbl prepared French mustard mashed with 1½ oz. softened butter

Salt and pepper

Away from heat, swirl the mustard-butter by spoonfuls into the casserole, and add a sprinkling of salt and pepper.

Salt and pepper   **3 tbl chopped parsley**

Rapidly cut the kidneys into crosswise slices ⅛ inch thick. Sprinkle with salt and pepper and put them and their juices into the casserole. Sprinkle on the parsley. Shake and toss them over a low heat for a minute or two to warm them through without allowing the sauce to come near simmering point.

Hot plates

Serve immediately on very hot plates.

VARIATIONS

Rognons de Veau Flambés

[Veal Kidneys Flamed in Brandy—Cream and Mushroom Sauce]

This extremely good combination is one which is often prepared beside your table at a good restaurant. If you are making it at home in a chafing dish, have all the sauce ingredients, including the sautéed mushrooms, at hand in separate containers. Kidneys cooked this way are best as a separate course, served with hot French bread, and a full, red Burgundy wine.

For 4 to 6 people

3 veal kidneys, peeled and trimmed   **2 oz. butter**
   of fat   **A fireproof casserole or chafing dish**

Cook the kidneys for about 10 minutes in hot butter as described in the master recipe.

⅛ pt. cognac   **A hot plate and cover**

Pour the cognac over the kidneys. Avert your face and ignite the cognac with a lighted match. Shake the casserole or chafing dish and baste the kidneys for a few seconds until the flames have subsided. Remove the kidneys to a hot plate, and cover them.

¼ pt. brown sauce, page 58, or ¼ pt.   **⅛ pt. Madeira**
   beef bouillon mixed with 1 tsp
   cornflour

Pour the brown sauce, or bouillon and cornflour, and the wine into the casserole. Boil for a few minutes until reduced and thickened.

½ pt. cream   **Salt and pepper**
½ lb. sliced fresh mushrooms
   sautéed in butter with 1 tbl
   chopped shallots or spring onions,
   page 473
   N

Stir in the cream and mushrooms and boil a few minutes more. Sauce should be thick enough to coat the spoon lightly. Season to taste with salt and pepper.

½ tbl prepared French mustard
   blended with 1 oz. softened
   butter and ½ tsp Worcester sauce

Away from heat, swirl in the mustard–butter.

Salt and Pepper   **Hot plates**

Rapidly cut the kidneys into crosswise slices ⅛ inch thick. Season with salt and pepper, and put them and their juices into the sauce. Shake and toss the kidneys over a low heat for a moment to reheat them without bringing the sauce near simmering point. Serve immediately on hot plates.

Rognons de Veau à la Bordelaise

[Veal Kidneys in Red Wine Sauce with Marrow]

Sauce à la bordelaise is a reduction of red wine, brown sauce, shallots, and herbs into which poached marrow is folded just before serving. It goes very well with kidneys. With sautéed potatoes and braised onions or buttered peas, this would make a fine main course served with a red Burgundy wine.

For 4 to 6 people

3 veal kidneys, peeled and trimmed   A fireproof casserole or chafing
   of fat   dish
2 oz. butter   A hot plate and cover

Cook the kidneys for about 10 minutes in hot butter in a casserole or chafing dish as described in the master recipe, page 384. Remove them to a hot plate and cover them.

2 tbl chopped shallots or spring   Big pinch each of thyme, pepper,
   onions   and powdered bay leaf
¼ pt. good, young, red wine such
   as a Burgundy or Mâcon

Stir the shallots or spring onions into the casserole and cook for 1 minute. Pour in the wine, add seasonings, and boil until reduced by half.

½ pt. brown sauce or ½ pt. beef   Salt and pepper
   bouillon, mixed with ½ oz.
   arrowroot or cornflour

Then pour in the brown sauce or bouillon and arrowroot or cornflour. Simmer for 3 to 4 minutes until lightly thickened. Correct seasoning.

Salt and pepper
2 oz. diced beef marrow softened
for 2 to 3 minutes in hot water,
page 15

2 to 3 tbl fresh parsley
Hot plates

Rapidly cut the kidneys into crosswise slices $\frac{1}{8}$ inch thick, and season with salt and pepper. Mix them and their juices in with the sauce. Fold in the marrow. Shake and toss for a moment over a low heat to reheat the kidneys without bringing the sauce near simmering point. Sprinkle with parsley and serve on very hot plates.

CHAPTER EIGHT

VEGETABLES

Légumes

Anyone who has been fortunate enough to eat fresh, home-cooked vegetables in France remembers them with pleasure. Returning voyagers speak of them with trembling nostalgia: 'Those delicious little French beans! They even serve them as a separate course. Why I'll never forget the meal I had . . . ,' and so forth. Some people are even convinced that it is only in France that you can enjoy such experiences because French vegetables are somehow different. Fortunately this is not the case. Any fine, fresh vegetable in season will taste just as good in Britain or anywhere else if the French vegetable-cooking techniques are used.

The French are interested in vegetables as food rather than as purely nutrient objects valuable for their vitamins and minerals. And it is in the realm of the green vegetable that French methods differ most radically from British. The French objective is to produce a cooked green vegetable so green, fresh-tasting, and full of flavour that it really can be served as a separate course. They do not hesitate to peel, boil, squeeze, drain, or refresh a vegetable, which is often upsetting to those very Britons who weep in delighted remembrance of vegetables in France. For many Britons have been taught that by performing any of these acts one is wickedly 'throwing away the best part'.

BLANCHING

You will note that before anything else in the way of cooking or flavouring takes place, all the green vegetables in this chapter are blanched—dropped into a very large pan of rapidly boiling salted water. This is the great secret of French green-vegetable cookery. Success is entirely dependent on having a great quantity of boiling water: 6 to 7 quarts for 2 to 3 pounds of vegetables. The more water you use in proportion to your vegetables, the quicker the water will return to the boil after the vegetables have gone in, and the greener, fresher, and more full of flavour they will be. Bicarbonate of soda is never necessary when you cook green vegetables this way.

REFRESHING

A second important French technique is that of refreshing. As soon as green vegetables have been blanched, and if they are not to be served immediately or are to be served cold, they are plunged for several minutes into a large quantity of cold water. This stops the cooking immediately, sets the colour, and preserves the texture and flavour. If the vegetables are not refreshed in this manner and are left steaming in a saucepan or colander, their collective warmth softens and discolours them, and they lose their fresh taste. Following the refreshing technique, then, you can cook all your green vegetables well in advance of a party, and have only the final touches left to do at the last minute.

OVERCOOKING

A cardinal point in the French technique is: *Do not overcook*. An equally important admonition is: *Do not attempt to keep a cooked green vegetable warm for more than a very few moments*. If you cannot serve it at once, it is better to leave it aside and then to reheat it. Overcooking and keeping hot ruin the colour, texture, and taste of green vegetables—as well as most of the nutritive qualities.

SCOPE OF VEGETABLE CHAPTER

This chapter does not pretend to offer a complete treatise on vegetables. The French repertoire is so large that we have felt it best to go into more detail on a selection than to give hints on all. Most of our emphasis is on green vegetables. There is a modest but out-of-the-ordinary section on potatoes. Other vegetables rate only one or two recipes—but good ones—and some we have not mentioned at all.

GREEN VEGETABLES

ARTICHOKES

Artichauts

A fresh, desirable artichoke is heavy and compact, with fleshy, closely clinging leaves of a fine, green or greenish-purple colour all the way to the tips. The stem is also fresh and green.

*Cooked Artichoke Filled
with Hollandaise Sauce*

All the following recipes are based on the large, 10- to 12-ounce artichoke which is about 4½ inches high and 4 to 4½ inches at its largest diameter.

SERVING SUGGESTIONS

Hot or cold boiled artichokes are served as a separate course, either at the beginning of the meal or in place of a salad. Most wine authorities agree that water should be served with them rather than wine, for wine changes its character when drunk with this vegetable. But, if you insist, serve a strong, dry, chilled white wine such as a Mâcon, or a chilled and characterful *rosé* such as a Tavel.

PREPARATION FOR COOKING

One at a time, prepare the artichokes as follows:

Remove the stem by bending it at the base of the artichoke until it snaps off, thus detaching with the stem any tough filaments which may have pushed up into the heart.

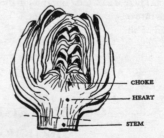

*Sectional View of
Artichoke*

CHOKE
HEART
STEM

Break off the small leaves at the base of the artichoke. Trim the base with a knife so that the artichoke will stand solidly upright.

Lay the artichoke on its side and slice three-quarters of an inch off the top of the centre cone of leaves. Trim off the points of the rest of the leaves with scissors. Wash under cold running water.

*Trim off Ends of Leaves
with Scissors*

Rub the cut portions of the artichoke with lemon juice. Drop it into a basin of cold water containing 1 tablespoon of vinegar per quart of water (acidulated water). The acid prevents the artichoke from discolouring.

---

* *ARTICHAUTS AU NATUREL*

[Whole Boiled Artichokes—Hot or Cold]

Artichokes should be boiled in a large pan so that they have plenty of room. It is not necessary to tie the leaves in place. Because they must cook a comparatively long time, artichokes turn an olive green. Any Frenchman would look with disfavour on a bright green boiled artichoke, knowing that bicarbonate of soda had been added to the water.

6 artichokes prepared for cooking as in the preceding directions	1½ tsp salt per qt. of water
A large pan containing 6 to 7 qts. of rapidly boiling water	Washed cheesecloth

Drop the prepared artichokes into the boiling salted water. To help prevent discolouration, lay over the artichokes a double thickness of cheesecloth; this will keep their exposed tops moist. Bring the water back to the boil as rapidly as possible and boil slowly, uncovered, for 35 to 45 minutes. The artichokes are done when the leaves pull out easily and the bottoms are tender when pierced with a knife.

A slotted spoon   **A colander**

Immediately remove them from the pan with the spoon and drain them upside down in a colander.

Boiled artichokes may be served hot, warm, or cold.

If you have never eaten an artichoke before, here is how you go about it. Pull off a leaf and hold its tip in your fingers. Dip the bottom of the leaf in melted butter or one of the sauces suggested further on. Then scrape off its tender flesh between your teeth. When you have gone through all the leaves, you will come to the heart, which you eat with a knife and fork after you have scraped off and discarded the choke or hairy centre growth.

It is not necessary to remove the choke, but it makes a nicer presentation if you wish to take the time. To do so, gently spread the leaves apart enough so that you can reach into the interior of the artichoke. Pull out the tender centre cone of leaves in one piece. Down in the centre of the artichoke, at the point where you removed the cone of leaves, is the choke or hairy growth which covers the top of the heart. Scrape off and remove the choke with a spoon to expose the tender flesh of the artichoke heart. Sprinkle salt and pepper over the heart. Turn the cone of leaves upside down and place it in the hollow formed by the top of the artichoke.

Sauces for Hot or Warm Artichokes

Beurre Fondu, melted butter.
Beurre au Citron, lemon butter sauce, page 88.
Sauce Hollandaise, page 70. If you have removed the choke, you may wish to spread the leaves apart enough to expose the heart, then heap 3 or 4 spoonfuls of the hollandaise into it, and top with a sprig of parsley.

Sauces for Cold Artichokes

Vinaigrette, French dressing, page 85.
Sauce Ravigote, vinaigrette with herbs, capers, and onions, page 85.
Sauce Moutarde, mustard sauce with olive oil, lemon juice, and herbs, page 86.
Sauce Alsacienne, soft-boiled egg mayonnaise with herbs, page 84.
Mayonnaise, page 77.

---

* *ARTICHAUTS BRAISÉS À LA PROVENÇALE*

[Artichokes Braised with Wine, Garlic, and Herbs]

Most of the many recipes for braised artichokes follow the general lines of this one. You may, if you wish, add to the casserole ¼ pound of diced tomato pulp, or 3 ounces of diced ham, and, 10 minutes before the end of the cooking, ½ pound of sautéed mushrooms. Another suggestion with different vegetables follows this recipe. Braised artichokes go well with roast or braised meats, or they can constitute a first course. As they are rather messy to eat with the fingers, guests should be furnished with a spoon as well as a knife and fork, so that the flesh may be scraped off the artichoke leaves.

For 6 to 8 people

6 large artichokes	1½ tsp salt per qt. of water
A large pan containing 6 to 7 qts. of rapidly boiling water	

Prepare the artichokes for cooking as directed at the beginning of this section, but cut off the leaves so that the artichokes are only about 1½ inches long. Then slice the artichokes into lengthwise quarters and cut out the chokes. Drop the quarters in boiling water and boil for 10 minutes only. Drain.

Preheat oven to 325° F., Mark 2.

4 oz. diced onions	2 large cloves chopped garlic
5 tbl olive oil	Salt and pepper
A 10- to 11-in. covered fireproof casserole large enough to hold the artichokes in one layer	

Cook the onions slowly in olive oil in the casserole for 5 minutes without letting them colour. Stir in the garlic. Arrange the artichoke quarters in the casserole. Baste with the olive oil and onions. Sprinkle on salt and pepper. Cover casserole and cook slowly over a low heat for 10 minutes, not allowing artichokes to brown.

⅛ pt. wine vinegar	A herb bouquet: 4 parsley sprigs,
¼ pt. dry white wine or dry white vermouth	½ bay leaf, and ¼ tsp thyme tied in cheesecloth
¾ pt. stock, beef bouillon, or water	A round of greaseproof paper

Pour in the vinegar and wine. Raise heat and boil until liquid is reduced by half. Then pour in the stock, bouillon, or water. Add the herb bouquet. Bring to simmering point, then lay the greaseproof paper over the artichokes. Cover casserole and place it in the middle of the preheated oven. Casserole should simmer slowly for 1¼ to 1½ hours, or until the liquid has almost entirely evaporated.

(*) If not to be served immediately, leave casserole aside, its cover askew. Reheat when needed.

N*

2 to 3 tbl chopped parsley

Discard herb bouquet. Serve from casserole or on a warm serving dish. (The artichokes may be surrounded with baked tomatoes and sautéed potatoes.) Sprinkle with parsley before bringing to the table.

VARIATION

Artichauts Printaniers

[Artichokes Braised with Carrots, Onions, Turnips, and Mushrooms]

Except for the addition of other vegetables, this recipe is the same as the master recipe. You may wish to use butter instead of olive oil, cut down on the garlic, and omit all or part of the vinegar, increasing the wine accordingly.

Ingredients for the preceding braised artichokes, including diced onions, oil (or butter), wine, stock, and seasonings
12 small onions, about 1 in. in diameter, peeled

3 or 4 carrots, scraped, quartered and cut into 1½ in. lengths
3 or 4 white turnips, peeled and quartered

Following the preceding recipe, quarter and blanch the artichokes, and cook the diced onions in the olive oil (or butter). Then add the artichokes and place the whole onions and the other vegetables around the edge of the casserole. Baste with the diced onions and oil (or butter), and season with salt and pepper. Proceed with the recipe.

12 to 18 mushroom caps lightly sautéed in olive oil or butter

About 10 minutes before the end of the cooking, add the mushroom caps. Finish the sauce and serve the casserole as in the preceding recipe.

ARTICHOKE HEARTS OR BOTTOMS
Fonds d'Artichauts

An artichoke heart is the tender, meaty bottom of the artichoke; all the leaves and the choke have been removed. The heart is even more of a delicacy in this country, owing to the price of artichokes, than it is in France. Artichoke hearts are delicious braised in butter or served with a sauce. Or they may be filled with mushrooms or other vegetables and served as a garniture or a first course. Topped with poached eggs they make a good entrée. Artichoke hearts are also eaten cold filled with shellfish and mayonnaise or *à la Grècque*. Their preparation is rather exacting; the lower leaves must be broken off from the artichoke bottom in such a way as to lose as little of the meat as possible. Then the heart is trimmed and given a preliminary cooking in a *blanc* to preserve its whiteness. But all of this may be done a day or two before serving.

HOW TO PREPARE ARTICHOKE HEARTS

Choose the largest artichokes you can find. Ideally they should be 4½ inches in diameter, which will do for one serving. Otherwise, allow two per person. Prepare them one at a time.

Break the stem off close to the base of the artichoke. Holding the artichoke base up, bend a lower leaf back on itself until it snaps, then pull it off. Continue all around the artichoke until you have gone beyond the curve of the heart, and the leaf structure folds inward.

Slice off the rest of the leaves just over the top of the heart. Immediately rub cut parts with lemon juice. The choke and leaf ends are removed after cooking.

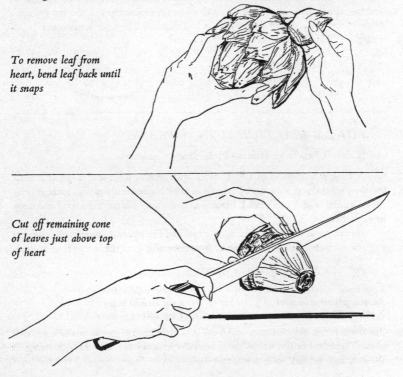

To remove leaf from heart, bend leaf back until it snaps

Cut off remaining cone of leaves just above top of heart

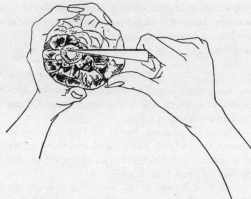

*To trim base of heart,
rotate it against sharp
knife blade*

Holding the heart base up, rotate it slowly with your left hand against the blade of a knife held firmly in your right hand, to remove all pieces of green and to expose the whitish surface of the heart. Frequently rub the cut portions with lemon juice. Drop each heart as it is finished into acidulated water (1 tbl vinegar or lemon juice per quart of water).

*Trimmed heart ready to cook;
choke is removed after
cooking*

FONDS D'ARTICHAUTS À BLANC

[Cooked Artichoke Hearts—Preliminary Cooking]

A *blanc* is a solution of salted water with lemon juice and flour. It is used for the preliminary cooking of any food which discolours easily, such as artichoke hearts, salsify, calf's head. Flour and lemon juice blanch the food and keep its whiteness.

Never cook artichoke hearts in anything but enamel, ovenglass, stainless steel, or earthenware. Aluminium or iron pans will give them a greyish colour.

For 6 to 8 large artichoke hearts

1 oz. flour	1½ pts. cold water
An enamelled saucepan	2 tbl lemon juice
A wire whisk	1 tsp salt

Put the flour in the saucepan and beat in a little cold water to make a smooth paste. Then beat in the rest of the water, the lemon juice, and the salt. Bring to the boil and simmer for 5 minutes.

Add the artichoke hearts. Bring the liquid again to the boil, then simmer for 30 to 40 minutes or so until the hearts are tender when pierced with a knife. Be sure they are completely covered with liquid at all times. Add more water if necessary.

Allow them to cool in their liquid. If they are to be refrigerated for a day or two, film the top of the liquid with oil.

Cooked Artichoke Heart,
Choke Removed

Just before using the hearts, remove them from the liquid and wash them under cold water. Delicately remove the choke with a spoon and trim off the remaining leaf ends.

---

* *FONDS D'ARTICHAUTS AU BEURRE*

[Buttered Artichoke Hearts, Whole]

This is the method for heating cooked artichoke hearts which are to be filled with hot vegetables, poached eggs, *béarnaise* sauce, truffles, or whatever is called for.

Preheat oven to 325° F., Mark 2.

6 cooked artichoke hearts (see preceding recipe)
Salt and white pepper
2 oz. butter
A covered fireproof casserole (enamelled, ovenglass, stainless steel or earthenware) just large enough to hold the hearts in one layer

A round of buttered greaseproof paper

Season the artichoke hearts with salt and pepper. Heat the butter in the casserole until it is bubbling. Remove from the heat. Baste each heart with butter as you place it upside down (to keep the centre moist) in the casserole. Lay the buttered paper over the artichoke hearts. Reheat the casserole, then place it in the middle of the preheated oven for about 20 minutes, or until the hearts are well heated through. Do not overcook.

The artichoke hearts are now ready to receive any filling your recipe directs.

VARIATIONS

Quartiers de Fonds d'Artichauts au Beurre

[Buttered Artichoke Hearts, Quartered]

This is basically the same as the preceding recipe, except that the artichoke hearts are cut into quarters, and shallots or onions are included with the butter. Use quartered artichokes as a vegetable garnish or combine them with other vegetables such as braised carrots and onions, or sautéed mushrooms. The artichoke hearts go well with veal, chicken, and egg dishes.

6 cooked artichoke hearts, page 396

Cut the artichoke hearts in quarters, and preheat oven to 325° F., Mark 2.

2 oz. butter	Salt and pepper
A 2½-pt. casserole	A round of greaseproof paper,
2 tbl chopped shallots or spring	buttered
onions	2 tbl chopped parsley

Melt the butter in the casserole. Stir in the shallots or spring onions, then fold in the artichokes. Season with salt and pepper, and lay over them the round of buttered paper. Cover the casserole and bake in the middle of a preheated oven for about 20 minutes, or until the vegetables are well steeped in the butter. Do not overcook. Sprinkle with parsley before serving.

(*) May be cooked in advance.

Fonds d'Artichauts Mirepoix

[Buttered Artichoke Hearts with Diced Vegetables]

This is particularly good if the artichoke hearts are to be served as a separate vegetable.

1 oz. each: finely diced carrots, onions, and celery	Ingredients for the preceding buttered artichoke hearts
¾ oz. finely diced, lean, boiled ham	

Cook the carrots, onions, celery, and ham for 8 to 10 minutes in the butter called for in the preceding recipe. When the vegetables are tender but not browned, add the rest of the ingredients listed, and proceed with the recipe.

Fonds d'Artichauts à la Crème

[Creamed Artichoke Hearts]

Serve creamed artichoke hearts with roast veal or chicken, or sautéed brains or sweetbreads. They also go with omelettes.

Ingredients for 6 quartered artichoke
   hearts cooked as in either of the
   two preceding variations
¾ pt. cream

Salt and pepper
1 tsp lemon juice, more if needed
A hot vegetable dish
2 tbl chopped parsley

While the artichoke hearts are cooking as directed in either of the two preceding
recipes, boil the cream in a small saucepan until it has been reduced by half.
Season to taste with salt, pepper, and lemon juice. When the artichokes are done,
fold the hot cream into them. Simmer for a moment on top of the stove to blend
flavours. Turn into a hot vegetable dish and sprinkle with parsley.

Fonds d'Artichauts Mornay

[Artichoke Hearts *Gratinéed* with Cheese Sauce]

Serve *gratinéed* artichoke hearts with roast chicken or veal, sautéed chicken,
veal scallops, or liver. Or you could use them as a hot first course or luncheon
dish; in this case, you might fold into the artichoke hearts before saucing them
¼ pound of sautéed mushrooms, diced boiled ham, or diced cooked chicken.

Ingredients for 6 buttered artichoke
   hearts, quartered, page 397
¾ pt. *sauce mornay* (béchamel with
   cheese), page 54
A lightly buttered baking dish

about 8 ins. in diameter and 2 ins.
   deep
3 tbl grated Swiss cheese
½ oz. butter

While the artichoke hearts are cooking, make the *sauce mornay*. When the
artichokes are done, spread one-third of the sauce in the dish and arrange the
artichoke hearts over it. Pour on the rest of the sauce, sprinkle on the cheese, and
dot with butter.

About 30 minutes before serving, place in upper part of a preheated, 375° F.,
Mark 5 oven to heat through thoroughly and brown the top of the sauce lightly.
Serve as soon as possible.

FONDS D'ARTICHAUTS AU GRATIN

[Stuffed Artichoke Hearts *au Gratin*]

Stuffed artichoke hearts make an attractive hot first course or luncheon dish.

For 6 people

6 large artichoke hearts cooked in   3 oz. grated Swiss cheese
    a *blanc*, page 396   ¾ oz. butter
A buttered baking dish
½ to ¾ pt. of one of the creamed
    fillings on pages 183 to 185, such
    as ham, chicken, mushrooms or
    shellfish

Arrange the cooked artichoke hearts in the baking dish. Place several spoonfuls of the filling in each, heaping it into a slight dome. Sprinkle with cheese and dot with butter. About 20 minutes before serving, bake in upper part of a preheated 375° F., Mark 5 oven until thoroughly warmed through and the cheese has browned lightly.

ASPARAGUS

Asperges

Cooked green asparagus should be tender yet not limp, and a fresh, beautiful green. Fresh white asparagus is prevalent in Europe, and is prepared and cooked in the same way as green asparagus. The French method of cooking asparagus is to peel it, tie it in bundles, plunge it into a very large pan of rapidly boiling, salted water, boil it slowly until it is just tender; and to drain it immediately. Peeled asparagus cooks more quickly than unpeeled asparagus, retains its colour and texture, and can be eaten usually all the way down to the butt. We have tested every asparagus cooking method we have heard of— peeled, unpeeled, boiled butts, steamed tips—and can say categorically that the freshest, greenest, and most appetising asparagus is cooked by the French method.

SERVING SUGGESTIONS

Whole boiled asparagus, hot or cold, is served as a separate vegetable course either at the beginning of the meal, or in place of a salad. With hot asparagus serve a not too dry, chilled white wine such as a Graves, Barsac, Pouilly-Fumé, or Vouvray. No wine should accompany cold asparagus with a vinegar-based sauce, as the vinegar will spoil the taste of the wine.

CHOOSING ASPARAGUS

Select firm, crisp stalks, moist at the cut end, and with tips which are compact and closed. Fat spears are just as tender as thin spears; as long as the asparagus must be peeled, the fat ones are easier to handle and less wasteful. Loose asparagus is preferable to asparagus in bundles, since you may examine each spear and choose ones all of a size. Plan on 6 to 10 fat spears per person, depending on your menu.

PREPARATION FOR COOKING

You will find that a vegetable peeler is not useful for this operation because it does not go deep enough. Asparagus is peeled not just to remove the skin, but to shave off enough of the tough outer flesh (particularly around the lower part of the spear) to make just about the whole cooked spear edible. Peeling is therefore economical.

Hold an asparagus spear with its butt end up. Peel off the outer skin with a sharp, small knife, going as deep as $\frac{1}{16}$ of an inch at the butt in order to expose the tender, moist flesh. Gradually make the cut shallower until you come up to the tender green portion near the tip. Shave off any scales which cling to the spear below the tip. Wash the peeled asparagus spears in a large basin of cold water. Drain.

Line up the tips evenly and tie the asparagus in bundles about $3\frac{1}{2}$ inches in

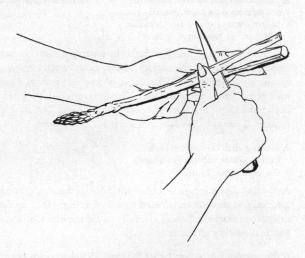

Peel asparagus with a small, sharp knife

diameter, one string near the tip, one near the butt. Leave one spear loose to be used as a cooking test later. Cut a bit off the butts if necessary, to make the spears all the same length.

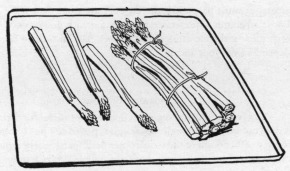

*Make two ties to
secure each bundle*

If not cooked immediately, place bunches upright in ½ inch of cold water. Cover the asparagus with a polythene bag and refrigerate.

---

* *ASPERGES AU NATUREL*

[Boiled Asparagus—Hot or Cold]

A large saucepan or oval casserole   1½ tsp salt per qt. of water
   containing 6 to 7 qts. rapidly
   boiling water (for 4 to 6 bundles
   of prepared asparagus spears)

Pan must be wide enough to hold the asparagus bunches horizontally. Lay the asparagus bundles in the rapidly boiling salted water. Bring water to boil again as quickly as possible. When boil is reached, reduce heat and boil slowly, uncovered, for 12 to 15 minutes. The asparagus is done when a knife pierces the butt-end easily. The spears should bend a little, but should not be limp and droopy. Taste the loose spear as a test for being done.

A serving dish covered with a
   folded white napkin (to absorb
   the asparagus liquid)

As soon as the asparagus is tender, lift it out of the water, bundle by bundle, with 2 forks, one slipped under each round of string. Hold up for a few seconds to drain, then place the bundle carefully on the napkin. Cut and remove the strings. Proceed quickly to the next bundle.

If the asparagus is not to be served immediately, it will keep warm for 20 to 30 minutes covered with a napkin. Place the dish on top of the pan of hot asparagus cooking water. The asparagus will lose a little of its texture as it waits because it will continue to exude moisture, but it will retain its taste and colour.

Sauces to Serve with Hot Asparagus

Allow 3 to 4 tablespoons of sauce per person.

Sauce Hollandaise, page 70. You may beat 3 or 4 tablespoons of puréed cooked asparagus spears into the hollandaise if you wish.

Sauce Mousseline, hollandaise with cream, page 74.

Sauce Maltaise, hollandaise with orange flavouring, delicious with asparagus, and makes a nice change, page 75.

Sauce Crème, béchamel with cream and lemon juice, page 52.

Beurre au Citron, lemon butter sauce, page 88.

COLD ASPARAGUS

To serve cold asparagus, spread the cooked spears in one layer on a double thickness of clean cloth so that the asparagus will cool rapidly. When thoroughly cold, arrange on a serving dish.

Sauces to Serve with Cold Asparagus

Allow 2 to 4 tablespoons of sauce per person.

Sauce Vinaigrette, French dressing, with herbs and mustard, page 85.

Sauce Vinaigrette à la Crème, vinaigrette with cream and herbs, page 86.

Sauce Ravigote, vinaigrette with herbs, shallots, and capers, page 85.

Sauce Moutarde, mustard sauce with herbs, page 86.

Sauce Alsacienne, soft-boiled egg mayonnaise with herbs, page 84.

Mayonnaise, page 77. 2 to 3 tablespoons of green herbs, or 4 to 6 tablespoons of puréed cooked asparagus spears may be stirred into the mayonnaise if you wish.

ASPARAGUS TIPS
Pointes d'Asperges

Asparagus tips are the part of the spear from the tip as far down as the asparagus is green and still tender. Asparagus tips are served as a separate vegetable or as part of a vegetable garnish and go well with chicken breasts, veal scallops, brains, sweetbreads, scrambled eggs, and omelettes. They are also used in a sauce to fill tarts, tartlets, or artichoke hearts, or can be served as a cold vegetable or as part of a vegetable salad.

PREPARATION FOR COOKING

Chose thin asparagus spears $\frac{1}{4}$ to $\frac{3}{8}$ of an inch in diameter. Hold each by its butt end and, moving your fingers up toward the tip, bend the spear until it snaps in two, usually at about the half-way point. (Place the butt ends aside; they may be peeled and cooked, and are good for soups or purées.) Scrape off all the scales below the tip and wash the asparagus. Cut the tips off so that each is $1\frac{1}{2}$ inches long and tie in bundles about 2 inches in diameter. Dice the remaining stalks.

---

* *POINTES D'ASPERGES AU BERRE*

[Buttered Asparagus Tips]

For 4 to 6 people as a vegetable garnish

Blanching

2 lbs. asparagus tips prepared as directed in preceding paragraph	5 qts. rapidly boiling water 2 tbl salt

Drop the diced asparagus stalks in the boiling salted water and boil for 5 minutes. Then add the asparagus bundles and boil slowly for 5 to 8 minutes more, or until just tender. Remove the bundles carefully and drain; drain the diced stalks.

(*) If you are cooking the asparagus in advance or wish to serve it cold, plunge for a minute or two in cold water to stop the cooking and set the colour. Drain.

Braising in butter

Preheat oven to 325° F., Mark 2.

A covered baking dish or fireproof baking and serving dish $\frac{1}{2}$ oz. softened butter	Salt and pepper 2 oz. melted butter A round of greaseproof paper

Smear the baking dish with softened butter. Arrange the diced asparagus stalks in the bottom; season with salt, pepper, and part of the melted butter. Remove the strings and arrange the asparagus tips over the stalks. Season with salt, pepper, and butter, and lay the greaseproof paper on top. Heat for a moment on top of the stove; cover the casserole and place in middle of the oven for 10 to 15 minutes or until asparagus is heated through. Serve immediately.

VARIATION: SAUCES

Sauces for hot and cold asparagus are listed on page 403. If you are serving a hot sauce, you may wish only to blanch the asparagus tips and omit the braising-in-butter step in the preceding recipe.

FROZEN ASPARAGUS

Frozen asparagus will always be limp however you cook it; the following method is as good as any we have found. Allow the asparagus to thaw partially before cooking so that the spears can be separated and will cook more evenly. If you are doing more than two packets at a time, use two wide saucepans in order that the cooking water will boil away by the time the asparagus is done.

For each 10-oz. packet of frozen asparagus, partially thawed:	A cover
¼ pt. water	Pinch of pepper
⅛ tsp salt	A hot vegetable dish
½ oz. butter	Melted butter or one of the
A wide enamelled saucepan or frying pan	sauces listed on page 403

Bring the water, salt, and butter to the boil in the saucepan or frying pan. Add the asparagus, cover, and boil slowly for 5 to 8 minutes or until the asparagus is tender. Remove cover, raise heat, and quickly boil off any remaining liquid. Correct seasoning. Arrange in vegetable dish, pour on sauce or pass it separately, and serve as soon as possible.

TIMBALES D'ASPERGES

[Asparagus Mould]

This asparagus custard is served unmoulded as a first course or luncheon dish, or may be served with roast or sautéed veal or chicken. The custard mixture may be prepared hours in advance of cooking, and the cooked mould may be kept warm for a considerable time or reheated. You can mould the custard in individual dishes if you wish.

NOTE: Chopped, cooked Brussels sprouts, broccoli, cauliflower, spinach, or puréed green peas may be cooked in the same way; substitute about a pint of any of these vegetables for the asparagus.

For 6 people

Flavourless salad oil	¾ oz. stale, white breadcrumbs
A 2½ pt. soufflé dish	

Preheat oven to 325° F., Mark 2. Oil the dish. Roll breadcrumbs in it to cover the entire inner surface. Knock out excess crumbs.

2 oz. finely chopped onions	½ oz. butter

Cook the onions slowly in butter for about 10 minutes in a covered saucepan, not allowing them to colour.

A 5-pt. mixing bowl   2 oz. stale, white breadcrumbs
Big pinch of white pepper   5 eggs
¼ tsp salt   ½ pt. milk brought to the boil with
Pinch of nutmeg   2 oz. butter
2 oz. grated Swiss cheese

Scrape the onions into the mixing bowl. Stir in the seasonings, cheese, and
breadcrumbs. Beat in the eggs. In a thin stream of drops, beat in the hot milk
and butter.

3 lbs. boiled, fresh asparagus, or   Salt and pepper
  1 lb. cooked frozen asparagus,
  or tinned asparagus

Cut the tender portion of the asparagus spears into ½-inch pieces. Fold the
asparagus into the custard mixture. Correct seasoning.

(*) May be prepared ahead to this point.

A baking tin of boiling water
  large enough to hold the dish
  easily

Turn the custard into the prepared dish and place dish in a baking tin of
boiling water. Place in lower part of preheated oven and bake for 35 to 40
minutes, regulating the heat so that the water remains just below simmering point. Custard is done when a knife, plunged through the centre, comes
out clean.

A warm serving dish

Remove dish from the water and allow to settle for 5 minutes. Run a knife
around the edge of the custard and reverse on to a warm serving dish. Surround
with one of the sauces listed, and serve.

(*) If custard is not served immediately, do not unmould it, but leave in its tin
of hot water, reheating the water from time to time, if necessary. Unmould
when you are ready to serve.

Sauces for Asparagus Mould

Prepare 1 to 1½ pints of one of the following:
Sauce Chivry, béchamel with cream and green herbs, page 55.
Sauce Mornay, béchamel with cheese, page 54.
Sauce Mousseline, hollandaise with cream, page 74.

FRENCH BEANS
Haricots Verts

French beans, green beans, string beans, or whatever you wish to call them, are of many varieties: some are flat, others are round, still others are a mottled green rather than a uniform colour. Most of those on the market today are stringless. Whichever you buy, look for beans which are clean, fresh-looking, firm, and which snap crisply and contain immature seeds. If possible, select beans all of the same circumference so that they will cook evenly. A diameter of not more than ¼ inch is most desirable.

Fresh beans take time to prepare for cooking, but have so much more flavour than frozen beans that they are well worth the trouble. The cooking itself is easy; however, beans demand attention if they are to be fresh-tasting, full of flavour, and green. Although their preliminary blanching may be taken care of hours in advance, the final touches should be done only at the last minute. It is fatal to their colour, texture, and taste if they are overcooked, or if they are allowed to stand around over heat for more than a few minutes after they are ready to be eaten.

SERVING SUGGESTIONS
French beans will go with almost any meat dish, or may constitute a separate vegetable course.

AMOUNT TO BUY
One pound of beans will serve 2 or 3 people depending on your menu.

PREPARATION FOR COOKING
Snap the tip of one end of a bean with your fingers and draw it down the length of one side of the bean to remove any possible string. Do the same thing with the other end, pulling it down the other side of the bean.

Beans of not much more than ¼ inch in diameter are cooked whole, and retain their maximum flavour. If they are large in circumference, you may slice them diagonally to make several 2½-inch lengths per bean. Sliced beans never have the flavour of whole beans.

Wash the beans rapidly in very hot water immediately before cooking.

HARICOTS VERTS BLANCHIS

[Blanched French Beans—Preliminary Cooking]

Whatever recipe you choose for your beans, always give them a preliminary blanching in a very large pan of rapidly boiling salted water. Depending on what you plan to do to them later, boil them either until tender or until almost tender, and drain immediately. This essential step in the French art of bean cookery always produces a fine, fresh, green bean of perfect texture and flavour.

For 6 to 8 people

3 lbs. French beans, trimmed and washed	1½ tsp salt per qt. of water
A large pan containing at least 6 to 7 qts. of rapidly boiling water	

A handful at a time, drop the beans into the rapidly boiling salted water. Bring the water back to the boil as quickly as possible, and boil the beans slowly, uncovered, for 10 to 15 minutes; test the beans frequently after 8 minutes by tasting one. A well cooked bean should be tender, but still retain the slightest suggestion of crunchiness. Drain the beans as soon as they are done.

For Immediate Serving

Turn the beans into a large, heavy-bottomed saucepan and toss them gently over a moderately high heat by flipping the pan, not by stirring them. This will evaporate their moisture in 2 to 3 minutes. Then proceed with one of the following recipes.

For Later Serving or to Serve Cold

Run cold water over the beans for 3 to 4 minutes. This will stop the cooking immediately and the beans will retain colour, taste, and texture. Drain, spread them out on a clean cloth, and pat dry. The beans may then be left aside in a colander, or put in a covered bowl in the refrigerator where they will keep perfectly for 24 hours.

To Reheat: Depending on your recipe, either drop the beans into a large pan of rapidly boiling, salted water, bring quickly again to the boil, then drain immediately. Or toss the beans in a tablespoonful or two of hot butter or oil, season them, cover the pan, and let them warm thoroughly for 3 to 4 minutes over a moderate heat. Then proceed with your recipe.

TWO RECIPES FOR BUTTERED FRENCH BEANS

Buttered French beans go with almost anything, and particularly roast or grilled lamb, beef, chicken, veal, and liver. They may also be served as a separate course.

Haricots Verts à l'Anglaise

[Buttered French Beans I]

For 6 to 8 people

3 lbs. hot, blanched French beans (preceding recipe)	Salt and pepper A hot serving dish
A wide, heavy-bottomed, enamelled saucepan or frying pan	2 to 4 oz. butter, cut into pieces or formed into shells

Toss the hot beans in the saucepan or frying pan over a moderately high heat to evaporate their moisture. Toss briefly again with salt and pepper to taste. Turn them into the serving dish, distribute the butter over them, and serve at once.

Haricots Verts à la Maître d'Hôtel

[Buttered French Beans II—with Lemon Juice and Parsley]

For 6 to 8 people

3 lbs. hot, blanched French beans (preceding master recipe)	3 to 4 oz. softened butter cut into 4 pieces
A wide, heavy-bottomed, enamelled saucepan or frying pan	2 to 3 tsp lemon juice A hot vegetable dish
Salt and pepper	3 tbl chopped parsley

Toss the hot beans in the saucepan or frying pan over a moderately high heat to evaporate their moisture. Toss briefly again with salt, pepper and a piece of butter. Add the rest of the butter gradually while tossing the beans; alternate with drops of lemon juice. Taste for seasoning. Turn into the vegetable dish, sprinkle with parsley, and serve immediately.

TWO RECIPES FOR FRENCH BEANS IN CREAM

Serve creamed French beans with plain roast lamb, veal, or chicken, grilled or sautéed chicken, lamb chops, sautéed liver, or veal chops or scallops.

Haricots Verts à la Crème

[Creamed French Beans I]

For 6 to 8 people

3 lbs. French beans, trimmed and washed	Salt and pepper to taste 1½ oz. softened butter
A wide, heavy-bottomed, enamelled saucepan or frying pan	¾ pt. cream A lid for the pan

Blanch the beans in 6 to 7 quarts of rapidly boiling salted water as described on page 407, but drain them 3 to 4 minutes before they are tender. Toss the beans in the pan over a moderately high heat to evaporate their moisture. Then toss with the salt, pepper, and butter. Pour in the cream, cover the pan, and boil slowly for 5 minutes or so, until the beans are tender and the cream has reduced to half. Correct seasoning.

A hot vegetable dish
3 tbl fresh chopped savory,
  tarragon, or parsley

Turn into hot vegetable dish, sprinkle with herbs, and serve at once.

Haricots Verts, Sauce Crème

[Creamed French Beans II]

This is less rich than the pure cream treatment in the preceding recipe.

For 6 to 8 people

3 lbs. French beans, trimmed and washed	**A wide, heavy-bottomed enamelled saucepan or frying pan**

Blanch the beans in 6 to 7 quarts of boiling salted water as described on page 407, but drain them 3 to 4 minutes before they are tender. Toss the beans in the pan over a moderately high heat to evaporate their moisture.

Salt and pepper to taste	**A lid for the pan**
1½ oz. softened butter	
3 tbl chopped shallots or spring onions	

Then toss them with the seasonings, butter, and chopped shallots or spring onions. Cover the pan and let them cook slowly for 3 to 4 minutes.

1¼ pts. boiling *sauce crème* (béchamel with cream), page 52	**A hot vegetable dish**
Salt and pepper	**3 tbl fresh chopped savory, tarragon, or parsley**

Delicately fold the hot sauce into the beans. Cover the pan and simmer slowly again for 3 to 4 minutes, or until the beans are tender. Correct seasoning. Turn into a hot vegetable dish, sprinkle with herbs, and serve at once.

A GOOD ADDITION

½ to 1 lb. sliced mushrooms sautéed
  in butter

Fold the sautéed mushrooms into the beans with the sauce.

HARICOTS VERTS GRATINÉS, À LA MORNAY

[French Beans *Gratinéed* with Cheese Sauce]

This is a good method for ahead-of-time preparation. Serve with the same meats suggested in the preceding recipes for French beans in cream.

For 6 to 8 people

3 lbs. French beans, trimmed and washed

Blanch the beans as described on page 407 until they are just tender. Drain, refresh in cold water, and dry on a cloth.

1¼ pts. *sauce mornay* (béchamel with cheese), page 54
A lightly buttered baking dish

Salt and pepper to taste
1½ oz. grated Swiss cheese
½ oz. butter cut into pea-sized dots

Spread a third of the sauce in the baking dish. Season the beans and arrange them over the sauce. Pour on the rest of the sauce. Sprinkle with cheese, dot with butter, and leave aside uncovered.

Half an hour before serving time, bake in upper part of a preheated 375° F., Mark 5 oven until beans are well heated through and the sauce has browned lightly on top.

HARICOTS VERTS À LA PROVENÇALE

[French Beans with Tomatoes, Garlic, and Herbs]

These full-flavoured beans go wonderfully with roast lamb or beef, steaks, chops, or grilled chicken. Tossed with diced, sautéed ham, they can serve as a main-course luncheon or supper dish. Frozen beans react nicely to this treatment.

For 6 to 8 servings

½ lb. thinly sliced onions
¼ pt. olive oil
An enamelled saucepan or frying pan large enough to hold the beans

Cook the onions slowly in the olive oil until they are tender and translucent but not browned, about 10 minutes.

4 to 6 large, firm, ripe, red tomatoes   ¼ pt. liquid: juice from the tomatoes
    peeled, seeded, juiced, and   plus water or water only
    chopped, page 465   Salt and pepper to taste
2 to 4 cloves mashed garlic
A medium herb bouquet with
    cloves: 4 parsley sprigs, ½ bay
    leaf, ¼ tsp thyme, and 2 cloves
    tied in cheesecloth

Add all the ingredients above, and simmer for 30 minutes. Then remove the
herb bouquet.

3 lbs. French beans   1 oz. chopped parsley, or a mixture
Or: 3 packets partially defrosted   of green herbs such as basil,
    cut French beans added directly   savory, and tarragon plus
    to the cooked tomato mixture   parsley
Salt and pepper

While the tomatoes are cooking, blanch the beans in 6 to 7 quarts of boiling
salted water as described, page 407; however, drain them for 3 to 4 minutes before
they are tender. Toss them in the pan with the onions and tomatoes. Cover and
simmer slowly for 8 to 10 minutes, tossing occasionally, until they are tender.
Most of the liquid should have evaporated by this time; if not, uncover, raise
heat, and boil off the liquid rapidly, tossing the beans. Correct seasoning, toss in
the herbs, and serve.

FROZEN FRENCH BEANS

Frozen beans cook more evenly if they are partially thawed and not stuck
all together in a solid block. When you are doing more than two packets, use
two saucepans; if too many beans are cooked in one pan, the liquid will not
evaporate by the time the beans are tender.

For each 10-oz. packet of beans: ¼ tsp salt
¼ pt. chicken stock, chicken broth,   ½ oz. butter
    tinned mushroom broth, or water   A heavy-bottomed, enamelled
1 tbl chopped shallots or spring   saucepan or frying pan with
    onions   cover

Bring the liquid, shallots or spring onions, salt, and butter to the boil in the
saucepan. Add the partially thawed beans. Cover and boil slowly for 5 to 6
minutes, tossing occasionally, until the beans are just tender. Remove cover and
rapidly boil off any remaining liquid. Correct seasoning.

The beans may now be used in any of the preceding French bean recipes.
If they are to be simmered in cream or in a sauce, use half the amount of liquid

for their preliminary cooking, and cook only until partially tender. They will finish cooking in the sauce.

If you wish to do the preliminary cooking in advance, spread the cooked beans out in one layer in a big cold saucepan or dish so that they will cool rapidly.

If the beans are to be served cold, use olive oil rather than butter in the preceding recipe, and spread the beans out afterward in one layer to cool rapidly.

BRUSSELS SPROUTS
Choux de Bruxelles

Cooked Brussels sprouts should be bright green, fresh-tasting, and have the slightest suggestion of crunch at the core. Overcooked sprouts become yellowish, mushy, and develop the flavour of stale cabbage.

Choose firm, healthy, fresh, rounded heads all of the same size with bright green leaves. Soft-headed sprouts are overmature, tasteless, or unhealthy, and will cook into a pulp.

AMOUNT TO BUY
About 1 pound will serve 4 people as a vegetable garnish.

SERVING SUGGESTIONS
Buttered Brussels sprouts go well with roast duck, goose, turkey, beef, pork, liver, ham, and sausages. Creamed Brussels sprouts may be served with any of these, and also with roast chicken or veal.

PREPARATION FOR COOKING
Trim the base of each Brussels sprout with a small knife; pierce a cross in it for quick cooking. Remove any wilted or yellowish leaves. Discard any sprouts which are soft-headed, yellowish, or worm-eaten. Wash the trimmed vegetables rapidly in a large basin of water, and drain.

CHOUX DE BRUXELLES BLANCHIS

[Blanched Brussels Sprouts—Preliminary Cooking]

Brussels sprouts, whether they are to be served with melted butter and seasonings or are to be simmered or braised, always receive a blanching in a large pan of boiling salted water. This preliminary may be accomplished hours before the final cooking is to take place.

1 to 2 lbs. Brussels sprouts, trimmed   1½ tsp salt per qt. of water
   and washed
A large pan containing 6 to 7 qts.
   of rapidly boiling water

Drop the Brussels sprouts into the rapidly boiling salted water. Bring to the boil
again as rapidly as possible.

Partially cooked

A perforated spoon   **A colander**

If the vegetables are to be partially cooked and finished off later as directed in
most of the following recipes, boil them slowly, uncovered, for 6 to 8 minutes,
or until almost tender. Immediately remove vegetables with a perforated spoon
and drain in a colander.

Fully cooked

If they are to be fully cooked, and served at once with melted butter *à l'anglaise*,
boil them slowly, uncovered, for a total of 10 to 12 minutes. They are done
when a knife pierces the stem of a sprout easily; cut one in half and taste it, to be
sure. Drain immediately, as described above.

AHEAD–OF–TIME BLANCHING

If the Brussels sprouts are not to be used at once, as soon as they have been
drained spread them out in one layer, not touching one another, on a double
thickness of clean cloth. This lets the air circulate around them and cools them
quickly, so that they retain their colour and texture. (You may plunge them
into cold water instead, if you wish, but we think the one-layer cooling gives
a better texture.) When the Brussels sprouts are thoroughly cold, they may be
refrigerated and will keep perfectly for 24 hours. Complete the cooking as
directed in any of the following recipes.

---

* *CHOUX DE BRUXELLES ÉTUVÉS AU BEURRE*

[Brussels Sprouts Braised in Butter]

Serve braised Brussels sprouts with roast turkey, pork, duck, or goose,
steaks, chops, hamburgers, or sautéed liver. You may dress up braised Brussels
sprouts with cream, cheese, or chestnuts as suggested in the variations at the
end of the recipe.

For 6 people

¾ oz. softened butter
A 4-pt., fireproof, covered casserole
  or baking dish large enough to
  hold the Brussels sprouts in 1 or
  2 layers

Preheat oven to 350° F., Mark 4, and smear the butter inside the casserole or baking dish.

1½ lbs. blanched Brussels sprouts   Salt and pepper
  (partially cooked), page 413   1 to 2 oz. melted butter

Arrange the blanched Brussels sprouts heads up in the casserole or baking dish. Sprinkle lightly with salt and pepper, and with the melted butter.

A round of lightly buttered
  greaseproof paper

Lay the paper over the Brussels sprouts. Cover and heat on top of the stove until vegetables begin to sizzle, then place in the middle of a preheated oven. Bake for about 20 minutes, or until the sprouts are tender and well impregnated with butter. Serve as soon as possible.

VARIATIONS

Choux de Bruxelles Étuvés à la Crème

[Creamed Brussels Sprouts]

Serve these with veal, chicken, or turkey.

For 6 people

1½ lbs. Brussels sprouts   ½ to 1 oz. butter cut into pea-sized
¼ pt. boiling cream   dots
Salt and pepper

Braise the Brussels sprouts as in the preceding recipe, but use only 1 ounce of butter. After the casserole has been in the oven for 10 minutes, pour on the boiling cream and continue baking for 10 more minutes or until the vegetables are tender. They will have absorbed most of the cream. Correct seasoning, dot with butter, and serve as soon as possible.

Choux de Bruxelles aux Marrons

[Brussels Sprouts Braised with Chestnuts]

This recipe is particularly good with roast turkey, duck, or goose.

For 6 people

1½ lbs. Brussels sprouts braised in   ½ lb. braised chestnuts, page 479
   butter

Follow the preceding master recipe for braising the Brussels sprouts but add the
braised chestnuts to the casserole to cook with them.

Choux de Bruxelles à la Mornay, Gratinés

[Brussels Sprouts *Gratinéed* with Cheese Sauce]

Serve these with roast chicken or veal, or as a luncheon or supper dish.

For 6 people

1½ lbs. Brussels sprouts braised in   1 oz. grated Swiss cheese
   butter   ½ oz. butter cut into pea-sized dots
¾ pt. hot *sauce mornay* (béchamel
   with cheese), page 54
A lightly buttered baking dish
   about 9 ins. diameter and 2 ins.
   deep

Follow the preceding master recipe for braising the Brussels sprouts; you may
use only 1 ounce of butter if you wish. Prepare the sauce, and spread one-third
of it in the baking dish when the sprouts are done. Arrange the Brussels sprouts
over the sauce, spoon the rest of the sauce over them, and sprinkle with cheese
and dots of butter. Place under a moderately hot grill for 2 to 3 minutes to
brown lightly, and serve at once.

Choux de Bruxelles à la Milanaise

[Brussels Sprouts Browned with Cheese]

These cheese-coated Brussels sprouts are good with steaks and chops.

For 6 people

1½ lbs. Brussels sprouts braised in   1 oz. melted butter
   butter
2 oz. grated Swiss cheese mixed
   with 2 oz. grated Parmesan
   cheese

Follow the preceding master recipe for braising the Brussels sprouts, but when
they have been in the oven 10 minutes, turn them into a bowl. Reset oven to
425° F., Mark 7. Sprinkle 2 to 3 tablespoons of cheese in the casserole or baking
dish to coat the bottom and sides. Return the Brussels sprouts, spreading the
rest of the cheese over each layer. Pour on the melted butter. Place uncovered in
upper part of oven for 10 to 15 minutes, to brown the cheese nicely.

CHOUX DE BRUXELLES À LA CRÈME

[Brussels Sprouts Chopped and Simmered in Cream]

Serve this dish with steaks or chops, roast beef or lamb, pork, duck, or goose.

For 6 people

1½ lbs. Brussels sprouts, trimmed and washed

Follow the recipe for blanched Brussels sprouts, page 413, but boil them for 5 minutes only. Drain. If you are not proceeding at once with the rest of this recipe, let them cool in one layer. Chop them roughly.

1½ oz. butter   **¼ tsp salt**
A 10-in. enamelled frying pan   **Big pinch of pepper**

Heat the butter to bubbling in the frying pan. Add the chopped Brussels sprouts and season with salt and pepper. Shake them over a moderately high heat for several minutes to evaporate their moisture but not to brown them.

¼ pt. cream   **Salt and pepper**

Pour in the cream. Bring to simmering point. Cover the frying pan and cook at a slow simmer for 8 to 10 minutes or until the vegetables have almost entirely absorbed the cream and are tender. Correct seasoning.

½ to 1 oz. softened butter   **2 tbl chopped parsley**
A hot vegetable dish

Reheat to simmering point just before serving. Away from heat, fold in the butter. Turn into a hot vegetable dish, sprinkle with parsley, and serve.

TIMBALE DE CHOUX DE BRUXELLES

[Brussels Sprouts Mould]

This is a purée of Brussels sprouts mixed with eggs, milk, cheese, and breadcrumbs, cooked in a mould, then unmoulded and served with a cream sauce. It makes an unusual luncheon dish, or a fine accompaniment to roast veal or chicken. Use the same method and ingredients as for the asparagus mould, page 405, substituting blanched, chopped Brussels sprouts for asparagus.

o

FROZEN BRUSSELS SPROUTS

This recipe is for fully-cooked Brussels sprouts. If you wish to substitute partially cooked frozen sprouts for fresh ones in any of the preceding recipes, use half the amount of water indicated here, and cook the sprouts until they are almost but not quite tender, 3 to 4 minutes. (When you are cooking more than two packets, use two saucepans; if too many vegetables are cooked in one pan, the liquid will not evaporate by the time they are tender.)

For each 10-oz. packet frozen	¼ tsp salt
Brussels sprouts:	½ oz. butter
¼ pt. water	Salt and pepper

Allow the frozen Brussels sprouts to thaw just enough so that you can separate them. Boil the water with the salt and butter in a saucepan. Add the vegetables, cover, and boil slowly for 6 to 8 minutes or until the sprouts are tender. Uncover the saucepan and rapidly boil away any remaining liquid. Correct seasoning.

(*) If not to be used immediately, spread them out in one layer in a large, cold saucepan or dish.

BROCCOLI

Choux Broccoli—Choux Asperges

Broccoli, for some reason, is rarely seen in France though it abounds next door in Italy. We shall therefore not give it full-dress treatment, though we think it a delicious and useful vegetable.

PREPARATION FOR COOKING

Fresh broccoli will cook much more rapidly and stay greener if you divide it into flowerets about 3 inches long and then peel the thin, green skin off the stalks. Peel the cut-off butt ends deeply enough to expose the whitish, tender flesh, and cut into diagonal lengths.

BLANCHING

Blanch the prepared broccoli in a large pan of boiling, salted water; first put in the pieces of stem and boil for 5 minutes, then add the flowerets. Because it is a fragile vegetable, broccoli is easier to handle if you place it in a vegetable rack which you may put into the boiling water, and lift out with the broccoli when it is done. If the broccoli is to be partially cooked then braised, or simmered in a sauce, boil the flowerets for about 5 minutes or until almost tender. Fully-cooked broccoli that is to be served with melted butter or a sauce such as hollandaise requires 8 to 10 minutes of cooking, or until a knife pierces the stems easily. Drain immediately.

Cook frozen broccoli in the same manner as frozen Brussels sprouts, page 418.

SAUCES FOR PLAIN, BOILED BROCCOLI
Sauces for hot or cold broccoli are the same as those suggested for asparagus, page 403.

OTHER COOKING METHODS
Broccoli may be substituted for Brussels sprouts in any of the following recipes in the Brussels sprouts section:

Braised in Butter, page 414.
Creamed, page 415.
Gratinéed with Cheese Sauce, page 416.
Browned with Swiss and Parmesan Cheese, page 416.
Chopped and Simmered in Cream, page 417.
Baked in a mould with eggs, milk, and cheese, then unmoulded. See the master recipe for asparagus moulds on page 405.

SERVING SUGGESTIONS
Hot or cold broccoli with a sauce such as hollandaise or vinaigrette may be served, like asparagus, as a separate vegetable course. Creamed broccoli goes with roast or grilled chicken, roast veal, or sautéed veal scallops. Broccoli with melted butter or browned with cheese goes with sautéed liver, steaks, chops, and grilled chicken.

CAULIFLOWER
Chou-fleur

Choose cauliflowers with hard, clean, white heads containing firm, compact, flower clusters. The leaves surrounding the head should be fresh, healthy, and green.

AMOUNT TO BUY
A trimmed cauliflower head about 8 inches across will serve 4 to 6 people as a vegetable garnish.

SERVING SUGGESTIONS
Cauliflower *gratinéed* or served with a sauce may constitute a separate vegetable course. All types of cauliflower dishes go with roast turkey, chicken, lamb, beef, pork, and with steaks or chops.

PREPARATION FOR COOKING
Cauliflower cooks more evenly if you divide it into flowerets; we therefore always advise that you do so. Pull the outside leaves off the cauliflower and cut

the stem off close under the head. The smaller leaves and the peeled stem may be used for soup. Cut the flowerets off the central stalk, and peel the thin skin off their stems with a knife. Cut a slit in any stems larger than ¼ inch in diameter, so that they will cook quickly. Peel the central stalk deeply enough to expose its tender flesh, and cut it in diagonal pieces. Wash the cauliflower rapidly in a large basin of cold water. Drain.

---

* CHOU-FLEUR BLANCHI

[Blanched Cauliflower—Preliminary Cooking]

1 or 2 heads of cauliflower, cut into flowerets	A vegetable rack placed in the pan is useful
A large pan containing 6 to 7 qts. of boiling water	Optional: add ½ pt. of milk to pan for each 5 pts. of boiling water,
1½ tsp salt per qt. of water	to keep cauliflower white

Drop the washed cauliflower into the rapidly boiling water; use a vegetable rack if you have one. Bring back to the boil as quickly as possible. Boil slowly, uncovered, for 9 to 12 minutes. The cauliflower is done when a knife pierces the stems easily. Taste a piece to be sure. It should be tender but retain the merest suggestion of crunchiness at the core.

As soon as it is done, carefully remove the cauliflower with a spoon and drain in a colander, or remove the rack with cauliflower in it.

Refreshing Blanched Cauliflower

When cooked cauliflower is not to be served immediately or is to be served cold, it should be refreshed in cold water as soon as it is blanched. This stops the cooking so that the cauliflower retains its fresh taste and texture. Plunge the colander or vegetable rack holding the hot cauliflower into a large basin of cold water for 2 to 3 minutes. Drain.

Reheating

If the refreshed cauliflower is to be served hot with melted butter or sauce, steam it in a covered colander over boiling water for 4 to 5 minutes until hot through. Then season with salt and pepper, and it is ready for saucing and serving.

How to Mould Cooked Cauliflower into its Original Shape

It is not necessary, of course, to mould the cooked flowerets back into the shape of a whole head, but it makes an attractive presentation.

Select a bowl slightly smaller than the width and depth of the cauliflower head before it was cut into flowerets. Place the bowl over simmering water to warm it. When the cauliflower heads have been blanched and drained, one by one place the longest flowerets in the bottom of the bowl, heads down and stems converging at the centre of the bowl. Continue with the rest of the flowerets, arranging their heads around the sides of the bowl until it is filled. Place the cooked pieces of stem on top. Then turn a warm, round, serving dish upside down over the bowl. Reverse the bowl on to the dish and remove the bowl; the cauliflower will stand moulded in approximately its original shape.

SAUCES FOR HOT CAULIFLOWER

Here is a list of sauces to serve with hot cauliflower; about ½ to ¾ pint is sufficient for an 8-inch head. If the cauliflower has been moulded, spoon ⅓ of the sauce over the stems before reversing the bowl.

Beurre au Citron, lemon butter sauce, page 88.

Beurre Noir, brown butter sauce, page 88. You may brown 1½ ounces of fresh, white breadcrumbs with the butter. Sieved hard-boiled egg yolks and chopped parsley mixed into the butter and breadcrumbs turn the cauliflower into *chou-fleur à la polonaise*.

Sauce Crème, béchamel with cream, page 52.

Sauce Bâtarde, mock hollandaise, page 57.

Sauce Hollandaise, page 70.

Sauce Mousseline, hollandaise with cream, page 74.

Sauce à la Crème

[Fresh Cream Sauce]

For an 8-inch cauliflower

¾ pt. cream	1 oz. softened butter
A small saucepan	A wire whisk
Salt and white pepper	Parsley sprigs
Lemon juice	

Simmer the cream in the saucepan until reduced by half. Season to taste with salt, pepper, and drops of lemon juice. Leave aside until ready to use, then reheat. Remove from heat and beat in the butter a dessertspoon at a time and pour the sauce over the hot cauliflower. Decorate with parsley and serve.

CHOU-FLEUR À LA MORNAY, GRATINÉ

[Cauliflower *au gratin* with Cheese]

Cauliflower *au gratin* may be prepared for the oven well in advance of serving, and goes with all kinds of roasts, chops, and steaks. You may, if you wish, mould the cauliflower in a bowl before saucing it, page 420, so that it will preserve its round shape.

For 4 to 6 people

An 8-in. cauliflower cut into flowerets

Following the directions on page 420, blanch the cauliflower in 6 to 7 quarts of boiling, salted water for 9 to 12 minutes, refresh in cold water, and drain.

1 pt. *sauce mornay* (béchamel with cheese), page 54	Salt and pepper
A lightly buttered baking dish about 8 ins. in diameter and 2 ins. deep	2 tbl fine, dry, white breadcrumbs mixed with 2 tbl grated Swiss cheese
	1 oz. melted butter

Spread ⅓ of the sauce in the baking dish. Arrange the cauliflower over it and season with salt and pepper. Pour on the rest of the sauce and sprinkle the top with breadcrumbs and cheese. Pour on the melted butter.

(*) Leave aside, covered loosely with greaseproof paper, until ready to bake.

About 30 minutes before serving time, place in upper part of a preheated 375° F., Mark 5 oven to warm through thoroughly and to brown lightly. Serve as soon as possible.

CHOU-FLEUR AUX TOMATES FRAÎCHES

[Cauliflower *Gratinéed* with Cheese and Tomatoes]

This dish is particularly good with steaks, chops, and hamburgers.

For 4 to 6 people

An 8-in. head of cauliflower, cut into flowerets

Following the directions on page 420, blanch the cauliflower in boiling salted water for 9 to 12 minutes, refresh in cold water, and drain.

1 lb. firm, ripe, red tomatoes, peeled, seeded, and juiced, page 465

Cut the tomato pulp into strips ½ inch wide.

A shallow 10-in. buttered baking
dish
¼ tsp salt
Big pinch of pepper

4 oz. melted butter
1½ oz. fine, dry, white breadcrumbs
mixed with 1 oz. each grated
Swiss and Parmesan cheese

Arrange the cauliflower in the centre of the dish. Place the tomatoes around the edge of the dish. Season the vegetables with salt, pepper, and half the melted butter. Spread the cheese and breadcrumbs over the vegetables, and pour on the rest of the melted butter.

(*) Leave aside until ready to bake.

About 30 minutes before serving time, place in the upper part of a preheated 375° F., Mark 5 oven to warm through thoroughly and brown the cheese nicely. Serve as soon as possible.

CHOU-FLEUR EN VERDURE

[Purée of Cauliflower and Watercress with Cream]

Serve this delectable purée with roast veal, chicken, or turkey, grilled or sautéed chicken, chicken breasts, or veal scallops.

For 4 to 6 people

An 8-in. head of cauliflower
A bunch of fresh watercress
A pan containing 6 to 7 qts. of
rapidly boiling water

1½ tsp salt per qt. of water

Separate the cauliflower head into flowerets; peel off and discard the tough skin of the central stalk and chop the stalk. Cut off the bunch of watercress just above the point where the stems join the leaves (stems may be used for soup). Wash and drain the vegetables. Drop the cauliflower into the boiling, salted water and boil slowly for 6 minutes. Then add the watercress leaves and boil for 4 to 5 minutes more, or until cauliflower is just tender. Drain.

A moulinette
A 5-pt. mixing bowl
A rubber spatula
¾ pt. thick béchamel sauce, page 50
(2 oz. butter, 1½ oz. flour, ¾ pt.
boiling milk, salt, and pepper)

¼ pt. cream
2 oz. grated Swiss cheese
Salt and pepper

Purée the cauliflower and watercress through the moulinette and place purée in mixing bowl. Fold in the béchamel sauce. By spoonfuls, fold in the cream but do not thin out the purée too much; it should just hold its shape when a little is lifted on the spatula. Fold in the cheese, and season to taste with salt and pepper.

A lightly buttered baking dish 8 to 9   1 oz. melted butter
   ins. in diameter and 2 ins. deep
2 tbl fine, dry, white breadcrumbs
   mixed with 2 tbl grated Swiss
   cheese

Heap the purée in the baking dish. Sprinkle on the cheese and breadcrumbs, then
the melted butter.
(*) Leave aside until ready to bake.

About 30 minutes before serving, place in upper part of a preheated 375° F.,
Mark 5 oven to heat through thoroughly and brown the cheese and breadcrumbs. Serve as soon as possible.

TIMBALE DE CHOU-FLEUR

[Cauliflower Mould]

    This is a purée of cooked cauliflower mixed with eggs, breadcrumbs,
cheese, and milk. It is baked in a soufflé dish, unmoulded, and surrounded with
a sauce. Use the recipe for asparagus mould on page 405, substituting cauliflower
for the asparagus. Other sauces to serve besides those suggested in the recipe are:
    Coulis de Tomates, fresh tomato sauce with herbs, page 69.
    Sauce au Cari, béchamel with curry and onions, page 55.

GREEN PEAS

Petits Pois

    The tenderest, freshest, and sweetest peas have bright green pods that are
rather velvety to the touch. The pods should be fairly well filled. A perfect raw
pea will taste tender and sweet. As peas mature they become larger, harder, and
less sweet; but even a quite tough pea will make good eating if it is cooked in the
right way. Choose, if possible, pods of equal size with peas all at the same stage
of development so that they will cook evenly.
    As we have not the space in this book to cover every aspect of pea cookery,
we have felt it would be most useful to present one fundamental recipe each
for the small tender pea, the large tender pea, the tough pea, peas *à la française*,
and frozen and tinned peas.

AMOUNT TO BUY

    One pound of small, tender peas will usually furnish about ½ pound shelled
peas.

One pound of large peas will usually furnish about ¾ pound peas.

½ pound of shelled peas will serve from 1 to 3 people depending on your menu. We have based our recipes on 2 people per ½ pound.

Beautifully cooked peas make a delicious separate vegetable course, and they may accompany almost anything from eggs to roasts and stews.

THREE RECIPES FOR BUTTERED PEAS

Each of the three recipes here is designed for peas of a particular quality, from sweet and tender to rather tough. Pick the recipe which corresponds to the type of peas you are to cook.

Petits Pois Frais à l'Anglaise

[Buttered Peas I—for very tender, sweet, fresh, green peas]

Anyone who has eaten a plateful of small, tender, fresh, green peas in Italy or France in the springtime is not likely to forget the experience. These best-of-all peas are always cooked by blanching in a very large pan of boiling salted water. They are served at once *à l'anglaise*, meaning they are merely seasoned, turned into a vegetable dish, and topped with pieces of butter. This simple and fundamental treatment preserves, unadulterated, their colour, texture, and taste.

For 6 people

3 lbs. of very tender, sweet, young, fresh green peas (1½ lbs., shelled) A large pan containing 6 to 7 qts. of rapidly boiling water	1½ tsp salt per qt. of water

Drop the shelled peas into the rapidly boiling salted water. Bring the water to the boil again as quickly as possible. Boil slowly, uncovered, for 4 to 8 minutes, testing the peas frequently by tasting them. They will have more taste and be greener if they are drained at the point where they are tender but still retain a suggestion of texture. But this is a matter of personal taste, and they may be boiled for a few more minutes if you wish.

A colander A heavy-bottomed saucepan Salt and pepper ½ to 1 tbl granulated sugar (depending on sweetness of peas)	A hot vegetable dish 3 oz. butter, formed into little shells or cut into pieces

Drain the peas immediately. Place in the saucepan with the seasonings and roll them gently over moderate heat for a moment or two to evaporate all their

o*

humidity. Correct seasoning. Turn the peas into a hot vegetable dish, arrange the butter over them, and serve at once.

Petits Pois Étuvés au Beurre

[Buttered Peas II—for large but tender fresh green peas]

This is for the larger pea, the kind you usually find at your greengrocer's.

For 6 people

2 lbs. large but tender fresh green peas (1½ lbs. shelled)	1½ tsp salt per qt. of water
A pan containing 6 to 7 qts. of rapidly boiling water	A colander

Drop the peas in the boiling salted water and boil uncovered for 5 to 10 minutes or until the peas are almost but not quite tender. They will finish cooking later. Drain.

(*) If the peas are not to be served immediately, refresh them in cold water for 3 to 4 minutes to stop the cooking and to retain their colour and texture. Drain.

A heavy-bottomed, 3- to 4-pt. enamelled saucepan	Big pinch of pepper
1 to 2 tbl granulated sugar (depending on the sweetness of the peas)	3 oz. softened butter
	Optional: 1 to 2 tbl chopped fresh mint leaves
¼ tsp salt	Salt and pepper
	A hot vegetable dish

Roll the peas in the saucepan over a moderate heat for a moment or two to evaporate their moisture. Then roll them with the sugar, salt, pepper, butter, and optional mint. When the peas are well coated with butter, cover and cook over a very low heat for about 10 minutes, tossing occasionally, until they are tender. Correct seasoning, turn into a hot vegetable dish, and serve as soon as possible.

Petit Pois aux Oignons

[Buttered Peas with Onions]

12 to 18 small, peeled onions
   boiled in salted water until
   almost tender; Or: 3 to 5 tbl
   chopped shallots or spring onions

Prepare the peas as in the preceding recipe, but add boiled onions or diced shallots or spring onions to the saucepan with the peas and seasonings for the final, 10-minute cooking period.

Pois Frais en Braisage

[Buttered Peas III—for large, rather tough, fresh green peas]

This is for large, mature, end-of-season peas. They remain green after cooking, become tender, and have a fine flavour though they will look a bit wrinkled.

For 6 people

A heavy-bottomed, 2-qt.
   enamelled saucepan
2 lbs. of large, mature, fresh peas
   (1½ lbs., shelled)
1 large head of lettuce, shredded

½ tsp salt
2 tbl granulated sugar
4 tbl chopped spring onions
3 oz. softened butter

Place in the saucepan the peas and all the rest of the ingredients. Squeeze the peas with your hands rather roughly to bruise them slightly, and to mix them thoroughly with the butter, lettuce, onions, and seasonings. Add enough cold water to cover the peas by ¼ inch.

A hot vegetable dish

Cover the saucepan and place over a moderately high heat. Boil rapidly for 20 to 30 minutes; test the peas frequently by tasting one after 20 minutes, to see if they are tender. Add 2 to 3 tablespoons more water if it evaporates before the peas are done. When they are tender, uncover and quickly boil away any remaining liquid. Taste for seasoning. Turn into a hot vegetable dish, and serve.

(*) If not served immediately, leave aside uncovered. Shortly before serving, add 2 to 3 tablespoons of water, cover, and boil slowly until the peas are well warmed through and the water has evaporated.

PETITS POIS FRAIS À LA FRANÇAISE

[Peas Braised with Lettuce and Onions—for medium sized, tender, fresh peas]

This dish is considered the glory of pea cookery; it should really be served as a separate course and eaten with a spoon. If you wish to have a wine with the peas, serve a chilled white that is not too dry, such as Traminer or Graves, or a chilled *rosé*.

For 4 to 6 people

1½ firm, fresh heads of lettuce   **White string**

Remove wilted leaves, trim the stems, and wash the lettuce heads carefully so that they will not break apart. Cut into quarters. Wind several loops of string about each quarter to keep it in shape as much as possible during the cooking.

3 oz. butter
¼ pt. water
1 tbl granulated sugar
½ tsp salt
¼ tsp pepper
A heavy-bottomed, 2½-qt.
   enamelled saucepan
3 lbs. medium sized, tender, fresh
   green peas (1½ lbs. shelled)

8 parsley stems tied together with
   white string
12 spring onion bulbs about 1 in.
   in diameter; Or: small white
   onions boiled for 5 minutes in
   salted water

Bring the butter, water, and seasonings to the boil in the saucepan. Then add the peas and toss to cover them with the liquid. Bury the parsley in their midst. Arrange the lettuce quarters over them and baste with the liquid. Cut a cross in the root ends of the onions (for even cooking) and disperse them among the lettuce quarters.

A domed lid or a soup plate

So that the cooking steam will condense and fall back on to the peas, invert a lid over the saucepan and fill it with cold water or ice cubes; or use a soup plate. Bring the peas to the boil and boil slowly for 20 to 30 minutes or until tender. Several times during this period, remove the cover and toss the peas and vegetables to ensure even cooking. As the water warms up and evaporates in the cover or soup plate, refill with ice cubes or cold water.

Salt and pepper

When the peas are tender their cooking liquid should have almost entirely evaporated. Correct seasoning.

1 oz. softened butter   A hot vegetable dish

Discard the parsley and the lettuce strings. Just before serving, toss the peas and onions with the butter. Turn them into the vegetable dish, place the lettuce around the edge of the dish, and serve at once.

FROZEN PEAS

This method of cooking frozen peas gives them the character they often lack. Use two saucepans when you are cooking more than two 10-ounce packets; if too many peas are cooked in one pan, the cooking liquid will not evaporate by the time the peas are done.

For each 10-oz. packet of frozen   ¼ tsp salt
   peas: Pinch of pepper
½ oz. butter   ¼ pt. chicken stock or tinned
1 tbl chopped shallots or spring   chicken or mushroom broth, or
   onions   water

Allow the peas to thaw enough so that they can be separated. Bring the butter, shallots or spring onions, seasonings, and liquid to the boil in a saucepan. Add the peas, cover, and boil slowly for 5 to 6 minutes or until the peas are tender. Uncover and rapidly boil away any remaining liquid. Correct seasoning.

TINNED PEAS

Here is a way to improve the flavour of tinned peas.

For each tin of peas (1¼ lbs.):

Turn the peas into a sieve and run cold water over them. Drain.

1½ tbl chopped shallots or spring   Salt and pepper to taste
   onions   3 tbl stock or mushroom broth
1 oz. butter

Cook the shallots or spring onions in the butter for a moment. Add the peas and seasonings and toss them in the butter. Then add the stock or broth, cover the peas, and boil slowly for a few moments until the peas are warmed through. Uncover, raise heat, and rapidly boil away any remaining liquid.

SPINACH

Épinards

Spinach is an excellent vegetable when it is cooked properly. Except for the tenderest and freshest garden variety which may be simmered slowly in seasonings, butter, and its own juices, spinach is first blanched in a large pan of boiling salted water; then all the water is pressed out of it, and it is simmered in butter and meat stock or cream. In addition to its role as a vegetable, it can serve as a bed for poached eggs, fish, or breasts of chicken. It is also used in various stuffings, and makes an excellent soufflé, tart, or mould.

SERVING SUGGESTIONS

Spinach goes with almost everything, eggs, fish, chicken, sweetbreads, ham, roasts, steaks, chops, sautés. Or it may constitute a separate vegetable course. The *gratins* may also serve as entrées, luncheon, or supper dishes. If it is a separate course, a dry white wine such as a Riesling goes with spinach braised in butter or in stock. Serve a less dry white wine, such as a Graves, with spinach braised in cream.

AMOUNT TO BUY

One pound of fresh spinach yields about 8 ounces of cooked spinach, and we shall consider that enough for 2 people.

PREPARATION FOR COOKING

If the spinach is young and tender, the stems are usually removed at the base of the leaf. For more mature spinach, fold the leaf vertically, its underside up, in the fingers of one hand; grasp the stem in the other hand and rip it off toward the tip of the leaf, thus removing with the stem the tough tendrils which are attached to the underside of the leaf. Discard any wilted or yellow leaves. Whether or not it is claimed that the spinach is washed, plunge it into a large basin of cold water and pump it up and down for several minutes with your hands. Lift it out into a colander, leaving any soil in the bottom of the basin. Wash the spinach several times more, if necessary, until there is no soil to be seen in the bottom of the basin. Drain, and the spinach is ready for cooking.

ÉPINARDS BLANCHIS

[Blanched, Chopped Spinach—Preliminary Cooking]

For 1½ pounds of blanched, chopped spinach

3 lbs. fresh spinach

Prepare and wash the spinach as described in the preceding paragraph.

A large pan containing at least 6 to 7 qts. of rapidly boiling water	**1½ tsp salt per qt. of water**

A handful at a time, drop the spinach into the boiling salted water. Bring back to the boil as rapidly as possible and boil slowly, uncovered, for about 5 minutes, or until the spinach is almost tender. Test it by tasting a piece.

A large colander

At once, place the colander, curved side down, in the pan. Protecting your hands with a cloth, hold the colander firmly clamped to the sides of the pan as you tilt the pan and pour out the water. Still with the colander in place, run cold water into the pan for several minutes to refresh the spinach. This will preserve its colour and texture. Remove the colander and lift the spinach out of the water into the colander, thus leaving any possible grains of soil in the bottom of the pan.

A small amount at a time, squeeze the spinach in your hands to extract as much water as possible—last drops of water from each squeeze may be saved for soup·

**A stainless steel chopping knife
or a moulinette**

Chop the spinach with a big knife on a chopping board, or, if you want a fine purée, put it through a moulinette. The spinach is now ready for further cooking and flavouring.

(*) May be done several hours or a day in advance. Cover and refrigerate.

WARNING

Spinach quickly picks up an astringent and metallic taste if its final cooking is in iron or aluminium utensils. For the following recipes, use only enamel, ovenglass, earthenware, or stainless steel saucepans or baking dishes, and serve the spinach in enamel or porcelain, not silver.

---

* *PURÉE D'ÉPINARDS SIMPLE*

[Cooked Chopped Spinach—Purée of Spinach]

This is the last step in preparing spinach for use in soufflés, *quiches*, custards, *crêpes*, stuffings, or for final cooking in any of the following recipes. The directions on page 437 also bring frozen spinach to this point.

For 1½ pounds, or for 6 people

1 oz. butter	Salt and pepper
A 2-qt. heavy-bottomed, enamelled saucepan	Pinch of nutmeg
1½ lbs. blanched spinach, chopped or puréed (directions in preceding recipe)	

When the butter is bubbling in the saucepan over a moderately high heat, stir in the spinach. Continue stirring for 2 to 3 minutes until all the moisture from the spinach has boiled off—the spinach will begin to adhere to the base of the pan. Season to taste, and the spinach is ready to use.

RECIPES FOR COOKED CHOPPED SPINACH

Épinards Étuvés au Beurre

[Spinach Braised in Butter—Buttered Spinach]

Serve this deliciously buttery spinach with steaks, chops, roasts, ham, or sautéed liver. Use it also in any recipe calling for a bed of buttered spinach.

For 6 people

1½ lbs. cooked chopped spinach (the preceding recipe), in a heavy-bottomed enamelled saucepan	2 oz. butter Salt and pepper to taste

After you have followed the directions in the preceding recipe (stirring the spinach over a moderately high heat with butter and seasonings until its moisture has evaporated), stir in the additional 2 ounces of butter listed here. Cover the saucepan and cook very slowly for 10 to 15 minutes, stirring frequently, until the spinach has absorbed the butter and is very tender. Correct seasoning.

(★) If not served immediately, leave aside uncovered. Reheat when needed.

1 oz. softened butter	A hot porcelain serving dish

Remove from the heat, fold in the additional butter, and turn the spinach into the hot serving dish.

Épinards au Jambon

[Spinach with Ham]

4 oz. finely diced ham, sautéed briefly in butter The preceding spinach braised in butter	12 *croûtons* (triangles of white bread sautéed in clarified butter) page 181

Stir the ham into the spinach 2 to 3 minutes before the end of the cooking. After arranging the spinach on its serving dish, place the *croûtons* around the edge of the dish.

* *Épinards au Jus*

[Spinach Braised in Stock]

* *Épinards à la Crème*

[Spinach Braised in Cream—Creamed Spinach]

This is an alternative to the preceding recipe for buttered spinach. Whether to use cream or stock for the braising depends on your judgment of which goes best with the rest of your menu. Creamed spinach would contrast well with sautéed ham, liver, brains, sweetbreads, chicken, or veal; spinach braised in stock would be preferable if you served any of these meats in a cream sauce. Spinach braised in stock or cream may also be *gratinéed* with cheese or be used as a filling for *crêpes* as suggested in the variations following the recipe.

For 6 people

1½ lbs. cooked chopped spinach, page 431, in a heavy-bottomed enamelled saucepan	½ oz. flour, sifted to remove any lumps

After you have stirred the spinach over a moderately high heat with butter and seasonings to evaporate its humidity, as directed in the recipe for cooked chopped spinach, lower the heat to moderate. Sprinkle on the flour and stir for 2 minutes more to cook the flour.

½ pt. brown stock, beef bouillon, or cream	Salt and pepper

Remove from the heat and stir in two-thirds of the stock, bouillon, or cream by spoonfuls. Bring to simmering point, cover, and cook very slowly for about 15 minutes. Stir frequently to prevent spinach from sticking to the base of the pan, and add more liquid by spoonfuls if the spinach becomes too dry. Correct seasoning.

(*) If not to be served immediately, leave aside uncovered, and film the top with a tablespoon of stock or cream. Reheat when needed.

½ to 1 oz. softened butter A hot porcelain serving dish	Optional: 1 or 2 sieved or sliced hard-boiled eggs

Remove spinach from the heat, fold in the butter, and turn into the serving dish. Decorate with optional egg.

VARIATIONS

Épinards Gratinés au Fromage

[Spinach *Gratinéed* with Cheese]

Serve this *gratinéed* spinach with steaks or chops, roast veal or chicken, or sautéed liver. It also goes well with grilled fish.

For 6 people

3 oz. grated Swiss cheese
1½ lbs. spinach braised in stock (the preceding recipe)
A lightly buttered baking dish 8 ins. in diameter and 1½ ins. deep

2 tbl fine, dry, white breadcrumbs
¾ oz. melted butter

Stir two-thirds of the cheese into the spinach and turn it into the baking dish, heaping it into a slight dome. Mix the rest of the cheese with the breadcrumbs and spread over the spinach. Sprinkle on the melted butter.

About 30 minutes before serving, place in upper part of a preheated, 375° F., Mark 5 oven to heat through thoroughly and brown the top lightly.

Canapés aux Épinards

[Spinach and Cheese Canapés]

Serve these canapés as a hot first course or luncheon dish, or make them smaller than directed here and serve as cocktail appetizers.

For 6 people

12 slices of white bread, 3½ by 2½ ins. and ⅜ in. thick
1½ oz. butter and 1 tbl oil, more if needed
3 oz. grated Swiss cheese

1½ lbs. spinach braised in stock (the preceding master recipe)
2 tbl fine, dry, white breadcrumbs
1 to 1½ oz. melted butter

Cut off the crusts and sauté the bread in hot butter and oil in a frying pan until lightly browned on each side. Stir two-thirds of the cheese into the braised spinach and heap 2 or 3 tablespoons on each piece of sautéed bread. Sprinkle with the remaining grated cheese, the breadcrumbs, and the melted butter.

Just before serving, place under a moderately hot grill to heat through and brown lightly.

Épinards à la Mornay, Gratinés

[Spinach Gratinéed with Cheese Sauce]

Serve this gratinéed spinach with roasts, steaks, or chops, or as a hot first course or luncheon dish.

For 6 people

¾ pt. sauce mornay (béchamel with cheese), page 54
A lightly buttered baking dish 8 ins. in diameter and 1½ ins. deep
1½ lbs. spinach braised in stock or in cream, page 432

Optional: ½ lb. sliced mushrooms sautéed in butter, page 473
3 tbl grated Swiss cheese
¾ oz. melted butter

Spread a third of the sauce in the bottom of the baking dish. If you are using the optional mushrooms, fold them into the spinach. Heap the spinach in the dish over the sauce, and spoon the rest of the sauce over it. Sprinkle with the grated cheese and melted butter.

About 30 minutes before serving, place in upper part of a preheated, 375° F., Mark 5 oven to heat through thoroughly and brown lightly on top.

Épinards en Surprise

[Spinach Hidden under a Giant *Crêpe*]

This is an amusing presentation; the spinach is heaped in a serving dish and a large French pancake is spread over it, hiding it completely. Serve it as a main course luncheon or supper dish and, if you wish, mix ¼ pound of sautéed, diced ham or mushrooms into the spinach.

For 6 people

2 oz. grated Swiss cheese
1½ lbs. spinach braised in stock or in
    cream, page 432
A hot, lightly buttered porcelain
    serving dish about 8 ins. in
    diameter

A French pancake, large enough to
    cover the spinach completely,
    page 173

Just before serving, stir the cheese into the hot, braised spinach and heap it in the serving dish. Then cover with the pancake.

PETITES CRÊPES D'ÉPINARDS

[Spinach Pancakes]

Spinach pancakes may be folded in quarters to garnish a roast, steaks, or chops. Filled as suggested in the *Crêpe* section, pages 173 to 178, they may be served as a hot first course, or luncheon or supper dish.

For about 12 crêpes 6 inches in diameter

Ingredients for ⅓ the recipe for
    crêpes, page 173

½ lb. blanched spinach, page 430

If you are making the *crêpe* batter in an electric liquidizer, you may purée the blanched spinach at the same time. Otherwise, purée the spinach in a moulinette and combine with the *crêpe* batter. Let batter rest for 2 hours before using. Cook spinach pancakes like ordinary pancakes, according to directions following those for the batter.

TIMBALE D'ÉPINARDS

[Spinach Mould]

This is a purée of spinach mixed with eggs, milk, cheese, and breadcrumbs, baked in a soufflé dish, unmoulded, and surrounded with a sauce. Use the recipe for asparagus mould on page 405, substituting spinach purée, page 431, for asparagus. Other sauces besides those with the asparagus mould recipe are:

Sauce Tomate or Coulis de Tomates, tomato sauce, pages 68 to 69.
Sauce Aurore, velouté or béchamel sauce with tomato flavouring, page 54.

ÉPINARDS À LA BASQUAISE

[Gratin of Spinach and Sliced Potatoes with Anchovies]

Serve this with steaks, roast beef, roast lamb, or with grilled fish such as mackerel, herring, or sardines.

For 6 people

2 oz. grated Swiss cheese
1½ lbs. spinach braised in stock,
  page 432

Stir the cheese into the braised spinach.

1 lb. boiling potatoes

Peel the potatoes and cut them into slices ⅛ inch thick. Boil them in salted water for 5 to 6 minutes, or until tender. Drain.

A lightly buttered baking dish
  2 ins. deep and 9 ins. in diameter
2 tbl mashed anchovies (or 1 tbl
  anchovy paste) blended with
  2 oz. softened butter and a pinch
  of pepper

Spread half of the potatoes in the bottom of the baking dish. Cover with half of the anchovy mixture. Spread half of the spinach over the potatoes. Repeat with the remaining potatoes, anchovy mixture, and spinach.

1½ oz. grated Swiss cheese mixed
  with 3 tbl dry, white breadcrumbs
1 oz. melted butter

Spread the cheese and breadcrumbs over the top of the spinach and pour on the melted butter.

About 30 minutes before serving, place in upper part of a preheated, 375° F., Mark 5 oven to heat through thoroughly and brown the top nicely.

FROZEN SPINACH

Although it never has quite the lovely taste of fresh spinach, frozen spinach is certainly one of the great inventions. When you have given it the following preliminary treatment, you may use it in any of the preceding recipes. If you are cooking more than two packets at once, use two saucepans; when too much is in one saucepan, the liquid will not evaporate quickly enough and the spinach will overcook.

A heavy, stainless steel chopping knife

Whether the frozen spinach is whole, chopped, or puréed, it will cook most successfully if you unwrap and defrost it just enough so that you can slice it by pressing down on the block with a heavy knife. If the spinach is already chopped or puréed, cut the slices roughly into half-inch pieces. If the spinach is whole, chop the slices into small bits.

For each 10-oz. packet of
spinach:
¾ oz. butter
A heavy-bottomed, enamelled
saucepan or frying pan

¼ tsp salt
Pinch of pepper
Small pinch of nutmeg

Melt the butter in the saucepan or frying pan, then stir in the chopped spinach and seasonings. Cover and cook very slowly for a minute or two, until the spinach has thawed and released its juices. Uncover, raise heat, and stir for 2 to 3 minutes until all moisture has evaporated.

This may now be substituted for the cooked chopped spinach on page 431, and used in any of the recipes calling for it or blanched spinach.

CARROTS, ONIONS, AND TURNIPS
Carottes, Oignons, et Navets

Carrots, onions, and turnips à la française are all cooked in substantially the same manner, so we have grouped them together.

CARROTS
Carottes

Carrots develop their maximum flavour if they are cooked in a covered saucepan with a small amount of liquid, butter, and seasonings until the liquid has evaporated and the carrots are beginning to sauté in the butter.

Buttered or glazed carrots go well with all kinds of roasts, and combine with other vegetables to make many of the classic garnitures which may surround a meat dish. One of the more elaborate of these is *à la bouquetière* which includes glazed carrots and turnips, diced French beans, peas, cauliflower bouquets, and potato balls sautéed in butter. Creamed carrots are particularly good with veal and chicken.

AMOUNT TO BUY

One pound of carrots minus their tops will serve 3 or 4 people.

PREPARATION FOR COOKING

Trim off the stems and scrape the carrots with a vegetable peeler. Depending on their size and the effect you wish, slice them horizontally, or halve or quarter them lengthwise, then cut the lengths into 2-inch pieces. These pieces may, if you wish, be trimmed into the form of long garlic cloves; in French this is termed *tourner en gousses* or *en olives*.

(For tough old carrots only: If you happen to have end-of-season carrots, quarter them lengthwise, then cut out and remove the woody central section, and use only the reddish outer portion which French recipes call *rouge de carotte.* Then before proceeding with any of the following recipes, blanch the carrots by boiling for 5 to 8 minutes in salted water.)

---

* CAROTTES ÉTUVÉES AU BEURRE

[Carrots Braised in Butter]

This is the basic recipe for cooked carrots; they may be served with a sprinkling of parsley, simmered in cream, mixed with other vegetables, or puréed.

For 6 people

A heavy-bottomed, 3-pt. enamelled saucepan	¾ pt. water
	¾ oz. butter
1½ lbs. carrots, scraped, and sliced or quartered	½ tsp salt
	Pinch of pepper
1 tbl granulated sugar (to develop their flavour)	

In the saucepan, bring the carrots to the boil with the sugar, water, butter, and salt. Cover and boil slowly for 30 to 40 minutes or until the carrots are tender and the liquid has evaporated. Correct seasoning.

(*) If they are not to be served at once, leave aside uncovered and reheat when needed.

VARIATIONS

Carottes aux Fines Herbes

[Braised Carrots with Herbs]

1½ lbs. carrots braised in butter   A hot vegetable dish
1 oz. softened butter
2 tbl chopped parsley, chervil and
    chives, or parsley only

Just before serving and away from heat, toss the carrots with the butter and herbs. Turn into a hot vegetable dish.

Carottes à la Crème

[Creamed Carrots]

½ to ¾ pt. cream   Salt and pepper
1½ lbs. carrots braised in butter

Bring the cream to the boil in a saucepan and pour in enough to cover the carrots. Boil slowly, uncovered, for 15 to 20 minutes or until the cream has been almost entirely absorbed by the carrots. Correct seasoning.

1 oz. softened butter   A hot vegetable dish
2 tbl chopped parsley, chervil and
    chives, or parsley only

Just before serving and away from heat, gently toss the butter and herbs into the carrots. Turn into a hot vegetable dish.

Carottes à la Forestière

[Braised Carrots with Artichoke Hearts and Mushrooms]

½ lb. quartered fresh mushrooms   ¾ oz. butter
1 dsp oil   Salt and pepper

In a frying pan, sauté the mushrooms in hot oil and butter for 4 to 5 minutes until very lightly browned. Season with salt and pepper.

2 tbl chopped shallots or spring   1½ lbs. carrots braised in butter
    onions
3 or 4 cooked fresh artichoke
    hearts cut into quarters, page 396

Stir the shallots or spring onions and the cooked fresh artichoke hearts into the mushrooms and toss for 2 to 3 minutes over a moderately high heat. Fold or toss the artichoke hearts and mushrooms into the carrots.

$\frac{1}{8}$ **pt. good brown stock or beef**   **Salt and pepper**
    bouillon

Pour the stock or bouillon into the vegetables. Cover and boil slowly for 4 to 5 minutes until the stock has almost completely evaporated. Correct seasoning.

A hot vegetable dish
2 tbl chopped parsley, chervil, and
    chives, or parsley only

Turn into a hot vegetable dish and sprinkle with the herbs.

CAROTTES GLACÉES

[Glazed Carrots]

Glazed carrots receive the same type of cooking process as braised carrots; the only difference is that they are cooked in stock instead of water, and more butter and sugar are used so that the liquid reduces to a syrupy glaze in the bottom of the pan. Just before serving, the carrots are rolled about in the liquid so that each piece is shiny with glaze.

For 6 people

$1\frac{1}{2}$ **lbs. carrots, scraped, quartered**   **2 tbl granulated sugar**
    and cut into 2-in. lengths   **Pinch of pepper**
A 2-qt., heavy-bottomed,   **3 oz. butter**
    enamelled saucepan with cover   **Salt and pepper**
$\frac{3}{4}$ **pt. good brown stock or beef**
    bouillon

Boil the carrots slowly in the covered saucepan with the stock or bouillon, sugar, pepper, and butter for 30 to 40 minutes until the carrots are tender and the liquid has reduced to a syrupy glaze. Correct seasoning.

A hot vegetable dish   **2 tbl very finely chopped parsley**

Reheat just before serving and roll the carrots gently in the pan to coat them with glaze. Turn into a hot vegetable dish or arrange them around your roast, and sprinkle with parsley.

CAROTTES VICHY

[Carrots Vichy]

The recipe for carrots Vichy is exactly the same as that for the preceding glazed carrots except that in place of stock you would use bottled Vichy water.

The assumption is that non-calcareous bottled water produces a more delicate carrot.

CAROTTES À LA CONCIERGE

[Casserole of Creamed Carrots with Onions and Garlic]

This hearty dish of carrots goes nicely with red meats, pork, sausages, or plain roast chicken. It can also constitute a meatless main-course dish.

For 6 people

1½ lbs. carrots, scraped and cut into ¼-in. slices	3 tbl olive oil
½ lb. sliced onions	A 2-qt., heavy-bottomed, enamelled saucepan with cover

Cook the carrots, onions, and olive oil slowly in the covered saucepan, tossing occasionally, for about 30 minutes. The vegetables should be tender but not browned.

A large clove mashed garlic

Add the garlic for the last 5 minutes of cooking.

½ oz. flour

Toss the vegetables with the flour and cook 3 minutes more.

¼ pt. boiling brown stock or beef bouillon	Salt and pepper to taste
¼ pt. boiling milk	1 tsp granulated sugar
	Pinch of nutmeg

Away from heat, fold in the boiling stock or bouillon, then the milk, and finally the seasonings. Simmer uncovered for about 20 minutes or until the liquid has reduced to about a third of its volume and has thickened into a light cream. Correct seasoning.

2 egg yolks blended with ⅛ pt. cream	A hot vegetable dish
A rubber spatula	2 tbl chopped parsley

Away from heat and just before serving, use the spatula to fold in the egg yolks and cream. Shake and swirl saucepan over a low heat until the egg yolks have thickened but be careful not to bring them near to simmering point or they may coagulate. Turn into a hot vegetable dish and sprinkle with parsley.

ONIONS
Oignons

It is hard to imagine a civilization without onions; in one form or another their flavour blends into almost everything in the meal except the dessert. We shall concentrate here on the small, whole onions which are so often called for as a vegetable garnish. When they are used in stews and fricassees it is generally advisable that they be cooked separately so that you are sure they will be tender and retain their shape.

AMOUNT TO BUY
One pound of small onions will serve 3 or 4 people if they constitute a principal vegetable dish. If they are used as a garnish or in a mixture with other vegetables, count on 3 or 4 small onions per person.

PREPARATION FOR COOKING
The quickest, neatest, and least tearful way to peel small onions is to drop them into a saucepan of rapidly boiling water and leave them for 5 to 10 seconds, just long enough for their skins to loosen. Drain. Run cold water over them. Trim off the top and bottom portions, removing only a little piece so as not to disturb the onion layers. Then slip off the outside skin and the first onion layer with your fingers. Pierce a cross in the root ends so that the onions will cook evenly without bursting.

If the onions are old and very strongly flavoured, or if for digestive reasons you wish to make them milder, drop them into boiling, salted water and boil slowly for 5 minutes before proceeding with a recipe.

To remove onion flavour from your hands, wash them in cold water, rub them with salt, rinse again in cold water, then wash in soap and warm water.

---

* *OIGNONS GLACÉS À BLANC*
[White-braised Onions—Glazed Onions]

White-braised onions may be served as they are, or they may be simmered for a moment in a good sauce. Use them also as a garnish for fricassees or *blanquettes*.

For 18 to 24 peeled onions about
1 in. in diameter:

A heavy-bottomed, enamelled
saucepan or frying pan which
will just hold the onions in one
layer

¼ pt. white stock, chicken broth,
dry white wine, or water

1 oz. butter

Salt and pepper to taste

A small herb bouquet: 2 parsley
sprigs, ⅛ tsp thyme, and ½ bay
leaf tied in cheesecloth

Place the onions in the saucepan or frying pan with the liquid, butter, seasonings, and herb bouquet. Cover and simmer very slowly, rolling the onions in the saucepan from time to time, for 40 to 50 minutes. The onions should not colour, and should be perfectly tender yet retain their shape. If all the liquid evaporates during the cooking, add more by spoonfuls as necessary. Remove herb bouquet.

(*) May be cooked several hours in advance, reheated, and served as in the following suggestions.

TO SERVE

Petits Oignons Persillés

[Parslied Onions]

These go particularly well with chicken, veal, or fish in cream sauce.

1 oz. softened butter
A warm vegetable dish

2 tbl chopped parsley

Just before serving the onions, correct seasoning. Away from heat, roll them with the softened butter. Turn into a warm vegetable dish and sprinkle with parsley.

Petits Oignons à la Crème

[Creamed Onions]

Serve creamed onions with roast veal, chicken, or turkey, chops, steaks, or hamburgers, sautéed veal, chicken, or liver.

(For 2 pounds of white-braised onions, serving 6 people.)

¾ pt. *sauce crème* (béchamel with
cream), page 52

Salt and pepper

½ to 1 oz. softened butter
2 tbl chopped parsley
A hot vegetable dish

Fold the cream sauce into the braised onions and simmer for 5 minutes. Correct seasoning. Away from heat, fold in the butter. Turn into a hot vegetable dish and sprinkle with parsley.

* *OIGNONS GLACÉS À BRUN*

[Brown-braised Onions]

Brown-braised onions are used whenever you wish to have a brown effect, such as in brown fricassees like *coq au vin* and *boeuf bourguignon*, or in a mixture with other vegetables.

For 18 to 24 peeled onions about 1 in. diameter:	1 tbl oil
¾ oz. butter	A 9- to 10-in. enamelled frying pan

When the butter and oil are bubbling in the frying pan, add the onions and sauté over a moderate heat for about 10 minutes, rolling the onions about so that they will brown as evenly as possible. Be careful not to break their skins. You cannot expect to brown them uniformly.

Then either braise them as follows:

¼ pt. of brown stock, beef bouillon, dry white wine, red wine, or water	A medium herb bouquet: 4 parsley sprigs, ½ bay leaf, and ¼ tsp thyme tied in cheesecloth
Salt and pepper to taste	

Pour in the liquid, season to taste, and add the herb bouquet. Cover and simmer slowly for 40 to 50 minutes until the onions are perfectly tender but retain their shape, and the liquid has evaporated. Remove herb bouquet. Serve them as they are, or follow one of the suggestions at the end of the recipe.

Or bake them as follows:

Transfer the onions and their sautéing fat to a shallow baking dish or casserole just large enough to hold them in one layer. Place uncovered in upper part of a preheated 350° F., Mark 4 oven for 40 to 50 minutes, turning them over once or twice. They should be very tender, retain their shape, and be a nice golden brown. Remove herb bouquet. Serve them as they are or according to one of the following suggestions.

(*) The onions may be cooked hours in advance, and reheated before serving.

TO SERVE

Petits Oignons Persillés

[Parslied Onions]

½ to 1 oz. softened butter	1 tbl chopped parsley
A hot vegetable dish	

Roll the hot onions gently in the butter. Turn into a hot vegetable dish or place them around the roast, and sprinkle with parsley.

Petits Oignons en Garniture

[Vegetable Mixtures]

Braised onions go nicely mixed with other vegetables such as glazed carrots, sautéed mushrooms, artichoke hearts, and sautéed potatoes.

TINNED ONIONS

All the brands of tinned 'small boiled onions' we have tried have tasted, to us, rather unpleasantly sweetish and over-acidulated; they also need more cooking to make them tender. However, they are so useful in an emergency that we offer the following treatment, which improves them considerably.

For each No. 2 tin of small boiled onions (1¼ lbs.):
1 oz. butter
⅛ pt. stock, beef bouillon, or mushroom broth

Salt and pepper to taste
A small herb bouquet: 2 parsley sprigs, ⅛ bay leaf, and ¼ tsp thyme tied in cheesecloth

Drain the onions. Drop them into boiling water, bring back to the boil and boil 1 minute. Drain. This removes some of the tinned taste. Then simmer them slowly in a covered saucepan for 10 to 15 minutes with the butter, stock, seasonings, and herb bouquet until they are very tender and the liquid has evaporated.

SOUBISE

[Braised Rice and Onions]

This is a savoury mixture of sliced onions, rice, and butter cooked slowly together until they melt into a purée. The natural moisture of the onions is sufficient to cook the rice; no other liquid is needed. *Soubise* is particularly good with veal or chicken, or boiled leg of lamb *à l'anglaise*. It may be turned into a *sauce soubise* by puréeing it with a *sauce béchamel* or *velouté* and enriching it with cream.

For 6 people

Preheat oven to 300° F., Mark 1.

4 oz. rice
3 qts. rapidly boiling water
1 tbl salt

Drop the rice into the boiling salted water and boil for 5 minutes exactly. Drain immediately.

2 oz. butter $\frac{1}{2}$ tsp salt
A 2$\frac{1}{2}$-qt. fireproof casserole $\frac{1}{8}$ tsp pepper
2 lbs. thinly sliced onions   Salt and pepper

When the butter is foaming in the casserole, stir in the onions. As soon as they are well coated with butter, stir in the rice and seasonings. Cover and cook very slowly in the 300° F., Mark 1 oven for about 1 hour, stirring occasionally. The rice and onions should become very tender and will usually turn a light golden yellow. Correct seasoning.

(*) May be cooked several hours in advance and reheated later.

$\frac{1}{8}$ pt. cream   A hot vegetable dish
1 oz. grated Swiss cheese   1 tbl chopped parsley
1 oz. softened butter

Just before serving, stir in the cream and cheese, and then the butter. Taste again for seasoning. Turn into a hot vegetable dish and sprinkle with parsley.

TURNIPS

Navets

The turnip is a wonderful vegetable when given the treatment required to bring out its delicious qualities. It wants and needs to absorb butter or meat fats, which is why turnips are particularly succulent when finished off in a stew or a braised dish, or in the juices of roasting meat. In France swedes are practically unheard of as food for humans, but they may be used interchangeably with white turnips.

SERVING SUGGESTIONS

The full flavour of turnips goes well with pork, sausages, ham, goose, and duck.

AMOUNT TO BUY

One pound of turnips without tops will serve 3 or 4 people.

PREPARATION FOR COOKING

Small, tender, early-crop turnips, usually sold in bunches with their tops attached, are trimmed, peeled, and placed to cook with no preliminary blanching. The older and stronger winter turnips and swedes, always sold without tops, are peeled fairly deeply with a knife, and are cut into slices or quarters. Quarters may be trimmed into neat ovals the shape of large garlic cloves, called in French *tourner en gousses* or *en olives*. Any turnips which are woody or fibrous should be discarded.

PRELIMINARY BLANCHING

After peeling and cutting winter turnips or swedes, place them in a saucepan with salted water to cover them by 2 inches, bring to the boil and boil for 3 to 5 minutes or until they are partially tender. Drain them. This removes some of their very strong taste. The following recipes are based on winter turnips; omit the blanching step if the turnips are young and tender.

---

* NAVETS À L'ÉTUVÉE

[Turnips Braised in Butter]

Braised turnips may be served by themselves or combined with other vegetables. Their final cooking may be done around a roast or in a braised dish or a fricassee.

For 6 people

2 lbs. turnips, peeled and quartered
A heavy-bottomed, 2½-qt. enamelled saucepan
1 oz. butter

½ to ¾ pt. stock, beef or chicken bouillon, or water
Salt and pepper to taste

Blanch the turnips for 3 to 5 minutes in boiling salted water to cover. Drain, and place them in the saucepan with the butter and enough liquid barely to cover them. Season lightly. Cover and boil slowly for 20 to 30 minutes or until they are tender but retain their shape. If the liquid has not evaporated, uncover and boil it off. Correct seasoning.

(*) May be cooked several hours in advance of serving.

TO SERVE

Navets Persillés

[Parslied Turnips]

1 oz. softened butter
Optional: Drops of lemon juice to taste

2 tbl chopped parsley
A hot vegetable dish

Just before serving, toss the hot turnips gently with the butter, optional lemon juice, and parsley. Turn into the vegetable dish.

VARIATION

Purée de Navets Parmentier

[Turnip and Potato Purée]

Serve this purée with roast turkey, duck, goose, ham, pork, or pork chops or sausages.

For 6 people

2 lbs. turnips braised in butter (the preceding master recipe)	Salt and pepper
1 lb. warm mashed potatoes	A hot vegetable dish
2 oz. softened butter	2 tbl chopped parsley

Purée the turnips and beat them into the mashed potatoes. Beat the purée in a saucepan over a moderate heat to evaporate moisture and to heat thoroughly. Remove from heat and just before serving, beat in the butter. Season to taste with salt and pepper. Turn into a hot vegetable dish and sprinkle with parsley.

---

* NAVETS GLACÉS À BRUN

[Glazed Turnips]

Glazed turnips are used to garnish a roast, or may be served as a separate vegetable. It is essentially the same procedure as that for braised turnips, except that they are browned before being simmered, and are cooked with sugar and more butter to reduce the liquid to a glaze.

For 6 people

2 lbs. turnips, peeled and quartered

Blanch the turnips for 3 to 5 minutes in boiling salted water to cover. Drain, and dry them in a cloth.

A 10- to 12-in. enamelled frying pan	½ to ¾ pt. stock or beef bouillon
1 oz. butter and 1 tbl oil, or 3 tbl rendered fresh pork or goose fat	1 oz. butter
	3 tbl granulated sugar

Sauté the turnips in hot butter and oil, or in fat, for 3 to 4 minutes to brown them lightly. Pour in enough stock or bouillon barely to cover them. Add the butter and sugar. Cover and boil slowly for 20 to 30 minutes or until the turnips are tender but retain their shape. Correct seasoning.

(*) When cooked in advance, leave aside uncovered. Before serving, add a tablespoon of water, if necessary, and reheat in covered saucepan.

A hot vegetable dish   **2 tbl very finely chopped parsley**

If the liquid has not reduced to a syrupy glaze, uncover and boil it down rapidly. Gently toss the turnips to coat them with the glaze. Turn them into a hot vegetable dish or heap them around your roast, and sprinkle with parsley.

NAVETS À LA CHAMPENOISE

[Turnip Casserole]

People who disdain the turnip almost invariably revise their opinion after tasting this dish. It goes admirably with roast pork, beef, duck, goose, turkey, ham, or grilled sausages. (Yellow turnips or swedes do well here.)

For 6 to 8 people

2½ lbs. turnips, peeled and cut into quarters

Blanch the turnips for 3 to 5 minutes in boiling salted water to cover. Drain.

A ¼-lb. chunk of streaky bacon

Remove the rind and cut the bacon into ¼-inch dice. Simmer for 10 minutes in a quart of water. Drain.

A 5-pt. fireproof casserole about   ½ oz. butter
2 ins. deep   3 oz. finely diced onions

Sauté the bacon in the butter for several minutes until very lightly browned. Stir in the onions, cover, and cook slowly for 5 minutes without browning the onions.

½ oz. flour

Blend in the flour and cook slowly for 2 minutes.

¼ pt. stock or beef bouillon   Salt and pepper
¼ tsp sugar   ¼ tsp sage

Away from heat, blend in the stock or bouillon, seasonings to taste, and the sage. Simmer for a moment, then fold in the turnips. Cover and simmer slowly for 20 to 30 minutes or until the turnips are tender. If the sauce is too liquid, uncover and boil slowly for several minutes until it has reduced and thickened. Correct seasoning.

(*) May be cooked several hours in advance and reheated later.

2 tbl chopped parsley

Sprinkle with parsley and serve.

P

BRAISED VEGETABLES
Légumes Braisées
LETTUCE, CELERY, CHICORY, AND LEEKS
Laitues, Céleris, Endives, et Poireaux

The braising of lettuce, celery, chicory, or leeks requires a relatively long, slow cooking, usually of an hour and a half or more, before the desired interchange of flavours between the vegetable and its braising medium can take place. It is this culinary osmosis which gives them the delicious flavour they should always have. Any one of these vegetables may be braised, left aside uncovered to cool, then covered and reheated several hours or even a day later.

LAITUES BRAISÉES
[Braised Lettuce]

Plain boiled lettuce is dreadfully uninteresting, but lettuce braised slowly in stock and herbs is a marvellous dish. It goes well with roast veal, roast beef, and roast chicken. It can also be combined with other vegetables such as grilled tomatoes and sautéed potatoes to garnish a meat dish.

Lettuce and endive are equally good for braising. Count on one 6- to 8-inch head per person.

For 6 people

6 heads of lettuce, 6 to 8 ins. in diameter

Trim the stems of the lettuce and remove wilted leaves. Two at a time, hold each head by its stem and plunge up and down gently in cold water to remove all traces of soil.

A large pan containing 6 to 7 qts. of boiling water	**1½ tsp salt per qt. of water** **Salt and pepper**

Plunge three of the heads in the boiling salted water. Bring rapidly back to the boil and boil slowly, uncovered, for 3 to 5 minutes until the heads have wilted. Remove and plunge for 2 to 3 minutes in a large basin of cold water. Repeat with the remaining lettuce. A head at a time, squeeze gently but firmly in both hands to eliminate as much water as you can. Slice each head in half lengthwise. Sprinkle with salt and pepper. Fold in half crosswise and shape with your hands to make fat triangles.

Preheat oven to 350° F., Mark 4.

6 thick slices of streaky bacon   **A 4-in. square of bacon rind**

Simmer the bacon and rind in a quart of water for 10 minutes. Drain, rinse in
cold water, and dry.

A 12-in., fireproof, covered casserole   **2 oz. sliced carrots**
2 oz. sliced onions   **1½ oz. butter**

In the casserole cook the onions and carrots slowly with the butter until tender
but not browned. Push them to the sides of the casserole and arrange the lettuce
triangles in the bottom, closely pressed against each other. Spread part of the
vegetables over the lettuce, then the bacon and bacon rind.

About ¾ pt. good beef stock or   **A round of buttered greaseproof**
  beef bouillon, plus, if you wish,   **paper**
  ¼ pt. dry white wine or dry white
  vermouth
A medium herb bouquet:
  4 parsley sprigs, ¼ tsp thyme, and
  ½ bay leaf tied in cheesecloth

Pour in enough liquid barely to cover the lettuce. Add the herb bouquet. Bring
to simmering point on top of the stove. Place the buttered paper over the lettuce,
cover the casserole, and place in lower part of preheated oven. Regulate heat so
that lettuce simmers slowly for 1½ hours.

A lightly buttered serving dish

Remove the lettuce to the serving dish and keep it warm. Quickly boil down
the braising liquid until it has reduced to the consistency of syrup (about ¼ pint).

1 oz. butter   **2 to 3 tbl chopped parsley**

Away from heat, swirl the butter into the sauce, then strain it over the lettuce,
sprinkle with parsley and serve.

(*) If made in advance, do not sauce the lettuce until the last moment. Boil
down the braising liquid and strain it into a saucepan. Reheat the lettuce by
covering with buttered foil and placing it for about 15 minutes in a 350° F.,
Mark 4 oven. Just before serving, butter the sauce and pour it over the lettuce.

CÉLERIS BRAISÉS

[Braised Celery]

Except for slight differences at the beginning and at the end, celery is
braised in the same way as lettuce, so we shall not give it a full recipe. Serve
braised celery with chops, steaks, roast beef, turkey, goose, duck, pork, or lamb.

For 6 people

6 heads of tender, practically stringless celery about 2 ins. in diameter	1½ tsp salt per qt. of water White string
A pan containing 6 to 7 qts. boiling water	

Trim the roots, and cut off the tops to make each celery head 6 to 7 inches long. Wash thoroughly, using warm water if necessary: spread the stalks apart gently while running water all the way down to the root to remove all grit. Drop into the boiling, salted water and boil slowly for 15 minutes. Drain. Plunge for 2 to 3 minutes in a basin of cold water. Drain, and gently extract as much water as possible by pressing each head in a cloth. Tie each with 2 or 3 loops of white string to keep the stalks in place while braising.

The same ingredients as for braised lettuce (preceding recipe)	A lightly buttered baking or serving dish

Following the method for the preceding braised lettuce, arrange the celery in a casserole or baking dish large enough to hold it in one layer. Cover with blanched bacon strips and cooked vegetables. Add the wine and enough stock just to cover the celery. Season lightly and add the herb bouquet. Cover, bring to simmering point, and bake for 1½ hours in a 350° F., Mark 4 oven. Then uncover the casserole, raise oven heat to 400° F., Mark 6, and bake 30 minutes more, basting 2 or 3 times, until the celery has browned lightly. Drain the celery, remove strings, cut heads in half lengthwise, and arrange in dish. Cover and keep warm if to be served immediately.

½ oz. arrowroot (or potato flour or cornflour) blended with 2 tbl Madeira, port, stock, or bouillon

Strain the braising liquid into a saucepan and boil it down rapidly until it has reduced to ½ pint. Away from heat, beat in the starch mixture. Simmer for 3 to 4 minutes. Correct seasoning.

1 oz. softened butter	2 tbl chopped parsley

Remove from heat and just before serving, beat the butter into the sauce. Pour it over the hot celery and sprinkle with parsley.

(*) May be cooked ahead; see preceding recipe for braised lettuce.

VARIATION

Cold Braised Celery

Degrease the braising liquid thoroughly before you reduce it. Omit the starch and the enrichment butter.

CÉLERI-RAVE BRAISÉ

[Braised Celeriac—Turnip-rooted Celery]

Celeriac, a delicious winter vegetable, is not nearly as common in British shops as it should be. Besides braising it in stock as in the following recipe, you may treat it exactly like the turnips on page 447, cooking it slowly in a small amount of liquid, butter, and seasonings, and serving it with butter and parsley, or puréed with mashed potatoes. Celeriac may accompany roast goose, duck, pork, ham, or turkey.

For 6 people

2 lbs. celeriac

Peel the celeriac and cut it into slices ½ inch thick. Drop it into a saucepan with boiling salted water to cover, and boil slowly for 5 minutes. Drain.

Preheat oven to 350° F., Mark 4.

**A ¼-lb. chunk of streaky bacon, rind
  removed**

Cut the bacon into ¼-inch dice. Simmer for 10 minutes in 1½ pints of water. Drain.

3 oz. chopped onions	**Optional: ¼ pt. dry white wine or**
½ oz. butter	**dry white vermouth in place of**
A 2½-qt. fireproof casserole	**¼ pt. stock**
½ to ¾ pt. brown stock or beef	**Salt and pepper**
** bouillon**	

Cook the onions and bacon in butter slowly in the casserole for 10 minutes without browning. Arrange the celeriac in the casserole and spread the onions and bacon over it. Pour in enough liquid barely to cover the celeriac. Season lightly.

**A round of buttered aluminium foil   2 tbl chopped parsley
A bulb baster**

Bring to simmering point on top of the stove. Cover loosely with the foil. Place in upper part of preheated oven and bake for about 1 hour, basting 2 or 3 times with a bulb baster. The celeriac is done when it is very tender, has browned lightly, and the liquid has almost evaporated. Serve sprinkled with parsley.

---

* ENDIVES À LA FLAMANDE

[Braised Chicory—Belgian Endive or Witloof]

Chicory is one of the better winter vegetables. The plain butter-braise is, in our opinion, the most delicious way of cooking chicory. It emerges a beautiful light golden colour and its characteristic flavour is enhanced by its slow absorption of the butter. Chicory goes particularly well with veal.

For 6 people

Preheat oven to 325° F., Mark 2.

**12 firm, medium-sized chicory
  heads with tightly closed leaves**

Trim the bases of the chicory. Discard any withered leaves. Wash one by one rapidly under running cold water. Drain.

$2\frac{1}{2}$ oz. butter	1 tbl lemon juice
A 2- to $2\frac{1}{2}$-qt. enamelled casserole	$\frac{1}{8}$ pt. water
$\frac{1}{4}$ tsp salt	

Smear $\frac{3}{4}$ ounce butter in the casserole. Lay the chicory in it in two layers. Sprinkle each layer with salt and lemon juice, and dot with butter. Pour in the water. Cover and boil slowly for 10 minutes. Uncover and boil rapidly for about 10 minutes or until the liquid is reduced to 2 or 3 tablespoons.

A round of buttered paper	**Or:**
Either:	**A shallow baking dish**
2 tbl chopped parsley	**1 oz. melted butter**
A hot vegetable dish	**2 tbl chopped parsley**

Lay the paper over the chicory, cover the casserole, and bake in middle of a preheated oven for 1 hour. Remove casserole cover but leave paper in place, and bake 30 minutes more or until chicory is a nice golden yellow. *Either* arrange the chicory in a hot vegetable dish or around your roast, and sprinkle with parsley, *or*, for a more golden effect, arrange them in a baking dish, baste with melted butter, and brown briefly under the grill. Sprinkle with parsley just before serving.

VARIATION

Endives Gratinées

[Chicory *Gratinéed* with Cheese]

Butter-braised chicory is also good when sauced and browned under the grill. For a main-course dish, wrap each head in a thin slice of boiled ham before saucing. See also the *quiche aux endives* on page 137, and the *gratin d'endives* on page 141.

For 6 people

¾ pt. *sauce crème* or *sauce mornay*
  (béchamel with cream, page 52,
  or with cheese, page 54
A shallow, lightly buttered baking
  dish

12 chicory heads butter-braised as in
  the preceding recipe
2 to 3 tbl grated Swiss cheese
½ oz. butter cut into pea-sized dots

Spread a third of the sauce in the baking dish. Arrange the braised chicory over it, and pour on the rest of the sauce. Sprinkle with cheese and dot with butter.

Shortly before serving, place under a moderately hot grill to reheat thoroughly and brown the cheese lightly.

---

* POIREAUX BRAISÉS AU BEURRE

[Braised Leeks]

Braised leeks are a fine accompaniment to roast beef, steaks, or turkey.

For 6 people

12 fine fresh leeks about 1½ ins. in
  diameter
A covered, fireproof casserole or
  baking dish, square or oval,
  and long enough to hold the
  trimmed leeks

1¼ to 1½ pts. water
3 oz. butter
1 dsp salt

Trim off the roots, remove any withered leaves, and slit the green part of the leeks lengthwise two ways. Wash thoroughly under running water, spreading leaves apart. Cut off a portion of the green tops to leave the leeks about 7 inches long. Lay the leeks in the casserole, making 2 or 3 layers. Pour in enough water to come two-thirds of the way up the layers of leeks. Add the butter and salt.

Place over a high heat and bring to the boil. Partially cover, leaving a $\frac{1}{16}$-inch gap to allow steam to escape, and maintain liquid at a fairly fast boil. As the leeks soften, the water will just cover them. In 30 to 40 minutes, the white part of the leeks should be tender when pierced with a knife, and the liquid should have almost evaporated.

**A shallow, fireproof baking and
  serving dish**

Transfer the leeks to the baking dish, and pour the remaining cooking juices over them.

Aluminium foil   **2 to 3 tbl chopped parsley**

Half an hour before serving, cover loosely with aluminium foil and set in the middle of a preheated, 325° F., Mark 2 oven for 20 to 30 minutes or until the leeks have taken on a light golden colour. Sprinkle with parsley and serve.

(*) After their baking, the leeks may be left aside uncovered, and reheated later.

VARIATIONS

Poireaux Gratinés au Fromage

[Leeks Browned with Cheese]

The preceding braised leeks   **1½ oz. melted butter**
2 oz. grated Swiss, or Swiss and
  Parmesan cheese, or mixture of
  cheese and breadcrumbs

After the braised leeks have browned lightly in the oven, sprinkle them with the cheese or cheese and breadcrumbs. Pour the butter over them. Place for 2 to 3 minutes under a moderately hot grill to brown the cheese lightly.

Poireaux à la Mornay, Gratinés

[Leeks Browned with Cheese Sauce]

The braised leeks in the preceding   **1 oz. grated Swiss cheese**
  master recipe   **½ oz. butter cut into pea-sized dots**
1 pt. sauce mornay (béchamel with
  with cheese), page 54

After the braised leeks have browned very lightly in the oven, pour the *sauce mornay* over them, sprinkle on the cheese, dot with the butter. Place under a moderately hot grill for 2 to 3 minutes to brown the top of the sauce lightly.

RED CABBAGE AND SAUERKRAUT
Chou Rouge et Choucroute

Both braised red cabbage and braised sauerkraut need 4 to 5 hours of slow cooking for them to develop their full flavour. Once they have been placed in the oven they need little or no attention, and are even better when cooked in advance and reheated the next day.

CHOU ROUGE À LA LIMOUSINE

[Braised Red Cabbage with Red Wine and Chestnuts]

Red cabbage braised in this fashion is a fine dish to serve with roast goose, duck, pork, or venison. Or you may cook the meat in the casserole with the cabbage. See the recipe for duck on page 255. All red vegetables must be cooked with something acid to retain their colour; thus the presence of the tart apples and red wine in the following recipe.

For 6 people

Preheat oven to 325° F., Mark 2.

A ¼-lb. chunk of streaky bacon

Remove the rind and cut the bacon into *lardons* (strips 1½ inches long and ¼ inch across). Simmer for 10 minutes in 1½ pints of water. Drain.

2 oz. thinly sliced carrots
¼ lb. sliced onions
2 tbl rendered fresh goose or pork fat, or butter

A 4- to 5-qt., covered, fireproof casserole

Cook the bacon, carrots and onions, in fat or butter slowly in the covered casserole for 10 minutes without browning.

2 lbs. red cabbage leaves cut into ½-in. slices

Stir in the cabbage leaves and when well covered with the fat and vegetables, cover and cook slowly for 10 minutes.

¾ lb. diced tart apples
2 cloves mashed garlic
¼ tsp ground bay leaf
⅛ tsp clove
⅛ tsp nutmeg

½ tsp salt
⅛ tsp pepper
¾ pt. good, young red wine (claret, Mâcon, or Chianti)
¾ pt. brown stock or beef bouillon

Stir in all the ingredients listed above. Bring to simmering point on top of the stove. Cover and place in the middle of a preheated oven. Regulate heat so that cabbage bubbles slowly for 3 to 3½ hours.

24 peeled chestnuts, page 478   **Salt and pepper**

Add the chestnuts to the cabbage, cover and return casserole to the oven for 1 to 1½ hours more, or until the chestnuts are tender and all the liquid in the casserole has been absorbed by the cabbage. Taste carefully for seasoning, and serve as follows:

(*) If not served immediately, leave aside uncovered. Reheat slowly before serving.

P*

4 or 5 sprigs of parsley   **A hot vegetable dish**

Turn into a vegetable dish or heap around your meat, and decorate with parsley.

CHOUCROUTE BRAISÉE À L'ALSACIENNE

[Braised Sauerkraut]

In France before sauerkraut is braised with wine, stock, aromatic vegetables, and spices, it is always drained and soaked in cold water for 15 to 20 minutes to remove all but a suggestion of its preserving brine. If you have never cared much for the sour flavour of most sauerkraut dishes, this recipe may well change you into an enthusiast. Sauerkraut makes a most savoury accompaniment to duck, goose, pheasant, pork, ham, or sausages, any of which may even be cooked along with the sauerkraut and give it that much more flavour.

For 6 people

**2 lbs. fresh sauerkraut (tinned raw
sauerkraut may be used, but it is
never as good as the fresh)**

Drain the sauerkraut (either fresh or tinned) and soak it in a large basin of cold water for 15 to 20 minutes or more, changing the water three times. Taste the sauerkraut, and when as much of the briny flavour as you wish has been removed, drain it. Taking it by small handfuls, squeeze out as much water as you can. Pick it apart to separate the strands.

A ½-lb. chunk of streaky bacon

Remove the rind and slice the bacon into ½-inch pieces about 2 inches long. Simmer it in 3 pints of water for 10 minutes. Drain.

Preheat oven to 325° F., Mark 2.

2 oz. thinly sliced carrots   **A 2- to 2½-qt., covered, fireproof**
¼ lb. sliced onions   **casserole**
3 tbl rendered fresh goose or pork
fat, or butter

Cook the bacon, carrots, and onions in fat or butter slowly in the covered casserole for 10 minutes without browning. Stir in the sauerkraut and when it is well covered with the fat and vegetables, cover and cook slowly for 10 minutes more.

The following tied in washed   ¼ pt. dry white wine or ⅛ pt. dry
  cheesecloth: white vermouth
4 sprigs of parsley   ¾ to 1 pt. white stock, brown
1 bay leaf   stock, or beef or chicken
6 peppercorns   bouillon
10 juniper berries (or add ⅛ pt.   Salt
  gin to the casserole)   A round of buttered paper

Bury the herb and spice bag in the sauerkraut. Pour in the wine, and sufficient stock or bouillon just to cover the sauerkraut. Season lightly with salt. Bring to simmering point on top of the stove. Lay on the round of buttered paper. Cover and place in middle of preheated oven. Regulate heat so that the sauerkraut bubbles slowly for 4½ to 5 hours, and until all the liquid has been absorbed by the sauerkraut. Taste carefully for seasoning.

(*) If not served immediately, leave aside uncovered. Reheat slowly before serving.

TO SERVE

Choucroute Garnie

[Sauerkraut Garnished with Meat]

Braised sauerkraut may be used as a bed for sliced roast pork, pork chops, ham, or browned sausages, or with roast goose, duck, or pheasant. The dish is usually accompanied with boiled potatoes and either a chilled Alsatian wine such as Riesling or Traminer, or beer.

If you wish to cook your meats in the sauerkraut, brown them first in a frying pan in hot fat; then bury them in the casserole while the sauerkraut is braising, timing the meats so that they and the sauerkraut will be done together. See the recipe for duck braised in sauerkraut on page 255.

CUCUMBERS

Concombres

* ## CONCOMBRES AU BEURRE

[Baked Cucumbers]

If the natural moisture content is not withdrawn beforehand, cucumbers exude so much water as they are heated that you usually end up with a tasteless mush and swear never to attempt cooked cucumbers again. Blanching for 5 minutes before cooking will remove unwanted water, but also most of the cucumber flavour. A preliminary stand in salt draws out the water and also the bitterness, if they are of the bitter type, yet leaves the flavour, which a little vinegar and a pinch of sugar accentuates. We have found the following method delicious, and suggest it for all cooked cucumber recipes. Baked cucumbers go with roast, grilled, or sautéed chicken, roast veal, veal chops or scallops, and sautéed brains or sweetbreads.

For 6 people

6 cucumbers about 8 ins. long

Peel the cucumbers. Cut in half lengthwise; scoop out the seeds with a spoon. Cut into lengthwise strips about ½ inch wide. Cut the strips into 2-inch pieces.

2 tbl wine vinegar	**A 2-qt. porcelain or stainless steel**
1½ tsp salt	**bowl**
⅛ tsp sugar	

Toss the cucumbers in a bowl with the vinegar, salt, and sugar. Let stand for at least 30 minutes or for several hours. Drain. Pat dry on a cloth.

Preheat oven to 375° F., Mark 5.

A baking dish 12 ins. in diameter	**½ tsp dill or basil**
and 1½ ins. deep	**3 to 4 tbl chopped spring onions**
1½ oz. melted butter	**⅛ tsp pepper**

Toss the cucumbers in the baking dish with the butter, herbs, spring onions, and pepper. Place uncovered in the middle of the preheated oven for about 1 hour, tossing 2 or 3 times, until the cucumbers are tender but still have a suggestion of crispness and texture. They will barely colour during the cooking.

(*) Leave aside uncovered; reheat before serving as in the following suggestions.

TO SERVE

Concombres Persillés

[Parslied Cucumbers]

A hot vegetable dish   **2 tbl chopped parsley**

Turn the baked cucumbers into the vegetable dish, sprinkle with chopped parsley, and serve.

Concombres à la Crème

[Creamed Cucumbers]

¼ pt. cream   **1 tbl chopped parsley**
Salt and pepper

Boil the cream in a small saucepan until it has reduced to half. Season with salt and pepper, fold into the hot, baked cucumbers, sprinkle with parsley, and serve.

Concombres aux Champignons et à la Crème

[Creamed Cucumbers with Mushrooms]

½ lb. fresh mushrooms
An enamelled frying pan
½ pt. cream
1 tsp cornflour mixed with 1 tsp
  water

Salt and pepper to taste
2 tbl chopped parsley

Trim, wash, and quarter the mushrooms. Dry in a cloth. Place them in the dry frying pan and toss over a moderately low heat for 5 minutes. Pour in the cream and cornflour mixture; boil slowly for 5 minutes or so, until the cream has reduced and thickened. Stir in salt and pepper, simmer for a moment and check seasoning. Fold into the hot baked cucumbers, sprinkle with parsley, and serve.

Concombres à la Mornay

[Cucumbers with Cheese Sauce]

1 pt. *sauce mornay* (béchamel with
  grated cheese), page 54

2 to 3 tbl grated Swiss cheese
½ oz. butter cut into pea-sized dots

Fold the cheese sauce into the hot, baked cucumbers. Sprinkle with cheese, dot with butter, and place under a hot grill for 2 to 3 minutes to brown top delicately.

AUBERGINES

Aubergines

Aubergines, like cucumbers, contain a considerable amount of water which must be removed before cooking; in their raw state they also have a bitter, astringent quality. The most satisfactory way to remove both moisture and bitterness yet retain flavour is to let them stand in salt for about half an hour.

AUBERGINES FARCIES DUXELLES

[Aubergines Stuffed with Mushrooms]

This excellent aubergine dish goes with roast lamb, lamb chops, or roast, sautéed, or grilled chicken. Or it may be a separate vegetable course. Preparation is somewhat long, as it is for many good things, but you may have the dish ready for the oven several hours or even the day before baking it.

For 6 people—12, if the aubergines are divided as they are served

**3 aubergines about 6 ins. long and
   3 ins. in diameter**

Remove the green stem covering and cut the aubergines in half lengthwise. Cut grooves an inch apart in the flesh, going down to within ¼ inch of the skin. Preheat grill in time for paragraph three.

1 tbl salt   **2 tbl olive oil**

Sprinkle the flesh with salt and lay the aubergines flesh down on a cloth for half an hour. Gently squeeze them to extract as much water as possible. Dry them, then pour the oil over them.

**A shallow roasting tin large enough
   to hold aubergine halves in one
   layer**

Place them flesh-side up in a roasting tin and pour ⅛ inch depth of water around them. Place them so that their flesh is 4 to 5 inches below preheated, moderately hot grill for 10 to 15 minutes, until tender, and lightly browned on top.

A 2½-qt. mixing bowl

Leaving the skin intact, remove all but ¼ inch of the aubergine meat with a spoon. Chop it and place it in a mixing bowl.

NOTE: In the following stuffing, you may, if you wish, substitute for part of the mushrooms 3 ounces of rice steamed in butter, page 488.

¼ lb. finely chopped onions   **A 9- to 10-in. enamelled frying pan**
1 tbl olive oil or butter   **Salt and pepper**

Cook the onions slowly in the oil or butter in a frying pan for about 10 minutes until very tender but not browned. Season lightly and add to the aubergine meat in the mixing bowl.

1 lb. finely chopped fresh   **1 tbl olive oil**
**   mushrooms**   **Salt and pepper**
1½ oz. butter

Following the recipe for mushroom *duxelles* on page 475, twist the mushrooms, a handful at a time, in the corner of a cloth to extract their juice. Sauté them in butter and oil until very lightly browned (5 to 6 minutes). Season and add to the mixing bowl.

| 5 oz. cream cheese | $\frac{1}{2}$ tsp basil or $\frac{1}{4}$ tsp thyme |
| 4 tbl chopped parsley | |

Mash the cheese with a fork, then beat it into the mixing bowl. Beat in the herbs and taste carefully for seasoning.

Preheat oven to 375° F., Mark 5.

3 tbl grated Swiss cheese mixed	1 to 1$\frac{1}{2}$ oz. melted butter
with 3 tbl fine, dry, white bread-	
crumbs	

Fill the aubergine shells with the mixture. Top with cheese and breadcrumbs, and baste each half with melted butter.

(*) May be prepared ahead to this point.

About 40 minutes before serving, arrange in a roasting tin and surround with $\frac{1}{8}$ inch depth of water. Bake in upper part of preheated oven for 25 to 30 minutes to heat thoroughly and brown the cheese and breadcrumbs.

RATATOUILLE

[Aubergine Casserole—with tomatoes, onions, peppers, and courgettes]

Ratatouille perfumes the kitchen with the essence of Provence and is certainly one of the great Mediterranean dishes. As it is strongly flavoured it is best when it accompanies plain roast or grilled beef or lamb, *pot-au-feu* (boiled beef), or plain roast, grilled, or sautéed chicken. Equally good hot or cold, it also makes a fine accompaniment to cold meats, or may be served as a cold hors d'œuvre.

A really good *ratatouille* is not one of the quicker dishes to make, as each element is cooked separately before it is arranged in the casserole to partake of a brief communal simmer. This recipe is the only one we know of which produces a *ratatouille* in which each vegetable retains its own shape and character. Happily a *ratatouille* may be cooked completely the day before it is to be served, and it seems to gain in flavour when reheated.

For 6 to 8 people

$\frac{1}{2}$ lb. aubergines	1 tsp salt
$\frac{1}{2}$ lb. courgettes	
A 2$\frac{1}{2}$-qt. porcelain or stainless steel	
mixing bowl	

Peel the aubergines and cut into lengthwise slices $\frac{3}{8}$ inch thick, about 3 inches long, and 1 inch wide. Scrub the courgettes, slice off the two ends, and cut the courgettes into slices about the same size as the aubergine slices. Place the vegetables in a bowl and toss with the salt. Let it stand for 30 minutes. Drain. Dry each slice in a cloth.

A 10- to 12-in. enamelled frying   **3 tbl olive oil, more if needed**
pan

One layer at a time, sauté the aubergines, and then the courgettes, in hot olive oil for about a minute on each side to brown very lightly. Remove to a side dish.

½ lb. thinly sliced onions   **2 cloves mashed garlic**
2 sliced green peppers   **Salt and pepper to taste**
2 to 3 tbl olive oil, if necessary

In the same frying pan, cook the onions and peppers slowly in olive oil for about 10 minutes, or until tender but not browned. Stir in the garlic and season to taste.

1 lb. firm, ripe, red tomatoes,   **Salt and pepper**
peeled, seeded, and juiced, page
465

Slice the tomato pulp into ½-inch strips. Lay them over the onions and peppers. Season with salt and pepper. Cover the frying pan and cook over a low heat for 5 minutes, or until the tomatoes have begun to render their juice. Uncover, baste the tomatoes with the juices, raise heat and boil for several minutes, until juice has almost entirely evaporated.

A 2-qt. fireproof casserole about   **3 tbl parsley**
2½ ins. deep

Place a third of the tomato mixture in the bottom of the casserole and sprinkle over it 1 tablespoon of parsley. Arrange half of the aubergines and courgettes on top, then half the remaining tomatoes and parsley. Put in the rest of the aubergines and courgettes, and finish with the remaining tomatoes and parsley.

Salt and pepper

Cover the casserole and simmer over a low heat for 10 minutes. Uncover, tip the casserole and baste with the rendered juices. Correct seasoning, if necessary. Raise heat slightly and cook uncovered for about 15 minutes more, basting several times, until the juices have evaporated, leaving a spoonful or two of flavoured olive oil. Be careful of the heat; do not let the vegetables scorch in the bottom of the casserole.

(*) Leave aside uncovered. Reheat slowly at serving time, or serve cold.

MOUSSAKA, a mould of aubergines and lamb, is in the Lamb section, page 319.

TOMATOES
Tomates

Many recipes calling for tomatoes direct that they be peeled, seeded, and juiced. This applies to tomato sauces, to the tomato *fondues* which are used in egg dishes, to various Basque or Provençal recipes, and to the diced tomato pulp which may be poached in a soup or a sauce. One pound or 4 or 5 medium tomatoes will yield about ¾ pound of pulp.

TO PEEL TOMATOES

Use firm, ripe, red tomatoes. Drop the tomatoes one or two at a time into boiling water to cover, and boil for exactly 10 seconds. Remove. Cut out the stem. Peel off the skin starting from the stem hole.

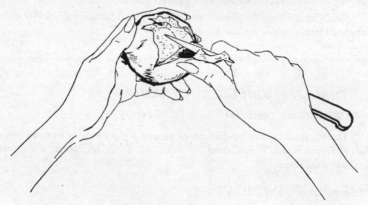

After a 10-second blanching, tomato skin is loosened and peels off easily

TO SEED AND JUICE TOMATOES
(for illustration, see next page)

Cut peeled or unpeeled tomatoes in half crosswise, not through the stem. Squeeze each half gently to extract the seeds and juices from the centre of the tomato. If they are to receive a cold stuffing, sprinkle the interior with salt which will draw more juices out, then invert them in a colander.

Gently press the
juice and seeds out
of the tomato half

DICED, SLICED, OR CHOPPED TOMATO PULP

Dice, slice, or chop the peeled, seeded, and juiced tomato halves. Roughly chopped tomato pulp is *tomates concassées*.

TOMATES GRILLÉES AU FOUR

[Whole Baked Tomatoes]

These make an attractive decoration around a meat dish, or surrounding a dish of French beans. They should be baked only at the last minute if they are to retain their shape.

Preheat oven to 400° F., Mark 6.

Firm, ripe, red tomatoes, all of the same size and not more than 2 ins. in diameter	**Olive oil**
	An oiled roasting tin just large enough to hold the tomatoes
Salt and pepper	**easily**

Wash and dry the tomatoes. Cut out the stems, leaving as small a hole as possible. Sprinkle salt and pepper into the stem hole. Brush the tomatoes with olive oil, then place them stem-end down in the roasting tin. Do not crowd them together.

Bake in the middle of the preheated oven for about 10 minutes. Keep an eye on them; they are done when the skins break a little, but they should not be baked so long that they burst.

Salt and pepper
Chopped, mixed green herbs or
  parsley

Baste them with the tin juices. Season lightly with salt and pepper, and sprinkle herbs or parsley over them. Serve as soon as possible.

---

* TOMATES À LA PROVENÇALE

[Tomatoes Stuffed with Breadcrumbs, Herbs, and Garlic]

One of the most savoury ways of serving tomatoes is *à la provençale*. These tomatoes go well with many things—steaks, chops, roast beef, lamb, roast or grilled chicken, grilled mackerel, sardines, or herrings. They may also be a hot hors d'œuvre, or accompany egg dishes.

For 6 people

Preheat oven to 400° F., Mark 6.

5 firm, ripe, red tomatoes about 3 ins. in diameter	**Salt and pepper**

Remove the stems, and cut the tomatoes in half crosswise. Gently press out the juice and seeds. Sprinkle the halves lightly with salt and pepper.

1 to 2 cloves mashed garlic	**Big pinch of pepper**
3 tbl chopped shallots or spring onions	**⅛ pt. olive oil**
3 tbl chopped fresh basil and parsley, or parsley only	**1½ oz. fine, white, dry breadcrumbs**
⅛ tsp thyme	**A shallow, oiled roasting tin just large enough to hold the tomatoes easily in one layer**
¼ tsp salt	

Blend all the ingredients above in a mixing bowl. Correct seasoning. Fill each tomato half with a spoonful or two of the mixture. Sprinkle with a few drops of olive oil. Arrange the tomatoes in the roasting tin; do not crowd them.

(*) May be prepared ahead to this point.

Shortly before you are ready to serve, place them in the upper part of the preheated oven and bake for 10 to 15 minutes, or until the tomatoes are tender but hold their shape, and the breadcrumb filling has browned lightly.

VARIATION

Tomates Farcies Duxelles

[Tomatoes Stuffed with Mushrooms]

Follow the preceding recipe, but use the mushroom filling described in the recipe for stuffed mushrooms on page 476.

CULTIVATED MUSHROOMS
Champignons de Couche—Champignons de Paris

Fresh, cultivated mushrooms are an essential element of French *cuisine* and appear not only as a vegetable or in a garnish, but as an important flavour factor in numerous dishes, sauces, and stuffings. Mushrooms should never be submitted to prolonged cooking or they will lose most of their taste and texture. Therefore if they are to go into a sauce they are usually cooked separately, then added to the sauce to simmer a moment and blend their flavour with the sauce.

CHOOSING MUSHROOMS

It is always advisable to buy mushrooms in bulk rather than in a packet, so that you can hand-pick each one. Some varieties of cultivated mushrooms are creamy white, others have brownish caps. The freshest of fresh mushrooms are closed on the underside of the cap so that you cannot see the gills. Caps and stems should be smooth, unblemished, fresh looking, and fresh smelling. As a mushroom ages in the shop, the cap expands to expose the gills, the mushroom darkens, and begins to dry out.

If you are not going to use fresh mushrooms immediately, refrigerate them in a polythene bag and they will keep perfectly for two to three days.

PREPARATION FOR COOKING

Trim the base of the stems. If the gills are even partially exposed, break the stem off inside the cap so that you will be able to wash out any soil which may have lodged in the gills.

Just before using them, drop the mushrooms in a large basin of cold water. Rapidly rub them between your hands for several seconds to dislodge dirt particles. Immediately lift them out into a colander. If there are more than a few grains of soil left in the bottom of the basin, wash the mushrooms again. Dry them in a cloth.

HOW TO CUT MUSHROOMS

After they have been washed and dried, here are the various ways in which mushrooms may be cut.

To chop or dice

Place the mushrooms in a heap on the chopping board. Chop them with a big, sharp, straight-edged knife, holding an end of the blade in the fingers of each hand. Use rapid up and down movements, and repeatedly brush mushrooms back into a heap with the knife. Chop until the pieces are less than $\frac{1}{8}$ inch.

Chop mushrooms with a big chef's knife held between the thumb and forefinger of each hand

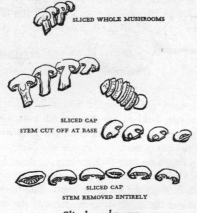

SLICED WHOLE MUSHROOMS

SLICED CAP
STEM CUT OFF AT BASE

SLICED CAP
STEM REMOVED ENTIRELY

Sliced mushrooms

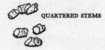

Quartered mushrooms

To flute mushroom caps

Fluted mushroom caps may be stewed or grilled, and are used as decorations. It takes a little practice to master the technique of fluting, but it is quite a nice professional touch to have at your command.

Fluted caps

Hold the mushroom, cap up, in the fingers of your left hand. Its blade pointing away from you, hold a very sharp, small knife rigidly in your right hand. Rest the thumb of your right hand on the mushroom cap to act as a guide. Then rotate the cap toward you against the blade of the knife starting at the crown, thus removing a very shallow strip, or flute, down one half of the cap. Note that the knife remains stationary; the mushroom cuts itself as it rotates against the blade. It is your left hand, controlling the mushroom's movement, which determines the depth and direction of the cut. Continue in the same manner all around the cap.

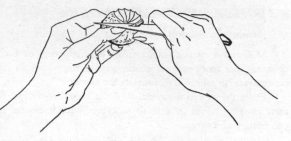

*Starting at crown,
rotate mushroom
toward you against
rigidly held knife
blade*

*Left hand guides
mushroom against
knife blade and
regulates cut*

CHAMPIGNONS À BLANC

[Stewed Mushrooms]

When mushrooms are used in white sauces, or in a garniture in which they must remain white, they are cooked this way.

¼ lb. fresh mushrooms
⅛ pt. water
⅛ tsp salt
½ tbl lemon juice (which helps keep
   mushrooms white)

½ oz. butter
A 1½- to 2½-pt. enamelled saucepan

Trim and wash the mushrooms; cut as directed in your recipe, or as shown in the preceding illustrations. Bring the water, salt, lemon juice, and butter to the boil in the saucepan. Add the mushrooms and toss to cover them with the liquid. Cover and boil moderately fast, tossing frequently, for 5 minutes. Put aside until ready to use.

FUMET DE CHAMPIGNONS

[Mushroom Essence]

Mushroom essence results from the reduction or boiling down of the cooking juice from stewed mushrooms or tinned mushrooms. It is used as a concentrated mushroom flavouring for sauces.

Drain the stewed mushrooms of the preceding recipe. Rapidly boil down their cooking liquid in a small saucepan until it has reduced almost to the consistency of a syrup.

(*) If not used immediately, refrigerate or deep-freeze it.

CHAMPIGNONS GRILLÉS

[Grilled Mushroom Caps]

Grilled mushroom caps are used as a garniture, usually on steaks. They may also be served as a separate vegetable, or as a hot hors d'œuvre on toast.

Fresh mushrooms of whatever size you wish

Preheat grill to moderately hot. Separate the mushroom caps from the stems. Wash and dry the caps. Stems may be chopped and turned into a *duxelles*, page 475.

Melted butter   **Salt and pepper**
A shallow, buttered baking dish

Paint the mushroom caps with melted butter. Arrange them hollow-side up in the baking dish. Sprinkle lightly with salt and pepper. Place 4 to 5 inches from heat, and grill rather slowly for 5 minutes. Turn the caps, and grill for 5 minutes more or until the caps are tender and lightly browned.

Optional: *Beurre Maître d'Hôtel* (butter mixed with lemon juice, parsley, and seasonings), page 92   **Or:** *Beurre pour Escargots* (butter mixed with herbs, shallots, and garlic), page 92

The caps may then, if you wish, be filled with parsley butter into which you also incorporate finely chopped shallots with or without a little mashed garlic. Spread the butter in the caps, filling them by about a third.

Just before serving, heat them for a moment or two under the grill until the butter is bubbling.

* *CHAMPIGNONS SAUTÉS AU BEURRE*

[Sautéed Mushrooms]

Use these mushrooms either as a vegetable alone or in a combination with other vegetables, or as an integral part of such dishes as *coq au vin, boeuf bourguignon, poulet en cocotte*. Successfully sautéed mushrooms are lightly browned and exude none of their juice while they are being cooked; to achieve this the mushrooms must be dry, the butter very hot, and the mushrooms must not be crowded in the pan. If you sauté too many at once they steam rather than fry; their juices escape and they do not brown. So if you are preparing a large amount, or if your heat source is feeble, sauté the mushrooms in several batches.

A 10-in. enamelled frying pan	½ lb. fresh mushrooms, washed,
1 oz. butter	well dried, left whole if small,
1 dsp oil	sliced or quartered if large

Place the frying pan over a high heat with the butter and oil. As soon as you see that the butter foam has begun to subside, indicating that it is hot enough, add the mushrooms. Toss and shake the pan for 4 to 5 minutes. During this the mushrooms will at first absorb the fat. In 2 to 3 minutes the fat will reappear on their surface, and the mushrooms will begin to brown. As soon as they have browned lightly, remove from the heat.

**Optional: 1 to 2 tbl chopped
shallots or spring onions**

Toss the shallots or spring onions with the mushrooms. Sauté over a moderate heat for 2 minutes.

(*) Sautéed mushrooms may be cooked in advance, put aside, then reheated when needed. Season to taste just before serving.

VARIATIONS

Champignons Sautés à la Bordelaise

[Mushrooms Sautéed with Shallots, Garlic, and Herbs]

These may garnish a meat or vegetable dish.

½ lb. fresh mushrooms, whole if	1 dsp oil
small, quartered if large	1 oz. butter

Sauté the mushrooms in oil and butter until lightly browned.

3 tbl chopped shallots or spring   3 tbl fine, white, dry breadcrumbs
   onions
Optional: 1 small clove chopped
   garlic

Stir in the shallots or spring onions, optional garlic, and breadcrumbs, and toss over moderate heat for 2 to 3 minutes.

Salt and pepper to taste
3 tbl chopped fresh parsley, chervil,
   chives, and tarragon, or parsley
   only

Just before serving, season to taste, and toss with the herbs.

Champignons Sautés à la Crème

[Creamed Mushrooms]

Creamed mushrooms may garnish canapés, little *vol-au-vents*, tartlet shells, artichoke bases, or may accompany such foods as omelettes, poached eggs, sweetbreads, or chicken.

½ lb. fresh mushrooms, whole if   1 dsp oil
   small, sliced, quartered, or   2 tbl chopped shallots or spring
   chopped if large   onions
1 oz. butter

Sauté the mushrooms in hot butter and oil for 4 to 5 minutes, but do not allow them to brown any more than necessary. Add the shallots or spring onions and toss over a moderate heat for 2 minutes.

1 tsp flour

Stir in the flour and cook slowly for 2 minutes more, stirring.

¼ to ½ pt. cream   Pinch of pepper
⅛ tsp salt   Optional: 1 to 2 tbl Madeira

Away from heat, blend in the cream and seasonings. Then boil down rapidly until the cream has reduced and thickened. Add the optional wine, and boil for a moment to evaporate its alcohol. Correct seasoning.

(*) May be put aside and reheated later.

½ to 1 oz. softened butter

Remove from heat and just before serving, fold in the butter.

Champignons Sautés, Sauce Madère

[Sautéed Mushrooms in Brown Madeira Sauce]

Another appetizing way of using mushrooms is in a brown Madeira sauce. You may smother a *filet mignon* with them, or fill tartlets, or combine the mushrooms with sautéed chicken livers and ham to fill a rice ring. If you do not have on hand one of the classic, flour-thickened, long-simmered brown sauces, you may use a quick brown sauce made of very good bouillon thickened with arrowroot or cornflour, as suggested in the recipe.

½ lb. mushrooms, sliced, quartered, or chopped	1 dsp oil
1 oz. butter	1 tbl chopped shallots or spring onions

Sauté the mushrooms in butter and oil, adding chopped shallots or spring onions at the end. Remove to a side dish.

⅛ pt. Madeira

Pour the Madeira into the sautéing pan and boil it down rapidly until it has reduced to half.

½ pt. brown sauce
  (the flour-thickened sauces,
  Numbers 1 or 2, pages 59 to 62,
  or the quick sauce, Number 3,
  page 62)

Add the sauce and simmer for 2 to 3 minutes. Then stir in the sautéed mushrooms and simmer for a moment more to blend flavours. Correct seasoning.

(*) May be made ahead of time. Dot top of sauce with butter and leave aside.

½ to 1 oz. butter

Reheat just before serving. Away from heat, stir in the enrichment butter.

DUXELLES

[Mushroom *Duxelles*—Chopped Mushrooms Sautéed in Butter]

Duxelles is a dry, mushroom flavouring for many kinds of stuffings and quick mushroom sauces; once made it will keep for several weeks under refrigeration or may be deep-frozen. The juice is squeezed out of the raw chopped mushroom so that the cooked *duxelles* will be as dry as possible; if the *duxelles* were wet it would dilute and soften a stuffing.

For about ¼ pound

½ lb. finely chopped fresh
  mushrooms, whole or just stems

A handful at a time, twist the mushrooms into a ball in the corner of a cloth to extract as much juice as possible. (Juice may be saved to go into a sauce or soup.)

An 8-in. enamelled frying pan	1 oz. butter
2 tbl chopped shallots or spring	1 dsp oil
onions	

In the frying pan, sauté the mushrooms and shallots or spring onions in butter and oil over a moderately high heat, stirring frequently. After 6 to 8 minutes the mushroom pieces should begin to separate from each other and brown lightly.

Salt and pepper to taste
Optional: ⅛ pt. Madeira and ⅛ pt.
  brown stock or beef bouillon

Season to taste with salt and pepper. Add the optional wine and stock, and boil down rapidly until the liquid has reduced to nothing.

(*) If not to be used immediately, allow to cool. Pack in a covered jar, and refrigerate or deep-freeze.

___

CHAMPIGNONS FARCIS

[Stuffed Mushrooms]

Stuffed mushrooms make a good hot hors d'œuvre or a garnish for a meat dish.

Preheat oven to 375° F., Mark 5.

12 fresh mushroom caps 2 to 3 ins.	A shallow, lightly buttered roasting
in diameter, stems removed	tin
1 to 1½ oz. melted butter	Salt and pepper

Brush the mushroom caps with melted butter. Place them, hollow-side up, in the roasting tin. Sprinkle lightly with salt and pepper.

3 tbl finely chopped onions	Stems from the mushroom caps,
1 oz. butter	finely chopped and squeezed in
1 dsp oil	a cloth to extract their juice
3 tbl chopped shallots or spring	
onions	

Sauté the onions in butter and oil for 3 to 4 minutes without browning. Then add the shallots or spring onions and mushroom stems. Sauté as in the preceding *duxelles* recipe.

Optional: ⅛ pt. Madeira

Add the optional Madeira and boil it down rapidly until it has almost entirely evaporated.

3 tbl fine, white, dry breadcrumbs	**½ tsp tarragon**
1 oz. grated Swiss cheese	**Salt and pepper**
1 oz. grated Parmesan cheese	**• 2 to 3 tbl cream**
4 tbl chopped parsley	

Away from heat, mix in the breadcrumbs, cheeses, parsley, tarragon, and seasonings. A spoonful at a time, blend in just enough cream to moisten the mixture but keep it sufficiently stiff to hold its shape in a spoon. Correct seasoning.

¾ oz. grated Swiss cheese   **1 oz. melted butter**

Fill the mushroom caps with the stuffing. Top each with a pinch of cheese and drops of melted butter.

(*) May be done ahead to this point.

Bake in upper part of a preheated, 375° F., Mark 5 oven for 15 to 20 minutes, or until caps are tender and stuffing has browned lightly on top.

TINNED MUSHROOMS

Tinned mushrooms will have more flavour in sauces or garnitures if you follow the procedure outlined here. (If they are to be browned, drain them, dry in a cloth, and sauté quickly in butter and oil with chopped shallots or onions.)

For ¼ lb. drained, tinned mushrooms:	**1 oz. butter**
	Salt and pepper
1 tbl chopped shallots or spring onions	**Optional: 1 to 2 tbl port or Madeira**

In a small enamelled saucepan, cook the shallots or spring onions slowly in the butter for 2 minutes without browning. Add the mushrooms and seasonings, and toss them in the butter. Add the optional wine. Cover and cook slowly for 2 minutes.

NOTE: The juice from the tin may be boiled down in a saucepan until reduced to a third of its volume or less. Use as a sauce flavouring.

CHESTNUTS
Marrons

Fresh raw chestnuts are in season in the winter months. Choose heavy nuts with tight-fitting shells—indications that they are fresh and will have their maximum flavour.

Chestnuts have a traditional affinity for roast turkey, goose, venison, wild duck and pheasant; they also go with pork and with sausages. Chestnut purée is used as a starchy vegetable to accompany any of these meats. Whole braised chestnuts are often combined with other vegetables such as red cabbage, Brussels sprouts, mushrooms, onions, or carrots. Whole partially-cooked chestnuts go into stuffings, particularly sausage stuffings for goose and turkey.

Chestnuts have an outside shell and a bitter inside skin, both of which must be removed before the chestnuts can be used. Peeling off the inside skin is a chore whatever method you adopt. To our mind, and we have tried them all, the following is the most satisfactory, especially if you want the chestnuts to remain whole.

With a small sharp knife, peel a ⅛-inch strip of shell off one side of each chestnut. Place the chestnuts in a saucepan of cold water, bring to the boil and boil for 1 minute; remove from heat. Then three at a time, with a slotted spoon, ladle the chestnuts out of the water and peel off the shells and inner skins. (Leave aside until later any recalcitrant chestnuts. Drop them all later into boiling water for a moment, then peel them one by one.) The whole peeling process must be a continuous operation and done while the chestnuts are still warm.

PURÉE DE MARRONS

[Chestnut Purée]

For 6 to 8 people

A 2½-qt. heavy-bottomed saucepan
3¼ pts. peeled chestnuts
2 stalks celery
A medium herb bouquet: 4 parsley sprigs, ½ bay leaf, and ⅛ tsp thyme tied in cheesecloth

1¼ pts. good brown stock or ¾ pt. beef bouillon and ½ pt. water
A moulinette

Place in the saucepan the chestnuts, celery stalks, and herb bouquet. Pour in enough stock, or bouillon and water to cover the chestnuts by 1½ inches.

Simmer very slowly and uncovered for 45 to 60 minutes, or until the chestnuts are cooked through. Do not overcook and allow them to become mushy. Drain immediately; remove celery and herb bouquet. Purée the chestnuts in the moulinette, then return them to the saucepan.

| 1½ to 3 oz. softened butter | Pinch of sugar, if needed |
| Salt and pepper | |

Beat in the butter. If the purée is too thick, beat in spoonfuls of the cooking liquid. Season to taste with salt and pepper, and a pinch or two of sugar if you feel it necessary.

(*) If not to be used immediately, instead of beating in the butter, spread it over the surface of the purée. To reheat, cover and place over boiling water, beating occasionally.

MARRONS BRAISÉS

[Whole Braised Chestnuts]

Preheat oven to 325° F., Mark 2.

24 peeled chestnuts	¾ pt. good brown stock or beef
A heavy, fireproof casserole or	beef bouillon and ¾ pt. water
baking dish just large enough to	Water, if necessary
hold the chestnuts in one layer	1½ oz. butter
½ oz. arrowroot or cornflour	
mixed to a paste with 1 tbl port,	
Madeira or water	

Place the chestnuts in the casserole or baking dish. Beat the starch mixture into the stock or bouillon and pour it over the chestnuts. There should be enough liquid to cover them by ½ inch; add water, if necessary. Add the butter. Bring to simmering point, cover, then place in lower part of preheated oven. Regulate heat so that the liquid simmers very slowly for 45 to 60 minutes or until chestnuts are tender.

(*) If not to be served immediately, leave aside uncovered. Cover and reheat slowly on top of stove before proceeding.

If the liquid has not reduced to a syrupy glaze at the end of the cooking, drain it off and boil it down in a saucepan. Pour it back into the casserole and roll the chestnuts gently around in it to cover them with the glaze.

Serve sprinkled with parsley, or combined with other vegetables as directed in whatever recipe you are using.

POTATOES
Pommes de Terre

Out of the vast store of French potato dishes, we have selected an unusual version of mashed potatoes, some excellent grated potato pancakes, a series of good regional recipes for scalloped potatoes, and one for potatoes sautéed in butter.

KIND OF POTATOES TO BUY

We shall not classify potato varieties by name. We shall merely specify baking potatoes when we mean the type of white potato which turns floury after cooking, and boiling potatoes when we are talking about the white potato which retains its shape. It is particularly important that you use the right kind of potato for such dishes as scalloped potatoes, for the potato must not disintegrate during cooking.

PURÉE DE POMMES DE TERRE À L'AIL

[Garlic Mashed Potatoes]

Two whole heads of garlic will seem like a horrifying amount if you have not made this type of recipe before. But if less is used, you will regret it, for the long cooking of the garlic removes all of its harsh strength, leaving just a pleasant flavour. Garlic mashed potatoes go with roast lamb, pork, goose, or sausages. Although both garlic sauce and potatoes may be cooked in advance, they should be combined only at the last minute; the completed purée loses its nice consistency if it is left too long over the heat, or if it is cooked and then reheated.

For 6 to 8 people

2 heads garlic, about 30 cloves

Separate the garlic cloves Drop into boiling water, and boil 2 minutes. Drain. Peel.

A 1½ pt. heavy-bottomed   **2 oz. butter**
saucepan with cover

Cook the garlic slowly with the butter in the covered saucepan for about 20 minutes or until very tender but not browned.

1 oz. flour   **Pinch of pepper**
½ pt. boiling milk   **A sieve and wooden spoon, or an**
¼ tsp salt   **electric liquidizer**

Blend in the flour and stir over a low heat until it froths with the butter for 2 minutes without browning. Away from heat, beat in the boiling milk and seasonings. Boil, stirring, for 1 minute. Rub the sauce through a sieve or purée it in the electric liquidizer. Simmer for 2 minutes more.

(*) May be done ahead of time. Dot top of sauce with pieces of butter to keep a skin from forming. Reheat when needed.

2½ lbs. baking potatoes	2 oz. softened butter
A 2-qt. enamelled saucepan	Salt and white pepper
A wooden spoon	

Peel and quarter the potatoes. Drop into boiling salted water to cover, and boil until tender. Drain potatoes immediately and put through a sieve. Place the hot purée in the saucepan and beat with the spoon for several minutes over a moderate heat to evaporate moisture. As soon as the purée begins to form a film in the bottom of the pan, remove from heat and beat in the butter a tablespoon at a time. Beat in salt and pepper to taste.

(*) If not used immediately, leave aside uncovered. To reheat, cover and place over boiling water, removing cover and beating potatoes frequently.

3 to 4 tbl cream	A hot, lightly buttered vegetable
4 tbl chopped parsley	dish

Shortly before serving, beat the hot garlic sauce vigorously into the hot potatoes. Beat in the cream by spoonfuls but do not thin out the purée too much. Beat in the parsley. Correct seasoning. Turn into the hot vegetable dish.

CRÊPES DE POMMES DE TERRE

[Grated Potato Pancakes]

These are excellent with roasts, steaks, or chops. As a bed for fried or poached eggs, they may be topped with a cheese or tomato sauce. Or roll them around a filling of mushrooms, chicken livers, or ham, top with a sauce, and brown under the grill.

For 18 crêpes *about 3 inches in diameter, or 8* crêpes *made in individual 6-inch* crêpe *pans*

8 oz. cream cheese	A 2½-qt. mixing bowl
1½ oz. flour	

Mash the cream cheese with the flour, in the mixing bowl.

2 eggs	⅛ tsp pepper
½ tsp salt	

Mix in the eggs and seasonings and beat until smooth.

Q

**6 oz. Swiss cheese cut into ⅛-in.
  dice**

Stir in the Swiss cheese.

2½ lbs. baking potatoes   A grater

Peel the potatoes and rub them through the large holes of the grater. A small
handful at a time, twist them into a ball in the corner of a cloth to squeeze out
as much of their water as you can. Stir the grated raw potatoes into the egg and
cheese mixture.

**3 to 6 tbl cream
Optional: 3 oz. diced boiled ham, or
  3 oz. sautéed mushrooms, chicken
  livers, or onions, 3 to 4 tbl fresh
  herbs, such as parsley, chives,
  chervil**

Stir in the cream by spoonfuls to make a mixture of the consistency of a thick
batter—not runny. Add optional ingredients. Taste carefully for seasoning.

**A 10-in. frying pan   A large spoon or ladle
⅜ oz. butter, more as needed   A hot dish
1 dsp oil, more as needed**

Place frying pan over a moderately high heat with the butter and oil. When you
see the foam begin to subside, ladle 3 lots of batter into the frying pan to form
3 *crêpes* approximately 3 inches in diameter and ½ inch thick. Regulate heat so
that the *crêpes* are lightly browned on the bottom and bubble holes have appeared
on the surface in about 3 minutes. Then turn and brown on the other sides for
about 3 minutes. Transfer to the dish and keep warm in one layer while making
the remaining *crêpes*.

(*) If not served immediately, arrange *crêpes* in one layer on a baking sheet.
Leave aside uncovered. Reheat for 4 to 5 minutes in a 400° F., Mark 6 oven.

---

* *GRATIN DAUPHINOIS*

[Scalloped Potatoes with Milk, Cheese, and a Pinch of Garlic]

There are as many 'authentic' versions of *gratin dauphinois* as there are of
bouillabaisse. Of them all, we prefer this one because it is fast, simple, and
savoury. It goes with roast or grilled chicken, turkey, and veal. With roast beef,
pork, lamb, steaks, and chops you may prefer the *gratin savoyard* which follows,
since it is cooked with stock rather than milk. Although some authorities on

le vrai gratin dauphinois would violently disagree, you may omit the cheese. If you do so, add 1 ounce more of butter.

For 6 people

Preheat oven to 425° F., Mark 7.

2 lbs. boiling potatoes

Peel the potatoes and slice them ⅛ inch thick. Place in a basin of cold water. Drain when ready to use.

A fireproof baking-serving dish	**2 oz. butter**
about 10 ins. in diameter and	**1 tsp salt**
2 ins. deep (if recipe is increased,	**⅛ tsp pepper**
dish must be wider but no deeper)	**4 oz. grated Swiss cheese**
½ clove unpeeled garlic	**½ pt. boiling milk**

Rub the baking dish with the cut garlic. Smear the inside of the dish with ½ ounce of the butter. Drain the potatoes and dry them in a cloth. Spread half of them in the bottom of the dish. Divide over them half the salt, pepper, cheese, and butter. Arrange the remaining potatoes over the first layer, and season them. Spread on the rest of the cheese and divide the butter over it. Pour on the boiling milk. Place baking dish over heat and when simmering, place in upper part of preheated oven. Bake for 20 to 30 minutes or until potatoes are tender, milk has been absorbed, and the top is nicely browned. (As the oven is hot, and the dish shallow, the potatoes will cook quickly.)

(*) It could wait for half an hour, loosely covered, over simmering water. For a longer wait, stop the initial cooking just before all the milk has evaporated. Leave aside uncovered. Shortly before serving, dot with 1 ounce butter, reheat on top of the stove, and place in a 425° F., Mark 7 oven for 5 to 10 minutes to finish cooking.

VARIATIONS

Gratin Savoyard

[Scalloped Potatoes with Meat Stock and Cheese]

For 6 people

Ingredients for the preceding *gratin*	**½ pt. brown stock or beef bouillon**
***dauphinois* with the following**	**instead of milk**
exceptions:	**3 rather than 2 oz. butter**

Follow the recipe for *gratin dauphinois*, but substitute stock for milk, and increase the butter proportions as indicated above.

Gratin Jurassien

[Scalloped Potatoes with Cream and Cheese]

Potatoes baked in cream are mouth-watering with roast lamb, chicken, turkey, veal, beef, or pork. An important point in this recipe is that you must never let the cream come quite to simmering point during the baking; thus it will not curdle.

For 6 people

Preheat oven to 300° F., Mark 1.

2 oz. butter
A 10-in. fireproof dish 2 ins. deep
2 lbs. boiling potatoes, sliced ⅛ in. thick

1 tsp salt
⅛ tsp pepper
¼ lb. grated Swiss cheese
½ pt. cream

Smear ½ ounce of the butter in the baking dish. Arrange layers of potatoes in it, seasoning each layer with salt, pepper, cheese, and dots of butter. End with a sprinkling of cheese and butter dots. Pour on the cream and bring slowly almost to simmering point on top of the stove. Then place in the middle of a preheated oven and bake for 1 to 1¼ hours, regulating oven heat throughout baking so that the cream never quite bubbles. The *gratin* is done when the potatoes are tender and have absorbed the cream, and the top is lightly browned.

Gratin de Pommes de Terre Crécy

[Scalloped Potatoes and Carrots with Cream]

This mixture of potatoes, carrots, and cream is delicious with veal or chicken. It is the same as the preceding *gratin jurassien* but the potatoes are interspersed with sliced, braised carrots prepared as follows:

½ lb. carrots sliced ⅛ in. thick
¼ oz. butter
¼ tsp salt
2 tbl finely chopped shallots or spring onions

¼ pt. water
A 1½- to 2-pt., heavy-bottomed, enamelled saucepan with cover

Boil the carrots slowly with the butter, salt, shallots or spring onions, and water in the covered saucepan for 20 to 30 minutes or until the liquid has evaporated and the carrots are tender. Then continue as for the preceding *gratin jurassien*, but alternate carrot slices with the potato slices.

Gratin de Pommes de Terre Provençale

[Scalloped Potatoes with Onions, Tomatoes, Anchovies, Herbs, and Garlic]

This casserole with its full-bodied Mediterranean flavour goes with roast lamb or beef, steaks, chops, or grilled mackerel. It is also good served cold. The potatoes need no other liquid than that rendered by the tomatoes as they cook together.

For 6 people

Preheat oven to 400° F., Mark 6.

½ lb. thinly sliced onions	1½ lbs. tomatoes, peeled, seeded,
2 dsp olive oil	and juiced, page 465
A small saucepan	¼ tsp salt

Cook the onions and olive oil slowly together in the saucepan until the onions are tender but not browned. Cut the tomato pulp into strips ½ inch wide. Fold the tomatoes and salt into the onions. Leave aside.

6 tinned anchovies packed in olive	¼ tsp thyme
oil, drained	⅛ tsp pepper
2 cloves mashed garlic	1 tbl olive oil (include as part of this
¼ tsp basil	the oil from the anchovy tin)

In a small mixing bowl, mash the anchovies into a paste with the garlic, herbs, pepper, and oil.

An oiled baking dish about 10 ins.	1 oz. grated Parmesan or Swiss
in diameter and 2 ins. deep	cheese
2 lbs. boiling potatoes sliced ⅛ in.	1 tsp olive oil
thick	

Spread one-quarter of the tomatoes and onions in the baking dish. Over them arrange half the potato slices, then half the anchovy mixture, then half the remaining tomatoes and onions. Spread over this the rest of the potatoes and the anchovy mixture; top with the last of the tomatoes and onions. Spread on the cheese, and sprinkle with olive oil.

Aluminium foil, if necessary

Place in the middle of a preheated oven and bake for about 40 minutes, or until the potatoes are tender and have absorbed all of the juice from the tomatoes. If the top browns too much during cooking, cover very loosely with a sheet of foil.

(*) Keep warm or reheat as for the *gratin dauphinois*, page 482.

* POMMES DE TERRE SAUTÉES
POMMES DE TERRE POUR GARNITURE
POMMES DE TERRE CHÂTEAU

[Potatoes Sautéed in Butter]

Although we rationed ourselves strictly on potato recipes, potatoes sautéed in butter appear as a garnishing suggestion in so many of the main-course dishes that we are including directions for doing them. The following recipe demands that the potatoes be sautéed raw, which produces a delectable result. But the cooking is rather exacting as raw potatoes will stick to the sautéing pan unless certain precautions are taken.

PREPARATION FOR COOKING

If you were living in France, you would buy smooth oval potatoes 2 to 2½ inches long, with yellowish flesh, *pommes de terre de Hollande*. You would peel them neatly, and sauté them whole. Elsewhere, choose small boiling potatoes or new potatoes. Peel them, and cut them into elongated olive shapes all the same size, 2 to 2½ inches long and 1 to 1¼ inches at their widest diameter. Cut them smoothly, so that they will roll around easily and colour evenly when they are sautéed. (You might save the cuttings for the good leek and potato soup, page 31.) Do not wash the potatoes; simply pat them thoroughly dry in a cloth. If you peel them some time in advance of their cooking, roll them in a damp cloth; dry them in a fresh cloth just before sautéing.

For 4 to 6 people

**2 lbs. boiling potatoes or new
  potatoes**

Cut the potatoes according to the directions in the preceding paragraph. Remember they are not to be washed, merely well dried in a cloth.

**1½ to 2 oz. clarified butter, page 12,
  or 1 oz. butter and 1 tbl oil,
  more if needed**

**A 10- or 11-in. heavy frying pan
  large enough to hold all the
  potatoes easily in one layer**

Add enough clarified butter or the butter and oil to the frying pan to film it by 1/16 inch and place over a moderately high heat. When the clarified butter is very hot but not colouring, or when the butter foam in the butter and oil mixture begins to subside, put the potatoes into the frying pan. Leave them for 2 minutes, regulating the heat so that the butter is always very hot but not colouring. Then shake the frying pan back and forth to roll the potatoes and to sear them on another side for 2 minutes. Continue thus for 4 to 5 minutes more until the potatoes are a pale golden colour all over, indicating that a seared, protective film has formed over them, so that they will not stick to the pan.

¼ tsp salt

Then sprinkle the potatoes with salt and roll them again in the frying pan.

**A heavy, close-fitting lid for the
frying pan**

Lower the heat, cover the frying pan and cook the potatoes for about 15 minutes, shaking them every 3 to 4 minutes to prevent their sticking to the frying pan, and to ensure an even colouring.

They are done when they yield slightly to the pressure of your finger, or when a knife pierces them easily; they should be a nice, fairly even, golden brown colour. Hold the cover slightly askew over the frying pan, and pour out the sautéing fat.

(*) If not to be used immediately, place cover askew to allow for air circulation, and place frying pan on an asbestos mat over a very low heat. The potatoes can be kept thus for about half an hour. Reheat just to sizzling hot before serving.

1 to 1½ oz. softened butter   **Big pinch of pepper**
2 to 3 tbl chopped parsley, chives,   **A hot vegetable dish**
** or fresh tarragon, or a mixture of**
** fresh green herbs**

Then away from heat, add the butter and herbs, sprinkle on the pepper, and roll the potatoes in the frying pan so that they glisten with herbs and butter. Arrange the potatoes around your meat dish, or turn them into a vegetable dish.

VARIATIONS

Pommes de Terre Parisiennes

[Potato Balls Sautéed in Butter]

Pommes de Terre Sautées en Dés

[Diced Potatoes Sautéed in Butter]

Use exactly the same system as that in the preceding recipe, but form the raw potatoes into balls with a potato-ball cutter, or cut them into ½-inch dice.

RICE

Riz

Whatever method you use for rice the grains should emerge whole, tender, and separate. Although raw rice is not difficult to cook, many people are so afraid of it that they dare to attempt only the pre-cooked or treated varieties, thus limiting their scope of rice dishes and denying their skill as good cooks. Two factors contribute to the gumminess of badly cooked rice. One is over-cooking. The other is failure to deal with the floury coating which clings to raw rice and becomes sticky and gluey unless the rice is washed or sautéed in butter or oil.

TYPES OF RICE

Types of raw, white rice usually available in shops are: *patna*, a long, thin, hard grain, *Carolina*, a long and somewhat plumper grain, and *Java*, with shorter and flatter grains. Occasionally you may find the short, fat-grained, imported Italian rice, which has a fine, chewy quality. Although any of these types may be used in any recipe, patna and Carolina are particularly suited to boiling and steaming, while Italian rice is especially nice for braising. Remarks on packaged, pre-cooked rice and wild rice are on pages 493-4.

AMOUNT TO BUY

Rice will about triple in quantity after cooking. Half a pound of raw rice will serve 4 to 6 people.

---

* *RIZ À L'INDIENNE*
RIZ À LA VAPEUR

[Steamed Rice]

There are many ways of arriving at plain boiled or steamed rice, and most cooks choose one which best suits their temperaments. We find the following to be a foolproof system. The rice may be cooked hours ahead of time and reheated when needed. The large amount of water used for boiling the rice gets rid of its floury coating, and the washing of the rice after this preliminary blanching is an added precaution. The final steaming finishes its cooking, leaving the grains dry, fluffy, and separate.

For cooked rice serving 6 people

Preliminary blanching

¾ lb. clean, unwashed, raw rice   **1½ tsp salt per qt. of water**
A large pan containing 6 to 7 qts.
  of rapidly boiling water

Gradually sprinkle the rice into the boiling salted water, adding it slowly enough
so that the water does not drop below the boil. Stir it up once to be sure none of
the grains are sticking to the bottom of the pan.

A large colander

Boil uncovered and moderately fast for 10 to 12 minutes. Start testing after 10
minutes by biting successive grains of rice. When a grain is just tender enough to
have no hardness at the centre but is not yet quite fully cooked, drain the rice in
the colander.

Fluff it up under hot running water for a minute or two to wash off any traces
of flour.

    Final steaming. (See an alternative method, Buttered Rice III, page 490,
where the rice is steamed in butter for its final cooking.)

3 thicknesses of cheesecloth, or a
  clean cloth or napkin, well washed
  and rinsed so that there is no
  odour of soap or bleach

Wrap the blanched rice in the damp cheesecloth, towel, or napkin.

Either place the bundle of rice in a colander, cover, and place over boiling water
to steam for 20 to 30 minutes until the rice is tender;

Or place the bundle in a heated casserole, cover, and place in a 325° F., Mark 2
oven for 20 to 30 minutes until the rice is tender.

(*) If the rice is not to be served immediately, fluff it with a fork, rewrap it, and
leave it aside away from heat. Steam the bundle again for 5 minutes or so to
reheat it, and serve as in one of the following suggestions:

TO SERVE

Riz à l'Anglaise

[Buttered Rice I]

A hot vegetable dish   **1 to 2 oz. butter**
Salt and white pepper

Turn the hot rice into a hot vegetable dish. Fluff it with a fork, adding salt and
pepper to taste. Distribute the butter over it.

    Q*

Riz au Beurre

[Buttered Rice II]

1½ to 2 oz. butter	Salt and pepper
An 8-in. enamelled frying pan or saucepan	

Melt the butter in the frying pan or saucepan. When foaming, add the hot, steamed rice and fluff it with a fork to impregnate it with the butter. Fluff in salt and pepper to taste.

(*) May be left aside and reheated later.

Riz Duxelles

[Buttered Rice with Mushrooms]

¼ lb. finely diced fresh mushrooms	Salt and pepper to taste
1 oz. butter	½ to 1 oz. more butter
1 tbl oil	2 to 3 tbl chopped parsley
1 to 2 tbl chopped shallots or spring onions	

Following the procedure for *duxelles* on page 475, twist the mushrooms, a handful at a time, in the corner of a cloth to extract their juice. Sauté the mushrooms in butter and oil for 6 to 8 minutes until very lightly browned. Stir in the shallots or spring onions and cook slowly for 2 minutes more. Mix in the hot, steamed rice with a fork and season to taste. Fluff in the rest of the butter and the parsley.

(*) May be left aside and reheated later.

RIZ ÉTUVÉ AU BEURRE

[Buttered Rice III]

This is an alternative method for the final cooking of blanched rice. If you want to serve buttered rice, this is easier than steaming.

For 6 people

Preheat oven to 350° F., Mark 4.

¾ lb. unwashed raw rice

Blanch the rice for 10 to 12 minutes in 6 to 7 quarts of boiling salted water until barely tender as described on page 489. Rinse under hot water.

1½ oz. butter   **A round of buttered, greaseproof**
¼ tsp salt   **paper**
Big pinch of pepper
**A 2½-pt. covered casserole set in a
    pan of boiling water**

While the rice is blanching, melt the butter with the seasonings in the casserole over the boiling water, and prepare the round of greaseproof paper. As soon as the rice has been rinsed in hot water, turn it into the hot casserole and fluff it with a fork to blend with the butter and seasonings. Lay the paper over the rice, cover the casserole, and place it, still in its pan of boiling water, in the lower part of the preheated oven. Bake for 20 to 30 minutes or until the rice is tender. Fluff it with a fork. Correct seasoning.

(*) Rice may be kept hot in the casserole placed over barely simmering water. Or it may be put aside, then reheated over boiling water when needed.

---

* RIZ AU BLANC

[Boiled Rice for Hors d'Œuvres and Salads]

If you are using rice in hors d'œuvres or salads, it need not be steamed. Simply boil it as directed on page 489, but for 18 to 20 minutes, testing it frequently until it is tender. Drain it in a colander, fluff it under cold running water, and allow it to drain thoroughly before using it.

RISOTTO
PILAF
PILAU

[*Risotto*—Braised Rice]

This is the standard French method for braised rice, meaning rice sautéed in fat and onions, then cooked in seasoned liquid. Whether the final dish is labelled *risotto*, pilaf, or pilau it is usually done in this manner regardless of the traditional techniques of other rice-eating nations. A good *risotto* is simple to make if you bear the following points in mind that apply to a plain *risotto* as well as to one which includes vegetables, chicken, or sea foods.

SAUTÉING

The rice must first be sautéed slowly in butter for 2 to 3 minutes until it turns a milky colour. This cooks the rice-flour coating and prevents the rice from becoming sticky.

PROPORTIONS

Use the correct amount of liquid: ¾ pint for each ½ pound of raw rice.

HEAT

Regulate the heat so that the liquid is entirely absorbed in 18 to 20 minutes. This means, try to maintain the liquid at a very slow boil; if it is absorbed too quickly, the rice will not be tender. If it is absorbed too slowly, the rice becomes gummy, the grains disintegrate, and the flavour of the rice is impaired.

STIRRING

Do not stir the rice until all the liquid has been absorbed.

For 6 people

Preheat oven to 375° F., Mark 5.

1 oz. finely chopped onions
2 oz. butter
A 2½-pt. fireproof casserole about
8 ins. in diameter with a tight-
fitting cover

Cook the onions and butter slowly in the casserole for about 5 minutes until tender but not browned.

¾ lb. clean, unwashed, raw rice

Blend the rice into the onions and butter and stir over a moderate heat for several minutes, not letting the rice brown. The grains will at first become translucent, then will gradually turn a milky colour.

1¼ pts. boiling liquid, depending on
what your *risotto* is to be served
with:
Chicken stock or tinned chicken
broth
Brown stock or beef bouillon
Mushroom broth and water
White wine fish stock

White wine or white vermouth,
and water
Or: water only
Salt and pepper
A small herb bouquet: 2 parsley
sprigs, ⅓ bay leaf, and ⅛ tsp
thyme tied in cheesecloth

As soon as the rice looks milky, pour in the boiling liquid. Add the herb bouquet, and salt and pepper to taste. Bring to simmering point, stir once, cover the casserole, and place in lower part of preheated oven. As soon as the liquid maintains itself at a very slow boil, in 4 to 5 minutes, reduce heat to 350° F., Mark 4; the boil should be regulated so that the liquid has been absorbed by the rice in 18 to 20 minutes. Do not touch the rice for a total of 18 minutes. Then uncover. Tilt casserole and lift rice with a fork to see if all liquid at the bottom of the casserole has evaporated. If not, return to the oven for 2 to 3 minutes more. Then remove the casserole from the oven. If you wish the rice to be slightly *al dente*, uncover it. If you wish it to become a little more tender, leave it covered for 20 minutes. Discard herb bouquet. Fluff the rice with a fork and correct seasoning.

(*) If not to be used immediately, keep warm over barely simmering water. Or leave aside, and reheat casserole over boiling water when needed.

VARIATION

Riz en Couronne

[Rice Ring]

This is how to make a ring of rice which is to be filled with creamed shellfish, sautéed chicken livers with ham and mushrooms, buttered peas, or whatever luscious sauced titbits you wish.

For 6 people

Preheat oven to 350° F., Mark 4.

A 2½-pt. ring mould, smeared with ¼ oz. butter	A lid to cover the mould
The preceding *risotto*	A pan of boiling water to hold the mould
A round of greaseproof paper	

Turn the *risotto* into the buttered mould, patting down the rice lightly; it should fill the mould exactly. Lay the greaseproof paper over the *risotto*. Cover with the lid, and place the mould in the pan of boiling water. Place in lower part of preheated oven for 10 minutes.

A round serving dish, heated and lightly buttered

Just before serving, remove paper, turn dish upside down over mould and reverse the two, to unmould the rice ring on to the dish.

(*) If the *risotto* is not to be served immediately, leave it in its mould, covered, and over barely simmering water.

PACKAGED TREATED OR PRE-COOKED RICE

This is the type of rice which has been treated or pre-cooked and is very useful for those who dare not attempt raw rice. To make it more interesting gastronomically, follow the printed directions but add cooked onions and herbs and, instead of water, use one of the flavoured liquids suggested on p. 492.

WILD RICE

Wild rice has hardly been heard of in France, but you can cook it deliciously in the French manner by using a modified *risotto* technique.

For 6 to 8 people

Preheat oven to 350° F., Mark 4.

¾ lb. wild rice	1 tbl salt
2½ qts. boiling water	

Drop the rice in the boiling salted water and boil uncovered for 5 minutes. Drain thoroughly.

3 tbl each: finely chopped carrots, onions, and celery	¾ pt. brown stock or beef bouillon
2 oz. butter	1 bay leaf
A 2-qt. fireproof casserole with cover	¼ tsp thyme
	Salt and pepper

While the rice is boiling, cook the chopped vegetables slowly in the butter in the casserole for 5 to 6 minutes until tender but not browned. Then add the drained rice and stir over a moderate heat for 2 minutes to impregnate it with the butter. Add the stock or bouillon, bay leaf, thyme, and seasonings to taste. Bring to the boil. Cover the casserole and place in lower part of the preheated oven for 30 to 35 minutes or until the rice is tender and has absorbed all the liquid. Add a few drops more liquid if all has been absorbed before the rice is tender. The rice grains should emerge separate and lightly filmed with butter. Discard the bay leaf. Fluff rice with a fork and correct seasoning.

(*) May be cooked in advance and reheated when needed.

CHAPTER NINE

COLD BUFFET

Préparations Froides

Cold vegetables, composed salads, aspics, moulded mousses, *pâtés*, and *terrines*, any of these may be served as a first course for a dinner, or be the mainstay of a summer meal. And a collection of such dishes on a buffet table can be most inviting. Recipes for various salad dressings are in the Sauce chapter under vinaigrettes starting on page 85, and mayonnaise starting on page 77.

COLD VEGETABLES

Légumes Servis Froids

* *LÉGUMES À LA GRECQUE*

[Vegetables Cooked in Aromatic Broth]

Vegetables *à la Grecque*, a refreshing idea for any time of the year, are simmered in an aromatic *court bouillon* of water, oil, herbs, and seasonings. After the vegetables have been removed to a serving dish, the *court bouillon* is boiled down to concentrate its flavour, and is poured over the vegetables. When the vegetables are cold, serve as hors d'œuvre, or combine them with other vegetables for a composed salad.

Court Bouillon

[The Aromatic Broth]

For 1 pound of vegetables

¾ pt. water
⅛ pt. olive oil
⅛ pt. lemon juice
½ tsp salt
2 tbl chopped shallots or spring
  onions
The following (tied in cheesecloth
  if you wish):
  6 sprigs parsley including roots if
    available
  1 small celery stalk with leaves
    or ⅛ tsp celery seeds

1 sprig fresh fennel or ⅛ tsp fennel
  seeds
1 sprig fresh thyme or ⅛ tsp dried
  thyme
12   peppercorns
6 coriander seeds
A 2-qt. enamelled or stainless steel
  saucepan with cover

Place all the ingredients above in the covered saucepan and simmer for 10 minutes.

Champignons à la Grecque

[Mushrooms à la Grecque]

1 lb. fresh mushrooms, button
  size if possible

1 pt. simmering *court bouillon*
  (preceding recipe)

Trim and wash the mushrooms. Leave them whole if they are small, quarter if large. Add them to the simmering *court bouillon*, tossing them to cover with the liquid. Cover and simmer for 10 minutes.

A slotted spoon
A serving dish

Salt and pepper

Remove the mushrooms from the saucepan with the slotted spoon, and arrange them in a serving dish. Rapidly boil down the *court bouillon* until it has reduced to about ⅛ pint. Correct seasoning, and strain it over the mushrooms.

(*) When cold, the mushrooms may be covered and refrigerated, and will keep for 2 to 3 days.

2 to 3 tbl chopped parsley or
  mixed green herbs

Sprinkle with herbs just before serving.

VARIATIONS: OTHER VEGETABLES À LA GRECQUE

Any of the following vegetables may be prepared à la Grecque. In each case, make a *court bouillon* as directed in the preceding recipe, prepare and simmer the vegetables as indicated for each kind in the list, then drain and arrange on a serving dish. Boil down court bouillon until it has reduced to about ⅛ pint, pour it over the vegetables, and chill. Sprinkle with chopped, fresh green herbs just before serving.

Fonds d'Artichauts à la Grecque

[Artichoke Hearts à la Grecque]

Before cooking, trim the artichoke hearts as described on page 396. The choke is removed after cooking. Simmering time is from 30 to 40 minutes.

Céleris à la Grecque

[Celery à la Grecque]

Buy heads labelled 'celery hearts'. Remove any tough outside stalks. Cut off the tops of the heads to just below the main body of leaves. Halve or quarter the heads lengthwise, wash thoroughly under running water, and arrange them in a baking dish. Pour on the simmering court bouillon, adding more water if necessary to cover the celery. Cover the dish, bring to simmering point, and bake in a preheated 350° F., Mark 4 oven for 30 to 40 minutes or until tender.

Concombres à la Grecque

[Cucumber à la Grecque]

Peel, cut in half lengthwise, and scoop out the seeds with a spoon. Cut the halves into ½-inch strips, then into 2-inch pieces. Toss with ½ teaspoon of salt for each pound of cucumber pieces, and let them stand in a bowl for 20 minutes. Drain thoroughly, and proceed with the recipe. Simmering time is about 10 minutes.

Aubergines à la Grecque

[Aubergine à la Grecque]

Peel the aubergine, cut into serving pieces, and let them stand for 20 minutes in ½ teaspoon of salt and 1 teaspoon of lemon juice for each pound of aubergine pieces. Drain thoroughly and proceed with the recipe. Simmering time is about 10 minutes.

498 CHAPTER NINE: COLD BUFFET

Fenouil à la Grecque   Endives à la Grecque

[Fennel or Chicory à la Grecque]

Quarter or halve the fennel or chicory lengthwise, wash under cold, running water, then proceed with the recipe. Simmering time is 30 to 40 minutes.

Poireaux à la Grecque

[Leeks à la Grecque]

Trim off the roots, make two lengthwise cuts in the green part, remove a portion of the green tops to leave the leeks about 7 inches long. Wash thoroughly under cold, running water, being sure you get off all the grit from each leaf. Arrange the leeks in a fireproof dish, pour on the simmering *court bouillon*, and add boiling water, if necessary, to cover the leeks. Cover the baking dish, bring to simmering point on top of the stove, then bake in a preheated, 350° F., Mark 4 oven for 30 to 40 minutes or until the leeks are tender. Drain off the *court bouillon*, boil it down to ⅛ pint, pour over the leeks, and chill.

Oignons à la Grecque

[Onions à la Grecque]

Buy small onions about an inch in diameter. Drop them for 1 minute in boiling water to cover, drain and peel them, then cut a cross in their root ends to ensure even cooking. Proceed with the recipe. Simmering time is 30 to 40 minutes.

Poivrons à la Grecque

[Red or Green Peppers à la Grecque]

Halve the peppers lengthwise, remove the seeds and ribs, and slice or quarter the peppers. Proceed with the recipe. Simmering time is about 10 minutes.

CÉLERI-RAVE RÉMOULADE

[Celeriac in Mustard Sauce]

Celeriac or celery root prepared in this manner makes a typically French hors d'œuvre. The root must first be softened in some way. You may drop it in boiling water for a minute before dressing it, or steep it in salt and lemon juice, then dress it several hours before serving. We have suggested the latter system as it removes the slight bitterness of celeriac, softens it, yet preserves its flavour and freshness of taste.

NOTE: *Céleri-rave rémoulade* has nothing to do with *sauce rémoulade*, a mayonnaise with pickles, capers, and other ingredients.

1 lb. celery root	1½ tsp salt
A 3-pt. mixing bowl	1½ tsp lemon juice

Peel the celery root and cut it into julienne matchsticks as illustrated on page 22. Toss in a bowl with the salt and lemon juice, and leave to steep for 30 minutes. Rinse the pieces in cold water, drain, and dry them in a cloth.

4 tbl prepared French mustard	⅛ to ¼ pt. olive oil or salad oil
3 tbl boiling water	2 tbl wine vinegar
A wire whisk	Salt and pepper

Warm the mixing bowl in hot water. Dry it. Add the mustard and beat in the boiling water drop by drop with a wire whisk. Then beat in the oil drop by drop to make a thick creamy sauce. Beat in the vinegar by drops, and season to taste.

2 to 3 tbl chopped mixed green
  herbs or parsley

Fold the celery root into the sauce, and allow it to marinate for 2 to 3 hours or overnight. Decorate with herbs before serving.

POMMES DE TERRE À L'HUILE

[French Potato Salad—sliced potatoes in oil and vinegar dressing]

French potato salad is prepared while the boiled, sliced potatoes are still warm, so that they absorb the dressing. The salad may be eaten warm with grilled sausage, or cold. Mayonnaise may be folded into the potatoes if you wish. Be sure to use potatoes which may be boiled and sliced without crumbling.

For about 1½ pounds

2 lbs. boiling potatoes (8 to 10 medium potatoes)	A 5-pt. mixing bowl

Scrub the potatoes. Drop them in boiling salted water to cover, and boil until the potatoes are just tender when pierced with a small knife. Drain. As soon as they are cool enough to handle, peel, and cut them into slices about ⅛ inch thick. Place them in the mixing bowl.

**4 tbl dry white wine, or 2 tbl dry
white vermouth and 2 tbl stock
or bouillon**

Pour the wine or vermouth and stock or bouillon over the warm potato slices
and toss very gently. Leave aside for a few minutes until the potatoes have
absorbed the liquids.

**2 tbl wine vinegar, or 1 tbl vinegar
  and 1 tbl lemon juice
1 tsp prepared mustard
¼ tsp salt
A small bowl and wire whisk**

**5 tbl olive oil or salad oil
Pepper
Optional: 1 to 2 tbl chopped
  shallots or spring onions**

Beat the vinegar or vinegar and lemon juice, mustard, and salt in the small bowl
until the salt has dissolved. Then beat in the oil by drops. Season to taste, and
stir in the optional shallots or onions. Pour the dressing over the potatoes and
toss gently to blend.

**2 to 3 tbl chopped mixed green
herbs or parsley**

Serve them while still warm, or chill. Decorate with herbs before serving.

COMPOSED SALADS
Salades Composées

Here are three recipes and several suggestions for salad mixtures. Green
vegetables will lose their fresh colour if they are left in a vinaigrette for more
than half an hour; therefore prepare each component of the salad in a separate
dish. Just before serving, season each with dressing, and put together the salad in
its serving bowl.

SALADE NIÇOISE

[Mediterranean Combination Salad]

Salmon, anchovies, tomatoes, potatoes, French beans, hard-boiled eggs, and
lettuce are the usual elements for this appetizing combination, and you may
arrange the salad in any manner you wish. Serve as an hors d'œuvre or as a
main-course summer salad.

For 6 to 8 people

¾ lb. cold, blanched, French beans,
    page 407 (see also directions for
    frozen beans, page 412)
3 or 4 quartered tomatoes
½ pt. vinaigrette (French dressing)
    with herbs, page 85
1 head lettuce, separated, washed,
    drained, and dried
A salad bowl
¾ lb. cold French potato salad
    (preceding recipe)

8 oz. tinned salmon chunks,
    drained
3 oz. stoned black olives, preferably
    the dry Mediterranean type
2 or 3 hard-boiled eggs, cold,
    peeled, and quartered
6 to 12 tinned anchovy fillets,
    drained
2 to 3 tbl chopped, fresh green
    herbs

Just before serving, season the beans and tomatoes with several spoonfuls of vinaigrette. Toss the lettuce leaves in the salad bowl with ⅛ pint of vinaigrette, and place the leaves around the edge of the bowl. Arrange the potatoes in the bottom of the bowl. Decorate with the beans and tomatoes, interspersing them with a design of salmon chunks, olives, eggs, and anchovies. Pour the remaining dressing over the salad, sprinkle with herbs, and serve.

SALADE DE BOEUF À LA PARISIENNE

[Cold Beef and Potato Salad]

This is an attractive way to use cold boiled or braised beef as a main-course summer dish or on a cold buffet table. We shall not give proportions because they depend on how much meat you have.

Thinly sliced, cold, boiled or
    braised beef
Vinaigrette (French dressing) with
    herbs, page 85
Thinly sliced rings of mild onion
A serving dish
French potato salad, page 499

Lettuce or watercress
Quartered hard-boiled eggs
Quartered tomatoes
Optional: cold cooked French
    beans, broccoli or cauliflower;
    beetroot
Chopped fresh green herbs

In separate bowls, marinate the beef and the onion rings in vinaigrette for half an hour or longer. When ready to serve the salad, arrange the beef on the dish, alternating the slices with onion rings. Decorate the dish with the rest of the ingredients, spoon a little vinaigrette over them, and sprinkle with herbs.

---

* SALADE À LA D'ARGENSON

[Rice or Potato and Beetroot Salad]

When rice or potatoes are marinated with beetroot in a vinaigrette for a sufficient amount of time, the whole mass becomes beetroot-coloured. Then it can be tossed in a herbal mayonnaise, and all sorts of cooked vegetables, meat, or fish leftovers can be mixed into it to make a nourishing hors d'œuvre, a main-course dish, or an attractive addition to a picnic.

8 oz. boiled rice, *riz au blanc*, page 49, Or: 8 oz. of warm boiled potatoes, peeled and diced	4 tbl chopped shallots or spring onions
½ lb. diced cooked or tinned beetroots	A 3-pt. bowl ¼ pt. vinaigrette (French dressing), page 85

Toss the rice or potatoes, beetroots, and shallots or spring onions in a bowl with the vinaigrette. Season to taste. Cover, and refrigerate for at least 12, preferably 24, hours.

½ to ¾ pt. mayonnaise with green herbs, page 80, or the recipe following it, for green mayonnaise	A salad bowl Decorate with any or all of the following:
Salt and pepper	Green or black olives, anchovies,
¼ lb., one or a mixture of the following:	sliced hard-boiled eggs, watercress or parsley sprigs
Cooked green peas, or cooked and diced French beans, cauliflower, broccoli, carrots, turnips, or asparagus; diced cooked beef, pork, poultry, or fish; flaked tinned salmon; diced raw apples; grated raw carrots; walnuts	

Shortly before serving, fold in the mayonnaise and other ingredients. Season carefully. Arrange the salad in the bowl and decorate with the suggestions listed.

ASPICS

Préparations Froides en Aspic

Cold chicken decorated with tarragon leaves and shimmering with jelly, a moulded aspic of chicken livers, or a *boeuf mode en gelée*—these are lovely summer dishes, and fun to do if you enjoy decorating. You may be very elegant with your designs, or amusing, and, after a little experience, very professional.

DEFINITIONS: *GELÉE*, JELLY, ASPIC

Gelée is the French culinary term for beef, veal, chicken, or fish stock which stiffens when cold because it contains natural gelatine, or because gelatine has been added to it. Liquid or jelled, it is always spoken of as *gelée*. We shall refer to *gelée*, whether hot or cold, liquid or set, as jelly or jellied stock. Aspic, in French, usually refers not to the jelly, but to the whole decorated dish of various elements coated with or moulded in jelly.

RECIPES FOR JELLY

Directions for home-made jellied stock are on page 101 in the Stocks and Aspic section. These stocks are almost always clarified, meaning that they are rendered clear and sparkling through a simmering with egg whites; directions for clarification are on page 100. Cubed bouillons and consommés are turned into jelly by the addition of powdered gelatine, as described on page 102; following this are directions for wine flavourings.

HOW TO WORK WITH JELLY

Never fail to test out the jelly before you begin to work with it: Pour $\frac{1}{2}$ inch of jelly into a small, chilled saucer, and refrigerate for about 10 minutes or until set. Then break it up with a fork and let it stand at room temperature; the pieces should hold their shape but not be rubbery. Further information and gelatine proportions are on page 102.

Allow yourself plenty of time and cracked ice, for the jelly must be given full opportunity to set; it cannot be hurried. A complicated decoration need not be completed in one continuous operation. Successive coats of jelly may be spooned over the dish whenever you have time, and the process may go on in spurts all one day and on into the next.

COATING FOODS WITH ASPIC   Jellied stocks set very quickly once they are cold. To avoid continual warmings of the whole amount when you are to coat foods with successive layers of jelly, heat just what you will need at one time in a small saucepan. Stir over cracked ice until the liquid turns syrupy, indicating it is about to congeal. Then remove the pan immediately from its bed of ice, and spoon a layer of jelly over the chilled food. Refrigerate the dish for about 10 minutes to set the layer of jelly, and repeat the process two or three times until you have built up a coating of jelly almost $\frac{1}{8}$ of an inch thick.

DECORATIVE ELEMENTS

CHOPPED JELLY   When you spoon jelly over foods arranged on a dish, you will usually need to fill up empty spaces or cover dribbles of jelly that have run off the edges of the food. Chopped jelly is an easy solution, and is made as follows: Pour a $\frac{1}{2}$-inch layer of jelly into a plate or tin and chill until set. Then make narrow cross-hatches through the jelly with a knife to cut it into small pieces $\frac{1}{8}$ inch or less in size. Either force the jelly through a forcing bag to outline the food or to fill up the dish, or heap it into place with a spoon.

JELLY CUTOUTS   These make nice decorations around the edge of a dish. Chill a $\frac{1}{4}$-inch layer of jelly in a plate or tin, then cut it into squares, triangles, or diamonds, and it is ready to use.

DESIGNS AND COLOURS   You can make fanciful decorations of curlicues, sprays, branches and flowers, or geometric patterns out of the ingredients listed below. Use them as follows: First spoon two or three layers of jelly over the chilled food; chill the decorative materials and cut them into various shapes. Then, holding them with two trussing needles or skewers, dip them into almost-set jelly and arrange them over the food. Refrigerate the dish of food to set the designs, then give a final coating or two of jelly to cover the decorations with a transparent film.

FOR BLACK: Use thin slices of truffle or black olives.

FOR RED: Use thin strips, dice, or dots of tinned red pimento. The pulp of peeled, seeded, and juiced tomatoes, page 465, may be diced or sliced, or twisted in the corner of a cloth to make little balls.

FOR YELLOW: Use hard-boiled egg yolks, mashed with softened butter, and pushed through a piping tube to make dots or fluted designs.

FOR ORANGE: Use cooked carrots sliced, diced, or cut into strips.

FOR GREEN: Use fresh or pickled tarragon leaves, dropped in boiling water for 30 seconds, refreshed in cold water, and dried on a cloth. Cooked green peppers cut into strips or dice. The green tops of leeks or spring onions simmered in water for several minutes until softened, refreshed in cold water, and dried; cut into thin strips, these can then be formed into curlicues, or made to look like branches of mimosa (use dots of 'yellow' for the flowers).

FOR WHITE: Use hard-boiled egg white, thinly sliced and cut into strips, dice, or shapes.

OEUFS EN GELÉE

[Poached Eggs in Aspic]

Serve eggs in aspic as a first course or luncheon dish, or arrange them around a dish of cold meats, fish, or vegetables.

For 6 eggs

1½ pts. jelly (jellied stock, page 101, or tinned consommé with gelatine, page 102)

6 round or oval moulds of ¼ pt. capacity, preferably of metal as they are easier to unmould

Pour ⅛ inch of jelly in the bottom of each mould and refrigerate for about 10 minutes or until set.

12 tarragon leaves, fresh or preserved in vinegar

Drop the tarragon leaves into boiling water for 30 seconds. Refresh in cold water, drain, dry, and chill. Dip them in a little almost-set jelly, and arrange

them in a cross over the jelly in the bottom of each mould. Chill for a few
minutes to set the tarragon.

6 chilled poached eggs, page 104

Place an egg in each mould, its least attractive side up. Pour in almost-set jelly to
cover the eggs. Chill for an hour or so, until the jelly is well set.

Chilled plates   Lettuce leaves

At serving time, dip each mould for 3 to 4 seconds in hot water. Run a knife
around the edge of the jelly, turn the mould upside down and, giving it a sharp
knock on the base, unmould on a chilled serving plate over a bed of lettuce
leaves.

OTHER DECORATIONS

Lay a thin slice of ham over the cross of tarragon leaves. Or make designs
of truffle in the bottom of the mould, top with a slice of *foie gras*, then add the
poached egg and the rest of the jelly.

---

* *FOIES DE VOLAILLE EN ASPIC*

[Chicken Livers in Aspic]

Chicken livers sautéed in butter, simmered in wine, then moulded in aspic
make a delicious hors d'œuvre, and are most simple to do.

For six ¼ pint moulds

1½ pts. jelly (jellied stock, page 101,   6 round or oval moulds of ¼ pt.
   or tinned consommé with gelatine,   capacity, preferably of metal
   page 102)

Pour a ⅛-inch layer of jelly into the bottom of each mould and chill until set.

6 large whole chicken livers

Look over the chicken livers, and cut out any blackish or greenish spots. Dry
the livers thoroughly.

An 8-in. enamelled frying pan   2 tbl finely chopped shallots or
1 oz. butter   spring onions
1 tbl oil

Place the frying pan over a moderately high heat with the butter and oil. When
you see that the butter foam has almost subsided, add the chicken livers. Stir and

toss for 2 minutes to brown the livers very lightly. Add the shallots or spring onions and toss for 5 seconds more. Hold a cover askew over the frying pan and drain out all the sautéing fat.

Big pinch of salt	**¼ pt. Madeira or port, or ⅛ pt.**
Pinch of pepper	**cognac**
Pinch of allspice	

Sprinkle seasonings over the livers; pour in the wine or cognac. Cover the frying pan and simmer very slowly for 8 minutes, then remove the livers to a side dish. Rapidly boil down the cooking juices until reduced to a syrupy consistency. Remove from heat, roll the livers in the frying pan to cover with the juices, and chill.

Optional: 6 slices of truffle	**Lettuce leaves**
Chilled plates or dish	

Place a slice of truffle (optional) over the jelly layer in each mould, and arrange a chicken liver over it. Fill the moulds with the remaining jelly, which should be like syrup and almost set. Chill for an hour or so. Unmould on chilled serving plates or a dish, over lettuce leaves.

VARIATION

Homard, Crabe, ou Crevettes en Aspic

[Lobster, Crab, or Shrimps in Aspic]

The preceding system may also be adapted for lobster, crab, or shrimp meat in aspic.

POULET EN GELÉE À L'ESTRAGON

[Chicken Tarragon in Aspic]

Also for: turkey, pigeons, guinea hen, and pheasant.

Chicken in tarragon jelly is one of the simplest and best of the cold poultry dishes. The chicken may be poached by complete immersion in tarragon-flavoured stock which is then clarified and turned into jelly, or you may follow the simpler version here.

For 6 people

Cooking the chicken

A 3-lb. ready-to-cook roasting
  chicken

⅛ tsp salt, ¼ oz. butter, and 3 sprigs
  fresh tarragon or ½ tsp dried
  tarragon for inside the chicken

1 oz. butter and 1 tbl oil for
  browning the chicken

A heavy, covered, fireproof
  casserole

¼ tsp salt

3 sprigs fresh tarragon or ½ tsp
  dried tarragon for the casserole

Following the procedure for casserole-roasted chicken with tarragon, page 225,
season the cavity with salt, butter, and tarragon. Truss and butter the chicken,
then brown it on all sides in hot butter and oil in a casserole. Salt the chicken,
add the tarragon, cover the casserole, and roast in a preheated 325° F., Mark 2
oven for 1 hour and 10 to 20 minutes. Remove the chicken, and let it cool to
room temperature. Then chill it.

The tarragon jelly

2 or 3 sprigs fresh tarragon or 1 tsp
  dried tarragon

1½ pts. jelly (jellied stock made
  from brown chicken stock,
  page 101, or tinned consommé
  with gelatine, page 102)

An enamelled saucepan

Stir the tarragon into the jelly; bring to simmering point, cover, and leave it to
steep over a very low heat for 10 minutes.

4 to 5 tbl Madeira or port

A chilled saucer

Remove from the heat, and stir in the wine by spoonfuls, tasting, until you have
achieved the flavour you wish. Strain through a very fine sieve or several
thicknesses of washed cheesecloth. Test a little of it in a chilled saucer in the
refrigerator, to be sure it will jell to the right consistency.

Decorating the chicken

An oval serving dish about 16 ins.
  long

Pour a ⅛-inch layer of jelly into the dish, and chill in the refrigerator until set.

Carve the chicken and arrange it over the layer of jelly. Return the dish to the
refrigerator.

A small saucepan

A bowl of cracked ice

Pour ½ pint of jelly into the saucepan and stir over ice until it has acquired a
syrupy consistency. Immediately remove from the ice, and spoon the almost-set

jelly over the chicken; this first layer will not adhere very well. Chill the chicken for 10 minutes, and spoon another layer of almost-set jelly over it. Repeat.

20 to 30 fresh tarragon leaves or   **A saucer of almost-set jelly**
    tarragon leaves preserved in
    vinegar
2 trussing needles or skewers, or a
    small pointed knife (for picking
    up the tarragon leaves)

Drop the tarragon leaves in boiling water for 10 seconds. Refresh in iced water, and dry. Dip each leaf in the almost-set jelly, and arrange in a decorative pattern over the chicken. Chill. Then spoon on a final layer of almost-set jelly.

A tin or dish

Pour the remaining jelly into the tin or dish and chill until set. Chop the jelly into $\frac{1}{8}$-inch pieces and distribute it around the chicken.

Refrigerate. Unless the weather is very warm, remove the chicken from the refrigerator half an hour before serving; it will have more flavour if it is not too cold.

---

* *SUPRÊMES DE VOLAILLE EN CHAUD-FROID, BLANCHE NEIGE*

[Breast of Chicken in *Chaud-froid*]

Here is a decorative, delicious, and easy-to-execute aspic which lends itself to numerous variations as suggested at the end of the recipe. The cold cream sauce for this, which congeals into an aspic covering over the chicken breasts, looks like the classic *sauce chaud-froid*—flour-based, jellied *velouté* with cream. The sauce *chaud-froid blanche neige* used here is purely a reduction of tarragon-flavoured stock and cream in which gelatine has been dissolved; it is much lighter and better in texture than the classic sauce, we think. Serve chicken breasts in *chaud-froid* as a luncheon dish, or as part of a cold buffet.

For 6 people

6 *suprêmes* (the skinless and boneless   **A serving dish**
    breast-halves from 3 frying   **Greaseproof paper**
    chickens)

Poach the chicken breasts in butter as described at the beginning of the recipe, *suprêmes de volaille à blanc*, page 243. Drain them, and let them cool to room temperature. Arrange them in a serving dish, cover with greaseproof paper, and chill.

½ pt. cream	1 sprig fresh tarragon or ¼ tsp dried
¾ pt. excellent white chicken stock, page 213; Or, chicken broth simmered for 20 minutes with 2 tbl thinly sliced carrots, 2 tbl thinly sliced onions, and a pinch of thyme	tarragon Salt and white pepper

Simmer the cream, chicken stock or broth, and tarragon slowly in the saucepan for about 10 minutes, until the mixture has reduced to ¾ pint. Correct seasoning, and strain.

¼ oz. gelatine	3 tbl dry white vermouth

Soften the gelatine in the vermouth for a few minutes. Then beat it into the cream mixture and stir over a low heat until the gelatine has dissolved completely. Cool, or stir over cracked ice, until the sauce has thickened slightly and is just about to congeal.

Spoon a layer of sauce over the chilled chicken breasts, and refrigerate until the sauce has set. Repeat with successive coats of almost-set sauce until all but enough for a final layer has been used.

A handful of fresh tarragon leaves or tarragon leaves preserved in vinegar; Or, thinly sliced or finely diced truffle	Watercress or parsley

Drop the tarragon leaves in boiling water for 30 seconds, refresh in iced water, and dry. Immediately after coating the chicken with the final layer of sauce, decorate with the tarragon leaves or truffles. Surround the edge of the dish with watercress, or sprigs of parsley, and refrigerate again until serving time.

AN ELABORATION

After the tarragon leaves or slices of truffle have set, the chicken breasts may be given one or two coats of almost-set jelly, as in the preceding recipe for chicken tarragon, and the dish may be decorated with chopped jelly or jelly cutouts.

VARIATIONS

Suprêmes de Volaille en Chaud-froid à l'Écossaise

[Breast of Chicken in *Chaud-froid* with Diced Vegetables]

Ingredients for the master recipe
1½ oz. each: finely diced carrots,
   celery, and onions cooked until
   tender in ¾ oz. butter

1 or 2 finely chopped truffles, or
   1 oz. diced mushrooms cooked
   in butter

Proceed as for the master recipe, but stir the cooked carrots, celery, and onions into the chicken stock and cream mixture as it is reducing. Mix in the truffles or mushrooms, then the gelatine called for in the recipe, and continue as directed. With this sauce, the chicken breasts need no other decoration.

Suprêmes et Mousse de Volaille en Chaud-froid

[Breasts of Chicken and Mousse of Chicken in *Chaud-froid*]

When you wish to make something wonderful for an elaborate buffet, such as a wedding breakfast, here is a good idea. Directions for chopped jelly, jelly cutouts, and other decorative elements are at the beginning of this section on aspics. We shall not note the number of servings for this recipe, as it is designed primarily to give you an indication of how to go about such a dish.

Ingredients for chicken breasts in
chaud-froid (the master recipe)

Cook and chill the chicken breasts and prepare the *chaud-froid* sauce as directed in the master recipe. The chicken breasts may be cut in halves or in thirds, if you wish.

A mousse of chicken, page
   517, or of chicken livers,
   page 516
A chilled serving dish

Sufficient jelly for glazing and for
   other decorations (jellied stock,
   page 101, or consommé with
   gelatine, page 102)

Unmould the mousse on the dish and pour around it a ⅛-inch layer of almost-set jelly. Chill.

Place the chilled chicken breasts on a rack placed over a tray, and coat the breasts with several layers of *chaud-froid* sauce, chilling between each layer. Decorate with truffles, tarragon leaves, or whatever else you wish; then chill and glaze with coats of almost-set jelly. With two knives lift each breast off the rack and arrange on the dish around the mousse. Decorate dish with chopped jelly or jelly cutouts. Chill until shortly before serving time.

Crabe ou Homard en Chaud-froid, Blanche Neige

[Crab or Lobster in *Chaud-froid*]

Crab or lobster in *chaud-froid* follows the general method of chicken breasts in *chaud-froid*, and makes a decorative cold first course or summer luncheon dish. Directions for steaming live lobster (which also apply to crab) are at the beginning of the lobster *Thermidor* recipe on page 199; boil down the steaming-liquid afterward, and use it in place of the fish stock called for in the following recipe.

For an hors d'œuvre serving 6 people

1 lb. cooked lobster or crab meat	⅛ tsp dry mustard
1½ oz. butter	Pinch cayenne pepper
An enamelled frying pan	Salt and pepper
2 tbl chopped shallots or spring onions	3 tbl cognac

Dice or flake the shellfish meat. Heat the butter to bubbling in the frying pan, then stir in the shallots or spring onions and shellfish meat, and cook slowly for 2 minutes. Stir in the mustard and cayenne pepper, and season to taste. Then pour in the cognac, and boil rapidly for a minute or two, shaking the frying pan, until the cognac has reduced almost completely. Chill.

½ pt. cream	1 sprig fresh tarragon or ¼ tsp dried
½ pt. white-wine fish stock	tarragon
(shellfish steaming-liquid, or the white-wine stock on page 103)	¼ oz. gelatine softened in 3 tbl dry white vermouth

Following the recipe for breast of chicken in *chaud-froid*, page 508, simmer the cream and stock together with the tarragon until reduced to ¾ pint. Dissolve the gelatine completely in the hot sauce, strain, correct seasoning, and cool until the sauce is almost set.

6 crab, lobster, or scallop shells, or porcelain or glass shells of about ¼ pt. capacity	Optional: ½ pt. almost-set jellied stock, page 101
Crab or lobster claws, scalloped shellfish meat, truffle slices, or blanched tarragon leaves (enough to decorate the shells)	

Fold ½ pint of the almost-set sauce into the chilled shellfish meat. Arrange the mixture in the shells, and coat with the remaining sauce. Decorate with shellfish claws, shellfish meat, truffle slices, or tarragon leaves. Then, if you wish, chill, and coat with a layer of jellied stock. Chill until shortly before serving time.

VOLAILLES EN ESCABÈCHE

[Cold Fowl in Lemon Jelly]

For: chicken, pigeon, mature pheasant and partridge.

The Paris restaurateur from whom we borrowed this recipe makes a speciality of *escabèche* in late autumn when partridge are no longer young, and have turned from *perdreau* to *perdrix*. The birds are slowly simmered in wine, stock, olive oil, vinegar, aromatic vegetables, herbs, garlic, and slices of lemon. They are cooled in this liquid which, because of the pectin in the lemon and the gelatine in the poultry bones, turns into a very light jelly. If you want a stiffer jelly, you can add powdered gelatine to the liquid after the birds are cooked. *Escabèche*, which is Spanish in origin, is usually associated with fish, but it is also extremely successful for elderly poultry as the lemon and vinegar help to tenderize the flesh. Simmering times for various birds are as follows:

Cut-up frying chicken, 1 hour.
Cut-up roasting chicken, 1½ hours.
Cut-up boiling chicken, 2½ hours or more.
Whole pigeon weighing about 1¼ pounds, 1½ hours.
Mature, whole partridge, 2 to 2½ hours.
Mature, cut-up pheasant, 2 to 2½ hours.

For 1 cut-up, 4-lb. boiling chicken (or 1 cut-up, 4-lb. pheasant, or 2 whole partridges, simmered according to the preceding time-table)

2 oz. each: thinly sliced onions,   A 3-pt. saucepan
   carrots and celery   ¼ pt. olive oil
6 cloves peeled garlic

Place the vegetables and garlic in the saucepan and cook slowly with the olive oil for 10 minutes without browning.

¼ pt. dry white wine or ¼ pt. dry   ¼ tsp rosemary
   white vermouth   ½ bay leaf
⅛ pt. wine vinegar   2 parsley sprigs
½ lemon cut into ⅛-in. slices   5 peppercorns
2 oz. thinly sliced green or red   ¾ pt. white stock or chicken broth
   peppers   Salt
¼ tsp thyme

Stir in all the ingredients above and simmer for 10 minutes. Taste for seasoning, and salt lightly if necessary.

A cut-up boiling chicken, plus the   A slotted spoon
  neck, heart, and peeled gizzard
A heavy, covered, fireproof
  casserole just large enough to
  hold the chicken

Place the neck, heart, and gizzard in the bottom of the casserole. Arrange the
dark meat over them. With a slotted spoon, distribute half the cooked vegetables
and lemon slices over the dark meat. Then put in the white meat, cover with
the rest of the vegetables, and pour on the cooking broth. Add water if necessary,
so that the chicken is just covered with liquid.

Bring to simmering point on top of the stove, cover, and simmer very slowly
either on the stove or in a preheated 300° F., Mark 1 oven for $2\frac{1}{2}$ hours, or until
the chicken is very tender but the meat does not fall from the bones. Uncover,
and allow the chicken to cool in the stock for half an hour. Remove any loose
bones.

A serving dish deep enough to hold   Salt and pepper
  chicken and sauce

Arrange the chicken in a deep serving dish. Ladle out the vegetables and lemon
slices and distribute them on and around the chicken. Skim the fat and oil off the
cooking stock and boil the stock down rapidly if necessary until it has reduced
to $\frac{3}{4}$ pint. Correct seasoning, and strain over the chicken. Allow the dish to cool
to room temperature, then cover and refrigerate. When chilled, the sauce will
thicken into the consistency of a jellied soup.

BOEUF MODE EN GELÉE

[Cold Braised Beef in Aspic]

The braised beef on page 283 can be turned into a splendid cold dish with
very little trouble. If you are going to make the traditional recipe, the proceedings must be started at least the day before you are to serve; the beef needs 24
hours of marination, 5 hours for browning and braising, and 4 to 6 hours for
chilling in jelly. Once made, it may be covered and kept under refrigeration
for 2 to 3 days. A light red wine and French bread would go very well with it.

For 10 to 12 people

Ingredients for the marination and   boneless beef, page 283, including
  braising of a 5-lb. piece of   the braised carrots and onions

Marinate and braise the beef, and braise the carrots and onions according to the
recipe, but omit the final sauce-thickening step. Remove the meat to a carving
board.

R

½ oz. gelatine   Salt and pepper
1¼ pts. cold brown stock or tinned   ⅛ pt. port or brandy
   consommé   A chilled saucer

Degrease the braising liquid thoroughly, then boil it down until it has reduced
to 1½ to 2 pints. Soften the gelatine in the cold stock or consommé, pour it into
the braising liquid and stir over a low heat until the gelatine has dissolved
completely. Correct seasoning carefully. Pour in the port or brandy and strain.
The liquid has now become a jelly; test a little of it in a chilled saucer as described
on page 103.

For a simple arrangement in a mould

A rectangular mould, *terrine*, or
** baking dish large enough to hold**
** the sliced meat and vegetables**

Slice the beef into serving pieces and arrange in the mould, interspersing the
slices with the braised carrots and onions. Pour in the jelly, which need not be
cold. Chill for 4 to 6 hours, or until well set.

A chilled serving dish
Watercress, parsley, or leaves of
** lettuce**

When ready to serve, dip the mould in hot water for several seconds. Run a
knife around the edge of the aspic. Turn dish over mould, reverse, and give a
sharp jerk to unmould aspic on dish. Decorate dish with watercress, parsley, or
lettuce.

For a more elaborate arrangement on a dish

Cut the beef into serving pieces and chill. Chill the braised onions and carrots.

An oval serving dish

Pour ⅛ inch of the jelly into the serving dish and chill until set. Then arrange the
chilled meat and vegetables on the layer of jelly.

A small saucepan set in a bowl of
** cracked ice**

Pour ¾ pint of jelly into the saucepan and stir over cracked ice until the jelly is
of a syrupy consistency, and on the point of setting. Spoon a layer over the meat
and vegetables. Chill for 10 minutes. Repeat with 2 or 3 more layers of almost-
set jelly, chilling the meat between each. Chill the remaining jelly, chop into
⅛-inch pieces, and arrange it around the dish.

MOULDED MOUSSES
Mousses Froides—Mousselines

A beautifully flavoured and moulded creation glittering in aspic is always impressive as a first course, as a luncheon dish, or on a cold buffet table. All of the following are purées of chicken liver, poultry, ham, or fish mixed with wine and seasonings and, in all but one recipe, jellied stock. Softened butter or lightly whipped cream is combined with them to give body and what the French call *moelleux* or a velvety texture. An electric liquidizer is a great time-saver. If you do not have one, pass meat twice through the mincer (fish may be puréed in a moulinette) then beat in the liquids.

The first recipe in this section may be packed into a decorative bowl and served just as it is; the rest must be moulded. If they are moulded plain, without a jelly lining in the mould, they should be glazed with jelly after they are unmoulded, or with a type of *chaud-froid* sauce such as the one described for the fish mousse on page 519. They may then be decorated with truffles, tarragon leaves, jelly cutouts, or, if it is a fish mousse, with designs of shellfish meat.

HOW TO *CHEMISER UN MOULE* OR LINE A MOULD WITH JELLY

A mould lined with jelly is one which contains a fairly stiff coating of jellied stock about ⅛ inch thick all over its inside surface. The mousse is packed into the lined mould, and chilled. When unmoulded, the mousse is encased in a shell of jelly. The jelly should be made from clarified stock so that it will be clear, glistening, and transparent. Recipes for stock, clarification, home-made jellied stock, and jellies made from tinned consommé begin on page 95.

You can roll a mould over cracked ice with spoonfuls of jellied stock until an adequate layer of jelly has been built up inside the mould, or you can use the following method which we find easier.

1½ pts. clarified jelly (jellied stock,   **A bowl of cracked ice**
   page 101, or consommé with
   gelatine, page 102)

The jelly should be fairly stiff; be sure to test it as directed in the recipe for jellies before you line the mould. Chill the jelly over cracked ice until of a syrupy consistency and almost set.

A 1½ pt. mould, preferably of metal
   as it is easier to unmould

Then pour the almost-set jelly into the mould and place the mould in cracked ice. Watch it carefully, and as soon as a ⅛-inch layer of jelly has set around the edges of the mould, pour out the unset jelly. If there is too thick a layer of jelly in the bottom of the mould, scoop it out with a spoon dipped in hot water.

Chill the mould for about 20 minutes until the jelly lining is stiff. Then pack the cold mousse into the mould as directed in whatever recipe you are following.

DECORATIONS

If you wish to decorate the bottom of a mould, begin by pouring into it a $\frac{1}{16}$-inch layer of jelly and chill until firm. Choose any of the decorative suggestions on pages 503-4, or sliced poultry meat, ham, tongue, shrimp, or lobster; cut into shapes and chill. Dip into almost-set jelly, and arrange on the jelly in the bottom of the mould. Chill until set, then proceed to line the mould with jelly as described in the preceding directions.

HOW TO UNMOULD AN ASPIC

Dip the mould in very hot water for 3 to 4 seconds (a non-metal mould will require a few seconds longer). Quickly wipe it dry. Invert a chilled serving dish over it, and turn it upside down. Give it a sharp downward jerk to dislodge it from the mould to the dish.

Another method is to invert the mould on a chilled dish, and surround the mould with a cloth wrung out in very hot water. As soon as the aspic drops, remove the mould.

MOUSSE DE FOIES DE VOLAILLE

[Chicken Liver Mousse]

The following mousse may be packed into a decorative jar and used as a spread for cocktail appetizers, or moulded in aspic for an hors d'œuvre. It is easy to make in an electric liquidizer; if you do not have one, purée the liver in a mincer or moulinette.

For about 1 pound

1 lb. chicken livers	1 oz. butter
2 tbl chopped shallots or spring onions	A frying pan
	An electric liquidizer

Look the livers over and remove any greenish or blackish spots. Cut the livers into $\frac{1}{2}$-inch pieces. Sauté with the shallots or spring onions in hot butter for 2 to 3 minutes, until the livers are just stiffened, but still rosy inside. Scrape into the liquidizer jar.

$\frac{1}{8}$ pt. Madeira or cognac

Pour the wine or cognac into the sauté pan and boil it down rapidly until it has reduced to 3 tablespoons. Scrape it into the liquidizer jar.

⅛ pt. cream   ⅛ tsp pepper
½ tsp salt   Pinch of thyme
⅛ tsp allspice

Add the cream and seasonings to the liquidizer jar. Cover and blend at top speed
for several seconds until the liver is a smooth paste.

4 oz. melted butter

Then add the melted butter and blend several seconds more.

A fairly fine-meshed sieve   Salt and pepper
A wooden spoon

Force the mixture through the sieve and taste carefully for seasoning.

A decorative bowl or jar   Greaseproof paper

Pack into the bowl or jar, cover with greaseproof paper, and chill for 2 to 3
hours. Or chill until almost set, then pack into a mould lined with jelly as
described on page 515; chill for several hours before unmoulding.

---

* *MOUSSELINE DE VOLAILLE*

[Mousse of Chicken, Turkey, Duck, or Game]

This is an excellent way to use up cold fowl, and you may mix several
kinds together if you wish. *Foie gras*, liver *pâté*, or chicken livers, a good stock,
wine, and careful seasoning give character to the blandness of the meat. If you
do not have an electric liquidizer, purée the ingredients with a mincer.

To serve 8 to 10 people

3 tbl chopped shallots or spring   ½ oz. gelatine softened in ⅛ pt. dry
  onions   white wine or vermouth
½ oz. butter   An electric liquidizer
A 1½-pt. saucepan
¾ pt. well flavoured poultry stock
  or white stock; Or: chicken broth
  simmered for 20 minutes with
  2 tbl of thinly sliced carrots,
  celery, and onions, and a herb
  bouquet, then strained

Cook the shallots or spring onions slowly with the butter in the saucepan for 2
minutes without browning. Add the stock and the gelatine mixture, and simmer
for 1 minute. Pour into the liquidizer jar.

1 lb. chopped, cooked chicken,	A 2½-qt. mixing bowl
turkey, duck, or game-bird meat	
2 oz. *foie gras* (goose liver), or	
liver paste; Or: 2 oz. chicken	
livers lightly sautéed in butter	

Add the poultry meat and *foie gras*, liver paste, or sautéed livers to the liquidizer. Cover and blend at top speed for a minute or two until the ingredients are puréed. Pour into the bowl.

| 2 to 3 tbl cognac or Madeira | Pinch of nutmeg |
| Salt and pepper | |

Beat in the cognac or wine to taste, and overseason slightly as the cream, which comes later, will mask the flavour a little. Cover and chill until almost set, stirring occasionally.

¼ pt. chilled cream	A 2½-pt. mould, lightly oiled;
A chilled bowl	Or: a 3-pt. mould lined with
A chilled wire whisk	jelly, page 515
Optional: 1 or 2 chopped truffles	

Following directions on page 535, beat the cream until it has doubled in volume and holds its shape softly. Fold the cream and optional truffles into the cold chicken mixture. Pack into the mould. Cover with greaseproof paper and chill for several hours before unmoulding.

VARIATIONS

Mousse de Jambon

[Ham Mousse]

Use the same recipe and ingredients as for the preceding chicken mousse, but substitute 1¼ pounds of lean, chopped, boiled ham for the chicken and *foie gras*; a tablespoon of tomato paste may be added for colour. Either 1 or 2 diced truffles or 2 ounces chopped mushrooms sautéed in butter may be folded into the mousse with the cream.

Mousse de Saumon

[Salmon Mousse]

Use the same recipe and ingredients as for the master recipe, chicken mousse, but with 1¼ pounds of cooked or tinned salmon instead of chicken and *foie gras*, and use a white-wine fish stock, page 103, instead of white stock.

* MOUSSELINE DE POISSON, BLANCHE NEIGE

[Fish Mousse—with shellfish and *chaud-froid* sauce]

This is a handsome cold dish for a first course or luncheon, and looks well on a cold buffet table. It is important, however, that you season the mixture with care, and use an excellent stock for your jelly, or the flavour of the mousse will not be interesting. Instead of moulding the mousse, you may heap it into individual serving shells, then sauce and decorate them as suggested in the recipe.

If you do not have an electric liquidizer, purée the cooked fish in a moulinette.

To serve 8 to 10 people

1¼ pts. very good white-wine fish stock, page 103 (note that ½ pt. is to be reserved for sauce at end of recipe)

6 oz. skinless and boneless sole, turbot, or brill fillets

A small herb bouquet: 2 parsley sprigs, ⅓ bay leaf, and ⅛ tsp thyme tied in cheesecloth

A 2-qt. enamelled saucepan

Place ¾ pint of the fish stock with the fish and herb bouquet in the saucepan. Bring slowly almost to simmering point, cover, and poach the fish at just below simmering point for about 8 minutes, or until just tender when pierced with a fork.

An electric liquidizer

A slotted spoon

Remove the fish to the liquidizer jar with a slotted spoon. Discard herb bouquet.

½ lb. diced fresh mushrooms

Add the mushrooms to the fish stock in the saucepan. Boil slowly for 8 minutes. Strain, leave mushrooms aside, and return liquid to saucepan.

½ oz. gelatine softened in 4 tbl dry white vermouth

Salt and white pepper

A 2-qt. mixing bowl

Stir the gelatine mixture into the liquid in the saucepan and simmer a moment to dissolve the gelatine completely. Pour into the liquidizer jar with the fish. Cover and blend at top speed for a minute or two until puréed. Taste very carefully for seasoning. Pour into a bowl, stir in the mushrooms, and chill. Stir occasionally until cold and almost set.

¼ pt. chilled cream, lightly beaten, page 535

A 2½-pt. lightly oiled ring mould

A chilled serving dish

Fold the cream into the cold fish mixture, and turn into the oiled mould. Cover with greaseproof paper and chill for several hours to set. When ready to decorate, unmould the mousse on the dish and cover with the following sauce.

Sauce chaud-froid, blanche neige ($\frac{3}{4}$ pint)

The remaining fish stock from	**$\frac{1}{4}$ oz. gelatine softened in 3 tbl dry**
first paragraph ($\frac{1}{2}$ pt.)	**white vermouth**
$\frac{1}{2}$ pt. cream	**Salt and white pepper**
$\frac{1}{4}$ tsp tarragon	**A bowl of cracked ice**

Simmer the stock, cream, and tarragon in a saucepan until reduced to $\frac{3}{4}$ pint. Stir in the gelatine mixture and simmer a moment to dissolve it completely. Correct seasoning, and strain. Stir over cracked ice until the sauce thickens lightly and is about to set.

$\frac{3}{4}$ lb. cooked shrimp, lobster, or	**Thin slices of truffle or any of the**
crab meat warmed in $\frac{1}{8}$ pt. dry	**decorative suggestions on pages**
white wine or vermouth, seasoned	**503-4**
with salt and pepper, then chilled	

Fold $\frac{1}{4}$ pint of the sauce into the chilled shellfish, and place in the centre of the mousse. Coat the mousse and shellfish with several spoonfuls of sauce. Chill for 10 minutes, and repeat with layers of almost-set sauce. Immediately after the last application of sauce, decorate the mousse with truffles or whatever else you have chosen. Chill until serving time.

VARIATION

Mousseline de Crustacés, Blanche Neige

[Shellfish Mousse]

Substitute cooked shellfish meat for the sole in the preceding recipe, but omit the simmering of fish in stock, paragraph one.

PÂTÉS AND TERRINES
Pâtés et Terrines

The memory of a good French *pâté* can haunt you for years. Fortunately they are easy to make and you can even develop your own special *pâté maison*. Do not expect a top-notch mixture to be inexpensive, however, for it will contain minced pork, pork fat, and usually veal, as well as cognac, port, or Madeira, spices, strips or cubes of other meats, game, or liver, and often truffles. If the mixture is cooked and served cold in its baking dish it is called either a *terrine* or a *pâté*. If it is moulded in a pastry crust, it is a *pâté en croûte*. A boned chicken, turkey, or duck filled with the same type of mixture is a galantine.

Pâtés and *terrines* will keep for about 10 days under refrigeration; they are fine to have on hand for cold impromptu meals, since all you need to serve with them is a salad and French bread.

Wines to serve with *pâtés* include the dry whites such as Chablis or Mâcon, *rosés*, or one of the light regional red wines such as Beaujolais or Chinon.

A NOTE ON PORK FAT

Fresh pork fat is an essential ingredient for the type of meat mixture which goes into a *pâté*. Blended with the meats, it prevents them from being dry and gives them a lighter texture. Cut into thin sheets, *bardes de lard*, it is used to line the inside of the baking dish. The best type is fat back—*lard gras*. This comes from the back of the pig next to the skin. It is firm and does not disintegrate as easily as fat from other parts of the animal. Fresh fat back is best. Alternatives are fat salt pork simmered for 10 minutes in water to freshen it and remove the salt, or fat trimmed from fresh leg, or from around a fresh loin of pork. Thick strips of fat bacon, simmered for 10 minutes in water to remove the smoky taste, may be used to line a baking dish.

BAKING DISHES

Pâtés may be cooked in almost any kind of a baking dish from a special rectangular or oval mould called a *terrine*, to a soufflé dish, casserole, or bread tin. The best materials are glazed pottery, porcelain, enamelled iron, or oven-glass. Cover the meat mixture with aluminium foil, and the dish with a heavy lid; old recipes call for a cover held in place with a thick band of flour and water paste.

STORAGE

Pâtés, *terrines*, and galantines may be deep-frozen, but they will never again have their original texture. Once you have compared the two, you will always recognize the somewhat damp quality of thawed *pâté*. If a *pâté* is to be kept for 10 days or more under refrigeration, it should be unmoulded after it has been chilled and the meat jelly wiped off its surface. It may then be wrapped airtight in greaseproof paper and foil, or returned to its *terrine* and covered with melted pork fat.

ASPIC

(Recipes for aspics are on pages 101 to 103; instructions for lining and decorating moulds start on page 502.)

To serve a *pâté* in aspic unmould the *pâté* after it has been chilled, and scrape off the layer of pork fat surrounding it. Line the bottom of a slightly larger mould with a ⅛-inch layer of jellied stock and chill until set. Place the *pâté* in the mould, and pour almost-set jellied stock around and over it. Chill. Unmould on a chilled dish.

R*

Another system is to slice the chilled *pâté*, arrange it on a dish lined with jellied stock, and then glaze the slices with jelly as for the *boeuf mode en gelée* on page 513.

FARCE POUR PÂTÉS, TERRINES, ET GALANTINES

[Pork and Veal Stuffing]

This good general-purpose meat mixture we shall refer to as a stuffing, for that is a translation of the French generic term *farce*. It can be used as the basis for any type of *pâté*, *terrine*, or galantine you wish. Mixed with chestnuts, it can also serve as a filling for roast goose or turkey. The pork gives flavour, the veal gives lightness. The proportions may be changed according to your own ideas, and sautéed liver, minced poultry, or game may be beaten into it. Chopped truffles are always a good addition, and you can include such things as pistachios, or strips or cubes of pork fat, tongue, or ham to give a pattern to the meat when it is sliced.

For about 2 pounds

4 tbl very finely chopped onions	A large mixing bowl
1 oz. butter	

Cook the onions slowly with the butter in a small frying pan for 8 to 10 minutes until they are tender and translucent but not browned. Scrape them into the mixing bowl.

¼ pt. port, Madeira, or cognac

Pour the wine into the frying pan and boil it down until reduced by half. Scrape it into the mixing bowl.

¾ lb. each, lean pork and lean veal and ½ lb. fresh pork fat, all finely minced together	⅛ tsp pepper
	Big pinch of allspice
2 lightly beaten eggs	½ tsp thyme
1½ tsp salt	Optional: 1 clove mashed garlic
	A wooden spoon

Add all the ingredients above, and beat vigorously with a wooden spoon until the mixture has lightened in texture and is thoroughly blended. Sauté a small spoonful and taste. Then beat in whatever additions you feel are necessary. It should be perfectly flavoured. If not to be used immediately, cover and refrigerate.

* TERRINE DE PORC, VEAU, ET JAMBON

[Pork and Veal *Pâté* with Ham]

A pork and veal *pâté* with decorative strips of veal and ham buried in its slices is the most classic of all *pâté* mixtures; the three elements blend themselves in a very savoury manner.

For about 3 pounds

Marinating the veal strips

½ lb. lean veal from the round or fillet cut into strips ¼ in. thick

Optional: 2 or 3 tinned truffles cut into ¼-in. dice, and juice from tin

A bowl

3 tbl cognac

Big pinch of salt and pepper

Pinch of thyme

Pinch of allspice

1 tbl finely chopped shallots or spring onions

Marinate the veal and optional truffles and their juice in a bowl with the cognac and flavourings while preparing the other ingredients. Before using, drain the strips, and reserve the marinade.

Moulding the pâté

Preheat oven to 350° F., Mark 4.

A 3½-pt. rectangular or oval *terrine*, baking dish, casserole, or loaf tin

Sheets of fresh pork fat back ⅛ in. thick, or blanched fat salt pork, or blanched fat bacon, page 12

The preceding pork and veal stuffing (about 2 pounds)

½ lb. lean boiled ham cut into strips ¼ in. thick

1 bay leaf

A sheet of pork fat or strips of blanched bacon to cover the *pâté*

Line the bottom and sides of the *terrine* with the pork fat or bacon. Beat marinade into stuffing; divide stuffing into three parts. Dip your hands in cold water, and arrange the first third of the stuffing in the bottom of the *terrine*. Cover with half the strips of marinated veal alternating with half the strips of ham. If using diced truffles, place a row down the centre. Cover with the second third of the stuffing, and a final layer of veal and ham strips, and optional truffles. Spread on the last of the meat stuffing. Lay the bay leaf on top, and cover with a sheet of pork fat or bacon strips.

Baking the pâté

Aluminium foil

A heavy lid for the *terrine*

A pan of boiling water

Enclose the top of the *terrine* with aluminium foil, cover, and place in the pan of boiling water. The water should come about half-way up the outside of the *terrine*; add boiling water during cooking, as necessary. Place in lower part of preheated oven and bake for about 1½ hours depending on the shape of the *terrine*; a long loaf shape will cook faster than a round or oval shape. The *pâté* is done when it has shrunk slightly from the sides of the *terrine*, and the surrounding fat and juices are clear yellow with no traces of rosy colour.

Cooling and chilling

Take the *terrine* from the water and place it on a plate. Remove lid, and on top of the foil covering the *pâté* put a piece of wood, a pan, or a casserole which will just fit into the *terrine*. On or in it, place a 3- to 4-lb. weight or parts of a mincer; this will pack the *pâté* into the *terrine* so there will be no air spaces in the meat. Allow the *pâté* to cool at room temperature for several hours or overnight. Then chill it, still weighted down.

Serving

Serve the *pâté* from its *terrine*, slicing down through it with a knife. Or unmould it and serve on a dish, or decorate in aspic as suggested on page 521.

VARIATIONS

Pâté de Veau et Porc avec Gibier

[Game *Pâté*]

For rabbit, hare, partridge, pheasant, duck, and other game

1 lb. boneless, skinless, raw game
Ingredients for the preceding pork
    and veal *pâté*, minus the veal
    strips and ham strips

Following the preceding recipe, cut the game meat into strips ¼ inch wide, and marinate them in cognac and seasonings. Mince the smaller pieces and beat them into the stuffing mixture; then proceed with the recipe.

Pâté de Veau et Porc avec Foie

[Pork and Veal *Pâté* with Liver]

Ingredients for the pork and veal   **1 lb. liver: chicken, calf, lamb,**
    ***pâté* in the preceding master**   **pork, or beef**
    recipe, minus the veal strips and
    ham strips

Follow the master recipe, but after cooking the onions for the meat stuffing, cut the liver into ⅛-inch pieces and sauté with the onions for 2 to 3 minutes until the liver is slightly stiffened but still rosy inside. Scrape into the mixing bowl, and proceed with the recipe. (The cognac and other ingredients listed in the recipe as a marinade may be beaten into your meat stuffing, if you wish.)

A NOTE ON GALANTINES

The boned and stuffed duck in the following recipe would be a *galantine de canard* rather than a *canard en croûte* if it were stuffed, then wrapped in a damp cloth, poached in meat stock, cooled with a weight over it, chilled, and glazed with jellied stock. The same system may be used also for large roasting chickens and turkeys.

PÂTÉ EN CROÛTE

[*Pâté* Baked in a Crust]

The recipe we have chosen to illustrate *pâté en croûte* is boned duck stuffed, reformed, surrounded with decorated pastry, and baked. The same method may be used for any of the *pâté* mixtures previously described, and they do not have

Canard en Croûte

to be enclosed in duck skin. You may simply heap the mixture into a loaf on an oval of pastry and enclose it with a second oval. Or you may line a hinged mould with pastry, pack the mixture into it, and cover with more pastry. All *pâtés en croûte*, in other words, follow the same general outline for forming and baking.

HOW TO BONE A DUCK, TURKEY, OR CHICKEN

You may think that boning a fowl is an impossible feat if you have never seen it done or thought of attempting it. Although the procedure may take 45 minutes the first time because of fright, it can be accomplished in not much more than 20 on your second or third try. The object is to remove the flesh with the skin from the carcass bones without piercing the skin except at the back where the bird is slit open, and at the natural openings at the vent and neck. This skin, which is laid flat on a board, is to serve as the container. The *pâté* mixture is heaped on to it, then the skin is folded over the *pâté* mixture and sewed in place. When baked in a *terrine* and unmoulded, or baked in a crust, the sutures are on the bottom, and the *pâté* appears to be enclosed in an un-broken, browned casing—which is the skin. It is always an impressive sight. The important thing to remember is that the cutting edge of your knife must always face the bone, never the flesh, thus you cannot pierce the skin.

To begin with, cut a deep slit down the back of the bird from the neck to the tail, to expose the backbone. With a small, sharp knife, its edge always cutting against the bone, scrape and cut the flesh from the carcass bones down one side of the bird, pulling the flesh away from the carcass with your fingers as you cut. When you come to the ball joints connecting the wings and the second joints to the carcass, sever them, and continue down the carcass until you reach just the ridge of the breast where skin and bone meet. Then stop. You must be careful here, as the skin is thin and easily slit. Repeat the same operation on the other side of the bird. By the time you have completed half of this, the carcass frame, dangling legs, wings, and skin will appear to be an unrecognizable mass of confusion and you will wonder how in the world any sense can be made of it all. But just continue cutting against the bone, and not slitting any skin, and all will come out as it should. When you finally arrive at the ridge of the breastbone on this opposite side, stop again. Then lift the carcass frame and cut very closely against the ridge of the breastbone to free the carcass, but not to slit the thin skin covering the breastbone. Chop off the wings at the elbows, to leave just the upper wing bones attached.

Then arrange this mass of skin and flesh on a board, flesh side up. You will now see, protruding from the flesh, the pair of ball joints of the wings and of the two second joints. Scrape the meat from the bones of the wings and pull out the bones. Repeat for the second joints, severing them from the ball joints of the drumsticks; the drumstick bones may be left in place if you wish. Discard any bits of fat adhering to the flesh, and the bird is ready to become a *pâté* or a galantine.

PÂTÉ DE CANARD EN CROÛTE

[Boned Stuffed Duck Baked in a Pastry Crust]

For 12 people

Stuffing the duck

A 5-lb. ready-to-cook roasting duckling	**2 tbl cognac**
½ tsp salt	**2 tbl port**
⅛ tsp pepper	**Optional: 2 or 3 diced tinned**
Pinch of allspice	**truffles and their juice**

Bone the duck as described in the preceding paragraphs, and lay the boned bird skin-side down on a board. Slice off the thickest layers of breast and thigh meat, and cut into cubes about ½ inch across. Place the cubes back on the duck, season, and sprinkle with cognac and port. Add the optional truffles and their juice. Roll up the duck, place it in a bowl, and refrigerate.

2 lbs. pork and veal stuffing,
page 522

Prepare the meat stuffing and mix into it the cubed duck meat, optional truffles, and marinade.

A trussing needle   **White string**

Spread the boned duck on a board, skin-side down. Heap the stuffing in the centre and shape it into a loaf. Bring the duck skin up over the loaf to enclose

Boned duck
with stuffing

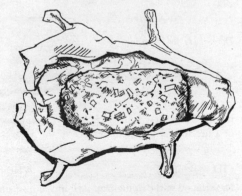

NOTE: *In this and following drawings, wing bones and drumsticks have not been removed.*

NINE: COLD BUFFET

Duck skin folded around stuffing

Sewing the duck

Duck ready for browning

it completely. Sew it in place with a trussing needle and white string. Make 3 or 4 ties around the circumference of the duck to give it a cylindrical shape.

3 tbl cooking oil   **A large frying pan**

Heat the oil in the frying pan until it is almost smoking. Then brown the duck slowly on all sides. Remove, and allow it to cool. The trussing strings remain on the duck to hold its shape while baking.

Forming the crust

1¼ lbs. plain white flour
2 oz. lard
4 oz. butter
1½ tsp salt

¼ tsp sugar
2 eggs
About ¼ pt. cold water

Following directions on page 126, prepare chilled pastry with the ingredients above.

Preheat oven to 400° F., Mark 6.

A greased baking sheet
A pastry brush

1 egg beaten with 1 tsp cold water
in a small bowl

Roll two-thirds of the pastry dough into an oval ⅛ inch thick. Lay it on the baking sheet. Place the duck on the oval, breast up. Bring the pastry up around

Duck in bottom pastry oval

the duck, patting it into place. Roll out the rest of the dough ⅛ inch thick and cut it into an oval to fit over the top of the duck. Paint the edges of the bottom

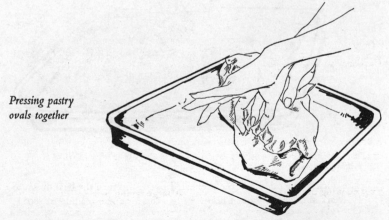

*Pressing pastry
ovals together*

pastry oval with a pastry brush dipped in beaten egg, and press the top oval in place. Flute or pinch the edges together to seal them.

Make circles or ovals with a 1½-inch biscuit cutter in the remaining pastry, and press fan-shaped lines into them with the back of a knife.

Pastry cutouts

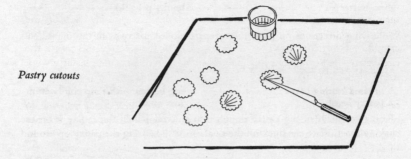

Paint the top pastry oval with beaten egg, and press the pastry cutouts over it in a decorative design. Paint with beaten egg.

Make a ⅛-inch hole in the centre of the pastry and insert a brown paper or foil funnel; this will allow cooking steam to escape. Insert a meat thermometer into the hole through the funnel, and down through the duck skin into the *pâté*.

*The duck
is ready
for the
oven*

Baking the pâté

Place the duck in the middle of the preheated oven, and turn the heat down to 350° F., Mark 4. Bake for about 2 hours, or to a thermometer reading of 180° F.

Remove from oven and allow to cool for several hours; the crust will soften if the *pâté* is refrigerated too soon. Then chill.

TO SERVE

A little preliminary work in the kitchen will enable you to present your duck with the elegance and drama it deserves. Before bringing it to the table, then, cut around the crust just under the seam of the top pastry oval; lift the oval off carefully so as not to break it. The duck will have shrunk from the crust during its baking, so you can lift it out of the bottom crust. Remove the circular trussing strings from around the duck, then cut and pull out the sewing strings underneath the duck.

If carving is to take place at the table, put the duck back into the bottom crust and replace the top pastry oval. The carver will then decide whether to remove the duck from the crust and carve it as suggested farther on, or whether to cut right down through the crust and through the duck, making crosswise slices of duck with crust.

If the duck is to be carved before serving, follow either of the two methods in the next paragraph, then reconstruct the duck in its bottom crust, and replace the top pastry oval.

To carve the duck after removing it from the crust, either make crosswise slices as though you were cutting a sausage, or make a deep incision the length of the breast, and cut lengthwise slices angled towards the centre of the duck on each side.

OTHER COLD DISHES

Here is a list of dishes which are described as hot elsewhere in the book, but which you may also serve cold.

Eggs

Oeufs brouillés pipérade, scrambled eggs garnished with a *pipérade* (the cooked green peppers, onions, and tomatoes used for *omelette pipérade* on page 124). The *pipérade* is mixed into the eggs after they have been scrambled; the eggs are chilled, and used to fill tomato cases.

Poultry

Poulet grillé à la diable, chicken with herbs, mustard, and breadcrumbs, page 241.

Poulet sauté and *poulet sauté aux herbes de Provence*, either of these two recipes for sautéed chicken beginning on page 229, without the sauce.

Poulet poêlé à l'estragon, casserole-roasted chicken with tarragon, page 225. This is one of the best ways to cook a whole chicken that is to be served cold.

Caneton à l'orange, duck with orange, page 251, or with the other fruits suggested in the recipes following it. The sauce is made according to the directions in the recipe but, instead of thickening the sauce with arrowroot, dissolve gelatine in it (¼ ounce for each ¾ pint), and glaze the duck as in the recipe for *poulet en gelée à l'estragon*, page 506.

Beef

Daube de boeuf, casserole of beef with wine, herbs, and vegetables, page 296.

Lamb

Moussaka, lamb and aubergine baked in a mould lined with aubergine skins, then unmoulded, page 319. This makes a handsome cold dish, and is an excellent way to use up cold roast lamb.

Pork and Veal

Veau poêlé or *rôti de porc poêlé*, casserole-roasted veal with herbs, page 323, or pork, page 349. Both of these are good cold, and if you wish to dress them up, slice the meat and spread each slice with *beurre Montpellier* (green herb mayonnaise with butter, anchovies, pickles, and capers, page 81), reform the roast, and spread with a covering of the mayonnaise. Chill before serving.

Veau Sylvie or *porc Sylvie*, veal marinated in wine then stuffed with ham and cheese before roasting, page 328, or pork treated in the same manner, page 353.

Ham

Jambon braisé au Madère, ham braised in Madeira wine, page 361. See also the recipes following it, for ham braised with mushroom stuffing, and ham in a pastry crust. All of these are good cold, and a pleasant change from plain cold, baked or boiled ham.

Sweetbreads and Brains

Ris de veau braisés or *cervelles braisées*, braised sweetbreads, page 376, or brains, page 382. Either may be dressed with vinaigrette and herbs and used as a cold meat dish, or as part of a combination salad.

Artichokes

Artichauts au naturel or *fonds d'artichauts à blanc*, cold boiled artichokes, page 391, or cooked artichoke hearts, page 396. Either of these may be served with vinaigrette or mayonnaise. You may fill cold, cooked artichoke hearts with vegetables, meat, poultry, or fish in mayonnaise; you could also fill them with one of the aspics or mousses described in this chapter.

Aubergine

Aubergines farcies duxelles, aubergine cases stuffed with mushrooms, page 461. These go well with cold, roast lamb.

Ratatouille, aubergine casserole with tomatoes, onions, and courgettes, page 436. This dish is just as good cold as it is hot, and is especially recommended with cold roast lamb, beef, pork, chicken, and fish. A little leftover *ratatouille* may be passed through a moulinette with hard-boiled egg yolks to make a filling for stuffed eggs or stuffed tomatoes.

Celery and Leeks

Céleris braisés and *poireaux braisés*, braised celery, page 451, braised leeks, page 455. Either of these may be part of a cold vegetable combination, or be served with cold meats.

Potatoes

Gratin de pommes de terre provençale, potato and tomato casserole with anchovies, page 485. Serve this with cold meats or fish.

CHAPTER TEN

DESSERTS AND CAKES

Entremets et Gâteaux

FUNDAMENTAL TECHNIQUES
AND INFORMATION

ONE OR SEVERAL of the following processes will be a part of almost any dessert or cake recipe you encounter. Some can be accomplished by machine, others are better performed by hand. None is difficult, but all contribute to the success of your dish and must be done precisely.

EGG WHITES

Innumerable desserts, as well as soufflés and all the spongecakes, call for stiffly beaten egg whites. Successful cooking of any of these dishes is usually dependent on how voluminous and stiff you have beaten the egg whites, and how carefully you have folded them into the rest of the ingredients. As they are so important, we shall continually put in little reminders and warnings about them. Directions and illustrations for egg whites begin on page 143, in the Entrée chapter. You will note that in all the recipes for beaten egg whites in this chapter a tablespoon of sugar is whipped into them near the end of the beating; this gives them an added bit of stiffness and body. You will also note that egg whites may be folded into either a hot or a cold sauce or batter; unlike whipped cream, which liquefies when it comes in contact with hot ingredients, egg whites are not affected.

BEATING EGGS AND SUGAR TO FORM THE RIBBON

Whenever egg yolks and sugar are beaten together the recipe will say to continue beating 'until the mixture is pale yellow and forms the ribbon'. This prepares the egg yolks so that they can be heated without turning granular. To accomplish it, add the sugar gradually to the egg yolks in a mixing bowl while beating with a wire whisk or an electric beater; continue beating for 2 to 3 minutes. The mixture will turn a pale, creamy yellow, and thicken enough so that when a little is lifted in the beater, it will fall back into the bowl forming a slowly dissolving ribbon on the surface of the mixture. Do not beat beyond this point or the egg yolks may become granular.

WHIPPED CREAM

As used in French cooking, whipped cream should double in volume, and be light, smooth, and free from granules. Much the same principles apply to it as to the beating of egg whites, in that you must incorporate as much air as possible. The stationary electric beater never produces as smooth and light a cream as could be wished; the electric liquidizer is not recommended at all. Chilled double cream beaten at a leisurely pace of 2 strokes per second with a chilled wire whisk in a chilled bowl will easily mount in 2 to 3 minutes. If you cannot bear the thought of not using your electric beater, circulate it by hand, starting at a slow speed and gradually increasing it to moderate, while lifting as much air as possible into the cream.

Warning

If whipped cream is to be folded into other ingredients, be sure the other ingredients are cold; otherwise the cream will lose its stiffness and thin out.

A note on French cream

Although French *crème fraîche* and British dairy cream both contain approximately the same amount of butter fat, the consistency of French cream is thicker because it is slightly fermented. It must be thinned before whipping by the addition of 1 part of cold milk, iced water, or shaved ice for every 3 parts of cream.

Crème Chantilly

[Lightly Beaten Cream]

This is lightly beaten cream, which is usually specified for such desserts as Bavarian cream, and for dessert sauces.

For about ¾ pint

½ pt. chilled cream
A chilled 2½-qt. bowl

A chilled wire whisk or chilled blades of electric beater

Pour the cream into the chilled bowl and beat it slowly until it begins to foam, while circulating the beater all around the bowl and lifting the cream as you whip it. Gradually increase the beating speed to moderate and continue until the beater leaves light traces on the surface of the cream. A little cream lifted and dropped on the surface will softly retain its shape.

Stiffly beaten cream

For desserts which require more body, continue beating a few seconds more until the cream is a little stiffer and forms soft peaks. Do not beat beyond this stage or the cream will become granular, and then begin to turn into butter.

Storing whipped cream

Once cream is whipped, it will keep for several hours under refrigeration. As it usually exudes a bit of liquid, it is a good idea to turn it into a fine-meshed sieve and place the sieve over a bowl. This allows any seeping liquid to drop out of the cream.

Flavoured whipped cream

Before serving, fold in 2 tablespoons of sifted icing sugar and a tablespoon or two of brandy, rum, or sweet liqueur, or a teaspoon or two of vanilla extract.

CREAMING BUTTER AND SUGAR

Numerous dessert and cake recipes direct that butter and sugar be creamed together; this may be accomplished either by machine or by hand.

Electric Beater. Use the pastry-blender attachment if you have one; you may use the regular beater, but the blades will become clogged. Cut the butter into ½-inch pieces. Warm the large mixing bowl in hot water. Dry it, add the butter and sugar, and beat at a moderate speed for several minutes. The mixture is ready to be used when it is light, fluffy, and a pale ivory colour.

Hand Beating. If the butter has been left at room temperature for an hour to soften, simply beat the butter and sugar together in a bowl for several minutes until they form a light, fluffy mass. For cold, hard butter, use the following system: Cut the butter into ½-inch pieces and place it with the sugar in a mixing bowl placed over barely simmering water. Beat with a wooden spoon for several seconds until the butter softens. Then place the bowl in a basin of cold water and beat for a minute or two until the mixture is light, fluffy, and a pale ivory colour.

MELTED CHOCOLATE

Because chocolate burns easily, you should watch it carefully while it melts. To melt chocolate, break it into small pieces or use chocolate drops. Place the chocolate in a small saucepan with ½ to 1 tablespoon strong coffee, rum, or water per ounce. Place the pan over hot but not simmering water and stir constantly with a wooden spoon for several minutes until the chocolate has melted to a perfectly smooth cream. Keep the saucepan in warm water until you are ready to use the chocolate.

ALMONDS

Whole, slivered, and ground almonds have many uses in French pastries and desserts. You will note that all the recipes which use almonds also call for a little almond extract to bring out the almond taste. This is not necessary in France: one or two bitter almonds are always included. Bitter almonds have a pronounced almond flavour, but also contain a small amount of prussic acid, a poison. It is thus best to rely on almond extract; but as it is a strong concentrate, a few drops or a quarter teaspoon are enough in most recipes.

Blanched Almonds. Drop shelled almonds into boiling water and boil 1 minute. Drain. Squeeze each almond between the thumb and forefinger, and the almond will slip out of its skin. Spread the blanched almonds in a roasting tin and dry them out for 5 minutes in a 350° F., Mark 4 oven.

Pulverized Almonds. If you do not have an electric liquidizer, pound the almonds with a little granulated sugar in a mortar, or pass them through a mincer with granulated sugar and a few drops of water. If you have a liquidizer, pulverize them 3 ounces at a time at top speed for about 30 seconds.

Toasted or Grilled Almonds. Spread whole, slivered, or ground almonds in a roasting tin and place in a 350° F., Mark 4 oven for about 10 minutes. Stir them up frequently and keep an eye on them so that they do not burn. They should emerge an even, light, toasty brown.

Pralin

[Caramelized Almonds]

This delicious ingredient is quickly made and can be stored for weeks in a screw-topped jar. It is used in desserts and sauces, as a sprinkling for ice cream, and as a flavouring for cake icings and fillings. In France, *pralin* is also made with hazel nuts or a mixture of hazel nuts and almonds.

3 oz. slivered or powdered almonds

Toast the almonds in a 350° F., Mark 4 oven as previously described.

3 oz. granulated sugar   **An oiled marble slab or large baking**
2 tbl water   **sheet**

Boil the sugar and water in a small saucepan until the sugar caramelizes (see directions for caramel farther on). Immediately stir in the toasted almonds. Bring just to the boil, then pour on to the marble or baking sheet. When cold in about 10 minutes, break the hardened mass into pieces. Pulverize in the electric liquidizer, pound to a coarse powder in a mortar, or put it through a mincer.

Pulverized Macaroons

Pulverized stale macaroons may be substituted for *pralin*. Break macaroons into small pieces, spread them in a roasting tin, and place in a 200° F., Mark ¼ oven for about an hour. Remove them when they are fairly dry and lightly browned; they will crisp up as they cool. When crisped, pulverize them in the electric liquidizer, pound in a mortar, or put them through a mincer. Store in a screw-topped jar where they will keep for weeks.

Caramel
[Caramel]

Caramel is sugar syrup cooked until it turns a light, nut brown. It is used as a flavouring or colouring, or for coating a mould.

4 oz. granulated sugar or crushed sugar lumps	**⅛ pt. water**
	A small, heavy saucepan

Place sugar and water in a saucepan and swirl (shake pan slowly) over moderately high heat until the sugar has dissolved completely. Then let the sugar boil, swirling the pan occasionally, until the syrup turns a light, nut brown. This will take 3 to 4 minutes.

Remove the saucepan from the heat as soon as the desired colour is reached; if it is allowed to darken too much, it will have a bitter taste. Use immediately, as directed in your recipe.

Caramel Syrup

Pour ⅛ pint of water into the preceding caramel and simmer, stirring, until the caramel has dissolved.

HOW TO LINE A MOULD WITH CARAMEL

Un Moule Caramelisé
[A Caramel-lined Mould]

Custard desserts are often baked in a mould lined with caramel so that the dessert will be covered with a brown glaze when unmoulded. You may make the caramel directly in the mould when you are using a metal one such as the *charlotte* illustrated for soufflés on page 147. If you are using porcelain, make the caramel separately. Metal takes a caramel lining more evenly than porcelain, and the dessert is usually easier to unmould. We therefore suggest you buy metal moulds if you plan to do many desserts of this type. After unmoulding the dessert, you will be directed by your recipe to add a little liquid to the mould and simmer it to dissolve the remaining caramel; place the mould over an asbestos mat, if you are using fireproof porcelain, or omit this step.

For a 2½-pint metal mould

3 oz. granulated sugar or crushed sugar lumps	A pan of cold water
2 tbl water	A plate

Boil the sugar and water in the mould over a moderate heat, swirling the mould frequently, until the syrup caramelizes. At once, dip the mould in the cold water for 2 to 3 seconds to cool it very slightly. Then tilt the mould in all directions to film the bottom and sides with caramel. When the caramel has ceased to run, turn the mould upside down over a plate. This is now a caramelized mould.

For a fireproof porcelain mould (or cup-custard moulds or ramekins)

Make the caramel in a saucepan. While it is cooking, warm the porcelain mould in a pan of hot water; remove it as soon as the caramel is done. Pour in the caramel and tilt the mould in all directions to film the base and sides. When the caramel has ceased to run, reverse the mould on a plate.

Charlotte Malakoff

HOW TO LINE A MOULD WITH SPONGE FINGERS

Some of the grand desserts such as the *charlotte Malakoff*, page 558, the *diplomate*, page 564, and the *charlotte Chantilly*, page 561, call for a mould lined with sponge fingers. Any kind of a cylindrical mould or dish will do for the operation, but the dessert will be more spectacular if your mould is the *charlotte* type 3½ to 4 inches deep, like that illustrated in the Soufflé section on page 147. Some recipes direct that the sponge fingers be dipped first in diluted liqueur; others do not. The procedure for lining the mould is the same in either case.

Warning

Do not attempt any dessert calling for a mould lined with sponge fingers unless you have sponge fingers of best quality—dry and light, not spongy and limp. Inferior sponge fingers, unfortunately the only kind usually available in bakeries, will debase an otherwise remarkable dessert. The recipe for home-made sponge fingers is on page 617.

*Lining the base of
the mould*

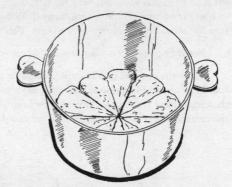

Cut the sponge fingers into a design of wedges to fit the base of the mould exactly. Lay them in the mould, their curved sides down.

*Lining the sides
of the mould*

Place a row of sponge fingers upright and pressed together, their curved sides against the sides of the mould. If your mould slants outward, you may have to trim the edges of the sponge fingers to make them slightly wedge-shaped.

The mould is now ready for filling, as directed in your recipe.

HOW TO UNMOULD A DESSERT

Many other desserts in this chapter, besides those with sponge fingers in the preceding paragraphs, are formed or baked in a mould, and are unmoulded for serving. The easiest way to unmould them is: place a serving dish upside down over the mould and reverse the two quickly so that the dish rests over a flat surface, give a sharp, downward jerk to dislodge the dessert, then remove the mould.

Vanilla

We have specified vanilla extract in all of the dessert and cake recipes. If you prefer to use the bean, steep it for 20 minutes in whatever hot liquid you are using. Sugar with a mild vanilla flavour is made by burying a vanilla bean for a week or so in a screw-topped jar with 1 pound of granulated sugar. For a strong flavour, pulverize ½ ounce or 2 whole vanilla beans in a mortar with 4 ounces of sugar lumps. When very finely granulated, pass through a very fine-meshed sieve. If you use an electric liquidizer for this, allow the pulverized mixture to stand in a closed jar for a week or so before sieving it.

Glazed Orange or Lemon Peel

This provides a nice decoration and is easy to make.

For about 2 ounces

5 lemons or 3 bright-skinned oranges	**A vegetable peeler**
	1½ pts. of simmering water

Remove the coloured part of the lemon or orange skin with a vegetable peeler. Cut into julienne strips 1½ inches long and ⅟₁₆ inch wide. Simmer in water for 10 to 12 minutes or until just tender when bitten. Drain. Refresh in cold water. Dry.

6 oz. granulated sugar	**A jam thermometer, if possible**
⅛ pt. water	**1 tsp vanilla extract**

Boil the sugar and water in a small saucepan to the thread stage (230° F.). Remove from the heat. Stir in the drained peel and the vanilla. Let the peel stand in the syrup for at least 30 minutes. Drain when ready to use. Under refrigeration, the peel will keep in the syrup for several weeks.

SWEET SAUCES AND FILLINGS

Sauces Sucrées et Crèmes

Crème anglaise, a light custard sauce, and *crème pâtissière*, a thick custard filling, are fundamental to French desserts and pastries. Both are quick to do, and should definitely be in anyone's repertoire.

CRÈME ANGLAISE

[Light Custard Sauce]

This sauce is a blend of egg yolks, sugar, and milk stirred over heat until it thickens into a light cream. If it comes near simmering point, the yolks will scramble. Although it can be omitted, a very small amount of starch in the sauce acts as a safeguard just in case the heat becomes too much for the egg yolks. Some recipes direct that the sauce be cooked in a double boiler; this is slow work and quite unnecessary if you concentrate on what you are doing, and use a heavy-bottomed saucepan. A jam thermometer is a useful guide.

Vanilla is the basic flavouring for *crème anglaise*; others are added to the vanilla if you wish, such as coffee, liqueurs, or chocolate. The sauce is served either warm or chilled, depending on your dessert. Less rich than cream, *crème anglaise* is used on fruit desserts, moulded creams, puddings, ice cream, or accompanies any dessert where it could be substituted for cream. With additional egg yolks and with double cream, it becomes the custard used for ice creams. Also with more egg yolks, plus gelatine, whipped cream, and flavouring, it is ready to be a Bavarian cream.

For about ¾ pint

3 oz. granulated sugar	A 2½-qt. mixing bowl
4 large or 5 standard egg yolks	A wire whisk or electric beater

Gradually beat the sugar into the egg yolks and continue beating for 2 to 3 minutes until the mixture is pale yellow and forms the ribbon, page 534.

Optional: 1 tsp cornflour or potato flour

Beat in the optional starch.

¾ pt. boiling milk

While beating the yolk mixture, very gradually pour on the boiling milk in a thin stream of drops so that the yolks are slowly warmed.

A clean, heavy-bottomed enamelled   Optional but recommended: a jam
  or stainless steel saucepan   thermometer
A wooden spatula or spoon

Pour the mixture into the saucepan and place over a moderate heat, stirring
slowly and continuously with a wooden spatula or spoon, and reaching all over
the base and sides of the pan, until the sauce thickens just enough to coat the
spoon with a light, creamy layer. Do not let the custard come anywhere near
simmering point. Maximum temperature is 165° F. on the thermometer (170°
if you have used starch). Then beat the sauce away from the heat for a minute
or two to cool it. Strain it through a fine sieve, and beat in one of the flavourings
below.

Flavourings

1 dsp vanilla extract   Or: 2 or 3 oz. of plain chocolate
Or: 1 tsp vanilla extract and 1 tbl   melted in the boiling milk, and
  rum, kirsch, cognac, orange   1 tsp vanilla extract stirred into
  liqueur, or instant coffee   the finished sauce

To serve hot: Keep the sauce over warm but not hot water. If you wish, beat in
1 to 2 tablespoons of unsalted butter just before serving.

To serve cold: Place the saucepan in a pan of cold water, and stir frequently until
cool. Then cover and chill.

Crème Brûlée

Although many people think of it as a French dessert, *crème brûlée* is
actually Creole. Make the basic cream exactly like the preceding *crème anglaise*,
but use half the amount of sugar, and cream instead of milk. Chill in a serving
dish. Rather than glazing the top of the cream with brown sugar, try spreading
a ⅛-inch layer of *pralin*, page 537, over the cream. This would then be a *crème
anglaise pralinée*, and is good as a dessert either by itself or served with strawberries.

CRÈME PÂTISSIÈRE

[Custard Filling]

This custard is also made of egg yolks, sugar, and milk, but unlike *crème
anglaise*, it contains flour so it may be brought to the boil, and is much thicker.
The proportions of flour vary according to the use of the filling; the following
recipe is designed as a base for fruit tarts. With the addition of beaten egg

whites it becomes a *crème Saint-Honoré* and may be used as a filling for cream puffs, or may be mixed with fruit to make a quick dessert like the *plombières* on pages 548-9.

For about 1 pint

6 oz. granulated sugar
5 egg yolks

A 2½-qt. mixing bowl
A wire whisk or electric beater

Gradually beat the sugar into the egg yolks and continue beating for 2 to 3 minutes until the mixture is pale yellow and forms the ribbon, page 534.

2¾ oz. sifted flour

Beat in the flour.

¾ pt. boiling milk

Beating the yolk mixture, gradually pour on the boiling milk in a thin stream of drops.

A clean, heavy-bottomed, 2-qt.
**   enamelled saucepan**

A wire whisk

Pour into the saucepan and place over a moderately high heat. Stir with wire whisk, reaching all over the base of pan. As sauce comes to the boil it will get lumpy, but will smooth out as you beat it. When boil is reached, beat over a moderately low heat for 2 to 3 minutes to cook the flour. Be careful the custard does not scorch in base of the pan.

½ oz. butter
   Flavourings
1½ tbl vanilla extract
Or: 2 tsp vanilla extract and 2 to 3
**   tbl rum, kirsch, cognac, orange**
**   liqueur, or instant coffee**
Or: 3 oz. plain chocolate melted
**   with 2 tbl rum or coffee and 2**
**   tsp vanilla extract**

Or: 3 oz. pulverized almonds,
**   page 537, or pulverized macaroons,**
**   page 538, ¼ tsp almond extract,**
**   and 2 tsp vanilla extract**

Remove from the heat and beat in the butter, then one of the flavourings above. Then if the custard is not used immediately, clean it off the sides of the pan, and dot top of custard with softened butter to prevent a skin from forming over the surface. *Crème pâtissière* will keep for a week under refrigeration, or may be deep-frozen.

CRÈME SAINT-HONORÉ

[Custard Filling with Beaten Egg Whites]

A *crème pâtissière* with the addition of stiffly beaten egg whites is used as a filling for tarts and cream puffs, and as a dessert cream. It is flavoured with chocolate, liqueurs, grated orange peel, *pralin*, or whatever your recipe calls for.

1 pt. crème pâtissière	**Big pinch of salt**
8 egg whites	**2 tbl granulated sugar**

Make the *crème pâtissière* as directed in the preceding recipe. Beat in the flavourings you have chosen. Beat the egg whites and salt together until soft peaks are formed; sprinkle on the sugar and continue beating until stiff peaks are formed, page 144. Stir one-quarter of the egg whites into the hot custard, fold in the rest. If the cream is to be served cold, chill it in the refrigerator.

FRANGIPANE

[Almond Custard Filling]

This is a very thick type of *crème pâtissière* with crushed macaroons or ground almonds. Use it as a filling for *crêpes* or tarts. Any leftover *frangipane* may be mixed with an equal amount of *crème pâtissière* and used as a filling.

For about 1¼ pints

A wire whisk or electric beater	**4 oz. granulated sugar**
1 egg	**2 oz. sifted flour**
1 egg yolk	**½ pt. boiling milk**
A 2½-qt. mixing bowl	

Beat egg and yolk in the mixing bowl, gradually adding the sugar, until mixture is pale yellow and forms the ribbon, page 534. Beat in the flour. Then beat in the boiling milk in a thin stream of drops.

A clean, heavy-bottomed, 2-qt.	**A wire whisk**
enamelled saucepan	**A wooden spoon**

Pour into saucepan and place over a moderate heat. Stir slowly with the whisk, reaching all over the base of the pan. When the mixture begins to coagulate into lumps, beat it vigorously until it smooths and thickens into a stiff paste. Then over a moderately low heat, beat it with a wooden spoon for 2 to 3 minutes to cook the flour thoroughly. Be careful the custard does not scorch on the bottom of the pan.

S

1½ oz. butter   **Optional: 2 to 3 tbl kirsch**
2 tsp vanilla extract
¼ tsp almond extract
3 oz. pulverized macaroons, page
   538, or pulverized almonds, page
   537

Away from heat, beat in the butter, then the flavourings, macaroons or almonds, and optional kirsch. If not used immediately, clean custard off the sides of the pan and dot top with softened butter to prevent a skin from forming on the surface. *Frangipane* will keep for a week under refrigeration, or may be deep-frozen.

FRUIT SAUCES

Fruit sauces are made from purées of fresh or frozen fruits, or from fruit jams and jellies. They are used with ice creams, custard desserts, and various puddings.

Sauce aux Fraises

[Fresh Strawberry Sauce]

Sauce aux Framboises

[Fresh Raspberry Sauce]

For about ¾ pint

1 lb. fresh strawberries or   **An electric liquidizer or an electric**
   raspberries   **beater**
A sieve and wooden spoon   2 to 3 tbl kirsch, cognac, or lemon
6 to 8 oz. castor sugar   juice

Hull, wash, drain, and sieve the fruit. Add sugar to taste. Either whisk for 2 to 3 minutes in a liquidizer, or beat for 10 minutes with an electric beater. The sugar should dissolve completely; the purée will be quite thick. Beat in kirsch, cognac, or lemon juice to taste.

Made with frozen berries

Thaw the berries and drain them thoroughly. Force them through a sieve, and beat in some of their syrup to thin out the purée. Flavour with kirsch, cognac, or lemon juice.

Made with jam, preserves, or jelly (for ½ pint)

¼ pt. strawberry or raspberry
    jam and ¼ pt. red currant jelly
Or: ¼ pt. orange marmalade and ¼ pt.
    apricot preserves
	2 to 3 tbl kirsch or cognac
	A sieve and wooden spoon

Stir the mixture in a saucepan over a moderate heat until melted. Simmer for a moment with the liqueur, then force through a sieve.

STRAINED APRICOT PRESERVES

Before using apricot preserves (jam or marmalade) stir it over heat, if necessary, until it has melted, then rub it through a sieve to leave the pieces of skin behind. If not used immediately, it will keep almost indefinitely in its original container.

GLAZES

Either apricot preserves or red currant jelly contains enough pectin so that when boiled to between 225° and 228° F. it will stiffen slightly as it cools and not be sticky to the touch. You may then use it as a glaze, paint it over the top of a tart to give brilliance and glitter, spread it over a cake to act as a simple icing, or paint it inside a baked pastry shell to provide a light water-proofing before the filling goes in.

Abricot

[For Apricot Glaze]

Gelée de Groseilles

[For Red Currant Glaze]

For about ¼ pint

¼ pt. apricot preserves, forced
    through a sieve; Or: ¼ pt. red
    currant jelly
2 tbl granulated sugar
	A small saucepan
	A wooden spatula or spoon
	Optional: a jam thermometer

Stir the strained apricot preserves or currant jelly with the sugar over a moderately high heat for 2 to 3 minutes until thick enough to coat the spoon with a light film, and the last drops are sticky as they fall from the spoon (225° to 228° F. on a jam thermometer). Do not boil beyond this point or the glaze will become brittle when it cools. Apply the glaze while it is still warm. Unused glaze will keep indefinitely in a screw-topped jar; reheat again before using.

CUSTARDS, MOUSSES, AND MOULDS

Crèmes et Mousses

* CRÈME PLOMBIÈRES PRALINÉE

[Caramel Almond Cream—a cold dessert]

A *crème plombières* is a custard filling into which beaten egg whites and a flavouring or fresh fruits are folded. It is spooned over sponge fingers or spongecake, then chilled. For the few minutes it takes to assemble, *crème plombières* makes a surprisingly attractive dessert.

For 6 servings

6 squares of stale spongecake or sponge fingers, about 1½ ins. across and ½ in. thick

A 3-pt. serving bowl about 4 ins. deep or 6 sweet dishes
2 tbl rum mixed with 2 tbl coffee

If the squares of cake or sponge fingers are not stale, dry them out for about an hour in a 200° F., Mark ¼ oven. Arrange the pieces in the serving bowl, or place one in each sweet dish. Sprinkle with the rum and coffee.

4 egg yolks
2 oz. granulated sugar
1½ oz. flour
1 pt. boiling milk

1 tbl vanilla extract, or 2 tsp vanilla and 3 tbl rum
½ oz. butter

Following the procedure for *crème pâtissière*, page 543, beat the egg yolks and sugar in a mixing bowl until they are pale yellow and form the ribbon. Beat in the flour. Then beat in the boiling milk by drops. Pour into a clean saucepan and, stirring with a wire whisk, boil slowly for 2 minutes. Remove from heat and beat in the vanilla or rum, then the butter.

4 egg whites
Pinch of salt
1 tbl granulated sugar

3 tbl *pralin* (caramelized almonds), page 537, or the pulverized macaroons, page 538

Beat the egg whites and salt until soft peaks are formed; sprinkle on the sugar and beat until stiff peaks are formed, page 144. Fold the egg whites and the *pralin* or macaroons into the hot *crème pâtissière*.

2 tbl *pralin* or pulverized macaroons

Spoon the cream into the serving bowl or sweet dishes and chill for 2 to 3 hours, or until serving time. Just before serving, sprinkle with the rest of the *pralin* or macaroons.

VARIATIONS

Crème Plombières au Chocolat

[Chocolate Cream]

Use the ingredients and method in the master recipe, but substitute chocolate for all or part of the *pralin* as follows:

**3 oz. chocolate melted with 3 tbl
rum or strong coffee, and 2 tsp
vanilla extract**

Beat the smooth melted chocolate into 1¼ pints of hot *crème pâtissière*. Then fold in the beaten egg whites.

**1 oz. grated or shaved
plain chocolate**

Just before serving, sprinkle chocolate over the cream.

Crème Plombières aux Fruits

[*Plombières* with Fresh Strawberries or Raspberries]

Use the ingredients and method in the master recipe, but substitute fresh strawberries or raspberries for the *pralin*. Instead of soaking the cake in rum, use kirsch or cognac diluted with water; and use kirsch or cognac plus vanilla for flavouring the cream.

You may substitute defrosted frozen fruits for fresh fruits here, but the look rather limp, especially when used for a decoration on top.

**½ lb. sliced fresh strawberries or
whole raspberries** **2 tbl castor sugar**

Sprinkle fruit with sugar and leave to stand for 10 minutes, or until ready to use. Fold into the cream with the egg whites.

**12 to 18 whole strawberries or
½ lb. raspberries** **2 tbl castor sugar**

Sprinkle the berries with sugar, leave to stand for 10 minutes. Arrange over dessert just before serving.

Crème Plombières à l' Ananas

[*Plombières* with Pineapple]

Follow the ingredients and method in the master recipe, but substitute pineapple for the *pralin*. And instead of soaking the cake in rum, use kirsch or cognac diluted with water; use kirsch or cognac, plus vanilla for flavouring the cream.

An 8-oz. tin crushed pineapple in
heavy syrup

Drain the pineapple. Boil ⅛ pint of the syrup in a small saucepan for 5 minutes. Add the crushed pineapple and boil for 5 minutes. Drain. Stir 2 tablespoons of the syrup into the *crème pâtissière*. Fold in the egg whites and all but 1 ounce of the pineapple. Reserve remaining pineapple to decorate dessert just before serving.

---

* *BAVAROIS À L'ORANGE*

[Orange Bavarian Cream—a cold dessert]

Bavarian cream is a mould of *crème anglaise* (custard sauce) with gelatine, beaten egg whites, lightly beaten cream, and a flavouring. It is unmoulded after it has been chilled, and makes a dessert as beautiful to see as it is to eat. When properly made, it has a most lovely, light, creamy, velvety quality and ranks as one of the best of the moulded desserts.

We were curious to try out some recipes for Bavarian cream which claimed to produce masterpieces in seconds, so we experimented with the electric liquidizer, raw egg yolks, cracked ice, and so forth. We also rang various changes of our own, such as substituting frozen fruits or ice cream for cracked ice. Though the moulded results looked handsome, their flavour and consistency were disappointing. We have concluded that this particular masterpiece cannot be achieved in seconds; a cooked custard, well-dissolved gelatine, stiffly beaten egg whites, properly whipped cream, perfect flavouring, and then the right blending of one element into another at the right time seem to be the requisites for a true Bavarian cream. The classical method below is certainly far from difficult, and the whole dessert may be prepared the day, or even two days, before serving.

Orange Bavarian cream is our favourite. Other flavourings are suggested at the end of the recipe.

For 8 to 10 people

The orange flavouring

2 large, fine, bright-skinned oranges   A 3-qt. mixing bowl
2 large sugar lumps

Wash and dry the oranges. One at a time, rub the sugar lumps over them until all sides of each lump are impregnated with orange oil. Mash the sugar lumps in the mixing bowl. Grate the orange part of the skins into the bowl.

| A measuring jug | ½ oz. gelatine |
| A strainer | |

Squeeze the juice of the oranges into the jug, to make ¼ pint of strained juice. Sprinkle the gelatine over the orange juice and leave aside to soften.

The custard sauce

| 7 egg yolks | 6 oz. granulated sugar |
| A wire whisk or electric beater | 2 tsp cornflour |

Following the procedure for *crème anglaise*, page 542, add the egg yolks to the orange sugar in the mixing bowl. Gradually beat in the granulated sugar and continue beating for 2 to 3 minutes until mixture is pale yellow and forms the ribbon. Beat in the cornflour.

| ¾ pt. boiling milk | A wooden spoon |
| A 3-pt. enamelled saucepan | Optional: a jam thermometer |

Beat the milk in a thin stream of drops into the egg yolk mixture. Pour into the saucepan and place over a moderate heat. Stir with wooden spoon until mixture thickens enough to coat the spoon lightly (170° F.). Do not overheat or egg yolks will scramble. Remove from the heat and immediately add the orange juice and gelatine mixture, beating for a moment or two until gelatine has dissolved completely. Rinse out the mixing bowl and pour in the custard.

The egg whites

| 5 egg whites | 1 tbl castor sugar |
| Pinch of salt | A rubber spatula |

Beat the egg whites and salt until soft peaks are formed; sprinkle on the sugar and beat until stiff peaks are formed, page 144. Using the rubber spatula, fold the egg whites into the hot custard. Put in refrigerator. Fold delicately with spatula several times while mixture is cooling, to keep it from separating. When cold and almost but not quite set, proceed with recipe.

The whipped cream and final flavouring

| ¼ pt. chilled cream | A chilled beater |
| A chilled mixing bowl | 2 tbl orange liqueur |

Beat the cream lightly, until doubled in volume and beater leaves faint traces on the surface, page 535. Fold the whipped cream and orange liqueur into the custard.

A 3-pt. cylindrical mould or ring	Lightly oiled greaseproof paper
mould, preferably of metal as	
unmoulding is easier	

Rinse mould in cold water and shake out excess. Turn the Bavarian cream into the mould. Cover with the greaseproof paper. Chill for 3 to 4 hours or overnight.

Unmoulding and serving

A long, thin knife . **A chilled serving dish**

Remove greaseproof paper. Dip mould in very hot water for 1 second (a second or two longer for a porcelain mould), run knife around the edge of the cream, and reverse on a chilled serving dish. (May be unmoulded and refrigerated several hours before serving.)

**Peeled orange segments sprinkled
  with orange liqueur and sugar**

Serve surrounded with the orange segments.

VARIATIONS

Bavarois au Chocolat

[Chocolate Bavarian Cream]

Use the same method and ingredients as for the master recipe for Bavarian cream, but omit the orange flavouring and make the following changes.

5 egg yolks instead of 7

Fewer egg yolks are needed for the custard when chocolate is used.

¼ pt. strong coffee   **2 tsp vanilla extract**

Soften the gelatine in coffee and vanilla rather than in orange juice.

3 oz. plain chocolate

Grate the chocolate into the ¾ pint of milk destined for the custard sauce. Heat slowly to simmering point, beating with a wire whisk to blend the chocolate smoothly. Proceed with the custard sauce, beating in the coffee and gelatine at the end. Fold in the beaten egg whites and refrigerate, folding occasionally, until cool but not set.

2 tbl dark rum or orange liqueur

Rum is a more usual flavouring with chocolate, but orange liqueur may be used if you wish. Fold it in with the whipped cream, and fill the mould.

**¾ to 1 pt. *crème anglaise* (custard
  sauce), page 542, or *crème Chantilly*
  (lightly whipped cream), page 535**

Serve chocolate Bavarian cream with *crème anglaise* or with *crème Chantilly*.

Bavarois Praliné

[Almond Bavarian Cream]

Use the same ingredients and method as for the master recipe for Bavarian cream, page 550, but omit the orange flavouring and substitute the following.

¼ pt. cold strong coffee

Soften the gelatine in coffee rather than in orange juice.

3 oz. *pralin* (caramelized almonds),
   page 537, or pulverized macaroons
   page 538

Fold the *pralin* or macaroons into the custard with the beaten egg whites. Chill, folding occasionally, until cool but not set.

1 tbl vanilla extract and ¼ tsp
   almond extract; Or: 1 tsp vanilla
   extract, ¼ tsp almond extract,
   and 2 tbl dark rum

Fold the flavouring into the custard with the whipped cream.

2 tbl *pralin* or pulverized macaroons
¾ to 1 pt. *crème anglaise* (custard
   sauce), page 542, or *crème Chantilly*
   (lightly whipped cream), page 535

Sprinkle the top of the Bavarian cream with *pralin* or macaroons just before serving. No sauce is necessary, but you may serve with it *crème anglaise* or *crème Chantilly*.

Bavarois aux Fruits

[Strawberry or Raspberry Bavarian Cream—and other fruits]

This recipe calls for raspberries or strawberries. Other fruit purées may be substituted, such as apricot, peach, or caramelized pears. Use the method and ingredients in the master recipe for Bavarian cream, page 550, but omit the orange flavouring and make the following changes.

5 egg yolks instead of 7

The fruit purée gives body to the custard, so fewer egg yolks are needed.

s*

¼ **pt. strawberry or raspberry juice,
or orange juice**

If you are using frozen berries, dissolve the gelatine in ¼ pint of the juice. Otherwise use orange juice.

½ **lb. fresh strawberries or
raspberries; Or: 1 lb. frozen
berries, thawed and well drained**

Force the fruit through a sieve; measure out a bare ½ pint of purée. (Any leftover purée may go into your sauce.) Fold measured purée into the custard along with the whipped cream.

¾ **to 1 pt. strawberry or raspberry
sauce
Or: ½ lb. fresh strawberries or
raspberries, hulled and sprinkled
with sugar**

Serve this Bavarian cream with strawberry or raspberry sauce, or surround the dessert with fresh berries.

Cold Soufflés

Many of the recipes you will see for cold soufflés are not cold soufflés at all, but Bavarian creams. They look like soufflés because they appear to have risen several inches up beyond the rim of the mould. This effect is achieved by surrounding the mould with a paper collar which holds the cream in place until set; the paper is removed just before serving time. You may mould any of the preceding Bavarian creams this way, as well as the chocolate mousse on page 557, or the almond-cream filling for the *charlottes Malakoff* starting on page 558. Two recipes for actual cold soufflés are the rum and macaroon soufflé on page 573, and the caramel and almond soufflé on page 574.

RIZ À L'IMPÉRATRICE

[Bavarian Cream with Rice and Fruits—a cold dessert]

Riz à l'Impératrice is one of the grand old standbys of the classic French *cuisine*, and has no relation, fortunately, to the dreadful rice puddings of one's youth. It is velvet to the tongue, and is always accompanied by a decorative fruit sauce.

For 8 to 10 people

Preheat oven to 300° F., Mark 1.

4 oz. finely diced glacé fruits of
   various colours, such as cherries,
   angelica, orange peel

4 tbl kirsch or cognac
½ oz. gelatine

Mix the fruits in a small bowl with the kirsch or cognac. Sprinkle on the gelatine and leave aside until needed.

4 oz. white rice

3 qts. boiling water

Sprinkle the rice into the boiling water and boil 5 minutes. Drain thoroughly.

¾ pt. boiling milk
2 oz. granulated sugar
1 oz. butter
A 1½-pt. covered, fireproof casserole

1 tsp vanilla extract
A round of buttered greaseproof
   paper

Bring milk, sugar, and butter to boil in the casserole. Stir in the rice and vanilla. Bring to simmering point on top of the stove. Lay paper over the rice, cover casserole, and place in preheated oven to cook very slowly for 35 to 40 minutes, until the milk has been absorbed and the rice is very tender.

5 egg yolks
A 2- to 3-qt. mixing bowl
A wire whisk or an electric beater
4 oz. granulated sugar
1 tsp cornflour
¾ pt. boiling milk
A heavy-bottomed enamelled
   saucepan

A wooden spoon
Optional: a jam thermometer
1 tsp vanilla extract
3 tbl apricot preserves forced
   through a sieve

Meanwhile, following the procedure for *crème anglaise*, page 542, place egg yolks in mixing bowl. Gradually beat in the sugar and continue beating until mixture is pale yellow and forms the ribbon. Beat in the cornflour, then the boiling milk by drops. Pour into the saucepan and stir over a moderate heat until custard coats the spoon lightly (170° F.). Do not bring near simmering point or egg yolks will curdle. Remove from heat and immediately stir in the glacé fruits and gelatine mixture, stirring until gelatine has thoroughly dissolved. Add the vanilla and apricot preserves. Stir the rice into the custard, a spoonful at a time if rice is hot. Chill, stirring occasionally, until cold but not set.

Flavourless cooking oil
A 2½-pt. cylindrical mould about
   3½ ins. deep, or a ring mould

A round of oiled greaseproof
   paper

Lightly oil the inside of the mould and line the base with oiled greaseproof paper.

½ pt. chilled cream   A chilled beater
A chilled bowl   A round of oiled greaseproof paper

When the rice custard has cooled, beat the cream until doubled in volume and beater leaves light traces on the surface, page 535. Fold the cream delicately into the rice custard, and turn the mixture into the mould. Cover with oiled greaseproof paper. Refrigerate for 4 hours or overnight.

¾ pt. strawberry or raspberry sauce,
    page 546
A chilled serving dish
Optional: 1 oz. glacé fruits,
    diced or cut into fancy shapes,
    and steeped in 1 tbl kirsch or
    cognac

Remove greaseproof paper. Dip mould in very hot water for 1 second (a few seconds more if mould is not of metal). Run a knife around the custard, and unmould on chilled serving dish. Surround with the sauce.

NOTE: After dessert has been unmoulded, you may decorate it with glacé fruits.

MOUSSE À L'ORANGE

[Orange Mousse—a cold dessert]

A becoming way to serve this delicate mousse is in the scooped-out halves of oranges.

For 6 people

3 tbl orange liqueur   ½ lemon
A 1-pt. measuring jug   Orange juice
3 or 4 bright-skinned oranges

Pour the liqueur into the measuring jug. Grate the coloured part of the skins of 3 oranges and the ½ lemon into the jug. Strain in enough orange juice so that liquid measures ¾ pint.

6 egg yolks   A 2-qt., heavy-bottomed, enamelled
3 oz. granulated sugar   saucepan
A 2-qt. mixing bowl   A wooden spoon
A wire whisk or electric beater   Optional: a jam thermometer
2 tsp cornflour

Beat the egg yolks and sugar in a mixing bowl until mixture is pale yellow and forms the ribbon, page 534. Beat in the cornflour and the orange juice mixture.

Pour into the saucepan and stir over a moderate heat with wooden spoon until mixture heats through and thickens, but does not come to simmering point, or a temperature of more than 170° F. It should coat the spoon lightly. Remove from heat and beat a moment to stop the cooking.

6 egg whites	1 tbl castor sugar
Pinch of salt	A rubber spatula

Beat the egg whites and salt in a separate bowl until soft peaks are formed; sprinkle in the sugar and beat until stiff peaks are formed, page 144. Fold the egg whites into the hot orange mixture and refrigerate until thoroughly chilled, folding occasionally so that the custard will not separate.

¼ pt. chilled cream	Glazed orange peel, page 541,
6 orange-shell cups, or sweet	angelica cut into leaf shapes,
dishes, or a serving bowl	mint leaves, or whipped cream

Beat the cream until stiff, page 535, and fold into the chilled mousse. Turn into orange-shell cups, sweet dishes, or the bowl. Chill for at least 2 hours.

Decorations
Decorate the dessert just before serving.

MOUSSELINE AU CHOCOLAT
MAYONNAISE AU CHOCOLAT
FONDANT AU CHOCOLAT

[Chocolate Mousse—a cold dessert]

Among all the recipes for chocolate mousse this is one of the best, we think; it uses egg yolks, sugar, and butter, and instead of cream, beaten egg whites. The orange flavouring suggested here is delicious with chocolate. An interchangeable version is *charlotte Malakoff* on page 558, made of butter, chocolate, and ground almonds. Either may be unmoulded after chilling, or served in a bowl, or in sweet dishes, or in little covered pots.

For about 2 pints, serving 6 to 8 people

A 2-qt. porcelain or stainless steel	⅛ pt. orange liqueur
mixing bowl	A pan of not-quite-simmering
A wire whisk or electric beater	water
4 egg yolks	A basin of cold water
4 oz. castor sugar	

Beat the egg yolks and sugar together until mixture is thick, pale yellow, and falls back upon itself, forming a slowly dissolving ribbon. Beat in the orange

liqueur. Then place the mixing bowl over the not-quite-simmering water and
continue beating for 3 to 4 minutes until the mixture is thick and too hot for
your finger. Then beat over cold water for 3 to 4 minutes until the mixture is
cool and again forms the ribbon. It will have the consistency of mayonnaise.

6 oz. plain chocolate	**6 oz. softened unsalted butter**
3 tbl strong coffee	**Optional: 1 oz. finely diced, glazed**
A small saucepan	**orange peel, page 541**

Melt the chocolate with coffee over hot water. Remove from the heat and beat
in the butter a little at a time, to make a smooth cream. Beat the chocolate into
the egg yolks and sugar, then beat in the optional orange peel.

4 egg whites	**1 tbl castor sugar**
Pinch of salt	

Beat the egg whites and salt until soft peaks are formed; sprinkle on the sugar and
beat until stiff peaks are formed, page 144. Stir a quarter of the egg whites into
the chocolate mixture. Fold in the rest.

Turn into serving dish, sweet dishes, or *petits pots*. Refrigerate for at least 2 hours
or overnight.

¾ pt. vanilla-flavoured *crème anglaise*
   (custard sauce), page 542, or
   lightly whipped cream sweetened
   with icing sugar, page 535

Pass the sauce or whipped cream separately.

Moulded Mousse

Turn the preceding mousse into a lightly oiled, 2½-pint ring mould. Cover
with oiled, greaseproof paper. Chill for 3 to 4 hours until well set. Remove
paper, dip mould for 1 second in very hot water, and unmould on a chilled
serving dish. Fill centre of mousse with *crème anglaise* or lightly whipped cream.

Or use the following *charlotte Malakoff* system, lining a cylindrical mould
with sponge fingers dipped in orange liqueur.

---

* CHARLOTTE MALAKOFF AUX FRAISES

[Almond Cream with Fresh Strawberries—a cold dessert]

This delectable almond cream is relatively quick to assemble if you have
sponge fingers on hand—but they must be of excellent quality, not the soggy,

baking-powder variety. If you cannot buy them, or have not the time to make them, omit the sponge fingers altogether and turn the almond cream into a ring mould as described in the preceding paragraph, or into a serving dish, or into individual sweet dishes. Although the dessert cannot then be called a *charlotte Malakoff*, it will still be delicious, and can be nicely decorated with fresh strawberries.

For 8 to 10 people

Preparing strawberries and lining mould

1 lb. fresh strawberries	A cake rack

Hull the strawberries. Wash them quickly if necessary, and place on the cake rack to drain thoroughly.

A 3-pt. cylindrical mould, about 4 ins. high and 7 ins. in diameter	A round of greaseproof paper

Line the base of the unbuttered mould with the round of unbuttered greaseproof paper.

¼ pt. orange liqueur	A cake rack
¼ pt. water	
A soup plate	
24 single sponge fingers, 4 ins. long and about 2 ins. wide, page 617	

Pour orange liqueur and water into soup plate. Dip in the sponge fingers, one by one, and drain on the rack. Line sides of mould with sponge fingers as described on page 539. Reserve the remaining dipped sponge fingers.

The almond cream

A 3-qt. mixing bowl	¼ pt. orange liqueur
An electric beater or wire whisk	¼ tsp almond extract
½ lb. softened unsalted butter	6 oz. pulverized almonds,
6 oz. castor sugar	page 537

Cream butter and sugar together for 3 to 4 minutes, until pale and fluffy, page 536. Beat in orange liqueur and almond extract. Continue beating for several minutes until sugar is completely dissolved. Beat in the almonds.

¾ pt. chilled cream	A chilled beater
A chilled bowl	

Whip the cream until the beater, drawn across the top of the cream, leaves light traces, page 535. Fold the cream into the almond and butter mixture.

Moulding and serving

A round of buttered greaseproof
paper
A saucer which will just fit into
the mould

A 1-lb. weight, or pieces of a
mincer

Turn a third of the almond cream into the lined mould. Arrange over it a layer of strawberries, heads down. Cover them with a layer of sponge fingers. Repeat with another layer each of almond cream, strawberries, and sponge fingers. Fill the mould with the rest of the almond cream and a layer of sponge fingers if there are any left. Trim off sponge fingers around edge of mould, and press the trimmed-off pieces into the top of the cream. Cover mould with the greaseproof paper, place saucer over the paper, and place the weight on it. Refrigerate for 6 hours or overnight. The butter must be chilled firm, so that dessert will not collapse when unmoulded.

A chilled serving dish
The remaining strawberries, more
if needed

¾ pt. *crème Chantilly* (lightly
whipped cream), page 535, or
strawberry sauce, page 546

Remove greaseproof paper. Run a knife around the inside of the mould, and reverse the dessert on a chilled serving dish. Peel greaseproof paper from top, and refrigerate dessert until serving time. Decorate with strawberries and accompany with whipped cream or strawberry sauce.

VARIATIONS

Use the same method and proportions as in the preceding master recipe for *charlotte Malakoff*, but make the following changes for these variations:

Charlotte Malakoff aux Framboises

[Almond Cream with Raspberries]

Substitute fresh raspberries for strawberries in the preceding recipe.

Charlotte Malakoff au Chocolat

[Almond Cream with Chocolate]

Ingredients for the master recipe
but without the strawberries
4 oz. plain chocolate melted in
⅛ pt. strong coffee
⅛ pt. rather than ¼ pt. orange liqueur
for the almond cream

¾ pt. *crème Chantilly* (lightly
whipped cream), page 535, or
***crème anglaise* (custard sauce),**
page 542

Following the master recipe, line the mould with sponge fingers dipped in diluted orange liqueur. Make the almond cream as directed, but fold the melted chocolate into it, and only ⅛ pint of orange liqueur. Cool before folding in the whipped cream, and complete the recipe. Serve with whipped cream or custard sauce.

Charlotte Basque

[Almond Custard with Chocolate]

This is lighter than the *charlotte Malakoff* because the base is a custard and no whipped cream is folded into it.

For 8 to 10 people

1½ pts. *crème anglaise* (custard
   sauce), page 542, flavoured with
   chocolate

Prepare a chocolate-flavoured custard sauce and beat over cold water, or refrigerate, until almost cold.

½ lb. unsalted butter
6 oz. pulverized almonds, page 537
½ tsp almond extract
2 to 3 tbl rum, kirsch, cognac, or
   orange liqueur

A 3-pt. mould lined with sponge
   fingers, and extra sponge fingers
   as described in master recipe
¾ pt. *crème Chantilly* (lightly
   whipped cream), page 535

Cream the butter and almonds together in a mixing bowl. Gradually beat in the cool custard sauce. Beat in the almond extract, and rum or liqueur to taste. Turn into lined mould, alternating with layers of sponge fingers, and chill until set. Serve with lightly whipped cream.

CHARLOTTE CHANTILLY, AUX FRAISES
CHARLOTTE CHANTILLY, AUX FRAMBOISES

[Strawberry or Raspberry Cream—a cold dessert]

Here is another handsome moulded dessert; this one is also relatively quick to execute. But unless the egg yolks are well thickened, and then chilled before the cream is folded in, the dessert will collapse rather quickly. If you do not wish to serve it unmoulded, turn the cream into a serving bowl or into sweet dishes. You may use frozen fruit instead of fresh, but be sure the fruit is well thawed and most thoroughly drained, otherwise the purée will be too liquid.

For 8 to 10 people

A round of greaseproof paper
A 3-pt. cylindrical mould about 4
    ins. high and 7 ins. in diameter,
    lined with sponge fingers, page 617

Place the round of greaseproof paper in the bottom of the unbuttered mould. Then line the sides of the mould (not the bottom) with upright sponge fingers as described in the directions.

¾ lb. fresh strawberries or rasp-
    berries

Hull, wash, and drain the berries. Force them through a sieve and into a bowl. Measure out ¾ pint of purée. Chill.

A wire whisk or electric beater	**A pan of not–quite–simmering**
A 2-qt. stainless steel mixing bowl	**water**
4 oz. castor sugar	**A basin of cold water**
8 egg yolks	

Beat the sugar into the egg yolks and continue beating until mixture is pale yellow and falls back on itself, forming a slowly dissolving ribbon. Then place the mixing bowl over the not–quite–simmering water and beat until mixture has thickened into a cream and becomes uncomfortably hot for your finger. Put the bowl in cold water and beat until the mixture is cold and falls back upon itself, forming a slowly dissolving ribbon on the surface. Chill.

1 pt. chilled whipping cream   **A chilled beater**
A chilled bowl

When the egg yolk mixture has chilled, beat the cream until doubled in volume and forms soft peaks, page 535.

Extra sponge fingers, if needed   **A round of greaseproof paper**

Fold the chilled strawberry or raspberry purée into the chilled egg yolk mixture, then fold in the whipped cream. Turn into the mould. Place sponge fingers over the cream to fill the mould almost completely. Trim off any protruding sponge fingers around the edges of the mould. Cover with greaseproof paper and refrigerate for at least 6 hours or overnight.

A chilled serving dish
¼ to ¾ lb. fresh strawberries or
    raspberries

Just before serving, remove greaseproof paper, run a knife around the edge of the mould, and reverse dessert on to a chilled serving dish. Remove greaseproof paper. Decorate the top of the dessert with fresh berries and, if you wish, place more berries around the dessert.

* CRÈME RENVERSÉE AU CARAMEL

[Caramel Custard, Unmoulded—warm or cold]

French custards are usually unmoulded, and therefore call for more eggs and egg yolks than custards served directly from their baking dishes.

For a 1½ pint mould serving 4 to 6 people

The custard mixture

Preheat oven to 350° F., Mark 4.

A 1½-pt., fireproof, cylindrical mould lined with caramel, page 538	1 pt. milk Optional: 1 vanilla bean

Line the mould with caramel as directed. Bring the milk with the optional vanilla bean to just below simmering point in a saucepan, cover, and let the bean steep in the milk while you prepare the rest of the custard ingredients.

3 oz. granulated sugar 3 eggs 3 egg yolks A 2-qt. mixing bowl	A wire whisk 1 tsp vanilla extract, if you have not used a vanilla bean A fine-meshed sieve

Gradually beat the sugar into the eggs and egg yolks in the bowl until well mixed, light, and foamy. Continue beating while pouring on the hot milk in a thin stream of drops. Stir in vanilla extract, if you have not used a vanilla bean. Strain the mixture through a sieve into the caramel-lined mould.

Baking the custard

Place the mould in a tin and pour enough boiling water around mould to come half-way up its sides. Place in lower part of preheated oven and turn heat down to 325° F., Mark 2. Regulate oven so water in tin never quite comes to simmering point during baking; if it simmers or boils, the interior of the custard will be grainy. Bake for about 40 minutes, or until a trussing needle or knife, plunged down through the centre of the custard, comes out clean.

Unmoulding and serving

If you wish to serve the custard warm, place the mould in a tin of cold water for about 10 minutes to firm it up; otherwise chill in the refrigerator. To unmould, run a knife between custard and edge of mould, place a serving dish upside down over the mould, quickly reverse the two, and remove the mould from the custard. If you wish, simmer 2 to 3 tablespoons of water in the mould to dissolve the remaining caramel; strain around the custard.

VARIATIONS

To serve individual unmoulded custards, use the custard mixture in the preceding master recipe, and mould the custards as follows:

Petits Pots de Crème

[Cup Custards, Unmoulded]

1½ pts. caramel custard mixture, the master recipe
8¼ pt. caramel-lined ramekins, page 539

A tin containing enough boiling water to come half-way up outside of ramekins

Divide the custard mixture among the ramekins and place them in the tin of boiling water. Bake for about 20 minutes in lower part of preheated, 325° F., Mark 2 oven. Cool; unmould when ready to serve.

Crème Sainte-Anne au Caramel

[Macaroon Cup Custards, Unmoulded]

½ oz. butter
8 caramel-lined ramekins, ¼ pt., page 539
6 oz. pulverized macaroons, page 538

1½ pts. caramel custard mixture, the master recipe

Butter the insides of the caramel-lined ramekins and sprinkle 2 tablespoons of pulverized macaroons in each. Fill with the custard mixture. Place in a tin of boiling water and bake for about 20 minutes in lower part of preheated, 325° F., Mark 2 oven. Cool; unmould when ready to serve. You may garnish the custards, if you wish, with one of the suggestions below.

Optional garnishings

Crème anglaise (custard sauce), page 542
Or: strawberry or raspberry sauce, page 546

Or: fresh or tinned peach halves, coated with caramel syrup, page 538

DIPLOMATE
POUDING DE CABINET

[Custard with Glacé Fruits, Unmoulded—a warm or cold dessert]

This delicious and most classical of French desserts does not take too long to prepare, and can be baked the day before your dinner party. The custard is baked in a mould lined with sponge fingers which must be of best quality, tender and dry, not spongy.

For 8 people

2 oz. small, seedless raisins	3 tbl dark rum or kirsch
A saucepan of boiling water	
A small bowl	
3½ oz. finely diced, mixed, glacé	
fruits, such as cherries, angelica,	
apricots, pineapple	

Drop the raisins into the boiling water and leave to stand for five minutes. Drain, and place in the bowl. Stir in the glacé fruits, the rum or kirsch, and leave to stand until ready to use.

A round of buttered greaseproof paper	A 2½-pt. cylindrical mould about 3½ ins. high

Place the buttered paper in the bottom of the mould.

⅛ pt. dark rum or kirsch	A cake rack
¼ pt. water	
A soup plate	
About 40 single sponge fingers,	
3½ ins. long and 2 ins. wide	
(recipe for home-made sponge	
fingers is on page 617)	

Pour the rum or kirsch and water into the soup plate. One by one, dip 20 to 25 sponge fingers (or enough to line the mould) into the liquid. Drain on cake rack. Following directions on page 539, line the base and the sides of the mould with the dipped sponge fingers.

2 eggs	A wire whisk
3 egg yolks	¾ pt. milk, brought to the boil with
3 oz. granulated sugar	the grated rind of 1 orange
A 2-qt. mixing bowl	

Beat the eggs, egg yolks, and sugar in a mixing bowl until light and foamy. Gradually beat in the boiling milk. Strain in the kirsch or rum from the glacé fruits.

Preheat oven to 350° F., Mark 4.

¼ pt. apricot preserves forced
    through a sieve

Spoon a ladleful of custard into the prepared mould. Over it sprinkle a small handful of the glacé fruits, then 2 to 3 tablespoons of apricot preserves. Cover with 2 or 3 sponge fingers, and spoon a little custard over them. Wait for a moment for the sponge fingers to absorb the custard, then continue with layers of fruit, apricot preserves, sponge fingers, and custard until the mould is filled. Trim off protruding sponge fingers around edge of mould.

A tin of boiling water

Place mould in a tin of boiling water, and place in lower part of oven. Immediately reduce heat to 325° F., Mark 2. Bake for 50 to 60 minutes, making sure water in tin never comes to simmering point. When centre of custard has risen very slightly and a needle or knife plunged to the base of the mould comes out clean, custard is done. Remove from tin of water and let cool. (May be served slightly warm, or chilled.)

A serving dish   **¾ pt. strawberry sauce, page 546**

Run a knife around the edge of the custard and reverse on a serving dish. Remove round of paper, and surround the dessert with the sauce.

SWEET SOUFFLÉS
Soufflés Sucrés

Many people consider the dessert soufflé to be the epitome and triumph of the art of French cookery, a glorious and exciting finish to a great meal. Although sweet soufflés are lighter and airier than entrée soufflés, the general idea is the same: a flavoured sauce base into which stiffly beaten egg whites are incorporated. All the points discussed in the Entrée chapter regarding soufflés, pages 142 to 148, apply also to sweet soufflés; these include soufflé moulds, placement in the oven, testing, and serving. The discussion in that section on how to beat egg whites is of particular importance. Though you will get a soufflé of some sort no matter what you do, you will achieve magnificence only if your egg whites are beaten so they mount smoothly and stiffly to about seven times their original volume, and are then folded carefully into the sauce base so that their maximum volume is retained.

THE SAUCE BASE OR *BOUILLI*

Of the three standard methods for making a soufflé base, the béchamel with its cooked *roux*, the *crème pâtissière* with its cooked egg yolks, and the *bouilli* used in the following recipes, we prefer the *bouilli* for lightness. A *bouilli* is milk, sugar, and flour or starch, boiled for a few seconds until thickened. After it has cooled slightly, egg yolks, butter, and flavouring are beaten in, then beaten egg whites are incorporated. Although you can make a soufflé without the flour or starch thickening, as in the lemon soufflé tart on page 597, you will find that it does not have quite the tender texture of the soufflés in this section.

SOUFFLÉ MOULDS

Be sure to read the illustrated section on soufflé moulds, pages 146–7 in the Entrée chapter.

TIMING

The following recipes for hot soufflés are based on a 2½-pint mould, and, except for the chocolate soufflé, take 30 to 35 minutes to bake. Since you may fill your mould and cover it with an empty pan as suggested on page 146, you can let it wait for about an hour before baking. Thus you can time it quite accurately to coincide with dessert if you are also able to estimate the general eating-speed for the rest of the meal. In any case, no guest who knows a soufflé is in the oven should mind waiting a few minutes for dessert.

Soufflés made in a 1-pint mould take 15 to 20 minutes to bake; those in a 3-pint mould, 40 to 45 minutes. Moulds larger than 3-pint capacity are difficult to time, and the soufflé is so large that it may not rise satisfactorily.

---

* *SOUFFLÉ À LA VANILLE*

[Vanilla Soufflé]

All of the sweet soufflés with the exception of chocolate may be made according to the following vanilla soufflé formula. A fairly quick operator can make any of them ready for the oven in 20 minutes.

For 4 people

Preparing the soufflé mould
Preheat oven to 400° F., Mark 6.

¼ oz. softened butter	**Granulated sugar**
A 2½-pt. mould, preferably one 3½ ins. deep like the *charlotte*. See illustrations on page 147	

Measure out the ingredients. Butter the entire inner surface of the mould. Roll granulated sugar around in it to coat the sides and bottom evenly. Knock out excess sugar.

The bouilli sauce base

A wire whisk   **¼ pt. milk**
¾ oz. flour   **2 oz. granulated sugar**
A 2-qt. enamelled saucepan

Beat the flour in the saucepan with a little milk until well blended. Beat in the
rest of the milk, and the sugar. Stir over a moderately high heat until the
mixture thickens and comes to the boil. Boil, stirring, for 30 seconds. The sauce
will be very thick. Remove from heat and beat for 2 minutes to cool slightly.

4 eggs   **A wire whisk**
A bowl for beating egg whites

Separate one egg, dropping the white into the bowl, and the yolk into the centre
of the sauce. At once beat the yolk into the sauce with the wire whisk. Continue
with the rest of the eggs, one by one.

1 oz. softened butter   **A rubber spatula**

Beat in half the butter. Clean the sauce off sides of pan with the rubber spatula.
Dot top of sauce with the rest of the butter to prevent a skin from forming on
the surface.

(*) If made in advance, beat over a gentle heat only until sauce is barely warm
to your finger, not hot. Then proceed with the recipe.

The egg whites

5 egg whites (4 left over from the   Pinch of salt
** yolks and 1 extra white)   1 tbl granulated sugar**

Beat the egg whites and salt together until soft peaks are formed. Sprinkle on the
sugar and beat until stiff peaks are formed. (Directions for beating egg whites are
on page 144.)

The flavouring

2 tbl vanilla extract
(Or see Vanilla, page 541, if you
prefer the bean)

Beat the vanilla into the sauce base. Stir in a quarter of the beaten egg whites.
Delicately fold in the rest. (Illustrated directions for folding are on page 146.)

Filling the mould

Turn the soufflé mixture into the prepared mould, leaving a space of at least
1¼ inches between the top of the soufflé and the rim of the mould. If the mould
is too full, the soufflé will spill over as it rises.

(*) If soufflé is not to be cooked immediately, place an empty pan upside down
over the mould. Filled mould can now wait for about an hour before baking.

Baking the soufflé

Icing sugar in a shaker

Place the mould in the middle of the preheated oven, and immediately turn down to 375° F., Mark 5. In 20 minutes, when the soufflé has begun to puff and brown, quickly sprinkle the top with icing sugar. After a total of 30 to 35 minutes of baking, the top of the soufflé should be nicely browned, and a trussing needle, or long, thin knife, plunged into the soufflé through the side of the puff, should come out clean.

Serve immediately.

VARIATIONS

All of the following variations are based on the preceding master recipe, using the same method and ingredients except for changes in flavour.

Soufflé à l'Orange

[Orange Soufflé with Cointreau, Curaçao, Grand Marnier, etc.]

1 bright-skinned orange	**2 large sugar lumps**

Use the master soufflé formula. Before making the *bouilli* sauce base, rub the sugar lumps over the orange to extract the oil. Mash the sugar lumps, grate the orange part of the peel, add to the saucepan with the granulated sugar, and proceed with the sauce base.

1 dsp vanilla extract instead of 2 tbl	**3 to 4 tbl orange liqueur**

Beat the vanilla and the orange liqueur into the sauce base just before incorporating the beaten egg whites. Complete the recipe.

Soufflé Rothschild

[Soufflé with Glacé Fruits and Kirsch]

3½ oz. diced, mixed glacé fruits	**⅛ pt. kirsch**

Let the glacé fruits stand in the kirsch for half an hour.

1 dsp vanilla extract instead of 2 tbl

Using the master soufflé formula, prepare the *bouilli* sauce base. Just before incorporating the beaten egg whites, drain the fruits and beat their kirsch maceration into the sauce base with the vanilla.

Turn a third of the soufflé mixture into the prepared mould. Sprinkle half of the glacé fruits on top. Cover with half the remaining soufflé mixture, then with the rest of the fruits, and finally the last of the soufflé mixture.

Soufflé au Café

[Coffee Soufflé]

Use the master soufflé formula on page 567, but before making the *bouilli* sauce base:

Either: 3 tbl coffee beans   **Or: 1 tbl instant coffee**

Blend 3 tablespoons of the milk into the flour for the *bouilli*. Then *either* bring the rest of the milk to the boil with the coffee beans, cover and steep for 5 minutes, and strain into the *bouilli* paste, beating thoroughly; *or* beat instant coffee into boiling milk, then combine with the *bouilli*.

1 dsp vanilla extract rather than
   1 tbl

Then proceed with the recipe, beating the vanilla into the sauce base before incorporating the beaten egg whites.

Soufflé Praliné
Soufflé aux Macarons

[Soufflé with Caramelized Almonds or Macaroons]

Use the master soufflé formula on page 567.

1 dsp vanilla extract rather than   **3 oz. *pralin*, page 537, or the**
   2 tbl   **pulverized macaroons, page 538**

Stir the vanilla and the *pralin* or macaroons into the *bouilli* sauce base just before incorporating the beaten egg whites.

Soufflé aux Amandes

[Almond Soufflé]

Almonds may be added to any soufflé, and are especially good with coffee, orange, or chocolate, as well as with vanilla.

Use the master soufflé formula on page 567.

2 tbl vanilla extract   **3 oz. pulverized toasted almonds,**
¼ tsp almond extract   **page 537**

Stir the vanilla and almond extracts and almonds into the *bouilli* sauce base just before incorporating the beaten egg whites.

Soufflé Panaché

[Half-and-half Soufflé]

For two kinds of soufflé cooked in the same mould, use vanilla, and coffee, *pralin*, or orange. Chocolate will not do, as it cooks in a different manner.

The *bouilli* sauce base, master recipe,   **Two 3-pt. bowls**
  page 568
Divide the sauce base into the two bowls.

5 egg whites   **1 tbl granulated sugar**
Pinch of salt
Beat the egg whites and salt together until soft peaks are formed; sprinkle on the sugar and beat until stiff peaks are formed.

1 tbl vanilla extract
Beat the vanilla flavouring into one bowl, and fold in half the beaten egg whites.

½ tsp vanilla extract
2 tsp instant coffee mixed with
  1 tbl boiling water
Beat the vanilla extract and coffee into the other bowl, and fold in the remaining egg whites.

A 2½-pt. soufflé mould prepared as
  in the master recipe
2 oz. pulverized macaroons, page
  538, moistened with 2 tbl orange
  liqueur
Turn half the vanilla soufflé mixture into the prepared mould. Sprinkle with a third of the macaroons and liqueur mixture. Spread half of the coffee soufflé over this, then sprinkle on more macaroons. Continue with the remaining vanilla soufflé, macaroons, and the last of the coffee soufflé.

Bake for 30 to 35 minutes in a preheated, 375° F., Mark 5 oven as for the master recipe.

SOUFFLÉ AU CHOCOLAT

[Chocolate Soufflé]

Cooked chocolate is heavy in itself, and requires special treatment to avoid a heavy, pudding-like soufflé. Therefore, instead of making the soufflé with a flour and milk *bouilli* sauce-base, you will use a base of potato flour, rice flour, or cornflour and milk, and 3 rather than 4 egg yolks. Chocolate soufflés also take 10 to 15 minutes longer to cook than other soufflés. Although the general method is essentially the same as for the vanilla soufflé, we give a full recipe because there are slight differences in technique.

For 4 people

Preheat oven to 375° F., Mark 5.

¼ oz. softened butter A 2½-pt. soufflé mould	2 to 3 tbl flour

Butter the soufflé mould and roll flour in it rather than sugar; knock out excess. Measure out the ingredients.

3½ oz. plain chocolate 2 tbl strong coffee	A small saucepan placed over almost simmering water

Stir the chocolate and coffee over the almost simmering water until chocolate is melted and smooth. Remove from stove and keep over hot water until ready to use.

A wire whisk 1 oz. potato flour, rice flour, or cornflour	½ pt. milk A 1½-pt. saucepan 2 oz. granulated sugar

Beat the starch and 3 tablespoons of the milk in the saucepan until blended and smooth. Beat in the rest of the milk, and the sugar. Stir over a moderate heat until the boil is reached. Boil and stir 3 seconds; this will be very gluey, especially if you use potato flour. Away from heat, beat in the hot melted chocolate until well blended.

A rubber spatula	1 oz. softened butter

Clean away from the sides of the saucepan and divide the butter over the sauce. Allow it to cool until it is tepid.

5 egg whites Pinch of salt	1 tbl granulated sugar

Beat the egg whites and salt together in a separate bowl until soft peaks are formed; sprinkle on the sugar and beat until stiff peaks are formed. (Directions are on page 144.)

A 2-qt. mixing bowl A rubber spatula	3 egg yolks

Scrape the chocolate sauce into the mixing bowl. Beat in the three egg yolks, which may be added all at once. Stir in one-quarter of the egg whites; delicately fold in the rest. Turn the soufflé into the prepared mould, leaving at least 1¼ inches between the top of the soufflé and the rim of the mould.

Icing sugar in a shaker

Bake in middle of the preheated oven. In about 35 minutes, or when soufflé has risen about an inch over the top of the mould, rapidly sprinkle top with sugar. Bake another 10 minutes, making about 45 minutes in all. Soufflé is ready when a knife, plunged into the side of the puff, comes out clean.

Optional, ¾ pt.:   **Or: *crème fraîche*, page 13**
  crème anglaise **(custard sauce),**
  page 542
Or: lightly whipped cream
  flavoured with sugar and vanilla,
  page 535

Serve at once, and accompany with a sauce or cream, if you wish.

SOUFFLÉ DÉMOULÉ AUX MACARONS

[Rum and Macaroon Soufflé, Unmoulded—a cold dessert]

For 6 to 8 people

Preheat oven to 350° F., Mark 4.

1 tsp butter
A 3-pt., fireproof, cylindrical
  mould lined with caramel, page 538

Butter the inside of the caramel-lined mould.

A wire whisk or electric beater   **A 2-qt. mixing bowl**
8 oz. pulverized macaroons,   **¼ pt. milk brought to the boil with**
  page 538   **1½ oz. granulated sugar**
⅛ pt. dark rum

Beat the macaroons and rum together in the mixing bowl while pouring on the hot milk and sugar, and continue beating for 1 minute.

4 egg yolks

One by one, beat in the egg yolks until blended with the macaroons.

4 egg whites   **1 tbl granulated sugar**
Pinch of salt

Beat the egg whites and salt in a separate bowl until soft peaks are formed; sprinkle on the sugar and beat until stiff peaks are formed, page 144.

A rubber spatula

Fold the egg whites into the macaroon mixture, being sure that the mixture, which is very liquid, is thoroughly but delicately blended with the egg whites. Turn into prepared mould which will be filled by about two-thirds.

A tin containing enough boiling
 water to come half-way up
 outside of mould

Place mould in tin of boiling water; place in lower part of preheated, 350° F., Mark 4 oven for 15 minutes. Then reduce heat to 325°F., Mark 2, and continue baking about 35 minutes more. Soufflé will rise about to the top of the mould. It is done when it shows a faint line of shrinkage from the sides of the mould.

A serving dish
1 pt. chilled, coffee-flavoured
 ***crème anglaise* (custard sauce),**
 page 542

Refrigerate for 3 to 4 hours. The soufflé will sink down as it cools, and shrink more from the mould. When chilled, reverse on to the serving dish. Simmer 2 tablespoons of water in the mould to dissolve the remaining caramel; allow to cool for a moment, then pour the caramel syrup over the soufflé. Surround with the sauce, and serve.

ÎLE FLOTTANTE

[Caramel Almond Soufflé, Unmoulded—a cold dessert]

French floating island is an unmoulded soufflé of beaten egg whites, sugar, and flavouring, surrounded by a sauce so that it looks as though it were floating. Those little mounds of egg whites floating on custard which are usually called floating island in English are the French dessert, *oeufs à la neige*.

For 6 to 8 people

Preheat the oven to 350° F., Mark 4.

¼ oz. softened butter   2 to 3 tbl sugar
A 3-pt., fireproof, cylindrical
 mould, preferably 4 ins. high

Butter the mould, roll sugar in it, and knock out excess.

8 egg whites	A 2-qt. bowl
⅛ tsp salt	A large wire whisk or an electric
6 oz. castor sugar	beater
2 oz. *pralin* (caramelized almonds), page 537	

Beat the egg whites and salt until soft peaks are formed. Then start beating in the sugar, sprinkling 2 tablespoons at a time, alternating with the *pralin*. Continue beating until all sugar and *pralin* have been added, and the egg whites form stiff peaks.

A tin containing enough boiling
   water to come half-way up
   outside of mould

Turn the mixture into the prepared mould, and place in tin of boiling water. Place in lower part of preheated oven for about 40 minutes. Soufflé is ready when it shows a faint line of shrinkage from the sides of the mould.

A serving dish	Or: 1 pt. strawberry or raspberry
2 tbl *pralin*	sauce, page 546
¾ pt. chilled *crème anglaise* (custard sauce), page 542, flavoured with vanilla, chocolate, or coffee	

Refrigerate for 3 to 4 hours. Soufflé will sink as it cools. Run a knife around the edge of the dessert and reverse on the serving dish. Sprinkle with *pralin*, and surround with one of the sauces.

FRUIT DESSERTS

Entremets aux Fruits

CHARLOTTE AUX POMMES

[Apple Charlotte, Unmoulded—a hot or cold dessert]

This extremely good dessert is a thick, rum- and apricot-flavoured apple purée piled into a cylindrical mould which has been lined with butter-soaked strips of white bread. It is baked in a very hot oven until the bread is golden brown, and is then unmoulded. For the sake of drama, the mould should be 3½ to 4 inches high. Be sure your apple purée is very thick indeed, or the dessert will collapse when unmoulded.

For 6 to 8 people

6 lbs. crisp eating or cooking apples	**A wooden spoon**
A heavy-bottomed enamelled pan (saucepan, casserole, or frying pan) 10 to 12 ins. in diameter	

Quarter, peel, and core the apples. Slice them roughly into $\frac{1}{8}$-inch pieces. Place in pan, cover, and cook over very low heat for about 20 minutes, stirring occasionally, until tender.

$\frac{1}{4}$ pt. apricot preserves, forced through a sieve	**2 tsp vanilla extract**
6 oz. granulated sugar	**$\frac{1}{8}$ pt. dark rum**
	$1\frac{1}{2}$ oz. butter

Uncover and beat in the apricot preserves, sugar, vanilla, rum, and butter. Raise heat and boil, stirring almost continuously, for about 10 minutes or until the water content has almost entirely evaporated. The purée should be a very thick and fairly stiff paste which holds itself in a solid mass in the spoon.

Preheat oven to 425° F., Mark 7.

10 to 12 slices of home-made type white bread, 4 ins. square and $\frac{1}{4}$ in. thick	**A $2\frac{1}{2}$-pt. fireproof, cylindrical mould about $3\frac{1}{2}$ ins. high**
	8 oz. clarified butter, page 12

Remove crusts. Cut a square and 4 semi-circles of bread to fit the base of the mould exactly. Sauté to a very light golden colour in 3 or 4 tablespoons of the clarified butter. Fit them into the base of the mould. Cut the rest of the bread into strips $1\frac{1}{4}$ inches wide. Dip in clarified butter and fit them, overlapping each other, around the inner circumference of the mould. Trim off protruding ends.

Pack the apple purée into the mould, allowing it to form a dome about $\frac{3}{4}$ inch high in the middle. (It will sink as it cools.) Cover with 4 or 5 butter-dipped bread strips. Pour any remaining clarified butter over the ends of the bread around the edges of the mould.

A tin	**A serving dish**

Place in a tin (to catch butter drippings) and bake in middle of preheated oven for about 30 minutes. Slip a knife between bread and sides of mould; if bread is golden brown, the charlotte is done. Remove from oven and cool for 15 minutes. Reverse the mould on to a serving dish and lift the mould up a few inches to see if the sides of the dessert will hold. If there is any suggestion of collapse, lower the mould over the dessert again; it will firm up as it cools. Test after 5 minutes or so, until the mould can safely be removed.

¼ pt. apricot preserves, forced
    through a sieve
3 tbl dark rum
2 tbl granulated sugar
Optional: ¾ pt. *crème anglaise*
    (custard sauce), page 542, or
    ¾ pt. lightly whipped cream
    flavoured with rum and icing
    sugar, page 535

Boil the apricot preserves, rum, and sugar until thick and sticky. Spread over the charlotte. Serve the dessert hot, warm, or cold, with the optional sauce or cream.

POMMES NORMANDE EN BELLE VUE

[Apple-sauce Caramel Mould—a warm or cold dessert]

This is a much lighter dessert than the apple charlotte, and also much easier to prepare.

For 6 people

4 lbs. crisp cooking or eating
    apples
A heavy-bottomed enamelled pan
    (saucepan, casserole, or frying
    pan) about 10 ins. in diameter

A wooden spoon

Peel and core the apples. Slice them roughly into ⅛-inch pieces. Place them in the pan; cover and cook over a very low heat for about 20 minutes, stirring occasionally, until tender.

Preheat oven to 400° F., Mark 6.

¼ tsp cinnamon
The grated peel of 1 lemon

3 oz. granulated sugar

Beat the cinnamon, lemon peel, and sugar into the apples. Raise heat and boil, stirring, for 5 minutes or so, until the apples have reduced to a thick purée which will hold its shape in the spoon.

⅛ pt. rum, cognac, or excellent
    apple brandy
2 oz. butter

4 eggs
1 egg white

Remove from heat and stir in the rum or brandy, then the butter. One by one, beat in the eggs, then the egg white.

    T

A 2½-pt., fireproof, cylindrical   A lid or a plate
   mould lined with caramel,   A deep saucepan
   page 538   Boiling water

Turn the apple mixture into the caramel-lined mould. Cover with a lid or plate, and set in the saucepan. Pour boiling water around the outside of the mould to come up to the level of the apple mixture. Place in lower part of preheated oven. Regulate oven heat to maintain water almost at simmering point. The dessert is done in 1 to 1½ hours, when it begins to shrink from the sides of the mould and the top, all except for a small area in the very centre, is set.

A serving dish

To serve warm, remove the mould from the saucepan and allow the dessert to cool for 20 minutes. Then reverse it on a serving dish. To serve cold, chill the dessert 4 to 5 hours or overnight. Then run a knife around the edge of the dessert and reverse on a serving dish; in a few minutes it will dislodge itself from the mould.

3 tbl rum, cognac, or apple brandy
¾ pt. lightly whipped cream
   flavoured with icing sugar and
   rum or brandy, or ¾ pt. *crème*
   anglaise (custard sauce), page 542

Simmer the rum or brandy in the mould to dissolve any remaining caramel, and strain over the dessert. Surround the dessert with the whipped cream or sauce.

POUDING ALSACIEN

[*Gratin* of Sautéed Apples—a cold dessert]

This simple apple dessert is always better if prepared the day before it is eaten, as a good 24 hours are needed for a slow blending of flavours.

For 6 to 8 people

2½ lbs. crisp eating or cooking
   apples

Quarter, core, and peel the apples. Cut into ¼-inch lengthwise slices.

2 to 2½ oz. butter
A 10- to 12-in. frying pan
A lightly buttered baking dish,
   8 to 9 ins. in diameter and 2 ins.
   deep

Sauté the apples, one layer at a time, in hot butter until they are very lightly browned on both sides and tender, but retain their shape. As they are done, place them in the baking dish.

| ¼ lb. plum jam, forced through a sieve | 2 tbl rum
A rubber spatula |

Melt the plum jam in the frying pan with the rum. Delicately fold into the apples, and smooth the apples in the dish.

Preheat oven to 325° F., Mark 2.

2 oz. butter	½ tsp cinnamon
3 oz. granulated sugar	2 oz. fresh whole wheat or rye
3 egg yolks	breadcrumbs
¼ oz. flour	

Cream the butter and sugar together in a mixing bowl until light and fluffy, page 536. Beat in the egg yolks, then the flour and cinnamon, and finally the breadcrumbs.

| 2 egg whites | ½ tbl granulated sugar |
| Pinch of salt | |

Beat the egg whites and salt until soft peaks are formed; sprinkle on the sugar and beat until stiff peaks are formed (page 144). Fold the egg whites into the breadcrumb mixture and spread evenly over the apples.

Icing sugar in a shaker

Bake in middle of preheated oven for 20 to 25 minutes, or until top has puffed slightly and has just begun to colour. Sprinkle liberally with icing sugar and continue baking another 20 to 25 minutes; the top should be a nice golden brown under the sugar.

Allow to cool, then chill, preferably for 24 hours.

ASPIC DE POMMES

[Rum-Flavoured Apple *Aspic*, Unmoulded—a cold dessert]

Because the apples for this simple dessert are boiled in a heavy sugar syrup, they set when chilled and can be unmoulded on a serving dish. It makes a pretty effect with its decoration of glacé fruits. Once made, the *aspic* may be kept moulded or unmoulded under refrigeration for at least 10 days.

For 6 to 8 people

3 lbs. cooking apples

Quarter, core, and peel the apples. Cut into lengthwise slices ½ inch thick.

A heavy 12-in. enamelled frying	**1¼ lbs. sugar**
** pan**	**1 tbl lemon juice**
¼ pt. water	

Bring water, sugar, and lemon juice to the boil, stirring until sugar has dissolved. Add the apples and boil over a moderately high heat, stirring frequently to keep them from sticking and burning, for about 20 minutes. They should become an almost transparent mass.

A 1½-pt. cylindrical mould	**A round of greaseproof paper**
1 tsp tasteless salad oil	

While the apples are cooking, rub inside of mould with oil; oil the greaseproof paper and place in the base of the mould.

**4 oz. glacé fruits, such as red
  cherries, angelica, orange peel**

Make a decorative design in the bottom of the mould with half the fruit. Dice the rest and add it to boil with the apples for 2 to 3 minutes at the end of the cooking.

3 tbl dark rum

When the apples are done, remove from the heat and stir in the rum. Spoon into the mould and chill for 4 to 6 hours, or until set. Serve as follows:

**A chilled serving dish
¾ pt. _crème anglaise_ (custard sauce),
  page 542**

Surround the mould with a hot cloth for 10 to 15 seconds. Run a knife around edge of mould, and reverse the aspic on to a chilled serving dish. Surround with the sauce and serve.

POMMES À LA SÉVILLANE

[Apples Braised in Butter, Orange Sauce—a hot or cold dessert]

For 6 people

Preheat oven to 325° F., Mark 2.

6 crisp, unblemished, cooking or eating apples	**A mixing bowl containing 3 pts. water and 2 tbl lemon juice**

One by one, peel and core the apples, and drop into the acidulated water.

A covered fireproof baking dish just large enough to hold the apples easily in one layer **2 oz. butter** **4 oz. granulated sugar** **¼ pt. dry white wine or dry white vermouth**	**¼ pt. water** **2 tbl cognac** **A round of buttered greaseproof paper**

Smear inside of baking dish with half the butter. Drain the apples and place them upright in the dish. Sprinkle with sugar and place a teaspoon of butter in the centre of each apple. Pour the wine, water, and cognac around the apples. Lay the round of buttered paper on top. Bring just to simmering point on top of the stove. Cover and bake in lower part of preheated oven for 25 to 35 minutes; it is important that you maintain the liquid at the merest simmer to prevent the apples from bursting. When a knife pierces them easily, they are done. Be careful not to overcook them.

2 or 3 brightly coloured oranges	**A vegetable peeler**

While apples are cooking, remove the orange part of the skin with vegetable peeler. Cut into strips 2 inches long and ⅛ inch wide. Simmer 10 to 12 minutes in water until tender. Drain, rinse in cold water, and dry.

6 canapés (rounds of white bread sautéed in clarified butter), page 181	**A serving dish** **A slotted spoon**

Also while the apples are baking, prepare the canapés, and arrange on serving dish. When apples are done, place a drained apple on each canapé.

¼ pt. red currant jelly	**3 tbl cognac**

Beat the jelly into the apple cooking liquid and boil down quickly over a high heat until thick enough to coat a spoon lightly. Stir in the cognac and the cooked orange peel, and simmer for a moment. Spoon the sauce and orange peel over the apples.

½ to ¾ pt. cream or *crème anglaise* (custard sauce) page 542

Serve them hot, warm, or cold, and pass the cream or sauce separately.

ORANGES GLACÉES

[Glazed Oranges—a cold dessert]

This recipe calls for whole, peeled oranges, placed in a bowl, then glazed with syrup and decorated with glazed orange peel. If you prefer sliced oranges, allow one to a serving, slice them crosswise, re-form the oranges horizontally in the serving dish, and glaze them.

For 6 people

6 large, brightly coloured navel oranges	A small bowl
A vegetable peeler	2 tbl orange liqueur

Remove the orange part of the skins with a vegetable peeler and cut into strips ⅛ inch wide and 2 inches long. Simmer in water for 10 to 12 minutes or until tender. Drain, rinse in cold water, dry, and place in a small bowl to stand with the liqueur.

A serving dish 2 ins. deep

Cut the white part of the peel neatly off the oranges to expose their flesh. Cut a bit off one end of each, so it will stand up. Arrange oranges in the serving dish, with the flattened ends on the bottom.

¾ lb. granulated sugar	A small saucepan
¼ pt. water	Optional: a jam thermometer

Boil the sugar and water in the saucepan until it reaches the firm ball stage (244° F.). Stir 3 tablespoons into the cooked orange peel. A spoonful at a time, glaze the oranges slowly with the rest of the syrup. Chill for several hours.

Optional: green-coloured glacé fruit cut into leaf shapes

Before serving, strain the orange peel. Decorate the glazed oranges with the peel and optional glacé fruit. Pour the orange-peel maceration around the oranges.

PÊCHES CARDINAL

[Compote of Fresh Peaches with Raspberry Purée—a cold dessert]

This is an especially nice dessert when both peaches and raspberries are in season. Though the taste is not quite as good, you can substitute fresh apricots or

pears for the peaches, or use tinned fruit. Frozen raspberries do not make as
thick a sauce as fresh ones, but are good anyway.

For 10 people

2½ pts. water   A 12-in. saucepan
1 lb. granulated sugar
2 tbl vanilla extract or a vanilla
   bean

Simmer the water, sugar, and vanilla extract or bean in the saucepan and stir
until sugar has dissolved.

10 firm, ripe, unblemished, fresh   A cake rack
   peaches about 2½ ins. in diameter   A serving dish 2 ins. deep
A slotted spoon

Add the unpeeled peaches to the simmering syrup. Bring again to simmering
point, then maintain at just below the simmer for 8 minutes. Remove pan from
heat and allow peaches to cool in syrup for 20 minutes. (Syrup may be used
again for poaching other fruits.) Drain peaches on rack; peel while still warm,
and arrange in serving dish. Chill.

1 lb. fresh raspberries, and ½ lb.   An electric liquidizer (or electric
   granulated sugar   beater)
Or: 1½ lbs. frozen raspberries,
   thawed and well drained, and
   4 oz. sugar

Force the raspberries through a sieve and place the purée in the jar of an electric
liquidizer along with the sugar. Cover and blend at top speed for 2 to 3 minutes,
or until purée is thick and sugar has dissolved completely. Chill. (Or beat purée
and sugar for about 10 minutes with an electric beater.)

Optional: fresh mint leaves

When both purée and peaches are chilled, pour the purée over the peaches and
return to refrigerator until serving time. Decorate with optional fresh mint
leaves.

POIRES AU GRATIN

[Pears Baked with Macaroons—a hot or cold dessert]

For 6 people

Preheat oven to 400° F., Mark 6.

2 lbs. fresh ripe pears or drained
   tinned pears
A baking dish about 2 ins. high and
   8 ins. in diameter, smeared with
   1 oz. butter

Peel, quarter, and core the pears. Cut into lengthwise slices about $\frac{1}{2}$ inch thick. Arrange in overlapping layers in the baking dish.

$\frac{1}{8}$ pt. dry white wine or dry white $\frac{1}{8}$ pt. apricot preserves, forced
   vermouth, or tinned pear juice   through a sieve

Beat the wine or pear juice and apricot preserves together and pour over the pears.

3 oz. pulverized macaroons,   1$\frac{1}{2}$ oz. butter cut into very small
   page 538   pieces

Sprinkle on the macaroons and distribute the butter over them.

Bake in middle of preheated oven for 20 to 30 minutes, or until top has browned lightly. Serve hot, warm, or cold.

FLAN DES ÎLES

[Pineapple Custard, Unmoulded—a cold dessert]

For 6 to 8 people

1$\frac{1}{4}$ lbs. drained, tinned, crushed   A 2$\frac{1}{2}$- to 3-pt. saucepan
   pineapple, and $\frac{3}{4}$ pt. syrup (30
   to 32 oz. tinned fruit in syrup)

Boil the pineapple syrup for 5 minutes in the saucepan. Add the pineapple, bring again to the boil, and boil slowly 5 minutes more.

A wire whisk   A 5-pt. mixing bowl
$\frac{1}{4}$ oz. flour $\frac{1}{8}$ pt. kirsch or cognac
3 tbl lemon juice   5 eggs

Beat flour and lemon juice in the mixing bowl until blended, then beat in the kirsch or cognac, and the eggs. Gradually beat in the hot pineapple mixture in a thin stream of drops.

A 2$\frac{1}{2}$-pt., fireproof, cylindrical   A deep saucepan
   mould lined with caramel,   Boiling water
   page 538

Pour the pineapple custard into the caramel-lined mould, and place mould in a deep saucepan. Pour boiling water around the outside of the mould to come up to the level of the custard. Bring to simmering point on top of the stove, and maintain water barely at simmering point, always on top of the stove, for $1\frac{1}{4}$ to $1\frac{1}{2}$ hours. Custard is done when it begins to shrink from the sides of the mould. A little circle in the centre of the custard will remain creamy.

Remove mould from water, let cool, then chill for 3 to 4 hours or overnight.

A serving dish $\frac{3}{4}$ **pt. chilled *crème anglaise* (custard**
2 tbl kirsch or cognac   **sauce), page 542**

Reverse on to a serving dish. Simmer kirsch or cognac in mould to dissolve remaining caramel. Strain it into the chilled *crème anglaise*, and pour the sauce around the custard.

DESSERT TARTS
Tartes Sucrées

French dessert tarts, like French entrée tarts and *quiches*, are open faced and stand supported only by their pastry shells. They should be beautiful to look at, especially the fruit tarts which lend themselves to glittering arrangements of rosettes and overlapping circles.

THE PASTRY

The pastry for dessert tart shells is moulded and baked in a *flan* ring or a false-bottomed cake tin so that the shell may be unmoulded. You may use either sweet short crust pastry, which is ordinary short crust pastry with sugar added, or *pâte sablée*, sweet flan pastry, which, besides flour and butter, contains eggs and usually more sugar. We give proportions for both here, and refer you to the illustrated directions in the Entrée chapter for their moulding and baking.

Pâte Brisée Sucrée

[Sweet Short Crust Pastry]

Sweet short crust pastry is made exactly like normal short crust pastry except that sugar is mixed into the flour before you begin. (If you are not using British or French flour, be sure to read the notes in paragraph one, page 126.)

Proportions for each 5 ounces of flour

(This is sufficient for an 8- to 9-inch shell. Use $1\frac{1}{2}$ times this amount for a 10- to 11-inch shell.)

T*

5 oz. plain white flour
A mixing bowl
1½ tbl. castor sugar
⅛ tsp salt

4 oz. chilled butter cut into ½-in.
   pieces
4 to 4½ tbl cold water

Place the flour in the bowl, mix in the sugar and salt, then proceed to make the dough and mould the shell as described and illustrated on pages 126-31.

Pâte Sablée

[Sweet Flan Pastry]

This is particularly good with fresh fruit tarts, like the strawberry tart on page 592. It is more delicate than sweet short crust pastry shells because of the eggs and additional sugar. The more sugar you mix in, the more difficult it is to roll and mould the pastry because it is sticky and breaks easily; the larger proportion of sugar, however, makes a delicious crust, actually a biscuit dough.

For a 9- to 10-inch shell

7 oz. plain white flour
3 to 7 tbl castor sugar (see remarks
   in preceding paragraph)
⅛ tsp double-action baking powder
3½ oz. chilled butter

A 2½-qt. mixing bowl
1 egg beaten with 1 tsp water
½ tsp vanilla extract
A pastry board
Greaseproof paper

Place the flour, sugar, butter, and baking powder in the mixing bowl. Rub the fat and dry ingredients together rapidly with the tips of the fingers until the fat is broken into pieces the size of small oatmeal flakes. Blend in the egg and vanilla, and knead the dough rapidly into a ball. Place on a pastry board and with the heel of your hand, not the palm, rapidly press the pastry by two-spoonful pieces down on the board and away from you in a firm, quick smear of about 6 inches. (This final blending of fat and flour is illustrated on page 127.) The dough will be quite sticky if you have used the full amount of sugar. Form again into a ball, wrap in greaseproof paper, and chill for several hours until firm.

Mould the pastry in a flan ring or false-bottomed cake tin as described and illustrated on page 129. Work rapidly if you have used the full amount of sugar, as the dough softens quickly.

FULLY and PARTIALLY BAKED PASTRY SHELLS

Sweet Short Crust Pastry Shells

Sweet short crust pastry shells, made from the formula in the first of the two preceding recipes, are baked exactly like normal short crust pastry shells, directions for which are on page 131. You will note in these directions that shells may be fully or partially baked. Partial baking is for shells which are filled and baked again; this preliminary cooking sets the dough, and is a safeguard against soggy based crusts. A fully baked shell may be used for fresh fruit tarts, and is an alternative to the sweet flan pastry shell.

Flan Pastry Shells

These are usually fully baked, and must be watched while in the oven as they burn easily if the full sugar proportions have been used. Because the dough is collapsible until it has firmed in the oven, it is essential that the dough be held in place against the sides of the mould by a lining of foil and beans or a bean-filled mould, as illustrated in the directions for moulding on page 131.

Bake the shell in the middle of a preheated, 375° F., Mark 5 oven for 5 to 6 minutes until the dough is set. Then remove the lining, prick the bottom of the pastry with a fork in several places, and bake for 8 to 10 minutes more. The shell is done when it has shrunk slightly from the mould and begins to brown very lightly. Immediately remove the mould from the shell and slip the shell on to a rack. It will become crusty as it cools.

LEFTOVER PASTRY DOUGH and BISCUITS

Leftover dough, securely wrapped, will keep for several days in the refrigerator or may be deep-frozen. Or use it for biscuits in the following recipe:

Galettes Sablées

[Sugar Biscuits]

Leftovers from either or both of the 2 preceding pastries	**Optional: cinnamon**
A 1¼ in. biscuit cutter	**1 egg beaten in a small bowl with 1 tsp water**
Granulated sugar	**A pastry brush**
A baking sheet	**A cake rack**

Roll out the dough to a thickness of ¼ inch, and cut into rounds 1¼ inches in diameter. Spread a ¼-inch layer of granulated sugar on your pastry board, lay a round of dough over it, and heap sugar on top. Roll the round into a sugar-coated oval about 2½ inches long and place on the ungreased baking sheet. When all the biscuits have been formed, sprinkle them with cinnamon if you wish. Paint tops with beaten egg. Bake in middle of a preheated, 375° F., Mark 5 oven for 10 to 15 minutes, until lightly browned. Cool on a rack.

TARTE AUX POMMES

[Apple Tart—warm or cold]

The classic French apple tart consists of a thick, well-flavoured apple sauce spread in a partially cooked pastry shell. Over it thinly sliced apples are placed

Apple Tart

in an overlapping design of circles. After baking, it is coated with apricot glaze.

For 8 people

**A 10-in. partially cooked pastry
shell placed on a baking sheet,
page 586**

Use the sweet short crust pastry on page 585 for your pastry shell.

**4 lbs. crisp cooking or eating
apples**
1 tsp lemon juice	**2 tbl granulated sugar**
A 3-pt. mixing bowl

Quarter, core, and peel the apples. Cut enough to make ¾ pound into even ⅛-inch lengthwise slices and toss them in a bowl with the lemon juice and sugar. Reserve them for the top of the tart.

**A 10-in. heavy-bottomed pan:
enamelled saucepan, frying pan
or casserole**
A wooden spoon
**⅛ pt. apricot preserves, forced
through a sieve**
**⅛ pt. Calvados (apple brandy),
rum, or cognac; or 1 tbl vanilla
extract**	**4 oz. granulated sugar**
1½ oz. butter
**Optional: ⅛ tsp cinnamon, and/or
the grated rind of 1 lemon or
orange**

Cut the rest of the apples into rough slices. You should have about 2 pounds. Place in the pan and cook, covered, over a low heat for about 20 minutes, stirring occasionally, until tender. Then add the remaining ingredients above.

Raise heat and boil, stirring, until apple sauce is thick enough to hold in a mass in the spoon.

Preheat oven to 375° F., Mark 5.

Spread the apple sauce in the pastry shell. Cover with a neat, closely overlapping layer of sliced apples arranged in a spiral, concentric circles, or as illustrated at the beginning of this recipe.

A cake rack or serving dish	**¾ pt. cream, or *crème fraîche***
¼ pt. apricot glaze, page 547	**page 13**

Bake in upper part of preheated oven for about 30 minutes, or until the sliced apples have browned lightly and are tender. Slide tart on to the rack or serving dish and spoon or paint over it a light coating of apricot glaze. Serve warm or cold, and pass with it, if you wish, a bowl of cream.

---

* *TARTE NORMANDE AUX POMMES*

[Custard Apple Tart—to be served hot]

While this creamy apple tart may be eaten cold, it is at its best when hot or warm. It can be reheated.

For 6 people

**An 8-in. partially baked pastry
  shell placed on a baking sheet,
  page 586**

Use the sweet short crust pastry on page 585 for the pastry shell. Preheat oven to 375° F., Mark 5.

1 lb. crisp cooking or eating apples	**½ tsp cinnamon**
2 oz. granulated sugar	

Quarter, core, and peel the apples. Cut into ⅛-inch lengthwise slices. You should have about ¾ pound. Toss them in a bowl with the sugar and cinnamon, then arrange them in the pastry shell. Bake in upper part of preheated oven for about 20 minutes, or until they start to colour and are almost tender. Remove from oven and allow to cool while preparing the custard.

1 egg	**¼ pt. cream**
2 oz. granulated sugar	**3 tbl Calvados (apple brandy) or**
1 oz. sifted flour	**cognac**

Beat the egg and sugar together in a mixing bowl until mixture is thick, pale yellow, and falls back on itself forming a slowly dissolving ribbon. Beat in the flour, then the cream, and finally the brandy. Pour the mixture over the apples. It should come almost to the top of the pastry shell.

Icing sugar in a shaker

Return to oven for 10 minutes, or until cream begins to puff. Sprinkle heavily with icing sugar and return to oven for 15 to 20 minutes more. Tart is done when top has browned and a needle or knife plunged into the custard comes out clean.

A cake rack or serving dish

Slide tart on to a rack or serving dish, and keep warm until ready to serve.

VARIATION

Tarte aux Poires

[Pear Tart]

Using the same method and proportions, substitute sliced pears for the apples.

LA TARTE DES DEMOISELLES TATIN

[Upside-down Apple Tart—hot or cold]

This is an especially good tart if your apples are full of flavour. It is cooked in a baking dish with the pastry on top of the apples. When done, it is reversed on to a serving dish and presents a lovely mass of caramelized apples.

For 8 people

4 lbs. crisp cooking or eating apples	2 oz. granulated sugar Optional: 1 tsp cinnamon

Quarter, core, and peel the apples. Cut into lengthwise slices ⅛ inch thick. Toss in a bowl with the sugar and optional cinnamon. You should have about 2½ pounds of apples.

1 oz. softened butter A baking dish 9 to 10 ins. in diameter and 2 to 2½ ins. deep (ovenglass is practical, as you can see when the tart is done)	3 oz. granulated sugar 3 oz. melted butter

Butter the baking dish heavily especially on the base. Sprinkle half the sugar in the base of the dish and arrange a third of the apples over it. Sprinkle with a third of the melted butter. Repeat with a layer of half the remaining apples and butter, then a final layer of apples and butter. Sprinkle the rest of the sugar over the apples.

Preheat oven to 375° F., Mark 5.

Chilled sweet short crust pastry,
  page 585

Roll out the pastry to a thickness of $\frac{1}{8}$ inch. Cut it into a circle the size of the top of the baking dish. Place it over the apples, allowing its edges to fall against the inside edge of the dish. Cut 4 or 5 holes about $\frac{1}{8}$ inch long in the top of the pastry to allow cooking steam to escape.

Aluminium foil, if needed

Bake in lower part of preheated oven for 45 to 60 minutes. If pastry begins to brown too much, cover lightly with aluminium foil. Tart is done when you tilt the dish and see that a thick brown syrup rather than a light liquid exudes from the apples between the crust and the edge of the dish.

A fireproof serving dish   **Icing sugar, if needed**

Immediately unmould the tart on to serving dish. If the apples are not a light caramel brown, which is often the case, sprinkle rather heavily with icing sugar and put below a moderately hot grill for several minutes to caramelize the surface lightly.

$\frac{3}{4}$ pt. cream, or _crème fraîche_,
  page 13

Keep warm until serving time, and accompany with a bowl of cream. (May also be served cold, but we prefer it warm.)

---

* *TARTE AUX ABRICOTS*
  TARTE AUX PÊCHES

[Fresh Apricot or Peach Tart—warm or cold]

For 6 people

An 8-in. partially cooked pastry
  shell placed on a baking sheet,
  page 586

For the shell use the sweet short crust pastry on page 585.

| 8 to 10 fresh apricots or 3 or 4 | **Boiling water** |
| peaches | |

Drop the fruit in boiling water for 10 to 15 seconds. Peel, halve, and remove stones. Slice the fruit if you wish.

Preheat oven to 375° F., Mark 5.

4 oz. granulated sugar
1 oz. butter cut into very small
   pieces

Sprinkle 3 tablespoons of sugar in the base of the pastry shell. If the fruit is sliced, arrange it over the sugar in a closely overlapping layer of concentric circles. If it is halved, place the halves, domed side up, closely together in the shell. Spread on the rest of the sugar. Dot with the butter.

Bake in middle of preheated oven for 30 to 40 minutes, or until fruit has coloured lightly and the juices have become syrupy.

| 1½ oz. slivered almonds | ¼ pt. apricot glaze, page 547 |

Slip the tart on to a rack. Decorate with the slivered almonds, and spread on the apricot glaze.

Serve warm or cold.

VARIATIONS

Use the same system with plums, pears, or tinned fruit. A nice combination is slices of tinned apricots alternating with slices of banana.

Tartes Flambées.   Any of these tarts may be flamed with liqueurs as they are brought to the table, as described in the recipe for cherry tart, page 595.

---

*   TARTE AUX FRAISES*

[Fresh Strawberry Tart—cold]

Fresh fruit tarts are easy to make, pretty to look at, and refreshing to eat. They consist of a fully baked tart shell which is lined with liqueur-flavoured *crème pâtissière* (custard filling). The fresh fruit is arranged over the filling and topped with apricot or red currant glaze. Other suggestions follow this recipe.

For 8 people

Fresh Strawberry Tart

**A 10-in. fully baked pastry shell,
page 586**

Use either the sweet short crust pastry, or the flan pastry for your tart shell.
Recipes begin on page 585.

1 lb. large, ripe, handsome   **A cake rack**
   strawberries

Hull the strawberries. If necessary to wash them, do so very quickly, and drain
them on a rack.

½ pt. red currant jelly   **Optional: a jam thermometer**
2 tbl granulated sugar   **A pastry brush**
2 tbl kirsch or cognac

Boil the currant jelly, sugar, and liqueur in a small saucepan until last drops from
spoon are sticky (228° F.). Paint the interior of the shell with a thin coating of
the glaze and allow to set for 5 minutes. This will give the shell a light water-
proofing. Reserve the rest of the glaze for the strawberries. Warm it briefly if it
has hardened.

¾ pt. chilled *crème pâtissière* (custard
   filling), page 543, with 2 to 3 tbl
   kirsch or cognac

Spread a ½-inch layer of *crème pâtissière* in the base of the pastry shell.

Arrange a design of strawberries over the cream. Put the largest strawberry in
the centre, and graduate down in size, placing the berries closely together, their
stem ends in the cream. Spoon or paint over them a thin coating of the glaze,
and the tart is ready to serve.

(*) Because of the glazed waterproofing in the base of the shell, the filled tart
may be left for an hour or so.

VARIATIONS

Using the same method as that for the preceding strawberry tart, substitute a layer of peeled and seeded grapes, sliced bananas, raspberries, or poached or

Mixed Fruit Tart

tinned peaches, apricots, plums, or pears. Follow the above illustration for design.

TARTE AUX POIRES À LA BOURDALOUE

[Pear and Almond Tart—tepid or cold]

For 6 people

1½ to 2 lbs. firm, ripe, unblemished pears	¾ pt. cold water and 1 tbl lemon juice in a mixing bowl

Peel and halve the pears. Neatly stem and core them with a grapefruit knife.

Pear Tart

Drop each half, as it is prepared, into the acidulated water to keep it from discolouring.

¾ pt. claret
2 tbl lemon juice
5 oz. granulated sugar
1 stick or ½ tsp cinnamon

A 2½-qt. enamelled saucepan
A slotted spoon
A rack

Bring the wine, lemon juice, sugar, and cinnamon to the boil in the saucepan. Drain the pears, and drop into the boiling syrup; bring liquid to just below simmering point for 8 to 10 minutes or until pears are tender when pierced with a knife. Do not overcook; they must hold their shape. Remove saucepan from heat and allow pears to cool in the syrup for 20 minutes. Drain the pears on a rack.

Optional: a jam thermometer
⅛ pt. red currant jelly in a small
    saucepan

A wooden spoon

Rapidly boil down the syrup to the thread stage (230° F.). Measure out ⅛ pint of syrup and simmer it with the red currant jelly until jelly has dissolved and the syrup coats the spoon with a light glaze.

A 10-in. fully cooked flan pastry
    shell, page 586

Paint the inside of the shell with a thin layer of the pear and jelly glaze.

1 pt. chilled *frangipane* (almond
    custard), page 545, with 2 tbl
    kirsch

Spread the *frangipane* in the pastry shell. Cut the pears into crosswise or length-wise slices and arrange them over the custard.

Optional: 1 oz. slivered almonds

Decorate with the optional almonds. Spoon a light coating of the glaze over the top of the tart.

TARTE AUX CERISES, FLAMBÉE

[Cherry Tart *Flambée*]

For a spectacular entrance, sprinkle sugar over a cooked fruit tart, cara-melize it briefly under the grill, pour on liqueur, and ignite it as you enter the dining room. The following recipe is for cherries; you may use the same technique for the apricot or peach tart on page 591, and for the variations following it.

The Cherries

You may use tinned cherries instead of fresh for this recipe. In this case, omit the first step in the directions, drain the cherries thoroughly and allow them to stand for at least half an hour with 3 tablespoons of kirsch or cognac and as much sugar as you feel they need. Drain them again just before using, and beat their kirsch or cognac into the cream filling.

For 6 people

¾ lb. fresh black cherries	6 tbl granulated sugar
½ pt. claret	A 3-pt. enamelled saucepan
2 tbl lemon juice	

Wash and stone the cherries. Bring the wine, lemon juice, and sugar to the boil. Drop in the cherries, and bring the liquid to just below simmering point for 5 to 6 minutes or until cherries are tender, but retain their shape. Allow cherries to cool in the syrup for 20 to 30 minutes. Drain.

**An 8-in. fully cooked pastry shell,
   page 586, set in a fireproof serving
   dish**

Use either of the sweet pastry recipes beginning on page 585. If you wish to fill the tart shell some time before serving, paint the interior with a thin coating of red currant glaze, page 547.

**¾ pt. cold *crème pâtissière* (custard
   filling), page 543, or *frangipane*
   (almond custard), page 545, with
   2 tbl kirsch or cognac**

Fold the drained cherries into the custard, and spread the mixture in the tart shell.

Preheat grill to moderately hot.

**3 tbl granulated sugar
⅛ pt. kirsch or cognac, warmed in
   a small saucepan**

Immediately before serving, sprinkle the sugar over the surface of the tart and place it under the grill for 2 to 3 minutes to caramelize the sugar lightly; be careful it does not burn. Just before entering the dining room, pour the warm liqueur over the hot caramelized surface. Avert your face and ignite the liqueur with a lighted match; bring the flaming tart to the table.

TARTE À L'ANANAS

[Pineapple Tart]

For 6 people

20 oz. tinned, sliced, cut or crushed
pineapple (12 oz. drained fruit;
¼ to ½ pt. syrup)

Drain the pineapple. Boil the tinned pineapple syrup for 5 minutes in a saucepan. Add the pineapple and boil for 5 minutes more. Drain the pineapple, and allow it to cool.

¼ pt. red currant jelly   **Optional: a jam thermometer**
2 tbl kirsch or cognac

Boil the pineapple syrup with the jelly and liqueur until it reduces to a glaze (last drops are sticky when dropped from a spoon, 228° F.).

A pastry brush   **½ to ¾ pt. chilled *crème pâtissière***
An 8-in. fully cooked, flan pastry   **(custard filling), page 543, with**
shell, page 586   **2 to 3 tbl kirsch or cognac**

Paint the interior of the shell with a coating of the pineapple glaze. Spread the *crème pâtissière* in the pastry shell.

Optional: 1 oz. diced red and green
glacé fruit and 1 oz. slivered
almonds

When the pineapple is cold, arrange it over the filling. Decorate with the optional glacé fruits and almonds. Spoon a light coating of pineapple glaze over the top.

TARTE AU CITRON
TARTE AUX LIMETTES

[Lemon or Lime Soufflé Tart—hot]

This delicious, light tart is really a soufflé. The same filling is also attractive in little tart shells served for afternoon tea. Speaking of these, see also the lemon butter filling on page 626.

For 8 people

**A 10-in., cooked, flan pastry shell
   placed on a baking sheet,
   page 586 (use only 3 tbl sugar in
   the pastry)**

When you bake the shell allow it to barely colour so that it will not brown too much when it goes again into the oven.

Preheat oven to 325° F., Mark 2.

A wire whisk or electric beater   **3 tbl lemon juice or lime juice**
A 2- to 3-qt. stainless steel bowl   **A pan of not-quite-simmering**
3 oz. granulated sugar   **water**
4 egg yolks   **A wooden spoon**
The grated rind of 1 lemon or   **Optional: a jam thermometer**
**   2 limes**

Gradually beat the sugar into the egg yolks and continue beating until the mixture is thick, pale yellow, and falls back on itself, forming a slowly dissolving ribbon. Beat in the rind and juice. Place bowl over not-quite-simmering water and stir with wooden spoon until mixture is too hot for your finger (165° F.), and thickens enough to coat the spoon lightly. Be careful not to overheat it and scramble the egg yolks.

4 egg whites   **2 oz. granulated sugar**
A pinch of salt

Beat the egg whites and salt until soft peaks are formed; sprinkle on the sugar and continue beating until stiff peaks are formed (page 144). Fold the egg whites delicately into the warm lemon or lime mixture and turn into the tart shell.

Icing sugar in shaker

Bake for about 30 minutes in middle of preheated oven. When tart has begun to puff and colour, sprinkle with icing sugar. It is done when top is lightly brown, and a needle or knife plunged into the centre comes out clean.

If you cannot serve it immediately, leave in turned-off hot oven with the door ajar. It will sink slightly as it cools. (May be served hot, warm, or cold but we think it is best hot.)

TARTE AU CITRON ET AUX AMANDES

[Lemon and Almond Tart—cold]

For 6 people

**An 8-in., cooked, flan pastry shell
  placed on a baking sheet, page 586
  (use only 3 tbl sugar in the pastry)**

When you bake the shell, allow it to barely colour so that it will not brown too much when it goes again into the oven.

3 lemons   **A vegetable peeler**

Remove the yellow part of the lemon skin with a vegetable peeler; cut into julienne strips $\frac{1}{16}$ inch wide and $2\frac{1}{2}$ inches long. Simmer 10 to 12 minutes in water. Drain thoroughly.

$\frac{3}{4}$ lb. granulated sugar   **A small saucepan**
$\frac{1}{4}$ pt. water   **Optional: a jam thermometer**
1 tsp vanilla extract

Boil the sugar and $\frac{1}{4}$ pint of water to the thread stage (230° F.); add the vanilla and lemon peel. Allow to stand for 30 minutes.

Preheat oven to 325° F., Mark 2.

An electric beater or wire whisk   **3 oz. granulated sugar**
2 eggs   **A 5-pt. mixing bowl**

Beat the eggs and sugar in a mixing bowl for 4 to 5 minutes, or until the mixture is thick, pale yellow and falls back on itself forming a slowly dissolving ribbon.

4 oz. pulverized almonds, page 537   **A rack**
$\frac{1}{4}$ tsp almond extract
**The grated rind and strained juice
  of $1\frac{1}{2}$ lemons**

Beat in the almonds, almond extract, lemon rind, and lemon juice. Pour this almond cream into the pastry shell and bake in middle of preheated oven for about 25 minutes. Tart is done when the cream has puffed, browned very lightly, and a needle or knife plunged into the cream comes out clean. Slide tart on to rack.

Drain the strips of lemon peel and strew them over the tart. Boil their syrup down until it is a glaze (last drops are sticky when they fall from a spoon, 228° F.), and spoon a thin coating over the top of the tart. This tart is usually served cold, but may be eaten warm if you wish.

* TARTE AU FROMAGE FRAIS

[Cream Cheese Tart—hot or cold]

This is really a *quiche*, and very simple indeed to make.

For 6 people

**An 8-in. partially baked pastry
   shell placed on a baking sheet,
   page 586**

Use the recipe for sweet short crust pastry on page 585.

Preheat oven to 375° F., Mark 5.

½ lb. cream cheese	A wooden spoon or electric beater
4 oz. softened unsalted butter	2 eggs
4 oz. granulated sugar	Big pinch of nutmeg
A 5-pt. mixing bowl	

Cream the cheese, butter, and sugar together in a mixing bowl. Beat in the eggs and nutmeg. Turn into pastry shell and bake in upper part of preheated oven for 25 to 30 minutes. Tart is done when it has puffed and browned, and a needle or knife plunged into the centre comes out clean.

Tart will sink slightly as it cools. It may be served hot and puffed, or warm, or cold. It may also be reheated, but will not puff again.

VARIATION

Tarte au Fromage Frais et aux Pruneaux

[Cream Cheese and Prune Tart]

3 oz. prunes	¼ tsp almond extract
3 oz. pulverized almonds, page 537	

Soak prunes in hot water until tender. Drain, remove stones, and dice the prunes. Stir prunes, almonds, and almond extract into tart mixture after the eggs have been beaten in.

DESSERT CRÊPES

Crêpes Sucrées

Dessert *crêpes*, especially if they are for *crêpes Suzette*, should be as thin and delicate as possible. There are numerous varying recipes for making them; some use egg yolks, others use whole eggs, and still others specify cream rather than milk. The lightness of *crêpes* made from the following recipe can be attributed to the use of milk diluted with water. If you wish a heavier *crêpe*, use all milk, or light cream. The batter for dessert *crêpes*, like that for entrée *crêpes*, must be left for at least 2 hours before using.

METHOD FOR COOKING CRÊPES

The procedure for cooking *crêpes* is described and illustrated in the Entrée chapter on page 173. You may wish to sauté them in clarified butter, page 12, rather than in oil and butter. As dessert *crêpes* are fragile, you will probably find it best to lift them with your fingers to turn and cook them on the other side.

Crêpes may be made several hours before serving time. Pile them in a dish, cover with greaseproof paper and a plate to keep them from drying out.

CRÊPES FINES SUCRÉES

[Light Batter—for *crêpes* Suzette]

(If you do not have an electric liquidizer proceed as follows: Gradually work the egg yolks into the flour with a wooden spoon, beat in the liquids by drops, then strain the batter through a fine sieve.)

For 10 to 12 crêpes *6 inches in diameter, or 16 to 18* crêpes *4 to 5 inches in diameter*

¼ pt. milk	5 oz. flour
¼ pt. cold water	2½ oz. melted butter
3 egg yolks	An electric liquidizer
1 tbl granulated sugar	A rubber spatula
3 tbl orange liqueur, rum, or brandy	

Place the ingredients in the liquidizer jar in the order in which they are listed. Cover and blend at top speed for 1 minute. If pieces of flour adhere to sides of jar, dislodge with a rubber spatula and blend for 3 seconds more. Cover and refrigerate for at least 2 hours or overnight.

CRÊPES À LA LEVURE

[Yeast Batter—for stuffed *crêpes*]

The addition of yeast makes a more tender and slightly thicker *crêpe*.

Ingredients for the preceding *crêpe*   ¼ oz. fresh or dry yeast
    batter

Warm ⅛ pint of milk to tepid (not over 90° F.) and allow the yeast to dissolve in it. Add it to the rest of the ingredients in the liquidizer and proceed with the recipe.

Cover the batter with a cloth and allow it to stand at room temperature for about 2 hours, or until the yeast has worked and the batter looks bubbly on top. Use immediately, or the yeast will over-ferment.

CRÊPES SOUFFLÉES

[Raised Batter—for stuffed *crêpes*]

Beaten egg whites folded into the batter makes the *crêpes* puff slightly.

Ingredients for one of the preceding   **3 egg whites**
    ***crêpe* batters, either plain or with**   **Pinch of salt**
    yeast

After the batter has rested for 2 hours, and just before you wish to make the *crêpes*, beat the egg whites and salt until stiff. Fold half into the batter, fold in the other half, then make the *crêpes*.

CRÊPES SUZETTE

[*Crêpes* with Orange Butter, *Flambées*]

Every chef has his own recipe for *crêpes Suzette*; of the many we have tried, we find this one especially good. Obviously if you plan to perform in public with a chafing dish, it is a good idea to practise on your family until you become adept at folding and flaming. *Crêpes* 4 to 5 inches in diameter are a convenient size, and three of these per person is the usual serving.

For 6 people

The orange butter

4 large lumps of sugar   **A vegetable peeler**
2 bright-skinned oranges

Rub the sugar lumps over the oranges until all sides of the lumps have absorbed oil. Remove the orange part of the skin of both oranges with a vegetable peeler.

1½ oz. granulated sugar   **A 5-pt. mixing bowl**

Mash the sugar lumps on a chopping board. Add the orange peel and granulated sugar and chop with a heavy knife until peel is very finely shredded. Scrape into a mixing bowl.

½ lb. softened unsalted butter
**An electric beater or a wooden
spoon**

Cream in the softened butter, beating until mixture is light and fluffy. (An electric beater is fine for this.)

¼ pt. strained orange juice   **3 tbl orange liqueur**

By drops, beat the orange juice and orange liqueur into the butter, making a thick cream. Cover and refrigerate until ready to use.

   The chafing dish finish

18 cooked *crêpes* 4 to 5 ins. in
  diameter

Use the recipe for *crêpes fines sucrées*, page 601.

**A chafing dish placed over an
alcohol flame**

Place the orange butter in the chafing dish and heat until it is bubbling.

A spoon and fork

Dip both sides of a *crêpe* in the butter. Its best-looking side out, fold it in half and in half again, to form a wedge. Place it at the edge of the chafing dish. Rapidly continue with the rest of the *crêpes* until all have been dipped, folded, and arranged.

2 tbl granulated sugar   **⅛ pt. cognac**
⅛ pt. orange liqueur

Sprinkle the *crêpes* with the sugar. Pour over them the orange liqueur and cognac. Avert your face and ignite the liqueur with a lighted match. Shake the chafing dish gently back and forth while spooning the flaming liqueur over the *crêpes* until the fire dies down. Serve.

CRÊPES FOURRÉES ET FLAMBÉES

[*Crêpes* with Orange-almond Butter, *Flambées*]

These *crêpes* are stuffed with orange-flavoured almond butter, and may be flamed in a chafing dish, or brought flaming to the table as suggested here.

For 6 to 8 people

The orange-almond butter

3 oz. pulverized almonds, page 537, or pulverized macaroons, page 538	¼ tsp almond extract The orange butter in the preceding recipe

Beat the almonds or macaroons and almond extract into the orange butter.

Filling the crêpes

18 cooked *crêpes* 4 to 5 ins. in diameter	A lightly buttered baking dish suitable for serving

Use any of the 3 *crêpe* recipes starting on page 601. Spread the butter on the less good side of each cooked *crêpe*, and fold into wedge shapes, or roll them, to enclose the butter filling. Arrange in the baking dish.

(*) If not to be heated immediately, cover with greaseproof paper and refrigerate.

Flaming the crêpes

3 tbl granulated sugar

Shortly before serving time, sprinkle with sugar and place in a preheated, 375° F., Mark 5 oven for 10 to 15 minutes until dish is very hot and *crêpes* are beginning to caramelize on top.

⅛ pt. orange liqueur and ⅛ pt. cognac warmed in a small sauce-pan	A long-handled serving spoon

Just before entering the dining-room, pour the warm orange liqueur and cognac over the hot *crêpes*. Avert your face, ignite *crêpes* with a lighted match, and bring them blazing to the table. The server tilts the dish and spoons the flaming liqueur over the *crêpes* until the fire dies down.

CRÊPES FOURRÉES, FRANGIPANE

[*Crêpes* with Almond Cream]

This is a much lighter filling than the preceding orange-almond butter. It may be set aflame if you wish, or served with chocolate as suggested in the recipe.

For 6 people

12 cooked *crêpes* 6 ins. in diameter

Use any of the three recipes for *crêpes* beginning on page 601.

½ pt. *frangipane* (almond custard), page 545	2 oz. plain chocolate
A lightly buttered baking-serving dish	1 oz. melted butter
	1 tbl granulated sugar

Spread 2 tablespoons of *frangipane* on the less good side of each *crêpe*. Fold the *crêpes* into wedge shapes, or roll them, to enclose the filling, and arrange in the baking dish. Grate the chocolate over the *crêpes*, sprinkle on the melted butter, then the sugar.

About 20 minutes before serving, place in a preheated, 350° F., Mark 5 oven until the chocolate has melted. Serve hot or warm.

GÂTEAU DE CRÊPES À LA NORMANDE

[Mound of *Crêpes* with Apples, *Flambé*]

Instead of stuffing each *crêpe* separately, you can pile them one upon the other with a layer of filling between each, as in this recipe.

For 6 to 8 people

2 lbs. crisp cooking or eating apples	**A wooden spoon**
A heavy-bottomed, 2½-qt. pan: saucepan, casserole, or frying pan	3 oz. granulated sugar, more if needed

Quarter, core, and peel the apples. Chop them roughly. Cook in a covered pan over a low heat for about 20 minutes, stirring occasionally, until apples are tender. Uncover, add sugar, raise heat and boil, stirring, for 5 minutes or more. Apple sauce should reduce and be thick enough to hold itself in a fairly solid mass in the spoon. Add more sugar while the apples are cooking if you feel it necessary.

2 tbl cream	**2 tbl Calvados (apple brandy),**
¼ tsp almond extract	cognac, or dark rum

Stir the cream, almond extract, and brandy or rum into the apple sauce.

10 to 12 cooked *crêpes* 6 ins. in diameter

Use the raised batter recipe for *crêpes soufflées* on page 602.

A lightly buttered baking-serving   2 tbl slivered almonds or pulverized
   dish   macaroons
3 oz. pulverized almonds, page 537,   1 oz. melted butter
   or pulverized macaroons, page   2 tbl granulated sugar
   538

Centre a *crêpe* in the base of the dish. Spread a layer of apples over it and sprinkle
with a bare tablespoon of almonds or macaroons. Continue with layers of *crêpe*,
apples, and almonds, ending with a *crêpe*. This will look like a many-layered
cake. Sprinkle the almonds or macaroons over the last *crêpe*. Pour on the butter
and sprinkle with the sugar.

About 30 minutes before serving, place in the upper part of a preheated, 375° F.,
Mark 5 oven to heat through thoroughly. The sugar on top of the mound
should almost begin to caramelize. Serve as follows:

¼ pt. Calvados (apple brandy),   A long-handled serving spoon
   cognac, or dark rum, warmed
   in a small saucepan

Just before entering the dining-room, pour the warm brandy or rum over the
hot mound of *crêpes*. Avert your face, set liqueur aflame with a lighted match,
and bring the blazing dessert to the table. The server should spoon the flaming
liqueur over the dessert until the fire subsides, then cut portions from the mound
as from a cake.

OTHER FILLINGS FOR CRÊPES

Here are some other ideas following the general method in any of the
preceding recipes. Flame the *crêpes* or not, as you wish.

Fresh Fruits

Let strawberries, raspberries, or sliced bananas stand in a bowl with a
sprinkling of sugar and kirsch, orange liqueur, or cognac for an hour, then use
as a filling.

Stewed Fruits

Any of the following may be folded into an equal amount of *crème
pâtissière* (custard filling), page 543, and then used for stuffed *crêpes* or a mound
of *crêpes*:

Apples, peeled, sliced, sautéed in butter, then sprinkled with sugar and
cinnamon.

Pears, peeled, poached in red-wine syrup, as in *tarte aux poires à la Bour-daloue*, page 594, then diced and sprinkled with crumbled macaroons.

Peaches, apricots, or plums poached in syrup, using the system for poaching peaches in *pêches cardinal*, page 582, then drained, peeled, and diced.

Pineapple (crushed, tinned pineapple), drained, the syrup boiled for 5 minutes, then the pineapple boiled in the syrup for 5 minutes more and drained.

Jams, Preserves, and Jellies

These simple fillings make a delicious dessert when the *crêpes* are flamed with liqueur. To prepare them, mix a little kirsch, cognac, or orange liqueur into red currant jelly, or raspberry, strawberry, apricot, or cherry jam or preserves. Stir in also, if you wish, some crumbled macaroons. Spread the filling on the *crêpes*, roll, fold them, or pile them into a mound in a fireproof dish. Sprinkle with melted butter and granulated sugar, and place in a preheated, 375° F., Mark 5 oven until thoroughly heated. Flame with warmed liqueur just as you bring them to the table.

FRUIT FLANS
Clafoutis

* CLAFOUTI

[Cherry Flan]

The *clafouti* (also spelled with a final 's' in both singular and plural) which is traditional in the Limousin during the cherry season is peasant cooking for family meals, and about as simple a dessert to make as you can imagine: a pancake batter poured over fruit in a fireproof dish, then baked in the oven. It looks like a tart, and is usually eaten warm.

(If you have no electric liquidizer, work the eggs into the flour with a wooden spoon, gradually beat in the liquids, then strain the batter through a fine sieve.)

For 6 to 8 people

Preheat oven to 350° F., Mark 4.

¾ lb. stoned black cherries

Use fresh, black, sweet cherries in season. Otherwise use drained, tinned, stoned cherries.

½ pt. milk
2 oz. granulated sugar
3 eggs
1 tbl vanilla extract

⅛ tsp salt
2½ oz. sifted flour
An electric liquidizer

Place the ingredients above in the liquidizer jar in the order in which they are listed. Cover and blend at top speed for 1 minute.

A 3- to 4-pt. lightly buttered,
fireproof baking dish or ovenglass
pie plate about 1½ ins. deep

An asbestos mat, if necessary
2 oz. granulated sugar

Pour a ¼-inch layer of batter in the baking dish or pie plate. Place over a moderate heat for a minute or two until a film of batter has set in the bottom of the dish. Remove from heat. Spread the cherries over the batter and sprinkle on the sugar. Pour on the rest of the batter and smooth the surface with the back of a spoon.

Icing sugar in a shaker

Place in middle of preheated oven and bake for about an hour. The *clafouti* is done when it has puffed and browned, and a needle or knife plunged into its centre comes out clean. Sprinkle top of *clafouti* with icing sugar just before bringing it to the table. (The *clafouti* need not be served hot, but should still be warm. It will sink down slightly as it cools.)

VARIATIONS

The *clafouti* in the preceding master recipe is the simple and classic version. Here are some variations:

Clafouti à la Liqueur

[Cherry Flan with Liqueur]

Ingredients for the preceding
clafouti

⅛ pt. kirsch or cognac
2 oz. granulated sugar

Follow the master recipe but first let the cherries stand for 1 hour in the kirsch or cognac and sugar. Substitute this liquid for part of the milk called for in the batter; omit the sugar near the end of the recipe.

Clafouti aux Poires

[Pear Flan]

Ingredients for the master *clafouti*
with changes as indicated
1¼ to 1½ lbs. peeled, cored, and
sliced pears

⅛ pt. sweet white wine, kirsch, or
cognac
2 oz. granulated sugar

Follow the master recipe with these changes: Substitute pears for cherries, and allow to stand for 1 hour in wine, kirsch, or cognac and sugar. Substitute this liquid for part of the milk called for in the batter; omit the sugar near the end of the recipe.

Clafouti aux Pruneaux

[Plum Flan]

Ingredients for the master *clafouti* with changes as indicated	⅛ pt. orange liqueur, kirsch, or cognac
1 lb. firm, ripe plums	2 oz. sugar
Boiling water	

Follow the master recipe with these changes: Substitute plums for cherries, and drop them in boiling water for exactly 10 seconds. Peel. Slice them or leave whole. Allow to stand in liqueur, kirsch, or cognac and sugar for 1 hour. Substitute this liquid for part of the milk called for in the batter; omit the sugar near the end of the recipe.

Clafouti aux Pommes

[Apple Flan]

Ingredients for the master *clafouti* with changes as indicated	An enamelled frying pan
About 1¼ lbs. crisp eating or cooking apples	⅛ pt. Calvados (apple brandy), dark rum, or cognac
1½ to 2 oz. butter	⅛ tsp cinnamon
	2 oz. sugar

Follow the master recipe with these changes: Substitute apples for cherries; peel, core, and cut them into lengthwise slices ¼ inch thick. Sauté to brown very lightly in hot butter, then allow to stand in the frying pan for ½ hour with the brandy or rum, cinnamon, and sugar. Substitute this liquid for part of the milk called for in the batter; omit the sugar near the end of the recipe.

Clafouti aux Mûres

[Blackberry Flan]

Ingredients for the master *clafouti* or the variation following it with changes as indicated	1¼ lbs. stemmed and washed blackberries

Follow the master recipe or the variation after it with these changes: Substitute berries for cherries and, because berries are very juicy, increase the flour for your batter from 2¼ ounces to 4 ounces.

U

Clafouti à la Bourdaloue

[Cherry or Pear Flan with Almonds]

Ingredients for either of the 2   **3 oz. blanched almonds**
cherry flans, or for the pear flan   **1 tsp almond extract**

Follow the master recipe for cherry flan, or the variation after it, or the recipe
for pear flan, but purée the almonds in the liquidizer with the milk called for in
your batter. Add the almond extract, and proceed with the recipe.

BABAS AND SAVARINS

Babas et Savarins

Babas and *savarins* always seem to delight guests, and they are not difficult
to make if you have any feeling at all for doughs and baking. They may be
cooked a day or two ahead. They deep-freeze perfectly; all you need to do to
make them ready to imbibe their syrup is to pop them from the freezer into a
300° F., Mark 1 oven, to warm through for about 5 minutes.

Whenever you are working with yeast doughs, do so in a warm place free
from draughts; a sudden chill can cause the dough to fall. So that the dough will
rise in one to two hours, cover it with a damp cloth and place it where the
temperature remains between 80° and 100° F. If you can control the heat and
have a thermometer, put it in a plate-warming oven, or in a baking oven,
heating briefly every once in a while to maintain the correct temperature. Or
place the covered bowl on a pillow over the radiator. If you allow the dough
to rise too much, or too long, or at too warm a temperature, it will develop a
taste of over-fermented yeast.

---

* PÂTE À BABA ET BABAS

[*Baba* Paste and *Babas*]

For about 12 babas

Mixing the paste

2 oz. butter

Melt the butter, and let it cool to tepid while you are preparing the other
ingredients.

½ oz. fresh yeast   2 tbl granulated sugar
A fork or wire whisk   ⅛ tsp salt
A 2½-qt. mixing bowl   2 eggs

Mash the yeast with a fork or wire whisk in the bowl, then beat in the sugar and
salt until the mixture forms a wet paste. Beat in the eggs and blend well.

½ lb. flour   A wooden spoon

Mix in the flour and the cool melted butter with a wooden spoon.

Kneading the paste

Then with the fingers of one hand held together and slightly cupped, knead the
dough by lifting it, slapping it, and pulling it vigorously against the sides of the
bowl for about 5 minutes. It will be very sticky at first, but will gradually detach
itself from the bowl and from your hand. It has been worked to sufficient
elasticity and body when you can grasp it in both hands, pull it to a length of
10 to 12 inches, and give it a full twist without breaking it. (NOTE: If you are
doubling the recipe, you will have to remove the dough from the bowl and
knead it by pulling and slapping it between your hands.)

Preliminary rising in a bowl

1 tsp flour

Form it into a ball in the bottom of the bowl. Cut a cross an inch deep on top
and sprinkle the ball with the flour. Cover the bowl with several thicknesses of
damp cloth and allow it to rise in a warm place, 80° to 100° F., for 1½ to 2 hours,
or until the dough has doubled in bulk.

Again with the cupped fingers of one hand, gently deflate the dough by gathering it from the sides of the bowl to the centre.

Final rising in moulds

½ oz. softened butter
12 *baba* tins, about 2 ins.
   deep and 2 ins. in diameter

Butter inside of tins. Lightly break off about a tablespoon of dough, enough to
fill a third of a tin, and press it lightly into the bottom of the tin. Do not bother
to even the top of the dough as it will smooth out as it rises.

Place the tins, uncovered, again in a warm place and allow to rise 1 to 2 hours
more, or until the dough is ¼ inch over the rim of the tins.

Cylindrical Baba Mould,
2 Inches Deep and 2 Inches
in Diameter

Baking

As soon as the dough has risen this second time—and do not delay or it may collapse—bake in the upper part of a preheated, 375° F., Mark 5 oven for about 15 minutes. The *babas* should be nicely browned, and slightly shrunk from the sides of the cups. Unmould them on to a cake rack.

Babas au Rhum

[Rum *Babas*]

Both the *babas* and the rum syrup should be lukewarm but not hot before this operation begins. If the *babas* are cold, heat them briefly in the oven; warm the syrup if necessary. (NOTE: Some authorities use a stronger sugar syrup, 10 ounces of sugar to ¾ pint of water. We prefer the lighter syrup given here.)

For 12 babas

The sugar syrup

¾ pt. water	¼ pt. dark rum, more if needed
6 oz. granulated sugar	(Jamaican rum is recommended)
A 1½-pt. saucepan	

Bring the water and sugar to a boil. Remove from heat and stir until sugar has dissolved. When the sugar syrup has cooled to lukewarm, stir in the rum; you may add a few tablespoons more if you feel it necessary.

The babas imbibe the syrup

12 barely warm cooked *babas*, the preceding recipe	A skewer, trussing needle or sharp-pronged fork
A dish 2 ins. deep and just large enough to hold the *babas* easily	A cake rack placed over a tray

Arrange the barely warm *babas* in the dish, their puffed tops up. Prick tops in several places, pour the lukewarm syrup over them, and allow to stand for ½ hour, basting frequently with syrup. They should imbibe enough syrup so that they are moist and spongy but still hold their shape. Drain on rack for ½ hour.

TO SERVE

Babas au Rhum, Classique

[Rum *Babas*]

2 tbl dark rum	**12 glacé cherries**
A pastry brush	**A serving dish or frilled paper**
¼ pt. apricot glaze, page 547	**cups**

After the *babas* have drained, sprinkle the top of each with a few drops of rum. Paint them with the apricot glaze, and place a cherry on top of each. Arrange in a serving dish or in paper cups.

Babas aux Fruits

[Rum *Babas* with Fruit]

A serving dish
¾ to 1 lb. fresh strawberries
Leftover *baba* syrup
¾ to 1 pt. *crème Chantilly* (lightly
  whipped cream), page 535,
  flavoured with rum and icing
  sugar

Arrange the *babas* in the serving dish. Surround them with the berries which have stood for 10 to 15 minutes in leftover *baba* syrup. Pass the cream separately.

---

* SAVARIN

[*Savarin*]

Large Savarin *or Ring Mould, 7 to 9 Inches in Diameter. Small* Savarin *Mould, 2¼ to 4 Inches in Diameter*

The *savarin* uses the same paste or dough as the *baba*, but is baked in a ring mould, and its sugar syrup is flavoured with kirsch rather than rum. The centre is then filled with a cream or with fruits macerated in liqueur.

For 6 people

Filling the mould

½ oz. softened butter   **The master recipe for *baba* paste,**
A 1½- to 2-pt. ring mould 2 ins.   **page 610**
deep

Butter the ring mould. Make the *baba* paste as directed and allow it to rise in its
bowl until doubled in bulk. Deflate it by pressing it rapidly in several places
with the cupped fingers of one hand. Then break off a 2-tablespoon piece of the
paste and press lightly into the bottom of the mould. Continue rapidly with the
rest of the paste. The mould will be from a third to a half filled. Do not bother
to smooth the surface of the paste; it will even out as it rises. Place uncovered in
a warm place, 80° to 100° F., for 1 to 2 hours or until the paste has risen to fill
the mould. Proceed at once to the following step.

Baking the savarin

Preheat oven to 375° F., Mark 5 in time for this step.

Aluminium foil   **A cake rack**

Insert a cylinder of aluminium foil through the hole in the centre of the mould;
this will help the *savarin* rise evenly in the oven. Place in the middle of the oven
and bake for about 30 minutes. If top of *savarin* browns too much during baking,
cover lightly with aluminium foil. The *savarin* is done when it is toasty brown
and has begun to shrink a little from the sides of the mould. Remove from oven
and allow to cool for 5 minutes. Reverse rack over mould, reverse the two,
remove the mould. When savarin has cooled to tepid, proceed to the following
step.

(*) It may be baked a day or two in advance, then heated briefly to tepid in a
300° F., Mark 1 oven.

The savarin imbibes the syrup

¾ pt. sugar syrup (rum *baba* recipe),   A dish 2 ins. deep and just large
  page 612, but flavoured with ¼ pt.   enough to hold the *savarin* easily
  kirsch rather than rum   A cake rack
A skewer, trussing needle, or   A tray
  sharp-pronged fork

While the *savarin* is baking, make the same sugar syrup as that for the *babas*, but
perfume it with kirsch rather than rum. Allow it to cool until tepid. Prick the
puffed side of the barely warm *savarin* and place it puffed-side down in the dish.

Pour the tepid syrup over it and allow to stand for ½ hour, basting frequently
with the syrup. The *savarin* should be moist and spongy, but still hold its shape.
Then tilt the dish and pour out the remaining syrup (which may be reserved
for flavouring fruits). Turn the rack upside down over the dish and reverse the
dish on to the rack to unmould the *savarin*. Place rack on tray and allow the
savarin to drain for about ½ hour.

A serving dish

The *savarin* is now resting puffed-side up on the rack; it is usually served puffed-
side down. The safest way to get it from the rack to the serving dish is to turn
the dish upside down over the *savarin* on the rack; then reverse the rack on to the
dish.

1 tbl kirsch

Sprinkle the *savarin* with drops of kirsch before decorating and filling as directed
in one of the following suggestions:

TO SERVE

Savarins are usually painted with a glaze into which are pressed designs of
almonds and glacé fruits, or fresh strawberries or raspberries. The centre is filled
with whipped cream, custard filling, or fruits. The following recipe gives the
general procedure for glazing, decorating, and filling; other suggestions are
listed after it.

Savarin Chantilly

[*Savarin* with Whipped Cream]

The preceding savarin
⅛ **pt. apricot glaze, page 547**
A pastry brush
6 to 8 glacé cherries
A piece of angelica

8 to 12 blanched almonds
¾ **pt. *crème Chantilly* (lightly**
whipped cream), page 535,
flavoured with icing sugar and
kirsch

Paint the *savarin* with a light coating of apricot glaze. Cut the cherries in half,
and the angelica into small diamond shapes. Press the fruits and almonds over
the *savarin* in a decorative design and paint a little glaze over them. Fill the
centre of the *savarin* with the cream just before serving.

OTHER FILLINGS

Instead of whipped cream, you may use a custard or fruit filling. In the
case of fruit fillings, decorate glazed *savarin* with the fruits you are using rather

than with almonds and glacé fruits. Between ½ and ¾ pint of custard filling is sufficient. If you are using fruits, you will probably want more; fill the centre of the *savarin* with them, and heap the rest around the outside. The fruits are usually flavoured with 3 to 4 tablespoons kirsch for ¾ to 1 pound fruit, and several tablespoons of sugar, if necessary (or use leftover imbibing syrup).

Frangipane, custard filling with almonds or macaroons, flavoured with vanilla and kirsch, page 545.

Crème Saint-Honoré, *crème pâtissière* with beaten egg whites, flavoured with vanilla and kirsch, page 545.

Macédoine de Fruits, a mixture of cut-up fruits, such as cherries, pears, apricots, pineapple, either fresh, poached in syrup as for the *pêches cardinal* on page 582, or tinned. Allow to stand for ½ hour in kirsch, and sugar if necessary, before using.

Fresh strawberries or raspberries, which have been left for ½ hour with sugar and kirsch.

Cherries, poached in red wine syrup, as for the cherry tart on page 595.

VARIATION

Petits Savarins

[Small *Savarins*]

Small *savarins* are baked in the small moulds illustrated at the beginning of the *savarin* recipe; they range in diameter from 2¼ inches for tea parties to 3 or 4 inches for individual dessert servings.

MOULDING, BAKING, AND SYRUPING

Proceed exactly as for the large *savarin* on page 613, but omit the aluminium-foil funnel, and bake for only 10 to 15 minutes. Saturate them with kirsch-flavoured syrup as directed for the large *savarin*. The proportions in the recipe will furnish about 12 small *savarins* 2¼ inches in diameter or about 6 *savarins* 3 inches in diameter.

TO SERVE

You may paint small *savarins* with apricot glaze, page 547, decorate with glacé fruits cut into diamond shapes, and serve them as they are, or you may fill them. If you fill them and do not intend to serve them on dessert plates, it is best to place them on small rounds of baked flan pastry, page 586. Paint the rounds first with the apricot glaze, then glaze and decorate the *savarins*. Use any of the fillings suggested for the large *savarin* in the preceding list.

SPONGE FINGERS
Biscuits à la Cuiller

Biscuits à la cuiller are among the oldest of the French *petits gâteaux secs*. Before forcing bags were invented, the batter for sponge fingers was dropped on to baking sheets with a spoon, and this is how they acquired their French name.

Because shop-bought sponge fingers are usually so dreadful in taste and texture that they cannot be used in good cooking, it is useful to know how to make your own. They can be made quickly when you become familiar with the process and will keep at least 10 days in an airtight container or deep-freeze perfectly. With home-made sponge fingers on hand, you will find many of the spectacular desserts in the preceding pages not at all formidable. These include the *charlotte Chantilly* on page 561, the *charlotte Malakoff*, on page 558, and the *diplomate* on page 564. Then there are the easily assembled *plombières* on pages 548-9, which consist of custard filling, beaten egg whites, and sponge fingers dipped in liqueur. To serve sponge fingers with afternoon tea, you may hold them together back to back with a little butter cream, page 631.

The mixture for sponge fingers is of the spongecake type, with egg yolks and sugar beaten to a thick cream, then flour and stiffly beaten egg whites are folded in. You must be particularly careful to obtain a mixture which will hold its shape; this means expert beating and folding. A mixture that is too liquid will form flat rather than rounded sponge fingers. Be sure to read the illustrated directions on beating egg whites and folding which start on page 163.

BISCUITS À LA CUILLER

[Sponge Fingers]

For 24 to 30 sponge fingers

Preheat oven to 300° F., Mark 1.

Two 12- by 24-in. baking sheets
½ oz. softened butter
Flour
A forcing bag with a round nozzle
½ in. in diameter

4 oz. icing sugar in a sieve or a shaker

Prepare the baking sheets: butter lightly, dust with flour, and knock off excess flour. Assemble the forcing bag. Prepare the icing sugar. Measure out all the rest of the ingredients listed in the recipe.

U*

The batter

An electric beater or a wire whisk   **1 tsp vanilla extract**
3 oz. granulated sugar   **A 2½-qt. mixing bowl**
3 egg yolks

Gradually beat the sugar into the egg yolks, add the vanilla, and continue
beating for several minutes until the mixture is thick, pale yellow, and forms the
ribbon, page 534.

3 egg whites   **1 tbl castor sugar**
Pinch of salt

Beat the egg whites and salt together in a separate bowl until soft peaks are
formed. Sprinkle on the sugar and beat until stiff peaks are formed. (Directions
are on page 144.)

A rubber spatula
2 oz. sifted cake flour
** or plain flour returned to sifter**

Scoop one-quarter of the egg whites over the top of the egg yolks and sugar
mixture. Sift on one-quarter of the flour, and delicately fold in until partially
blended. Then add one-third of the remaining egg whites, sift on one-third of
the remaining flour, fold until partially blended, and repeat with half of each,
then the last of each. Do not attempt to blend the mixture too thoroughly or
you will deflate it; it must remain light and puffy.

Forming the sponge fingers

Scoop mixture into forcing bag. Squeeze out even lines on to the prepared
baking sheets, making finger shapes 4 inches long and 1½ inches wide, spaced
1 inch apart. Sprinkle with a $\frac{1}{16}$-inch layer of icing sugar. To dislodge some of
the excess sugar, hold baking sheet upside down and tap the back of it gently;
the sponge fingers will not budge unless you are rough with them.

Baking the sponge fingers

Bake in middle and upper parts of preheated oven for about 20 minutes.
The sponge fingers are done when they are a very pale brown underneath their
sugar coating. They should be slightly crusty outside, and light but dry inside.
If they are not baked enough, they will become soggy when they cool; over-
baking makes them dry. As soon as they are done, remove from baking sheets
with a spatula and cool on cake racks.

To serve

Sponge fingers may be served as they are, with tea or fruit desserts. Or you
may make double sponge fingers by sticking the two flat sides together with
apricot glaze, page 547, or one of the butter creams starting on page 631.

FIVE FRENCH CAKES
Cinq Gâteaux

Here are five unusually good and typically French cakes. They are all made in very much the same way, but as there are slight differences in mixing and in how each should look in the oven, we give full recipes for all five. After you have practised with one or two, you will find that they can all be made very quickly; any one of them may be prepared for the oven in about 20 minutes. An electric beater is a help in mixing but is far from essential, because a large wire whisk does the work almost as quickly.

PRELIMINARY REMARKS

Before you begin the cake

Preheat the oven, prepare the cake tin as in the following directions, and measure out all your ingredients. Then the mixture may be prepared and baked in one continuous operation.

Preparing the cake tin

To prepare the tin for the cake mixture, rub the entire inner surface with a thin film of softened butter. Then roll flour around in the tin to cover the sides and base; knock out excess flour by banging the tin, upside down, on a hard surface. A light dusting of flour should adhere all over the inner surface of the tin; this will make the cake easy to remove after baking.

Flour

In all of the following recipes, we have specified cake flour, and given plain flour as second choice. Cake flour is more finely granulated than plain flour, and will produce a lighter and puffier cake. Be sure to measure your flour with the utmost accuracy, as the balance of proportions in cakes is delicate.

Eggs

All the cake recipes are based on the 2-ounce egg. The yolk weighs $\frac{1}{2}$ ounce, or slightly less than a standard tablespoon; the white weighs 1 ounce.

Egg yolks, sugar, and butter

Directions for beating egg yolks and sugar until they form the ribbon are on page 534. Directions for creaming butter and sugar are on page 536.

Egg whites

You will note that no baking powder is used in any of the cakes; their lightness is due to the careful folding of perfectly beaten egg whites into the mixture. As this is one of the most important aspects of successful cake making, be sure to read the illustrated directions on egg whites in the Entrée chapter starting on page 143.

Temperature

Oven temperature must be correct if the cake is to bake and rise as it should. Check your thermostat with an oven thermometer.

Removing from tin

After the cake is done, your recipe will usually direct you to let it remain in its tin for a few minutes; it will settle, and shrink slightly from the sides of the tin. Remove the cake as follows: Run a thin knife between the cake and the edge of the tin. Then, if you are using a one-piece tin, turn a cake rack upside down over the tin, reverse the two, and give a short, sharp, downward jerk to dislodge the cake on to the rack. For a false-bottomed tin, either use the same general system, or place the tin over a jar to release the rim from the false bottom; remove the cake from the false bottom to a rack with a spatula, or reverse the cake on to a rack. [Directions in recipes refer to a one-piece tin.]

Icings

A cake must be thoroughly cold before it is iced; if you ice a warm or even a tepid cake with butter cream, the icing will soften and usually dribble down the sides of the cake. Illustrated directions for filling and icing cakes are in the pair of recipes beginning on page 623.

Storage

After any of the following cakes has been baked and thoroughly cooled, but before it has been covered with icing, it may be stored for several days in an airtight container, or may be securely wrapped and deep-frozen. Cakes iced with butter-creams should be stored in the refrigerator.

BISCUIT AU BEURRE

[Butter Spongecake]

This fine, light spongecake may be served with a sprinkling of icing sugar, and goes well with tea, or with fruit. It is also delicious as a strawberry short-cake. Or you may fill and decorate it as suggested at the end of the recipe.

For a 10-inch cake serving 10 to 12 people

Preheat oven to 350° F., Mark 4.

A round cake tin, 10 ins. in diameter and 2 ins. deep

Butter and flour the cake tin, page 619. Measure out the ingredients.

2 oz. butter

Melt the butter and leave aside to cool.

A 2½-qt. mixing bowl	**4 oz. castor sugar**
An electric beater or large wire	**4 egg yolks**
whisk	**2 tsp vanilla extract**

Gradually beat the sugar into the egg yolks, add the vanilla, and continue beating for several minutes until mixture is thick, pale yellow, and forms the ribbon, page 534.

4 egg whites	**A rubber spatula**
Pinch of salt	**3½ oz. sifted cake flour (or plain**
2 tbl castor sugar	**flour) returned to sifter**

Beat the egg whites and salt together in a separate bowl until soft peaks are formed; sprinkle on the sugar and beat until stiff peaks are formed. (Directions are on page 144.) Scoop one-quarter of the egg whites over the top of the egg yolks and sugar mixture. Sift on one-quarter of the flour, and delicately fold in until partially blended. Then add one-third of the remaining egg whites, sift on one-third of the remaining flour, fold until partially blended, and repeat with half of each, then the last of each and half of the tepid, melted butter. When partially blended, fold in the rest of the butter but omit the milky residue at the bottom of the pan. Do not overmix; the egg whites must retain as much volume as possible.

Turn into prepared cake tin, tilting tin to run to the rim all around. Place in middle of preheated oven and bake for 30 to 35 minutes. Cake is done when it has puffed, is lightly brown, and has just begun to show a faint line of shrinkage from the edges of the tin.

A cake rack

Remove from oven and allow to stand in the pan for 6 to 8 minutes. It will sink slightly and shrink more from the edges of the tin. Run a knife around the edge of the tin, and reverse on cake rack, giving the tin a sharp little jerk to dislodge the cake. If cake is not to be iced, immediately reverse it so its puffed side is uppermost. Allow to cool for an hour or so.

TO SERVE

Sucre Glace

[Icing Sugar]

Shake icing sugar over the cake.

Glaçage à l'Abricot

[Apricot Glaze with Almonds or Glacé Fruits]

A pastry brush   **1 oz. slivered almonds or glacé**
¼ pt. apricot glaze, page 547   **fruits**
3 oz. pulverized almonds, page 537

Follow the general procedure for icing a cake illustrated on page 625: Brush crumbs off top and sides of cake, paint cake with apricot glaze. Brush almonds against the sides and decorate top with slivered almonds or with glacé fruits cut into dice or fancy shapes.

Glaçage à la Crème ou au Chocolat

[Butter-cream or Chocolate Icing]

The spongecake may be iced, or filled and iced. Follow the recipe for orange-butter filling on page 623, or that for the orange butter-cream, page 625. Or, using the same procedure, follow one of the recipes for butter-cream starting on page 631, or for the chocolate-butter icing on page 634.

GÂTEAU À L'ORANGE

[Orange Spongecake]

For a 9-inch cake serving 8 people

Preheat oven to 350° F., Mark 4.

A round cake tin 9 ins. in diameter
and 1½ ins. deep

Butter and flour the cake tin, page 619. Measure out the ingredients.

A large wire whisk or an electric   **The grated rind of 1 orange**
beater   **⅛ pt. strained orange juice**
4 oz. granulated sugar   **Pinch of salt**
4 egg yolks   **3½ oz. sifted cake flour (or plain**
A 2½-qt. mixing bowl   **flour)**

Gradually beat the sugar into the egg yolks and continue beating until the mixture thickens to form the ribbon, page 534. Add the grated orange peel, orange juice, and salt. Beat for a moment or two until mixture is light and foamy. Then beat in the flour.

4 egg whites   **1 tbl castor sugar**
Pinch of salt

Beat the egg whites and salt together in a separate bowl until soft peaks are formed. Sprinkle on the sugar and beat until stiff peaks are formed. (Directions are on page 144.) Stir one-quarter of the egg whites into the mixture, delicately fold in the rest.

Immediately turn into prepared cake tin and run the mixture up to the rim all around. Bake in middle of preheated oven for 30 to 35 minutes. Cake is done when it has puffed and browned, and shows a faint line of shrinkage from the edge of the mould.

A cake rack

Allow it to cool for 6 to 8 minutes. Run a knife around the edge of the tin and reverse cake on a rack. If not to be iced, immediately reverse again, puffed side up. Allow to cool for an hour or two. When cake is cold, sprinkle it with icing sugar, or fill and ice the cake according to one of the two following recipes:

DIRECTIONS FOR FILLING AND ICING A CAKE

Gâteau Fourré à la Crème d'Orange

[Spongecake with Orange-butter Filling]

This orange-butter filling may be used for cakes, or as a filling for tartlets or biscuits. When softened butter is beaten into it, as described in the variation at the end of the recipe, it may also serve as an icing.

For about ¾ pint, enough to fill a 9- to 10-inch cake

The orange-butter filling

3 oz. unsalted butter	⅛ pt. strained orange juice
10 oz. castor sugar	1 tbl orange liqueur
2 eggs	A 2½-pt. enamelled saucepan
2 egg yolks	A wire whisk
The grated rind of 1 orange	Optional: a jam thermometer

Place all the ingredients above in at the saucepan and beat with wire whisk over a low heat or not-quite-simmering water until mixture thickens like honey and is too hot for your finger (160° to 163° F. on a jam thermometer). Do not overheat or the eggs will scramble.

A pan of cold water

Then place saucepan in cold water and beat for 3 to 4 minutes until filling is cool.

(*) May be refrigerated for 10 days, or may be deep-frozen.

Filling the cake

A 9- to 10-in. cake: the preceding   **A long, sharp, thin knife**
orange spongecake or the
butter spongecake on page 620

Cut a tiny vertical wedge up the edge of the cake; this will guide you in re-
forming it later. Slice the cake in half horizontally.

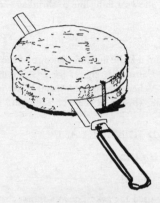

Splitting the cake in half

A flexible blade-spatula

Using a spatula, spread enough orange–butter filling on the lower layer of the
cake to make a ⅛-inch coating.

Icing the bottom layer

*Replace top layer, lining
up with wedge*

Decorating the cake with apricot glaze and almonds

A pastry brush
¼ pt. apricot glaze, page 547
5 oz. pulverized almonds, plain or
toasted, page 537

A dish for the almonds
A cake plate
Optional: 1 oz. glazed orange peel
page 541

Brush off any crumbs, and paint the cake with a coating of apricot glaze. When
the glaze has set slightly, brush the almonds against the sides of the cake; not
more than one-quarter of them will adhere, but you need a large amount for
easy manipulation. Place the cake on the plate; decorate top with optional
orange peel.

*Hold cake over almonds
and brush them against
sides with free hand*

VARIATIONS

Crème au Beurre à l'Orange

[Orange Butter-cream Icing]

For a richer filling, or for an icing, you may turn the preceding filling into
a *crème au beurre*, which resembles the butter cream on page 633. In the following
recipe, we have suggested that you use half the original orange-butter filling
for inside the cake, and beat butter into the rest to make a butter-cream icing.

For a 9- to 10-inch cake

¾ pt. orange-butter filling, the
preceding recipe
A 2½-qt. mixing bowl

A wire whisk or an electric beater
¼ lb. softened, unsalted butter,
1 to 1½ oz. more if necessary

Use half of the filling to spread inside your cake as described in the preceding recipe. Re-form the cake. Place the rest of the filling in the mixing bowl and gradually beat in the softened butter. The mixture should thicken into a smooth, mayonnaise-like cream; if it looks grainy, beat in more butter a little at a time. Chill until firm but still of spreading consistency.

NOTE: Be sure cake is thoroughly cold before you begin this operation.

Icing the cake

A flexible blade-spatula
A cake plate

Optional: 1 oz. glazed orange peel,
page 541

Brush crumbs off cake. Hold the cake in the palm of your hand as illustrated (or ice it on its serving plate). Spread on the icing with the spatula, starting at the top of the cake, and finishing with the sides. Place the cake on the plate. Decorate, if you wish, with pieces of glazed orange peel. Refrigerate the cake until ready to serve.

(*) Leftover butter-cream may be refrigerated for about a week, or may be deep-frozen. Before using, allow it to warm at room temperature until it can be beaten into spreading consistency.

Spread icing on top of cake first, then smooth it around sides

Crème au Citron

[Lemon-butter Filling]

Crème au Beurre au Citron

[Lemon Butter-cream Icing]

Use the same method and proportions as in either of the two preceding recipes, but substitute grated lemon rind and lemon juice for orange.

GÂTEAU À L'ORANGE ET AUX AMANDES

[Orange and Almond Spongecake]

This delicious cake may be served with a sprinkling of icing sugar, with a glazing of apricot, or with a filling and icing.

For a 9-inch cake serving 8 people

Preheat oven to 350° F., Mark 4.

**A round cake tin 9 ins. in diameter
and 1½ ins. deep**

Butter and flour the cake tin, page 619. Measure out all the ingredients.

¼ lb. butter

Melt the butter and leave aside.

**A wire whisk or electric beater
4 oz. granulated sugar
3 egg yolks
A 2½-qt. mixing bowl
The grated rind of 1 orange
⅛ pt. strained orange juice**

**¼ tsp almond extract
4 oz. pulverized almonds, page 537
2 oz. sifted cake flour (or plain flour)**

Gradually beat the sugar into the egg yolks and continue beating until the mixture is thick, pale yellow and forms the ribbon, page 534. Add the grated orange rind, orange juice, and almond extract. Beat for a moment or two until mixture is light and foamy. Then beat in the almonds, and finally the flour.

**3 egg whites
Pinch of salt**

1 tbl castor sugar

Beat the egg whites and salt together in a separate bowl until soft peaks are formed; sprinkle on the sugar and beat until stiff peaks are formed. (Directions are on page 144.)

A rubber spatula

Using a rubber spatula, fold the cool, melted butter into the cake mixture, omitting milky residue at bottom of butter pan. Stir one-quarter of the egg whites into the mixture, delicately fold in the rest.

Immediately turn into prepared cake tin and run the mixture up to the rim all around. Bake in middle of preheated oven for 30 to 35 minutes. Cake is done when it has puffed, browned lightly, top is springy when pressed, and a needle plunged into the centre of the cake comes out clean.

A cake rack

Remove from oven and allow to stand for about 10 minutes, until cake begins
to shrink from sides of tin. Run a knife around the edge of the tin and reverse
the cake on to the rack, giving it a small, sharp, downward jerk to dislodge it
from the tin. If it is not to be iced, reverse the cake immediately so that it will
cool puffed-side up. Allow to cool for an hour or two.

TO SERVE

Serve with a sprinkling of icing sugar, or with apricot glaze and almonds,
page 625, or with the orange-butter filling or butter-cream icing described for
the orange spongecake and starting on page 623.

REINE DE SABA

[Chocolate and Almond Cake]

This extremely good chocolate cake is baked so that its centre remains
slightly underdone; overcooked, the cake loses its special creamy quality. It is
covered with a chocolate-butter icing, and decorated with almonds. Because of
its creamy centre it needs no filling. It can be made in the same manner as the
preceding cakes, starting out with a beating of egg yolks and sugar, then proceeding with the rest of the ingredients. But because the chocolate and the
almonds make a mixture so stiff it is difficult to fold in the egg whites, we have
chosen another method, that of creaming together the butter and sugar, and
then incorporating the remaining items.

For an 8-inch cake serving 6 to 8 people

Preheat oven to 350° F., Mark 4.

A round cake tin 8 ins. in diameter and $1\frac{1}{2}$ ins. deep	4 oz. plain chocolate melted with 2 tbl rum or coffee

Butter and flour the cake tin, page 619. Melt the chocolate over very hot water;
be sure it is smooth and creamy. Measure out the rest of the ingredients.

A $2\frac{1}{2}$-qt. mixing bowl	$\frac{1}{4}$ lb. softened butter
A wooden spoon or an electric beater	$\frac{1}{4}$ lb. castor sugar

Cream the butter and sugar together for several minutes until they form a pale
yellow, fluffy mixture, page 536.

3 egg yolks

Beat in the egg yolks until well blended.

3 egg whites   **1 tbl castor sugar**
Pinch of salt

Beat the egg whites and salt in a separate bowl until soft peaks are formed; sprinkle on the sugar and beat until stiff peaks are formed. (Directions are on page 144.)

A rubber spatula   **¼ tsp almond extract**
2 oz. pulverized almonds,   **2 oz. sifted cake flour (or plain**
  page 537   **flour)**

With a rubber spatula, blend the melted chocolate into the butter and sugar mixture, then stir in the almonds and almond extract. Fold in one-quarter of the egg whites. When partially blended, sift on one-quarter of the flour, and continue folding, alternating with more egg whites and more flour until all is used.

Turn the mixture into the cake tin, pushing the mixture up to its rim with a rubber spatula. Bake in middle of preheated oven for about 25 minutes. Cake is done when it has puffed, and 2½ to 3 inches around the circumference are set so that a needle plunged into that area comes out clean; the centre should move slightly if the tin is shaken, and a needle comes out oily.

A cake rack

Allow cake to cool in the tin for 10 minutes. Run a knife around the edge of the tin, and reverse cake on the rack. Allow it to cool for an hour or two; it must be thoroughly cold if it is to be iced.

TO SERVE

Use the chocolate-butter icing on page 634, and press a design of almonds over the icing.

LE MARQUIS

[Chocolate Spongecake]

For an 8-inch cake serving 6 to 8 people

Preheat oven to 350° F., Mark 4.

A round cake tin 8 ins. in
   diameter and 1½ ins. deep

Butter and flour the cake tin, page 619. Measure out the ingredients.

3½ oz. plain chocolate	A wooden spoon
2 tbl coffee	2 oz. softened butter
A small saucepan placed over	
very hot water	

Stir the chocolate and the coffee in the saucepan over very hot water until the chocolate is melted and smooth. Away from heat, beat in the butter in blocks to make a creamy mass. Allow to cool until tepid while proceeding with recipe.

A wire whisk or electric beater	A 2½-qt. mixing bowl
3 egg yolks	3 oz. granulated sugar

Beat the egg yolks in the mixing bowl, gradually adding the sugar, until mixture is thick, pale yellow and forms the ribbon, page 534.

3 egg whites	1 tbl castor sugar
Pinch of salt	

Beat the egg whites and salt together in a separate bowl until soft peaks are formed; sprinkle on the sugar and beat until stiff peaks are formed. (Directions are on page 144.)

2 oz. sifted cake flour (or plain	A rubber spatula
flour) returned to sifter	

Fold the tepid chocolate and butter into the mixture, then fold in one-quarter of the egg whites. When partially blended, sift on one-quarter of the flour and continue folding, alternating with more egg white and more flour until all is used.

Immediately turn into prepared cake tin and run the mixture up to the rim all around. Bake in middle of preheated oven for about 30 minutes. Cake will puff about ¼ inch above rim of tin and top will crack. It is done when a needle plunged into the centre of the cake comes out clean.

A cake rack

Remove from oven and allow to cool in tin for 5 minutes. Cake will sink slightly and top will wrinkle. Run a knife around inside of tin, and reverse cake on rack. Allow to cool for about 2 hours; it must be thoroughly cold if it is to be iced.

To serve

You may serve the cake with a sprinkling of icing sugar, fill and ice it with one of the following butter-creams, or fill with butter-cream and cover with the chocolate-butter icing on page 634. Illustrated directions for filling and icing a cake begin on page 623.

THREE BUTTER CREAMS

Trois Crèmes aux Beurre

Butter creams consist of egg yolks, sugar, butter, and flavouring which are beaten together into a creamy mass of spreading consistency. There are half a dozen ways of arriving at them; one is the orange butter-cream on page 625. Here are three more recipes. The first of these is quick and easy but always slightly grainy, because the sugar never completely dissolves. The second is made with sugar syrup in which egg yolks are poached before the butter is beaten in; it makes a fairly firm cream good in hot weather. Custard sauce and butter make up the third cream, which is lighter in texture than the other two and better in cold weather than in hot. Any of these butter-creams may be used both as fillings and as icings.

STORAGE AND LEFTOVERS

Butter creams may be refrigerated for several days, or deep-frozen for several weeks. To use again, allow the cream to warm at room temperature until it can be beaten into a spreading consistency. If it begins to separate or turn grainy, beat in a tablespoon or two of tepid, unsalted, melted butter.

FILLING AND ICING

Illustrated directions for filling and icing cakes are in the pair of recipes starting on page 623.

CRÈME AU BEURRE, MÉNAGÈRE

[Butter-cream I—with icing sugar]

For about ½ pint

This should be made with an electric beater; it is heavy work by hand.

A 2-qt. mixing bowl
2 egg yolks
2 oz. sifted icing sugar
2 tbl kirsch, rum, orange liqueur
    or strong coffee; Or: 1 tbl
    vanilla extract; Or: 2 oz. melted
    plain chocolate

6 oz. softened, unsalted butter
An electric beater (or a wire whisk)

Rinse the bowl in hot water, dry it, and place in it all the ingredients listed. Beat at a moderate speed for about 5 minutes to obtain a smooth cream. Chill until the cream is cold but still malleable, then fill and ice your cake.

CRÈME AU BEURRE, AU SUCRE CUIT

[Butter-cream II—with sugar syrup]

You may use either a wire whisk or an electric beater for most of the steps in this recipe. We find, however, that a large whisk, such as that illustrated for beating egg whites on page 144, is the quickest and most effective instrument for the beating of egg yolks and sugar syrup step.

For about ¾ pint

Preliminaries

A wooden spoon or an electric
    beater

A 2-qt. mixing bowl
½ lb. unsalted butter

Cream the butter until it is light and fluffy. (Directions are on page 536.) Leave aside.

5 egg yolks; Or: 1 egg and 3 yolks
A 2-qt. mixing bowl

A large wire whisk (or an electric
    beater)

Place the egg yolks (or egg and yolks) in the bowl and beat a few seconds to blend thoroughly. Leave aside.

The sugar syrup

4 oz. granulated sugar
3 tbl water

A small, heavy saucepan
Optional: a jam thermometer

Boil the sugar and water in the saucepan, shaking pan frequently, until the sugar has reached the soft ball stage (236° to 238° F. on jam thermometer).

Beating the egg yolks with the syrup

At once beat the boiling syrup in a stream of drops into the egg yolks, using your wire whisk (or electric beater).

| A pan of not-quite-simmering water, large enough to hold the bowl | A basin of cold water |

Place the mixing bowl in the pan of not-quite-simmering water, on the stove, and continue beating the yolk and sugar mixture at a moderate speed, lifting in as much air as possible. In 4 to 5 minutes the mixture will be light, foamy, doubled in bulk, and feel very hot to the finger. When this stage is reached, place the bowl in cold water and continue beating for several minutes until mixture has cooled to tepid, and when a little is lifted, it falls back forming a slowly dissolving ribbon on the surface of the mixture.

Combining with the butter

| A wooden spatula or spoon, or an electric beater
2 to 3 tbl kirsch, rum, orange liqueur, or strong coffee; Or:
1 tbl vanilla extract; Or: 2 oz. melted plain chocolate | 1 to 2 oz. softened, unsalted butter, if needed |

Then beat the egg mixture by spoonfuls into the bowl of creamed butter. Beat in the flavouring. The *crème au beurre* should be a smooth, homogeneous, creamy mass. If it looks grainy or has a tendency to separate, beat in softened butter by tablespoons. Chill until cold but still malleable, then fill and ice your cake.

CRÈME AU BEURRE, À L'ANGLAISE

[Butter-cream III—with custard base]

This final recipe is simpler to make than the preceding one with its sugar syrup and its poaching of egg yolks. The custard base here is that most familiar of custard sauces, *crème anglaise* which, when cooled, receives the butter.

For about 1 pint

The crème anglaise (custard sauce)

| A wire whisk or electric beater
4 oz. castor sugar
4 egg yolks
A 2-qt. mixing bowl
¼ pt. boiling milk
A 1½-pt., heavy bottomed, enamelled saucepan | A wooden spoon
Optional: a jam thermometer
A basin of cold water
A sieve |

Following the general procedure in the master recipe for *crème anglaise* on page 542, gradually beat the sugar into the egg yolks in the bowl until the mixture is thick, pale yellow, and forms the ribbon. Then beat in the boiling milk by drops.

Pour into saucepan and stir with wooden spoon over a moderately low heat until mixture thickens enough to coat spoon with a light cream (165° F. on jam thermometer). At once place saucepan in cold water and beat until custard has cooled to barely tepid. Rinse out mixing bowl and strain custard back into it.

Beating in the butter

A wire whisk or electric beater
½ lb. softened, unsalted butter,
**   more if needed**
2 to 3 tbl kirsch, rum, orange
**   liqueur, or a strong coffee; Or:**
**   1 tbl vanilla extract; Or: 2 oz.**
**   melted plain chocolate**

Beat the softened butter into the barely tepid custard by spoonfuls, using whisk or beater. Beat in the flavouring. If cream looks grainy or has a tendency to curdle, beat in more softened butter by tablespoons. Cream should be smooth, thick, and homogeneous. Chill until cold but still malleable, then fill and ice your cake.

CHOCOLATE ICING
Glaçage au Chocolat

This simple chocolate icing is butter beaten into melted chocolate, and forms a tender coating over a white or chocolate cake, or over a thoroughly chilled butter-cream icing.

GLAÇAGE AU CHOCOLAT

[Chocolate-butter Icing]

For an 8-inch cake

A wooden spoon
2 oz. plain chocolate
1 tbl rum or coffee
A small saucepan set over very hot
**   water**

2 oz. unsalted butter
A bowl of cold water
A small, flexible blade-spatula, or
**   a table knife**

Stir the chocolate and rum or coffee in the saucepan over the hot water until chocolate has melted into a very smooth cream. Remove saucepan from hot water, and beat the butter into the chocolate, a tablespoon at a time. Then beat over cold water until chocolate mixture is cool and of spreading consistency. At once spread it over your cake with the spatula or knife.

INDEX

x